Property Management

Eighth Edition

Robert C. Kyle
Marie S. Spodek, DREI
Floyd M. Baird, RPA/SMA
Consulting Editors

Dearborn™
Real Estate Education

This publication is designed to provide accurate and authoritative information in regard to the subject matter covered. It is sold with the understanding that the publisher is not engaged in rendering legal, accounting, or other professional advice. If legal advice or other expert assistance is required, the services of a competent professional should be sought.

President: Dr. Andrew Temte
Chief Learning Officer: Dr. Tim Smaby
Vice President, Real Estate Education: Asha Alsobrooks
Development Editor: Chris Kugler

PROPERTY MANAGEMENT 8TH EDITION
© 2010 by Kaplan, Inc.®
Published by DF Institute, Inc., d/b/a Dearborn™ Real Estate Education
332 Front St. S., Suite 501
La Crosse, WI 54601
www.dearbornRE.com

Printed in the United States of America
11   12   10   9   8   7   6   5   4
ISBN: 978-1-4277-2141-9 / 1-4277-2141-6
PPN: 1551-1008

CONTENTS

PREFACE

First published in 1979, *Property Management* quickly became a standard as an introduction to the rapidly expanding property management field. By 1988, several states required that property managers obtain a special license, so the third edition was tailored to meet those requirements. Now, *Property Management* is the premier introduction both to the field and the license preparation manual.

The eighth edition continues to provide an overview of the profession and the essentials for those who wish to specialize. As in previous editions, each chapter concludes with "real-life" case studies, challenges that are designed to provoke class discussion and individual thought. Rationales for every answer to the end-of-chapter multiple-choice questions have been included.

Study aids that emphasize key anecdotal, policy, and/or procedural information in the text are identified by the icon on the left, featured at the beginning of the paragraph.

The eighth edition of *Property Management* includes information on environmental concerns; expanded information concerning Internet and Web-based material; updated software information to assist users in managing their time and reporting; and increased focus on security issues in the wake of 9/11 and the 2003 power outage on the East Coast and lessons learned from Hurricane Katrina in 2005.

As in each of the earlier editions, *Property Management*, eighth edition, provides a comprehensive introduction for those seeking to enter the field, those already in the management field, and real estate practitioners seeking to broaden their education beyond listing and selling.

■ ABOUT THE AUTHORS

Robert C. Kyle, MA, MBA, DBA, principal author, recently retired as president of Dearborn™ Financial Publishing, Inc., the parent company of Dearborn™ Real Estate Education, one of the nation's largest publishers of real estate textbooks.

As founder of Real Estate Education Company (now Dearborn™ Real Estate Education), Mr. Kyle was instrumental in developing its full curriculum of real estate textbooks, starting with *Modern Real Estate Practice*, a book he coauthored and that has now sold over 3 million copies in 16 editions.

Mr. Kyle was a founder and past president of Real Estate Educators Association (REEA), a national professional organization of individuals from universities, colleges, proprietary schools, real estate firms, trade associations, and regulatory agencies concerned with education within the industry. He received the Award Emeritus from that organization. For many years, he also served on the board of directors of Grub & Ellis Company, the San Francisco based NYSE company, and was chairman of both the executive committee and compensation committee.

In the summer of 1998, Dearborn™ Publishing Group was sold to Kaplan Educational Centers of the Washington Post Company. Mr. Kyle remains chairman of CTS Financial Publishing, a Florida-based former subsidiary of Dearborn™ that was spun off to shareholders prior to the Kaplan sale. CTS is a subscription-based provider of financial information to traders with a heavy presence on the Internet.

Marie S. Spodek, DREI, consulting editor, was awarded the first Jack Wiedemer Distinguished Career in Real Estate award in 2001 by REEA. She served three terms on REEA's board of directors and became a Distinguished Real Estate Instructor (DREI) in 1988. As a senior instructor of REEA's Instructor Development Workshop (IDW), she wrote REEA's Course Development Workshop (CDW) in 1999. In 1996, Marie developed REEA's course for real estate instructors, "Taking the Risk out of Radon," for which she received a commendation from the U.S. Environmental Protection Agency (EPA). REEA named her course, *Caught on Camera: Antitrust in the 21st Century*, an Education Program of the year for 2004.

Ms. Spodek's involvement with property management began in 1987 when South Carolina instituted license requirements for property managers. While owner/director of the Professional School of Real Estate in Charleston, South Carolina, she developed a licensing class using Robert C. Kyle's first edition of this text and was a critical reviewer for subsequent editions. For the sixth edition, she revamped the material and expanded the text by including extensive information about federal laws that have an impact on the profession. She worked closely with the Greater Charleston Apartment Association (GCAA) and had the highest enrollment of property management students and one of the highest pass rates in the state.

Ms. Spodek's credentials include several books and supplements for Dearborn™ Real Estate Education. *Sustainable Housing and Building Green: What Agents Should Know* is the fifth in her series of continuing education materials for the real estate industry. She is coauthor of *Environmental Issues In your Real Estate Practice*; *Man-*

ufactured and Modular Housing; Insurance for Consumer Protection; and *Mortgage Fraud and Predatory Lending.* Additionally, she is the consulting editor for *Nevada Property Management,* and contributing editor for the compendium of *Language of Real Estate* products.

Floyd M. Baird, AB, JD, DREI, consulting editor, practiced law for several years before his property management career began in 1958. In that year he became executive vice president of a privately owned company owning multifamily, commercial, and industrial properties in several states. His activity in real estate education included serving as an adjunct instructor in property management at Tulsa Junior College and the Continuing Education Center of the University of Oklahoma. Dr. Baird was also a real estate broker and an instructor licensed by the Oklahoma Real Estate Commission, for which he authored continuing education monographs in property management and basic real estate subjects.

His involvement in real estate education was recognized by the National Real Estate Educators Association in 1983, when he was named a Distinguished Real Estate Instructor (DREI). As a lawyer admitted to the bar in three states as well as the U.S. Supreme Court, Dr. Baird brought both legal and practical knowledge to the property management profession.

■ ACKNOWLEDGMENTS

The following reviewers have provided invaluable contributions to this edition: Theodore Highland, California Community College Real Estate Educators Association; Edward J. Smith, Senior Broker, First Choice Business Brokers, Las Vegas, Nevada; and Angela M. Waller, NAHP-e, SHCM, FHC, CPO, Ambling Management Company, Summerville, South Carolina.

1

PROFESSIONAL PROPERTY MANAGEMENT

■ KEY TERMS

Asset management
  services
Building Owners and
  Managers Association
  (BOMA)
Code of Ethics
Commercial property
Corporate property
  manager
Industrial property

Institute of Real Estate
  Management (IREM)
National Affordable
  Housing Lenders
  Management
  Association
  (NAHMA)
National Apartment
  Association (NAA)

National Association of
  Home Builders Multi-
  Family Council
National Association of
  Residential Property
  Managers (NARPM)
Office property
Residential property
Retail property
Special-purpose property

■ LEARNING OBJECTIVES

At the end of this chapter, the student will be able to

1. state three goals of a property manager;

2. discuss several developments that changed the face of cities and caused suburban areas to grow;

3. list four classifications of real property and give examples of each;

4. explain the difference between office property and retail property;

5. recognize the importance of identifying the owner's objectives;

6. list at least three professional organizations and name at least one designation offered by each; and

7. summarize the value of ethical conduct in property management.

■ OVERVIEW

A property manager's role is far more complex than simply showing space, signing leases, and collecting rents. In reality, the property manager attempts to generate the greatest possible net income for the owners of an investment property over the economic life of that property. Thus, the property manager has three goals:

1. Achieve the objectives of the property owners.

2. Generate income for the owners.

3. Preserve and/or increase the value of the investment property.

Current Challenges

Property management, one of the fastest-growing areas of specialization within the real estate industry, is emerging as a managerial science. Today, property managers must possess the communication skills and technical expertise required for dynamic decision making.

Versatility Increasingly, more varied skills are required of the property manager who is called on to act as a market analyst, advertising executive, salesperson, accountant, diplomat, or even maintenance engineer. Moreover, the manager is expected to interact competently with many professionals in related fields: attorneys, accountants, environmental inspection companies, and so forth. The manager must acquire and refine a wide range of interpersonal skills in order to work effectively with owners, prospects, tenants, employees, outside contractors, and others in the real estate business.

Types of Property Specialists are needed to manage various types of properties. Commercial properties can include multistory office buildings, regional shopping malls, strip shopping centers, ministorage centers, and large warehouses. Residential properties vary from large multifamily apartment communities to scattered single-family dwellings. Commercial property to be managed may also include condominiums/cooperatives and town houses. Other opportunities for specialization include the management of subsidized or affordable housing, manufactured home parks, elderly housing, and military housing. The most recent specialty is managing REOs, bank-owned real estate as a result of so many housing foreclosures.

Nonstandardized Titles

■ In the property management profession, each organization uses its own system for defining job categories, with responsibilities varying according to the type and extent of properties managed. A property manager with the title Vice President–Director of Real Estate, for example, may perform the duties of a facility manager or an asset manager. One property manager may manage a number of buildings with several tiers of staff to supervise, while another property manager may take care of only a few single-family dwellings.

■ DEVELOPMENT OF THE PROPERTY MANAGEMENT PROFESSION

The demand for effective, professional property management began in the 1800s with several advancements that contributed to a radical transformation in the nature of urban real estate: steel frame buildings, the electric elevator, development of suburban areas, and increasing investment opportunities.

Steel Frame Buildings and the Electric Elevator

The structural advantages of the steel frame building, coupled with the perfection of the electric elevator in 1889, made it possible to build tall buildings on relatively small parcels of scarce urban land. This led to taller office buildings and construction of all types of multifamily apartment buildings, especially in the 1920s.

Development of Suburban Areas

The expansion of public transportation and the increase in automobile ownership following World War II enabled young couples to purchase their own homes in the suburbs. As the population shifted, suburban shopping centers were built outside the city, thereby decentralizing the traditional downtown concentration of commerce. As a result, office buildings and light industry were built away from the city core. Note, however, that these trends are being modified in some areas by the revitalization of central cities.

■ In recent years, the realignment and centralization of ownership of investment properties by large institutions and groups of investors have continued to increase the demand for professional property management.

■ CLASSIFICATION OF REAL PROPERTY

The definition of *real property* begins with the surface of a parcel of land and moves on to the owner's rights to the air above the surface and the soil and minerals beneath the surface, as well as anything permanently attached to this land, either by nature or by human hands. Man-made, permanent attachments are called *improvements*.

For example, because minerals and agricultural crops are considered to be part of real estate, the management of mines and farms could be considered real property management. In these cases, though, the process of mining or farming is more significant than the management of the land itself. Likewise, large enterprises with extensive holdings of real estate, such as hotel and motel chains, groceries, and other specialized retailers, will have a property management department staffed with experienced property managers. Activities of this nature represent specialized business enterprises and will not be covered in this text.

Most professional property management involves structures built on real property that are not intrinsic to the operation of a business or industry. For the purposes of studying specialized property management, real estate can be divided into four major classifications:

1. Residential

2. Commercial

3. Industrial

4. Special-purpose

Each type of property requires a different combination of knowledge and skills on the part of the manager.

Residential Property

Residential real estate, including privately owned residences as well as government and institutional housing, satisfies the basic shelter needs of the population. **Residential property** is the largest source of demand for the services of professional property managers.

Single-family homes Freestanding, single-family homes are still the most popular form of residential property in the United States. According to the U.S. Census Bureau, 60 percent of U.S. housing is made up of single-family owner-occupied homes that do not require professional management. Nevertheless, more than 10 percent of single-family homes are used as rental properties. While these often are managed directly by the owner, there is a growing trend toward hiring professional management for these properties.

Manufactured home parks Manufactured homes are built in factories according to Department of Housing and Urban Development (HUD) specifications. Although permanently attached to a chassis that, in theory, permits them to be moved, fewer than 5 percent of manufactured homes are moved a second time. About $\frac{1}{3}$ of the homes are sited in rental communities, and their value comes from the desirability of the community. Many localities designate certain areas for these homes. The landowner rents space to the owner of the manufactured home or rents such a home to a tenant. Many retirees in the Sun Belt states choose to live in manufactured home parks (see Chapter 12). Many of these communities have been designated "senior" living (near elderly is older than 55, elderly older than 62); that, coupled with the low acquisition cost and low maintenance, has contributed to their popularity.

FIGURE 1.1
Residential Real Estate Categories

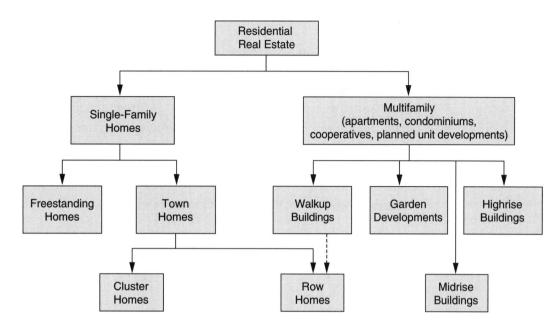

Multifamily residences Rising construction costs and a decrease in the availability of usable land have increased the popularity of multifamily developments such as town homes (or row houses), condominiums, and cooperatives, many of which are individually owned. The economy of design and land usage inherent in multifamily housing allows for a lower per family cost of construction, although these costs also have increased, in part because of legal requirements for handicapped accessibility. Structurally, multifamily residences have many classifications—among them are garden developments, walkup buildings, and high-rise buildings. Each type is unique in its location, design, construction, services, and amenities. Figure 1.1 illustrates the interrelationships of several types of residential structures.

Multifamily residences can be held under various forms of ownership. Small properties of two to six units often are owner-occupied and owner-managed, whereas most large apartment complexes are professionally managed for their investor-owners. Cooperative and condominium apartments are largely owner-occupied buildings governed by boards of directors elected by the owners. These boards usually hire professional managers for their properties.

Facilities for the Aging Increasingly, people are living long beyond what was once considered retirement age, forcing a rethinking of housing needs for those who are retired and semiretired. There has been a tremendous increase in the number of retirement communities, homes for the aged, convalescent care facilities, and independent living facilities. Housing for the elderly is often exempt from certain laws, such as the lead-based paint notification and the fair housing law protecting families with children against discrimination based on familial status. On the other hand, construction costs are often higher in order to comply with handicapped accessibility. Whether for-profit or not-for-profit, most communities require specialized, professional management.

Commercial Real Estate

Commercial real estate includes various types of income-producing properties, such as office buildings, shopping centers, stores, gas stations, and parking lots. A **commercial property** is generally considered to be a "public accommodation"—a private entity that provides goods, services, facilities, or accommodations to the public. Thus, even though commercial premises are privately owned, the public has certain rights to use them.

Essentially, either services or goods are provided to the public, and that determines the two principal categories of commercial real estate:

1. Office property, where the occupants provide services
2. Retail property, from which goods are sold

The general categories of commercial real estate are illustrated in Figure 1.2.

Management of these properties is discussed in Chapters 13 and 14.

Office property   **Office property** can consist of low-rise (walkup) offices; high-rise complexes; or office parks (also called business parks). Whether an office property is situated in a downtown commercial district or in a suburban development, its success is determined by its location relative to the prospective workforce, transportation facilities, and other business services.

Office property can be occupied by several tenants or a single occupant who may or may not be the owner. A number of major corporations occupy their own real estate for business purposes. Such real estate is often referred to as *institutional property* and is sometimes under the supervision of the corporation's own property or facilities management department. Some multiple-tenant office properties accept any financially qualified business or organization, whereas others cater to one type of business. Medical complexes, dental complexes, and trade centers are examples of multiple-occupancy, single-use properties. Trade centers cater to one type of merchandise, and usually only wholesalers are allowed to enter and buy.

Retail property   **Retail property** includes freestanding buildings; traditional shopping centers designated by size (strip centers, neighborhood centers, community centers, regional shopping centers, and superregional malls); and specialized centers, such as off-price stores, factory outlets, and specialty centers. The freestanding, single-tenant building is often owner-occupied and owner-managed. Strip centers usually consist of 4 to 10 stores located on a corner of a main thoroughfare and are designed primarily for convenience shopping. Neighborhood centers are the next

FIGURE 1.2
Commercial Real Estate Categories

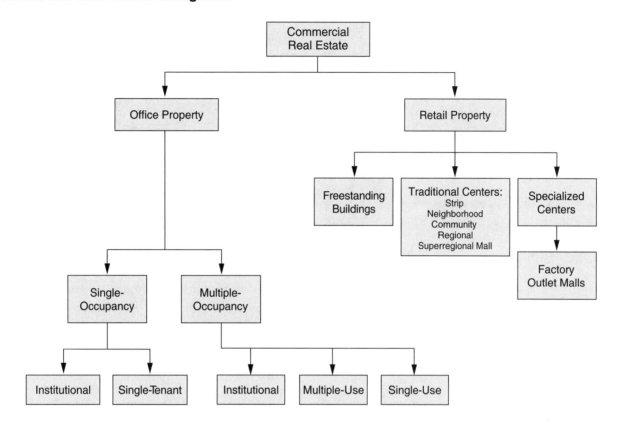

largest, containing 15 to 20 retail outlets. Community centers may consist of 20 to 70 stores and serve an even larger area.

As regional shopping centers, superregional malls, and factory outlets that offer brand names at discounted prices have located in suburban areas, the centralized urban commercial district has all but disappeared. Professional management is a necessity due to the size of these shopping centers and their diverse tenant mix. The success or failure of a shopping center often hinges on the property manager's ability to assess the market, to conduct sales promotion and public relations, and to act swiftly and decisively.

Research parks   Research parks are often located in the same locale as universities with active graduate schools; tenants may specialize in certain fields, such as high-tech computers or engineering. Research parks may also include spaces for beginning companies, called *incubator spaces*. The traditional separation between office space and manufacturing or warehouse facilities is breaking down in many business and industrial parks. Many parks now offer combinations of office and industrial space or buildings that are divided into differently sized units. These incubator spaces are designed to be adapted to the changing needs of a growing company.

FIGURE 1.3
Industrial Real Estate Categories

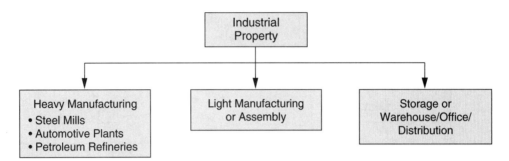

Industrial Property

The industrial process converts raw materials into finished products, comprising all activities involved in the production, storage, and distribution of goods. **Industrial property** includes all land and facilities used for heavy and light manufacturing, for storage, and for the distribution of goods. The diagram in Figure 1.3 shows the various types of industrial property.

Heavy manufacturing   Very large industrial plants, such as steel mills, automotive plants, and petroleum refineries, and smaller facilities must be accessible to transportation facilities, an adequate source of raw materials, and a skilled labor supply. Because property for heavy industry must be designed with the specific needs of potential users in mind, such plants are generally occupied and managed by the owner.

Light manufacturing   Assembly or warehousing, on the other hand, can usually be performed in smaller buildings requiring fewer unique specifications. As a result, light industrial buildings can often be utilized by more than one type of enterprise—a fact that has stimulated some real estate speculators to build this type of facility for future lease to industrial concerns.

Industrial parks   The migration of the population away from the urban centers and the development of freeway systems to facilitate the flow of workers, materials, and finished goods have stimulated the need for industrial parks. Located in suburban areas, these parks, designed for light industry, have enjoyed rapid growth over the past 30 years, while the number of urban manufacturing facilities has declined. Some industrial tenants need extensive office space as an integral part of their facilities. Because of greater land availability, industrial parks in suburban areas can provide the advantages of one-story plant and warehouse design, ample parking, and extensive landscaping. These developments are often called business parks, particularly if they have a high ratio of office space.

Loft buildings   Multistory, low-rent buildings, once used for manufacturing, are reminders of the former concentration of industrial activity in the central urban areas of older cities. They are now being converted into various combinations of manufacturing, office, residential, and storage space. The thousands of square feet in loft buildings that remain to be converted and leased offer unique possibilities for the creative and ambitious property manager.

Distribution facilities   To relieve the traffic congestion of the central city, distribution facilities or warehouses are being built in suburban industrial parks. Although the larger warehouses usually are owner-occupied, more and more are being built by investors for lease to industrial users with different space requirements. By the very nature of their use, warehouses require minimal management. Depending on the terms of the lease, management responsibilities are often shared by landlord and tenant. Some creative property managers are converting many older warehouses in some central city areas into shopping malls, condominium apartments, and office space.

Ministorage facilities   Rising construction costs and scarce land have contributed to another modern development, ministorage facilities, storage areas not specifically designed to meet the needs of industry. The primary purpose is to provide extra storage space for homeowners and apartment dwellers. However, businesses may also rent space in ministorage facilities to store files, extra supplies, and surplus equipment. As a result, many ministorage facilities are now also located in commercial areas as well as near apartment projects. To provide security, on-site resident managers for ministorage are common.

Enterprise zones   Usually, enterprise zones are created through state statutes, and consist predominantly of warehousing, light manufacturing, or assembly zones. Local governments may grant certain tax concessions to business enterprises in return for the creation of new jobs. Some port cities have created free trade zones, where imported goods may be stored in selected warehouses until sometime in the future when import duties are paid.

Special-Purpose Property

Hotels, motels, clubs, resorts, nursing homes, theaters, schools, colleges, government institutions, and places of worship are considered **special-purpose property.** Their common denominator is the fact that the activity in these buildings is a special business or organizational undertaking that dictates the design and operation of the buildings themselves. Thus, management of these properties is usually provided internally by members of the particular business or organization. These individuals must be skilled in the techniques of professional property management and knowledgeable in their specific fields of endeavor.

Some single-occupant property is often termed *institutional*, particularly if the purpose served is religious or charitable. The designation is also coming into common usage to categorize property owned by pension trusts and life insurance companies. This is a result of referring to financing from such sources as "institutional."

Retirement communities that combine independent living facilities with assisted living and nursing-home care are a fast-growing segment of special-purpose property. As the population ages and health care advances keep people alive longer, there is a growing need for housing for this segment of the population.

■ SPECIALIZED OPPORTUNITIES IN PROPERTY MANAGEMENT

Aside from choosing among the various types of property that can be managed, property managers can also choose to offer one or more of the many specialized facets of property management.

Concierge Services

A fixture in French hotels for decades, the *concierge* is traditionally defined as a doorkeeper or lobby attendant. Originally, a concierge ordered tickets for the theater, sporting events, and other attractions; made dinner reservations; and arranged for messengers or deliveries and limousines or taxis, among other services.

Routinely placed in office buildings, condominium developments, shopping centers, and apartment complexes, enterprising concierges now offer a greatly expanded list of available services.

For example, concierges now offer fax, courier, and secretarial aid; cater in-office lunches and arrange conferences; and provide rental service for little-used office equipment, such as audio or visual aids. Personal services—dry cleaning, laundry, shopping, automobile care, gift shopping and wrapping, or repair of small appliances—may also be offered.

Companies now specialize in training and staffing concierges in office buildings and other settings; but a property manager, with proper research into concierge services, can supply this service as a profit center. If a building will not support a full-time concierge, property managers often hire one concierge to split time between several buildings.

Asset Management Services

Asset management in a real estate management context generally refers to financial management of a sizable number of investment properties. Real property asset managers deal with numerous large properties, monitor financial performance, study local markets, and compare individual properties against a norm as well as with other like properties in the portfolio.

A real estate asset manager supervises and is responsible for a portfolio of properties rather than managing directly an individual property or the properties in a particular area. Generally, while the manager may not make a final buy-and-sell decision, he or she is critical to the overall real estate investment process at the ownership level. In providing **asset management services** the asset manager may be called upon to recommend or decide any or all of the following:

- Whether to invest in real estate and in what localities
- In what type of real estate to invest, such as commercial or residential
- Which particular property to purchase
- Appropriate financing methods and sources
- When and if a particular property is sold or otherwise disposed of

A major difference between an asset manager and a traditional property manager is that ownership delegates to the asset manager the responsibility of monitoring the portfolio of properties in the same manner as a securities portfolio. Rent (dividends) must be collected; the performance of properties (individual issues) must be reviewed regularly; and types of properties (industries) must be analyzed. In addition, the asset manager must be knowledgeable about all markets where portfolio property is located. Like the financial asset manager, the real property asset manager usually has a strong voice in retention or disposition of property.

Corporate Property Managers

Some non–real estate corporations spend millions of dollars investing in and managing real estate assets. Their **corporate property managers** create facilities and manage properties for corporations that invest in real estate. Because real estate is not their main occupation, these corporations need property managers to develop and manage their real estate investments. These property managers are usually employees of the corporation, not independent contractors or consultants.

Current economic conditions have created the dual phenomena of *downsizing* and *outsourcing*. Corporations are reducing staff to save costs, hiring outside service providers (called *outsourcing*) to take up the slack. By outsourcing, a corporate real estate department can continue to provide essential services and remain responsive to the corporation's real estate needs. For example, if a corporation decides to sell a large property or properties, it can simply cancel its outsourced services rather than restructure or reduce its real estate department. Outsourcing also allows a corporation to save money in hiring and training costs.

Downsizing and outsourcing mean reduced opportunities for corporate managers. However, they also mean increased opportunities for property management companies in a position to offer corporations the real estate services they need.

Technology Expert

Smart buildings need smart managers; property managers must be on the cutting edge of constantly changing technology in order to adapt to cater to the needs of clients who require sophisticated space. Increasingly, developers are adding fiberoptics, Internet access, and other telecommunications options to residential buildings as well as office space. In fact, some buildings are installing antennas on the roof so that the occupants can tap into wireless technology.

Telecommuting is more commonly becoming an option for workers, thus cutting the spatial requirements of office buildings. Some sales organizations are able to significantly cut requirements for office space, particularly in downtown areas of cities.

An Internet Web site needs to provide information *now* to people interested in brokerage and leasing activities. Merely providing the address of the property is insufficient; the site needs to provide property information the viewer can access and analyze immediately. Web sites require site maintenance, and the property manager should keep up with technology and be aware of what the site manager knows in case the manager leaves the company.

Leasing Agents

Larger property management companies are utilizing the skills of specialty leasing consultants. Leasing agents move from property to property, on a month-to-month basis, leasing new or repositioned properties. In fact, there is a great concern about how to recruit and retain such individuals, who are generally paid by commission. One thing is sure: in a very competitive market, those who can lease are in high demand.

■ ROLES OF THE PROPERTY MANAGER

Most professional property managers work in one of two capacities: as employees of an owner of extensive properties or as an independent managers for several owners. The latter are often referred to as third-party managers.

Manager as Economist

A professional property manager must have a comprehensive understanding of the economic forces at work in the real estate market in order to evaluate the property in terms of operating income, forecast its potential for the future, and construct a management plan that reflects the owner's objectives. The plan must be flexible enough to adapt to future changes in the market. These topics are treated in detail in Chapters 2 through 10.

Manager as Involved Community Member

In addition to the tasks involved in property management per se, professional managers should take an interest in professional, social, and political organizations in their municipality. Their long-range goals will be more easily realized if property managers take on civic responsibilities and help implement plans for the growth and improvement of their communities.

Manager as Facilitator of Owner's Interests

■ As an agent for the owner, the property manager must work within the owner's guidelines, goals, and objectives. For that reason, it is imperative that the manager identifies what the owner wants to achieve. Most often, the owner wants to realize the most amount of income while preserving the value of the property.

Occasionally, a shortsighted owner will direct a property manager to operate a property to extract every possible dollar from the property without putting any money back into the property. Even if not actually expressed or even tacitly admitted, it occurs when an owner demands frequent payments of accumulated cash; refuses to make any repairs except those absolutely necessary to keep the property operating; and pays bills, and even taxes, at the last possible minute. This is called *milking* a property and those owners are referred to as *slumlords*.

A property manager in this position should meet with the owner and tactfully, but clearly, point out the ultimate loss that can occur as a result of following such a course of action. If the property owner, for financial or other reasons, continues to direct that the property be managed in this manner, the property manager should document the owner's direction with a confirming letter. The property manager should consider whether to continue managing the property under policies that may be illegal and would appear to doom the project to financial failure.

Property managers should also pay careful attention to owner attitudes regarding civil rights laws and other applicable laws and regulations affecting the property. If the property manager will suffer increased exposure to liability based on an owner's refusal to comply with such laws, the prudent course of action is to terminate the management agreement.

■ GROWTH OF PROFESSIONALISM IN PROPERTY MANAGEMENT

The Depression of the 1930s had a profound influence on the evolving property management profession. The numerous business failures and real estate foreclosures of this era placed much of the nation's real estate in the hands of mortgage-lending institutions, such as trust companies, insurance companies, associations, credit unions, and banks. These new owners soon learned that a landlord must do more than select tenants and collect rents; and as the need for more sophisticated management techniques became apparent, the property management profession gained stature.

Today, more than ever, the diverse types of properties now under professional management and the increasing variety of ownership entities employed by investors make the need for professional property management skills even more critical. Continued professional training is, therefore, a must if a property manager is to grow and succeed in this profession. A number of organizations have been formed to develop professional standards and offer educational programs.

Career Opportunities

Just as there are various types of real property, there are different classifications of property managers. A professional property manager may be an individual entrepreneur, a member of a real estate firm specializing in property management, or a member of the property management department of a large multiservice real estate company. The manager also may work within the trust department of a financial institution or within the real estate department of a large corporation or public institution.

Property managers pursue similar objectives regardless of their employment background. As the person in charge of maximizing the net income from a property, the property manager may be responsible for planning thorough budgeting and market analyses as well as advertising and space merchandising, screening tenants, negotiating leases, collecting rents, maintaining the interior and exterior of the premises, supervising security, obtaining insurance, paying taxes on the property, keeping accurate records, and making periodic reports to the property owner.

Management duties vary according to the specific situation and particular property; the successful manager therefore must be competent in all of these areas. The major functions of the property manager are discussed in Chapters 2 through 10.

Professional Organizations

Early in the 20th century, George A. Holt, owner and manager of a 16-story Chicago skyscraper, invited his colleagues to a dinner meeting, which led to the formation of the Chicago Building Managers Organization. In 1908, 75 people attended a national organizational meeting. By 1921, a number of groups had formed in the nation's larger cities and organizational changes were required: the **Building Owners and Managers Association (BOMA)** became a national federation of local and regional groups.

BOMA International   Most early BOMA members were office building managers, with some participation from apartment and loft building managers. Later, as chapters were organized in Canada, England, South Africa, Japan, and Australia, the name was changed to the Building Owners and Managers Association International. An independent organization, the Building Owners and Managers Institute (BOMI) was established in 1970 to provide educational programs for property owners and managers of commercial properties. Individuals with several years of experience in the field who have successfully completed the program's courses receive the professional designation of Real Property Administrator (RPA).

For training building maintenance personnel and facility managers, BOMI has developed courses of study for Systems Maintenance Administrators (SMA) and Facilities Management Administrators (FMA). To promote professionalism in the specialized field of retail property management, the International Council of Shopping Centers (ICSC) has developed a series of courses that lead to the designation of Certified Shopping Center Manager (CSM).

Institute of Real Estate Management (IREM)   In 1933, a group of property management firms created the **Institute of Real Estate Management** (IREM) as an affiliate group of the National Association of Realtors® (NAR). IREM offers not only opportunities for property managers to meet to share ideas but also offers programs to instruct those coming into the business. IREM offers the designation of Certified Property Manager (CPM)® to those who meet educational, experience, and examination requirements. The institute also grants qualified management firms the designation of Accredited Management Organization (AMO)®. Those who specialize in the management of residential properties can pursue the designation Accredited Residential Manager (ARM)®.

National Apartment Association (NAA)   Residential rental property was also affected by the 1930s depression. Apartment owners and managers in most of the larger cities formed their own associations during the 1930s. The **National Apartment Association (NAA),** created in 1939, sponsors courses for Certified Apartment Managers (CAM), Certified Apartment Maintenance Technicians (CAMT), and Certified Apartment Property Supervisors (CAPS).

Multi-Family Housing Council   The **National Association of Home Builders Multi-Family Housing Council** offers extensive training for those involved in managing larger apartment complexes. Its certification programs offer industry professionals a training path for complete career development. The Registered Apartment Manager (RAM) program is the oldest residential property management certification program in the United States and is HUD-approved as providing quality training to managers of multifamily rental, condominium, cooperative, subsidized, and market-rate housing. Other designations include Certified Leasing Professional (CLP); Advanced Registered Apartment Manager (ARAM); and the newest designation, Tax Credit Certification, to assist owners in reducing risk of tax credit recapture due to ineffective on-site management.

National Affordable Housing Lenders Management Association (NAHMA)   The **National Affordable Housing Management Association (NAHMA)** advocates on behalf of multifamily property managers and owners who are involved in affordable housing. NAHMA works with Department of Housing and Urban Development, Congress, the Department of Agricultures' Rural Development office, the Internal Revenue Service, state housing finance agencies, and housing credit monitoring agencies. Its members can participate in several certification programs including Specialist in Housing Credit Management (SHCM), national Affordable Housing Professional (NAHP), Certified Professional of Occupancy (CPO), Fair Housing/Section 504 Compliance (FHC), and others.

National   Association   of   Residential   Property   Managers (NARPM)   The **National Association of Residential Property Managers (NARPM)** was founded in 1988 as a permanent trade organization for property managers who specialize in managing single-family dwellings (about 10 percent of the nation's single-family homes are not owner-occupied). Members must have a real estate license and primarily manage single-family dwellings. They agree to abide by the professional and ethical standards of NARPM's Code of Ethics and bylaws. Several designations are offered—for individuals, Professional Property Manager (PPM) and Master Property Manager (MPM), and for companies that qualify, Certified Residential Management Company (CRMC).

Ethics While property managers must obey many laws regarding their fiduciary obligations to their clients and customers, ethical standards often go beyond the letter of the law and reflect social and cultural concerns. Ethics is a system of moral principles, or rules of conduct that refer to fidelity, integrity, and competency. Ethical behavior is often considered the equivalent of fairness, and professional ethics are a kind of business version of the Golden Rule. As agents for the owner, property managers should maintain unimpeachable ethical standards.

Honesty and integrity are as important to a property manager as skill, knowledge, and experience. Property managers must treat their clients, customers, and employees in an ethical manner, and they must also ensure that their employees behave in an ethical manner. Most property managers codify some sort of rules of ethical behavior in their written office policies. For example, some unethical practices that should be mentioned in the policy manual are prohibiting an employee from working on the manager's own property or from accepting gifts from suppliers.

Most of the professional trade associations previously mentioned embrace **Codes of Ethics** to which its members subscribe. The Institute of Real Estate Management has formulated its own Code of Ethics, based on the NAR Code of Ethics outlining standards of business conduct for all CPMs. One of the requirements for becoming a CPM is the successful completion of an ethics course.

Under the terms of most of the codes, the manager-agent pledges to act in the best interest of his or her principal and to handle all transactions involving the property with honesty and discretion. In essence, the property manager promises to uphold and promote the integrity of that occupation and the standards of the entire property management profession. Many of the standards of conduct required of the agent under specific articles of the code have been incorporated in the terms of most management contracts.

■ SUMMARY

The primary function of a property manager is to generate income while achieving the owner's objectives, always preserving the value of the property. Since the early 1900s, trends in urban and suburban development have sparked the increased demand for trained and skilled property managers.

For the purposes of professional property management, real estate can be divided into four major classifications: residential, commercial, industrial, and special-purpose property—each summoning a different combination of knowledge and skills from the manager.

Residential real estate is the single largest area of involvement for property managers. Single-family rental homes are often owner-managed, but professionals usually manage most apartment buildings and condominium and cooperative communities.

Commercial real estate consists of office buildings and retail properties. While some companies own, occupy, and manage their own buildings, most multiple-tenant office buildings are professionally managed. Retail properties include freestanding stores and restaurants, commercial strip centers, and shopping malls of various sizes.

Industrial property includes heavy and light manufacturing plants and warehouses for storage and distribution of the products. Most industrial property requires minimal outside management or the responsibility is shared jointly by the owner and the tenant.

Modern developments requiring specialized management include incubator spaces, ministorage facilities, research parks, free trade zones, concierge services, and asset management services.

The professional property manager must be able to assess the present and future value of a property based on net operating income, construct a management plan that will meet the owner's objectives, and remain flexible enough to respond to market fluctuations and other contingencies. Additionally, the professional property manager must be knowledgeable in advertising and marketing space, tenant psychology, the legal aspects of the landlord-tenant relationship, maintenance procedures, insurance, accounting, and financial reporting.

A professional manager may work either as an employee of an owner with many properties or an independent manager who works for several owners. The manager should make every effort to understand the owner's intentions and objectives, and if these objectives are shortsighted or illegal, the property manager should disengage from the agreement.

The educational arm of the Building Owners and Managers Association International encourages the ongoing professional development of property managers by offering education courses leading to four different designations. The Institute of Real Estate Management (IREM), an affiliate of the National Association of REALTORS® (NAR), provides education leading to a designation, certification, and/or accreditation. Other trade associations offer certifications and designations relevant to their specialties.

■ **CASE STUDY**

THE PROFESSIONAL PROPERTY MANAGER

Upon graduating from the University of Southern California, Jeff Lance went to work for a large commercial property management company as an assistant property manager, training in the management of office buildings. In his early training days, he was closely supervised by an experienced manager who assigned to him full responsibility for a small office building, in addition to assisting on other properties.

After a few months, Jeff found that he not only liked office building management, but he had demonstrated to himself and others a real talent for handling the many varied duties and responsibilities of a property manager. For example, he had observed that many areas of knowledge were involved in managing commercial property—housekeeping, lease preparation, building systems maintenance, roof repair, and exterior grounds upkeep.

Through contacts developed in professional organizations, Jeff was hired to manage a single-occupant landmark office building in San Francisco. After some years there—missing the variety of duties of managing multiple properties—he accepted a position as the chief asset manager for a large commercial investor that owned extensive rental properties throughout the western United States. Jeff now oversees the operations of dozens of property managers and a staff of several hundred.

1. Jeff, like most property managers, discovered that he preferred a specific type of property management. What are the advantages or disadvantages of working as an employee manager as opposed to working as a third-party manager?
2. List reasons why property owners would choose to hire a property manager rather than manage the property themselves.
3. Why should a property manager be concerned about ethics?

■ REVIEW QUESTIONS

1. The demand for professional property management that occurred in the late 1800s resulted primarily from
   a. reshaping the urban center by building tall buildings with elevators.
   b. increasing concentration of retail activity in downtown urban areas.
   c. increasing availability of land for development.
   d. declining opportunities for investments in real property.

2. The traditional concentration of retail property in downtown areas became decentralized as a result of
   a. development of light industry in the suburbs.
   b. development of multifamily apartment buildings.
   c. evolution of the suburban shopping center.
   d. expansion of public transportation.

3. The growth of shopping centers has been stimulated by
   a. population shifts to the suburbs.
   b. declining construction costs.
   c. urban renewal programs.
   d. the International Council of Shopping Centers.

4. All of the following should be goals of the professional property manager EXCEPT
   a. maintain 100% occupancy.
   b. generate income to the owner.
   c. increase value of the property.
   d. accomplish the objectives of the owner.

5. Which of the following professional organizations has the longest history?
   a. Building Owners and Managers Association International (BOMA)
   b. National Apartment Association (NAA)
   c. Institute of Real Estate Management (IREM)
   d. International Council of Shopping Centers (ICSC)

6. Incubator spaces are most likely to be found in
   a. loft buildings.
   b. research parks.
   c. ministorage areas.
   d. special-purpose properties.

7. Examples of special-purpose properties include
   a. manufactured home parks.
   b. loft buildings.
   c. enterprise zones.
   d. nursing homes.

8. Which of the following types of real estate properties utilizes more professional property managers?
   a. Industrial
   b. Commercial
   c. Special-purpose
   d. Residential

9. The professional property manager formulates plans to
   a. generate the most amount of money.
   b. maintain 100% building occupancy.
   c. enhance the prestige of the property.
   d. achieve the objectives of the owner.

10. The construction of multifamily unit ownership housing has been stimulated by
    a. the varieties of ownership means by which they may be held.
    b. government-assisted financing programs.
    c. rising land and construction costs.
    d. the invention of the steel frame building.

11. Income producing properties that offer services are known as
    a. government and charitable institutions.
    b. retail strip centers and regional shopping malls.
    c. retail space and regional malls.
    d. office property and business parks.

12. The ability of a property manager to assess a market and implement sales promotion is *MOST* critical when dealing with
    a. retail property.
    b. industrial property.
    c. office property.
    d. special-purpose property.

13. Ministorage, unlike many other types of industrial property, is
    a. not designed to meet the needs of any particular industry.
    b. located in downtown commercial areas.
    c. always designed for business clients.
    d. not managed by professional property managers.

14. Areas that are predominately warehousing, light manufacturing, or assembly zones and that are created under state statutes are called
    a. research parks.
    b. enterprise zones.
    c. special-purpose properties.
    d. business parks.

15. Which of the following would be classified as special-purpose property?
    a. Anything managed by a property management company
    b. Hotels, motels, theaters, schools, and places of worship
    c. Residential condominiums and cooperatives
    d. Buildings occupied by members of the medical profession

16. Which of the following offers a combination of home ownership and site rental?
    a. Manufactured home parks
    b. Housing for the elderly
    c. Loft buildings
    d. Condominiums

17. Messenger services, taxi services, fax services, and shopping are all services commonly offered by
    a. asset managers.
    b. third-party managers.
    c. concierges.
    d. managers of low-income housing.

18. Asset managers often have the task of
    a. repairing properties.
    b. selecting tenants.
    c. acquiring taxi services for tenants.
    d. monitoring the financial performance of a portfolio of properties.

19. If a property owner asks a property manager to manage the property in violation of current civil rights laws, the property manager should
    a. comply with the owner's wishes under protest.
    b. terminate the management agreement.
    c. comply immediately without complaint.
    d. comply but inform the building's tenants about what the owner is requesting.

20. Ethics conduct refers to
    a. legally required conduct.
    b. socially or culturally imposed rules of conduct that go beyond the letter of the law.
    c. opportunities to obey civil rights legislation.
    d. the property manager's obligation to supervise his or her employees.

CHAPTER TWO

2

PROPERTY MANAGEMENT ECONOMICS AND PLANNING

■ KEY TERMS

Business cycle
Cash flow
Comparables
Comparative income
 and expense analysis
Economic oversupply
Five-year forecast

Gross collectible rental
 income
Management plan
Market analysis
Neighborhood analysis
Operating budget
Operating costs

Optimum price
Optimum rents
Property analysis
Regional market analysis
Reserve funds
Technical oversupply

■ LEARNING OBJECTIVES

At the end of this chapter, the student will be able to

1. list four types of changes in the general economy that affect the real estate market;

2. name and explain the four business cycles in the economy (expansion, recession, contraction, and revival);

3. develop a management plan by reconciling the data collected from regional, neighborhood, and property analyses;

4. discuss the reasons behind an oversupply of space, whether technical or economic;

5. recognize the value of comparables when developing both a rental schedule and an operating budget for the subject property;

6. recognize the importance of the owner's objectives when formulating the management plan;

7. discuss the difference between an operating budget and a five-year forecast, and the value of each; and

8. explain how a comparative income and expense analysis can benefit the owner when planning any major capital expenditure for repairs, alterations, or improvements.

■ OVERVIEW

Since the 1930s, the real estate market has been recognized as a key component of the general economy. Economists, forecasters, and even stockbrokers eagerly wait for news of housing starts and sales from the previous month as an indication of the health of the economy. The two are so closely allied that the condition of one directly affects the condition of the other. Although much attention is given to real estate sales, rentals are just as important to the economy and are equally affected by local, state, and national economic trends.

In order to assist the owner, the property manager must first understand basic economic trends and their implications for the real estate market. This knowledge enables the property manager to assess the current and future potential of a property in order to develop a management plan for it.

A competent, professional management plan begins with a regional and neighborhood analysis, a thorough look at the potential rental income and expenses of the subject property, and a plan to help the owners reach their short-term and long-term goals. The management plan becomes a blueprint; its implementation provides direction for the property manager and the basis for evaluation by the owners.

■ THE GENERAL BUSINESS ECONOMY

In large part, the general economy is based on the activity, or lack of activity, in the various markets. A *market* is defined as a situation where willing sellers and willing buyers exchange goods and services. Many different kinds of markets exist—those that deal in consumer products; in professional services; and in commodities, stocks, and bonds. The real estate market is made up of the many scattered, unrelated transactions that occur between property buyers and sellers, and landlords and tenants.

The marketplace responds to a number of different factors, especially the principle of supply and demand. When the supply of any product is limited, and there is a demand for that product, prices rise because competing consumers are willing to pay more. On the other hand, when there is a greater supply of the product, and not very many interested consumers, prices are lowered in an effort to entice the consumer to buy or rent. In a perfect economy, the forces of supply and demand are always seeking to balance each other, which create a stable economy. In reality, however, supply and demand are rarely equal.

As supply and demand fluctuate, other events occur in the marketplace that may cause ripples throughout the general economy. Changes and trends fall into four different categories that may appear in the overall economy and in real estate markets singly, doubly, or all at the same time. These changes are classified as seasonal, cyclic, long-term, or random.

Seasonal Variations

Seasonal variations can occur at regular intervals either because of custom or nature. In the northern United States, for example, construction virtually stops during the winter months, a seasonal change affecting both the general and the real estate economy. A custom such as the nine-month school year has a seasonal effect on apartment vacancy rates in college and university towns. Each year, moreover, many retired persons flee cold weather, swelling the wintertime populations of many southern cities.

Obviously, it is impossible to eliminate seasonal trends. Because these changes are predictable, property managers can plan ahead to make any necessary adjustments to counter resulting economic shifts.

Cyclic Fluctuations

Historically, economists have concentrated on *cyclic fluctuations* in the general economy. **Business cycles** are usually defined as wavelike movements of increasing and decreasing economic prosperity. A cycle consists of four phases:

1. Expansion
2. Recession
3. Contraction
4. Revival

Figure 2.1 shows how the phases merge.

FIGURE 2.1

The Business Cycle

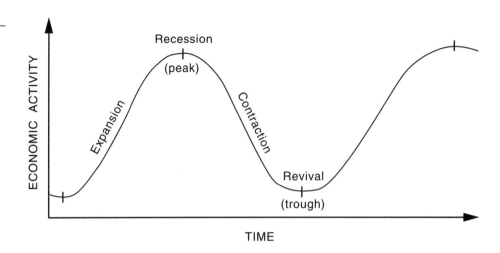

Expansion   Production increases in an expansion phase. The country is work-ing at near full-employment level, wages and consumer purchasing power climb to their highest point, and demand for goods increases. In this phase of the cycle, prices increase because of greater demand, the purchasing value of the dollar decreases, credit is eased, and more money becomes available for purchasing. At the same time, increased profits earned by business attract new capital for the con-tinued expansion of production facilities to meet product demand.

Recession   Recession occurs when supply meets and begins to surpass the demand for products and services. This is the peak of the cycle.

Contraction   Immediately after the recession phase or peak has been reached, there is less and less demand for products, so fewer products are made. The decrease in production, with its corresponding layoffs, brings about a general awareness that the peak has been reached and that a period of unemployment and retrench-ment is imminent. Confidence in the economy is shaken, and a downward spiral effect, or contraction, takes place. Consumers spend less in anticipation of lower earnings; prices of goods are lowered to attract buyers, the purchasing power of the dollar rises, and credit becomes harder to obtain. While cutbacks occur, the economy does not come to a complete halt. Essential activities will continue, because people must eat, wear clothes, have a place to live, and replace important appliances.

Revival   The revival phase of the general economy begins when consumers venture back into the market. Excess supplies of goods have been exhausted, major purchases can no longer be postponed, and consumers are lured into buying by lower prices.

Lull A lull or "trough" or hollow occurs between the two ridges of contraction and expansion. As business activity increases slightly, confidence begins to return. Slowly, production facilities gear up to meet consumer demand, capital begins to flow back into business enterprises, and additional employees are hired. Vacancies in industrial and other types of real estate decline. Finally, when the gradual increase in employment generates more spendable income and an increasing demand for more goods, the business cycle again enters the expansion phase.

Most discussions deal simply with expansion and contraction, measuring expansion from trough to peak and contraction from peak to trough. Business cycles are recurrent but not periodic; that is, they vary in duration and timing. Through empirical research, economists have observed cycles in the general economy vary from 1 to 12 years in length.

Specific cycles are wavelike movements similar to business cycles. They occur in specific sectors of the general economy, such as the real estate economy, and in individual sectors of the real estate economy, such as housing starts and real estate sales. Specific cycles do not always coincide with cycles of the general business economy, but the business cycle is actually a weighted average of all specific cycles.

Regardless of the state of the national economy, certain areas will boom in recessions and stagnate in prosperous times because local demand may run counter to current broad economic trends. Areas whose economies centered on the oil industry continued to prosper long after northeastern manufacturing towns were in trouble in the early 1980s; likewise, an influx of new residents and industries into central Florida kept that area building and growing when other areas of the country were experiencing housing declines.

Long-Term Movements Long-term movements of the general economy, usually measured over 50 years or more, reflect the overall direction the economy is taking. For example, the steady increase in goods and services produced per capita in the United States is a long-term movement upward. Such movements are believed to result from population growth and shifts, technological breakthroughs, the rate of savings and investment, and use of natural resources. Other political, bureaucratic, and contingency factors also influence a nation's growth rate. It is too early to estimate the overall effects of "outsourcing" technology, telemarketing, or manufacturing jobs overseas.

The growth pattern in specific industries is usually quite different from the national long-term growth pattern. New industries generally consist of firms that operate and experiment on a small scale. When effective standardized methodologies are established, the industry enters a rapid growth phase. Although the debate continues about the overall effects of "outsourcing" technology, telemarketing, or manufacturing jobs overseas, it is clear that the economies of the rust belt states have been negatively impacted when their heavy manufacturing companies moved. Today, many empty homes and businesses in cities like Detroit, Michigan, Duluth, Minnesota, and Gary, Indiana are testaments to the joblessness created when factories shut down.

Long-term movements in the real estate industry are often shorter, perhaps only five to ten years, because real estate activities occur at local levels at irregular intervals. But they follow the same basic pattern whenever a new land area is developed or an existing area redeveloped. Initially, few investors are willing to lend money for construction on raw land or rehabilitation of older property. After a few buildings have been constructed or renovated, more investors are attracted and building activity in the area increases rapidly. When all existing land has been put to its highest and best use, construction activity virtually ceases.

Random Changes

Random economic fluctuations may be caused by legislative and judicial decisions or by strikes, revolutions, wars, fires, storms, floods, terrorist attacks, or other catastrophes. These changes are impossible to predict or analyze and may affect one or more sectors of the overall economy. The only way to survive random fluctuations of the economy is to be alert to them and be adaptable enough to cope with events as they occur.

Following are some examples of random changes in regard to real estate:

- A national labor strike that halts construction activity

- A zoning ordinance change that allows undeveloped land to be used for industrial purposes, thus stimulating construction activity in that locality

- The imposition of rent control or code changes requiring retrofit of existing buildings

- Changes in government policies or changes in tax laws that cause marked random changes in real estate activity on a nationwide scale, such as occurred after the Tax Reform Act of 1986, the Revenue Reconciliation Act of 1993, and the Tax Reform Act of 1997

- A hurricane, earthquake, or extensive flooding that damages or destroys businesses, factories, and much housing

- Passage of the North American Free Trade Agreement (NAFTA), hailed as a step for free trade and globalization and also held responsible for loss of manufacturing jobs in the United States

- The 9/11/01 attacks on the World Trade Center in New York City, which particularly hit the airline industry, New York City's economy, and security issues nationwide

Government Influences

The government attempts to control major economic fluctuations by setting up a number of programs and regulatory agencies to buffer the effect of a severe economic downturn. Such programs include Social Security, welfare, Medicare, and unemployment benefits. Regulatory agencies, including the Federal Reserve Board, enact policies that seek to control runaway growth.

Other more indirect government actions that have a significant impact on business cycles include tax rates and policies, affordable housing programs, and the general spending and debt financing policies of the government. For example, when the government decreases taxes, people have more money to save or spend, and the general economy is expected to heat up as a result. Another example of indirect government influences is the cut in defense spending, resulting in the closure of many defense facilities. When a military base or defense industry closes down, the effect on the property values in the surrounding community can be dramatic. In 2009-2010, the federal foreclosure reduction programs and First Time Home Buyer Credits of up to $8,000 were attempts to stabilize and stimulate the real estate market.

■ THE REAL ESTATE ECONOMY

As discussed earlier, the real estate economy is a large, integral part of the general business economy and as such is subject to the same four types of fluctuations. Cyclic movements (specific cycles) can be observed in all phases of real estate: land development, building, sales, rentals, finance, investment rental, and redevelopment.

Factors Affecting the Value of Real Estate

General business cycles, such as a downturn in the general business economy, will mean that fewer people can afford to buy real estate, which then decreases the demand, causing prices to decline. On the other hand, when people cannot afford to buy a house, there is a greater demand for rental housing. In a healthy economy, if consumers have more money to spend, the demand for housing may, in fact, drive up housing prices, and there may be less demand for rentals.

The state of the national economy affects employment rates, housing affordability, the availability of credit, and interest rates, all of which influence the supply of and demand for real estate. Interest rates have a serious impact on the desirability of real estate as an investment. When interest rates decrease, mortgage loan payments become as affordable as rental payments, thus increasing the demand for sales, not rentals. On the other had, as housing prices increase, fewer people may be able to purchase homes, thereby increasing demand for rentals.

■ Since 2000, interest rates have dropped to the lowest in 30 or more years. The resulting cheap loans have turned many renters into buyers. By the year 2003, rental vacancy rates rose to nearly 10 percent, the highest level since the Census Bureau began keeping statistics in 1956. Rental rates have fallen as much as 10 percent in some markets. Unfortunately, many of these low-interest rate loans were made to unqualified buyers. Since 2006, high foreclosure rates have returned many of these same individuals to the status of tenants, thus reducing vacancy rates in the rental market.

Local population trends also change the value of real estate. A large influx of people into a community (because of increased job opportunities, for example) will cause the value of real estate to go up because of increase in demand. A decrease in population will have the opposite effect and will add to supply. The demographics of that population will also alter real estate values. For example, an increase in retirement-age citizens will increase the value of certain types of properties (retirement communities) while decreasing the value of other types of properties (large, high-maintenance, single-family homes).

Local government actions also affect real estate values. Community real estate values may decline with high property taxes or poor schools. It will be interesting to read the statistics as they emerge from the ten-year census conducted in 2010.

The Rental Market

Changes in the supply of and demand for residential, commercial, and industrial properties are important to the property manager. Because the real estate market lags behind the general economy in the short cycle, the general business economy often predicts trends that eventually affect the real estate market.

When the economy is heating up, the rental market for commercial property is generally good and vacancies are low. As properties continue to offer attractive returns to investors, more space is built. At the cycle peak, the supply of occupiable space equals and then often exceeds the demand. When that happens, rents fall and vacancy rates increase. During the contraction phase, vacancy rates are high, and property owners must compete for tenants, resulting in a drastic reduction in rents. As the cycle reaches the trough, the demand for space once again equals and begins to surpass the supply of available space, so rental rates as well as construction starts begin to increase.

Rental market trends for commercial property lag from six months to a year behind residential rental market trends. Commercial leases generally are longer and require more time to reflect current conditions.

The real estate rental market can undergo a severe and prolonged contraction phase, more so than with manufactured products. When the supply of a manufactured product exceeds the demand, the manufacturer can cut back on output, and merchants reduce inventory to balance supply and demand. However, property owners cannot reduce the amount of space that was constructed to accommodate business and consumer needs at the peak of the cycle. Vacancy rates climb and the downward trend becomes more severe.

Rental rates generally do not drop below a certain point, the minimum that must be charged in order to cover operating expenses. Some owners will take space off the market rather than lose money on it. A few, unable to subsidize the property, will sell at distress prices, and lenders will repossess others. These may then be placed on the market at lower rental rates, further depressing the market.

Economic trends and specific cycles in the real estate sector provide a background against which to view the specific conditions and characteristics of each property. By anticipating changes in the market and adjusting rentals and other factors within their control, property managers can minimize the effect of contractions in the real estate cycle and keep their vacancy rates as low as possible.

■ THE MANAGEMENT PLAN

A **management plan** is the financial and operational strategy for the ongoing management of a property. The manager must consider the income, operating costs, condition of the property, and owner's objectives, all in the context of the general market. In formulating a management plan, the property manager focuses on three factors:

1. Regional and neighborhood market analyses
2. Specific property analysis
3. Analysis of an owner's objectives

For a diagram of how these factors impact the management plan, see Figure 2.2.

On the basis of these three factors, the manager should be able to draw up a management plan and a budget that are feasible in terms of present and future business and real estate economic cycles. Critical market indicators are occupancy and absorption rates and new starts.

A comprehensive management plan will include a market analysis, an alternative analysis, and proposed financing, as well as any other conclusions and recommendations. Because creating a management plan requires time and effort, many managers write a management plan only if they will be paid for its development or if they have already signed a management contract. On the other hand, in today's competitive market, property management firms may be forced to complete a plan as part of the bidding process, for which they may or may not be compensated.

FIGURE 2.2
Management Plan Input

■ MARKET ANALYSIS

A market is created in real estate when two or more parties meet for the purpose of leasing or buying space. Depending on the persons or organizations involved, these transactions can occur at a national, regional, or local level and will involve office buildings, factories, warehouses, stores, houses, and apartments. Whatever the case may be, all real property is part of the national real estate economy and is subject to the same cyclic trends.

As the agent for the owner, the property manager is responsible for identifying major economic trends and their effect on the value of a specific property in that particular market level. This is true whether the property manager is managing a large retail mall; a business park; a large apartment building; or individual, scattered-site houses.

A comprehensive **market analysis** integrates information about the larger overall region with detailed information about the specific, local area where the property is located. Such specific information may include data regarding land use, availability of transportation and utilities and the local economy and its effect on supply and demand, as well as a discussion of neighborhood amenities and facilities.

Regional Market Analysis

The **regional market analysis** report should include demographic and economic information on the regional or metropolitan area in which the subject property is located. Information typically presented includes the following:

- Population statistics and trends
- Major employers in the area
- Average incomes and employment data
- Description of transportation facilities
- Supply and demand trends

- Economic base of the city
- Future economic prospects

As the overall regional economy affects availability of all tenants, a regional market overview is just as important for owners of multifamily buildings and for individual, scattered single-family dwellings as it is for commercial and industrial property owners. This analysis should be updated every year.

Neighborhood Market Analysis

Generally, property management is carried out at the local level. Before the property manager can determine the optimum income for a building, he or she must first determine the economic climate of the neighborhood real estate market.

Neighborhood analysis should begin with a tour of the area. Equipped with local maps, zoning ordinances, applicable building codes, and statistical data on the population, the property manager should assess six major factors in the neighborhood market area:

1. Boundaries and land usage
2. Local building codes and regulations
3. Transportation and utilities
4. Economy
5. Supply and demand
6. Neighborhood amenities and facilities

Boundaries and land usage   A neighborhood usually is defined as an area that has certain common population characteristics and land use. Boundaries, such as rivers, lakes, railroad tracks, parks, or major throughways often are used to define a neighborhood. In the absence of any obvious physical boundaries, the manager must use powers of observation to determine how much land is under common use and shares a similar population.

Additionally, there is no predetermined size for a neighborhood. For instance, in rural areas a neighborhood may encompass ten square miles, whereas a city neighborhood might include only five square blocks. Even shopping patterns may be used to define a neighborhood. A small mom-and-pop grocery store may serve only a few square blocks whereas some of the largest food stores that incorporate a pharmacy, dry cleaners, and other facilities will market to a much wider area.

Local building codes and regulations   Once the boundaries of a neighborhood have been established, the property manager should make special note of features that can restrict its future growth such as parks, recreational areas, freeways, railroad tracks, and rivers. Any variances or restrictions in zoning should also be noted; zoning regulations may have a positive or negative effect, depending on the type of property involved. For example, commercial and industrial enterprises would be adversely affected by a zoning restriction that limits the area to multifamily units, whereas a zoning ordinance favorable to industrial development would detract from the desirability of a residential neighborhood.

Generally, growth appears to be good for a community as it often promises additional businesses that hire more people, thus increasing the tax base. On the other hand, taxes may increase as more businesses and more people create a greater demand for community services, such as increased police and fire protection, upgraded sewers, better roads and streets, and perhaps even more classrooms.

Previously, existing property owners paid higher taxes to fund these services. Today, however, many communities impose "impact fees" on new development. Thus, the people or businesses that are creating the demand are "taxed up front" for additional services that their presence requires. Often bitterly opposed by developers, these impact fees can make or break some investment projects depending on how much they affect the bottom line.

Transportation and utilities Transportation facilities are crucial. Traffic counts are readily available from government traffic departments. Regional planning councils can supply valuable information concerning future roads, highways, and paths of growth. Proposed or scheduled widening of streets, opening or closing of bridges, or new highway construction may improve or injure a location.

Easy access to public transportation is a must for apartment dwellers in large cities, many of whom do not own cars, and for employees in office buildings, who often take public transportation to work. Access to and from major streets, traffic patterns, and the traffic count in a neighborhood are of concern to commercial ventures such as strip centers or shopping malls. Industrial enterprises must have access to transportation facilities to distribute their goods, so proximity to railroad terminals, major highways, and airports is important to industrial tenants.

Almost all property users—commercial, industrial, and residential—are concerned with the availability of parking. Commercial enterprises rely heavily on adequate parking facilities for their customers, and industrial concerns require dockside space for loading, as well as an area for employee parking.

The cost and quality of utility services will also affect the desirability of any real property. Residential and commercial buildings must offer certain basic amenities—electricity, gas, water, heat and, perhaps, air-conditioning—to attract individual and corporate tenants. Industrial users will be particularly concerned with heavy-duty power lines, sprinklers, separate sewerage systems, and other unique utility services called for in their businesses.

Economy The property manager can draw on several sources of statistical information for help in assessing the economic health of a neighborhood. Valuable information resources include real estate brokers and appraisers, local newspapers and the area chamber of commerce, and neighborhood financial institutions.

A neighborhood with a diversified, well-integrated business sector is in better economic condition than an area that depends on a single major industry for its support. If that company were to move, the economic framework of the area probably would collapse.

The property manager must also try to assess the potential for growth within the community. In the absence of natural or artificial boundaries, local zoning restrictions, or other growth controls, the opportunity for growth will depend on the amount of existing competition in the neighborhood and on the availability of loans for construction or expansion.

Supply and demand The occupancy rate for a particular type of property reflects the relationship between supply and demand for that type of space at its current rental level. Occupancy and vacancy rates continually fluctuate, reflecting supply and demand of the tenant population (whether residential properties or corporate office space).

The first step is to identify occupancy trends. With this information, the property manager can project the growth rate of the market.

Vacancy rate statistics can be obtained from the U.S. Census Bureau, from current regional housing reports published by the U.S. Department of Commerce, or from local owner-manager associations. Every year, the Building Owners and Managers Association (BOMA) publishes its *Experience Exchange Report,* the most authoritative survey of office buildings in nationwide use. Members of local real estate and civic associations are knowledgeable about specific localities. Rent control, if in effect in the area under investigation, must be taken into account as well.

Current rental rates are another sound indicator of the present rental real estate market. When space is in short supply, rents are high. The Consumer Price Index (CPI) published by the Bureau of Labor Statistics displays trends in rental schedules in 20 sample cities. Many Internet sites yield fascinating statistics that are invaluable to economists. Learning the number of inoperative gas and electric meters corresponds roughly to the amount of vacant space.

The property manager can survey comparable properties to find out if occupancy levels for a given type of property are rising or falling, and how rapidly. The amount of similar existing space and vacancy levels in the neighborhood must be inventoried according to building type, age, size, location, features, and rental schedule. New construction also must be noted, as well as any preleasing activity. In addition, sublease space should be taken into account.

The second step in analyzing occupancy trends is to match the local tenant population to the available space. A high occupancy rate indicates a shortage of space and therefore the possibility of rental increases. A low rate, as evidenced by many For Rent signs posted in the area, will result in tenant demands for lower rents, decorating or tenant alteration allowances, and other concessions on the part of the landlord, such as free rent or gifts of appliances.

The oversupply of space that results in low occupancy rates can be either *technical* or *economic* in nature. **Technical oversupply** occurs when there are more units available than potential tenants. **Economic oversupply** reflects the fact that potential tenants cannot afford to pay the price of the available space.

Neighborhood amenities and facilities   The final checkpoint in the manager's survey of a neighborhood is more relevant to residential property managers than to managers of commercial or industrial real estate. Nevertheless, any amenities that make the neighborhood attractive to potential residents will indirectly benefit business and industry by providing a local pool of potential consumers and employees. When touring the neighborhood, the manager notes the number and location of parks, playgrounds, theaters, restaurants, schools, colleges, places of worship, and any other social or cultural organizations that will be attractive to potential tenants.

Evaluating the Data

Once the regional and neighborhood market surveys are complete, the manager can begin to analyze the information. The analyses are as reliable as the judgments behind them. Only a manager who is knowledgeable about real estate economic cycles can begin to assess their impact on future trends in his or her own market.

When reviewing these data, the manager who specializes will focus on the following:

- Industrial: Opportunities for expansion, transportation facilities, special utility services, the availability of raw materials, and the potential workforce in the area

- Commercial: Traffic counts and patterns, the location of competitors, public transportation facilities, parking space, and the median income of the population

- Residential: Size of family units, the median income level, population trends, current employment rates, and the area's social and cultural facilities

By reconciling the data, the manager can arrive at the **optimum price** for a standard unit of that type within the market area. From this figure the expected base income for the property can be calculated.

■ PROPERTY ANALYSIS

A **property analysis** familiarizes the manager with the nature and condition of a particular building and with its position relative to similar properties in the neighborhood. The owner will need this analysis in order to make an informed decision before making any financial decisions.

A useful property analysis will include this information:

- A thorough description of the subject property
- Data on similar properties in the area
- Data to be able to estimate the average operating cost of the building
- What is needed to make the subject property competitive to the best available space

Leases

When taking over a new property, the manager begins by reading all leases and any other information in the file. The terms of each lease will disclose the amount and durability of rental income. To avoid any surprises, the manager should be alert for concessions, renewal options, and termination notices. If the property was built prior to 1978, the residential manager must look for the lead-based paint disclosure forms that should be in every tenant's file.

Vacancy and loss rates can provide insight into the previous management of the building. If leases have a low renewal rate (high tenant turnover), the quality of tenant services may be poor, or the rental rate may be above the going rate for the market. On the other hand, if there is no turnover, perhaps the rents are too low, and there may be an opportunity to raise the rents. Summarizing this information on a spreadsheet can assist the manager in organizing the material to provide a methodical analysis.

Physical Condition of the Premises

"You don't get a second chance to make a first impression" is especially true in property management. Prospective tenants form their initial impressions of the premises based on "curb appeal," what they see as they approach the building.

A thorough inspection of the building's exterior, common interior areas, and equipment should provide the property manager with additional data necessary to calculate maintenance and operating costs for the upcoming year.

Exterior The exterior inspection should begin with the overall outward appearance of the structure, including its age and style as well as the condition of its walkways and landscaping. If the subject building does not present as pleasing a facade as others in the area, the manager can suggest corrective measures to improve the initial presentation of the premises.

Access for the disabled and removal of architectural barriers may be necessary. In addition, the masonry, windows, eaves and trim, roof, porches, grounds, parking area, fire escapes, and any other common areas must be scrutinized for signs of deferred maintenance or defects for which improvements might require immediate attention and capital outlays.

Interior   Inside the building, the manager determines the total amount of usable space or number of individual rental units in the building. The ability to command optimum rents depends not only on the desirability of its design but also on the quality of its features and amenities.

Entrance ways, halls, basement, laundry rooms, boiler rooms, and other common interior areas are carefully noted. Redecorating or replacement expenses need to be estimated, along with expenses for personnel required to satisfy the routine housekeeping and maintenance requirements for these areas.

Equipment   The condition of the hardware, plumbing, walls, and electrical fixtures should not be overlooked whether the space is commercial, industrial, or residential. The manager's tour of the building's machinery, equipment, and amenities will disclose their condition and age, need for major repairs, and the amount of personnel and supplies required to keep them operating efficiently. Included in this tour are the heating, ventilating, and air-conditioning systems (HVAC); plumbing fixtures and water heaters; machinery such as snow removers and lawn mowers; elevators; and facilities such as cafeterias, swimming pools, and tennis courts.

The physical inventory will also reveal areas of deferred maintenance and curable obsolescence. It should show compliance with building, housing, and zoning codes.

Health or safety hazards   The property manager must recognize the importance of safety considerations when inspecting the property. For example, the manager should always find out if any lead paint, asbestos, underground storage tanks, radon, or other safety or environmental dangers are present. If the manager suspects that any portion of the property contains a contaminant or other safety hazard, he or she should raise the issue with the owner and require a full inspection by a professional agency or a complete cleanup before agreeing to manage the property. Sometimes an insurance company or the local fire marshal will conduct a safety and fire inspection on request at no charge.

Evaluating Comparables

The evaluation of comparable properties (**comparables**) provides insight into the competition faced by the manager's property. Things to consider include building size, rental rates, vacancy rates, location, construction, age, special features and amenities, condition of premises and size of the building staff, and if possible, operating expenses for comparable properties. Industry standards obtained from professional property management associations are also valuable. The Institute of Real Estate Management publishes a series of income and expense analyses for all types of properties including apartments, office, condo/co-op, retail, and subsidized housing.

Operating costs All of the following information gives the manager a good idea of the routine operating costs over the course of the year:

- Salaries for the building staff

- Cost of utilities not charged to the tenants

- Contract services, such as lawn maintenance, elevator maintenance, rubbish removal, and security guards

- Supplies and equipment

- Advertising and management expenses

The manager can now begin to develop both a rental schedule and an operating budget for the subject property's management plan, identifying and estimating expenditures needed to yield a net return that is in accord with the owner's objectives. Additionally, the owner should be advised of any estimates of any capital expenditures that may be required to make the building competitive with similar properties in the neighborhood, if this is consistent with the owner's goals. Finally, the manager can assist the owner by setting priorities for the proposed tasks.

■ ANALYSIS OF THE OWNER'S OBJECTIVES

The management plan cannot be completed until the manager has identified and analyzed the owner's goals, which will vary widely among the individual, corporate, fiduciary, and government owners. The management plan may suggest changing the current operation of the property through rehabilitation, alteration, and modernization.

Corporate and Institutional Objectives

Corporate owners can be divided into two broad classes: those who own real property as an investment, such as Real Estate Investment Trusts (REITs) and syndicates, and those who own and use real property for their own benefits. Most institutional and corporate investors have well-defined, written goals in the form of policy statements or investment guidelines that are readily obtainable by the property manager.

Cooperative corporations and condominium associations may not be concerned with tenant-attracting amenities. They do show an interest in making the expenditures necessary to maintaining their property values.

Fiduciary institutions become involved in real estate in two ways. One is through the services of their trust departments, which administer properties under testamentary and living trusts or as executors of estates. The other involves their investment divisions, which purchase income property. The prime concern of the trustee is maintaining the value of the property entrusted to its care while earning a reasonable income for the trust beneficiary.

Government Objectives

Government agencies, such as the U.S. Department of Housing and Urban Development and the General Services Administration, are interested mainly in preserving the value of the properties they administer. Most government-subsidized buildings are low-income housing developments that do not seek a high rental income. Social service and maintenance of property value are the main objectives of most government agencies involved in real estate.

Individual Owner's Objectives

Many individual owners are private entrepreneurs seeking profit or cash flow from their investment. Because most probably have never developed long-range plans, a property manager can make a real contribution by assisting the owner to commit to a set of written goals. The manager can lead the owner to establishing reserves and scheduling appropriate maintenance. Some owners are only interested in collecting rents, and not in preserving the property. This goal may be at the expense of the tenants' expectations and comfort. If the manager determines that this is the situation, the manager may wish to withdraw from the management of the property.

■ PREPARATION OF THE MANAGEMENT PLAN

Financial Planning Reports

In order to draft a management plan, the property manager should obtain from the owner a statement of the annual real estate taxes and special assessments on the property, the cost of debt service, and the premiums for insurance policies currently in effect. These figures, along with the manager's market analyses, study of comparables, and inspection of the property, provide the information needed to draft a management plan.

Preparing a management plan involves analyzing information from regional and neighborhood surveys and making a property analysis to formulate a management plan based on the owner's goals, as shown in Figure 2.2. Three different financial planning reports are a major part of the management plan:

1. Operating budget (usually for one year)

2. Five-year forecast

3. Comparative income and expense analysis

Information Required to Formulate Operating Budget

To formulate the financial planning reports, the following information must be determined:

■ Optimum rents

■ Gross annual scheduled rental income

- Anticipated revenue
- Income adjusted to reflect anticipated market trends
- Yearly operating costs
- Necessary reserve funds
- Cash flow in light of the owner's objectives

Optimum rents   After surveying other rentals, the manager can determine the **optimum rent** for a specific space—one-bedroom, one-bath; two-bedrooms, one-bath; two-bedrooms, two-baths, etc. However, each property has specific advantages and disadvantages that affect the rental potential, so the manager may have to increase or decrease rents to reflect differences such as these:

- If an apartment building is not convenient to public transportation routes, the optimum rental rate may have to be lowered.

- If the property provides amenities that are not standard for the area, such as tennis courts and a swimming pool, then the optimum rental figure can be raised.

- If a warehouse is easily accessible to an interstate interchange, the optimum rent may be raised.

- If office space is in an old building with concrete walls that hinder computer and telephone line installation, the optimum rent may have to be lowered.

After considering all the advantages and disadvantages, the resulting figure is the expected base rental for each type of space in the building. These rates, however, may not exceed the income capacity of potential tenants. If tenants cannot afford the space, the rates must be readjusted to a more realistic figure. The increases on rents on long-tem leases may be restricted, especially with industrial or commercial leases, so the manager will have to prepare the operating budget on contract rents, not market rents.

Gross rental income   **Gross rental income** is determined by multiplying the amount of space in the building by the base rental rate for that type of space. Making this determination is slightly different for residential versus commercial.

Apartment rentals are determined by room count, so the residential manager multiplies the number of studio, one-bedroom, and two-bedroom apartments by the price for each type of unit, keeping in mind the increased rental for certain units. Commercial space is measured by number of square feet, so the commercial property manager multiplies the square footage available on each floor of the building by the appropriate rental rate per square foot for that floor or area. The total of either estimate is the gross annual scheduled rental income for the entire property.

Total anticipated revenue   It is unrealistic to expect 100 percent occupancy and collections, so the manager must determine the percentage of probable rent loss resulting from vacancies, tenant defaults on leases, and tenant turnover. These estimates must be subtracted from the gross rental income figure. The resulting figure is the **gross collectible rental income** (gross adjusted rental income), because it represents monies that actually may be collected after rent loss.

The gross effective revenue includes the gross collectible income and other sources of income from the property. Additional potential income can be generated from a parking garage, vending machines, laundry rooms, and sale of utilities (where permitted under state law).

Operating costs   The next step is to calculate the yearly costs of operation based on operating expenses for comparable properties and on the maintenance needs of the subject property. The expense section of the **operating budget** reflects the manager's ability to project realistic, supportable estimates of operating expenses for that particular property. Before entering the operating costs, the manager must determine the percentage of increase that can be expected for each category during the year.

First, the manager estimates the **operating costs** for salaries, utilities, contract services, supplies, minor routine repairs and replacements, insurance, real estate taxes, administrative costs, and management costs. Average operating costs for similar properties in the area can be obtained from neighborhood and property analyses. Regional norms are available through trade associations, trade journals, local property owners' groups, and professional real estate management organizations. These figures should, of course, be modified based on the manager's experience.

Second, the manager can study the records of operating costs for the previous year. The manager can then compare the actual costs for the previous year with figures known to be normal for the space and the neighborhood, thus identifying any excessive operating charges and expenses that can and should be reduced in the coming year.

Reserve funds   In any budget forecast the **reserve fund** is placed in the expense category, either under maintenance or repairs. In large buildings, this figure is often estimated at 10 to 15 percent of the total cost of all supplies, maintenance, and repairs, but the actual amount of necessary reserves fluctuates greatly according to a property's size and age, among other features. Experience alone will teach the manager to calculate reserve funds realistically.

Property management professionals have a saying that "unexpected expenditures may be expected." Roof repair, boiler replacement, outside masonry repair, and expenses due to flood or other catastrophe not covered by insurance are only a few of the unforeseen contingencies that can arise. Many mortgage loans under federal government programs require establishing a reserve fund for replacement expenditures.

FIGURE 2.3

Annual Operating Budget

Income			
	3 studio @ $550	$ 19,800	
	6 one-bedroom @ $700/month	50,400	
	3 two-bedroom @ $850/month	30,600	
	Gross scheduled rental income less	100,800	
	5% Vacancy and rent loss	– 5,000	
	Gross collectible rental income	95,800	
	Income from other sources	3,500	
	Total anticipated income		$99,300

Expenses			
	Real estate taxes	$11,900	
	Salaries	18,800	
	Utilities	5,200	
	Supplies	700	
	Maintenance and repairs	3,500	
	Insurance	1,500	
	Administrative	1,200	
	Management @ 6% of gross income	5,700	
	Reserves	1,300	
	Total budgeted expenses		$49,800

Net Operating Income Before Debt Service			$49,500

Debt Service			
	$290,000 @ 8%	23,200	
Cash Flow			$26,300

Cash flow   **Cash flow** is the amount of money available for use after paying expenses and the debt service (mortgage). Cash flow is determined by subtracting the total adjusted operating expenses plus debt service from the anticipated revenue for the upcoming year. The cash flow figure should then be examined in terms of the owner's investment in the property. If the annual cash flow does not reflect the cost of the property and the desired return on investment, the operating budget will have to be modified if circumstances allow. For an explanation of how to calculate the return on an investment, see Chapter 9.

Operating Budget

Now the manager is ready to draw up a one-year projected operating budget for the property in its present condition, using all the aforementioned data. A sample operating budget for a three-story walkup apartment building consisting of 12 units is shown in Figure 2.3. The rental rates used are strictly for purpose of illustration and are not to be taken as typical of any locality.

Five-Year Forecast

A stronger picture of the property's income potential is a **five-year forecast,** a long-term projection of estimated expenditures and income based on predictable changes. The budget figures in Figure 2.4 are arrived at by calculating and averaging all income and expenses for each of the next five years. Figures are rounded to the nearest $100. Before preparing a long-term forecast, the manager should study the market trends affecting all income and expense sources. Before setting the median income for the forecasted period, the manager considers the current rate of rental increases in the area, the potential for growth or decline in the area, and rent increases stemming from any projected improvements to the property.

Depending on the general business economy during the next five years, operating expenses will vary, quite possibly increasing at different estimated rates. These expenses must be realistically estimated, based on observable trends. Major influences to take into account are the rate of inflation, increases in the cost of labor and supplies, tax hikes, and raises in insurance premiums.

A sample five-year forecast is shown as Figure 2.4. A five-year budget starts with the base year and figures increase each based on the shown percentages. Keep in mind that some items, like the debt service and the management fee, do not automatically increase—that is, they are fixed. However, they could be changed as in this illustration. The manager projects an increase in the management fee in year 3.

Comparative Income and Expense Analysis

The final component for the management plan is a **comparative income and expense analysis,** an estimate of the costs of improvements, alterations, or remodeling that are consistent with the owner's objectives and are needed to command optimum rentals. This analysis provides the owner with the potential income increase resulting from the proposed capital improvement and how long it will take to recoup the owner's initial capital expenditure. Any capital expenditures needed to remodel the space to make it competitive with other units in the area market or to convert the structure to meet area demand also should be projected.

The manager's estimates of capital expenditures must be based on accurate information on the costs of construction, materials, and labor involved for any proposed improvements. The manager must then compute the increase in rental income or decrease in expenses that will result from these improvements. The cash flow generated after improvement should be compared with the return on investment for the property in its "as-is" condition. With this comparative analysis, the manager can demonstrate to the owner how long it will take to recoup the proposed capital expenditures from the future benefits to be derived from them. The comparative analysis also shows the estimated additional annual income or cash flow to be generated by the improvement.

■ **EXAMPLE**   Using an apartment building as an example, here is what may be expected if the lobby is renovated, a laundry room installed, and a recreational area added, at a total cost of $15,000. Based on the improved appearance of

FIGURE 2.4
Five-Year Forecast

	Base Year	1st Year % Incr.	1st Year $ Amount	2nd Year % Incr.	2nd Year $ Amount	3rd Year % Incr.	3rd Year $ Amount	4th Year % Incr.	4th Year $ Amount	5th Year % Incr.	5th Year $ Amount
Income											
3 studio @ $550	$ 19,800	10.0%	$21,800	5.0%	$22,900	5.0%	$24,000	5.0%	$25,200	10.0%	$27,700
6 one-bedroom @ $700/month	50,400	10.0%	55,400	5.0%	58,200	5.0%	61,100	5.0%	64,200	10.0%	70,600
3 two-bedroom @ $850/month	30,600	10.0%	33,700	10.0%	37,100	5.0%	39,000	5.0%	41,000	10.0%	45,100
Gross scheduled rental income	100,800		110,900		118,200		124,100		130,400		143,400
Less 5% vacancy and rent loss	−5,000	0.0%	−5,500	0.0%	−5,900	0.0%	−6,200	0.0%	−6,500	0.0%	−7,200
Gross collectible rental income	95,800		105,400		112,300		117,900		123,900		136,200
Income from other sources	3,500	5.0%	3,700	5.0%	3,900	5.0%	4,100	5.0%	4,300	5.0%	4,500
Total anticipated income	99,300		109,100		116,200		122,000		128,200		140,700
Expenses											
Real estate taxes	11,900	7.0%	12,700	15.0%	14,600	5.0%	15,300	5.0%	16,100	5.0%	16,900
Salaries	18,800	4.0%	19,600	4.0%	20,400	4.0%	21,200	4.0%	22,000	4.0%	22,900
Utilities	5,200	8.0%	5,600	8.0%	6,000	8.0%	6,500	8.0%	7,000	8.0%	7,600
Supplies	700	10.0%	800	8.0%	900	10.0%	1,000	10.0%	1,100	10.0%	1,200
Maintenance and repairs	3,500	10.0%	3,900	5.0%	4,100	10.0%	4,500	8.0%	4,900	8.0%	5,300
Insurance	1,500	15.0%	1,700	10.0%	1,900	10.0%	2,100	10.0%	2,300	10.0%	2,500
Administrative	1,200	8.0%	1,300	8.0%	1,400	8.0%	1,500	8.0%	1,600	8.0%	1,700
Management @ 6% gross income	5,700	fixed 6.0%	6,300	fixed 6.0%	6,700	incr. to 6.5%	7,700	fixed 6.5%	8,100	fixed 6.5%	8,900
Reserves	1,300	10.0%	1,400	10.0%	1,500	10.0%	1,700	10.0%	1,900	10.0%	2,100
Total budgeted expenses	49,800		53,300		57,500		61,500		65,000		69,100
Net Operating Income Before Debt Service	49,500		55,800		58,700		60,500		63,200		71,600
Debt Service $290,000 @ 8%	23,200	fixed	23,200	fixed	23,200	fixed	23,200	fixed	23,200	fixed	23,200
Cash Flow	$26,300		$32,600		$35,500		$37,300		$40,000		$48,400

FIGURE 2.5

Comparative Income and Expense Analysis

	Property As Is	Property with Improvements
Income		
Rental	$41,000	$47,500
Other	2,000	4,000
Total	$43,000	$51,500
Expenses		
Real estate taxes	$5,000	$5,000
Salaries	8,500	8,500
Utilities	4,000	4,500
Supplies	500	500
Maintenance and repairs	1,500	1,500
Insurance	500	500
Administrative	200	200
Management @ 6% gross income	2,500	3,000
Reserves	300	300
Total	$23,000	$24,000
Net Operating Income Before Debt Service	$20,000	$27,500
Debt Service $90,000 @ 10% constant	$9,000	9,000
Cash Flow	$11,000	$18,500

Increase of $7,500 per year in cash flow. Initial investment of $15,000 to improve property will be returned within two years.

the building, the added convenience of a laundry room on the premises, and the recreational amenities, all rentals can be raised $45 per month. Income from the laundry room will be $2,000 annually, offset in part by the increased cost of water because the water bills are expected to increase by $500 a year. The management fee will increase as a percentage of the greater gross annual income from the property.

The increase in cash flow resulting from the improvements will average approximately $7,500 per year, so the initial investment of $15,000 will be returned within two years. After five years, the owner will have realized a profit of $22,500 on the investment in improvements. A comparative income and expense analysis showing the effect of this property improvement is illustrated in Figure 2.5.

Because different owners have different standards regarding an acceptable return on an investment, it is critical to present the analysis to the owner for decision. Some owners will not invest in an improvement that cannot be recouped within three years, whereas others may accept 7, 10, or even 15 years.

Presenting the Plan

The plan should be thoroughly and neatly prepared, for many owners will judge a property manager's ability by the appearance and accuracy of submitted documents. It may be useful to submit this plan for review to a qualified colleague before presenting it to the owner.

The manager's plan for the property may be received in one of several different ways depending on the owner's objectives. The owner may do any of the following:

■ Authorize all suggested repairs and alterations in an effort to increase long-term income or reduce taxes

■ Decide that only deferred maintenance should be performed to preserve the property's value without tying up additional working capital

■ Make no changes at all, preferring to get as much income as possible from the property in the short term without making any capital expenditures

Many owners prefer to finance improvements from the proceeds of the property but are unwilling to invest any additional capital in the property. The owner may decide to make no changes for a variety of reasons: lacks available resources, a pending zoning change, building has outlived its economic usefulness, or the land will be used for other purposes, such as a highway or new building.

Ultimately, the owner's objectives will be the deciding factor in the adoption of the management plan. One of the most challenging aspects of property management is that there is more than one answer to any given problem. Once the manager and the owner agree on a workable management plan for the property, a management contract is drawn up.

■ SUMMARY

The business economy moves in long-term cycles affecting the real estate market. During one full cycle, business activity progresses from a peak period, in which demand exceeds supply, to a time of depressed transaction, in which supply exceeds demand, and then gradually back to peak performance.

Owners of real property cannot reduce the amount of leasable space in their buildings when demand falls and vacancy rates rise. A manager who can analyze the real estate market, recognize trends, and anticipate their effects can hopefully shield the property from the impact of economic cycles.

The property manager must integrate specific studies (a regional analysis, a neighborhood analysis, and a property analysis) and then reconcile the data collected to formulate a management proposal. The regional analysis generally includes area demographic information, and available transportation and utility services. The neighborhood analysis studies the supply-and-demand ratio in the neighborhood of the subject property by analyzing similar existing space in the area.

In the property analysis, the manager studies the rental units of the subject building as well as the interior and exterior of the premises and any machinery or equipment and estimates the amount and cost needed to perform routine maintenance, cleaning, and operating chores. The property owner can provide the cost of debt service and insurance premiums. The analysis notes any improvements that can be made to make the premises more competitive. The completed property analysis indicates the expected operating costs for the subject property.

The manager develops the management plan based on the available capital resources and the income requirements of the owner. The first step is to draw up an operating budget for the property, as is, for the coming year. The five-year forecast should draw on every available resource to anticipate future market trends in the area and to estimate increases in both operating costs and rental income. The forecast should demonstrate future cash flow benefits to the owner.

Any recommendations for major capital expenditures, such as repairs, alterations, or improvements, should include a comparative income and expense analysis showing the potential increase in income. This analysis should project how long it will take to recoup the owner's initial capital expenditure.

The objectives of the property owner determine what action is eventually taken on the management plan. Individual and corporate owners are often profit oriented, but some are interested in tax shelter benefits. Condominium owners, cooperative apartment corporations, and the government usually are concerned with maintaining the value of the property and providing adequate housing for the resident-owners or tenants. Fiduciary trustees are typically interested in preserving value and generating a reasonable income stream.

■ CASE STUDY

THE PROPERTY MANAGER AS ECONOMIST-PLANNER

After graduating from college with honors and a master's degree in economics, Charles Gill was hired by the local urban renewal authority in his home town of approximately 500,000 people. His responsibilities were in the areas of statistics, financial planning, and research. When activities of the urban renewal authority began to wind down upon completion of a major downtown redevelopment project, one of the directors, a businessman who had acquired some real estate investment property, hired Charles to manage one of his residential rental properties.

The area's economy had slowed with the general downturn that occurred throughout the country and severely depressed the price of real estate in many areas, including property in Charles's town. In addition, a local defense factory had closed, leaving hundreds out of work. Charles saw there were suddenly many properties available that were priced far less than they had sold for just a few years before. Charles also saw that although the rental market was not booming, tenants were shifting where they could to buildings with lower rent.

1. Why is it important for Charles to note the area's economy when preparing a management plan for his new employer?
2. What does the shutdown of the local defense factory mean for Charles and the property he manages?
3. What does the decrease in local property values mean for Charles and the property he manages?

■ REVIEW QUESTIONS

1. Which of the following characterizes the expansion phase in the business cycle?
   a. Production increases.
   b. Prices of goods fall because of increased supply.
   c. Credit is tightened because the dollar can buy more.
   d. Businesses do not attract capital because alternative investments are more attractive.

2. At or just before the peak of the general business cycle,
   a. supply surpasses demand.
   b. the value of the dollar is at its highest.
   c. demand for goods decreases.
   d. it is difficult to obtain credit.

3. Movements of the general economy that usually are measured over 50 years or more are called
   a. peaks and valleys.
   b. long-term movements.
   c. random movements.
   d. specific cycles.

4. Cycles of the general business economy differ from those of the real estate market in that the
   a. general business economy is usually subject to more extreme oversupply and undersupply.
   b. trends in real estate lag significantly behind trends in the general economy.
   c. general business economy is cyclic on a predictable basis.
   d. real estate market is not subject to seasonal variation.

5. From an economic standpoint, the rental market as a segment of the economy
   a. has cycles in various types of construction that do not affect the property manager.
   b. is generally poor during a contraction phase.
   c. has relatively short contraction phases.
   d. has cycles in the rental market that correspond roughly to cycles in shopping center starts.

6. In the operating budget, what is the name of the expenditure that accounts for money for replacement expenditures?
   a. Cash flow
   b. Reserve funds
   c. Variable expenses
   d. Direct costs

7. When more space is available than potential tenants demand, it indicates a(n)
   a. demand market.
   b. technical oversupply.
   c. economic oversupply.
   d. upswing in the real estate market.

8. In market analysis, the specific goal of the property manager is to identify major economic trends and their
   a. effect on the region where the property is located.
   b. influences in the neighborhood where the property is located.
   c. effect on rental rates for various types of properties found in the market.
   d. effect on the value of a specific property at the manager's particular market level.

9. The objective in a market analysis is to
   a. identify all properties comparable to the subject property.
   b. determine the average rate for comparable rental units.
   c. establish vacancy rates for comparable property.
   d. determine the optimum rental price for a standard space in the area.

10. To avoid any surprises when taking over a new property, the manager should first
    a. have a third party audit the books.
    b. hire a building engineer to evaluate the structure.
    c. review the insurance policies.
    d. read all the leases.

11. When evaluating the data in a neighborhood market survey, a residential property manager will be MOST concerned with
    a. opportunity for expansion.
    b. special utility services.
    c. traffic counts.
    d. trends in population demographics.

12. Economic oversupply results when
    a. there are more tenants than available units.
    b. supply and demand are equal.
    c. tenants cannot afford the rents.
    d. the economy is based on one industry.

13. What should the manager do if the building is 100 percent occupied?
    a. Consider raising the rents
    b. Consider lowering the rents
    c. Cut back on amenities
    d. Ask for a raise

14. Prospective tenants form their initial impression of a rental property based on the
    a. personality of the manager or leasing agent.
    b. curb appeal of the property.
    c. appearance of the manager's office or quarters.
    d. inspection of the interior of the building.

15. After inspecting and analyzing the comparables, a property manager should be able to estimate the routine operating costs for the subject property and
    a. provide the owner with an estimate of the capital expenditures required to make the property competitive with similar properties.
    b. offer enough information to convince the owner that if he or she wants to use the property for a tax deduction, the owner will have to reduce annual operating costs.
    c. notify the local property manager's association of the new management plan for the building.
    d. immediately prepare a five-year budget.

16. A good management plan is based on a(n)
    a. income, expense, and loss analysis for all similar properties in the city.
    b. feasibility study.
    c. 15-year forecast.
    d. operating budget for one year.

17. What should a property manager keep in mind when setting goals and objectives?
    a. Institutions and corporations generally do not have well-defined goals.
    b. Individual owners do not develop long-range plans.
    c. A property manager may make a real contribution by assisting in establishing written goals.
    d. Alternate uses should not be explored with an owner in setting objectives.

18. Cash flow from a property is predicted by which of the following formulas?
    a. Gross rental income minus vacancies plus other income
    b. Gross rental income, adjusted by market trends, minus reserve funds
    c. Anticipated revenue minus total adjusted operating expenses and minus debt service
    d. Anticipated revenue minus total adjusted operating expenses and minus reserve funds

19. The determining factor in the acceptance or rejection of the management plan will be the
    a. property analysis.
    b. owner's objectives.
    c. neighborhood analysis.
    d. five-year forecast.

20. In preparing a management plan for the owner to review, the manager
    a. need be concerned only with contents and not appearance.
    b. will not benefit from having a colleague review it before presentation.
    c. should realize the owner's objectives will be the deciding factor in its adoption.
    d. need not consider the possibility of renegotiating the plan if it is not accepted as submitted.

3

OWNER RELATIONS

■ KEY TERMS

Agent	Fiduciary duties	Percentage fees
Employee	Flat (or fixed) fees	Principal
Employer	Management contract	

■ LEARNING OBJECTIVES

At the end of this chapter, the student will be able to

1. contrast the differences between employer-employee and principal-agent relationships;

2. discuss the fiduciary responsibilities of the agent to the principal, which are care, obedience, accounting, loyalty, and disclosure;

3. recognize that managers must comply with individual state statutes;

4. name six essential elements of the management contract;

5. summarize the responsibilities of management and those of the owner;

6. list the information required from the owner when taking over a new property; and

7. summarize the value of monthly reports and personal contact with the owner.

■ OVERVIEW

A property manager may have one of several different relationships with the owner(s) of the property. Although the property managers who are employed directly by owners of large, individual buildings may retain the right to act as agents for other owners as well, generally, they only work for one employer exclusively. In other situations, a management company may act as agent for numerous individual or corporate owners, and the manager represents the company.

Full-service real estate agencies offer their clients property management services in addition to leasing, insurance brokerage, sales, counseling, appraisal, financing, and mortgage banking. In these scenarios, the management firms and management divisions have an agent-principal relationship with the property owner(s), and the individuals who manage the properties are employees of the management organization.

After the property manager and the owner agree on principles, objectives, and a viable management plan, they must then agree on the structure of their relationship, their specific responsibilities and liabilities, the scope of the manager's authority, fees, and the duration of their relationship. The written management contract formalizes their decisions. In addition, the owner must turn over management records and other information to the manager to facilitate the operation of the property. The manager is expected to make every effort to establish and maintain a clear line of communication with the owner.

■ NATURE OF THE RELATIONSHIP

Three basic relationships can exist between a property manager and the individual or corporate owner of a building:

1. Employer-employee relationship

2. Formal fiduciary relationship (trust)

3. Principal-agent arrangement

Employer-Employee Relationship

The **employer-employee** relationship is found most often in banks, colleges, large corporations, and other private institutions that require managerial services for their properties. The employee-manager is directly responsible to the officers of the owner-employer corporation or institution, which may be the principal occupant of the property.

Although no formalized contract is necessary in an employer-employee relationship certain issues should be clarified in writing. In lieu of a contract, the manager should obtain from the employing corporation written authorization to sign binding leases. This authorization is sometimes limited in the dollar amount or length of lease or in the dollar amount of the repairs. Many lessees, especially government agencies and corporations, request a copy of this authorization from the employee-manager.

Trusts

A trust is a device by which one person or institution transfers legal ownership of property to someone else to hold or manage for the benefit of a third party. Trusts are created by written agreements that establish formal fiduciary relationships. For example, many banks, trust companies, and employee benefit and pension plans have acquired income property that they hold in trust, in addition to their conventional purchases of stocks and bonds. Also, many investors use established forms of trusts to help meet their investment goals. Thus, a need for property managers arises.

The property owner, called a trustor, transfers the legal title to property to a trustee (who will manage the property) and transfers the equitable title to one or more beneficiaries. Beneficiaries may include the trustor, members of the trustor's family, or third parties, such as organized charities or an employee group. The trustee takes charge of the property for the benefit of the owner(s) of the equitable title. If the trustee is a bank or other organization a property manager commonly will be an officer or an employee of the trustee. In any case, the property manager is an extension of the trustee and must manage the property (technically called the corpus of the trust) in accordance with fiduciary principles. A trust may be inter vivos, that is, set up during one's life, or it may be *testamentary*, established by will.

It is not possible to examine this form of ownership fully in this text because the trustee is governed by terms of the trust instrument itself and federal and state laws concerning trusts. If employee benefit plans are involved, the trustee is also regulated by the U.S. Department of Labor. Property managers who find opportunities in this area must take special precautions to learn and define the legal responsibilities and requirements of the relationship.

Principal-Agent Relationship

The most common owner-property manager relationship is that of principal-agent and is created by a written contract signed by both parties. *Agency* is the word used to describe the special relationship between the **principal** (the one who hires) and the **agent** (the one who does the work). The written agreement creating this relationship is called the management contract; it empowers the property manager, as agent, to act on behalf of the owner, or principal, in certain situations. The agent is regarded as an expert on whom the principal can rely for professional advice; the agent acts for the principal to bring him or her into legal relations with third parties. The agent is governed by the terms of the contract and by certain legal and ethical considerations based on the law of agency.

Scope of agency authority
Depending on the scope of the agent's authority, an agent may be either a general agent or a special agent. A *general* agent

may act on behalf of the principal on a range of matters and may obligate the principal to any contracts signed by the agent that are within the scope of that agent's duties. This relationship usually is long-term. A *special* agent is authorized to represent only the principal on a specific matter or transaction; the authority is both limited in scope and time. Once that transaction is concluded, the agency is terminated. Typically, a special agent has no authority to sign any contracts on behalf of the principal. For example, a real estate agent hired to sell a house usually is a special agent, while a property manager usually is a general agent.

Fiduciary duties Whether special or general, an agent has certain duties imposed by common law or statutory law. An agent has a fiduciary relationship to his or her principal, a confidential relationship marked by trust and confidence that requires the highest degree of loyalty on the part of the agent. Some states require that duties owed must be identified in writing in the management agreement. Some state follow common law duties implicit in a fiduciary relationship. **Fiduciary duties** include care, obedience, accounting, loyalty, and disclosure.

The *duty of loyalty* means that the property manager must always put the property owner's interests first, above his or her own interests. The property manager must act without self-interest. For example, if the property manager receives a commission for leasing an apartment, he or she cannot simply accept any tenant in order to get the fee. The property manager must screen the prospective tenant carefully to make sure leasing to him or her would be in the best interests of the property owner.

The duty of care requires the property manager to exercise a reasonable degree of skill while managing the property. If the property manager is careless in carrying out his or her duties, the property manager could be found negligent and be liable to the property owner for any damage caused by that carelessness.

The duty of *obedience* means that the property manager must carry out, in good faith, the property owner's instructions. However, if the property owner requires the property manager to do something that is illegal or unethical, the property manager should terminate the relationship immediately. For example, if the owner asks the manager to lease space only to those of a certain race or national origin, the property manager must refuse to comply and terminate the agency relationship immediately. The manager should also report this violation of the fair housing laws to the proper authorities.

The duty of *accounting* requires the manager to accurately report on the status of all funds received on behalf of or from the property owner (such funds are deposited into trust accounts). State real estate licensing laws typically include detailed accounting requirements in regard to trust funds that the property manager must follow explicitly. These laws virtually always prohibit commingling by the property manager—that is, combining trust funds with the property manager's business or personal funds.

The duty of *disclosure* imposes on the property manager the duty to keep the owner fully informed of all material facts regarding the management of the property.

> While agency law presumes many rights and responsibilities of the agent/property manager, the property manager's rights and responsibilities should be spelled out in detail in the property management agreement.

State statutes   Each state has licensing laws and regulations governing the conduct of persons and organizations acting as real estate agents. Although these laws apply mainly to those selling real estate, property managers should investigate the statutes of the states where they manage property to be sure they are in compliance with those laws. A few states have adopted statutes that apply solely to property managers. Specific, additional information can be obtained by calling the real estate commission (or division, as it is sometimes called) in the manager's state.

■ THE MANAGEMENT CONTRACT

The **management contract** is a dated agreement signed by both the manager and the owner (or the owner's authorized representative) that defines the relationship between the parties, serves as a guide for the operation of the property, and provides a basis for the settlement of any future disputes. Management contracts are as varied as the types of real property and the forms of real estate ownership. Specific circumstances aside, most management contracts share the following essential elements:

- Identification of the parties and the property
- Period over which the contract is to run
- Authority and responsibilities of the manager
- Responsibilities of the owner
- Fees and leasing/sales commissions
- Signatures of the parties

A typical management agreement is shown in Figure 3.1; it illustrates the kinds of issues that must be resolved before the manager accepts responsibility for the property.

Identification of the Parties and the Property

The owner's name ought to appear on the contract exactly as it does on the title or deed to the property. Required signatures vary depending on the type of ownership. The property must be unmistakably identified.

Parties vary   If the property is owned by a partnership, each partner's name should be stated in the contract and each should sign the document. With corporate ownership, the corporate name should appear on the contract, a duly

FIGURE 3.1
Management Agreement

AGREEMENT TO MANAGE AND LEASE REAL ESTATE
(This is a legally binding contract. If you do not understand it, seek legal advice.)

This agreement to manage and lease real estate is made and entered into as of this _____ day of _____, _____ by and between _____ hereinafter called the Owner and _____ hereinafter called the Broker.

Whereas, Owner is the owner of the property known as _____ located at _____ and legally described as _____ _____ _____

Owner hereby employs Broker exclusively to rent, lease, operate and manage said property subject to the terms and conditions of this agreement.

In consideration of the management and leasing functions to be performed by Broker under this agreement, Owner agrees to pay Broker a fee or fees for services rendered at the rates hereinafter set forth. Owner recognizes Broker as agent in any negotiations relative to said property or any part thereof, which may have been initiated during the term hereof, and if consummated, shall compensate Broker in accordance with the rates hereinafter set forth. Such compensation is due and payable on demand and may be deducted by Broker from gross receipts.

Management: _____(plus sales tax)
Leasing: _____(plus sales tax)

The term of this agreement shall commence on the _____ day of _____, _____ and expire on the _____ day of _____, _____. This agreement is automatically renewable, upon expiration, for annual periods unless terminated by either party giving 30-days' written notice to the other party in advance of such termination date. However, the termination of this agreement shall not affect the right of Broker to receive leasing commissions or fees which have accrued on the date specified in such notice and have not been paid.

As agent for Owner, Broker owes Owner the duties of loyalty, obedience, disclosure, confidentiality, reasonable care and diligence, and full accounting. Broker must disclose all known material facts about the property which could affect a tenant's use or enjoyment of the property, disclose information which could have a material impact on either party's ability to fulfill their obligations under the lease agreement, respond honestly and accurately to questions concerning said property, and deal honestly and fairly with all parties.

The duties and responsibilities of Broker in connection with the management of said property are as follows:

1. Broker shall take all reasonable steps to collect and enforce the collection of all rentals and other charges due Owner from tenants of said property in accordance with the terms of their tenancies.

2. From gross revenues collected from said property, Broker is hereby authorized to accrue and make disbursements from Owner's funds for contractual mortgage payments, property and employee taxes, salaries and any other compensation due and payable to the employees of Owner, special assessments, premiums for hazard and liability insurance and any other insurance required, and sums otherwise due and payable by Owner as operating expenses which are incurred pursuant to the terms of this agreement including management and other fees as provided herein.

3. Broker shall deposit gross revenues collected into a special trust account in a bank whose deposits are insured by the Federal Deposit Insurance Corporation. Broker shall have authority to endorse checks payable to Owner, deposit funds of Owner into said trust account, and to draw on such account any payment to be made by Broker to discharge any of the liabilities or obligations incurred by Broker pursuant to this agreement.

4. Broker shall arrange all repairs, replacements and decorating necessary to maintain said property it its present condition and for the operating efficiency of said property. The expense of any one item of maintenance shall not exceed the sum of $_____ unless authorized by Owner or unless Broker determines it to be an emergency. Owner approval is not required in the event of an emergency where immediate repairs are required to preserve the property, continue essential services to the property, avoid danger to life or property, or to comply with federal, state or local law.

5. Broker shall have the authority to negotiate, prepare and execute all leases and to cancel and modify existing leases as agent for Owner.

FIGURE 3.1 (CONTINUED)
Management Agreement

6. Broker shall advertise the availability for rent of the property or any part thereof and to display "For Rent" or "For Lease" signs thereon; to show property to prospective tenants; to execute leases, renewals or cancellations of leases relating to said property; to terminate tenancies and to sign and serve for Owner such notices as Broker deems appropriate: to institute legal actions in the name of Owner; to evict tenants and recover possession of said premises; to recover rents and other sums due, and to settle, compromise and release such actions.

7. Broker shall have authority to hire, supervise and terminate on behalf of Owner all independent contractors and property employees, if any, reasonably required in the operation of said property. All such property employees are employees of Owner.

8. Broker shall maintain accurate records of all moneys received and disbursed in connection with its management of said property, and such records shall be open for inspection by Owner at all reasonable times. Broker shall provide monthly financial statements to Owner.

Owner agrees to maintain a minimum balance of $_____ in Broker's trust account and in the event the amount falls below such minimum balance, Owner hereby agrees to pay such excess promptly upon the request of Broker.

Owner agrees to make available to Broker all data, records and documents pertaining to the property which Broker may require to properly exercise Broker's duties hereunder.

Owner shall complete and submit a lead-based paint disclosure if property is residential and built prior to 1978 as required by federal regulation.

Owner authorizes Broker to:
    a. cooperate with brokers who represent tenants and
    b. compensate cooperating brokers from Broker's fees
    c. compensate Broker's agent

Owner agrees to hold Broker harmless from all damage suits in connection with the management of said property and from liability from injury suffered by any employee or other person whomsoever and to carry, at Owner's expense, adequate public liability insurance and to name Broker as co-insured. Broker also shall not be liable for any error of judgement oR for any mistake of fact or law, or for anything which Broker may do or refrain from doing hereunder, except in cases of willful misconduct or gross negligence. If suit is brought to collect Broker's compensation or if Broker successfully defends any action brought against Broker by Owner, relating to said property, or Broker's management thereof, Owner agrees to pay all costs incurred by Broker in connection with such action, including reasonable attorney fees.

This agreement may be later amended or modified at any time by a written mutual agreement signed by Owner and Broker.

Broker will not discriminate based on race, color, creed, religion, sex, national origin, age, handicap or familial status and will comply with all federal, state and local fair housing and civil rights laws and with all equal opportunity requirements.

Broker accepts this exclusive employment and agrees to use due diligence in the exercise of the duties, authority and powers conferred upon Broker under the terms hereof.

Receipt of a copy of the contract by the owner has been acknowledged.

Owner	Date	Owner	Date
Social Security Number or Tax Identification Number		Social Security Number or Tax Identification Number	
Address		Phone Number	
City/State/Zipcode			

_____ by _____
            Broker   Agent

authorized corporate officer should execute the agreement, and, where required, the corporate seal should be affixed to the document.

When applicable, the management agency, rather than the specific individual who will be in charge of the property, should be listed on the contract. In many states, licensing laws require all listing and management contracts to be signed in the name of the broker. Laws in effect in the state where the property is located should be followed. If the manager represents a management firm, the manager will sign as the authorized representative of the firm.

Identifying the property   Although a full legal description usually is not required, the property must be described so as to leave no doubt concerning its identity, location, and extent. For individual houses, the street address of the property often is sufficient identification. With commercial property especially it is important to supply the street address plus a careful description of the exact land area and both main and auxiliary buildings to be managed. If the property has a special name, as is frequently the case with apartment complexes or shopping centers, that name should be specified in the contract.

Exclusions   Exclusions should also be noted. For example, if the owner of an office building that has a restaurant and bar on the first floor wants to deal directly with the restaurateur, the property description in the management contract should specifically exclude that particular area.

Contract Period

Next, the contract must stipulate a term of service. There is no single standard term for a management contract. Its length is a function of the size of the property, the responsibilities delegated to the manager, and the future intentions of the owner or owning body.

Terms vary   Long-term contracts are uncommon. Some owners want a provision for cancellation. Other owners may be thinking of selling their property in the near future and do not want to hinder the sale with a long-term management contract that cannot be canceled.

On the other hand, the manager who assumes responsibility for a large new property, exerting a considerable initial effort to lease the premises and set up a management system, wants sufficient protection as compensation for his or her extra effort. Therefore, management agencies usually will seek a minimum one-year contract period. The amount of additional time requested under the terms of the contract will depend on how much initial effort is needed to take over the management of the premises and obtain a profitable lease-up rate.

Thus, clauses in standard management contracts leave the length of the agreement open so that a mutually satisfactory number of years can be inserted in the appropriate blank. Contracts may be for a definite period of time or may also contain a provision for automatic renewal on a yearly basis unless notice of termination is given within the period set forth in the contract.

Termination   Generally, language is included to permit either the owner or the management agent to terminate the agreement by giving appropriate notice. Most agreements may be terminated before their expiration date by the agent if he or she may suffer damages or liability as a result of the owner's failure to comply with the requirements of any applicable statute, law, or government regulation. In such cases, cancellation takes effect when the owner is served with notice of the agent's intent to terminate the agreement.

Notice to terminate may be served in person or by registered mail to the address listed on the contract. Mail notices should be sent "Return Receipt Requested." Cancellation is considered to be effective when the notice is deposited in the mail. Termination by the agent due to an owner's illegal acts does not release the owner from his or her obligations under the contract terms.

The longer the agreement, the more likely things will change. Procedures for future amendments should be built into the management agreement to adapt the agreement to changed circumstances.

Management's Responsibilities

The manager is responsible for conveying to the owner information regarding the property. The following reports offer an idea of the status of the property and insight into the effectiveness of the owner.

Monthly reports and disbursements   The owner depends on the agent to prepare a monthly earnings statement itemizing income and expense for the owner's property. The management contract should specify the name and address of the person, corporation, or board of directors (as in the case of a cooperative or condominium) to receive the report; and the date on which it is to be submitted. The names, addresses, and percentage amounts for all recipients to whom the agent must dispense monthly payments usually are listed in the contract.

The contract should clarify how to deal with a month in which disbursements exceed receipts. Under some contracts, the manager is authorized to hold a certain sum of money in reserve to meet expenses that may come due between the time of disbursements and the time the next monthly rental income flow begins. The amount of this reserve fund should be proportional to the size of the property. Agents should not generally advance their own funds to cover a deficiency.

Surety bonds   As a rule, the property manager's employees who handle funds have to be covered by a surety bond, obtained at the manager's expense. A surety bond is a type of insurance that protects against loss in the face of employee theft.

Handling funds   Most contracts (and most state laws) require the manager to maintain a separate bank account for the owner's funds. That is, the owner's funds should never be commingled with the agent's personal or business funds. Traditionally, if the manager worked for more than one owner, the manager set up an individual account for each client. However, with today's software programs, the manager can easily track deposits and expenditures in one bank account without the necessity of multiple accounts, checks, and deposit slips.

Authority to rent, operate, and manage premises   The terms of the contract should list the agent's authority to lease, collect rents, terminate tenancies, return security deposits, evict tenants, and bring legal action for recovery of lost rents. The most important is the agent's authority to sign leases, for the statutes of fraud in most states do not consider an oral lease agreement of more than a certain duration (usually one year) to be enforceable. Some owners insert a clause in the contract limiting the agent's authority to sign leases to a certain dollar amount or to a maximum period, such as five years or less in the case of many commercial properties. Agents for residential properties generally have the authority to sign standard leases for the maximum term established by the owner's policy.

Expenditures   Expenditures for maintenance, personnel, and services are an inherent feature of property management, but the amount the agent may incur without consulting the owner must be stated in the contract. Some contracts contain a clause that gives the agent the power to enter into contracts not to exceed a certain amount for utility services, rubbish removal, window cleaning, or other recommended services. For the protection of the agent, such clauses should carry a caveat making the owner responsible for any such agreements upon termination of the contract.

Marketing costs   Advertising is considered part of the normal operating expense for many properties and, as such, is usually charged to the building and absorbed by the owner. The amount of the advertising budget is typically recommended by the management company and approved by the owner.

Agent's control over personnel   The management contract should also specify the agent's powers to hire and fire maintenance personnel for the premises. These powers will vary from contract to contract; as a general rule, though, the manager who is going to be responsible for the work done by building employees should also have the power to hire and supervise them. A manager who is permitted to hire the operating staff is usually expected not only to obtain liability and worker's compensation insurance for building personnel, but also to file returns and other reports required of the owner-employer by federal and state governments. The manager who hires and supervises employees must also decide whether the salaries of building employees and clerical staff will be charged to the building or to management operations. These expenses, which can have a major impact on financial statements and returns, should be clearly stated in the contract.

One difficult situation occurs when the owner reserves the right to hire, supervise, and fire employees who work at the property, particularly when building personnel have been employed by the owner for a long period of time. If this is the case, the property manager should seek protection through a clause stating that building personnel are employees of the owner, not the agent. This clause should explicitly set forth the owner's obligation to pay all settlements, judgments, damages, penalties, back-pay awards, court costs, attorneys' fees, and other costs arising from litigation of claims, investigations, or suits that may arise from alleged or actual violation of state or federal labor laws.

Owner's Responsibilities

The management agreement should spell out the owner's responsibility for miscellaneous management expenses. It should contain a clear statement designating the person responsible for each item of management and maintenance expenses, including the following:

- Payroll—maintenance, security, and supervision
- Insurance—employee and fidelity premiums
- Payments on owner's behalf
- Bookkeeping and auditing
- Building expenses and repairs
- Advertising for tenants
- Management fees

Payroll Unless previously agreed upon, the management contract should also clarify whether the manager or the owner is the employer of the maintenance employees. The employer may not actually be the same person who is responsible for hiring and supervising the employee.

Some management companies engage a third party to process all paperwork necessary to meet all statutory requirements governing the employer-employee relations, including payroll. The employees work for the employer; the third party simply exercises all human resource responsibilities.

Insurance The contract also should specify that the owner will carry, at his or her own expense, sufficient liability and workers' compensation insurance. The owner and the manager should be named as coinsureds on these policies, and the owner should provide the manager with certificates of evidence for such coverage. For the manager's protection, a stipulation should be included that the manager may purchase such insurance at the owner's expense if certificates of coverage are not produced within a reasonable period. It is in the manager's best interests to review the terms of these policies, for the owner usually looks to the manager to work closely with the insurance agency to settle any claims that might arise.

Purchasing   The owner should agree in the contract to give the agent a schedule of payments that must be made for debt service, taxes, special assessments, or insurance premiums. The manager can then budget or establish reserves for these items.

Building repairs   It is important for the management agreement to contain a clause that requires the owner to make any repairs and replacements necessary to keep the premises in their current condition and operating efficiently. Thus, the owner will be responsible for complying with the terms of the lease agreements, minimum housing codes, and any other applicable laws.

Advertising   The management contract should clarify advertising responsibility. Generally, it is the owner's responsibility with smaller, scattered site housing. As previously noted, advertising may be a management cost in very large apartment buildings and commercial properties. If it is an owner cost, limits should be set.

Management Fees

Management fees differ. Apartment buildings do not pose the same management problems as office buildings, and inner-city property has management needs that are different from those of suburban properties. Nonetheless, all contracts should specify the amount of the fee to be paid, when it is to be paid, and the manner of payment. Although no universal rule exists for establishing fees, two basic formulas will be discussed in detail in Chapter 9.

Flat or fixed fee versus percentage fee versus other fees   The type of property will determine the appropriate fee. A **flat fee** per unit may be most appropriate when managing a condominium or cooperative complex inasmuch as the owners want management to contain expenses, not increase them. The **percentage fee** is a wonderful incentive, on the other hand, for the manager to seek to improve the income of the building, although a minimum fee may be established to protect management fees if the building revenue drops.

Some owners are willing to pay a lump-sum fee or bonus when a new lease is executed or if the agent reaches certain lease-up goals.

Commissions to outside leasing agents   The management agent often is not the sole leasing agent for the property, especially for commercial property. Sometimes, the leasing fee is either split between the property manager and the leasing broker or wholly retained by the leasing broker. In other cases, the owner may agree to pay an additional amount when an outside broker or agent is involved. All possibilities should be discussed and agreed upon in the original management agreement.

Early termination   In all circumstances, the manager should see that the contract contains a clause that provides adequate compensation for the leases that the manager has already negotiated, should the owner wish to terminate the contract prior to its scheduled cancellation date. The owner should be able to terminate the management agreement upon service of proper notice as agreed to in the management contract, and the agent should receive payment for negotiating leases on behalf of the owner up to the date of termination. The contract should also contain a provision regarding current prospects with whom the management company is or has been in negotiation with and how the management company is to be compensated if those prospects become tenants.

Antitrust issues All fee structures must be negotiated between the owner and the manager, and terms should be kept between the two negotiating parties. Fees must not be discussed with other competing property management firms. If members of the property management profession try to impose uniform rates (or even appear as if they are trying to establish uniform rates), they will violate state and federal antitrust laws. Property managers must always be able to represent that the fees set by their firms have been established independently and must avoid any discussions with competing firms that may even hint at collusion. Penalties for antitrust violations include fines, imprisonment, or both.

■ TAKEOVER PROCEDURES

Once the contract between the owner and the property manager has been signed, the transfer of responsibilities for the property from the owner or the current manager should take place as soon as possible. The owner should take the responsibility for providing the manager or management agency with all data necessary for the efficient operation of the property. A takeover checklist for residential property, including a partial list of information needed by the manager, is shown as Figure 3.2. If at all possible, electronic files should be transferred as well. Also, the manager should personally inspect every inch of the property as part of the takeover procedure.

Minimum information At the minimum, the manager should obtain the owner's name, address, telephone number, Social Security or tax ID number, and state employment number, as well as the name, address, and telephone number of the owner's attorney, accountant, insurance broker, and any other consultants for the property. If the property is new, the manager should be given the name of the architect and the construction firm, as well as a complete set of "as built" building plans and specifications.

The owner should supply the name and address of any mortgagees, as well as mortgagors under any assumed mortgages on the property and the amount and due date of loan payments, real estate tax bills, and existing insurance policies. The owner also should furnish copies of all contracts for services, employment records, and federal and state employment reports. The records should include wages, pay periods, Social Security number, and fringe benefits for each employee. Finally, the manager must obtain the names, addresses, and telephone numbers of service contractors such as plumbers, electricians, suppliers, and on-site employees.

FIGURE 3.2
Takeover Checklist

Residential Property Takeover Checklist

Property address: _____

Title held as follows: _____

Owner's name: _____

Address: _____ Phone: _____

Original statements and vouchers sent to: _____

Additional statements to: _____

Property identification number: _____

Owner's attorney: _____

Owner's accountant: _____

Owner's insurance broker: _____

Construction firm: _____

Architect: _____

Copies of plans and specifications to: _____

Mortgagee: _____

Amount and due date of loan payments: _____

Washer and dryer service agency: _____

Percentage to building: _____

Electric account numbers: _____

Gas account numbers: _____

Water account numbers: _____

Scavenger service: _____

Exterminator service: _____

Other contractors (lawn, pool, HVAC, etc.): _____

_____

_____

_____

Secure current list of all rents, including:

❏ Secure all employment records.
❏ Obtain copies of prior tax pay-
   ments on employees.
❏ Secure current real estate tax bills.
❏ Power of attorney for taxes.
❏ Review accounts payable ledger.

❏ Building number
❏ Apartment size
❏ Rental rates
❏ Names of present
   tenants

❏ Copies of all leases
❏ Special lease clauses
❏ Security deposits
❏ Vacancies

Comments: _____

_____

_____

_____

_____

_____

Lease information   The manager must have a listing of all rental units, copies of all leases, and a schedule of rental rates for each space. Additionally, the manager will want to know layout plans, the names of the present tenants, all available financial data, the current dates to which rents have been paid, any present delinquencies, and the sources and amounts of additional income. In many cases, the manager will have to prepare these schedules from basic documents because some owners do not keep complete and well-organized records.

Accounts payable   The owner (or authorized representative of the owning corporation) and the manager should study the accounts payable ledger when the management agreement is executed and agree on each party's specific liabilities for expenses. Unpaid bills should be tended to and the parties should set an exact date on which the manager will become responsible for paying expenses from allotted funds.

After receiving the necessary information from the owner, the manager must set up accounting records. Notice of the takeover should be given to all suppliers, service contractors, on-site employees, and tenants.

Transfer of Working Capital Fund

A working capital fund for operating expenses is essential and should be an amount equal to one month's uncontrollable expenses, such as debt service and salaries. It is best for the owner to supply this fund. In other cases, working capital must be derived from current rental collections as the new manager takes over the building's assets and liabilities; this can be done by holding back the profits from the first few months' operation for contingency reserves.

Security Deposits

Accounting for tenant security deposit balances is an essential part of any takeover. In many states, failure to return deposits or pay interest when required is a violation of the landlord-tenant law and grounds for real estate licensee disciplinary action, and it may also incur costly monetary damages.

■ CONTINUING OWNER-MANAGER RELATIONS

Having assumed responsibility for the property, the manager must now begin to build a mutually satisfactory relationship with the owner. The owner (or the owner's authorized representative) should get to know the person or persons who will actually manage the property, who may or may not be the person who negotiated the agreement. However, in many large management firms, if a corporate officer executed the contracts, then it is wise to introduce the owner to the specific account executive for that property. To avoid confusion, from this point on, only one member of the management firm should deal with the owner. The account executive—the person most responsible for the property—can build a smooth and profitable working relationship between the owner and the management firm by being fully apprised of the particulars of the premises.

Monthly reports   Personal contact with the owner or owner's representative can be made by a short visit, telephone call, or e-mail. Letters and e-mail messages can be used to reach an owner who is out of town and to confirm decisions already reached through personal discussions or telephone conversations.

The monthly earnings report is often the principal means of regular communication between the manager and the owner or owning corporation. This report usually includes rental receipts, miscellaneous income, gross income, an itemized list of all disbursements and operating expenses, total expenses for the month, cash on hand at the beginning of the month, amount forwarded to the owner, and cash balance on hand. (Monthly income and expense reports are treated at some length in Chapter 9.)

Either in the monthly report or in a separate letter the manager also should inform the owner of delinquent accounts and other events pertaining to the operation of the property. Above all, the monthly report should be honest and intelligently written to assure the owner that the manager understands how all the variables interact to affect the revenue from the property.

The manager can demonstrate continuing personal interest in the property by always including a cover letter along with the financial report. In routine months, the letter will probably say nothing more than operations were normal. The manager should explain unusual items in either the expense or income columns. If the normal income is lower than the owner anticipated, it is likely that he or she will think that the manager has failed in some way unless the manager offers a reasonable, clear, and convincing explanation of market trends or other controlling factors. If the monthly revenue is greater than expected, the manager should explain unusual items in either the income or expenses of the property.

Ongoing contact   A successful property manager must have the ability to manage human relations, and effective communication is a large part of this facet of the property manager's job. The manager must know what kind and frequency of communication the owner wants and how to fulfill that need. The contacts may be by phone, printed documents by fax or U.S. mail, or by e-mail.

The manager's ability to care for the property, coupled with the goodwill arising from personal contact with the owner, will build a lasting and mutually profitable business relationship between the parties. The manager must know which types of information are important to which owners and make sure they are informed accordingly. Furthermore, the property manager must be able to deal effectively with a variety of personalities and temperaments. Different degrees of tactfulness or bluntness are required for different types of people, and maintaining a productive working relationship requires the ability to tell when each is to be used or avoided.

■ SUMMARY

Property managers may be involved in the real estate management profession in one of three major ways:

1. As individual managers, who are directly employed by owners of individual buildings

2. As employees of management firms, which hire property managers to oversee numerous buildings under their care

3. As employees of real estate agencies that offer a variety of services, including a property management division

Managers may be either employees or contractors (agents) of the owner. Those who work for management firms and real estate agencies are employees of the organization, which in turn is the agent of the owner or principal.

A property owner and manager may enter into one of three relationships:

1. Employer-employee

2. Trustor-trustee

3. Principal-agent

A principal-agent relationship is created with a written property management contract signed by both parties. Certain legal and ethical considerations due the owner from the manager are implicit in this agency relationship. As agent for the owner, the manager must be loyal and pledge to act in the best interest of the principal and to handle all transactions in regard to the property with honesty and discretion.

A properly drawn contract outlines the responsibilities of the property manager. Management contracts should contain most, if not all, of the following:

■ Identification of the property and the parties to the agreement

■ Term of the contract and provisions for extending or terminating early

■ Manager's authority to make expenditures for normal operation of the premise without consulting the owner

■ How to cover expenses in months when income is inadequate

■ Manager's power to rent and operate the premises

■ Manager's authority to sign leases

■ Manager's role and financial limit in contracting for utility services, rubbish removal, or other maintenance services

■ Manager's role to hire and fire building personnel

■ Manager's responsibility to obtain liability and workers' compensation insurance

■ Owner's responsibility to obtain liability and workers' compensation insurance

The contract should clearly state the amount of the fee, when it is to be paid, and in what manner. Independent agent managers may charge a flat fee or a percentage of gross collectible income. Sometimes an additional fee is paid to the manager for his or her leasing activities.

The transfer of responsibilities for the property should take place as soon as possible after the contract between the owner and manager has been signed. The owner should give the manager the names, addresses, and telephone numbers of all persons involved in the affairs of the property, along with the owner's Social Security or tax ID number, the employee record files, and all service contracts. The manager also should have a listing of all current tenants, rent schedules, and rental units, plus copies of leases, layout plans, income records, current tax bills, insurance policies, and outstanding bills. The owner may establish a fund of working capital to cover operating costs or authorize the manager to withhold the first few months' profits for a reserve fund.

The property manager must consistently communicate with the owner and usually does so through the monthly earnings statement. This statement should always be accompanied by a cover letter (either hard copy or by e-mail) explaining any unusual items in either the expense or income columns. The cover letter demonstrates the manager's personal interest in the property and knowledge of how market variables interact to affect the revenue from the property. Visits and phone calls are sometimes necessary, depending on the urgency of the situation and the personal preference of the owner.

■ CASE STUDY

THE OWNER RELATIONS MANAGER

Doug Connors, CPM, is the owner of an Accredited Management Organization, which manages property for individuals, pension funds, and trusts. He started his property management career as an employee of a company that managed investment properties for a large number of owners. The owner of this company was a dynamic individual who had built up the business over many years.

When the owner died, however, succeeding managers failed to maintain good relationships with the client property owners. After losing many clients, the company was forced to close. One disgruntled ex-client, for whom Doug had been the principal manager, encouraged him to set up his own company and subsequently transferred its holdings to him to manage.

1. To avoid a similar situation with his own company, what can Doug do?

2. How can Doug add clients to his own company?

■ REVIEW QUESTIONS

1. The law of agency requires the manager to
   a. deposit the property's tenant funds in the manager's business account.
   b. maintain confidentiality and loyalty to the owner's best interests.
   c. obey the owner's every instruction, even if it requires unethical behavior.
   d. act with self-interest in managing the property.

2. A property manager acting as an agent
   a. owes the duties of care, loyalty, obedience, accounting, and disclosure to the principal.
   b. need not maintain a separate bank account for the owner's funds.
   c. has the power to mortgage the property.
   d. has the exclusive right to sell the property.

3. A bank employee is asked to manage the properties owned by the bank. At the very least, the employee should be given
   a. a power of attorney.
   b. written authorization to sign leases.
   c. a management contract.
   d. permission to evict tenants.

4. The written agreement between the owner and the agent that specifies the duties of each is known as a
   a. lease.
   b. management contract.
   c. listing agreement.
   d. power of attorney.

5. In identifying the owner in a management contract, the owner's name should be identified
   a. as it is written on the building sign.
   b. as it is listed on an ad valorem tax statement.
   c. by the full name of the chief stockholder, if a corporation.
   d. as it appears on the title to the property.

6. Any employee who handles the owner's funds should be covered by
   a. an employer liability insurance policy.
   b. an errors and omissions insurance policy.
   c. worker's compensation.
   d. a surety bond.

7. Most property managers seek agreements with a term of at least
   a. one year.
   b. five years.
   c. ten years.
   d. twenty years.

8. Under what circumstances may an agent terminate the management contract early and not be subject to a claim for damages by the owner?
   a. If the tenants request that the agent be replaced
   b. If the agent takes a personal dislike to the owner or some member of the owner's staff
   c. If the owner causes the agent damages or liability by violating a law
   d. If the management contract becomes unprofitable because of high vacancies

9. If a property owner violates any applicable law or regulation, the property manager
   a. may sue for damages.
   b. should spend trust funds to correct the violation.
   c. must report the owner to the state real estate commission.
   d. may cancel the contract immediately upon serving the owner with notice of intent.

10. When disbursements exceed receipts for a certain month, the management agreement will usually provide that the manager
    a. advance funds to cover the deficit.
    b. petition the owner to make up the deficit.
    c. stave off creditors until the next rental payments come in.
    d. pay costs from a reserve fund established previously.

11. Managers usually prefer to have the authority to hire and fire property personnel because
    a. the additional responsibility increases their management fee.
    b. employees will develop more loyalty to the manager under these circumstances.
    c. the manager does not want the owner to violate labor laws.
    d. property owners are generally poor judges of good employees.

12. If an owner reserves the right to hire and fire personnel for the property, the property manager should
    a. make it clear in the agreement that the employees are the owner's, not the property manager's.
    b. not accept the assignment.
    c. report the situation to the state department of labor.
    d. cancel worker's compensation insurance coverage.

13. A property manager's agreement provides for a leasing fee plus $13,000 per year for managerial services. What kind of agreement is this?
    a. Straight commission
    b. Fixed fee per rental unit
    c. Flat-fee arrangement
    d. Percentage fee

14. To a property manager, a percentage fee is preferable to a flat fee
    a. just after the real estate cycle has peaked.
    b. when the agent can significantly increase the revenue of the building.
    c. when the agent manages multiple properties for one owner.
    d. if all other accounts managed are on a percentage fee basis.

15. As responsibility for the property is transferred, the manager should pay special attention to
    a. the accounts payable ledger.
    b. the mortgage payments.
    c. other sources of income besides rental.
    d. a start-up cash fund.

16. A monthly earnings report submitted by the manager to the owner
    a. eliminates the necessity for any other contact with the owner.
    b. should always be accompanied by a personal note.
    c. should be sent by certified mail.
    d. must be certified by an independent accountant.

17. A flat fee arrangement would be MOST appropriate when managing a(n)
    a. superregional mall.
    b. condominium community.
    c. office complex.
    d. retail store.

18. Who should be the primary contact with the owner on behalf of the agent?
    a. Building superintendent
    b. Person most responsible for the property
    c. Office manager
    d. Attorney or accountant for the agent

19. The manager should include a personal note with each monthly report to
    a. maintain a good relationship with the owner.
    b. keep the report from going astray.
    c. distract the owner from bad news.
    d. keep the owner from becoming confused by the figures.

20. A property manager had to begin an eviction action for one of the tenants. This kind of information
    a. should be given to the owner annually.
    b. should be given to the owner on a monthly basis, at least.
    c. is evidence of a breach of the manager's fiduciary duties.
    d. is bad news and should always be delivered in person.

CHAPTER FOUR

MARKETING

■ KEY TERMS

Broker cooperation   Leasing agents   Rental centers
Classified ads   Press release   Supply and demand
Display ads

■ LEARNING OBJECTIVES

At the end of this chapter, the student will be able to

1. name the two most important marketing principles;

2. list three categories of marketing activities and give examples for each;

3. name and summarize the influence of three factors that shape marketing objectives;

4. discuss the pros and cons of at least five advertising methods;

5. summarize the marketing value of maintaining good public relations with the real estate community, the press, and the public at large;

6. explain the importance of direct selling by the manager, and discuss how to qualify prospects, to create interest and desire, and how to handle objections;

7. discuss the pros and cons of using leasing agents and rental centers; and

8. analyze the cost-per-prospect-per-lease basis.

■ OVERVIEW

The principal responsibility of a property manager is to make sure that a property generates income. To find the best possible tenants, it is essential that the manager conduct a marketing campaign that reaches the greatest number of potential tenants while at the same time maintaining cost effectiveness. Knowing various lease agreements and utilizing effective tenant management techniques are of little practical use unless potential tenants are actively attracted to the property and the space is skillfully shown. Otherwise, it is unlikely that many tenants will be willing to sign leases or to pay the rent.

This chapter discusses a variety of advertising methods that managers may use to attract potential tenants. It also reviews selling skills that are useful to secure tenants who will stay for a long time and will faithfully pay the rent.

■ MARKETING PRINCIPLES

■ The basic principles of marketing are "Know the product" and "The best source of new business is your present customer base."

Thorough preparation is required to know the product and maximum use of referrals is essential to any marketing effort.

Know the Product

Before putting space on the market, the manager should preview it to make sure that everything is clean and in good condition. Cleaning, painting, and any repairs should be completed before the space is shown to prospects. The property should be inspected between showings, or periodically if it has not been shown recently.

While inspecting the unit, the manager should identify the unique features of the building and of the particular unit, as well as any advantages and amenities of the general area, in order to highlight these in all marketing efforts. The property manager may be working in conjunction with independent leasing agents (as is often the case with commercial and industrial properties). If so, the manager must provide adequate information about the features and layout to the cooperating agents. If an independent agent cannot give a suitable presentation of the premises, the lease and commissions may be lost altogether.

Use Present Customer Base

Recommendations from satisfied tenants are the best and least expensive method of renting property. Tenants are most likely to give referrals on the basis of their own satisfaction with a space, but a tangible or cash incentive is sometimes offered for a referral that yields a new tenant. The referral method of renting space is most effective with multitenant properties, and may be used for residential, commercial, and industrial space alike.

Real estate license laws in all states prohibit splitting of commissions with an unlicensed person. In some states, that has been interpreted as prohibiting referral fees to any source, including paying fees to tenants who have made the referral. The manager should be familiar with local and state laws.

At the very least, the manager should thank a tenant who supplies a lead on a prospect and should request permission to use the tenant's name when contacting the prospect. This can significantly improve the manager's chances of converting the prospect into a tenant. If the referred prospect signs a lease, the manager should personally thank the tenant who provided the lead, often with a small gift. This display of appreciation will encourage more referrals.

Civil Rights Compliance

Advertising content must comply with certain guidelines set forth in various federal and state statutes and county and city ordinances. This is to avoid the appearance of marketing to one type of tenant and not others, if the content is based on race, color, religion, national origin, familial status, and handicap. Although these laws have particular impact on residential property, the property manager must be familiar with them when marketing any type of property.

For example, display ads should display the equal housing logo and slogan. Failure to do so can be interpreted as prima facie evidence of discrimination. The logo is not required in a classified ad; however, the newspaper must carry an introductory paragraph to the housing classified section stating that the properties advertised are offered without regard to race, color, religion, national origin, sex, familial status, or handicap, and that the newspaper will not knowingly accept discriminatory advertising. (See Figure 4.1.) There are severe penalties for violations. Civil rights considerations are discussed in more depth in Chapter 10.

■ MARKETING ACTIVITIES

> As a rule, a good product backed by a well-designed advertising and promotional program will rent faster in the marketplace—and for a higher price—than its average competitor.

When the real estate climate is favorable, good property that is marketed effectively can be rented even at a premium rate. The following activities contribute to the property manager's goal of rapid rental to a good clientele at a profitable rate:

1. Advertising campaign strategy and methods

2. Promotional efforts

3. Personal selling activities

FIGURE 4.1
Equal Housing Opportunity Classified Ad

EQUAL HOUSING
OPPORTUNITY

All real estate advertised in this newspaper is subject to the federal and state Fair Housing Act which makes it illegal to advertise "any preference, limitation or discrimination based on race, color, religion, sex, handicap, familial status or national origin, or an intention to make any such preference, limitation, or discrimination."

The newspaper will not knowingly accept any advertising for real estate which is in violation of the law. All persons are hereby informed that all dwellings advertised are available on an equal opportunity basis.

■ ADVERTISING CAMPAIGN STRATEGY

Advertising campaigns refer to the media and marketing methods available to stimulate desire and action on the part of potential residents, commercial enterprises, and industrial firms. There is no right or wrong way to market specific rental properties, as each one is unique. Before deciding on any advertising, the manager needs to determine a detailed plan that is shaped by three factors:

1. The type of property

2. Supply and demand

3. Available financial resources

Type of Property

The strongest influence over the design of the marketing campaign is the kind of property, as residential, commercial, and industrial properties have unique pools of potential tenants. Also, new, empty properties require a more active initial lease-up campaign than older buildings, which already have most of their space occupied and enjoy an established reputation and referral clientele.

Industrial manufacturers in the market for warehouse space will probably consult an industrial broker rather than the classified section of the newspaper. They often let this broker, sometimes called a "straw broker," search and negotiate for them while keeping their identities secret. A large billboard located near an industrial area and easily visible from a major thoroughfare can help draw the attention of these potential tenants.

Commercial managers understand the importance of tenant mix and of traffic counts. These managers will often canvass businesses, even those in other locations, in order to find tenants for their own properties. These managers are involved with civic and trade organizations, and often network extensively with agents in other cities. A large sign posted on or near an office building or in the window of a vacant store might also attract commercial tenants, as will advertising in the weekly, special pull-out business sections promoted by many city newspapers.

On the other hand, a family looking for an apartment is more apt to comb the rental section of the newspaper, to canvass a neighborhood for vacancy notices, or, increasingly, turn to Web sites such as Facebook or *www.craigslist.com*. Because residential tenants are often looking for location (close to work, close to schools, etc.), the most effective way to advertise is often the most simple: a For Rent sign at the property.

Supply and Demand

The balance between **supply and demand** in an area can create two different marketing situations for a property. The manager must determine if there is a high or low vacancy rate in the areas, and plan accordingly.

Low vacancy rate   There is little need for a massive marketing program if the units are the size most in demand and if the consumers can afford the current rents.

If part of the general management plan includes raising rents, a well-planned promotional effort is required to enhance the prestige of the building, in order to generate consumer demand and a higher rental schedule. Impressive, well-designed, and often costly advertisements are needed to build an elite image for a low-vacancy property. The desired image can be projected to potential consumers through a modulated, evenly paced advertising campaign running for an extended period.

High vacancy rates   When the property has a high vacancy rate, it must be marketed to draw as many potential tenants to the premises as quickly as possible. Spending money on a major advertising campaign, and thus increasing expenses, runs counter to the natural instincts of some property managers, which is to cut expenses when business is bad. In fact, the best way to avoid further losses is to advertise and promote the property more heavily.

The focus, force, and frequency of advertisements used in a high-vacancy market will differ from those in a stable market. Attracting potential tenants for immediate occupancy of vacant units is a more urgent marketing concern than is upgrading the image of the property. The emphasis of the advertising campaign in the former situation will shift from quality to quantity, because short-term results are of greater economic import than long-range benefits.

Financial Resources

The financial status of the property usually has a direct effect on how much can be allocated to advertise and promote it. The strategies open to the manager may be limited if the total advertising budget is inadequate.

A fairly clear picture of the sources of potential tenants and the demand for a particular type of space in the area should have emerged from the market and property analyses that the manager performed before submitting a management proposal. This information and the amount budgeted for advertising and promotion give the manager all the data necessary to select the best techniques for reaching the most prospects at the least cost.

■ ADVERTISING METHODS

There is a saying in real estate: If prospects must call to ask the price, chances are they cannot afford the property. Likewise, if they must call to ask the location, they probably will not like the location. Effective advertising will offer both to cut out unwanted, time-wasting calls.

Subsequent chapters explain which techniques and which media are more effective for marketing specific kinds of property (residential, office, retail, and industrial). The marketing techniques reviewed and illustrated in this chapter are meant to clarify the manager's role in marketing space in general.

Promotional efforts are used to obtain publicity without paying direct advertising costs. Promotion includes good public relations, cooperation with outside brokers, and periodic press releases. The property manager can choose from a number of advertising and promotional methods and media to reach a target audience. The choice for any given market situation depends partially on the type of property involved.

Signs

All residential, office, and retail properties should exhibit a sign affixed to the premises identifying the management firm, the type of space, and the person to call for further information. For Rent signs should be clearly visible, simple, attractive, and in good taste. They should never include anything that could be considered discriminatory. Signs on the property are the least expensive, most effective method of advertising. However, their usefulness in filling vacancies differs depending on the type of property.

For Rent signs stating the type of unit presently vacant and the person to contact are often productive in front of residential buildings and in vacant store windows. They can also be useful in front of a single-family home in a residential neighborhood.

Highway billboards should be used when advertising larger industrial and commercial properties, because industrial users often drive around to observe buildings and call on people in the area they prefer. Billboards are directional in nature and should carry only basic information about the property and its location, and the person to contact. Larger residential and commercial properties should have a small office on the premises where tenants and prospects can make inquiries. The building directory in the lobby should list this office and its room number under several headings (Building Office, Management Office, or Rental Office, for example).

Newspaper Advertising

Newspaper advertising is divided into two types: **classified** and **display ads.** Classifieds are relatively inexpensive per line of copy and are the most prevalent method of advertising residential properties. Classified newspaper ads are listed alphabetically by subject and sometimes by area at the back or in a separate section of the paper. The sample residential classified shown in Figure 4.2 is brief yet informative.

FIGURE 4.2

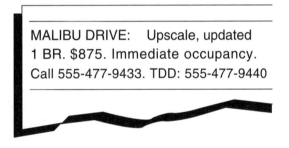

MALIBU DRIVE: Upscale, updated
1 BR. $875. Immediate occupancy.
Call 555-477-9433. TDD: 555-477-9440

Display ads carry greater visual impact than classifieds because they are larger and more elaborate in design. They also cost more. The display ad shown in Figure 4.3 effectively markets a variety of apartments and also plays up image and desirability. Display ads for industrial or commercial property often appear in the financial pages but may be placed in any section of the newspaper. Developers of large residential projects may promote new property complexes by inserting quarter-page or larger ads in the real estate sections of major papers.

An effective newspaper advertisement should be directed to a specific prospect. Such an ad attracts attention by stressing the benefits of the property and its services. The description of the advantages is followed by the location of the property, date of availability, times it can be seen, and names of people to contact.

Whether a small classified or a large display ad, two major themes can be used to attract attention quickly: use the word *free!* And give a reason for the prospective tenant to act now!

FIGURE 4.3
Display Ad

Source: Property managed by Seldin Company, Omaha, Nebraska.

For example, the residential manager can offer a *free* trip, *free* swimming lessons, *free* tennis lessons, *free* use of the clubhouse, etc. To encourage a prompt call, the ad might specify that the first six new approved residents will receive the first month's rent *free!* Or the offer should end at a specific time or date not to exceed ten days from the first day that the ad is published.

Internet Sites

Increasingly, prospective tenants are turning to the Internet to locate new properties. Every type of tenant is using the Internet: residential, commercial, and industrial. Even prospects interested in moving from one part of the city to another will first check the Web for housing options. Also, many print publications will reference a Web site. Thus, it is important that each management company maintain not only a company Web site, but also Web sites specific to each property. They should reference one another.

However, when developing a Web site, use caution; if the site is too fancy, prospects still using an older computer may not be able to download all the visuals, or will get tired of waiting and click to another site. As of the first quarter of 2010, on average, more than one-third of the country still does not have high-speed Internet. The percentages are higher for lower income, the disabled and elderly, and African Americans and Hispanics.

The manager should view other competitive sites to get a feel for what works and what does not. And, while the initial cost of setting up a Web site, ranging from $2,000 to $10,000 or more, may seem high, management should remember that the Web site is available 24/7—that is, night and day, worldwide. Moreover, no printing and mailing costs are involved. Once the Web site is established, every promotional piece, including signs, should reference the URL.

Web sites are constantly changing, so the following is only an overview. One particularly inviting site offered the following: an ongoing slide show of pictures of the outside of the property on the home page, which listed apartment availability, price, and amenities offered. The user could choose from any of the following: more photos (slide show format); maps/directions (linked to *Mapquest.com*); a virtual tour (like a movie trailer); floor plans; and a talking ad extolling the features of the property and the community in which it was situated. Some of these options would be difficult to use with a slow dial-up Internet connection.

Because of the immediacy when using the Internet, consumers expect that the information on the Web site is both current and reliable. Management should access the site frequently to ensure that the information on the site is the most current available. Also, users have the expectation that they will receive a response almost instantaneously. Someone in the office should be delegated to answer e-mail inquiries with a timely, appropriate response.

Many state real estate commissions have enacted rules and regulations specifically pertaining to Internet marketing by real estate licensees. Most simply state that the advertising be truthful and not misleading. The states that require more generally require the licensee to include his or her name, location of home office, and the states in which the licensee is licensed on every page controlled by the licensee (but not on linked sites not controlled by the licensee). Above all, advertising, whether in print or on the Internet, should never be discriminatory.

Periodicals and Other Publications

Regional magazines and trade journals are reliable and effective vehicles for advertising real estate, especially commercial and industrial properties. Most periodicals accept both classified and display ads.

Advertising in carefully selected nonregional journals can generate a list of qualified prospects, but the manager must be sure the property is large enough and has enough general nonregional appeal to merit this type of marketing. On a local level, properties can be advertised in programs distributed at sports events, plays, concerts, and other events. This method can be effective for residential, commercial, and industrial spaces.

Many metropolitan areas have apartment guides, apartment locators, and/or vacancy listings that are most effective for larger residential communities. These publications are usually distributed free at numerous high-traffic locations: supermarkets, airports, gas stations, and minimarkets. Apartment guides may be more expensive than newspaper advertising, but they can be quite useful for establishing a presence in the marketplace as they tend to encourage a steady stream of inquiries. These may be printed monthly or bimonthly, and many are linked to property Web sites. (For an example, see Figure 11.3.)

Radio

Radio advertising can be expensive. Though its audience is large, it is not select, which means many listeners are not potential buyers. Careful analysis of the cost per prospect is critical in broadcast advertising, for returns in many cases do not justify the expense. Radio is best employed on a community level for promoting large residential, commercial, and industrial developments. Local stations in major metropolitan areas can advertise available space in surrounding suburbs.

Television

The response to television advertising has varied throughout the country. The type of property and available budget will obviously have a great impact on any decision regarding the use of television. Because of its expense—television is the most costly of the media—managers should carefully research the success rate of previous television ads in their market areas. If comparable ads cannot be found to guide the manager, the initial financial obligation should be limited to a pilot program that can be used to gauge the success of further advertising.

Direct-Mail Advertising

Because of the expense involved to design, write, print, and mail a brochure or flyer, direct mail is effective only in cases where the mailing list contains well-qualified prospects. Industrial and commercial property owners and managers are most likely to use direct mail because they can compile a list of potential tenants for office, retail, or industrial space from the chamber of commerce and other local sources, such as the Yellow Pages. This marketing method can be cost-effective in terms of advertising expenditure per prospect.

The mailing list should include not only prospective tenants (major corporate executives in the case of commercial space) but also key brokers, either local or nationwide, depending on the property's appeal. In either case, the manager's objective is to make knowledgeable, active brokers aware that the property exists and that he or she is willing to cooperate with them in renting or leasing the space.

Brochures

Because of the high cost of development, brochures must be tailored to the recipients' interests and income level. Elaborate, expensive brochures randomly mailed to a broad readership will not provide the desired result; unsophisticated or inelegant handbills mailed to prestigious firms might actually provoke a negative response.

The more effective advertising brochure will have a central theme and will not try to cover every conceivable point about the property. This theme should run through the brochure's headlines, copy, and illustrations, as in the portions of the brochure used in mailing as shown in Figure 4.4. The brochure cover should set the themes of quality, convenience, and market. The other pages should appeal to the target market by showing how the facility will meet that market's needs.

If a direct mail advertisement is to stand out from all others, it must have special character and appearance. Layout should be kept simple, with lots of open space strategically arranged to guide the eye from the headline through the message to the name, address, and telephone number of the person or rental agent the reader is to contact. Short copy is best for quick and easy comprehension. Words should be used economically and all of the text should expand on the basic theme. Pictures can be effective—but use caution so that they are not perceived as discriminatory.

The regional market analysis discussed in Chapter 2 should outline vital selling points of the property. These are especially useful when designing brochures and mailing pieces to be sent to national and international tenants that require space in several major cities. Some large property management firms that cater to this type of tenant are geographically widespread; others use individual managers who travel widely. In either case, the information in the brochure and that gained from the market analysis can motivate the prospect to investigate a particular property.

Flyers

Flyers are less complicated, less formal, and less expensive than the brochures just mentioned since they can often be developed on the office computer. Flyers can be a very important marketing tool if presented correctly and to the right people, (i.e., present tenants, the best source of finding new residents). They can also be effective when distributed to human resource managers of nearby companies and managers of nearby convenience stores and motels.

The flyer should be designed to highlight the dollar amount, cash, or rent credit available to the present resident (if permitted by law), as well as any incentives to new tenants—for example, a discounted first month's rent to the approved new resident upon move-in. With little or no special expertise, someone in the office is often capable of using a software program to design an attractive flyer at little expense. Such a flyer should still be printed on good quality paper for the most professional look.

Mixed Media

An advertising campaign should not be limited to a single medium. For example, direct mail sent to a specially selected group of industries might be supplemented with a billboard placed at the side of a nearby freeway and a sign in the lobby of

FIGURE 4.4
Brochure

Highway 25
Folsom, Louisiana

~ Commercial Land for SALE in the Heart of Folsom ~
Five Commercial Lots For Sale
from 28,000 square foot to 5.48 acres
Grocery Store / Retail Sites / Commercial Use / with Outparcels
Zoned C-2

Exclusively Offered By: Duff Friend
(504) 555-9351 Phone
(504) 555-9336 Fax
www.latterblum.com   dfriend@latterblum.com

NAI / Latter & Blum
800 Common Street
Suite 1000
New Orleans, LA 70112

Source: Latter & Blum, Inc./REALTORS®, New Orleans, Louisiana.

the property itself. Creativity is especially important. For example, an architect's model of a large development displayed in a glass case at the airport along with supporting information might attract the interest of prospective tenants relocating from other cities. Whatever the media mix, the marketing campaign will be more successful if it is backed up with a permanent reference, such as a small sign on the premises identifying the management group or a listing in the Yellow Pages.

■ MANAGEMENT PROMOTIONAL EFFORTS

Community Involvement

Potential tenants are often attracted to a property because of the management firm's or the building's reputation, so it is important for a manager to maintain good relations with the real estate community, the press, and the public at large. This can be done by volunteering to address various interest groups and by sharing professional expertise.

Press Releases

Another way to enhance the reputation of the manager or the appeal of the property is through **press releases**, also called *news releases*. For personal publicity, an interesting factual article about a transaction, an idea the manager is implementing, an educational accomplishment, or a new trend in property management are always newsworthy themes. If the manager is not comfortable writing the news release personally, he or she should not hesitate hiring an advertising agency or freelance writer.

To attract attention to one particular property, a news release sent to local newspapers and publications should highlight the property's significant features—for example, size, amenities, historical importance, conversion or new usage, and striking architecture. This type of release can be particularly helpful in garnering publicity for the initial rental of large new commercial and residential developments. Depending on the topic, real estate journals and other trade magazines might be interested in writing an article from the information in the release (see Figure 4.5). Television coverage often can be arranged for new project announcements, ribbon cuttings, and open houses.

The primary advantage of publicity over advertising is that it is virtually free. It costs the manager only the time and effort spent to develop articles and press releases. News releases keep the name of a development or a management firm before prospective tenants and often have more credibility than paid advertising. The advantages of good publicity are so numerous that many large management companies engage independent public relations firms to work for them in this area.

FIGURE 4.5

Newspaper Article Developed from Publicity Materials

Randy Lenhoff, president and chief operating officer of Seldin Co., said the Ontario Place project is noteworthy because of its size and location in what has become a "midtown" area.

MATT MILLER/THE WORLD-HERALD

Apartments are result of long-term planning

◼ An Omaha company purchased the land for the complex more than 30 years ago.

BY GRACE SHIM
WORLD-HERALD STAFF WRITER

More than 30 years ago, the Seldin Co. purchased land on a site near Interstate 80 and South 72nd Street with plans to build apartments.

Ground finally was broken several weeks ago.

The Seldin Co. is owner of Ontario Place Apartment Homes, a 156-unit complex being built on the northeast corner of 74th Avenue and Ontario Street. The company said construction costs will exceed $5 million.

The 7.3-acre, five-building complex will have a clubhouse, a swimming pool, a health-and-fitness center and high-speed Internet access. The first building and the clubhouse are expected to be completed in late summer.

Randy Lenhoff, president and chief operating officer, said the characteristics that make this complex different from the 4,700 units managed in the Omaha area are its size and location in what has become a "midtown" area.

Despite Omaha's apartment occupancy rate, which is hovering around a several-year low of about 92.6 percent, Lenhoff said, a demand still exists in the part of the city in which Seldin is building.

See Seldin: Page 2

Ontario Place Apartment Homes
◼ **Location:** 74th Avenue and Ontario Street
◼ **Number of units:** 156.
◼ **Features:** Clubhouse, swimming pool, health-and-fitness center and high-speed Internet access.

Seldin: Apartments under way

Continued from Page 1
A recent market study showed strong demand for apartments in that area, and fewer concessions are being offered to prospective tenants, Lenhoff said.

"It'll be a year out when it's done, and we feel we're timing this (the construction of the project) pretty well," Lenhoff said. "It's a great location that's midway between west Omaha and downtown."

Lenhoff said that aside from the nearby Peony Village Apartments near 80th and Cass Streets, there hasn't been any major new construction of apartment complexes in the area.

A one-bedroom unit, with from 775 square feet to 1,000 square feet, will be rented for from $700 to $850. A two-bedroom apartment will have from 950 square feet to 1,500 square feet.

Two of the five buildings will have elevators, Lenhoff said, and 36 units will have attached garages.

Pat McNeil is president of McNeil & Co. Builders, the general contractor for the project. The exterior of the buildings will be brick and siding.

Some residents of the Westgate neighborhood have complained to the city that traffic from the complex will divert vehicles into their area and create a bottleneck at 72nd and Grover Streets.

Lenoff, however, said his company submitted a traffic plan for the development two years ago and the city approved it.

"We don't think it (the traffic) will cause a problem," he said.

The area has been zoned for apartments for 35 years, said Lenhoff.

Source: Omaha *World Herald*, Omaha, Nebraska.

◼ PERSONAL SELLING ACTIVITIES

Although all selling activities have as their ultimate goal the closing of a sale or lease, the property manager should take advantage of all opportunities to personally reach the customer. This means that sales efforts will be directed not only toward brokers and agents who can reach prospects but also toward prospective buyers and tenants.

Leasing with Broker Cooperation

◼ One of the most effective ways to market residential, commercial, or industrial space is to cooperate with outside brokers. Today, cooperation between managers and brokers is the rule, not the exception.

Broker cooperation can be especially beneficial when renting or leasing a new or very large development. Managers can alert key area brokers to available properties by mailing advertising pieces or newsletters, by sponsoring an open house, or by personal contact. Managers should indicate if they are willing to split the commission fees to be paid any further incentives offered by the owner.

Generally, the outside leasing broker with a qualified prospect will send a letter of registration stating his or her intent and the terms of the commission split before bringing the prospect to the manager's building. Many cooperating brokers will remain involved in the negotiations, as agent for the tenant. Obviously, the manager is representing the owner, so the manager will be obligated to work with a number of conflicting interests and parties.

Many professional real estate organizations constitute a built-in cooperative referral network. This marketing strategy is most practical for properties with more than local appeal, because it enables the manager to reach a target group over a broad geographic area. Members of the Society of Industrial and Office Realtors® and the National Association of Industrial and Office Parks can assist in leasing industrial space.

Managers of residential rental properties can and should make allies of residential real estate agents, since it is possible that the agents know of prospects who may not qualify for a 30-year home loan, but who certainly can afford to rent a house or apartment. Again, the manager should clearly indicate the referral fee to cooperating agents and should promptly pay those fees.

Direct Selling Skills

The first part of the marketing process, prospecting, is complete once the prospective tenant comes to the property manager's office or to the building. The manager's job is to convince this consumer, who has already expressed some interest in the property, that this space is more advantageous than any other available in the area. To do so, the manager needs selling skills.

Selling skills involve qualifying, dealing with objections, negotiating, and closing techniques. In a tight market, the manager could have an open house and, by creating the interest and desire, actually get the tenants to bid against each other. The manager must know how to show the premises and how to suggest judiciously that certain issues might be open to negotiation when the lease is drawn up. The manager also must be familiar with the space so as to answer questions, overcome objections, and point out relevant features to the prospective tenant. Finally, the terms of the lease must be negotiated, drawn up, and executed.

Qualifying the Prospect

Qualifying the prospect involves a number of factors: space needs, urgency, motivation for moving, and financial qualifications (which will be covered in Chapter 6). The manager is placed in a delicate position of learning more about the prospect and "selling" the prospect on the space, while making a decision as to whether this is the right tenant.

Space   Even before making an appointment to show the space, the manager should determine the prospect's needs and precise space requirements. For example, a commercial prospect might be asked the square footage that the prospect requires or a residential prospect might ask the number of bedrooms the prospect requires. The parties should discuss whether the prospect prefers a freestanding or multitenant building, desired price range, parking and transportation needs, the necessity for a traffic count, or other demographic information and any amenities the tenant requires. Although the questions are slightly different for commercial versus residential, the process is the same.

Sometimes prospects do not have an accurate idea of their needs, and the manager should be honest if the initial discussion suggests that the space is not suitable for that client. Rather than waste time showing the space, the manager should take the name and address of the prospect and check to see if a more suitable property is available. A prospect left with a good impression of the building and the management firm may call on the manager for a future transaction.

Urgency   A number of questions can be asked to understand the urgency or lack of urgency. Is relocation necessary or optional? When is the move planned? Why are they moving? Is this a temporary location or does the tenant see this as a long-term move?

Motives   The manager should study the prospect's motives and how they are expressed, because residential, commercial, and industrial tenants differ in their responses. Renting a residence tends to entail a much more emotional decision than selecting office space, so residential property managers must be attuned to the psychological nuances of a property's appearance. Commercial and industrial managers should be armed with facts when dealing with dollar-oriented commercial or industrial prospects (although an intangible, such as prestige, can enter into their decisions as well).

Decision making   An additional point to consider is whether the prospect is the decision maker or someone who is merely making initial inquiries. Particularly with commercial and industrial tenants, the manager must know who has the ultimate power to rent the space before entering into any serious negotiations. The corporate representative who first contacts the manager may or may not have that authority because leasing decisions are sometimes made by a board of directors. The manager should try to involve the primary decision maker in the transaction as soon as possible. This must be handled skillfully so as not to alienate the immediate contact, who may have considerable influence on the decision.

More detailed treatment of prospect qualification will be found in Chapters 11 through 15, which deal with managing specific types of properties. Financial qualification of the prospect is covered in Chapter 6.

Creating interest and desire

■ Talking about the property in great detail in the manager's office can sometimes be counterproductive. The prospect may visualize something totally different from the oral description and then be disappointed when actually viewing the property. There is no effective substitute for personally escorting the prospect on a tour of the premises.

Following are some basic rules to follow to present the property in the best possible way.

- **Getting there.** The manager should follow the most advantageous route from the office to the premises, using the drive time to point out amenities and services along the way. For example, during the drive to an industrial plant, the manager can show the prospective tenant transportation facilities located in the area. En route to an office complex or shopping center, the manager can describe other tenants on the premises to assure the client that there will be no close direct competition. Traffic patterns and other pertinent features of the neighborhood also can be seen from the car or on the walk to the space in question.

- **Play up positives.** During the tour, the manager can highlight the advantages of various features and how they might work for the prospect. Whether for commercial, industrial, or residential, the manager can comment on the excellent exterior condition of the building and describe the routine upkeep and operating procedures. Cleanliness of common areas, facilities the building affords its tenants, and management policy regarding tenant behavior are important points to raise with the client. Then the manager should permit the prospect to examine the premises alone.

- **Compare and contrast.** Unimproved commercial space presents the manager with a special problem. First, the prospect has to see the clean, vacant space that is available for lease; then, if possible, the prospect should be taken through comparable occupied spaces to see the effects of tenant alterations.

- **Determine the prospect's needs.** The manager should be selective about the number of units the prospect is shown. Care must be taken to involve the prospect in selecting the properties to view to avoid any appearance of steering (see Chapter 10). This is particularly true when showing residential properties. If too much space is shown, the decision-making process will become too complicated or the prospect may question the low occupancy. On the other hand, the manager must be able to assess the prospect's preferences and be willing to show additional space if the client is interested in a particular area or unit but is not quite convinced it is suitable.

Dealing with objections   Although the manager's job encompasses many different functions, understanding each prospect's requirements is among the most important. Questions and objections can be fielded quickly and intelligently if the manager has previewed the space and qualified the prospect in advance. If unable to answer a question, the manager should admit it, make a note of it, and then get back to the prospect with the information as soon as possible. The admission and the follow-up will demonstrate honesty and professionalism.

Some objections can be anticipated and handled before they are raised, particularly as to the condition of the property. The manager might reassure the prospect that such minor details as a leaking faucet will be taken care of prior to occupancy. More substantial requests, such as repainting an entire office area, could be negotiated in the lease terms. Problems such as these could be avoided simply by making sure that the available space is in the best possible condition before a showing.

Negotiating and closing   Negotiating and closing, critical points in the selling process, are treated in detail in Chapter 6. The property manager may find leasing agents and rental centers helpful as an aid in the whole process.

Leasing agents   In-house **leasing agents,** also called *real estate representatives* or *solicitors*, are sometimes retained by property managers as an integral part of the marketing campaign. These representatives disseminate information about the space to be marketed and follow up leads on prospective tenants. Their success hinges on their knowledge and personal selling skills, for they contact prospects directly in an attempt to stimulate interest in the property.

The advantage of in-house leasing agents over outside brokers is the additional control the property manager has over their activities. Leasing agents may be paid by a flat referral fee or a split-commission arrangement and may work full-time or part-time. Usually, the expense of compensating traveling or local agents is usually justified only for large, relatively expensive commercial and industrial properties. Some owners feel commission agents are expensive, but fees must be compared against total costs of full-time, in-house agents.

Rental centers   Despite the expense, a well-located, expertly staffed, smoothly operating **rental center** often is the best way to market large residential and commercial complexes. The rental center is a completely finished, attractively furnished space. It helps the prospect to "see" what the finished product will look like.

The decision to use a rental center should be based on the amount of available rental space, the expected rent-up period, anticipated turnover of tenants, and the sophistication of both clients and competitors. Rental centers are most appropriate for large developments, especially new or newly converted properties that must be rented initially. The higher the anticipated tenant turnover, the greater the utility of a rental center, because proper use of the center increases the ratio of new tenants to inquiries and uses time more effectively.

These centers are usually located directly within the project and include a display area, furnished models of the types of space available, a closing area, and, occasionally, the manager's office. Large directional signs should be positioned on the major thoroughfares throughout the area. Promotional aids such as brochures, site plans, floor plans, direct-mail flyers, photographs of the complex, and a scale model of the development to give the prospect an overall sense of the project and a better perspective on its buildings, interior layouts, and amenities can be displayed in the center.

Model space should be clean and attractive and the furnishings tailored to appeal to the target market. For example, traditional rather than contemporary furniture would be more appropriate for units that will be shown to conservative tenants. When decorating model offices, executive and clerical spaces should be highlighted and the arrangement should emphasize the flexibility of the units.

Managers have quickly and effectively marketed less-than-premium space with the following technique. The rental center is set up in one of the least attractive areas of the building or project and the models themselves are available for rental. When the rental center space is leased, another of the less appealing areas can be decorated as the rental center and subsequently rented.

A separate closing area with small tables and chairs should be set off from the rest of the rental center to offer prospective tenants property brochures, competent service personnel, and privacy. This part of the rental center forms the backdrop against which the selling process is culminated. In the event a rental center is not established, the manager should bring the prospect back to the office to discuss further details.

■ ECONOMICS OF MARKETING

Tracking Costs and Effectiveness

The prospect-generating cost of various advertising media, promotional efforts, and sales activities must be calculated to gauge the effectiveness of a marketing campaign. The expense of marketing property is often figured on a cost-per-prospect-per-lease basis. By keeping records, a property manager should be able to predict the number of prospects who must see the available space before a lease is signed and use these numbers to determine basic costs. Here are some examples to consider:

- A high-rise apartment that rents for $1,200 a month may have to be viewed by five prospects before it is leased. A small store in a strip shopping center might need 20 potential viewers. Suppose the manager of the high-rise apartment building spent $600 on a display ad in order to find a tenant. The cost per prospect would be a staggering $120 per prospect. However, the same $600 ad to find a tenant for the small store would cost only $30 per prospect, a more acceptable figure. (Of course, these examples assume that the $600 ad would produce the required number of prospects.)

- To rent the same high-rise apartment, the manager may run a $75 classified ad for five consecutive days to find a tenant. The total cost would be $375, which the building owner may consider quite high. However, the expense is justifiable because it results in a one-year lease worth $14,400 ($1,200/month × 12 months).

- Suppose the manager only advertises once a week, in the Sunday edition of the newspaper. The required five ads still only cost $375, but it will take five weeks to find a tenant for the property. So in addition to the $375 advertising costs, the manager is losing about $1,500 in rental payments. Under these circumstances, finding the new tenant will cost about $1,875. This is a considerable amount of money, and the manager may want to think about other ways to attract a tenant.

- The manager may be able to attract five prospects with one advertisement by lowering the rental by $100, to $1,100 a month. The cost of the rent reduction over the one-year lease period equals $1,200 ($100 × 12), and the ad costs $75. Using this method, the total cost to find a tenant is only $1,275, instead of the $1,875 discussed previously. This would mean a savings per tenant of about $600.

Obviously, it is imperative that the manager must use good judgment when making marketing decisions. Before deciding to lower the rent rather than spend more on advertising, the manager must also consider how decreasing the rental rate for one unit will affect similar space in the building. A rent reduction might jeopardize the entire rental schedule of the building.

■ SUMMARY

The marketing goal of the property manager is rapid rental to a good clientele at a profitable rental rate. To attain this goal, the manager must be adept at marketing, which includes preparation, advertising, promotion, and selling.

Designing an effective advertising and promotional campaign depends on three major factors: the type of property, supply and demand, and available financial resources. The method used to market a specific type of property is a function of the nature and number of potential tenants whose interest must be captured.

The supply and demand in the area may also determine the marketing strategy for a property. The focus, force, and frequency of advertisements used in a high vacancy market different from those geared to a stable market—this involves a shift from quality to quantity. In a stable market, a promotional program can enhance the prestige of the building, thereby generating consumer demand and allowing the owner to raise the rental rates. A high vacancy rate calls for a marketing campaign that draws many potential tenants to the property as quickly as possible.

The availability of financial resources is the third influence on the marketing strategy. In general, a marketing campaign should use several methods in combination, backed up with a permanent reference, such as a sign on the premises, or listing available property on your Web site. Depending on the type of property, advertising media may include signs, newspaper advertisements, periodicals, radio, television, direct mail and brochures, flyers, and an Internet Web site.

A property manager can increase rental ratios simply through good promotional efforts building on the reputation of the manager or the property itself. Press releases sent to local newspapers and journals are another efficient means of gaining virtually free publicity for specific properties.

Personal selling activities are directed toward brokers as well as toward individual prospects. Broker cooperation campaigns allow the manager to cooperate legally and financially with other key brokers when leasing new or very large developments. Employing in-house leasing agents can be cost-effective in marketing large properties.

Before showing the space, the manager should discuss the prospect's spatial and other requirements. If the property in question is not suitable for the prospect, the manager should seek to show space in another property managed by the same firm or at least take the prospect's name and address in case a suitable property becomes available. It is far better to make a good impression and lay the groundwork for future business contact than to waste the prospect's time. The prospect should also be qualified for urgency. Commercial and industrial property managers should determine whether the person they are dealing with has the authority to sign a lease and make decisions.

The manager can convince the prospect that the space in question is more advantageous than any other available space by skillfully showing the premises, by highlighting important features and benefits, and by knowing which issues may be open to negotiation. Managers working in conjunction with outside brokers should make certain that any broker who brings a prospect to the building is well acquainted with the space.

Although rental centers offer an effective way to show all types of property, they can be prohibitively expensive and staffing them can present problems. The manager should consider the size of the development, the number of units to be rented initially, and the expected tenant turnover before deciding to establish a rental center. Rental centers usually include a display area that contains promotional aids such as brochures, site plans, floor plans, photographs, and a scale model of the development as well as model units and a separate closing area.

The expense of marketing property is often figured on a cost-per-prospect-per-lease basis. Subject to market conditions and the specifications of the property, a definite relationship can be determined between the space for rent and the number of potential prospects required before one unit is actually leased. The management firm must keep accurate records of the number of prospects produced by the advertising and promotional efforts employed to calculate the prospect-generating cost of each in order to judge the effectiveness of a marketing campaign.

■ CASE STUDY
THE MARKETING MANAGER

Upon graduating from high school, Jon Milam enrolled in State College Business School with marketing as his intended major. In his second year of college, he married and he and his wife moved into an off-campus apartment project. When an opening was announced for assistant manager of this complex, Jon applied and was selected. He looked on the job as a way to get free rent while he finished college.

While earning his master's degree in marketing, Jon worked his way up to become manager of the complex, which belonged to a company that owned and managed numerous large apartment projects. The management of the company told Jon that they wanted him to improve the image of the apartment project and lower the vacancy rate.

1. What types of media might Jon consider using to meet the owner's two goals and why?
2. Create a brief outline of a marketing program Jon might develop to improve the image and prestige of the apartment project.
3. Would this be a good situation for the use of a rental center? Why or why not?

■ REVIEW QUESTIONS

1. All of the knowledge that the property manager has regarding lease agreements and the best management techniques are all wasted unless the manager can also effectively
   a. advertise the property.
   b. develop income from the property through marketing efforts.
   c. evict tenants.
   d. account for income and expenses.

2. Which of the following is a basic marketing principle?
   a. You can fool all of the people some of the time.
   b. You can fool some of the people all of the time.
   c. Money spent on marketing is better spent on improving the property.
   d. Your best source of new business is your present customer base.

3. Of the following, which shapes marketing strategies?
   a. Large numbers of vacancies; marketing is completely unnecessary when vacancy rates are normal.
   b. Property owner's ability to co-own certain forms of media.
   c. Extent of the owner's financial resources.
   d. Effectiveness of good leasing agents.

4. Which is the MOST accurate statement of the results to be expected from an effective marketing campaign?
   a. A good resident manager can keep a property well rented without a lot of advertising.
   b. Well-presented quality property cannot compete with poorly marketed property at a lower rate.
   c. Effectively marketing a property has no impact on its rental rate.
   d. A good product with well-designed advertising and promotion will rent faster and at a higher price than its average competitor.

5. A campaign to increase the prestige of a property logically should be undertaken
   a. when supply is high.
   b. if vacancy rates are increasing.
   c. in a stable market.
   d. when consumer pressure is great.

6. As the manager develops a marketing strategy, which of the following statements is the BEST guide?
   a. The kind of property to be promoted will not be a strong influence on the design of the marketing campaign.
   b. Each type of property requires certain advertising to reach the unique pools of potential tenants.
   c. If a marketing program is soundly conceived, the manager will not have to adjust rents for market fluctuations.
   d. New properties require a less active initial lease-up campaign than do established buildings with present clientele.

7. Other than signs on the property, the MOST popular medium for advertising residential property is
   a. billboards.
   b. classified ads.
   c. display ads.
   d. direct mail.

8. When developing advertising brochures, the property manager should begin by
   a. including comprehensive property information.
   b. keeping the layout simple.
   c. working around a central theme.
   d. gearing costs to target prospects.

9. Which of the following is the method *MOST* likely to be used by industrial tenants looking for warehouse space?
    a. Checking large billboards on or near the property
    b. Employing industrial brokers
    c. Hunting secretly through straw parties
    d. Checking the classifieds

10. When should For Rent signs be used?
    a. Carefully chosen times on all residential, retail, and office property
    b. Not generally useful in front of individual residential properties
    c. Used most productively when placed in vacant store windows
    d. Are not necessary if billboards are used

11. Which of the following statements is a *TRUE* statement about the effectiveness of each particular form of advertising?
    a. Regional magazines and trade journals are reliable vehicles for advertising commercial property for rent.
    b. Radio advertising is a cost-effective way of attracting new tenants.
    c. Response to television advertising has been negative throughout the country.
    d. Direct mail is favored when renting residential properties.

12. When planning an effective ad campaign, which of the following statements should the property manager remember?
    a. An advertising campaign need not employ more than one medium.
    b. Broker referral campaigns are too expensive to help with new or large properties.
    c. One advantage of in-house leasing agents is that the property manager has more control over them than over brokers.
    d. Referrals from satisfied tenants are the most expensive method of leasing property.

13. A property manager has been hired to market a new investment property. Of the following, the *BEST* way she can facilitate a broker referral campaign is to
    a. advertise in the Help Wanted classifieds.
    b. call the local office of the NAR.
    c. use signs on the property listing her number and saying "or call your broker."
    d. host a wine and cheese preview party for her fellow professional brokers in real estate organizations.

14. Which of the following is the *MOST* important action to take when showing a property to a new prospect?
    a. Be sure your personal appearance is appropriate.
    b. Learn the net worth of the prospect.
    c. Call and confirm the appointment.
    d. Inspect the property before you show it.

15. When a prospect comes to the manager's office in response to a marketing effort, the manager's job is to
    a. convince the prospect that the space is the most advantageous to the prospect.
    b. show the space without boring the prospect with a recital of special features.
    c. call in a trained salesperson.
    d. set up a later appointment to discuss lease terms if the prospect is interested.

16. Which of the following is a characteristic of a good rental center?
    a. Nominal investment and operating expense
    b. Best for small developments
    c. Needed in a strong market
    d. Often set up in the least attractive area for rent

17. Which factor below works against the establishment of a rental center?
    a. They are not really effective.
    b. They work only for residential property.
    c. They can be prohibitively expensive.
    d. Staffing them is a simple matter.

18. Which is the MOST effective ad on a per-lease basis?
     a. Display ad, inserted one time, costing $200, attracting 20 prospects before one lease
     b. Classified ad, inserted weekly four times, costing $100 per week, producing 16 prospects before one lease
     c. Radio commercial costing $50, resulting in five prospects before a lease
     d. Television spot costing $300, developing 30 prospects before one lease

19. A property manager is trying to market 4,000 square feet of retail space at $7 per square foot in an unfavorable market. The manager spent $2,000 this month in unsuccessful advertising. The owner would rather reduce the rent by $.50 a square foot and spend $500 advertising the space. If the manager takes the owner's advice,
     a. the entire rental structure of the building may be jeopardized.
     b. leasing the space will definitely cost less in the long run.
     c. the manager will make the owner happy and decrease the vacancy rate, both of which should be the manager's prime motivation.
     d. the manager should make sure that the $500 is spent on billboard advertising.

20. A $250-per-month apartment requires seven prospects before it is leased during active market conditions. If a $30 classified ad must be run for two days to attract this number of prospective tenants, the prospect-per-ad cost figure for this marketing effort would be
     a. $4.28.
     b. $8.57.
     c. $30.
     d. $60.

CHAPTER FIVE

LEASES

■ KEY TERMS

Actual eviction
Assignment
Constructive eviction
Escalation clause
Estate for years
Estate from period to
    period

Gross lease
Index lease
Net lease
Option to renew
Percentage lease
Restrictive clauses
Security deposits

Statute of frauds
Sublet
Tenancy at sufferance
Tenancy at will

■ LEARNING OBJECTIVES

At the end of this chapter, the student will be able to:

1. list and define four kinds of leasehold estates;

2. explain the differences between a gross lease, a net lease, and a percent-age lease;

3. name and explain at least five elements of a lease;

4. discuss the pros and cons of including the tenant's right to renew option;

5. summarize ways to protect the owner financially in a very long lease;

6. discuss why an owner should keep control of assignments and subletting; and

7. explain the importance of using attorneys to review all lease forms.

■ OVERVIEW

As explained in Chapter 3, the management contract formalizes the relationship between the property owner and the manager and specifies the rights and duties of each party. The lease sets up the rights and obligations of the landlord (owner/manager) and the tenant. This chapter discusses the estates and tenancies created by the lease as well as ways that rents are determined. As a lease is a contract, it must have certain essential elements, and additional common provisions are discussed.

All states and some cities have various laws regulating leases and the landlord-tenant relationship. Property managers must have a thorough understanding of those laws affecting the jurisdictions in which they operate.

Depending on the terms of the management contract, the property manager usually has responsibility for leasing the premises. Even those managers who have no active role in leasing should be consulted when drawing up the terms of the lease. Their knowledge of the costs and requirements for operating and maintaining the premises will have a direct impact on the lease terms.

Although the attorneys for the parties to the lease are responsible for its legal and technical details, property managers should be familiar with leasehold estates and basic lease clauses. It is most helpful to the transaction when property managers can cooperate knowledgeably with attorneys and leasing brokers.

Historically, leases favored the lessor because of the superior bargaining position of the landlord and the fact that attorneys representing the property owners and managers usually drafted the leases. This is changing, though, with revised legislation and judicial interpretation favoring the tenant.

■ LEASEHOLD ESTATES

A leasehold estate is of limited duration and is created when an owner or a property manager (acting as the owner's agent) grants a tenant the right to occupy the owner's property for a specified period of time in exchange for some form of consideration. The leasehold estate established a relationship that creates enforceable rights and duties for both parties.

Leases are contracts; contract rights are considered personal property rights. Either the landlord or tenant may transfer rights unless there is language in the contract that specifically prohibits such transfers. While the rights may be transferred, obligations usually remain with the original party, unless the obligations may be assumed by the new party. This is why most leases stipulate that the tenant cannot sell, assign, or pledge the leasehold interest without prior written approval of the property owner. A more common example is that of an owner who sells a leased-up apartment building. The new owner acquires not only the building but also the rights and obligations of the leases.

Although significant differences existed in the past, today, the terms *estate* and *tenancy* are generally used interchangeably. The following discussion of leasehold estates is based on common law characteristics. Property managers must consult state statutes for local law.

Estate for Years

An **estate** (or tenancy) **for years** is actually a misnomer. This tenancy is characterized as having a definite beginning and a definite end which can be as little as a week or as long as 99 years—or even longer. At the end of the lease, neither party is required to give notice that the lease is over. The tenant surrenders the property to the landlord. An estate for years is not terminated by the sale of the property or the death of either the tenant or the landlord. If either dies, the rights and obligations continue to their heirs.

Because an estate for years has a definite end, if the landlord wants notice that the tenant is planning to leave at the end of the term, the lease must contain a clause requiring the notice within a stated period. Although some states recognize an enforceable oral lease for less than a year, the prudent manager will put such agreements in writing.

Estate from Period to Period

An **estate from period to period**, or a periodic lease, is one that automatically renews unless either party gives notice of termination. These leases run week to week, or month to month, or year to year. Notice is often equal to the period, but the time of notice may vary from a minimum of one week to a maximum of six months prior to termination. This type of estate is not terminated by the sale of the property or the death of the owner or the tenant.

An estate from period to period may be created either by agreement or by operation of law. Express agreement is made when the owner actually leases his or her property to a tenant "to hold from year to year." Many residential leases are a combination of both an estate for years and a periodic lease. They begin as an estate for years (either a six-month lease or a one-year lease) and convert to a periodic lease.

A periodic estate arises by operation of law when a tenant has possession of the property and pays rent under an invalid lease or a lease that does not specify the duration of the tenancy. The frequency of rent payments in this case will determine the period of the estate. If rent is payable monthly, the tenancy is from month-to-month. The leasehold interest of a holdover tenant can be limited to a month-to-month extension by inserting an appropriate clause in the original lease agreement, and it is often in the property manager's best interests to do so.

An estate from period to period may also be created by operation of law when a tenant holding an estate for years remains in possession of the premises after the expiration of the lease. Acceptance of rental payments by the owner or property manager is considered legal proof of the owner's acquiescence to the holdover tenancy. Laws in most states consider a holdover tenant's leasehold interest to be of the same duration as that specified in the original lease agreement, up to a maximum term of one year.

Tenancy at Will

Tenancy at will is for an indefinite period of time. It exists only as long as both parties wish the estate to continue. In the past, an estate at will could be terminated without notice, but most states now require the party who wishes to terminate the tenancy at will to give some advance written notice. Property managers should consult their state statutes for the rights and obligations involved in tenancy at will. Unlike an estate for years or an estate from period to period, an estate at will is terminated by the death of either party.

Tenancy at Sufferance

Tenancy at sufferance occurs when a tenant obtains possession of the premises legally but then remains on the property after the expiration of the leasehold interest without the consent of the owner. This tenant has no right to possession. This tenancy continues until the owner brings legal action or the tenant voluntarily leaves.

An example of an estate at sufferance is the tenant who fails to surrender possession of the premises on the date specified in the lease agreement. The owner or the property manager, as the owner's agent, has two options when dealing with a tenant at sufferance. He or she may, under the common law, either evict the tenant without notice or acquiesce to the tenancy. The owner's acceptance of rent payments constitutes acquiescence and creates an estate at will or an estate from period to period. This is a complex issue and the property manager can sidestep costly legal entanglements by ensuring that the written leases conform to local laws and statutes. Special lease provisions can sometimes alter or clarify the rights and obligations of the parties. Again, always consult state statutes.

■ TYPES OF LEASE PAYMENTS

The three basic lease forms the property manager will be expected to administer are the gross lease, the net lease, and the percentage lease. The three types are differentiated by the manner in which rental compensation is computed and paid.

Gross Lease

Under a **gross lease,** sometimes called a straight lease, the tenant pays a fixed rental amount and the owner pays all other expenses for the property. Utility charges are generally paid by the tenant but may be negotiated between the parties. Most residential leases are gross leases.

Net Lease

Under a **net lease,** the tenant pays some or all of the expenses of the property in addition to the stated rent. Theoretically, there are three variations of the net lease: net, net-net, and triple net. The triple net leases usually run for longer terms, sometimes for periods of 50 years or more. A strict net lease obligates the tenant to pay utilities, real estate taxes, and other special assessments levied against the property in addition to the rent. The net-net lease generally requires the tenant to pay all items included under the net lease terms plus the insurance premiums agreed on in the contract. Agreed-on items of repair and maintenance are added to the net-net payments to determine the tenant's total payment obligations under a net-net-net, or triple net lease.

In practice, there is a great deal of overlap in the common usage of these terms. The differences between net and triple net leases are a matter of degree, i.e., how many extra expenses the tenant is required to pay. Therefore, the property manager should be explicit about the expenses the tenant will assume under any net leases and should call for a precise definition of net, net-net, or triple net lease whenever these terms arise. A net lease is shown in Chapter 15.

As property usage becomes more specialized, triple net leases are being more widely used, especially for industrial property. National franchising chains prefer net leases in leasing their retail outlets in order to control expenses and to ensure continuity from store to store. In another application, the owner of a tract of land may lease unimproved property to a tenant, who then constructs a plant or store on the site. The period covered by any such net lease must be long enough to make the tenant's building investment worthwhile. This type of lease is also called a ground lease, or land lease, and is one of the leases that might be recorded in the public records.

Percentage Lease

The **percentage lease,** sometimes called an overage lease, is commonly used for retail property. It usually provides for the payment of a fixed base rental fee plus a percentage of the tenant's gross income in excess of a predetermined minimum amount of sales. The advantage of a percentage lease from the tenant's point of view is that it is a long-term lease with a fair minimum rental, obligating the tenant to pay additional amounts only when the business volume justifies an increase. From the manager's and owner's point of perspective, the percentage lease implies that any new business is due to the location and management efforts.

Percentage leases are used quite commonly in malls. For example, management for malls will sponsor special shows to attract the widest range of potential shoppers. New cars, boats, craft fairs, and the like are brought in on a planned schedule and are varied to attract the widest range of people. The idea is that once people have entered the mall for the show, they will wander into the tenant's businesses and spend money. This is a win-win situation.

Although percentage payments may be prorated or paid monthly, payments are usually based on an annual computation. The percentage rate charged will vary greatly, depending on the nature and location of the property, the type of business occupying it, and the general economic climate. Percentage leases also may be based on a straight percentage of the tenant's gross sales, with no minimum, although this is rarely done. Chapter 14 contains a detailed discussion of a percentage lease, as well as a table showing some typical percentage ranges for various types of businesses.

To ensure that the owner receives the anticipated rental rate for the space, percentage leases often contain a recapture clause, which sets a minimum amount of rent that must be generated by the percentage of gross sales. If the minimum amount is not generated, the landlord may repossess, or "recapture," the premises. If the percentage actually generated by the tenant's business is below the minimum rental amount specified in the recapture clause, the tenant may be permitted to pay an extra rental fee so that the lease will not be canceled. This provision makes the recapture clause more equitable to the tenant. Most leases permit the manager/owner to audit the tenant's sales records to determine that proper payment is made.

Using software management   Tracking percentage lease payments is much easier using software. When setting up the property for the first time, in addition to the information required for most properties, the manager must include the percentage amounts on which the rent will be calculated. Often, the lease stipulates a certain base rent, and then adds on the percentage overage. Then, it simply becomes a matter of entering the reported monthly (or whatever term) income to start generating the monthly billing amount.

■ PROVISIONS OF A VALID LEASE

Statute of Frauds

The primary purpose of the **statute of frauds** is to prevent fraud or disputes over oral agreements. Written, oral, and implied leases are all covered by the statute of frauds of the state in which the property is located. The statutes usually require certain contracts to be in writing in order to be enforceable. Another provision of this statute requires any lease not fully performable within one year of its execution to be in writing to be legally enforceable. Although an oral lease agreement for less than one year is usually enforceable if the facts of the situation can be established to the satisfaction of the court, it is wise for the property manager to protect the interests of the owner by executing all leases in writing.

Essential Elements

Because a lease is a contract, the general requirements for a valid lease are similar to those for a legally enforceable contract. Both parties to the lease must have the legal capacity to enter into the agreement and must reach a mutual accord. As with any contract, the objectives of the lease must be legal in nature. The document should be dated and must provide for valid consideration to be paid.

The basic elements of a lease include

- complete and legal name and signatures of both parties;

- description of the property;

- term of the lease;

- consideration or amount of rent;

- time and method of payment;

- use of premises;

- rights and obligations of both parties; and

- possession of the premises.

Names and signatures   A lease is both a contract and a conveyance of an interest in real estate. It must contain the names of both the lessor and the lessee and must be signed by the property owner or a legal representative of the owner. As pointed out in Chapter 3, the power to execute leases can be delegated to the property manager under the terms of the management agreement. All parties should receive a copy of the agreed upon terms.

Some landlord-tenant laws permit an enforceable, unsigned lease in some circumstances. The manager should check local laws. If the tenant and all other involved parties have not signed the lease, the property manager may have problems enforcing the lease terms. Practically speaking, the manager should make sure that the tenant does not take possession of the premises until after the lease is signed. If the tenant is an organization or corporation, the lease must be signed by an authorized officer of the corporation and affixed with the corporate seal, if required by state law. The requirement for additional signatures from witnesses and an acknowledgment seal from a notary public varies from state to state, but witnesses and notaries generally are not required for leases of less than one year.

Description of the premises   If the rental property includes land, which might be the case when leasing industrial or commercial space, the lease agreement should include a legal description of the property. A lease for a portion of space in a particular building, such as an office or apartment, must accurately describe the bounds of the space itself. It is imperative that a ground lease contains an accurate legal description of the land.

The apartment number and the street address of the building are usually sufficient identification in an apartment lease. For commercial space, a floor plan showing the area to be leased should be appended to the lease.

It is a good idea to include both a description of the real estate or space and a statement of the tenant's right to use such common elements as stairways, elevators, halls, driveways, and alleys. An itemized list of furnishings or personal property and a description of their condition should be attached to the lease, if these are involved in the rental. Any supplemental space covered by the lease—a garage, storage area, or patio—also must be identified.

The lease should describe in detail any alterations that will be completed by the owner for the benefit of the tenant, a common concern with commercial and industrial properties. It should specify what improvements are to be made, how the expenses are to be divided, and who will arrange for the work.

For example, an office lease may stipulate that the owners provide interior partitions, doors, blinds, telephone jacks, outlets, and electric switches in the area to be rented. The lease could also detail the amount of painting and decorating, as well as the type of floor covering, heating, ventilating, and air-conditioning to be supplied. Blueprints, carpet samples, and pictures of fixtures usually accompany these specifications. Because this information makes the lease bulky and complex to renew, some managers describe all such tenant alterations in a separate contract that is contingent on the signing of the lease. This is legally valid and simplifies the lease by allowing the one-time alteration specifications to be agreed on independently.

Term of the lease   The lease should specify the beginning and termination dates, as well as a statement of the total period it covers. This can be done in a clause that reads, "for a term of 30 years beginning June 1, 20XX, and ending May 31, 20XX." It should be noted that residential leases are much briefer than those for commercial, industrial, or retail leases.

An option to renew is a clause that gives the tenant the right to extend the lease for an additional period of time on specified terms. To take advantage of this option, the tenant merely gives sufficient notice of intent. The option clause states the date by which the tenant must give notice, the form of notice, how and to whom it must be delivered, term of renewal and rate of compensation. It could read as follows:

> At the expiration of the term specified in Section _____, Article _____, said term shall be extended, at the option of the tenant, for an additional subsequent period of _____ years on the same terms, covenants, and conditions herein set forth, except as to renewals and except that the net yearly rental for this renewal term shall be $_____, payable in advance in equal monthly installments commencing on the first day of the first calendar month of

said renewal term. Tenant shall give landlord notice in writing of his or her desire to extend the original lease term six months prior to the expiration of such term.

Options to renew favor the tenant, so an owner often will insist on higher rental rates if the option is exercised. For example, an option to renew may provide for an increase in the rent that coincides with the increase in the consumer price index for the same period of time. Leases for indefinite periods are usually not valid unless the language of the contract and the circumstances involved clearly indicate that the parties intended to create such an agreement. The maximum term for any lease must conform to the statutes of the state in which the leased property is located.

Some leases include a clause allowing tenants to cancel the agreement before the expiration of the term if they pay a penalty. Other leases, especially those for industrial land on which tenants have constructed a plant, give them the option to purchase the property upon termination of the lease agreement.

Valuable consideration   All lease contracts must contain some type of valid and valuable consideration. Typically, consideration consists of the exchange of promises: the owner promises possession and the tenant promises to pay rent. Whether the lease is gross, net, or percentage, the amount and time of payment of rent must be clearly specified as must the amount of property. When rent is expressed or quoted on a square-foot basis, it is assumed the figure is "per square foot per year."

Possession of the premises   Property owners in most states are obligated by contract to give the tenant actual occupancy of the premises described in the lease. If the premises are still occupied by a holdover tenant on the date of the new lease, the property owner or an agent of the owner must take action to recover possession and bear the cost of this action. In other states, owners need only convey to the tenant the right of possession. In this case, it is the tenant's obligation to bring any court action necessary to secure actual possession.

The longer the lease, the more likely that operating costs, such as taxes and utility costs, will increase over the long haul. It is advisable to anticipate these possibilities under a long-term lease and to allow for adjustment of the rental rate when drafting the agreement. Certain clauses may be included in the original lease to allow for rental rate adjustments. This is an important consideration because most courts will not enforce an increase or reduction in the original amount of rent unless such changes were agreed to in the original contract. Rental rates may be increased by several methods.

Payment Options

Step-up clause   One method of adjusting rent is the step-up clause, found in both gross and net leases. Leases with step-up clauses are also called graduated or escalation leases. They provide for specific increases at specific times. A long-term lease for a luxury apartment, for example, might require monthly payments of $800 for the first two years, $900 during the third year, and $1,100 for the last two years. Step-up clauses are often used with commercial space to help a new business or professional get started. Following is a typical step-up clause:

> The LESSEE hereby covenants and agrees to pay to the LESSOR as rent for said premises during said term, the sum of SIXTY-EIGHT THOUSAND ONE HUNDRED Dollars ($68,100.00) per term payable at the office of LESSOR or of LESSOR's agent, in monthly installments, each in advance upon the first day of every calendar month during said term, payable as follows at the office of the Lessor or the Lessor's agent: EIGHT HUNDRED AND 50/100 DOLLARS ($850.00) per month for the first six (6) months; ELEVEN HUNDRED AND 00/100 DOLLARS ($1,100.00) per month for the next forty-two (42) months; FOURTEEN HUNDRED AND 00/100 DOLLARS ($1,400.00) per month for the last twelve (12) months.

Percentage lease   The percentage lease provides for a rise in the rental rate as the tenant's gross or net income increases.

Index lease   Because the income from professional offices, service firms, financial institutions, brokerage houses, and similar businesses cannot be reasonably and effectively adapted to the percentage lease pattern of rental payments, an increase or decrease in rent from such sources is often tied to a selected index of economic conditions. For this reason, such leases are called **index leases**. The index used in establishing the escalation clause must be reliable and published on a regular and continuing basis by an independent, reputable agency. It should bear a close relationship to the nature of the tenant's business. The most frequently used indexes are the consumer price index (cost-of-living index) and the wholesale price index. The escalation clause in Figure 5.1 uses terms based on the consumer price index.

The frequency and amount of the adjustments are matters for negotiation between the parties to the lease agreement. A lease might require a minimum rent of $1,200 plus a 1 percent increase for every point the consumer price index rises during the course of the year. If the index rises six points during the first year of the lease, the rental level for the next year will be $636 ($1,200 × 0.06 = $72 + $1,200 = $1,272).

Escalation clause   An **escalation clause** can be tied to outside factors other than economic indexes. Union pay scales, taxes, utility rates, and overall operating costs for the premises are common controlling factors. When operating costs are used as the basis for an escalation clause, the tenant usually is responsible only for expenses in excess of a negotiated amount per square foot. This provision is most

FIGURE 5.1

Escalation Clause

Commencing May 29, 20XX, the Lessee shall pay rent as follows:

A. Forty-eight Thousand Dollars ($48,000.00) per annum in equal monthly installments of Four Thousand Dollars ($4,000.00) per month, due on the first day of each month, subject to adjustments provided for in Subdivision "B" of this paragraph.

B. Tenant agrees that in the event the 1967 Consumer Price Index (Series A) for Urban Wage Earners and Clerical Workers (1967 = 100), for all items for U.S. City Average, issued by the Bureau of Labor Statistics of the United States Department of Labor (hereinafter called "Price Index") or successor or substitute index appropriately adjusted, reflects an increase in the cost of living over and above such cost reflected by the Price Index for the calendar month of May 19XX, the rent payable under Subdivision "A" shall be adjusted as follows:

(i) On June 1, 20XX, and every third year thereafter during the term of this lease on June 1st of each such third year, the monthly rent provided for in Subdivision "A" (hereinafter "Base Rent") shall be increased by an amount equivalent to the percentage of the increase, if any, of the Price Index for the calendar month of the March preceding the applicable June 1st (hereinafter "Current Index") over the Price Index of May 20XX, which is 120.8 (hereinafter "Base Index"), subject to the limitation hereinbelow set forth.

To illustrate the intent of the parties hereto as to the computation of the aforementioned adjustment, if any:

Assume the Current Index to be	157.04
Subtract the Base Index	120.80
Increase	36.24

The increase of 36.24 in the said Consumer Price Index would represent 30 percent of the Base Index and the Base Rent for the ensuing three-year period would, therefore, be increased by the application of that percentage equal to $14,400.00, making the total annual yearly rent for said three-year period $62,400.00.

(ii) In no event shall the Base Rent be reduced if the Current Index hereafter drops below the Base Index.

(iii) In the event the said Consumer Price Index shall hereafter be converted to a different standard reference base or otherwise revised, the determination of the Base Index and the Current Index shall be made with the use of such conversion factor, formula, or table for converting index figures as may be published by the Bureau of Labor Statistics or, if said Bureau shall not publish the same, then with the use of such conversion factor, formula, or table as may be published by Commerce Clearing House, Inc., or any other nationally recognized publisher of similar statistical information. In the event the Consumer Price Index shall cease to be published, then, for the purposes of this Section, there shall be substituted for such Consumer Price Index such other index as Landlord and Tenant shall agree on and there shall be substituted for the Base Index such figure as the Landlord and Tenant shall agree would have been derived under the substitute index for the month of May 20XX, and, if they are unable to agree on one or more of said matters within ninety (90) days after the Consumer Price Index ceases to be published, such matter or matters as to which they are not in agreement shall be determined by arbitration in accordance with the then-applicable rules of the American Arbitration Association.

commonly found in office building leases and is called an expense stop. When all operating expenses of a building are totaled and charged on a pro rata basis to all tenants, the computation is called a *passthrough*. Ceilings are sometimes imposed when escalation clauses permit rent increases based on the average increase of the other rental rates in the building.

Reappraisal lease   Another method of rental rate adjustment is found in a reappraisal lease. At set periods, usually five years, or at the end of a term followed by an option, the parties agree to accept a market rent that will be determined by independent appraisers.

Tax and insurance participation   The longer the lease, the more likely problems can arise from sudden and unanticipated increases in property taxes. As a result, many leases contain a provision for tax participation. These clauses require the tenant to pay, in addition to the monthly rental, a pro rata share of any increase in taxes or assessments in excess of those expenses for an established base year. Given the present economic climate, such tax participation provisions afford valuable protection for the owner's investment. A similar provision for insurance is becoming more common.

State and Lease-Specific Provisions

The lease provisions treated in the following discussion cover the major points that must be resolved to create an effective, mutually beneficial contract. The specific manner in which each of these issues is handled varies widely from lease to lease in response to the divergent needs of the parties and different state statutes. Property managers should discuss with the property owner and consult with state law to determine their latitude in regulating the use of the premises, subletting privileges, and related matters. The best leases leave no issue open to dispute or misinterpretation at a later date.

Use of the Premises

The property owner may restrict the use of the leased premises by including a special provision in the agreement. For example, **restrictive clauses** prevalent in office leases might restrict the tenant to using the premises "for the purpose of carrying on a general insurance agency only, and for no other purpose." Residential leases will state that the property is to be used for residential purposes only, not for a business (such as opening a child care center) or an illegal purpose (such as dealing drugs).

> The wording of restrictive clauses must be clear and unambiguous, for the courts will resolve any doubt as to the meaning of a restrictive clause in favor of the party who is restricted by it. In the absence of written restrictions, the tenant may use the premises for any lawful purpose.

Because of the growing number of properties that are being seized for illegal drug activities, it is wise to include a clause in the lease that states that any illegal drug activity is grounds for immediate termination of the tenancy. The following is a sample clause covering illegal drug activity:

> The Tenant, any member of the Tenant's household, or any person under the Tenant's control shall not engage in drug-related criminal activity on or near the leased premises. The term *drug-related criminal activity* means the illegal manufacture, sale, distribution, use, or possession with intent to manufacture, sell, distribute, or use a controlled substance. Tenant understands that such activity shall be cause for termination of such tenancy.

Rights and Obligations   The lease should set forth the rights and responsibilities of the landlord and the tenant. Briefly, the landlord is obligated to provide the property and usually reserves the right to re-enter and to collect rents.

Tenants can expect quiet enjoyment of the rental unit and are obligated to pay rent, not damage the property, and to respect the rights of other tenants. A more detailed discussion of rights and responsibilities follows.

Building rules   Most leases for multiple-occupancy buildings (residential or commercial) have an auxiliary section entitled "Building Rules." These rules are usually made part of the lease agreement by reference and provide a more detailed treatment of day-to-day matters, such as the tenants' use of common areas, parking spaces, and hours of building operations. They are designed to protect the condition, reputation, and safety of the property and to promote compatibility among the occupants.

Building rules apply to all tenants of the same type. They cannot be arbitrarily or selectively enforced, although rules for upper-floor residential tenants can differ from those for ground-floor commercial stores. The property owner reserves the right to add to or change these rules in a reasonable manner during the term of the lease, after giving proper notice. Many residential leases likewise will have a section entitled "Rules and Regulations" that contains guidelines for parking, housekeeping, guests, party noise, and other regulative items.

Condemnation   Most lease forms also include a clause providing for equitable cancellation of the agreement in the event that the tenant is denied use of the property because it has been either appropriated or condemned by a government agency.

Compliance clause   All leases should include a compliance clause that identifies which party is responsible for complying with any new local, state, or federal regulations. All leases should now contain language that allocates compliance with the Americans with Disabilities Act (ADA) between the parties.

Assignment and subletting provisions   Provided that the terms of the lease do not prohibit such activity, a tenant has the right to assign or **sublet** his or her interest in the property. **Assignment** of a lease transfers *all* of the tenant's remaining right in the property to a third party, whereas subletting transfers only *some* of the tenant's interest (transfer of part of the premises, transfer of the premises for part of the remaining term, or a combination of both). Most leases prohibit the tenant from assigning or subletting the rented space without the owner's prior written approval. This ensures that the owner has stable and financially secure tenants occupying the property. State statutes, however, have been passed in some jurisdictions modifying the unlimited right to prohibit assignment.

Fire and casualty damage   State statutes and lease provisions for fire loss, damage and property restoration vary widely. When drafting a lease, the manager should keep in mind the types and amounts of insurance to be carried on the property, who will pay the premium, and who will receive the proceeds if there is a loss. Insurance issues are discussed in greater detail in Chapter 16. It is very important to remember that landlords can only insure their buildings and cannot insure the tenants' property. Tenants must acquire their own renter's insurance.

Leases for agricultural land or for land upon which the tenant has constructed a building usually remain in force even when the buildings on the property are damaged or destroyed. By the same token, a tenant who is the sole occupant of the building is said to be leasing the underlying land as well. Under most state laws, this tenant's rental obligation continues even if the premises are damaged or destroyed.

When a multiple-tenant property is damaged or destroyed to such an extent that enjoyment of the premises is impaired, the tenant may vacate immediately and notify the owner in writing of the intent to terminate the lease as of the date possession was surrendered. The owner also may be given the option to repair the damage and make a rent allowance to the tenant for a certain period. If portions of the premises are still habitable, the tenant can vacate the unusable area and reduce the rent proportionately. If the destruction can be tied to negligence on the part of the owner, some state statutes even allow the tenant to recover damages.

For the owner's protection, the manager should be certain the lease includes a clause stating that damage caused by a tenant will be repaired without a rent abatement and that the owner may take legal action against a tenant. Most leases permit the owner to terminate the tenancy if fire completely destroys the property's usefulness.

Tenant's Obligations   Tenants are required by law to comply with local building and housing code provisions regarding health and safety. They should be required in the lease to take good care of the rented space, repair any damage they directly or indirectly cause, and comply with all applicable rules and laws. The terms of the lease should demand that tenants use all plumbing fixtures, elevators, and other facilities in a reasonable manner. Tenants should be prohibited from willfully destroying or damaging the premises, or allowing others to do so, and from disturbing the quiet enjoyment of other tenants.

Tenant improvements Tenants should not be allowed to make alterations without advance written consent from the owner, who must be informed of such alterations and protected from all liabilities arising from them. In general, most tenant improvements to property are classified as fixtures and become part of the real estate. However, a commercial or industrial tenant may be given the right to install *trade* or *chattel fixtures* for business use. These are the personal property of the tenant and may be removed before or upon expiration of the lease agreement, provided that the building is restored to the condition it was in when the tenant took possession.

The wording of the clause that allows the tenant to remove trade fixtures is crucial. Some lease forms stipulate that the property must be restored to the condition it was in as of "the tenant's taking of possession," whereas others require restoration only to the condition that prevailed "as of the beginning of the lease."

This minor difference in phraseology can have a major impact on the owner. As an example, one long-term tenant installed fixtures during the first lease and later removed them under the terms of the third lease, which required restoration only to the beginning of the lease. The tenant was obligated to restore only those alterations made under the third lease. Alterations made under the first lease were not covered by the terms of the last lease, so the owner had to bear the expenses for restoration.

Security deposit State laws vary regarding **security deposits,** particularly how they can be retained, what documentation is required, and the return within a certain period of time. While security deposits are not required by law, some states have imposed a maximum amount allowed for residential security deposits.

Prompted by the Uniform Residential Landlord and Tenant Act, many states have passed security deposit statutes. These are becoming more detailed and stringent, and managers must be aware of them to develop an equitable and legal policy. In some states landlords are required to keep security deposits in a federally insured financial institution based in the state where the property is located. In others, the amount of the deposit may be limited. Some states require that interest be paid on such deposits.

The lease should also list the amount and kind of security deposit due from the tenant, as well as the conditions under which it will be refunded. A security deposit may be cash, negotiable securities, or a surety bond. If the owner or manager retains any or all of the security deposit, he or she must document the reasons for retention (usually for unpaid rent and/or damages to the property).

Personal property

It is also in the best interests of the owner to include a clause that obligates the tenant to remove personal property from the premises and to clean the rented area at the termination of the lease. Any property left behind is considered abandoned and may be removed from the premises at the tenant's expense. The procedure for handling abandoned personal property in residential and commercial tenancies is often governed by specific state statutes.

Property Owner's Obligations

The landlord/manager also has certain obligations. Unless a net lease is involved, the owner generally is responsible for maintaining the property and to provide certain services, such as snowplowing, groundskeeping, and cleaning certain public areas.

Disclosure and billing On or before the beginning of a tenancy, the owner should disclose in writing the name and address of the property manager and of the person authorized to receive legal notice on behalf of the owner. The lease should provide that rent bills and other notices can be sent to the tenant by registered mail, left at the premises, or delivered personally, as long as they are submitted at the appropriate times.

Quiet enjoyment The owner or property manager grants the tenant a covenant for quiet enjoyment as one of the major benefits in the lease. This right to use also implies a right to possession. Because the tenant is thereby given the exclusive use and possession of the space, the terms of the lease must limit the cases in which the owner or manager is allowed on the premises. Most leases allow the owner to enter in emergencies and for necessary or agreed-upon repairs and to show the space to prospective tenants for a given period near the end of the lease. A clause should be included to permit showing prospective buyers the property, in the event the property is placed on the market for sale.

Managers leasing commercial and industrial property should reserve the right to enter and inspect the premises at will. This is the only way to ensure that lease provisions are not being violated, that the space is being used properly, and that no unauthorized building or alteration is underway. An astute property manager can predict a tenant company's expansion or impending failure from periodic inspections.

However, agents managing residential properties should be familiar with the state and local residential landlord tenant laws that may limit the agent's ability to enter the residence at will. The manager should be aware of all applicable notice requirements.

Maintaining the premises   The lease and state statutes often indicate repairs that are the responsibility of the owner. Most residential and commercial leases, and even some industrial leases, hold the owner responsible for all repairs necessary to keep the premises fit for use. The owner or the owner's agent must comply with local building and housing codes by maintaining in good operating condition all elevators and other facilities, as well as electrical, heating, and plumbing systems.

Unless the property is very small or under a net lease, the owner tends to the upkeep of common areas, trash removal, window cleaning, and other services promised in the lease terms. Running water, a reasonable amount of hot water, and heat during the required season are usually supplied by the owner unless the tenant has exclusive control over these installations or unless the building is not required by law to be equipped for these purposes.

Under some leases the owner must furnish utilities; in others, such as the triple net lease, the tenant has to pay for any or all utility services. If submetering is legal, the owner may buy utilities such as electricity at a lower rate and resell them to the tenants at the prevailing rate. This is common practice with office and retail space. In any case, the lease should outline the owner's and tenant's responsibilities for providing services and maintaining the property.

The manager should try to draft a lease that relieves the owner of responsibility for maintaining the premises and supplying service if compliance is prevented by conditions beyond his or her control. The lease should further state that if the property is sold, the obligations of the owner cease as of the date of sale, with the exception of the responsibility to return or transfer security deposits to the new owner.

Tenant's Remedies for Noncompliance

Tenants have rights when the landlord/agent cannot fulfill the lease obligations.

Noncompliance with rental agreement   If the property owner or manager fails to perform the required duties, the tenant may sue for damages or terminate the lease by giving the owner the specified notice for breach of contract. Many leases require the termination proceedings to stop if the owner or property manager begins a good faith effort to remedy the breach by the deadline stated in the termination notice. Remedies will vary depending on the lease. For example, under most residential leases, if the property owner or manager fails to perform the required duties, the tenant may sue for damages or terminate the lease by giving the owner the specified notice for breach of contract. The law may require the termination proceedings to stop if the owner or property manager begins a good faith effort to remedy the breach by the deadline stated in the termination notice. However, in commercial leases in which the landlord's covenants may be independent, the tenant may not have the right to terminate the lease for noncompliance by the landlord, but may be limited to a suit for damages.

If corrective action is not taken within the specified time, the tenant can sue for damages, obtain a court injunction directing the owner to remedy the breach, or terminate the tenancy. If the owner's noncompliance is willful, the tenant may also recover reasonable attorney's fees. Again, state statutes and the wording of the particular lease agreement in effect will affect the procedures and outcome in any situation.

Failure to deliver premises   Some states require the owner to convey only the right of possession of the leased premises to the tenant. In others, the owner must grant actual occupancy. If the right to possession or actual possession is not conveyed, the tenant does not have to pay rent. The tenant can terminate the rental agreement or sue for specific performance and thereby obtain possession, reasonable damages, and attorney's fees. It is not uncommon for a property manager to be unable to deliver possession because the previous tenant has not vacated the premises or because repairs and alterations have not been completed.

The manager should protect the owner's interests by including a covenant postponing the beginning of the term if necessary, waiving rental payments until the tenant is given substantial possession, and requiring the tenant to take the space, even if there is some delay. Such a clause might stipulate that:

> If tenant is not given substantial possession of the premises at the beginning of the term of the lease, this shall not be a basis for damages, nor shall it affect the validity and other terms of the lease, except that the lessor shall waive rentals until lessor can give substantial possession of the premises.

Failure to supply essential services   Constructive eviction occurs when the tenant must actually abandon the premises due to the owner's negligence in supplying essential services. Examples of constructive eviction include failure to supply heat or water, failure to repair premises, or other major material defaults that render the premises unusable by the tenant. Constructive eviction is recognized by most state courts as the basis for termination of the lease, for an action to recover possession, or for a suit for damages. For the owner's protection, the lease should require the tenant to give notice of any failure and allow the owner time to remedy the situation before the tenant claims constructive eviction. Some state statutes prohibit the cutoff of utilities to residential tenants even if rent or utility payments are owed to the owner.

Partial eviction occurs when a tenant has not physically moved out but is unable to use part or all of the premises for the purposes intended in the lease due to failure on the part of the owner. In cases of partial eviction, state statutes sometimes allow the tenant to give written notice of the breach of contract to the owner. After allowing time to correct the breach, the tenant can take appropriate measures to obtain the services needed and then deduct the cost from the rental payments. In other cases the tenant may simply be allowed to withhold rent until the breach of contract is corrected.

Owner's Remedies for Noncompliance

Tenants can lose their lease if they do not comply with the rental agreement, such as not paying their rent on time or not at all, seriously damaging the property, annoying other tenants by excessive sound, and so on.

Noncompliance with rental agreement   The owner is provided with certain remedies in case the tenant fails to meet the terms of the lease. According to most leases, the owner may deliver written notice to the tenant within a specified period, stating the nature of the contract breach and calling for a good faith effort on the tenant's part to repair the breach within a reasonable time to prevent termination of the lease. Sometimes the tenant has agreed in the lease to pay attorney fees as well.

The lease should further state that if the tenant's noncompliance can be remedied by the repair or replacement of damaged items and the tenant does not make such repairs within a reasonable time after notice is given, the owner or owner's agent may enter the premises and have the necessary work performed. An itemized bill for the actual and reasonable cost of the work then may be presented to the tenant, due with the next rental payment. The lease also should provide that if the owner chooses to terminate the lease, the bill comes due immediately on presentation.

Suit for eviction   Eviction proceedings can be brought against a tenant for several reasons: nonpayment of rent, illegal possession of the premises after termination of the lease, unlawful use of the premises, nonpayment of charges attributed to the tenant under the terms of the lease, and certain other breaches of the lease contract. When a tenant has failed to perform in one of these areas, the owner may file a court suit for recovery of the premises after giving the tenant required legal notice.

This proceeding is commonly known as a suit for eviction, a suit for possession, or a forcible entry and detainer suit. If the court issues a judgment decree for possession in favor of the owner, the tenant must peaceably leave or the owner can have the decree enforced by an officer of the court, who will then forcibly remove the tenant and the tenant's belongings. This process is known as **actual eviction.**

Default   Because statutes regarding a tenant's default under the terms of a lease vary from state to state, the lease should include a clause to the effect that if the tenant defaults on rent payments, the owner or manager can terminate the tenancy.

Bankruptcy   Because of changing federal bankruptcy laws and court decisions interpreting them, property managers should review bankruptcy default clauses in leases with an attorney. Advice should be sought to determine proper procedures to follow if a tenant declares bankruptcy.

Illegal activities Language in the lease should be very clear prohibiting certain activities such as drug trafficking, felony crimes, or threatening other tenants or the manager.

A thorough discussion of legal remedies available to residential landlords and tenants is found in Chapter 11.

Using software management Tracking rental payments and generating late notices is much simpler using software management. Of course, the timeliness and accuracy depends on correct inputting of the original information. For example, the manager initially lists all of the recurring charges, such as the monthly rental payment, pet fees, utility payments, and so forth. Then, the manager can specify the grace days enjoyed by the tenant until the payment(s) become overdue triggering a late charge, either a flat fee or a percentage.

The software can then automatically generate a notice that a late fee is due, and if not timely paid, will trigger an eviction notice. Of course, the eviction notice must be tailored to meet state and local requirements.

■ LEASE FORMATS

Standard lease forms usually are available through the Internet and local real estate and professional management organizations. These may be combined with riders and addenda to cover almost any leasing situation. Many larger management firms and property owners have developed standard leases that may be modified to cover most eventualities. Larger buildings, particularly commercial ones, may also utilize their own lease forms.

One advantage of employing a standard form is that the property manager can become thoroughly familiar with its provisions and legal ramifications. This benefits a manager who administers a single large property or several smaller properties. When employing standard leases, however, the manager must respect the opinion of the tenant's attorney and the special position of each prospective tenant.

Sometimes a standard lease may require considerable revision and may be out of date. Unless the manager is a lawyer, he or she should not write lease clauses or any form of legal statement that may bind the owner. The manager's or the owner's attorney should advise the parties about leases and riders.

■ SUMMARY

A landlord leases property to tenants granting tenants the right to occupy the premises for a specified period of time in exchange for some form of compensation and subject to certain responsibilities and restrictions. The tenant's right to occupy the property during the term of the lease agreement is called a leasehold estate, or interest, in the property.

There are four major kinds of leasehold estates. If the beginning and end of the lease term are clearly identified in the agreement, the leasehold interest is an estate for years. An estate from period to period occurs if the tenant leases the premises on a weekly, monthly, or yearly basis for an indefinite period of time. Both of these types are binding even if the property is sold or either party dies. Tenancy at will gives the tenant the right to possess the property with the consent of the owner for an indefinite period of time, and is terminated by the death of either party. Tenancy at sufferance occurs when a tenant obtains possession of the premises legally but then retains possession after the expiration of the leasehold interest and without the owner's consent.

The method by which the tenant pays rent determines the type of lease contract. The three basic lease forms are the gross lease, usually used with residential space; the net lease, common to office and industrial space; and the percentage lease, for most retail space.

Under a gross lease, the tenant pays a fixed rental amount and the owner pays the property expenses. Under the terms of a net lease, the tenant pays some or all of the expenses usually allotted to an owner, such as taxes, insurance, utilities, and maintenance, as well as a fixed rental payment. A percentage lease calls for the payment of a percentage of the tenant's gross income as rent.

The general requirements for a valid lease are similar to those for any legally binding contract. All parties should receive a copy of the agreed upon terms. The document itself must have legal objectives and provide for valid consideration to be paid. Leases for longer than one year must be in writing to be enforceable under the statute of frauds.

Because a lease is both a contract and a conveyance of an interest in real estate, it must contain the names and signatures of both the tenant and the property owner (or a legally designated agent of the owner). The lease must also be delivered and accepted.

A description of the premises is essential to the lease agreement. If the property to be rented includes land, the legal description should be included. For most residential leases, the apartment number and street address are usually sufficient.

When renting a portion of the leasable space, the space must be accurately described. A floor plan showing the dimensions of the space is sometimes attached to commercial leases. The lease should state the tenant's right to use common areas, itemize any personal property to be rented, and describe supplemental space, such as storage areas.

The term of a lease should be specified in the agreement. Other clauses may include an option to renew, an automatic extension clause, or a clause allowing the tenant to terminate the agreement prematurely upon payment of a penalty.

The amount of rent and time of payment must be clearly stated. The basic method of compensation determines the type of lease—gross, net, or percentage. Escalation leases provide for rental rate adjustments over the term of the lease. An index lease adjusts the rent based on outside economic statistics, such as the consumer price index. The owner usually retains the right to refuse any intended assignment or subletting of the leased premises by the tenant.

Commonly, leases include rules for occupancy and restrictions on the use of the premises. Building rules and regulations can be a separate attachment and should be reviewed by both parties to prevent misunderstandings. The tenant should have realistic expectations of the landlord's responsibilities. Managers and landlords should emphasize that the property may not be used for any illegal activities.

A management firm can develop its own standard lease forms that can be modified to cover most leasing situations or it may obtain them through local real estate organizations. One of the advantages of utilizing a standard lease is that the manager can become thoroughly familiar with its provisions and practical effects. Because any standard lease will probably have to be tailored to fit each specific situation, legal counsel should always be consulted for doing so.

■ CASE STUDY

THE LEASE MANAGER AND RECORD KEEPER

Patti Nielson recently joined the Baker Property Management firm. Within her first week on the job, Patti discovered that the owner of the One-Twenty Building, a property she was to manage, insisted on using a standard lease form dated 1989. She also got a call from Henry Arrow, a tenant in the One-Twenty Building, with a maintenance request.

After checking the lease form, Patti told Henry Arrow that the maintenance he requested was not the owner's responsibility. Henry disagreed. He said, "I know what the lease says, but I made a deal with the building's former owner, Edgar Sandifur, that he would pay for that part of maintenance. This came up just before we signed the lease and we did not want to pay the attorneys extra to redraft the lease, so Edgar just gave me a letter telling me he would take care of that."

"I have an extra signed copy that I will send to you if you can't find it." After checking with the current owner of the property, Patti learned that Arrow was correct about the side agreement.

1. Is it a good idea to agree to lease terms that are not included in the lease document? Why or why not?
2. What should Patti do about the maintenance agreement?
3. Can Patti present the owner of the building with a convincing argument as to why they should use a more current lease form? What points would she argue?
4. If the property owner refuses to change standard forms, what types of standard clauses should Patti suggest that an attorney draft to include into the standard form?

■ REVIEW QUESTIONS

1. The leasehold estate MOST commonly used by property managers is an estate
    a. for years.
    b. from period to period.
    c. at will.
    d. for percentage.

2. Leasehold estates that continually renew until either party gives notice to quit are called
    a. tenancy at will.
    b. tenancy at sufferance.
    c. estate from period to period.
    d. estate for years.

3. Which lease requires the tenant to pay all the expenses related to the property?
    a. Gross
    b. Percentage
    c. Triple net
    d. Recapture

4. Gross leases are most often used with
    a. apartments.
    b. retail space.
    c. office space.
    d. industrial property.

5. Net leases are commonly used with
    a. apartments.
    b. retail space.
    c. office space.
    d. industrial properties.

6. Percentage leases are most often used with
    a. apartments.
    b. retail space.
    c. office space.
    d. industrial property.

7. According to the statutes of frauds of most states,
    a. a lease must be in writing to be enforceable.
    b. leases for more than one year must be in writing to be enforceable.
    c. leases must comply with the Uniform Residential Landlord and Tenant Act.
    d. leases must be on standard forms.

8. A valid lease should
    a. clearly identify the property.
    b. be acknowledged.
    c. be on a standard form.
    d. be in compliance with the Uniform Residential Landlord and Tenant Act.

9. When describing the premises to be rented, an apartment lease should include the
    a. street address of the building.
    b. legal description of the property.
    c. dimensions of the space.
    d. floor plan of the building.

10. Leases often provide for automatic cancellation if the
    a. property is condemned.
    b. premises are partially damaged.
    c. lessee becomes unemployed.
    d. lessor becomes bankrupt.

11. Who are the parties to the lease?
    a. Tenant and manager
    b. Manager and owner
    c. Manager, tenant, owner
    d. Owner and tenant

12. Before being included, the "option to renew" clause must be carefully considered as it favors the
    a. tenant.
    b. manager.
    c. owner.
    d. tax assessor.

13. A lease should contain all of the following provisions EXCEPT
    a. use of the premises.
    b. building rules.
    c. permission to sublet.
    d. possession of the premises.

14. A retail establishment has a percentage lease at a rate of 2.5 percent of gross monthly sales. First-quarter sales were: January, $5,270; February, $4,500; March, $6,320. What was the total rent for the first three months?
    a. $244.25
    b. $270.50
    c. $289.75
    d. $402.25

15. What is it called when the tenant must vacate the premises because the landlord has failed to provide essential services?
    a. Constructive eviction
    b. Actual eviction
    c. Constructive notice
    d. Actual notice

16. What kind of lease provides for increases in the rental rates based on a selected index of economic conditions?
    a. Percentage
    b. Economic
    c. Index
    d. Cost-of-living

17. A lease may be assigned
    a. unless its terms prohibit assignment.
    b. only if it is a gross lease.
    c. so that the owner may be ensured that the tenant is stable and financially secure.
    d. only with consent of the owner.

18. A beauty shop owner finds that she has outgrown the space, even though her lease is effective for another three years. She has found a political party that is willing to take the space for the next year until the upcoming election. Such an arrangement is called a(n)
    a. sublet.
    b. assignment.
    c. passthrough lease.
    d. compliance lease.

19. If a tenant declares bankruptcy, the property manager should
    a. constructively evict the tenant.
    b. forcibly evict the tenant.
    c. complain to the bankruptcy court.
    d. ask an attorney to check the latest laws and cases to determine the owner's rights.

20. Which of the following lease forms is MOST recommended?
    a. Lease form drawn up by the attorney for the owner
    b. Preprinted forms taken from the Internet
    c. Lease used by the manager in his or her previous company
    d. Common lease used by local apartment association

CHAPTER SIX

LEASE NEGOTIATIONS

■ **KEY TERMS**

Closing techniques   Credit report   Noncompeting clause
Concessions   Expansion option   Qualifying process
Credit rating   Lease application   Rental history

■ **LEARNING OBJECTIVES**

At the end of this chapter, the student will be able to

1. discuss the role the manager and attorneys play in negotiating leases;

2. list at least four items that should be included on the lease application and discuss the value of each in the qualifying process;

3. explain the reason why knowledge of the prospect's rental history is useful;

4. summarize the information gained from a credit report and explain the rationale for validating the prospect's financial references;

5. list at least five owner concessions and itemize the pros and cons of each;

6. give examples of businesses that would desire a noncompetition clause and those that would not; and

7. discuss the value of establishing clear guidelines with tenants at the time the lease is signed.

■ OVERVIEW

All activities involved in marketing rental space are directed toward a single goal—the signing of a lease agreement between the owner or manager and the tenant. As the prospect weighs the advantages and disadvantages of the property, the manager is evaluating the prospect. Several steps are involved in this evaluation.

When the manager is confident that the space meets the prospect's needs and the prospect is qualified financially, the manager must then move to close the transaction. Negotiating the final details is a delicate act: too many concessions can hurt the owner in the long run, but being friendly, calm, and flexible is often required to convince the prospect that he or she wants to rent this facility. Basic closing techniques must be used, and these can be used singly or in combination, as the situation demands.

When the prospect does decide to act, the final step of the marketing program can be completed; that is, the terms of the lease agreement can be discussed and agreed on and the contract drawn up. The tenant signs the lease that is then referred to the owner for final approval. Once the manager or the owner signs the lease and delivers the lease to the tenant, the agreement is consummated and the marketing goal has been achieved.

■ QUALIFYING A TENANT

■ The process of **qualifying** a tenant (called the **qualifying process**) is essentially the same whether for a residential, commercial, or industrial prospect. Variations required for each are discussed in greater detail in subsequent chapters.

Visitor Registration

Every prospect walking in the door should fill out a Visitor Registration Form (see Figure 6.1). These completed forms are the starting point for discussion. It is possible that not everyone who registers will decide to fill out an application. These registration forms can be used to track leads as well as for documentation that all prospects are treated equally.

Lease Application

All interested prospects, whether residential, industrial, or commercial, should be required to complete a written **lease application.** The manager should retain these completed applications for the term of the tenancy. The forms should be saved even if the tenant does not lease as they can provide written evidence that the manager has accepted tenants based on sound business reasons, and not in an illegal discriminatory way. This is particularly important in residential leasing. The lease application form is critical as the manager requires additional information before making a final decision to lease to this particular applicant. The form

FIGURE 6.1
Visitor Registration Form

PROFESSIONAL PROPERTY MANAGEMENT, INC.

Leasing Consultant(s):   **visitor registration**

Thank You For Visiting Sun Prairie!
Please help us serve your rental needs by providing us with the following information:

Number of Occupants (see back for occupancy limits) _____ Today's Date_____ Date Needed _____ Size: Studio 1   2   3

Name (1)_____ Telephone: Home_____Work_____

Present Address_____City_____State_____Zip Code_____

Employer_____How long have you worked for them?_____Position Held?_____

Name (2)_____ Telephone: Home_____Work_____

Present Address_____City_____State_____Zip Code_____

Employer_____How long have you worked for them?_____Position Held?_____

How many bathrooms desired? _____Do you have an pets? ____ Yes ____ No (If yes, see back) What price range? $_____ to $_____

What features in an apartment are most important to you? _____

Combined income of all occupants will be: _____under $28,000_____$28-32,000 _____$32-36,000 _____$36-40,000 _____Over $40,000
(Please include all income such as SSI, disability, etc.)

How did you hear of our apartments?

_____**Present Resident**	_____**Sign/Drive By**	_____**Telecom Phone Book**	_____ **U.S West Phone Book**
_____**Former Resident**	_____**Newspaper**	_____**Internet**	
_____**Referred by Employer**	_____**Apt. Blue Book**	_____**Other (please explain)**	

What is your E-mail address? _____ , _____

♿ **ADA Issues-see back**   ⌂ **Equal Housing opportunity-see back**

PROFESSIONAL PROPERTY MANAGEMENT, INC. HAS A ZERO TOLERANCE TO DRUGS POLICY.
Any known or suspected drug related activity will be reported to the police.

Occupancy Limits:

# of Bedrooms	Maximum Occupancy
Eff.	1
1BR	2
2BR	4
3BR	6

Since we provide the heat, water, sewer, and guarantee the electricity, we charge $15 extra for each person over 2 persons in a 2 bedroom and 3 persons in a 3 bedroom.

Policy:
Pets are generally prohibited except fish. Animals that are medically necessary or necessary to assist someone with a disability will be permitted.

ADA Issues:
We strive to accommodate the needs of anyone with a disability. Many of the units have incorporated as standard features that make the unit more convenient for people with disabilities. Others units are designed so that changes can be made at either a modest cost or no cost.

Equal Housing Opportunity: Our apartments are made available, managed, and operated regardless of race, color, religion, sex, national origin, handicap, or familial status. IT IS OUR GOAL TO MAINTAIN A CONSISTENT PROCEDURE FOR SELECTING QUALIFIED APPLICANTS BASED UPON CLEAR OBJECTIVES AND TO COMPLY WITH ALL FAIR HOUSING GUIDELINES. IF YOU FEEL THAT YOU HAVE BEEN DISCRIMINATED AGAINST IN ANY WAY, PLEASE CONTACT CINDY JORGENSEN, VICE PRESIDENT OF PROFESSIONAL PROPERTY MANAGEMENT, INC., AT 201 S. 5TH STREET SUITE 202; AMES, IA; 50010. PHONE: (515) 232-5718.

PPM, Inc. is an agent for the Landlord and not an agent for the prospective tenants.

Office Notes	Second Visit?
	Leased
	Entered
	Thank You Card

Source: Professional Property Management, Inc., West Des Moines, Iowa.

should be clear, concise, and consistent and cover as many topics as necessary for the manager and owner to make an informed decision to accept or reject this applicant. When dealing with a company or organization, the manager should always attempt to work with the person who has authority to enter into contractual agreements on behalf of that company or organization.

Figure 6.2 is an example of a residential lease application. It gathers information and also includes acknowledgment from the tenant that the landlord may verify all information found on the application. The application includes permission to verify not only rental history but also court records and criminal records.

All tenants must be financially sound, but especially commercial and industrial tenants because of the greater net worth of the lease. The questions in the commercial lease application in Figure 6.3 are indicative of the kind of information requested from office, retail, and industrial tenants. The application asks for business location, organizational structure, and banking references.

Space requirements and any other special needs may have been discussed before starting the lease application.

Evaluation of Data

The property manager must thoroughly verify the accuracy of the lease application, not only the identity but also the financial representations. No one wins if the manager accepts a tenant who cannot pay the rental fees or who abuses the other tenants.

Identity It is important to verify the identity of a residential or commercial applicant. At the very least, the prospect must provide some form of identification (individually or as a company or organization), a rental history, financial status, and several references. Residential prospects can supply a government-issued picture ID. Business prospects may be asked for a summary of their long-range business objectives. Most lease applications include a request to allow the manager to check not only the applicant's credit history but also their criminal history.

In commercial real estate, particularly in retail, tenant compatibility also is vitally important. Tenant mix is especially important in retail malls. Moreover, the nature of the prospect's business will have a direct bearing on his or her compatibility with other tenants of the property. A pawnbroker would, for example, be out of place in a building occupied predominantly by attorneys. Moreover, some existing tenants may have leases containing noncompeting tenant restrictions. This is discussed in more detail in Chapter 14.

Fair housing Care must be taken when identifying prospects for residential properties. The manager must be vigilant in following the Civil Rights Act of 1968, also known as the Fair Housing Act. This federal law makes it illegal to deny a prospective purchaser or tenant on the basis of race, color, religion,

FIGURE 6.2

Sample Residential Lease

S/Seldin Company

Apt. Code

Residency APPLICATION/DEPOSIT Form
The undersigned hereby acknowledges and agrees that
we may contact persons listed below to verify information.

I hereby make application to rent Address:_____ Size_____

to be used as a dwelling and for no other purpose.

Rent to be pro-rated to date of lease.

I will sign a lease for_____ months, From_____ / _____ / _____ Move-in Date_____ / _____ / _____

Rental Rate: Basic_____, Market _____, Garage _____ Total_____

OCCUPANT NAME (1):_____ Soc.Sec._____ Date of Birth_____

PRESENT ADDRESS_____ Rate _____ How Long_____ Tele. No._____
Years

City/State_____ Zip_____ Apt. Complex_____

Reason for Moving_____

Landlord_____ **PRIOR ADDRESS**_____
Name   Home Phone/Wk. Phone

Landlord_____ Rate _____ How Long _____
Name   Home Phone/Wk. Phone   Years

EMPLOYER/INCOME SOURCE_____ ADDRESS_____

Tele. No._____ Ext._____ Position_____ How Long_____
Years

Monthly Income $_____ PREVIOUS EMPLOYER_____

ADDRESS_____ How Long_____
Years

Drivers License_____ (State)_____ Make of Vehicle_____ Year_____ License_____

EMERGENCY CONTACT_____
Name   Relation   Address   City/State   (Area) Phone

OCCUPANT NAME (2):_____ Soc.Sec._____ Date of Birth_____

PRESENT ADDRESS_____ Rate _____ How Long_____ Tele. No._____
Years

City/State_____ Zip_____ Apt. Complex_____

Reason for Moving_____

Landlord_____ **PRIOR ADDRESS**_____
Name   Home Phone/Wk. Phone

Landlord_____ Rate _____ How Long _____
Name   Home Phone/Wk. Phone   Years

EMPLOYER/INCOME SOURCE_____ ADDRESS_____

Tele. No._____ Ext._____ Position_____ How Long_____
Years

Monthly Income $_____ PREVIOUS EMPLOYER_____

ADDRESS_____ How Long_____
Years

Drivers License_____ (State)_____ Make of Vehicle_____ Year_____ License_____

EMERGENCY CONTACT_____
Name   Relation   Address   City/State   (Area) Phone

Occupancy _____ Adults_____ Children_____

Children's
Name(s)_____ Date of Birth   _____ Date of Birth

_____ Date of Birth   _____ Date of Birth

( ) check

As consideration, I deposit the sum of ( ) cash $_____ to be applied on the total deposit of $_____ and a $_____
non-refundable application fee. I hereby state and represent that the information provided in this application is complete and accurate. Verification or
re-verification of any information contained in the application will be retained by Landlord. I hereby authorize Tenant Data Services Inc. to obtain
information about me, including, but not limited to, this application, my credit, tenant history, my check writing history, any court records and/or my
criminal record, and I further authorize and instruct any entity or person contacted by Tenant Data Services Inc or the Landlord or Landlord's agents
to release such information to them. Upon request, Tenant Data will provide the name and phone number of the source of the information used in
the verification process. I understand that in the event a lease is entered into it may be cancelled by the landlord if any of the information provided in
the application is materially inaccurate or incomplete. If accepted, the above deposit is to be retained by you. If I should cancel on the application
after 3 days from date of application, $100.00 will be retained from the security deposit as termination charges. I also understand that pets are not
allowed to be kept on the premises (except as provided). I have inspected the premises and they are acceptable.

_____ _____ 1)_____ _____
Agent   Date   Applicant   Date

_____ _____ 2)_____ _____
Apt. Code   Complex   Telephone   Applicant   Date

Form 136 2/03

FIGURE 6.2 (CONTINUED)
Sample Residential Lease

RESIDENT SELECTION POLICY

This Resident Selection Policy is applied to everyone applying for or living in a Seldin Managed Property without regard to race, religion, national origin, familial status, handicap, age, or sex*

All information is held in confidence.

REQUIRED VERIFICATIONS FOR ACCEPTANCE:
1. Satisfactory landlord references required.
2. Satisfactory credit report required.
3. Employment and income is verified.
4. Satisfactory criminal background report required.

RENTAL PAYMENT:
1. Due on the 1st of month.
2. Delinquent rent subject to late charges and eviction as prescribed by applicable law.

PAY PROMPTLY TO PROTECT YOUR HOME AND CREDIT RATING

*As permitted under H.U.D. guidelines where applicable.

THANK YOU

FIGURE 6.3
Commercial Lease Application

Application For Commercial Lease

Date_____

Application is hereby made for lease of the following described premises:

Location _____ Square footage: _____

Use _____

By _____

Incorporation, State of _____

From _____ to _____

At a monthly rental of _____

Number of years in business: _____

Present locations: 1. _____

2. _____

3. _____

4. _____

Present landlords: 1. _____

2. _____

3. _____

4. _____

First bank reference: _____

Officer with whom business is done _____

Second bank reference: _____

Officer with whom business is done _____

Business references: 1. _____

2. _____

3. _____

4. _____

Personal references: 1. _____

2. _____

3. _____

4. _____

Applicant's name _____

Business address _____

Business telephone _____

Residence address _____

Residence telephone _____

Signature _____

national origin, sex, familial status, handicap, and other protected classes added by states and cities. Fair housing laws and exemptions are discussed in more detail in Chapter 10.

Many cities, counties, and states have added additional protected classes to those named here, making it imperative that the property manager be completely conversant with local requirements. As an example, the Iowa Fair Housing Law covers not just housing, but also commercial properties.

Rental history   The stability of the tenant's **rental history** will influence the manager's or owner's final decision. Unless there are valid reasons for doing so, a family or a company moving frequently is often considered a poor rental risk. It is expensive to have a constantly changing pool of tenants, so the manager should seek a family or company that will stay for a long time.

It is especially important that the prospect have a stable past record, particularly with commercial or industrial space, which often must be heavily modified to meet the tenant's specifications prior to occupancy. The manager should inquire about long-range business objectives to identify plans for future expansion that could influence a choice between several qualified occupants.

> ■ If there is a choice between several well-qualified tenants, the property manager should pay particular attention to rapidly growing companies. The space that is adequate now may be too small in a year or two, unless the manager can plan for or take steps to meet such a contingency. The property manager must evaluate such situations carefully and consider all the possible ramifications.

Financial status   It is in the owner's best interests to verify references given on the application. The rationale behind validating a prospect's financial references is simple. Slow or erratic payers generally retain this pattern when making mortgage or rental payments, whereas prompt and steady payers are consistent in meeting their obligations. A prospective tenant with a history of erratic and delinquent payments should be turned down. If there are only one or two lapses in an otherwise satisfactory record, though, the prospect should be invited to explain these lapses before a final decision is made.

Residential   Brief phone calls to banking and employment references used to be sufficient, but today most managers rely on a credit report. To avoid any appearance of any illegal discriminatory practices in violation of Fair Housing laws, the manager must show consistency. In other words, the manager should require a credit report from every applicant, if required of one.

A **credit report** may be obtained legally only with the applicant's consent and is a history of how a person pays his or her bills. Therefore the property manager must set up a procedure for obtaining permission (a permission form is usually completed as part of the application paperwork). Many managers charge a nonrefundable "application fee" to help defray the costs involved in obtaining a credit report.

The credit bureau will send the manager a report on the financial reliability of the prospect. This statement is an itemization of the status of the prospect's past and current accounts, usually identified by industry (e.g., bank and department stores). The report will note bankruptcies, collections, charge-off accounts, and current obligations. The quantity and dates of all payments are listed on the report along with an indication of their regularity. The letter indicates the type of account (open, revolving, installment) and the number refers to the payment pattern. A rating of 1 is the highest, given for payments made as agreed; bad debts that have been turned over to a collection agency receive a rating of 9.

Managers want to know even more about the prospect. A number of companies specialize in searching public records on behalf of the owner or property manager. These searches can include past rental performance history, nationwide credit reports, and outstanding bad check reports, as well as criminal history reports. Rental performance histories contain information such as evictions, past due balances, noise complaints, insufficient checks, and damages to the rental unit.

Nonresidential   Office, retail, and industrial lease applications emphasize the profit and loss record of the company over the past several years. The economic growth pattern of the tenant is of special significance when leasing retail space in a shopping center, where each business depends on the strength and success of its neighbors to generate the customer traffic needed to make a profit.

The financial status of commercial or industrial tenants can be ascertained by consulting a Dun & Bradstreet reference book or report. Dun & Bradstreet is an international business information company subscribed to by many large management firms. The reference book provides information on the nature and age of each listed firm, along with a composite **credit rating** and estimated financial strength. Dun & Bradstreet reports are more detailed analyses of a single company. They are supplied to Dun & Bradstreet subscribers on request and payment of a service fee. The reports list, among other things, assets, liabilities, and officers of all public (and some private) companies.

When a Dun & Bradstreet report is unavailable or inadequate, a credit report can be obtained from a national credit reporting service. The local chamber of commerce or Better Business Bureau may also have information relevant to the prospect's financial standing and reputation in the community. A follow-up check of major suppliers for the prospect's business can reveal other facts concerning the company's payment record.

There are many credit reporting companies other than Dun & Bradstreet. Check your local listings to determine the one that best suits your needs.

The corporate structure of a prospective commercial or industrial tenant is important when considering its financial capability. In some cases, a prospect may give information about the owning corporation when in fact this corporation will not guarantee the lease or be responsible for losses. Commercial and industrial property managers can avoid this pitfall by finding out whether any financial relationship exists between the franchisee and franchisor or between parent and subsidiary companies.

■ NEGOTIATING THE TERMS

The negotiating process begins when a prospect expresses definite interest in the space being marketed. Negotiation itself consists of bringing the prospective tenant to an agreement on lease terms that will be satisfactory to the owner. The goal is a signed lease beneficial to both tenant and owner. Because lease negotiations usually involve several steps amounting to a series of compromises on terms, the property manager must monitor the process continually.

Working with Others

Professionalism, the key to controlling the negotiating process, reassures both owner and tenant that the manager will effect a mutually satisfactory lease agreement. If the manager loses control, the transaction may never be completed. The process is the same whether for a residence, a retail establishment, or an industrial warehouse.

Part of the property manager's responsibility is to avoid personality conflicts that can prolong or even ruin a transaction. In many cases, the owner and the prospect should be kept apart, at least until negotiations are concluded and the lease is ready to be signed.

The leasing agent works directly with the prospect and *recommends* action to the owner. This allows more response time to analyze prospect requests and negotiate favorable compromises on major points. Many times the leasing agent can avoid a concession by simply stating, "Oh, the owner will never approve of that!"

Cooperating brokers An outside leasing agent often is involved in leasing office, retail, and industrial property. In some markets, real estate agents will refer residential prospects. This third-party interest can complicate the negotiation process unless the property manager coordinates efforts with the outside agent. Very early, the manager should attempt to be the party who communicates with the prospect in order to expedite direct negotiations with the prospect without affronting the cooperating broker. It is worthwhile to cultivate the loyalty of the prospect, especially in a tenant's market, for the cooperating broker will have no special allegiance to the manager, the owner, or the space in question. Cooperating brokers should be instructed to avoid quoting price and terms.

Role of attorneys The attorney's task is to formalize the agreement by translating it into legal terms after it has been established. Attorneys for the parties should review or draft leases that carry out the intentions of their clients. It is in the property manager's best interest to try to secure agreement on basic terms and conditions of a lease (for example, rent, years, and percentage) in negotiations between the owner and the prospect or between their agents before the lease goes to the attorneys. However, many owners and lessees expect that their respective attorneys will monitor each step in the negotiating process and will not act without their attorneys' guidance.

Security Deposits

Often a security deposit separate from the actual rent is held by the owner or manager to be used in the event that the tenant fails to pay the rent or causes expensive damage to the property. The amount of the security deposit is negotiable and depends on the length of the lease and the total dollar amount.

Many states require that the security funds be deposited in a trust or escrow account in a bank in that state, although in some states, exceptions are made for owners who hold the money. Because the money does not belong to the property manager under any circumstance, security amounts should be deposited directly into a trust account.

Also, the 1988 Fair Housing Amendments Act prohibits charging families with children and those with handicaps higher deposits or higher rents than other tenants.

Concessions

A **concession** is a benefit or boon to the tenant because the owner agrees to less than the original terms. Every concession costs the owner money and affects the total economic value of the lease to the owner. **Concessions** are granted in order to influence a prospect to become a tenant. A worthwhile concession alleviates a basic problem or specific financial pressure felt by the prospect. Nothing is gained by giving away something of little or no value to the recipient, regardless of its importance to the owner.

On the other hand, many concessions that may appear valuable to the tenant are in fact rather inexpensive to the owner. Thus, the importance of qualifying the client and knowing his or her needs is stressed. The manager should keep the owner's position in mind and must not negotiate for more than the owner can afford to deliver. Concessions should be granted reluctantly in all cases; this will increase their value in the eyes of the tenant. In addition, a concession granted to one may have to be given to all, including existing tenants.

A general rule to follow for industrial and commercial lease concessions (termed *inducements* in some markets) is that the larger the tenant and the longer the lease, the more acceptable the rent concessions. The owner's costs for preparing and altering the space to suit a new commercial or industrial user must be figured into the rental rate. These costs may even include interest on the money borrowed for tenant alterations. The rental schedule also should be such that the expense to the property owner will be completely amortized over the term of the lease, but no longer. Alteration costs for new tenants will be explained more fully later in this chapter.

Almost every item of the leasing contract is open to discussion. Depending on the relative strength of the manager's and the prospect's positions, any number of concessions might be made to induce the prospect to sign a lease agreement. Three factors can help a manager decide how far to go in granting concessions to attract tenants:

1. The owner's financial and strategic position (long-range goals and urgency to lease)

2. Competition in the area market

3. Urgency of the prospect's need to move

The following topics are possible concessions, with relative costs and advantages discussed.

Rent schedules and rebates   The rental rate is one of the most important and complex issues to negotiate. Although deviations from the basic rental schedule are undesirable from both a manager's and an owner's standpoint, they may become a necessity in a competitive market. In every situation, however, the manager must analyze the advantages and disadvantages of making a significant concession on rent.

All negotiations regarding rent reductions and rebates should be made on an individual basis. Not all tenants expect, nor do all deserve, the same rent concessions. Unfortunately, compromises with one tenant often necessitate compromises with the others as well. Rumors spread quickly throughout multitenant buildings (whether commercial or residential), creating ill will and an array of management problems. Failure to enforce the basic rental schedule, the manager soon learns, can result in a general downgrading of the rental structure and significant income loss.

Graduated rental structures calculated on a base standard rental rate are often used for office space, where the base standard rental is assessed on a per-square-foot basis. For example, standard rental rates in a high-rise office building usually ascend with each floor. Space on the quieter 35th floor might rent for $23.80 per square foot, whereas similar units on the less desirable 14th floor would go for

$21.20. Corner office space might cost an additional $2 per square foot above the base rent for any floor. An attractive view from one side of the building might enhance the base rent. The rental rate per square foot for retail and industrial space is likewise a function of the location.

In a very poor market, it might be better to leave space vacant for a period of time, then rent it at a higher rate later or rent month-to-month now. Accepting a tenant at a low rental rate that fails to cover operating expenses or under a long-term lease that provides little or no profit is more disadvantageous to the owner than vacancy.

Residential rental rates usually reflect the differing demand for particular areas of a building. A basic graduated rental structure facilitates a balanced rental of all space. For example, the manager of a walkup building might be able to charge $675 per month for the first-floor apartments but only $475 for similar third-floor units, which are less convenient in a walkup. The manager of a luxury high-rise should charge premium rates for corner units on the top floor that command a view and lower rates for apartments located in the center of the building.

Free rent   Temporary free rent is the major concession granted to balance the needs of the tenant and the prevailing market conditions. For example, if vacancy rates are high, the manager might offer the prospect two months' free rent as an inducement to sign the lease. Previously offered as "first month's free rent," the free rent has become more common at the back end of a lease to prevent a tenant from moving in, paying no money, and then continuing to live "free" during the eviction process.

The manager should attempt to remain within the basic rental schedule even when offering one-time rebates or other short-term concessions. Hopefully, the cost of temporary free rent is less than the loss resulting from a lower rental fee over the term of the loan. In addition, lower rental fees will lower the value of the property when measured on a rent-multiple basis.

Length of lease period   Tenant turnover costs money. It costs money every time that a unit has to be cleaned, redecorated, and refurbished, plus the loss of rent. Time and expense are involved in advertising, and qualifying, and negotiating with a new tenant, so it makes economic sense to negotiate longer leases. On the other hand, the owner can lose money on longer leases unless the lease has an escalation clause covering expense increases.

As a result, most residential leases are for terms of one year or less. Nonetheless, the manager of a newly renovated building in a newly upgraded area might very well be willing to give two-year or three-year leases to financially responsible tenants whose presence over a period of time will strengthen the reputation of the building and the neighborhood.

It is a different picture for office and retail leases, which generally have a minimum length of from 5 to 10 years, whereas industrial leases often run for periods of 10 to 25 years or more. Commercial property managers try to negotiate a lease term that is long enough to recover any monies expended to alter the space for a particular tenant. A long-term commercial lease with an escalator clause is definitely to the owner's advantage, but a manager may not want to grant a long-term percentage lease without a base rent unless the prospect is financially sound and has a proven reputation.

As discussed in Chapter 5, options to renew a lease for an additional term are sometimes granted as a concession to a tenant. The owner is more likely to renew tenants whose presence lends prestige or draws traffic to a commercial or industrial development. Other tenants may be granted such options as a trade-off for a higher rental rate or other point of negotiation.

During periods of high vacancy, tenants can sometimes insist on a cancellation option in the lease agreement, which provides that the tenant may cancel the lease at the end of a predetermined term. Tenants may also seek to reduce the total amount of rented space at the expiration of a set period. This option may or may not be accompanied by a penalty to the tenant. A contract with either of these options should also require the tenant to pay all or part of any remaining unamortized costs for alterations done for that tenant.

Tenant alterations New tenants have widely divergent requests for alterations or improvements before they move in. Negotiation usually involves trade-offs for certain items. Before granting concessions, the manager must consider not only the type of alteration required but also its total expense to the owner. An owner who pays for tenant alterations in essence is merely financing the costs, which ultimately will be charged back to the tenant in the form of rent. The lease should identify the nature and cost of the alterations and identify the party responsible for payment.

If a tenant wants a more luxurious or expensively finished space than the owner can provide, a tenant can be given a straight dollars-per-square-foot allowance. Tenant improvement should become an asset to the property, and no liens should arise as a result of a tenant's work in the building. The property manager must determine exactly what the tenant plans to do and make certain that the tenant can and will complete the space accordingly.

- **Residential tenant demands** usually are restricted to decorating expenses, such as painting, drapery cleaning, and new carpeting. The decision to redecorate an older building is usually tied to the market situation and the urgency of either the landlord's or tenant's situation. An apartment is usually painted before a tenant moves in, but if the vacancy rate in the area is low or if the tenant is anxious to occupy the unit, the landlord might agree to furnish the supplies, provided the tenant does the work. The manager should put the details in writing to prevent misunderstandings.

■ **Commercial and industrial tenant** alteration costs are a major point of negotiation since these tenants require highly customized space. Often, these buildings have established building standards—a specified number of outlets, light fixtures, windows, and such—that are provided in the rental space at the owner's expense. The tenant is required to pay for any equipment or facilities beyond the building standard, such as additional stairways, partitions, doors, truck docks, or sprinkler systems.

ADA compliance   Many businesses and governmental entities will refuse to rent in buildings that do not comply with the Americans with Disabilities Act (ADA); therefore, compliance with the ADA must be discussed with prospective tenants. Negotiations will determine whether the owner or the tenant will pay for the alterations, and specific details should be included in the lease.

Tax breaks are available to the party who makes these changes: $15,000 deduction and a tax credit of 50 percent of eligible access expenditures for small businesses. It is important to check figures with knowledgeable accountants, and make sure that any alterations made to the tenant space are in accordance with the ADA's requirements regarding new construction and alterations. The ADA mandates that alterations to existing buildings after January 26, 1992, must be made in such a manner that the altered portions are readily accessible to and usable by the disabled. This federal law is discussed in greater detail in Chapter 10.

Expansion options   Expansion options usually guarantee that a tenant may lease additional adjacent space in a property after a certain period of time. These options are not common in residential leases but may be worthwhile concessions to growing commercial and industrial firms. One downside to this concession is that it may be more difficult to rent the "held" space to another tenant who does not have any assurance as to how long he or she can remain. Obviously, the more fully tenanted a commercial or industrial property is, the less need there is for an expansion clause, because most of the space will already be leased or under option to other tenants.

Noncompeting tenant restrictions   Noncompeting clauses grant a tenant an exclusive right to operate without competition in the property. Most often found in commercial (especially retail) leases, the clause also may be relevant to service businesses that are seeking to build client loyalty, such as barber shops. In general, if a noncompeting tenant restriction can benefit the prospect without damaging the owner's interests or if the prospect is willing to pay a premium rental rate for it, the concession should be made. It should not be granted if it would exclude prospective tenants who might otherwise be valued occupants of the building.

Some professions do not mind being in close proximity to their competition. It is not uncommon for doctors to flock together; so do attorneys. Managers of large shopping malls should avoid granting exclusive rights at all costs. The total effect of many similar shops in large retail centers is to stimulate business and encourage competition.

Defraying moving expenses   One fairly inexpensive concession is offering to move the tenant from the old location to the manager's new location. A more indirect way to ease moving costs is to offer stationery and sign allowances to commercial and industrial tenants. An otherwise hesitant prospect might be convinced to make the move if letterhead stationery and advertising signs reflecting the firm's new address are supplied free of charge.

Lease buy-out, assumption, and subletting   In an effort to persuade a high-profile tenant, or to gain a long-term lease, the owner may buy out the tenant's existing lease or assume a tenant's unexpired lease. A lease buy-out, assumption, or subletting is most often used for long-term commercial and industrial rental agreements, *not* residential rental agreements.

Whether the landlord should assume the old lease will depend on the terms of the present lease, the period remaining, the possibility of subletting and the amount or value of space the prospect will be leasing in the manager's building. The existence of a cancellation penalty, an escalation clause, or any other provision could affect the cost of the lease to be assumed.

The manager should also consider the amount of space the tenant will occupy, the rental rate for the space, and the overall worth of the new lease over its term. Unless these factors more than compensate the manager for the effort and possible loss incurred in a lease assumption, the concession should not be made. As a general rule, a tenant whose lease has been bought or assumed should not expect to be given a rental rebate as well.

If economically feasible, this becomes a simple transaction between the tenant and the property owner (or manager as an agent). The latter agrees to take over the payments on the tenant's current lease, contingent on the tenant renting space in the manager's building.

■ SIGNING THE AGREEMENT

Once the tenant has responded favorably to the premises, the manager's action becomes very important. First, the manager verifies and evaluates the tenant's application. If the tenant meets the manager's standards, the economic viability of the negotiated lease terms must be considered. If the total value of the lease agreement justifies the cost of any concessions, the owner (or the manager as an agent of the owner) will sign the contract and return a copy to the tenant.

Prospect hesitancy   Before deciding whether or not to sign a lease, the prospect may pause trying to determine whether this is the right decision. The prospect is considering the following:

- Is this the best space available at the price?
- Do the concessions meet my needs?
- Should I act immediately?

Closing techniques   The manager's **closing techniques** can influence the prospect to respond positively to all three questions. A manager can use any of several closing techniques to guide a prospect to a successful close.

In one approach, often termed the question close, the manager asks direct questions aimed at eliciting an affirmative decision, for example, "Which space do you prefer?"

Another method closes with a summary of the benefits of the space and emphasizes the fact that the space satisfies the tenant's needs. The manager may need to summarize the benefits repeatedly throughout the showing and closing process to reassure an indecisive prospect that the space is ideal.

Follow-up   The manager must make sure that the new tenant is given a receipt for all advance charges, security deposits, and additional fees, indicating the purpose for which these payments are made. As noted earlier, any security deposit must be handled in accordance with applicable state law.

Many landlord-tenant misunderstandings can be avoided if the manager establishes clear guidelines from the beginning. The manager also should give the new tenant a copy of the building regulations and explain them fully. Questions concerning the obligations and rights of the parties under the terms of the lease should be settled before occupancy. When at last the lease has been signed, monies received, receipts given, and obligations outlined, the merchandising goal has been attained—the space is leased. From this point forward, responsibility for the success of the landlord-tenant relationship during the lease period will fall largely on the property manager.

■ SUMMARY

Although most prospects will be at least partially qualified before they apply for the lease, most decisions are based on information provided on the written application. The manager should determine the real estate needs, financial capability, and suitability of a prospective tenant before presenting the negotiated lease to the owner.

The manager should first verify the prospect's identity and the stability of the tenant's rental history. A number of companies can obtain not only credit reports but also criminal histories. The critical item in a credit report is the prospect's pattern of payment. Slow or erratic payers generally retain this pattern in their rental payments, whereas prompt and steady payers are consistent in meeting obligations.

Negotiation brings the prospect to an agreement on satisfactory terms for the lease. The manager must maintain control over the process by acting in a professional manner; establishing a direct relationship with all prospects (even when an outside broker is involved); and preventing undue complications stemming from premature involvement of either party's attorney.

Almost every item in the lease agreement is a potential point of negotiation. Depending on the relative strength of the manager's and prospect's positions, certain concessions might be made to induce the prospect to sign. Knowledge of the owner's financial and strategic position, market volatility, and the prospect's motivation will show the manager how many and what kind of concessions should be made to attract tenants. An owner is more likely to grant a concession for the tenant who requires more space and is willing to commit to a longer lease.

Concessions on rent should be used only in an extremely competitive market as they are financially costly to the owner. The manager's objective is to adhere to a basic rental schedule for the property. Free rent for a short period usually will cost the landlord much less than lowering the rent even a small amount over the term of the lease. Rental rebates are commonly given on a per-month basis and should be negotiated on an individual level.

Other lease terms often negotiated are the length of the lease period, renewal options, cancellation options, the amount and type of tenant alterations to be undertaken by the owner, expansion options, noncompeting tenant restrictions, and the defraying of some moving costs. The owner may agree to assume the unexpired lease on the prospect's current quarters, depending on the terms of the existing lease, the period remaining under the lease, the rentability of the space, and the value of the new lease to be executed.

Finally, the economic viability of the negotiated lease terms must be considered. If the total value of the lease agreement justifies the concessions given, the owner or the manager as the owner's agent should sign the contract and return a copy to the tenant. At this time the manager should collect the advance deposits and explain the lease terms and building regulations.

■ CASE STUDY

THE LEASE NEGOTIATOR

Harris Aimes recently took over the management of Building 2000, an office building. On reviewing the various leases for the tenants of Building 2000, Aimes realized that the lease terms were not particularly profitable for the owner. Because of a recent economic slump, the previous manager had leased several spaces to tenants at below-market rates and had paid for extensive remodeling. He had also leased a great deal of space to three large, rapidly growing businesses, all of which were trying to get out of their leases early because they had outgrown their space. Furthermore, because of the rapid growth of these three tenants, parking in the building lot had become a constant problem, and all the tenants were complaining.

1. What creative solutions can Aimes develop to alleviate the problem with the three expanding businesses and the requests for getting out of their leases?
2. What should he do about the resulting parking problems?
3. What should Aimes do to prevent these types of problems from occurring in the future?

■ REVIEW QUESTIONS

1. Before agreeing to the lease, the prospective tenant is asking himself or herself all of the following *EXCEPT*
   a. Is this the best price and space?
   b. Who else is considering the property?
   c. Are the concessions useful to me?
   d. Should I sign right now?

2. When renting or leasing space, good closing techniques include
   a. summarizing the benefits of the space and explaining how they satisfy the prospect's needs.
   b. direct questioning, such as, "Are you interested in renting this space?" to elicit a positive or negative response.
   c. saying to the prospect: "Think about it overnight."
   d. demanding a yes-or-no answer on the spot.

3. The marketing goal has been achieved when the prospect
   a. answers an advertisement.
   b. visits the premises.
   c. signs a lease.
   d. takes occupancy.

4. Qualifying a tenant includes examining the applicant's
   a. national origin.
   b. rental history.
   c. tenant improvements.
   d. educational background.

5. The property manager of a ten-unit strip shopping center is negotiating with a beauty shop owner. The beauty shop owner does not want the manager to rent to another beauty shop. What concession is the beauty shop owner asking for?
   a. Right to sublet
   b. Expansion option
   c. Tenant alterations
   d. Noncompete restriction

6. If an outside leasing agent is involved in lease negotiations, coordination of the transaction is the responsibility of the
   a. owner.
   b. tenant.
   c. outside leasing agent.
   d. property manager.

7. The proper role of an attorney in lease negotiations is to
   a. coordinate the negotiations.
   b. retard progress or kill the transaction.
   c. conduct the negotiations personally.
   d. formalize the agreement.

8. The manager can facilitate lease negotiations by
   a. securing agreement on basic terms and conditions before the attorneys are involved.
   b. encouraging the prospect and owner to get together and discuss important points.
   c. showing the property to two prospects at the same time.
   d. sending prospects to look at property without accompanying them.

9. All of the following are factors to decide how far to go in granting concessions *EXCEPT*
    a. the owner's financial and strategic position.
    b. the competition in the area market.
    c. the urgency of the prospect's need to move.
    d. the prospect's financial condition.

10. Concessions should always be granted to a prospective tenant
    a. willingly, to show a cooperative spirit.
    b. only on consent of the owner's attorney.
    c. reluctantly, to show how valuable the concession is.
    d. in a tight market.

11. When forced to make rental rate concessions during poor market conditions, the manager tries to
    a. lower the basic rental schedule by a very small amount.
    b. grant a temporary rental concession such as a few months' free rent.
    c. give the concession at the beginning of the term.
    d. match any concession being given by a competitor.

12. A long-term lease is generally to the owner's advantage when
    a. negotiating a commercial lease without an escalation clause.
    b. the owner has made significant alterations in the space to suit the tenant.
    c. the tenant has indicated that his or her business is unstable.
    d. the tenant has frequently changed locations in the past three years.

13. Before finally agreeing to the lease, the manager must determine that the tenant meets qualifying standards and that the
    a. owner has the finances to pay for the concessions.
    b. cash flow is sufficient to warrant making repairs.
    c. total value of the lease justifies the cost of the concessions.
    d. existing tenants will agree to the new tenant.

14. Tenant alteration costs
    a. should always be imposed on the tenant; the owner should never pay any portion of them.
    b. should be negotiated on a strict dollar basis with the prospective tenant.
    c. are a major negotiating point with commercial and industrial tenants.
    d. should never exceed the basic building standard.

15. The property manager should keep in mind that expansion options
    a. are usually advantageous to the owner.
    b. are not common with fully tenanted, established properties.
    c. may be given freely to encourage leasing.
    d. need not be coordinated with other tenant leases.

16. In an office building, who is responsible for complying with ADA accessibility requirements in each individual office?
    a. Property manager
    b. Building owner
    c. Tenant
    d. Whoever agrees in the lease

17. Many misunderstandings with tenants can be avoided by
    a. establishing clear guidelines at the beginning of the lease.
    b. waiting until there is a problem to review policies with tenants.
    c. threatening retaliation whenever a complaint is made.
    d. ignoring problems and concerns until absolutely necessary.

18. Alterations to residential property are often
    a. found in the rental agreement, which is typically drafted by the new tenant's attorney.
    b. paid for by the new tenant.
    c. performed by the property manager after being agreed to in writing.
    d. performed by the new tenant and may give rise to a lien against the property.

19. What is a building standard?
    a. Set of standard rules for all tenants
    b. Flagpole on top or in front of the building
    c. Basic base rental unit or the average-size unit
    d. Specific number of outlets, light fixtures, windows, etc., included in the rent

20. Which type of property should rarely have non-competing tenant restrictions in leases?
    a. Large shopping mall
    b. Industrial property
    c. Office building
    d. Residential property

CHAPTER SEVEN

7

TENANT RELATIONS

■ KEY TERMS

Eviction	Lease renewals	Rent increases
Eviction suit	Maintenance request	Security deposits

■ LEARNING OBJECTIVES

At the end of this chapter, the student will be able to

1. explain the importance of a move-in inspection sheet and visit;

2. discuss three methods of maintaining effective, ongoing communication with the tenants;

3. describe the value of requiring maintenance requests in writing and discuss how to handle excessive requests from tenants;

4. summarize methods that may be taken to encourage prompt and complete rental payments;

5. identify the value of stable tenants and list at least two concessions that may be utilized to retain good tenants;

6. discuss methods of presenting rental increases and list the steps that may be taken to avoid tenant revolt;

7. explain the steps to follow when the tenant does leave the property; and

8. list the legal steps that must be followed when terminating a tenancy in court.

■ OVERVIEW

The ultimate success of a property manager will depend greatly on his or her ability to maintain good relations with tenants. Dissatisfied tenants eventually vacate the property, and a high tenant turnover means greater expense for the owner in terms of advertising, redecorating, and uncollected rents.

An effective property manager will establish a good communication system with tenants. The manager will utilize intangible as well as tangible benefits to encourage tenant satisfaction by enforcing all lease terms and building rules and ensuring that maintenance and service requests are quickly dealt with. The property manager must be able to handle recalcitrant residents who do not pay their rents on time or those who break building regulations and breed dissatisfaction among other tenants. Careful record keeping will show whether rent is being remitted promptly and in the proper amount. Records of all lease renewal dates should be kept so that the manager can anticipate expiration and retain good tenants who otherwise might move when their leases expire.

If a manager is ineffective for long, the owner's profits will disappear as tenants move out, expenses increase, and unpaid past-due notices pile up. A good manager is tactful and decisive and will act to the benefit of both owner and occupants.

■ ESTABLISHING A SOUND LANDLORD-TENANT RELATIONSHIP

Landlords' and tenants' interests are not mutually exclusive and the two do not need to be in constant conflict. The foundation for good landlord-tenant relations begins with a clear understanding of the rules and regulations and the move-in inspection. Effective servicing of the lease throughout the term of the lease further contributes to sound landlord-tenant relationships.

Renewals are an important goal because they save the owner refurbishing costs, vacancy losses, leasing commissions, and renewed concessions. Tenants who are given diligent, fair, and equitable service will renew their leases for an additional term. These economic facts can be used to convince the owner that it is economically more advantageous to provide good service to tenants than to concentrate on short-term financial rewards.

■ Owners want a fair return on their investment in the property, based on current market conditions. Tenants, on the other hand, want the best value for their rental dollar and all the services promised during lease negotiations. Though the manager's first responsibility is to the owner, the successful property manager will encourage both parties to work together, because good tenants are an asset.

Move-in Inspections

At the beginning of the tenancy, the manager should inspect the premises with the tenant to determine if promised repairs or alterations have been made or are in progress. Inspecting with the tenant is a must, especially in a residential tenancy. At that time, the manager and tenant mutually agree to the condition of the premises and note any exceptions on the "move in/move out" checklist, an example of which is provided in Figure 7.1. Both the manager and tenant should sign this form, and both should have copies. The same form is then used at the time the tenant leaves. Putting it in writing helps avoid potential disagreements at the end of the lease.

Clear Understanding of Lease Terms

At the outset of each tenancy, the manager should establish a basic understanding with the tenant on all matters relating to the lease terms. A tenant brochure that outlines all policies and procedures should be given to and reviewed with each new tenant. The tenant should also be told of the penalties for failure to comply with building regulations.

The legal aspects of building regulations were discussed in Chapter 5; an example of typical rules for residential property is shown in Figure 7.2. The following topics should be addressed:

- Building rules and regulations
- Handling maintenance requests
- Procedures for paying the rent
- Penalties for late payments or no payments
- Terminating the tenancy
- Security deposits

Manager's Personal Efforts

The prerequisite for a sound manager-tenant relationship is reciprocal communication. No matter the management specialty, the manager demonstrates goodwill and availability by communicating regularly with tenants by telephone, e-mail, or in person. A newly appointed manager must make a special effort to meet each tenant personally as soon as possible.

Soliciting tenant input   On a regular basis, the manager should solicit tenants' comments on the amenities, services, maintenance, and general management of the building. Some managers do this very amicably by means of an annual or quarterly meeting or by a written questionnaire. Other managers have strong feelings against holding tenants' meetings, particularly in residential projects, preferring to maintain contact with tenants on an individual basis. One manager, on taking over a complaint-ridden complex, turned it around in a remarkably short time simply by appearing at poolside every Saturday morning with doughnuts and coffee to solicit tenants' comments.

FIGURE 7.1

Residential Checklist

Residential Move-In/Move-Out Checklist

Property: _____

Apartment:_____   Date _____

Tenant: _____

Tenant should complete this checklist on taking possession of the apartment. Please note existence and condition of each item and sign at bottom.

Keys _____	Keys _____
General cleanliness _____	General cleanliness _____
Kitchen tile _____	Kitchen tile _____
Stove _____	Stove _____
Refrigerator _____	Refrigerator _____
Ice trays _____	Ice trays _____
Countertop _____	Countertop _____
Sink _____	Sink _____
Cabinets _____	Cabinets _____
Dishwasher _____	Dishwasher _____
Disposal _____	Disposal _____
Tub _____	Tub _____
Basin _____	Basin _____
Commode _____	Commode _____
Medicine cabinet _____	Medicine cabinet _____
Bathroom tile _____	Bathroom tile _____
Light fixtures _____	Light fixtures _____
Wallpaper _____	Wallpaper _____
Paint _____	Paint _____
Windows _____	Windows _____
Screens _____	Screens _____
Floors _____	Floors _____
Fireplace _____	Fireplace _____
Air conditioning _____	Air conditioning _____
Thermostat _____	Thermostat _____
Other _____	Other _____
Tenant _____	Tenant _____
Manager _____	Manager _____
Date _____	Date _____

Manager should complete this checklist when tenant vacates premises.

FIGURE 7.2
Resident Regulations Form

Residents' Rules and Regulations

GENERAL

1. The resident is responsible for the proper conduct of family members and guests and for seeing that they understand and observe all rules and regulations.

2. While the buildings are well-constructed, they are not 100 percent soundproof. Reasonable consideration of one's neighbors is therefore important.

    a. No resident shall play, or allow to be played, any TV, radio, hi-fi, organ, piano or other musical instrument at a sound level that may annoy or disturb occupants of other units. Particular care must be exercised in this respect between the hours of 10:00 P.M. and 9:00 A.M.

    b. No resident shall make or permit any disturbing noises in the building or adjacent grounds by himself, his family or visitors, nor permit anything by such persons that will interfere with the rights, comforts or convenience of other residents.

    c. Hallways, laundry rooms and storage areas are not play areas for children and should not be used as such. They should be used only for the purpose for which they were originally intended.

3. The installation of aerials or antennas of any kind is not permitted outside of apartments or town houses.

4. Common areas of buildings such as stairs, stairwells, halls, lobbies, etc., are to be used only for the purpose intended. No articles belonging to owners should be kept in such areas. Boots and rubbers should not be left in corridors nor should doormats be placed outside the front doors.

5. To prevent water damage to their own or adjoining apartments, residents should close all windows tightly when leaving the apartment and building. When the resident is absent from the unit during the heating season, the thermostat shall be placed at a minimum 62-degree setting to avoid freezing pipes and resulting damage.

6. Residents shall not store anything in their apartment or storage room that can create a fire hazard.

7. Soliciting of any type will not be permitted in the buildings at any time, except by individual appointment with a resident.

PATIOS AND BALCONIES

1. Mops, cloths, rugs, brooms, vacuum cleaner bags, etc., must not be dusted nor shaken from apartment windows, halls or stairwells.

2. Residents shall not sweep or throw, or permit anyone to sweep or throw from apartments or balconies, any dirt, dust, cigarettes, cigars, ashes, water, paper or other material.

VEHICLES

1. No vehicle belonging to a resident or a member of the resident's family, guest or employee shall be parked in such a manner as to impede passage in the street or to prevent ready access through the adjoining alley.

2. Cars, trucks and motorcycles are not to be driven on the lawns or in any area other than parking areas, streets or driveways

---

Source: Reprinted with permission of Property Company of America Realty, Inc.

FIGURE 7.2 (CONTINUED)
Resident Regulations Form

Residents' Rules and Regulations

STORAGE ROOM

1. Each apartment has a numbered storage locker. If your storage locker has a lock on it or contents in it, call the office and the contents shall be removed.

2. All contents must be placed inside the locker. Anything left outside the lockers shall be removed.

3. Flammable liquids or gas-powered engines and empty boxes are not allowed in the storage areas by Fire Code.

4. It is recommended that all items be stored on wooden pallets or bricks in case of water leakage.

5. Valuable items should be not kept in the storage locker. Lockers are in a low-traffic area of the building and hence are more easily accessible to burglars. Report any suspicious person around the area to the police.

LAUNDRY FACILITIES

1. In consideration for other residents, common laundry facilities should be utilized only between the hours of 8:00 A.M. and 10:00 P.M.

2. Equipment failure or malfunction should be reported to the number posted on the machine so that prompt repairs may be made.

WINDOWS

All windows should be draped with curtains or drapes. Blankets and sheets are not suitable unless converted to drapes or curtains, not simply tucked or hung over drapery rods.

MISCELLANEOUS

Please note that although the fireplaces in many of the apartments were once functioning, they are no longer usable. Fires of any kind present extreme hazards to all residents due to the dangers of smoke and carbon-monoxide poisoning. For this reason, the fireplaces are decorative and NONFUNCTIONING. Do not attempt to burn in them. The chimneys have been sealed to prevent heat loss and to help us reduce our heating costs.

2.

Newsletters Monthly newsletters or notices are an excellent way of educating occupants about current market conditions, improvements being made to the property, building activities, and other events, such as the appointment or promotion of management personnel. Newsletters can be printed or distributed via e-mail. They can be simple or elaborate, but they should always be timely, accurate, and professional.

Cultivating a sense of pride The astute property manager—whether residential, industrial, or commercial—cultivates pride and a sense of community among the tenants. Living and conducting business in the building can be made as pleasant as possible by offering both tangible and intangible benefits. Amenities such as conference rooms, employee lunchrooms, child-care facilities, game rooms, swimming pools, and tennis courts are useful in marketing the space and in cultivating a stable tenancy.

However, the manager's personal efforts can generate friendliness and loyalty among the tenant population, even more than the amenities themselves. A little extra effort and creativity on the part of the manager can go a long way toward developing tenant pride and interest in the building.

For example, the manager can publicize building activities that encourage tenant identification with the building as a whole. By remembering the importance of prestige and aura of desirability, the manager can easily enhance the image of the property with such thoughtful gestures as providing free coffee in the office cafeteria or seasonal decorating for the lobby every year. A satisfied, stable tenant population solidifies the earning capacity of the property and improves the stability of the income, thus fulfilling the manager's primary obligation to the owner.

Handling Maintenance Requests

Maintenance is the single most important factor over which the property manager has control. The manager must make certain that the tenant understands the building's maintenance procedures and the proper division of this responsibility between tenant and owner. The tenant should be told what areas are covered under the terms of the lease agreement and also how and to whom to make service requests. Chapter 8 is devoted to the various types of maintenance and the implementation of management programs.

Requests in writing The most important step is to insist that all **maintenance requests** be submitted in writing. Then, a system should be developed to quickly and effectively channel service requests to the appropriate parties. One way is to use carbonless paper forms of three different colors: copies each for the manager, the serviceperson, and the tenant. A paper copy of the form used by Lincoln Property Company is shown as Figure 7.3.

Using software management Increasingly, managers are using software to track maintenance requests and to bill for such work. The work order command

FIGURE 7.3
Maintenance Request Form

LINCOLN PROPERTY COMPANY
Maintenance Request

No. 34456

	DEAD BOLT INFO.	RECEIVED	COMPLETED

APT. #

NAME

TELEPHONE NO.

UNABLE TO ENTER ☐

WORK REQUESTED:

PARTS TO BE ORDERED:

DATE ORDERED:

DELIVERY SCHEDULED:

REMARKS:

UNABLE TO COMPLETE BECAUSE:

☐ SPECIAL LOCK

☐ PET

☐ FILTER CHANGE

APARTMENT CONDITION

GOOD ☐   POOR ☐

ASSIGNED TO   COMPLETED BY   TAKEN BY

ORIGINAL

Source: Reprinted with permission of Property Company of America Realty, Inc.

provides the manager with a way of entering and tracking maintenance requests from tenants and owners. The work order can be broken down between materials and labor, and can even include comments from the worker. Additionally, any warranty may also be included in the software.

This software tracks work orders in progress, in addition to work order history. Once the work order has been completed, it can be automatically transferred into the maintenance history file. Work orders can be edited at any time.

Repairs can be performed in-house or by outside contractors, and billed appropriately. If the manager wants to create a bill for payment to the vendor, the software will automatically carry forward the information to the report to be printed.

Speedy response   The success of tenant relations also depends to a great extent on the speed of the landlord's response to the tenant's needs. Whenever a service request is made, the tenant should be told immediately when it will be taken care of. If the request is denied, the manager should be honest with the tenant and explain why. The best way to alienate a tenant is to allow him or her to expect something and then to procrastinate and evade the issue if delivery becomes impossible.

Excessive demands   One common management problem is excessive service demands from some tenants. The manager should listen courteously to requests and then explain to the tenant that providing extra services will necessitate a rent increase to cover the extra expenditures. Because the price of labor rises faster than that of any other commodity, service is becoming increasingly expensive; hence, service demands that call for additional personnel must ultimately result in disproportionately higher rents. Tenants who realize this will be more amenable to a compromise.

Role of maintenance personnel   No matter how responsible management is to tenant demands, good relations with tenants can be destroyed if tenants are made to feel their requests are an annoyance. Maintenance personnel, the superintendent, and the staff of the management office should handle tenant requests in a pleasant manner. Likewise, service personnel should speak courteously—especially on the telephone, where they are judged only by their voices. On-site maintenance people should be neatly groomed; in fact, service uniforms are a good idea if economically feasible. The property manager must set a good example in this regard.

Commercial and Industrial Variations

Although residential leases are generally uniform, commercial or industrial leases rarely have the same maintenance provisions. Therefore, a nonresidential property manager usually must consult the lease to verify whether the requested action is the responsibility of the tenant or of the owner. If the tenant is responsible, the tenant must be advised; otherwise, the manager should promptly service the request.

■ RENT COLLECTION

From the outset, the manager should be clear as to when rent is due, where it is to be paid, and the penalties for being late or not making payment. The manager must first serve the interests of the owner by setting up a viable system for collecting rent and dealing with uncooperative tenants. The tenant should never be accommodated at the expense of the owner. Whether the leased space is an office, a store, a warehouse, or an apartment, it is standard practice for rentals to be paid in advance.

When to Pay

For convenience, accuracy, and speed in rent collection and record keeping, most monthly rentals are due and payable on the first of the month. The promptness with which tenants pay their rent is directly related to the efficiency of the manager's collection policy. Timely communication with tenants and tracking their payment progress is very important. Tenants will lose respect for a manager who is apathetic about rent collection.

Encouraging Prompt Payments

There are many ways to elicit prompt payments from tenants. The most basic is to establish from the start a clear-cut understanding of the need for prompt payments. The requirements for prompt payment of rent and the provisions for default should be reviewed when the tenant signs the lease. The manager should explain in a firm but friendly manner that after a specified time, the tenant will be treated as delinquent and that appropriate legal action will be taken if necessary. The manager must not bluff, but should follow an established procedure that is rigidly adhered to without exception.

> Many tenants prefer to authorize regular, timely direct deposits. Direct deposits benefit both the tenant and the manager. An ideal program will notify the tenant that a withdrawal for the rent is going to be made, and then will notify the tenant when the withdrawal has been made and the manager when the deposit is made. Some companies even offer an incentive in the form of a discount to tenants to encourage direct deposits. A slight reduction in rent is more than made up in return for the savings realized by timely payments promptly deposited.

Late Fees

Two schools of thought exist concerning imposition of late charges on tenants who are delinquent in paying their rent. Some managers reject late charges, preferring instead to emphasize prompt payment and strict collection procedures; others maintain that late charges are necessary to affirm rigid collection taking charge. Payment habits of tenants are a direct reflection of the manager's attention to and enforcement of firm collection policies. A manager taking over an existing complex must establish a consistent policy immediately upon arrival. An alternative to late fees is a discount for payment on or before the due date. Another variation is giving a cash payment for a certain number of on-time payments.

Billing Notices

Whether tenants receive a rent bill for each payment period is a matter of building policy. Itemized, individual rent statements are a must for buildings whose tenants use variant services (net lease). For example, an office building manager might need to issue separate bills reflecting each occupant's share of the operating expenses based on that tenant's utility consumption during the billing period. Commercial tenants may also be billed separately for electricity, light bulbs, special janitorial services, special carpentry or plumbing jobs, and late charges. Machine or computer-operated accounting systems can print rent bills and receipts simultaneously, but these expensive systems are normally restricted to larger properties and management firms. Residential tenants rarely receive monthly bills and notices.

Using software management   First the manager must enter basic data about the rental payments. Each property often has its own time frame for what it designates as late rent. The program can track payments including the bank account, deposit date, and deposit number for maximum detail. If the payment is not received on the due date, a late notice with appropriate late fee is generated. Eventually, if no payment is received, an eviction notice is generated and that process can begin.

■ LEASE RENEWALS

■ Unless the lease agreement includes an automatic renewal clause, it will expire on the date specified in the contract. A tenant whose lease is expiring usually has no overwhelming need or desire to move to new quarters. Whether the tenant stays depends on the tenant-manager relationship and the terms of the new lease.

The Value of Stable Tenants

In a **lease renewal** situation, the manager must weigh one additional factor that was not present during the initial negotiations. A stable tenant with a history of timely rental payments is a proven quantity and an asset to the owner. Furthermore, the present tenant will probably make fewer demands for redecorating or other alterations than a new occupant would.

Bargaining Factors

Market conditions at the time of expiration will exert a strong influence over the concessions or terms granted under the new lease. In general, bargaining will center on

- the length of the new lease term;
- the extent of repairs, alterations, or redecorating to be done; and
- the amount of rent to be paid.

Concessions

The actual negotiation of lease renewals follows the same basic pattern as that used to obtain the initial rental agreement. If the general economic trend is inflationary, the manager should probably push for an increased rental rate and a short-lease term or for an escalation clause. During a deflationary trend the manager should favor a longer lease term to secure the current higher rental rate for as long as possible. The tenant usually will expect to receive other concessions in return for signing a longer lease at a fixed rent rate during a time of falling prices.

Construction   The extent of repairs, alterations, or redecorating to be done will be influenced by market conditions, particularly by the competition in the market, and the manager will have to be current on concessions being offered by competitors. If an alteration desired by a tenant will become a permanent improvement to the property, the manager may be able to charge it to a previously allocated fund, which could allow some flexibility in the rental rate.

Rental rate   One of the most important issues in lease renewals is the rental rate. Rent increases necessitated by rising operating costs are the most frequent cause for contract changes. With commercial property especially, the rent paid over the initial lease term may have included the cost of extensive preparation and tenant alterations. Because this work has been paid for by the time the lease is renewed, the rental rate may then revert back to the base rent, plus any increases deemed necessary by management. According to surveys made by BOMA and IREM, operating costs (excluding taxes and insurance) consume more than 43 percent of an office property's gross income and approximately 41 percent of an apartment building's income. Wages and taxes are currently increasing at a faster rate than rents in most areas.

Proper Notice

The manager can avoid the irritation, inconvenience, and legal complications of a holdover tenancy by communicating with the tenant well before the lease expires and discussing any changes desired by the owner. Residential tenants can be approached about 90 days before lease expiration, but commercial and industrial tenants should be contacted from six months to a year before the expiration date. The time interval generally depends on the tenant, the property, and the specific lease.

Competition

In commercial leasing and renewals, more independent brokers represent tenants. Sometimes these brokers expect their commissions to be paid by landlords; other times, they are paid by the tenant. Either way, the broker will survey the market and present a number of properties to the tenant. The broker may also favor a property other than the manager's. An alert manager, therefore, should try to contact the tenant before the broker becomes involved.

■ RENT INCREASES

Fact of Life

A 100-percent occupancy level may indicate that the rental schedule for the building is too low in comparison to the area market and that it is time for an increase. On the surface, both tenant and manager dislike **rent increases.** The former does not want to pay more; the latter fears a high vacancy rate will discredit him or her as a manager. On the other hand, wise tenants understand that economic realities probably dictate periodic increases. Managers may be more likely to support rent increases if their yearly bonus is tied into collected rent. In some cases, they will even recommend increases on available units and can help justify the increase if they were involved in the pricing decisions.

Before deciding on any increase, the manager should survey the market to establish a market rent schedule for the property (review the process of property analysis in Chapter 2). Although it may be easier to communicate rent increases to tenants based on increased expenses, ultimately, the tenant will tolerate the increase if pricing is competitive with the market.

Cutting expenses by eliminating certain services or maintenance activities (such as exterior upkeep) is a self-defeating proposition. Tenants may not complain about these cuts as vociferously as they would about a leaking faucet that was not repaired, but a cutback in exterior maintenance expenditures will detract from the general appearance of the property. In these situations, over a period of time, lower-quality occupants will replace the high-grade tenants, and the property will become even less desirable. The only effective method of strengthening a property's earning power is to raise rents while striving for better operating efficiency.

Avoiding Tenant Protest

The threat of organized tenant protest against rent increases is greatly overstated. Although the manager might receive an initial flurry of termination notices, the number of tenants who actually move after they have had a chance to shop the market will be considerably lower. Even if a few of the tenants do vacate, the higher rental schedule for the property will tend to absorb the brief vacancy loss until the units can be rented at the new rate. In fact, despite the loss of some tenants and a temporary increase in the vacancy rate, total income for the month immediately after the increase may sometimes exceed that for the previous month. Of course, this holds true only if the rent increase is justified in terms of the property and the area market.

Here's an example of how this might work: When the average rent for a 50-unit apartment building with full occupancy was increased about 9 percent, from $800 to $875, 20 percent of the tenants threatened to move. However, by the time the increase went into effect only three tenants had gone, for an overall occupancy level of 94 percent. Before the rent increase, the 50 units earned $40,000 per month. After the raise, even with a 6 percent vacancy factor, the 47 occupied units brought in $41,125—a monthly increase of $1,125 over the previous month at full occupancy.

Increase Services

When rents are increased, the manager should make sure that building maintenance and services either improve or remain at the same level. Often a simple cosmetic improvement will satisfy the tenants as to the owner's good intentions. Implementing a quickly completed improvement will help make a favorable impression on tenants at this critical time and allow the manager to postpone a more complicated project without losing tenant goodwill.

■ TERMINATING THE TENANCY

Required Notice

Notice of intent to vacate must be given within a certain period, which should be specified in the terms of most lease agreements. A letter from the manager outlining the procedures tenants should follow when terminating their tenancy can avoid many misunderstandings. Sometimes tenants are poorly informed as to the notice required and details they must follow when vacating their space. The letter should include a checklist for the tenant, detailing the expected cleaning, post-occupancy inspections, return of security deposit, etc.

If a good tenant decides to move, the manager should contact him or her immediately to find out whether the decision was prompted by any oversight on the part of management. If so, the manager should ascertain if the situation can be corrected, thereby retaining a valuable tenant. Even if the tenant's decision is irreversible, the manager should note the reasons behind it and file them for future reference.

Exit Interview

An exit interview between manager and tenant should be made in person, if possible, and should be a routine procedure; Figure 7.4 is a sample form for an exit interview. By analyzing the responses of all tenants who have moved recently, the manager can better understand the reasons behind the tenant turnover.

Fair Housing Compliance

The manager may refuse to renew a lease by giving the tenant appropriate notice of termination. This procedure can be used in lieu of the more expensive and time-consuming court eviction suit, provided the tenant's conduct is not too destructive and the remaining lease term is short.

■ To stay on firm legal footing, the manager who does not renew a lease should have demonstrable proof of just cause for the refusal. Such termination may not be based on the tenant's race, color, religion, national origin, sex, familial status, or handicap. Additionally, the manager is prohibited from serving notice in retaliation for the tenant's complaints to the authorities about building health and safety issues.

Inspection of the Premises

Whenever either party terminates a lease, the manager should inspect the space with the tenant after the tenant has removed all personal items. Whenever possible, the manager should use the same form used for move-in, the one that had been signed by both the tenant and the manager, to determine if any damage has been done to the property and if the unit is being returned in reasonable condition. Any deductions to be made from the security or cleaning deposits can be calculated at this time.

FIGURE 7.4
Tenant Exit Interview Form

Tenant Exit Interview

DATE: _____   PROPERTY: _____

NAME: _____   TITLE: _____

LENGTH OF TENANCY: _____   TYPE OF SPACE: _____

FORWARDING ADDRESS AND TELEPHONE NUMBER: _____

_____

_____

STATED REASON FOR MOVING: (Also details such as information on new location, size, rent, lease terms, purchased property, etc.): _____

_____

_____

_____

_____

_____

_____

_____

_____

COMMENTS/SUGGESTIONS: (How could we have served Tenant better? Cover any complaint or suggestion in detail.): _____

_____

_____

_____

_____

_____

_____

_____

_____

PERSONAL INTERVIEW? _____   TELEPHONE INTERVIEW? _____

COMPLETED BY: _____

Source: Floyd M. Baird, Temple, Texas.

When the unit is empty, the manager will have to determine what repainting and refurbishing will be needed before the space can be rented again. To facilitate this procedure, the manager might carry a checklist, similar to the move-in checklist (Figure 7.1) to note the condition of each room or area, repairs needed, and when they can be scheduled. Similar forms should be used for commercial space.

(At least one state, California, requires that the residential property manager must conduct a property inspection before the tenant vacates the property, if requested by the tenant.)

Return of the Security Deposit

Typically, state and/or local laws provide a detailed procedure for returning a **security deposit**. Generally, the landlord must account for how the security deposit is returned or retained within a certain period of time after the lease is terminated. Many states require that the reasons be documented in writing. A security deposit may usually be applied towards unpaid rent and/or damages or required repairs to the property. The landlord or manager must document in writing why any money is being retained. In some states, failure to do so will subject the landlord to legal penalties. State laws provide various ways to disburse unclaimed security deposits.

Retention for damages Acceptable grounds for retaining part or all of the security deposit typically include damages to the premises; unauthorized, nonstandard, or irreversible decorating; excessive cleaning expenses; and unauthorized alterations. Charges made against the security deposit must be documented to establish the case against the tenant, and an inspection checklist such as the one in Figure 7.1 is the best means of verification. Other documentation may include pictures of the damage or contractors' bills to clean or repair the premises.

Last month's rent In the past, residential tenants sometimes used security deposits as the last month's rent, but current legislation in some states forbids this practice. Even if it is not prohibited, leases should be written to prohibit it. One manager made the security deposit a different amount than the monthly rent; tenants stopped thinking of it as rent. Security deposit legislation also covers the handling of security deposits when the ownership of dwelling units changes. Under the law, the person holding a security deposit must either return the deposit to the tenant or transfer it to the new owner, while giving notice to the tenant. If a property manager is required by law to be licensed as a real estate broker, trust account laws and regulations governing brokers also apply to funds held by a property manager on behalf of tenants.

■ TERMINATING THE TENANCY IN COURT

Unfortunately, from time to time, tenants violate the building rules or do not pay their rents. Sometimes they are involved with criminal activities on the property. In these cases, the manager must take legal action on behalf of the owner. Allowing nonpaying tenants or tenants involved in illegal activities to stay will only prolong the problem.

Reasons for Eviction

In addition to nonpayment of rent, other permissible grounds for **eviction** of a tenant include breaches in the other terms of the lease agreement, as discussed in Chapter 5. If no written lease is in effect, grounds for eviction usually include noncompliance with building rules, misrepresentation or fraud, violation of the law, excessive occupants on the premises, excessive use of utilities, abuse of fixtures, illegal drug activity, unauthorized pets, and any miscellaneous activities that disrupt the other tenants.

Notice before Eviction Suit

If possible, before legal action can be taken, the tenant must always be given notice of the breach or improper conduct and an opportunity to rectify the situation. There may be some situations where this is not possible, such as assigning or subletting without consent or if the breach violates the law, as in illegal drug usage. Then, if the tenant fails to make a good faith effort to correct the situation, the manager may initiate dispossess proceedings and obtain a judgment decree for damages. (Note that many states have passed laws regarding the seizure and forfeiture of properties that are the sites of illegal drug activities, whether or not the owner knew of such activities. Special care should be taken when evicting tenants for illegal drug activities; it would be wise to consult an attorney.)

Although tenants have already been told that immediate action will be taken in the case of delinquency, it is good public relations for the manager to allow a reasonable period of time between the due date and the announcement of legal action for delinquency. This should be a fixed, predetermined period that in most cases should not exceed three to five days. During this grace period, the tenant should be sent a reminder notice that states the penalty and a warning that further action will be taken if payment is not received immediately. A sample past-due notice used in Iowa is shown as Figure 7.5. Any form used must conform to local laws and regulations.

Instead of a reminder letter, the manager can personally advise a delinquent tenant of the overdue obligation in person or by phone, thereby establishing two-way communication with the delinquent tenant. If the reminder (written or oral) does not generate a response from the tenant, the manager then can initiate a suit for eviction to regain possession of the premises (an available vacancy is better than an occupied space earning no rent).

The manager should be aware of not only state statutes but also the local rules that may apply. State statutes dictate the minimum number of days before suit can be filed, what notice must be given, and the forms that must be filed.

Eviction Suit

The process of eviction and repossession of property, particularly if the tenant resists the landlord's action, is highly technical and requires the guidance of an experienced attorney. As a general overview, to bring an **eviction suit,** the manager must fill out an eviction form (sometimes in triplicate). In this case, one copy

FIGURE 7.5
Three-Day Notice to Pay Rent or Quit

PROFESSIONAL PROPERTY MANAGEMENT, INC.
5901 VISTA DRIVE
WEST DES MOINES, IA 50266   PH: (515) 226-0000

NOTICE TO CURE / QUIT

TO: John Doe

ADDRESS: 1111 42nd St. 364 Des Moines, IA 50266

You are hereby notified that you have failed to comply with your written lease for non-payment of rent for the

premises located at the address stated above for the month of **March 1999**. There is a balance owing of:

$272.50. You are hereby notified that there is currently a balance owing to the Landlord for the **total amount of**

$272.50. Demand is hereby made upon you to pay the **total amount owed** within **THREE (3) DAYS** after this

notice is served.

THIS AMOUNT MUST BE PAID BY MONEY ORDER NO LATER THAN
March 22, 1999.
NO PARTIAL PAYMENTS OR PERSONAL CHECKS WILL BE ACCEPTED

IF YOU DO NOT PAY THE AMOUNT DUE AS SPECIFIED ABOVE WITHIN THE THREE(3) DAY PERIOD,
THE LANDLORD, PROFESSIONAL PROPERTY MANAGEMENT, INC., SHALL TERMINATE THE WRITTEN
LEASE AND SHALL BRING LEGAL PROCEEDINGS TO HAVE YOU REMOVED FROM THE PREMISES.

Time is of the essence with respect to this Notice! Not only will you be required to vacate the rental unit, but you
will be held responsible for any costs incurred by the Landlord plus any unpaid rent until the Landlord re-rents the
unit. Please therefore take notice and govern yourself accordingly.

_____
RESIDENT

_____   John Q. Adams, Accounting Specialist
DATE

                                  March 16, 1999
                                  DATE

Source: Professional Property Management, Inc., West Des Moines, Iowa.

is served on the tenant, another is given to the manager's attorney to be filed in court at a later date, and the third is retained by the manager.

Care must be taken when completing this form, as improperly drawn notices are frequently thrown out of court. An attorney familiar with local laws should draft this form. Precise eviction procedures are regulated by state statute. In some states, the manager must wait only three days after giving the eviction form to the tenant before allowing the attorney to file the notice in court; in other states, this period may be as long as ten days.

In many cases, a delinquent tenant will accept the landlord's notice to move from the rented premises, but in the event the tenant does not leave voluntarily, it will be necessary to file a legal action for possession. Under most statutes, this action is filed in the court of lowest jurisdiction, such as the small claims or magistrate's court. Depending on applicable state law, it may be necessary to have this action filed by an attorney. For example, in some states, if a corporation owns the property an attorney must be hired, whereas an individual property owner is allowed to file on his or her own behalf.

Process

Notice of the filing of an eviction suit must be served on the tenant, and service must be made according to applicable state law. In some states, the defendant must be served in person; in others, service may be made on certain members of the family or other persons residing on the premises. In still others, posting a copy of the summons on the property is valid service on the defendant. Although some tenants will ignore an owner's notice to quit the property, it has been the experience of many property managers that after the service of summons into court, the delinquent tenant generally will leave voluntarily. If the tenant fails to appear at the court hearing, a default judgment is given to the landlord. If a tenant appears in order to contest the notice, a trial must be held to determine the matter.

Actual Removal

Once the court gives a judgment returning possession to the landlord, or the landlord is successful at a trial, the property manager must determine whether the tenant has physically left the premises. If the tenant has moved out and left nothing of value behind, the owner may take possession and re-rent the property. If, as sometimes happens, a tenant leaves personal property behind, the landlord must follow local statutes with regard to its disposition. If the tenant refuses to vacate the property even after the court rules for the landlord, the landlord must secure a court order and the sheriff or constable serving the court will physically remove the tenant from the property.

■ SUMMARY

The effective property manager can establish personal but not unduly familiar relations with the tenant population, enforce all lease terms and building rules, and be able to handle residents who do not pay their rent on time. If a manager is ineffectual, the net operating income from the property will decline. The manager is responsible for maintaining communication and mutual understanding between the landlord and tenant. The manager should discuss rent payment and collection policies and building regulations with all new tenants.

Sound tenant relations are based on a good reputation for the management of the property. Tenants tend to renew their leases if they are getting the services and benefits they contracted for. Lease renewals eliminate the costs of high tenant turnover, and satisfied, long-term tenants take a personal interest in the upkeep of the property, thereby cutting the owner's maintenance costs.

The manager should make certain that the tenant knows the correct procedure for making service requests and what services the tenant can reasonably expect. When service requests are made, the tenant should be told immediately either when the job will be done or why it cannot be completed. All maintenance and management office personnel should be pleasant and accommodating in their dealings with tenants.

The manager can capitalize upon the fact that a tenant whose lease is expiring may have no specific need to move. Whether a tenant decides to renew a lease usually depends on the nature of the tenant-manager relationship and the terms of the new lease. Bargaining will center on the amount of rent, the extent of alterations or redecorating, and the length of the new lease term. Rising operating costs usually cause rent increases. The manager must look at the present market conditions and the value of a stable tenant when deciding whether to impose new lease terms.

Besides providing prompt, efficient service that will establish a management-tenant relationship conducive to lease renewals, the manager must also protect the owner's interests by setting up an effective system for collecting rent and coping with uncooperative tenants. When the tenant signs the lease, the lease terms should be reviewed and the tenant told about the penalties for failure to pay rent promptly and for noncompliance with other lease terms. The owner has the right to bring a court suit for eviction and a judgment for damages against any delinquent or disruptive tenant. Before initiating legal action, however, he or she must give the tenant sufficient legal notice and time to remedy the situation.

Under most lease agreements, tenants must give notice of intent to terminate within a specified period. The manager should question a valued tenant to determine whether the decision to move is based on any management oversight that can still be corrected. Even if the tenant's decision is final, the manager should note the reasons for the move. A compilation of the responses of all tenants who recently have moved should give the manager some insight into possible improvements that might be made in the management of the property. Security deposits must be administered according to local law.

■ CASE STUDY

THE TENANT RELATIONS MANAGER

Jennifer Chin manages a 75-unit apartment complex. One of her primary functions is to manage tenant relations. In one week, Chin had to deal with three unpleasant tenant situations. One tenant, White, has been chronically late with her rent. For the last three months, White has paid the rent only after receiving the landlord's official "pay or quit the premises" eviction notice. This month, White is late again.

A second tenant, Samuels, has made repeated requests for various services and repairs, most of which have not been the landlord's responsibility. Samuels just told Chin that he wants his apartment repainted. When Chin tactfully told him that the landlord was not obligated to repaint the apartment in the middle of his one-year tenancy, he became very upset and threatened to start a tenant revolt.

Juarez, who has been a model tenant for five years, just told Chin that she would not be renewing the lease when it expires in two months. When Chin asked her why not, she replied that she was uncomfortable with present management policies.

1. What can Chin do to solve the rent delinquency problem with White?
2. What can Chin do to head off the threatened tenant revolt?
3. How should Chin respond to Juarez's statement about present management policies?

■ REVIEW QUESTIONS

1. High tenant turnover means increases for the landlord in
   a. advertising expenses.
   b. utility costs.
   c. the value of the managed property.
   d. bad debts.

2. A record of lease renewal dates should be kept so that the property manager will know when to
   a. make plans for significantly decreased income.
   b. anticipate overuse and repairs of elevators.
   c. contact good tenants in an attempt to retain them.
   d. know when to watch for increased criminal activity.

3. The establishment of good tenant relations begins with which of the following?
   a. Tenant welcome party
   b. Joint inspection of the premises by manager and tenant before move-in
   c. Associating with tenants on a social basis
   d. Tenant association meetings

4. In which type of property is inspection of the premises with a new tenant the most important?
   a. Industrial
   b. Residential
   c. Commercial
   d. Agricultural

5. Which of the following is the most important in establishing tenant loyalty and friendliness?
   a. The manager's personal efforts
   b. Weekly informal coffees
   c. Features such as conference rooms, swimming pools, tennis courts, etc.
   d. Free continental breakfasts

6. Tenant relations can be aided by
   a. contacting tenants only on an emergency basis.
   b. saving brochures to distribute only when a problem arises.
   c. reviewing rent collection procedures with the tenant in a conference at the beginning of the lease.
   d. associating with tenants on a social basis.

7. The basic prerequisite for enlightened property maintenance is
   a. experienced maintenance crews.
   b. an experienced maintenance supervisor.
   c. on-call availability of maintenance specialists such as air-conditioning repairmen, journeyman plumbers, etc.
   d. getting the tenant's service requests to the appropriate parties.

8. What should be done when a tenant makes a service request?
   a. Forward it to the maintenance supervisor immediately
   b. If it is to be denied, the tenant should be told it will be forwarded to management
   c. Tenant should be told when it will be taken care of, or why it will not be
   d. Records should be checked to see if the requesting tenant is making excessive demands

9. What is the foundation of a good landlord and tenant relationship?
   a. Hard line regarding prompt rental payments
   b. Good reputation for maintenance and management
   c. Maintaining a proper distance from tenants and the building
   d. Prompt legal action at the first sign of tenant complaints

10. What should the manager do if a good tenant terminated the lease?
    a. Immediately contact the tenant to find out why he or she is moving and, if possible, correct the situation
    b. Accept the termination graciously and be grateful they stayed as long as they did
    c. Try to talk the tenants into staying
    d. Totally ignore the situation

11. The most critical factor in determining whether and how much of a rent increase to make is
    a. how many tenants will vacate.
    b. the total net increase in income after accounting for move-outs due to the increase.
    c. whether the manager has the ability to handle complaints because of the increase.
    d. whether the image of the project will be tarnished by bad publicity.

12. If rents are increased, the manager should
    a. schedule a vacation for the day the increase is announced.
    b. expect an organized tenant protest and hire extra security.
    c. learn the logic behind the increase so he or she can explain it to the tenants.
    d. decrease maintenance service.

13. An office building of 200,000 square feet has an average rental rate of $8.50 per square foot and an overall occupancy level of 97 percent. The manager determines from market and property analyses that if the rental rate is raised by $.20 per square foot, the occupancy level will drop by 2 percent. If the rental rate is raised by $.40 per square foot, the occupancy level will drop by 6 percent. Conversely, if the rental rate is decreased by $.30 per square foot, the occupancy level will increase to 100 percent. The optimum average rental rate per square foot for this office space would be
    a. $8.20.   c. $8.70.
    b. $8.50.   d. $8.90.

14. An apartment building of 75 units, each leased at $600 per month, enjoyed full occupancy. The property manager then instituted a 10 percent rent increase, and five tenants moved out. The month after the change, the gross rental income
    a. decreased by $1,550.
    b. increased by $1,200.
    c. was $45,000.
    d. was $49,500.

15. The BEST way to get prompt payment of rent is to
    a. file eviction suits if rent is not paid by the fifth day after it is due.
    b. have a clear-cut understanding of the requirements for payment and provisions for default.
    c. have a full-time professional collector.
    d. issue regular bills stating amount and date rent is due.

16. The time between the rent due date and the announcement of action for recovery should be
    a. three days.
    b. five days.
    c. adjusted according to the tenant's circumstances.
    d. a fixed, determined period.

17. Three copies of an eviction notice should be prepared—one for the tenant, one for the manager's attorney, and a third for the
    a. file 13.
    b. manager's file.
    c. tenant's attorney.
    d. sheriff's office.

18. Upon termination by a tenant, the property manager should
    a. contact the tenant immediately to get prospects for a new tenant.
    b. schedule an immediate discontinuance of utilities.
    c. inspect the space after the tenant has removed all personal property.
    d. make sure the tenant does not discuss plans for leaving with other tenants.

19. What form should the manager use when inspecting the property after the tenant has vacated?
    a.   Tenant exit interview form
    b.   Original lease
    c.   List of concessions previously made
    d.   Move-in/move-out checklist

20. In most states, detailed and stringent security deposit statutes have been passed. Which of the following is a provision of these statutes?
    a.   The landlord need not document any charges against the security deposit.
    b.   The landlord must itemize the deductions in a written statement.
    c.   Deductions are not authorized for nonstandard decorating, excessive cleaning charges, and damages to the premises.
    d.   The tenant may apply the deposit to the last month's rent.

CHAPTER EIGHT

MAINTENANCE
AND
CONSTRUCTION

■ KEY TERMS

Americans with
   Disabilities Act
   (ADA)
Competitive bids
Contract services
Corrective maintenance

Cost-plus bids
Deferred maintenance
Fast-track construction
Fixed-fee (flat-fee) bids
Negotiated contracts

New construction
   maintenance
Preventive maintenance
Retrofitting
Routine maintenance

■ LEARNING OBJECTIVES

At the end of this chapter, the student will be able to

1. list five kinds of maintenance operations and give an example for each;

2. determine whether to use on-site maintenance personnel or hire on a contract basis;

3. explain why the property manager should retain the right to hire and fire maintenance personnel;

4. discuss the need for ADA compliance when hiring personnel or making a building accessible;

5. explain the difference between competitive bids, negotiated bids, and fast track construction;

6. list the necessary steps to designing a preventive maintenance program;

7. give examples of long-term and short-term opportunities to save maintenance money; and

8. define life-cycle costing.

■ OVERVIEW

Maintenance is a continuous process of balancing services and costs; the manager must work to please the tenants and preserve the physical condition of the property while minimizing operating expenses and improving the owner's margin of profit. Efficient property maintenance demands an accurate assessment of the needs of the building and the number and kinds of personnel that will meet these needs.

Staffing and scheduling requirements will vary with the type, size, and regional location of the property, and the owner and manager should agree in advance on maintenance objectives for the property. In some cases, the most viable plan may be to operate with a low rental schedule and minimal expenditures for services and maintenance. Another property may be more profitable if kept in top condition and operated with full tenant services because it can then command premium rental rates. Specific maintenance requirements of each major classification of property are explored in Chapters 11 through 15. This chapter outlines the basic procedures for a sound maintenance program.

■ BASIC MAINTENANCE PROCEDURES

The successful property manager must be able to function effectively at four different levels of maintenance operations:

1. Routine maintenance

2. Preventive maintenance

3. Corrective maintenance

4. New construction

Routine Maintenance

Regular housekeeping chores are the most frequently recurring type of maintenance. For most multitenant buildings, residential or commercial, the common areas and the grounds around the buildings must be cleaned and patrolled daily.

Cleaning and housekeeping should be carefully scheduled and controlled, because costs can easily become excessive.

A major operating expense, **routine maintenance** can consume as much as 18 percent of the budget in commercial properties, as certain tasks like vacuuming elevators must be done several times a day. Other routine tasks, such as cleaning gutters and windows, are performed less frequently.

Preventive Maintenance

Regular maintenance activities and routine inspections of the building and its equipment should be scheduled on a predetermined basis. A good example of **preventive maintenance** is replacing air-conditioning filters on a regular basis or having the furnace inspected and tested at the beginning of the heating season. These inspections will disclose structural and mechanical problems before major repairs become necessary, hopefully eliminating or reducing corrective maintenance costs.

Corrective Maintenance

When something breaks, it must be fixed. **Corrective maintenance** involves the actual repairs that keep the building's equipment, utilities, and amenities functioning as contracted for by the tenants. Repairing a boiler, fixing a leaky faucet, and replacing a broken air-conditioning unit are examples of corrective maintenance.

The importance of corrective maintenance cannot be overly emphasized. Improperly handled (or worse, ignored) maintenance can quickly alienate tenants, causing them to leave. Delaying or ignoring needed repairs may also not only harm the reputation of the owner and the manager but also add more to the cost when repairs are finally performed.

New Construction Maintenance

New construction maintenance is often performed at the request and expense of the tenant; it is a category of maintenance closely tied to leasing and tenant relations. *Cosmetic maintenance* is designed to increase the marketability of the property. This may be as elementary as new wallpaper, light fixtures, and carpeting. If the new construction is extensive, it may be referred to as *upgrading*, which might include new entryways, the addition of a swimming pool, or converting storage space to a conference room. The preparation of a new building shell to accommodate a new tenant is termed *finish-out*. Similarly, renovation of a previously occupied space may be termed *makeready*. When the landlord redecorates or rehabilitates a space for a tenant as a condition of lease renewal, the space is *refurbished*.

Deferred Maintenance

Although not strictly a type of maintenance, **deferred maintenance** is a stock term in the property management business, and results when obvious repairs are postponed and are not made when needed. The building begins to lose value. This type of depreciation normally is curable by making the necessary repairs and improvements. It is sometimes called *curable physical depreciation* or *curable obsolescence*.

■ THE PROPERTY MANAGER AND MAINTENANCE PERSONNEL

As the property management field grows more sophisticated and building equipment becomes more complicated, managers who perform all four maintenance functions have become the exception rather than the rule. A property manager need not be a combination decorator, painter, roofer, and plumber, but he or she should understand the rudiments of all mechanical and electrical systems well enough to make intelligent decisions about their care and operation.

The manager must also be conversant with the economics, staffing, and scheduling involved in the smooth performance of maintenance tasks. The people who execute the work may be either building employees or outside personnel engaged on a contract basis. Depending on the size of the property, the amount of services required will determine whether to hire on-site maintenance staff or contract out each request for service. After determining the work to be done, and the time and expense involved, the property manager will make the decision on which is most cost-effective for the owner.

Resident Managers

Most residential properties of 16 units or more have a manager or an owner's representative on the premises at all times. These resident managers (who may be called superintendents or on-site managers) generally coordinate all maintenance operations for the building. Sometimes they may also be required to perform routine maintenance and simple corrective maintenance, such as replacing gaskets in a leaking faucet. Although a resident manager's responsibilities increase with the size of the building, this individual should report directly to the property manager.

A single property manager can stay abreast of the maintenance needs of several large buildings without becoming bogged down in the daily operating routine of each by regularly reviewing the reports submitted by resident managers. However, the property manager should still periodically visit each building regularly to gather information on necessary maintenance and repairs and to discover where operating costs can be cut.

On-Site Maintenance Staff

For most multitenanted buildings, minimum personnel requirements should be studied carefully to make sure that the full-time staff is large enough to meet the routine maintenance chores of the building. Understaffing can be just as expensive as overstaffing. Poor building maintenance will downgrade the premises, and when displeased tenants vacate, rental income drops.

Local union membership policies will also affect the composition of a building's maintenance staff. Semiskilled janitors, skilled general maintenance engineers, electricians, plumbers, and so on, belong to different unions, and union rules generally prohibit the hiring of nonunion workers. Therefore, when hiring a permanent building staff, the manager must consider the possible expense and inconvenience that might arise from mixing union and nonunion workers, or members of competing unions.

To avoid future misunderstandings, each newly hired employee should be shown the specific job responsibilities at the premises. Simple job descriptions listing the employee's various responsibilities can be helpful during the orientation period.

The manager will want to stress that each employee represents the owner, so members of the building staff must be pleasant, businesslike, and neat. Many knowledgeable managers provide service uniforms for maintenance personnel to enhance the prestige of the building and to strengthen employer-employee identification among the maintenance team.

Contract Services

Services performed by outside persons on a regular basis for a specified fee are known as **contract services**. Managers who represent several different owners, especially of scattered, single-family dwellings, will contract repairs on a case-by-case need basis. This simplicity enables the owners to be billed only for services performed on their buildings. The terms of the management agreement often set a ceiling on the service contracts the manager can execute without approval from the owner.

Before entering into any service contract, the manager should solicit competitive bids from several local contractors. If appropriate, the manager can then compare the cost of contracting out with the expense of using on-site personnel. In many situations, window cleaning, refuse and snow removal, pest control, and security are services that usually can be performed more efficiently and less expensively by outside contractors.

A contracting firm's references and work history should be checked out before it is hired; in fact, bids should not be solicited from contractors who have not been qualified in this manner. Part of qualifying a contractor is to verify that the contractor will maintain liability and worker's compensation insurances during the performance of the contract. The manager should obtain Certificates of Insurance that specify that the owner and manager are named as additional insured on the contractor's policy. The manager will also want to know whether the firm's employees are bonded and whether it has the necessary licenses or permits.

For the protection of both the manager and the owner, service contracts should always be in writing and contain a termination provision. The latter stipulation becomes important if service is not satisfactory or if the property is sold or destroyed. Before any payments are made to outside contractors, the manager should obtain mechanic's lien waivers or labor and material releases. Although different names are used for these documents, the intent is to provide proof that the work and materials were paid for and that the contractor paid the subcontractors.

Hiring and Firing Maintenance Employees

The approval of hiring and firing employees should be under the control of the property manager or the owner's agent and not left entirely to the discretion of the resident manager or superintendent. Nevertheless, the property manager should welcome the resident manager's opinion of the prospect's integrity, industry, and skills during the hiring process. The same is even more critical when termination is involved.

Each applicant for a maintenance position should complete an employment application. The appearance, demeanor, motivation, experience, education, reliability, and performance capabilities of the prospective employee should be the overriding factors. In addition, past employment references are important and should be checked. If a negative reference is received that contradicts the manager's evaluation of the applicant, the manager should try to determine whether a personality conflict caused the unfavorable report from a former employer, rather than the capabilities of the employee.

ADA Compliance

The Americans with Disabilities Act (ADA) applies to any management company that has 15 or more employees. More detailed information about ADA is covered in Chapter 10. Briefly, an employer may not ask applicants if they have a disability, or inquire into the nature or severity of a disability. The manager may ask if the applicant can perform the essential job functions as described.

A medical examination may be required after an offer has been made and before the employee actually starts work. The ADA does not encourage, authorize, or prohibit drug testing that is not considered a medical exam.

■ PREVENTIVE MAINTENANCE AND MAINTENANCE INSPECTIONS

Preventive maintenance has become a highly developed set of procedures. At its best, it involves carefully scheduled maintenance activities and prepared inspection forms that list the important physical elements and systems of the property.

> The purpose of preventive maintenance is twofold—to cut down on repair and replacement costs and to avoid interruptions in service to the tenants.
>
> Preventive maintenance programs should be implemented in all properties—whether residential or commercial, small or large properties—and may range from the efforts of a part-time maintenance worker to a full-time employee utilizing a sophisticated computerized program and headed by a full-time employee.

Routine Inspections

From a practical viewpoint, the manager's first responsibility is to be aware of the overall condition and operations of each property under his or her care. The manager's effectiveness as a maintenance administrator depends on thorough routine inspections and on the ability to pinpoint and correct laxness in the maintenance team. In addition to reviewing the preventive maintenance reports, the property manager should conduct spot checks and a tour of the premises, preferably once every four to six weeks. These inspection trips allow for a more extensive check of the systems, equipment, and condition of the building. Seasonal checks of the building's roofing and weatherproofing should be included in inspections.

Maintenance checks should be a routine procedure to find small problems before they get worse. The inspections are more comprehensive when the manager brings along checklists of the building features to be examined. If the checklists include the names of the maintenance personnel employed by the building and the tasks for which they are responsible, the manager can also rate the performance of building employees while touring the physical premises. The inspection checklist can help the manager explain to the owner any recommendations for repairs or replacements in addition to explaining expenditures that are made for maintenance service and repairs.

In general, the manager should inspect all interior and exterior features of each property and include comments on the condition of the grounds, walls, entrance steps, doorways, mailboxes, fire escapes, windows, eaves, and roofs. Regular walk-throughs offer the manager regular opportunities to note any potential possible breaches in security. When examining the interior of any property, the manager should observe the condition of the entranceway, stairwells, corridors, elevators, light fixtures, the lobby, and other common areas; heating and ventilating plant; hot water heater; and plumbing system and sewage disposal unit. Doors, locks, transoms, ceilings, baseboards, windows, light fixtures and switches, electrical outlets, floors, plumbing, and any permanent fixtures also should be inspected when checking recently vacated space.

Needed repairs and their anticipated cost should be noted on the checklist to help the manager set up a performance schedule and operating budget. Although it is not wise to become enmeshed in trivial daily maintenance problems, the property manager must be aware of all major concerns around the premises because he or she ultimately is accountable for all maintenance expenditures.

Maintenance Requests   The property manager should tell all tenants to report problems and maintenance needs immediately to the management or building office, preferably in writing. Making a three-part request form (see Figure 7.3) available to tenants will facilitate responses. Tenants should be personally thanked by the manager for passing on information about needed repairs in their rented space or public areas, even if the manager was already aware of the condition. Building employees should be alert to maintenance needs of the property and know how to report such problems.

■ SETTING UP A COST-EFFICIENT MAINTENANCE PROGRAM

A program to reduce maintenance costs is not easily engineered, implemented, or maintained. It requires the cooperation of all persons involved in the management of the property—from the resident manager or superintendent to the maintenance crew. On average, maintenance costs consume about 20 percent of the gross rental income for apartment buildings and more than 26 percent of the gross operating income for office properties. Since the beginning of the inflationary spiral in the early 1970s, expenditures for supplies, wages, contracted services, alterations, repairs, and other maintenance costs have risen steadily.

There is a definite need for both long-range and short-range planning techniques to control rising maintenance costs. Emergency planning should be included in any maintenance plan, because unanticipated emergencies are more costly if not responded to in an orderly, preplanned fashion.

Designing the Program   Software programs are particularly effective in designing a preventive maintenance program. Once the pertinent data is entered, reports can be generated on a regular basis to enable the manager to schedule repairs and to track their completion. There are five basic steps in designing a preventive maintenance program to fit the needs of a particular building:

1. Prepare an inventory of equipment and building.

2. Determine necessary maintenance tasks.

3. Calculate the cost.

4. Schedule the tasks.

5. Keep records.

Inventory   Make a complete inventory of all equipment that may have to be maintained. Each item should be listed and described, including its manufacturer, operating procedures, location in the building, date and place of purchase, and existing warranties. The inventory should indicate where to obtain parts and service and when each item needs to be lubricated, cleaned, or overhauled. Physical elements such as walls and supports should be listed by location and described. The manager can then decide what equipment and physical structures should be included in the preventive maintenance program.

Determine necessary maintenance tasks   The manager and the maintenance superintendent must decide what type of inspections and preventive maintenance tasks should be performed and how frequently. Structural items such as walls and roofs should be scheduled for inspection, painting, and patching. Equipment such as elevators, air-conditioning, heating plants, pumps, and motors also should be regularly inspected and serviced. Spare parts should be kept on hand to replace broken or worn machine parts. The exterior and interior of the building should be checked periodically. Some areas need to be checked daily, whereas others can be examined less frequently.

Calculate costs   Once the tasks have been determined, the manager must then calculate how much time, labor, and money the preventive maintenance program will require. The final figures must be realistic in terms of both the budget and the amount of work involved.

Schedule tasks   Because these tasks vary in frequency—weekly, bimonthly, or seasonally—a full year's schedule is easily determined in many software programs. Once scheduled, the manager can easily issue work orders and verify work completion. While all the areas must be checked on a regular basis, time must be set aside to complete unplanned emergency work.

Keep records   A complete set of such records will ensure systematic preventive maintenance, minimize interruptions in tenant services, and save the owner money. Figure 8.1 is a typical print form used to track preventive maintenance of certain elements of the heating and cooling system in a large regional shopping center. The resident manager or building superintendent should submit daily and weekly inspection reports to the property manager that are also entered into the maintenance history reports.

The manager must follow through on the program by keeping and regularly reviewing records on the results of preventive maintenance inspections and tasks for each piece of equipment. These reports eventually will show whether certain checks and activities can be performed less frequently, thereby saving labor and money, or whether certain items should be inspected more often. They also verify that maintenance personnel are actually performing these tasks and demonstrate the cost-effectiveness of the preventive maintenance program.

A well designed and implemented preventive maintenance program may not show significant results or savings for six months to a year. However, it will ultimately pay off in terms of increased efficiency and economy of operations.

Control Plans   Control techniques ensure an ongoing, cost-efficient maintenance program. Cost-reduction opportunities should be identified and ranked according to their ability to generate savings. Procedures for initiating work orders, timekeeping, control of materials, work scheduling, and control reporting then can be reassessed in light of new data gathered during the cost-reduction analyses.

The specific work executed by on-site or contracted maintenance personnel must be determined and planned by a maintenance administration staff. This administrative arm, which may consist of only the property manager and the resident

FIGURE 8.1
Cold Weather Inspection

Chiller Winter Inspection

| Ref. File |
| No. _____ |

| Sheet |
| ____ of ____ |

Unit No._____ Year_____ Division_____

MAINTENANCE CODE

TOP – test operation (observe, correct calibration, adjust as required)
VIS – visual inspection
LUB – lubricate (change oil)
CLN – clean as required
REP – replace

CONDITION CODE

G – good (minor deterioration)
F – fair (moderate deterioration)
P – poor (replace this inspection)

ITEM	MAINT. CODE	COND. CODE	SET POINT	DATE	ENGINEER INITIAL
condenser	VIS-CLN				
evaporator	VIS-CLN				
lube oil cooler	VIS-CLN				
control ampl. tubes	REP				
refr. filter/dryers	REP				
oil reservoir	LUB				
pur oper. contr.	VIS-TOP				
purge hi-limit contr.	VIS-TOP				
purge oil reservoir	LUB				
lube oil filter	REP				
cond. corrosion plugs	VIS				

Remarks:

_____

_____

_____

manager or of several highly trained employees, also should be responsible for budgeting, material control, and management reports.

Detailed plans are the foundation of effective maintenance supervision. Action plans should be designed for all repair, housekeeping, and construction tasks that maintenance personnel will perform. Although the degree of detail included in the advance planning program will vary from building to building, the more control the administrative arm exerts, the more effective and cost-efficient the actual maintenance program will be.

Short-term plans Redecorating, landscaping, and supplying stocks offer short-range opportunities to exercise cost control. Careful planning in these areas will result in a small but immediate reduction in expenses.

Bulk purchasing of supplies, also known as *volume buying,* is one of the most effective cost-control tools available to the manager. In some cases, it has increased the margin of profit on a property by as much as 3.5 percent. In order to buy in large lots, the manager must have storage space for at least a six-month supply of goods. An accurate inventory system enables the manager to identify items that are used infrequently or that have a short shelf life. These supplies should not be purchased in bulk, but rather as needed.

Security measures must be instituted to protect valuable stock from theft. One company solved the problem of expensive central control by maintaining small stocks of frequently used items at the offices of resident managers. Another way to deter theft is to purchase liquid supplies in drums and issue only the amounts needed for a pending job. Another system is known in other industries as "just-in-time" inventory—that is, ordering just what is needed, when it is needed. The success of JIT inventory depends on reliable and quick resupply. The cost of frequent inventories, supervision of issue, and other security measures necessary with large stocks has to be measured against the higher cost of smaller purchases. Computer software can simplify these tasks.

Long-term plans The first step in long-term cost-control planning is to identify opportunities to save on operational expenses. The property manager should study the functional alternatives for the property's major mechanical and electrical systems and examine ways to save on maintenance, labor, and wages. For example, it might be less costly to hire a handyman instead of a janitor. Although the salary for the former is higher, the extra expense is justified because the versatility of the handyman saves the wages that would otherwise be paid to contract personnel for repairs and other jobs.

Fuel and utility consumption costs, a large part of most properties' operating expenses, vary widely. The cost of running a heating plant and maintaining its equipment should be monitored over a period of time. Representatives of utility companies can provide helpful information on types of service and ways of decreasing utility costs.

▉ KEY TO SUCCESSFUL MAINTENANCE MANAGEMENT

▉ The key to successful maintenance is identifying what needs to be done, who is doing it, how much it costs, and whether the job was done right. It is useful to approach maintenance management from a customer service perspective rather than from only an engineering point of view. Tenants value quick responses to their requests; nevertheless, unlimited repairs and maintenance can quickly drain the financial coffers.

Information Required to Handle Maintenance Requests

Even the simplest maintenance plan should touch on seven basic points:

1. Scope of the job
2. Location of the job
3. Job priorities
4. Method to accomplish each job
5. Materials needed
6. Number of personnel
7. Hours of work performed

Scope and location of the job   The scope and location of the job should be accurately described. The instruction to "replace the grounding wire for the TV cable in 3C" is much more explicit than "fix the TV cable on the third floor." The maintenance crew sent out to perform the job will be able to determine in advance where they will be working and what tools they need for the job.

Job priorities   Job priorities are determined and assigned by the administration staff. The sequence in which the work for the day, the week, or the month is to be performed should be specified. Immediate problems such as a broken water pipe or window will take precedence over routine service checks and minor difficulties such as a leaking faucet.

Method to use and materials needed   The maintenance plan should also specify the best method of accomplishing each job. From this information, the administrative staff can determine the materials needed to complete the task and can have the appropriate supplies on hand. Employees will also recognize in advance the special tools, equipment, and safety requirements for a particular job.

Personnel and hours needed   To schedule maintenance crew time efficiently, the administrative staff should study all foreseeable jobs and project as far ahead as possible the number of personnel required and the hours of work that will be needed. Naturally, the scope of the job will dictate how detailed the data will have to be. Appropriate and realistic allocations of time and personnel should result in effective job performance at a reasonable cost, thereby avoiding tenant unrest due to inadequate service.

A well-planned maintenance program also protects the profit position of the owner by holding tenant turnover to a minimum and maintaining the physical integrity of the property. By skillfully assessing and balancing service needs and maintenance costs, the manager works for the mutual benefit of all concerned parties.

Choosing Computer Software

Software programs are the obvious solution to assist the manager when scheduling requested repairs, tracking time and cost of repairs, and scheduling regular preventive maintenance. Not all programs offer the same capabilities. Managers should determine how the software deals with any of the following situations:

- Handling temporary, one-of-a-kind work orders
- Scheduling work orders
- Retrieving work orders and reports
- Special requests from tenant
- Tenant responses to promptness and quality of work
- Invoicing for work done
- Scheduling work orders
- Ability to bill back charges to tenants
- Pay vendors
- Track costs of repairs
- Monitoring workers' performance and their pay
- Itemizing inventory and equipment
- Integrating maintenance information to the financial reports such as the general ledger, accounts payable, accounts receivable, etc.

Additionally, some programs monitor work orders through completion with continually updated inventory of supplies and materials. Some provide a module to inventory building and unit assets, such as stoves and refrigerators. Also useful is a database for purchase records, warranty information, maintenance contracts, and depreciation schedules. Some programs integrate budget control and purchase order modules that facilitate site purchasing and expense control. Fixed asset management becomes easier because the data allows the manager to decide when to repair and when to replace.

■ CONTRACTING FOR NEW CONSTRUCTION

Alterations

Construction activity stemming from tenant-requested alterations determines the hiring policy. If substantial tenant-required alteration is a regularly recurring event, as it often is in industrial and commercial space, a permanent staff of professional carpenters, electricians, and plasterers might prove cheaper and more efficient than using outside contractors on a steady basis. On the other hand, if a building's leasing policy is such that units are seldom restructured for tenants, then a full-time crew of experienced construction personnel would not be justified. In this case, it makes sense to hire outside contractors for major construction jobs and for smaller buildings that cannot bear the expense of a permanent staff.

New construction is sometimes required to protect the value of the property, improve its net income, increase its marketability, or meet the specifications of its tenants. The basic construction of a new building, especially a commercial one, often includes only the shell and the heating, ventilation, and air-conditioning (HVAC) systems. When space is rented, significant alteration is needed, both up to and beyond the building standard. Typically, the owner pays for improvements up to the building standard. The tenant pays for more extensive alteration and renovation, but such work is often arranged and handled by management as a convenience.

Building Conversions

Property managers also may be in charge of a building conversion, which often entails considerable remodeling, and perhaps some new construction.

Loft conversions are increasingly common. Lofts are so named because their interior floor space is not specialized. Each floor is a single open area, divided only by the support columns for the building. Loft buildings have been the albatrosses of many management firms. Beginning in the 1950s, many large lofts on the fringes of central business districts became vacant as light industries moved to the suburbs. Today, many loft structures are architectural nightmares and suffer from the dual woes of deferred maintenance and functional obsolescence. However, an imaginative professional manager in charge of this type of property can successfully convert it to one of several uses.

Lofts that are situated close to the downtown business district are the easiest to adapt to other uses. For example, lofts provide low-cost office space for businesses that do not need prestigious quarters for client reception. In other instances, particularly with high-tech start-ups, lofts can be the most "fashionably chic" spaces in the newly developing area of a city. Businesses requiring inexpensive facilities for large numbers of employees or for storage of materials may be able to use converted loft space. Some loft buildings in prime locations have been successfully converted into condominium apartments, shopping malls, restaurants, and bars. This conversion to a new use has been termed *adaptive reuse*.

Regardless of the approach adopted, substantial capital is needed to convert or adapt a neglected building to meet new tenants' needs. It is difficult for tenants to visualize how the space will look after renovation, so alteration may have to be completed before tenants are solicited and the space is shown.

General Contracting

The first task is to decide if the manager will hire a *prime* or general *contractor* who will then sublet the work out to various skilled trades and will supervise the project. When a prime contractor is used, only one set of plans and specifications is needed. Most large alteration and construction jobs are supervised by a prime contractor.

The alternative is for the manager to act in that capacity and assign the work directly to the necessary architects, engineers, carpenters, plumbers, and suppliers. A manager who performs this function can save money for the owner if he or she has the time, skill, and construction knowledge to supervise and settle differences among the various trades. A manager who acts as the prime contractor must develop and supply separate plans and specifications for each class of work, as well as schedule and coordinate each job.

Once the decision has been made whether to hire a general contractor or to contract with the various skilled trades separately, the manager must determine how to obtain the actual contracts. There are two types of contracts for construction: competitive bids and negotiated contracts.

Competitive bids   Competitive bids may be obtained from general contractors for all or part of the job or directly from representatives of skilled trades and suppliers. References should be requested in advance of allowing a contractor to bid, and then verified; if possible, the manager should see completed jobs. When comparing bids, the manager must ascertain that the bids are for comparable amounts and types of work. Taking all things into consideration, it is important to remember that sometimes neither the lowest bid nor the highest bid is the best bid.

Negotiated contracts   Managers who let many large construction projects often opt for another alternative, **negotiated contracts.** In this situation, the manager first chooses one general contractor or one reputable contractor in each field—plumbing, electrical, HVAC, etc. These contractors then submit a joint proposal estimating the total cost of the project. Even if a single general contractor is involved, the estimate should be the end result of collaboration between the plumbing contractor, electrician, hardware supplier, and other tradespeople.

The manager and the owner can accept this single bid and sign a contract or reject it and take further bids. Because contractors in a negotiated bid situation know that they have the manager's commitment to use their services if the price is acceptable, they often will do their best to shave costs. Thus, everyone—property manager, owner, and contractor—may benefit from negotiated contracts.

Fast-track construction   One development in the area of negotiated contracts is **fast-track construction.** Under this arrangement, the contractor begins work before final plans are completed. Obviously, such a procedure is feasible only when both the owner and the contractor trust each other and have a great deal of experience in construction.

Fee Choices

Although most construction contracts are negotiated on a **fixed-fee (fixed-fee bid)** or **flat-fee (flat-fee bid)** basis, a trusted contractor might ask to be paid on a **cost-plus (cost-plus bid) basis.** In this case, the contractor will furnish a preliminary estimate on the proposed job and will be paid the actual cost of the work plus a percentage for profit, usually around 15 percent. This method of payment is advisable only when dealing with established contractors. Various innovations have been introduced to cost-plus contracting, both to protect the owner and to provide incentives to the contractor. An owner will want to set a maximum *not-to-exceed* figure. The contractor will want to participate in savings effected through contracting skill and purchasing. An acceptable middle ground is for the owner and contractor to split any savings below the maximum figure.

Payment Timetables

Contracts for alterations, remodeling, and other construction should be scrutinized by the manager. The agreement should specify exactly when the contractors are to be paid. It is customary to pay about 40 percent of the costs when the job is half done, but at least 10 percent should be held back for a month after the work is completed in case additional service is necessary. It is important to obtain some kind of written verification that the subcontractors have, indeed, been paid. The contract should include a penalty for late completion of the work and might include a bonus for early completion.

The manager must remember that there is no substitute for personal inspection of the work in progress. On certain projects, the manager may want to engage an architect or engineer to review the contracts and inspect the work as it progresses.

Performance Bonds

A *performance bond* is a guarantee from an independent bonding company that the work will be completed despite any financial or other problems the contractor may experience. Many owners insist on performance bonds when assigning construction contracts, particularly when a substantial amount of money is involved. Should the contractor fail to complete the work, the bonding company will arrange for others to finish the job. Forms incorporating bond clauses are available from the American Institute of Architects (AIA), and a number of bonding companies offer bonds written on AIA bond instruments.

■ The nature and size of the project, as well as the contractor's reputation, experience, and financial standing help the owner determine whether to demand a performance bond.

Small contractors may be unable to secure performance bonds because of limited financial resources, in which case the owner or property manager will have to make a business judgment as to whether to proceed without a bond.

■ COMPLYING WITH THE AMERICANS WITH DISABILITIES ACT

The Americans with Disabilities Act (ADA), which became effective in January 1992, requires any business or other facility open to the public to be accessible to the disabled. This means that not only must physical barriers be removed whenever practical, but that policies and standards must be changed to make businesses more accessible. A detailed discussion of the ADA is found in Chapter 10.

Working within ADA parameters may come up anytime that new construction is contemplated or when modifications are made. No one expects the property manager to be an ADA expert, but he or she should be able to consult with an attorney or architect who specializes in this area. A property manager must be acutely aware of the necessity for strict compliance with the law and must be able to recognize when there may be problems with compliance. It is helpful if the manager has a good working relationship with the local municipalities to make sure they are in compliance with local ordinances as well.

■ ENERGY MANAGEMENT

Energy costs are increasing at a rapid pace, yet with effective planning and management, a property manager can demonstrate his or her professional ability and achieve dramatic savings. The manager should begin by meeting with maintenance personnel to solicit their recommendations.

Conservation Measures

Energy management experts agree that some of the greatest savings can be achieved by simple measures that cost either little or nothing. Others involve extensive programs of replacing or upgrading HVAC equipment (called **retrofitting**) that often are controlled and monitored by a computer. BOMA, in coordination with the Clinton Climate Initiative (CCI), has developed an energy performance-contracting model that allows the capital investments made to improve the building's environmental performance to be paid for by operational savings created by the improvements.

Among the simple energy-saving measures are reducing the size and number of electric lights, altering the types of light bulbs and fixtures, or installing storm windows. Timers or photocells are inexpensive and easy to install, and can effect real savings. Other ideas include reducing temperature settings, turning off lights and equipment when not in use, keeping the equipment properly maintained, and weatherstripping and caulking windows and doors.

Before redesigning or adding new controls to existing equipment, present HVAC equipment should be placed in top operating condition and kept in that condition with proper preventive maintenance. The ultimate in energy management is to take heat-producing articles in a building, such as electric lights, motors, and copy machines, and channel this wasted heat into areas where it can be utilized. Some managers have eliminated heating plants in their premises entirely by the use of this type of heat recovery system.

Instituting an Energy Management Plan

Whether conservation measures involve simple manual methods or complicated computerized controls, the basic steps in instituting an energy management plan or system are the same.

- Convert consumption costs into unit costs for each type of energy used. This may be watts of electricity, cubic feet of natural gas, gallons of fuel oil, or other measures. If possible, conversion to British thermal units (BTUs) will provide a common basis. This allows the manager to compare past and present consumption, without the distortion caused by fluctuating energy rates.
- Lighting, heating, refrigeration, etc., should be calculated separately.
- Select areas where savings appear possible.
- List various methods of effecting savings and determine the cost of each.
- Analyze each method to determine cost-effectiveness, using the payback method and life-cycle costing.
- Select the method to be used.
- Prepare a plan for implementation, including sequence and timing.
- Execute the plan.

To be successful, an energy management system must involve all the personnel in a company or an organization, as well as the tenants' conservation efforts. In large installations, conservation is accomplished through the use of automatic controls that are preset and cannot be altered except by management.

Gaining the Owner's Approval

When presenting an energy management plan to an owner for adoption, the property manager must explain the recommendations in terms of dollars and cents. In order to translate watts of electricity into dollars, the yearly cost of one watt of electricity must be obtained. The cost of each part of the plan must be calculated and the payback period established. Labor savings must be expressed in worker hours and worker days, again with savings set out in dollars. Graphs and pie charts help make recommendations easy to explain and understand.

■ LIFE-CYCLE COSTING

Computing the payback period for a remodeling project is discussed in Chapter 2, and equipment is evaluated by a similar computation. However, the cost of the equipment over its entire useful life, or life-cycle costing, must also be considered. *Life-cycle costing* simply means that both the initial and the operating costs of equipment over its expected life must be measured to compare the total cost of one type of equipment with that of another. Often, a higher-priced energy-efficient appliance may be the least expensive product because of its lower operating costs. If the property is covered by an investment tax credit, which varies according to the type of personal property, this must also be considered in life-cycle costing. The manager should consult with a knowledgeable accountant.

■ SUMMARY

To determine the property's maintenance demands, the manager must know the needs of the building and the number and type of personnel required to perform maintenance functions.

There are four types of maintenance operations:

1. Preventive maintenance attempts to preserve the physical integrity of the premises by routine scheduled inspections of the interior and exterior of the building and all equipment.

2. Corrective maintenance involves the actual repairs necessary to keep all structures, amenities, and utilities functional.

3. Routine housekeeping, including cleaning, is the most recurring maintenance task.

4. New construction includes finish out, remodeling, additions, and structural alterations made to satisfy tenants' specifications or to improve the marketability of the property.

A fifth type is referred to as deferred maintenance, when needed repairs are postponed. Eventually, postponed maintenance can cause the property value to decline.

The major benefits of a preventive maintenance program are decreased repair and replacement costs and improved service to tenants. The property manager should review preventive maintenance reports and oversee the program even if primarily coordinated by a resident manager or superintendent on the premises.

The basic steps in designing a preventive maintenance program are as follows:

1. Inventory all equipment and physical elements.
2. Decide on the nature and frequency of inspections and preventive maintenance tasks.
3. Calculate the time, labor, and money that will be involved.
4. Schedule the preventive maintenance tasks.
5. Keep records of the implementation of the program.

Software programs can track initial work orders, timekeeping, material control, work scheduling, and reporting. Action programs should include all the details of any job to be completed: scope, location, priority, method, materials, personnel, and hours of work.

The property manager should seek input from the resident manager or superintendent but retain control over the hiring and firing of employees and contractors. The hiring policy will depend on the cost differential between maintaining a permanent building staff and contracting for the needed services. Outside contractors may prove more economical in performing routine services such as window cleaning, refuse and snow removal, pest control, and security protection. The manager should always solicit competitive bids, check references, and make a cost comparison.

When contracting for new construction, the manager has at least three options:

1. Assign the project to a prime contractor, who will sublet the work to laborers and suppliers.
2. Let the work directly to the skilled trades and suppliers and supervise the construction.
3. Negotiate a contract in which there are one general contractor and/or one representative firm for each type of service or supply—carpentry, electrical work, plumbing, plastering, or hardware collaborate to submit a joint bid approximating the total cost of the proposed work.

With any new construction, maintenance, repair, and alterations, property managers must make sure that the property is in compliance with the Americans with Disabilities Act (ADA). The manager must also be aware that his or her own facilities must comply with the ADA.

Energy management measures must involve all personnel in the organization. Some inexpensive energy-saving steps can be taken by simple conservation, while others require large expenditures for retrofitting and computerizing heating and air-conditioning systems. Life-cycle costing is a method of measuring and comparing not only the initial cost of similar pieces of equipment but also the operating costs over the equipment's useful life to determine the cost-effectiveness of one particular brand of equipment over another.

■ CASE STUDY

THE MAINTENANCE MANAGER

Howard Blake manages a five-story office building. Blake has instituted a regular maintenance program that works very well in keeping the building in good condition. However, the maintenance program is quite expensive and the owner of the building has been complaining about the costs.

1. What steps can Blake take to reduce maintenance costs?
2. What are some of the elements of the building Blake should check for compliance with the ADA?

■ REVIEW QUESTIONS

1. The hiring and firing of maintenance personnel should be the responsibility of the
   a. property manager.
   b. owner.
   c. resident manager.
   d. leasing agent.

2. To command premium rental rates, a property manager might operate with
   a. minimal expenditures for services and maintenance.
   b. reasonable expenditures for services and maintenance.
   c. tenants supplying most of their services.
   d. all possible tenant services.

3. Preventive maintenance is aimed at
   a. making actual repairs to keep the facilities functioning.
   b. eliminating corrective maintenance costs.
   c. keeping common areas and grounds cleaned and patrolled daily.
   d. installing alterations requested by the tenant during occupancy to prevent a move-out.

4. The addition of a sauna to the common area of a multitenant development would be an example of
   a. corrective maintenance.
   b. tenant alterations.
   c. contract service.
   d. new construction.

5. Loss of building value resulting from postponing repairs, etc., is called
   a. preventive maintenance.
   b. deferred maintenance.
   c. cosmetic alteration.
   d. functional obsolescence.

6. The most critical factor in deciding whether to hire on-site maintenance personnel or contract out for certain services is
   a. the amount of construction required.
   b. union activity.
   c. required staff.
   d. the relative cost of each.

7. Which of the following is considered when hiring outside services on a regular basis?
   a. The race, color, or religion of the contractor
   b. Whether the contract should include a breach clause
   c. Whether the contractor is disabled
   d. Whether the cost of the contract service is greater than the cost of using in-house personnel

8. The first decision confronting the property manager when contracting for construction is to
   a. draw up a flat-fee contract.
   b. calculate the total cost of a cost-plus contract.
   c. decide whether to use competitive bidding or to hire the company that has the most employees.
   d. decide whether to act as the general contractor or to hire a prime contractor.

9. Which of the following is *TRUE* of negotiated contracts?
   a. They are far more prevalent than competitive bid contracts.
   b. They are often used in smaller construction contracts.
   c. Contractors often avoid sharing costs with subcontractors or the owner.
   d. The estimate of cost should be the end result of collaboration among various suppliers and subcontractors.

10. A type of construction that proceeds as plans are being drawn is called
    a. tenant finish-out.
    b. fast-track.
    c. competitive bid.
    d. retrofit.

11. A contract for construction work typically states that
    a. front money will be provided to contractors before the work is started.
    b. a percentage of the fee will be held back until all work has been completed.
    c. the contractor is to be the judge of the quality of the work.
    d. the owner will have hire and fire authority over workers on the site.

12. What is the first step in designing a preventive maintenance program?
    a. Read the instruction manuals that come with the building equipment.
    b. Make a complete inventory of all equipment.
    c. Confer with the maintenance superintendent to determine what types of inspection and what tasks are to be performed.
    d. Make a schedule of the tasks.

13. Of the following, which is the MOST important in determining the property manager's effectiveness as a maintenance administrator?
    a. His or her knowledge of detailed maintenance procedures and techniques
    b. Having an experienced and competent maintenance foreman
    c. Being able to perform many routine maintenance tasks personally
    d. The thoroughness of routine inspections and the manager's ability to pinpoint and correct omissions of the maintenance team

14. When the term *retrofit* is used in connection with energy management, it encompasses
    a. increasing the size or number of electric lights.
    b. repainting existing storm windows.
    c. monitoring air-conditioning and heating equipment currently in use in the building.
    d. replacing or upgrading heating and air-conditioning equipment.

15. Often, the greatest savings come from energy management systems or measures that
    a. involve computerization to eliminate human error.
    b. are simple and cost little or nothing.
    c. allow the property manager to demonstrate professional ability.
    d. are a result of retrofitting.

16. Life-cycle costing
    a. compares the salvage value of similar pieces of equipment.
    b. considers both initial and operating costs over the useful life of equipment.
    c. measures costs over the life of the average tenancy.
    d. compares estimated life of new equipment against actual life of equipment being replaced.

17. How are computers used in maintenance applications?
    a. Limited to certain maintenance functions
    b. Useful in monitoring, scheduling, controlling, and operating functions
    c. Declining use as they are a fad
    d. Only useful in multistory buildings

18. A type of building that is made up of nonspecialized interior floor space is called a(n)
    a. conversion.
    b. retrofit.
    c. loft.
    d. open building.

19. All of the following management situations would most likely have to comply with ADA *EXCEPT*
    a. single-family dwelling.
    b. commercial buildings.
    c. new high-rise apartment building.
    d. regional mall.

20. Which of the following protects the owner from a contractor who goes out of business before finishing the contract?
    a. Surety bond
    b. Negotiated contract
    c. Performance bond
    d. Fast-track construction

CHAPTER NINE

MANAGING THE OFFICE AND REPORTS

■ KEY TERMS

Break-even analysis
Capitalization rate
Cash flow report
Depreciation
Direct costs
Federal Insurance
   Contributions Act
   (FICA)

Form I-9
Federal Unemployment
   Tax Act (FUTA)
Hardware
Indirect costs
Management pricing
   worksheet
Operating budget

Return on investment
   (ROI)
Software
Workers' compensation
Work order bids

■ LEARNING OBJECTIVES

At the end of this chapter, the student will be able to

1. list five files that should be maintained in any property management office;

2. name at least three software functions and discuss how each is used in a property management office;

3. draw a flowchart for a typical management organization;

4. explain the difference between direct and indirect costs and give examples of each;

5. list three methods to determine an appropriate management fee and explain when each might be used;

6. explain the importance of the cash flow report and summarize how that information contributes to the profit and loss statement and the operating budget;

7. summarize the information contained in the tax records: EIN, W-4, I-9, 941, W-2, W-3, and 1099;

8. differentiate among FICA, disability workers' compensation, and FUTA; and

9. summarize methods of determining profitability: break-even analysis, capitalization rate, and return on investment.

■ OVERVIEW

The management office reflects the scope and nature of management operations and is staffed by individuals who see that the company meets its commitments to owners and tenants. This responsibility includes maintaining records and producing reports that provide overall information that guides both the management company and its client-owners in making business decisions.

The location and layout of the office is determined by the nature and duties of the manager and the management company, and may be on-site or located a distance from the managed properties. In smaller companies, several people often assume multiple responsibilities; in larger firms, a clear hierarchy can be found.

The management company must track its time and energy to competitively determine management fees by properly allocating direct and indirect costs related to each property it manages. Fees may be a per-unit cost, a percentage rate, or a fee derived from the management pricing worksheet.

Good record keeping is essential to providing for the easy collection, retention, and retrieval of records. Business decisions for a property will be based on the information in the reports.

Performance reports on the property's operations gauge the profitability of an owner's investment. The reports provide the owner with a clear picture of how the property was managed during the past year, what should be done differently, what can be expected for the upcoming year, whether the property is worth keeping, and how successful the manager has been.

The law requires that certain tax-related forms and reports be prepared and filed with local, state, and federal government departments. Operating license fees, inspection fees, and other fees also must be paid.

Many of these records are maintained electronically, and as previously mentioned, the proper software program is a major decision affecting operations for some time. All electronic records must be protected from loss, so it is critical that backups and duplicates are stored off-site.

■ ESTABLISHING THE MANAGEMENT OFFICE

Location and Layout

The location, organization, equipment, and staff of the management command post varies with the scope of the operation. Initially, the office may consist of only a property manager and a secretary. The most logical site for the manager's office is on the premises if most of the management operations are conducted there. Even if a manager has a home office elsewhere, a small office is often set up on the property for specific functions.

The office should not occupy space that has a specialized high rental value, such as the ground floor of an office building. Management firms and large real estate agencies in metropolitan areas often have main offices in prestigious high-rise quarters in the center of the business district. As business expands, they then establish smaller ground-level offices in outlying neighborhoods or in managed properties.

Office Design

Furnishings should be affordable, attractive, tasteful, uniform in style, and well arranged. The office should be designed to accommodate several different areas for specific uses including the following:

- Attractive reception area available for prospective clients and service personnel
- Space for comfortable private interviews with clients, potential employees, and businesspeople
- Accessible and private place for tenants to pay their rent, make service requests, or negotiate lease renewals
- Office space for administrative functions such as timekeeping, payroll, purchasing, billing, accounts receivable, bookkeeping, collections, and preparation of government reports
- Area large enough to prepare and store records for the properties

Files

The mark of an efficient management office is a good filing system. Data should be sorted and segregated into separate files for easy collection, retention, and retrieval of records. Even though much of the working information is stored electronically, certain paper documents will still have to be maintained. These paper files should be reviewed periodically and outdated material should either be shredded or moved to a storage center off-site. The boxes containing the files should be clearly labeled in the event that anything must be retrieved.

Whatever the size of the office, the records can be divided into five general filing categories:

1. Lease file

2. General correspondence file

3. Work estimates file

4. Financial file

5. Permanent file

Leases   The lease file should contain current lease instruments, as well as tenant credit and reference data. Leases usually are filed first by building and then by unit number. With a manual system, the manager can utilize a lease expiration list or tickler file of lease expiration dates to track leases coming up for renewal. Alternatively, lease expiration dates can be included in electronic tracking programs. Expired leases should be moved to a separate system and filed alphabetically by tenant name. These paper records may be stored off-site and then discarded after an appropriate time, such as ten years after the tenant vacates the property. Documents containing personal information about the tenant must be shredded to maintain privacy.

Correspondence   A general correspondence file should contain all communications with tenants. Correspondence usually is filed according to building, with each building then subdivided alphabetically according to tenant name. This file may be electronic and/or paper and should be updated annually. Typically, older documents may be discarded after three years. However, managers should check on their state laws for guidance.

Work order bids   When placing service contracts and contracting for new construction, the manager usually solicits **work order bids** from two or more contractors. These estimates should be filed according to the property involved. Even if the job is not placed with a particular bidder at the time of the solicitation, these bids can provide important comparison data when considering future projects. New files should be set up yearly because cost estimates do not remain current.

Financial files   Check registers, canceled checks, receipts, and disbursement records are usually retained for a ten-year period in a financial file organized by building. The file also organizes budgets, monthly income and expense reports, yearly profit and loss statements, and other financial records for each building and its employees. These basic documents should be retained for the duration of the management operation. Files generated electronically should be backed up at least weekly, if not daily. The backups should be stored in a fireproof safe and/or off-site.

Permanent files   These files are rarely referenced, but they need to be easily identifiable in the event of an emergency. A permanent file holds the management contract, mortgage and title information, labor contracts, a legal description of the property, and similar documents. Insurance policies on the property may be kept in this file, but it is preferable to have them in a separate folder with the coverage terms, policy limits, and expiration dates clearly visible on the outside for quick reference. A separate tickler list of policy expiration dates should be posted in the permanent file so that new entries can be made immediately and expiration dates monitored regularly. Expired insurance policies should be kept for five full years.

Equipment

Very few, if any, offices can run without the use of some equipment. Office equipment such as fax machines, copiers, postage scales, calculators, and computers are fundamental, not optional, once the business begins to grow. All information about the machines, such as training manuals and maintenance contracts, should be located where the information can be easily accessed.

■ COMPUTERS AND PROPERTY MANAGEMENT

The use of computers in small businesses has become commonplace, in large part because the initial cost is so low and because software companies have developed such "easy-to-use" software. Managers and clients should recognize that using a computer does not make life any easier. Computers simply provide more information on which to base decisions. Users can be overwhelmed by all of the information. Thus, the management company must look carefully at each segment of the organization to determine the information it requires and will actually use. Not every company needs all of the reports that can be generated. Plus, once the company begins to depend on the information supplied by the software, it is essential that someone is responsible for backing up all of the information at least weekly, if not daily. Whatever memory storage method is used, these backups must be protected and should be stored off-site.

Hardware

Matthew Ferrara, a technology consultant, suggests taking the "Goldilocks approach" when buying any technology, including computers, software, and phones. Remember Goldilocks in the three bears' house? She tried things that were too small or too large, and then one that was just right!

Some technology investments/tools are "too little."

Some technology investment/tools are "too big."

Some technology investments are "just right."

Any technology currently very much marked down in price may indicate hardware that will soon be out-of-date or lacking enough features to have an adverse effect on productivity (too small). Likewise, overkill investments do nothing to improve productivity as they have excess, unusable features incurred as an expense that cannot pay off (as Goldilocks could not eat the entire bowl of porridge, even though it "had more").

In every technology, products exist that are just right in combination terms of usefulness, features, and price.

Software

Today, various software companies offer software specifically for the property management industry to help property managers run their offices more effectively and manage their properties more easily. A company that does not want to take a risk buying a software program only to see the program become outdated can work with Web-based outsourcing companies. Web-based products are run on their servers, and the property manager client can access and use the products over the Internet.

With so many options, managers must do their homework before making the purchase. Several steps are involved:

1. Ask other management companies what program they use. Do they recommend it? What don't they like?

2. Attend a trade show and talk to various vendors.

3. Ask for and try out a "demonstration" (demo) version of the software.

4. Research the company to determine how helpful it will be if there are problems, and try to determine how stable it is.

5. Is the product specific for property management, or has it been adapted from a general accounting package?

6. Does it meet the manager's reporting needs?

7. Is it easy to learn?

**Basic Software
Functions**

One size does not fit all. Not every office needs all of the following functions. What follows is a general overview; the manager will have to make it specific.

Data sharing   At the very basic level, computers use two types of programs to make office lives easier: word processing and spreadsheet software.

- A *word processing* program (such as Microsoft Word) allows the user to key in (type) a letter, insert or delete characters, words, lines, paragraphs, or even pages of text, and merge that text with a mail list to generate mass mailings. New programs offer templates for late notices, eviction notices, lease termination, and letters on all types of problems (pets, excessive noise, garage usage, etc.). These form letters can be customized to meet the company's specific needs.

- A *spreadsheet* program (such as Microsoft Excel) takes the entered data and performs mathematical calculations. It can use these numbers to tie information together to produce a financial report.

With most programs, the user can expect to input data once, access that data at will, and easily move the data between a word processing document and a spreadsheet to make calculations and generate reports. For example, the tenant and lease information is keyed in at the beginning of the lease identifying rental due dates. Later, if the tenant is late in paying the rent, the program will automatically generate the appropriate late notice letter, thus relieving the office person from having to "remember." At the end of the month, all of this information will be "tied together" to produce the report indicating the percentage of late-paying tenants.

Financial record keeping   The accounting portion is a very sophisticated spreadsheet program. It should perform bookkeeping calculations automatically, including accounts receivable, accounts payable, payroll, inventory, and general ledger. Accounting programs can generate various reports that are valuable for financial planning and evaluations, including monthly budgets, cash flow studies, profit and loss statements, and reports to owners. Many even write and print a check, while entering that directly into the bank balance summary, thus maintaining even more up-to-the-minute control.

Tracking maintenance   As mentioned in Chapter 8, many software packages can integrate maintenance items with the appropriate and necessary financial records. Data processing software programs allow property managers to enter requests for maintenance, due dates, vendors, bids, completion dates, and more.

Internet   The Internet is a global system of interconnecting computer networks. The Internet has quickly become a vehicle for advertising, marketing, and communication. Savvy tenants use the Internet to locate communities before arriving in a new city. There are even mapping programs available that allow the user to merge a local map with information about properties and neighborhoods. Managers can very quickly do credit checks on prospective tenants and/or employees.

■ STAFFING THE MANAGEMENT OFFICE

The management operation will be successful if office personnel are efficient and loyal. The most basic qualification for an employee in the field of property management is *versatility*, because few management organizations are large enough to support a staff of specialists. The property manager and a secretary-bookkeeper may be the only staff during the early stages of a business, but larger established management firms or departments often employ several people in each of the positions described in the following sections. The most important point is that all of the functions must be completed, whether by 2 people or 20.

Property Management Executive

The chief property manager or property management executive often determines the success or failure of the operations. This person must be knowledgeable and experienced to control both the strategic and the operational aspects of property management.

During the growth years, the responsibilities can be classified as *executive* or *administrative*. The executive function includes preparing budgets; developing an advertising program; leasing; inspecting properties; communicating with tenants; contacting owners; contracting for services; hiring, training, and supervising both office and on-site employees; directing major repairs; and supervising all administrative functions. As part of the administrative function, the property management executive oversees collections, disbursements, payroll preparation, and recording; submits monthly operating reports; and keeps records in all areas.

As soon as the organization is large enough to make it economically feasible, the management executive should hire and train subordinates to assist with the work. Eventually, the property manager executive will supervise others in order to devote full attention to setting the general policy for the organization, developing new business, supervising operational costs and activities, and building employee morale and motivation.

Figure 9.1 illustrates the staffing pattern of a typical, large management firm department. A very large firm may add another level or two in the supervisory hierarchy, whereas a smaller firm may function as a one-person or two-person operation.

Property Supervisor (Field Manager)

The property supervisor takes care of the general administration, directs the daily operation of the property, and reports to the property management executive. Depending on variables such as condition of the property, problems, distance from the management office, and number of properties, one person can efficiently manage anywhere from 5 to 20 buildings, which should, if possible, be concentrated in one neighborhood.

FIGURE 9.1
Organization Flowchart

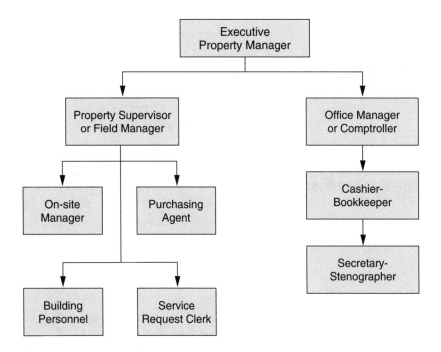

Part of the supervisor's responsibility is to establish a personal but businesslike relationship with the tenants and the owner. Besides seeing that all units are well maintained, competitively priced, and actively shown (if they are vacant), the property supervisor regularly inspects the premises and the activities of employees. Often the property supervisor sets hiring policy and salary levels for the resident manager and other building employees, so that the payroll will reflect the actual requirements of the premises.

The property supervisor usually has the added responsibility of comparing bids and obtaining outside contract services for corrective maintenance, housekeeping, and new construction. The supervisor monitors building and office employees, makes maintenance decisions, and approves purchase orders for supplies and services. When maintenance jobs are completed, the supervisor inspects the work and the materials.

On-Site Manager and Building Personnel

A carefully selected and qualified on-site manager is often authorized to hire custodians, handymen, and other maintenance workers, but the property supervisor will want to retain the right to approve the on-site manager's employment decisions. Often a leasing agent who has shown initiative and promise is promoted to either an assistant on-site manager or to the manager position.

Purchasing Agent

The purchasing agent is responsible for all purchases made by or through the management organization. Only large organizations can justify a full-time position for this function. In smaller management offices, the property supervisor or an accountant usually performs the job of the purchasing agent by compiling a list of preferred suppliers, contractors, products, and equipment, and making purchases.

Office Manager (Comptroller)

The office manager or comptroller interprets the income and expense reports, makes major decisions regarding new procedures, and submits profit and loss statements to the owner. A single comptroller is usually responsible for all of the properties managed by the firm. Because this is a crucial function, the executive property manager in a smaller operation will usually assume responsibility for it.

Cashier-Bookkeeper

Bookkeepers spend most of their time preparing rental bills, receiving and recording rent payments, keeping an account of monthly income and expenses for each property, and handling accounts payable and receivable. Regardless of the competence of the bookkeeping staff, it is wise for a management office to have an outside accounting firm audit its books semiannually or annually.

Bookkeepers also handle the payroll and maintain operating cost records for the management firm's operating costs. Depending on the owner's demand for detail and the type of accounting system in use (manual or computer), a single bookkeeper can usually handle eight to ten properties. This person may be able to handle more properties in a large management firm because the assumption of more properties justifies a more sophisticated accounting system, which requires less time and labor per property.

Clerical Personnel

Clerical personnel can be divided into two major groups, *secretaries* (or administrative assistants) and *service request clerks*. Secretaries are responsible for answering telephones, maintaining contact between the field managers and the central office, and handling the general correspondence of the management organization. General reception for the main office can be performed by these employees or by a special receptionist.

Service request clerks accept phone calls from tenants, easing the burden on the secretarial staff. These clerks provide a team of persons ready to respond promptly and patiently to tenant requests and can also act as liaisons between the main office and the building. They can notify the custodian of a service request, write the purchase order for items needed by the on-site staff and have it approved by upper management, then route the requisitioned material to the appropriate building when it arrives.

Branch Offices

As the management organization grows, branch offices may be opened in outlying areas to handle newly acquired business more efficiently. Traditionally, each outlying office is run by a property manager and a salesperson in charge of new accounts, assisted by a receptionist, bookkeeper, secretary, and possibly two accounting clerks (one for accounts receivable and another for accounts payable).

Isolated apartment properties should have a manager's representative on-site, if only part-time.

To avoid the problems of complete centralization, management functions integrally related to the neighborhood can be performed at branch offices, leaving the main office to take care of more standardized activities. Centralized accounting systems require only a property manager, a secretary-receptionist, and a salesperson who solicits local accounts at each branch. This arrangement can reduce the staffing needs of a branch office by 40 percent or more, actually increasing the overall efficiency and profit margin of the management company.

> Accuracy and uniformity of reports and records is a by-product of centralization. Perhaps the greatest benefit, however, is that new properties can be acquired and managed with fewer additional staff to the branch office and with minimum additions at the main office.

Licensing

The management company should determine which licenses it is required to obtain. Local ordinances may require that the company obtain a business license to operate. The state real estate regulatory agency may require that individuals performing certain activities, such as negotiating leases or collecting rents, hold either a property management license or a real estate license. In such circumstances, the ability to obtain a license could be a requirement when hiring certain personnel.

Mergers

In today's economic climate, many property managers are joining forces with other real estate professionals to increase their competitiveness. For example, property management firms may merge with real estate brokerages or auction firms.

■ DETERMINING MANAGEMENT EXPENSES

Before any management fees can be set, the management executive must first know how much it costs the organization to provide its management services. A budget that includes the direct and indirect costs of operation will show the total cost of doing business. Each management firm has the right to set its fees according to its needs. However, care should be taken so that setting of fees does not even appear to be in collusion with other firms, which would be in violation of antitrust laws (see Chapter 10).

Direct Costs

All costs incurred by an individual manager or management firm can be considered *direct costs*. If management operations are a division of a real estate agency, however, direct costs would include all expenses incurred during the performance of the management business that are not charged to or shared by another department of the parent company. General office expenses included in direct costs are the payroll for the management staff; depreciation on office furniture and equipment; equipment maintenance or rental; insurance premiums; legal, auditing, and other professional fees; stationery and postage; utilities; taxes; office supplies; and office rent. Business promotion and automobile expenses are also considered direct costs.

Indirect Costs

Indirect costs are incurred when a management department shares facilities and expenses with other divisions of the parent company or real estate agency. Although they may amount to 25 percent or more of the total cost of operating, they are less visible than direct costs and, therefore, are often ignored when drawing up a management department's budget. A proportionate share of occupancy costs, general office overhead, and accounting overhead should be assigned to the management department as its indirect costs.

■ CALCULATING THE MANAGEMENT FEE

When setting management fees, the pertinent variables must be evaluated and assigned an order of importance. Business will be lost if the estimated percentage rate is too high and is not competitive with the market rate. On the other hand, cutting back on necessary management services and staff to lower management operational expense, or accepting management contracts that will not cover costs, will only deteriorate the management organization's reputation, impair its financial structure, and hurt its business. A sound policy is to review all management contracts annually and raise fees on properties that are causing problems or consuming an inordinate amount of time without generating sufficient monetary compensation.

As mentioned earlier, most management fees are related to the property's gross collected income. Fees may range from as little as 2 percent to as much as 20 percent of the gross collectible income from a property, depending on the management risk, the size of the building, and the profit margin. Because of the numerous variables involved, there is no universally valid formula for the computation of management fees. In the last analysis, the local market and negotiation between the owner and the manager set the fees.

Residential property issues are quite different from those involved in managing industrial property. The size, condition, and location of the building, among other factors, also have an effect on the profitability rate for the management of the property. In general, however, there are several ways of computing management fees. One method bases the fee on the *per-unit cost* of management, which is derived from the operating budget for the management organization. A second method employs a standardized **management pricing worksheet**.

Per-Unit Cost Method

Essentially, the per-unit cost is a total of the total management costs, both **direct** and **indirect**, for one year divided by the number of units that the firm is capable of managing plus a percentage for profit. It is important to use the number of units the firm is capable of managing as opposed to the number of units the firm is actually managing currently or the per-unit cost will be unrealistically high and not competitive.

Although each management firm decides on its own profit margin, the typical range is from 10 percent to 20 percent. For example, a management firm with total operating expenses of $100,000 and the capability to handle 1,000 units will have a yearly per-unit cost of $100. Adding 20 percent for profit, the per-unit fee is $120. This figure represents the minimum per unit fee that must be obtained, regardless of the type or number of buildings or units being managed.

Adjustments to Per-Unit Fee

No standard method of setting a fee can possibly make allowance for every contingency. Therefore, the per-unit fee often has to be adjusted to reflect the economics of a particular situation. For example, one large building with 50 units may be cheaper to manage than five separate properties of ten units each. The travel time involved in field supervision of separate buildings is much greater, as is the total number of personnel and separate operational systems that must be inspected.

Any factor that adds to the time spent in caring for the premises should be reflected in the per-unit fee. The following illustrates some of the times that the fee should be increased:

- For a small ten-unit property to compensate for the inefficiency of decentralization

- For buildings with internal problems, a significant amount of deferred maintenance, or a pressing need for new construction or repairs

- For an owner who wants to be informed of every detail of operation (and this category often includes government agencies) taking more management time

- For properties located in depressed areas because of vandalism and related social ills

Percentage Rate

The percentage rate can be calculated by using the per-unit fee, the total number of units in the building, and the gross income of the property. First, multiply the per-unit fee as adjusted for the property by the total number of units to obtain the dollar amount of the management fee that must be recovered. Next, determine the gross collectible income for the property by subtracting a realistic vacancy and loss rate from the annual gross income. Finally, divide the dollar amount of the management fee by the gross collectible income. The resulting figure, when expressed as a percentage, is the base property management fee. Expressed as an equation, this calculation reads as follows:

$$\frac{\text{Adjusted per-unit fee}}{\text{Annual gross possible income}} \times \frac{\text{Total number of units}}{\text{Vacancy loss}} = \frac{\text{Dollar amount of fee}}{\text{Gross collectible income}} \times 100\% = \frac{\text{Percentage management fee}}{}$$

For instance, a 20-unit building has a gross income of $36,500 per year. Using the per-unit fee of $120 calculated in the previous example, the amount to be recovered for this property is $2,400 ($120 × 20 = $2,400). Assuming a 5 percent vacancy rate, the gross collectible income for the property would be $34,675 ($36,500 × .05 = $1,825; $36,500 – $1,825 = $34,675), so the percentage rate would be about 7 percent ($2,400 ÷ $34,675 = 0.069). The management fee for this property would be quoted at 7 percent of gross income.

Both owners and managers generally prefer a percentage fee to a flat rate because it gives the manager an incentive to increase the income of the property by raising rents and cutting operating costs, therefore maximizing the owner's profits. A flat fee may encourage a certain laxness in administrative and executive functions (especially rental) on the part of management because it is a constant that will change only through negotiation with the owner.

For some properties, though, a flat fee might be more appropriate, particularly when managing condominium associations or cooperatives. The owner/occupants certainly want the manager to maintain or lower the monthly maintenance fees, but a percentage fee might encourage the manager to raise those fees. In another example, a manager might want to consider a flat-fee agreement, at least initially, to compensate for extra work and lower profit for properties with much deferred maintenance, excessively high tenant turnover, or an undesirable tenant population that will have to be evicted.

Some management contracts provide for a management fee plus a separate fee for obtaining new rentals. This practice is prevalent when dealing with retail space. The disadvantage of this arrangement is that it may encourage the manager to allow or create a greater tenant turnover than is warranted. Many managers prefer to build the compensation for their leasing activities into the basic management fee by raising it slightly.

Management Pricing Worksheet

The management pricing worksheet relies on the same principles as the per-unit cost method, but the approach is completely different, as shown in Figure 9.2, a sample worksheet. The worksheet is particularly useful when dealing with condominiums and cooperatives, groups that often insist on many long and tedious meetings with the various owners on the board of directors and the manager. By listing the various services provided and putting a value on those services, including those meetings and travel time, the manager can more appropriately be compensated.

Section I   The first section estimates how many inspections, visits, meetings, and the like will be necessary for the particular property on a monthly basis. These figures, when multiplied by the number of hours each activity will consume, including time spent traveling to the site and preparing and checking reports, amount to the total number of hours the property supervisor must devote to the property per month. Then the figures in the "Total Hours" column should be multiplied by the cost of the property supervisor's time. In the example in Figure 9.2, the cost is $30 per hour. The total cost for each category is recorded in the far right-hand column. The total of these dollar amounts, plus travel expense, is the estimated total cost of the property supervisor's services.

Section II   The next section itemizes the executive property manager's activities with regard to the property. Total hours spent and total costs are calculated in the same manner as above, although the executive manager usually charges a higher fee per hour. On the sample management pricing worksheet, the fee is $100 per hour.

Sections III and IV   Section III allows the management firm to determine the total number of hours that will be spent monthly in credit and collections, accounts payable and receivable, payroll, preparation of financial statements, and related matters. The total number of hours spent in these activities should then be multiplied by the average hourly wage of accounting and clerical personnel ($15 an hour in the example) to calculate the total direct cost of these services. Section IV is a subtotal of all direct management costs.

Section V   The last section deals with overhead and profit. The management firm should know by experience what percentage of its income goes toward general overhead (office rental, utilities, phones, supplies) and marketing. The firm must also select an acceptable profit margin, usually from 10 percent to 20 percent. The next step is to multiply the percentage rates for overhead, marketing, and profit by the subtotal of costs in Section IV. These dollar amounts should be recorded in the far right-hand column in Section V.

Monthly management fee   The total of Sections IV and V, shown in Section VI, is actually the monthly management fee, expressed as a flat rate. If a percentage rate is desired, the dollar amount of the monthly fee must be divided by the average monthly gross collectible income less vacancy factor. The quotient is the estimated percentage management fee. The example in Figure 9.3 shows a gross monthly income of $89,600; $6,323 divided by $89,600 is approximately 7 percent.

FIGURE 9.2

Pricing Worksheet

Management Pricing

Property _____

No. of units ___300___ Residents ___1,200___ Offices ___1,200___ Stores ___1,200___ Boat slips _____

Age and present condition of property and improvements _____
_____ 15 years old; good condition _____

Miles from office _____20_____ Number of employees _____4_____

Gross common area charge _____

Management/Leasing _____ Leasing _____

	No. Per Month	Hours Each	Total Hours	Cost
I. Property Supervisor's Services				
Inspections	1	6	6	$180.00
Site visits	1	4	4	120.00
Capital improvement supervision	–	–	–	–
Owner/Investor/Association meetings	1	2	2	60.00
Travel time: $ _30_ per hr. × _4_ hrs.			4	120.00
Office hours per month			10	300.00
Travel expense: _100 mi._ × _33_ ¢ per mi.				33.00
Total				$813.00
II. Property Management Executive's Services				
Owner/Investor/Association meetings	1	2	2	$200.00
Site visits	–	–	–	–
Surveys and consultations	1	2	2	200.00
Inspections	1	4	4	400.00
Statement review	1	4	4	400.00
Budget preparation	–	–	–	–
Travel time: $ _50_ per hr. × _3_ hrs.			3	150.00
Travel expense: _75 mi._ × _33_ ¢ per mi.				24.75
Total				$1,374.75
III. Accounting and Clerical Services				
Receipts accounted for: days per mo.	4	8	32	
Disbursements: invoices, payments	4	8	32	
Monthly billing	1	10	10	
Payroll: checks issued	2	8	16	
Owner/Assn. statement preparation	4	4	16	
Resident statement and preparation	50	1	50	
Statement duplication	10	2	20	
Owner consultation	–	–	–	
Total				$2,640.00
IV. Subtotal Before Overhead and Profit				$4,827.75
V. Overhead and Profit	*Percent of Total*			
General overhead		10%		$483.00
Marketing		1%		48.00
Profit and contingencies		20%		966.00
VI. Total Monthly Fee				$6,324.75

$ _____ Fee ÷ Units = $ _____ each

$ _6,324.75_ Fee ÷ Units = $ _____ each

Compiled by _____ Approved _____

FIGURE 9.3

Budget Comparison Statement

	Surfside Apartments Fourth Month, 20XX					
	Current Month			**Year to Date**		
	Actual	**Budget**	**Variance**	**Actual**	**Budget**	**Variance**
Income						
Standard rent	$4,073.58	$3,835.00	$ (238.58)	$15,677.21	$15,985.00	$307.79
Miscellaneous income	0.00	5.00	5.00	100.00	20.00	(80.00)
Total Income	$4,073.58	$3,840.00	$ (233.58)	$15,777.21	$16,005.00	$ 227.79
Expenses						
Payroll and related	$ 0.00	$0.00	$ 0.00	$ 0.00	$ 0.00	$0.00
Administration	395.66	380.00	(15.66)	1,515.54	1,520.00	4.46
Maintenance and repair	1,880.71	852.00	(1,028.71)	5,634.59	3,498.00	(2,136.59)
Leasing expense	142.50	33.00	(109.50)	511.00	132.00	(379.00)
Utility expense	322.62	293.00	(29.62)	1,285.65	1,272.00	(13.65)
Taxes and insurance	0.00	0.00	0.00	250.00	250.00	0.00
Total Operating Expense	$2,741.49	$1,558.00	$(1,183.49)	$ 9,196.78	$6,672.00	$(2,524.78)
Net Operating Income	$1,332.09	$2,282.00	$ 949.91	$ 6,580.43	$9,333.00	$ 2,752.57
Capital expense	0.00	0.00	0.00	0.00	0.00	0.00
Debt service	0.00	0.00	0.00	0.00	0.00	0.00
Owner	1,332.09	0.00	(1,332.09)	6,538.91	0.00	(6,538.91)
Net Cash Flow	$0.00	$2,282.00	$ (382.15)	$ 41.52	$9,333.00	$ 9,291.48

■ OPERATING REPORTS

Before preparing any financial reports, the manager must set up a method of accounting for funds received and disbursed, keeping in mind the needs of the owner. Laws in most states prescribe rules for handling trust and operating accounts of licensed brokers.

An accounts receivable ledger is preferable because all cash receipts can be posted to the appropriate ledger card. Written orders should be issued for all purchases and purchase orders should be matched to incoming invoices before payment is made.

■ Automating these functions can take the sting out of preparing reports. After entering data once, a fully integrated accounting system can dramatically reduce the manager's time spent on accounting functions by generating reports at the touch of a button. Some of the best programs permit separate accounts for each property and owners, set up on a cash or accrual basis, calendar or fiscal year.

■ FINANCIAL REPORTS

The manager must be familiar with three different reports:

1. Budget comparison statement
2. Cash flow report
3. Operating budget

Although there is some similarity in terminology, form, and sequence of reports, successful property managers adapt their formats to suit each owner's requirements. Forms used in this text are for illustration and adaptation.

Budget Comparison Statement

The budget comparison for the property compares the actual results with the original budget drawn up either at the beginning of that period or at the time the manager assumed responsibility for the property. When maintained as an operating checklist, with ratios from the current period checked faithfully against past performance, trends may be detected that call for the property manager's attention. Without this comparison, they might go unobserved and uncorrected, causing problems later. A sample budget comparison statement is shown in Figure 9.3.

Cash Flow Report

The monthly **cash flow report** explains in much greater detail the financial status of the property for a given period as shown in Figure 9.4. The monthly report tells the owner the sources of income and expenses, and net operating income and net cash flow, and is the single most important financial report. It is usually accompanied by a note from the manager explaining any abnormal items.

Income The income portion includes gross rentals collected, delinquent rental payments, vending contracts, utilities, storage charges, and sale of extra services to tenants. Then, any losses incurred from evictions and from uncollected or delinquent rentals are deducted from the total gross revenue. The resulting figure is the total adjusted income from the property.

As a control measure, some owners require a property manager to list separate categories of items that are not producing income, such as

- vacant rental units;
- support space (for example, the manager's office or residence and maintenance or storage areas); and
- vacant space under major repair.

All rental space in a project should be considered when computing the gross possible income. The rental value of each space not producing income is deducted from the gross possible rental income to equal the *gross collectible (or billable) rental income*:

Total rentable space – All space not rented = Gross collectible rental income

FIGURE 9.4

Cash Flow Report

Cash Flow Report		
Property	**Period covered:**	**Date**
INCOME		
Gross possible rental income	_____	
Less space not rented (vacancy) loss	(_____)	
Gross collectible rental income	_____	
Service and repairs charged to tenants	_____	
Delinquent rental payments	_____	
Miscellaneous (including forfeited deposits)	_____	
Vending machines	_____	
Total income		_____
EXPENSES		
Routine operation and maintenance expenses		
cleaning	_____	
HVAC	_____	
elevator	_____	
general	_____	
administrative	_____	
electricity	_____	
fuel	_____	
water	_____	
telephone	_____	
Total operating expense	_____	
Alterations, decorating, repairs		
alterations—tenants' premises	_____	
decorating—tenants' premises	_____	
repairs—tenants' premises	_____	
Total alterations and decorating	_____	
Fixed charges		
insurance	_____	
taxes	_____	
Total fixed charges	_____	
Total expense		_____
NET OPERATING INCOME BEFORE DEBT SERVICE		
Debt service	_____	
Reserves	_____	
CASH FLOW TO OWNER		_____

Expenses Operating expenses may be direct or indirect expenses and fall into four general categories:

1. Wages paid to building personnel

2. General operating expenses (such as utilities)

3. Maintenance expenses

4. Administrative costs

Direct expenses do not fluctuate with rental income and can be either regularly recurring costs or periodic costs. *Regularly recurring costs* arise each month; examples include employee wages, basic operating costs, and maintenance expenditures. *Periodic costs* such as property taxes and insurance premiums recur at longer intervals. These costs are directly incurred by the building.

Specialized maintenance services such as roof repair, utility charges, refunds, and capital expenditures are *variable expenses*, and can be either *recurring* or *nonrecurring*. Decorating costs, minor repairs or replacements, and replenishment of supplies will predictably occur at varying intervals during the year. Landscaping and snow removal are examples. Variable operating expenses—capital improvements, additions, or repair of fire damage—may or may not occur in any given year.

When both *fixed* and *variable* expenses are deducted from total income, the resulting figure is the month's *net operating income* before debt service. Net operating income minus mortgage payments (another fixed expense) and deposits to reserve accounts equals the *cash flow* or *net receipts* remitted to the owner for that month.

The monthly cash flow report can be summarized in the following formula:

Gross rental income + Income from other sources – Losses incurred = Total income
Total income – Operating expenses = Net operating income before debt service
Net operating income before debt service – Debt service – Reserves = Cash flow

Profit and Loss Statement

Owners expect a profit and loss statement monthly, quarterly, semiannually, or annually. Monthly cash flow reports provide the raw data for these statements. Most such statements list gross receipts rather than itemized sources of income and the total of all operating expenses instead of individual expenditures.

The entire amount paid for debt service (mortgage payments) cannot be considered an expense on the profit and loss statement as it is on the monthly reports. Only the interest portion of each mortgage payment is considered an expense. The equity portion of each mortgage payment is actually applied toward retiring the total debt, thereby increasing the owner's equity in the property and accruing to his or her benefit. After the total mortgage payment has been deducted from the gross receipts, the mortgage loan principal must be added back in to obtain the net profit on the profit and loss statement.

The general formula for preparing a profit and loss statement for any type of property is as follows:

Gross receipts – Operating expenses – Total mortgage payment
+ Mortgage loan principal = Net profit

A sample profit and loss statement might look like this:

PROFIT AND LOSS STATEMENT

Period: January 1, 20XX, to December 31, 20XX

Receipts	$158,594.53
Operating Expenses	− 54,434.48
Operating Income	$104,160.05
Total Mortgage Payment	− 44,723.18
Mortgage Loan Principal Payments	+ 4,259.26
Net Profit (or Loss)	$ 63,696.13

Operating Budget

After developing the profit and loss statement for a specific period, the manager should compare the actual results with the original budget drawn up either at the beginning of that period or at the time the manager assumed responsibility for the property. After making the comparison, a new **operating budget** may be drawn up. A sample of an operating budget was illustrated in Chapter 2, Figure 2.3.

The budget gives the owner an idea of the cash yield to expect from the property during a fixed period, traditionally a year. The budget serves the manager as a guide for future operation of the property and as a measure of past performance. If the projected budget for a period does not agree with the actual monthly income and expense reports and the profit and loss statement for the same period, appropriate adjustments should be made in subsequent operating budgets or in operating procedures. In fact, many managers divide their annual operating budget into three-month segments so they can compare the budget with actual income and expenses on a quarterly basis. This helps pinpoint expense items that are out of line before a whole year has passed.

Estimate conservatively   The manager should resist setting unreasonably high goals for leasing agents or site managers to reach. Unreachable goals are self-defeating, if the organization morale suffers and competent personnel quietly seek other employment. Wise managers should set realistic goals that will allow the company to grow and prosper.

When preparing a budget forecast, the manager should use present rental rates for the estimates, rather than anticipated increases in revenue. Then, if the profit and loss statement at the end of the period shows a greater revenue than originally indicated on the budget projection, the manager will be able to point out what he or she contributed to the increase.

For example, a residential building with four two-bedroom apartments, each of which rents for $500 per month, billed $24,000 in rents during the past fiscal year (4 × $500 = 2,000 × 12 = $24,000), but actual rental collections amounted to $22,800. Based on these figures, the occupancy rate for the building can be calculated at 95 percent ($22,800 ÷ $24,000 = 0.95). In this case, when preparing the budget for the upcoming term, the manager should deduct 5 percent from projected gross rent receipts to allow for vacancies or loss of rent.

This method of computing an occupancy level can also be used for commercial and industrial properties that charge on a per-square-foot basis. For instance, an office building has 2,000 square feet of rentable space. The gross rent billed is $12 per square foot per year, or $24,000 for the entire building over a one-year period (2,000 × $12 = $24,000). Rental collections for the past year came to $18,000, so from these figures the occupancy rate for this building can be projected to be about 75 percent ($18,000 ÷ $24,000 = 0.75).

Examine discrepancies and prepare explanations   Before forecasting expenses for the new budget term, the manager should examine all discrepancies between anticipated costs as projected in the budget for the preceding year, and actual expenses incurred as shown on the income and expense reports from the same period. Substantial differences indicate either problem areas for management or items for which the projected estimates were unrealistic. If there is a decrease in the expected revenue, the manager should be prepared to explain why.

After determining the reason for the difference in costs, the manager should adjust either the operating policy or the forecast for the new budget period. An accumulation of budgets and comparative summaries over an extended period provides a valuable synopsis of recent trends and alerts the manager to areas of unfavorable progress.

The budget forecast should make allowances for vacancies and delinquent payments during the period to be covered. The cash flow reports for preceding months will tell the manager how much of an allowance to grant. The relationship between rentals billed and monies collected can be used to project an actual occupancy ratio for the property.

Allow for an evaluation of management skills   The owner can use the budgets and reports to judge the manager's skill in recognizing financial and market patterns and in coping with problem areas. The books and records of the management firm should be audited at least annually. Not only is this a proof of good faith, but many lenders and other parties require an audit before they will execute mortgages and other legal documents pertaining to properties under outside management.

■ INCOME AND EXPENSE STATEMENT FOR TAX PURPOSES

It is often the manager's responsibility to compute the tax liability for the property's revenue by drawing up an income and expense statement for the fiscal year even if an accountant prepares the owner's federal and state income tax returns. The income and expense statement adjusts the total net operating income from the property to allow for depreciation of the premises during the year. In addition, any expenses, such as tenant alterations that are considered capital improvements, are removed from the expense classification and are added to the property's depreciation schedule.

Depreciation

Depreciation accounts for the decline in value from physical deterioration, functional obsolescence, and economic obsolescence. For tax purposes, only depreciation from physical deterioration is deductible from the property's income. (Note that depreciation only applies to the improvements or the buildings on the land; the land itself does not depreciate.)

The rate to be used depends on applicable tax law, which will vary according to the date the property was placed in service. The property manager must consult with a qualified tax adviser before preparing any tax return. Material presented in this book is for the purpose of illustration only.

Pre-1981 properties   Property placed in service prior to 1981 may be utilizing several different recovery periods. Once the depreciation of a property has been calculated by a certain method, another method cannot be employed without authorization from the IRS. Formerly, there were three standard methods for computing the rate of physical deterioration:

1. Straight-line method
2. Declining balance method
3. Sum-of-the-years'-digits method

The *straight-line method* of computing depreciation assumes that the deterioration proceeds at a stable rate over the useful life of the building. The yearly percentage of the building's cost that is lost through depreciation (depreciation rate) is found by dividing 100 percent by the years of useful life of the building. For example, if a property can be expected to be used for 50 years with normal maintenance, the straight-line depreciation rate is 2 percent (100% ÷ 50 = 2%).

The annual depreciation rate is multiplied by the building cost to obtain the dollar amount of depreciation per year. This figure can be multiplied by the age of the building to find the total dollar amount of accrued depreciation. If the depreciable portion of the property in the previous example is worth $60,000 and is currently three years old, the dollar amount of depreciation would be $1,200 per year ($60,000 × 2%). The property would have depreciated by $3,600 ($1,200 × 3), and its depreciated cost would currently be $56,400 ($60,000 – $3,600).

The *declining balance method* and the *sum-of-the-years'-digits* methods are forms of accelerated depreciation. They are based on the premise that property depreciates more rapidly in its early years; hence, larger deductions are made in the first year of the property's economic life, with decreasing deductions throughout the later years.

The most common method of computing *accelerated depreciation* is the declining balance method, which adjusts the straight-line rate according to a percentage factor depending on the type of property. Common declining balance rates are 150 percent and 125 percent straight-line depreciation rate. For example, the 200 percent declining balance method doubles the straight-line rate. If the straight-line depreciation rate is 2 percent, the percentage multiplier used in the 200 percent declining balance method would be 4 percent.

For a building that cost $50,000,

$$\$50,000 \times .04 = \$2,000 \text{ depreciation for one year;}$$
$$\$50,000 - \$2,000 = \$48,000 \text{ undepreciated balance after one year;}$$
$$\$48,000 \times .04 = \$1,920 \text{ depreciation after two years; and}$$
$$\$48,000 - \$1,920 = \$46,080 \text{ undepreciated balance after two years.}$$

Accelerated Cost Recovery System (ACRS), 1981   Congress established the Accelerated Cost Recovery System (called "acres" from its acronym, ACRS) for property placed in service in 1981 to 1986. ACRS prescribes methods of recovery of expenditures through a depreciation allowance that varies according to the type of property being depreciated.

Tables published by the IRS set forth the ACRS percentages by property type and for the period the property is held. The tables for real estate are applied on a monthly basis in the first year the property is placed in service and allow recovery over prescribed periods of years. Percentages for real estate except low-income housing and percentages applicable only to low-income housing are shown in two separate tables.

Modified Accelerated Cost Recovery System, 1986   In 1986, ACRS was amended for property placed in service beginning in 1987 (called "makers" from its acronym, MACRS). Basically four new classes of property were added, two of which were classes of real property. Both must be depreciated on a straight-line method. Residential rental real estate was assigned 27.5 years of depreciable life and nonresidential real property was assigned 31.5 years.

Prescribed methods of depreciation were assigned to each class of property, rather than providing statutory tables, as was done in 1981. In some classes of property, a 200 percent declining balance method is prescribed, but the taxpayer is allowed to switch to the straight-line method if it will yield a larger depreciation. For other classes, the declining balance is set at 150 percent.

Revenue Reconciliation Act of 1993 For property placed in service on or after May 13, 1993, the new provision increased the recovery period of nonresidential property from 31.5 years to 39 years. Subsequent capital improvements to income-producing property may, with certain exceptions, be depreciated over the useful life of the improvements. Leasehold improvements are depreciated over the life of the lease unless the life of the property itself is extended by the improvements. In the case of extended life of the whole property, a longer schedule is required that reflects the true benefit of the improvements.

Depreciation rules must be applied with care regarding subsequent capital improvements because certain improvements may not be depreciated. Landscaping of shopping centers is an example of an improvement that may not be depreciated. Under the same rule, however, shrubbery and trees planted on apartment building grounds may be depreciated.

Investment tax credit Section 42 of the Internal Revenue Code addresses these issues for residential and multifamily housing. Federal income tax credits are allowed for certain depreciable property investments, and regulations vary for energy, antipollution, employee stock ownership plans, and other categories of property investments. Both the 1986 tax revision and the 1993 tax revision provide for tax credits to owners of low-income housing. If an investment tax credit is claimed and the property is sold or disposed of before a certain period of time, the investment tax credit must be repaid to the Internal Revenue Service.

Tax credits are available for qualified rehabilitated buildings and for the restoration of certified historic structures. Unlike depreciation, a tax credit is not an expense item for calculating taxable income but rather a direct offset against tax liability. There is a dollar-for-dollar credit on new construction of multifamily housing. Properties are unit-qualified using the median income for the entire area. This program has proven quite popular both with investors and tenant population that qualify for and benefits from subsidized rents. As tax laws frequently change, property managers and property owners should constantly check with qualified accountants for the most recent versions.

After-Tax Cash Flow The depreciation allowance is subtracted from the total net income from the property for the year. The resulting figure is the basis for the owner's tax liability on the profit from the property during that year. The actual tax due is taxable income times the appropriate percentage rate determined by the owner's tax bracket. Taxable income minus tax due, minus the principal add-back, plus depreciation equals the after-tax cash return on the property. The calculation of any report for an owner must conform to the owner's wishes. The formats used in this text are presented as methods that have found general acceptance; specialized situations will require adaptation.

For example, an apartment building valued at $600,000 when new has a gross annual income of $100,000 and average annual operating expenses of $60,000.

Mortgage payments amount to $30,000 annually, and $20,000 of this amount is payment on the principal balance. The property has a straight-line depreciation rate of 2 percent and is one year old on the principal balance. If the owner is in a 28 percent tax bracket, the cash flow would be calculated as shown in Figure 9.5.

Tax Reform Act of 1986   Losses (and credits) from passive trade or business activities, to the extent they exceed income from all such passive activities generally, may not be deducted against other income, such as salaries and wages, or interest and dividends. The one major exception is the ability of middle-income taxpayers to deduct up to $25,000 of rental losses from "actively managed" real estate.

To qualify as materially participating, a person must devote more than 50 percent of his or her personal services to real property trades or businesses during the tax year or devote more than 750 hours of service to these activities and be involved on a regular, continuous basis. Qualifying activities include development/redevelopment construction, reconstruction, acquisition, conversion, rental operation, management, leasing, or broker trade activities. Material participation is closely defined by the IRS, so again, anyone seeking this deduction should consult with an accountant.

Revenue Reconciliation Act of 1993   Beginning January 1, 1994, a taxpayer's rental real estate activities (RREAs) in which he or she *materially participates* are not subject to limitation under the passive loss rule if the taxpayer meets eligibility requirements relating to real property trades or businesses in which the taxpayer performs services. Real estate investors who qualify are now permitted to deduct their rental real estate losses from their current commissions, wages, interest, and dividends.

FIGURE 9.5
Statement of After-Tax Cash Flow

After-Tax Cash Flow Statement	
Gross annual income	$100,000
Operating costs	(60,000)
Annual income before debt service	$ 40,000
Debt service payments	(30,000)
Cash flow after debt service	$ 10,000
Mortgage principal add-back	+ 20,000
Net income before depreciation	$ 30,000
Depreciation allowance ($600,000 × .0364/yr × 1 yr)	(21,800)
Taxable income	$ 8,200
Taxes ($8,200 × 0.28)	(2,296)
Net income return after taxes	$ 5,904
Deduct principal add-back	(20,000)
Cash flow before depreciation add-back	$(14,096)
Depreciation add-back	+ 21,800
After-tax cash flow	$ 7,704

Tax laws are complicated and constantly changing. A property manager should be aware of these basic rules, as there is still misunderstanding among some owners and many would-be investors seeking tax shelters. However, it is imperative that property managers consult qualified tax specialists to get the most current, accurate tax information.

■ DETERMINING PROFITABILITY

The manager's monthly income and expense reports, profit and loss statements, and cash flow analysis help the owner decide whether the property is profitable enough to keep. In addition, they form a basis for judging the manager's competence. The owner and the manager may consider one or more of the following three methods:

1. Break-even analysis

2. Return on investment

3. Capitalization rate

Break-Even Analysis

In **break-even analysis** the primary method of calculating the profitability of a building is to determine its *break-even point*, the percentage of occupancy at which gross income is equal to fixed expenses. In large commercial projects, a break-even analysis is done to determine if a project is leased up to its "break-even point," often before a permanent lender will fund a takeout loan. When gross income exceeds the break-even point, the project will begin to be profitable. The formula for calculating a property's break-even point is as follows here:

$$BE = \frac{FC}{100\% - VCR}$$

BE = break-even point
FC = fixed costs (including mortgage payments)
VCR = variable costs ratio

By using the monthly income and expense reports for the property, the manager can first differentiate between the fixed costs (FC) and variable costs. Fixed costs remain the same whether or not a single unit is rented and include salaries, mortgage payment, insurance, and property taxes, and expenses related to new capital expenditures. Variable costs are those that change according the units rented; examples include management fees, maintenance expenses, utility costs, and so on.

Variable costs are usually expressed as a ratio to total rents. For example, a property with an annual income of $140,000 and annual variable cots of $28,000 has a variable cost ratio (VCR) of 20 percent (VCR = $28,000 ÷ $140,000 = .20 or 20 percent).

Finally, the break-even point is determined by dividing the fixed costs by the variable cost ratio.

Return on Investment

Return on investment (ROI), another measure of profitability, is the ratio of the property's net income after taxes to the money invested in the property (*investment*). In other words, this is what the owner paid, and this is the owner's return. This ratio can be converted into a percentage return on investment and measured against the owner's desired yield. In formula form, the return for a particular owner on the owner's investment

$$ROI = ATCF \div E \times 100\%$$

can be derived as follows:

ATCF = After-tax cash flow
E = Equity
ROI = Return on investment

For a property with a $15,000 after-tax cash flow in which the owner has an equity investment of $100,000, the rate of return is 15 percent ($15,000 ÷ $100,000 × 100 = 15%). Return on investment may also be quoted on a before-tax basis.

When an owner's cash investment is analyzed in this manner, it is often called a *cash-on-cash* return. In the foregoing example, a $100,000 initial cash investment yields a cash-on-cash return of 15 percent ($15,000 ÷ $100,000 × 100 = 15%). The term *cash-on-cash* may be quoted on either a before-tax or after-tax basis.

As a general rule of thumb, the rate of return should be equal to or above the rate of interest the owner could obtain with a savings account or a time note. If it is not, the owner is not receiving maximum return on the investment and should take steps to adjust operating costs, financing arrangements, depreciation rate, or taxes to increase the yield. The manager may be able to keep the local property taxes and special assessments on a property at a reasonable level by contesting its assessed valuation on behalf of the owner. If there is no way to improve the return on investment, perhaps the owner should consider selling the building in favor of a more profitable investment.

Capitalization Rate

The **capitalization rate** is another index of the profit on a particular property. An astute investor does not buy the bricks and mortar of a building but rather an investment property that has a projected net operating income (NOI). For comparison and measurement purposes, return is expressed through capitalization rates. Essentially, the capitalization rate converts future income to a present value; the rate is a number assigning a relationship between income and value. It is capitalizing the past and buying the future.

The general formula for calculating the capitalization rate is as follows:

$$R = I \div V \times 100$$

R = Capitalization
I = Net operating income before debt service
V = Value of property

The rates, which are not actually percentages, indicate a level of risk: the lower the risk, the lower the cap rate; the greater the risk, the higher the cap rate. For example, when purchasing a building with a 20-year lease with an insurance company, the investor might be content with a rate of 8. On the other hand, the investor might look to a higher rate of 12 when purchasing a multitenanted residential property with a higher risk and much more management.

The cash flow or income is going to stay the same regardless of what the investor pays. Here's how it works: On a property generating income of $100,000, the investor looking for a cap rate of 10 will expect to pay about $1 million. The investor who knows that the building and income are a bit riskier and more work will apply a rate of 12, and pay only $833,333. Another point of view is what is good for the buyer (cap rate of 12) is not necessarily good for the seller.

■ Here's a true story: An inexperienced manager who did not understand the differences advised his client/seller to ask for a higher cap rate. The astute buyer went along and "negotiated" an even higher cap rate, which was agreed upon, losing the seller thousands of dollars.

Making upgrades to reduce energy consumption can potentially increase value when determined by cap rate. ENERGY STAR estimates that every 10 percent decrease in energy use results in 1.5 increase in net operating income (NOI). After installing energy upgrades, reducing energy consumption, suppose that the income of the building was increased by 1.5 percent to $101,500. Assuming the same level of risk, apply the cap rate of 10; the building is now valued at $1,015,000. Often investors will compare capitalization rates of similar properties to determine the quality of the investment in the subject property. This is an estimate that depends on careful and objective selection of true comparables for its validity.

■ TAX RECORDS

The information given here is of a general nature because tax law is constantly changing. Property managers should obtain the latest IRS circulars and copies of state and local tax regulations and consult with competent tax counsel before filing any tax returns. However, the property manager should at least be familiar with the purpose of the various forms.

Property owners who pay people to work for them may be considered employers for federal and state income tax purposes and may be required to file certain reports with the appropriate government agencies. Most states have precise specifications as to the minimum number of persons on the job, total amount of wages paid, and working conditions that must exist before an owner is classified as an employer.

The difference between an employee and an independent contractor is also significant in terms of federal and state taxes. Workers are deemed to be *employees* if the person for whom they work has the right to direct and control when, where, and how the work is done and to define the desired end result of the work.

Independent contractors are able to control when, where, and how they perform the work and are hired to produce an end result. An agreement between owner and independent contractor must include a clause providing for the right of termination by either party on notice to the other. This is just one of the many fine distinctions that must be considered when contracting for work and when deciding whether a worker is to be considered an employee or a special (independent) contractor for tax purposes. Managers must not attempt to disguise employees as independent contractors if a bona fide independent contractor relationship does not actually exist, because the penalties from tax and liability standpoints can be severe.

Employee Documentation

Employer Identification Number (EIN)   If the workers at a building are employees under the law, the owner (or the property manager on the owner's behalf) must obtain a federal *employer identification number* from the IRS.

Employee's Withholding Allowance Certificate (W-4)   All employees must have a Social Security number and must fill out Form W-4, Employee's Withholding Allowance Certificate, stating the number of tax exemptions they intend to claim on their tax reports. The government charges the employer with the responsibility for obtaining these W-4 certificates and for complying with other important regulations concerning employees.

Employment Eligibility Verification (I-9)   Upon being hired, all employees must complete federal *Form I-9*, Employment Eligibility Verification, to establish they are lawfully able to work in the United States. The employee must complete and sign one section attesting to citizenship. A noncitizen employee must furnish evidence of lawful admittance for permanent residence or employment authorization.

The second part of the form requires the employer to review and verify the employee's statements, using documents furnished by the employee. The form must be presented for inspection to officers of the Immigration and Naturalization Service or Department of Labor upon request. Violation of this law is punishable by a civil monetary penalty.

Employer's Quarterly Tax Return (941)   In addition to providing all employees with W-4 forms, an employer must file Form 941, Employer's Quarterly Tax Return, for all income taxes withheld from employee wages. When filing Form 941 for the final quarter of the year, the employer must also transmit forms W-2 and W-3.

- Form W-2 is the Wage and Tax Statement for each employee, showing the total wages paid and amounts withheld during the year.

- Form W-3 is the Transmittal of Wage and Tax Statement. W-2 forms for all employees must be attached to the W-3 form, and the amount shown on the W-3 must equal the total of all the W-2 slips.

Property managers should follow the latest filing guidelines, published in *Circular E, Employer's Tax Guide*, by the Internal Revenue Service.

State obligations   To fulfill state income tax obligations, the employer must also register with the state in which he or she operates. These obligations and the specific forms used vary from state to state, but the W-2, W-3, and W-4 forms are generally used to document both state and federal income tax withholding liabilities.

Noncash compensation   When computing income for federal tax purposes, managers must indicate wages paid in any form other than money, at their fair market value. Included in this category are automobiles furnished to employees and living quarters provided for on-site managers. A qualified accountant or attorney must determine the proper treatment of any item of compensation given to an employee in lieu of salary. Different treatment and amounts are applicable, depending on the item and circumstances in each case. Under current regulations, the fair market value of living quarters furnished to a manager at the place of employment is not taxable to the employee, if the employee is required to reside on the premises as a condition of employment.

FICA insurance   The Federal Insurance Contributions Act (FICA) requires employers of one or more persons to pay tax into the Social Security retirement fund. The tax rate is set by Congress and shared by the employer and employee. The employer must withhold the proper amount from employees' paychecks and submit the total contribution from both parties to the federal government. The frequency of payment varies with the amount of the contribution; check the latest regulations available from local Social Security offices. When computing the FICA payment due, compensation other than wages (including a free apartment) must be shown as income at fair market value.

Disability and workers' compensation   In addition to Social Security, both disability insurance and **workers' compensation** insurance must be carried on all employees. Owners in some states obtain these through a government agency, whereas others use private insurance companies.

Statement of Miscellaneous Income (1099)   Employers must issue a Form 1099, Statement of Miscellaneous Income, to each independent contractor vendor who is not incorporated and was paid more than $600 in one year, and to each property owner stipulating the amount of rent the agent collected on the owner's behalf.

Unemployment taxes (FUTA)   A Federal Unemployment Tax Act (FUTA) return must be filed by every employer of one or more persons who work for some portion of a day for 20 weeks during the year or earn at least $1,500 during the year. The total tax levied will vary according to the amount of state unemployment tax paid by the employer for each employee. A credit against FUTA payments is given for any state unemployment taxes paid. Because the laws governing state unemployment taxes vary, the property manager must pay special attention to the applicable laws in his or her area.

■ SUMMARY

Whether located on-site or at another location, the office area and its furnishings must accommodate the basic functions of property management and create a good impression of the organization. There should be enough space for the firm's records and accounting system and for the reception of tradespeople and tenants.

Specialized property management software is readily available to perform financial analysis, planning, electronic filing, graphic design, word processing, and many specific business applications.

The property management executive is responsible for both strategic and operational management tasks. As the organization grows, the management executive can hire and delegate work to staff people. The property supervisor, or field manager, administers the properties and supervises resident managers, building personnel, and contract service or maintenance personnel.

A purchasing agent controls all purchases made by or through the management organization. The accounting department interprets the income and expense reports on properties, initiates new procedures, and provides the owner with profit and loss statements. The bookkeeping staff receives rents, handles credit and collections, and records accounts payable. Clerical personnel may be secretarial and/or service request clerks.

Two general methods of setting management fees are based on the organization's cost of doing business, including direct and indirect costs of operation. Many management fees are a percentage of the property's gross collectible income. The management pricing worksheet more accurately covers costs and profits.

The most functional reports generated for the owner are the monthly cash flow reports. Monthly income includes all rents actually collected plus any additional revenue from the property. Fixed and variable expenses are deducted from this amount.

Collectible income less operating costs leaves the month's net operating income before debt service. The net operating income minus the mortgage payment for the month equals the cash flow, the amount remitted to the owner along with the monthly cash flow report.

Monthly reports supply needed information to draw up a quarterly, semiannual, or annual profit and loss statement. Only mortgage interest may be deducted as an expense, not the amount paid on principal. An analysis of recent monthly cash flow reports should help the manager draw up a budget forecast for the year to come. At the end of the budget period, the forecasted figures can be compared to actual results.

The employer and/or manager is responsible for obtaining and filing various state and federal income tax forms and returns; computing, withholding, and paying Social Security, federal, state, and local payroll taxes; filing state and federal unemployment tax returns; and complying with a number of other regulations concerning employees. Specific rules as to working conditions, total amount of wages paid, and minimum number of persons to classify the owner as an employer vary from state to state.

If the workers at a building are termed *employees* under the law, the owner must obtain an employer identification number (EIN) from the Internal Revenue Service. All employees must have a Social Security number and fill out a Form W-4 (Employee's Withholding Allowance Certificate).

The manager draws on the income and expense statement for the fiscal year to compute the owner's tax liability for the revenue from the property. This statement adjusts the total net income from the property, as shown on the profit and loss statement, to allow the appropriate deduction for depreciation of the premises during the year. The income left after deducting the tax on the property from the adjusted income is the after-tax cash flow and represents the owner's profits from the property in that year. As tax rules change frequently, the manager should always communicate frequently with a professional accountant.

The owner can determine whether the manager is performing well and whether the property is profitable enough to keep by analyzing the after-tax cash flow with respect to comparable properties in the area and the desired yield from the investment. Other measures of a property's profitability include the break-even analysis, capitalization rate, and return on investment.

■ CASE STUDY

THE OFFICE MANAGER

Don Emerson has been assigned the task of bringing Professional Management, Inc.'s property management office up to date. He has worked for Professional Management for six months now as office manager and is well aware of the need to implement new office management systems. The filing system is disorganized, everything is done manually, and the clerical staff is overworked but unproductive. However, Emerson's boss is reluctant to spend a lot of money on a new computer system. She believes that computers are overrated—they end up generating more paperwork rather than less.

1. What should Emerson keep in mind as he sets up a new filing system?
2. Should Emerson try to convince his boss that a computer system is required? If so, how can he do this?
3. Assuming Emerson's boss agrees to computerize the office, what kind of system should Emerson get?

■ REVIEW QUESTIONS

1. The manager's office should be on the building premises when
   a. there is surplus space.
   b. most of the management operations are conducted there.
   c. the building is in a central location in the city.
   d. the building has good access to the interstate highway network.

2. Most property managers divide their office records into how many general categories for filing purposes?
   a. Three: in, out, and hold
   b. Four: lease, general correspondence, suspense, and permanent
   c. Six: lease, general correspondence, suspense, permanent, revolving, and "13"
   d. Five: lease, general correspondence, work estimates, financial, and permanent

3. The permanent property file should include
   a. the management contract.
   b. the yearly budgets.
   c. employment contracts.
   d. income tax records.

4. Which of the following should be considered when purchasing a computer system?
   a. Amount of space it takes up
   b. Ability to liquidate it quickly
   c. On-the-spot maintenance and repairs
   d. Popularity of brand name

5. An example of a direct cost would MOST likely be
   a. occupancy costs of the general management office.
   b. general office overhead.
   c. accounting overhead.
   d. payroll for the management personnel at the building.

6. If management operations are too limited to justify hiring a comptroller, the comptroller's tasks should be assumed by the
   a. purchasing agent.
   b. resident manager.
   c. bookkeeper.
   d. executive property manager.

7. In a large management organization, the general administration and daily operation of the property is performed by the
   a. field manager.
   b. on-site manager.
   c. office manager.
   d. property management executive.

8. Management fees may be computed on a percentage basis or
   a. on a square-foot by property-type basis.
   b. on a cost-plus basis.
   c. by the per-unit-cost method.
   d. by the BOMA or IREM systems.

9. In computing a management fee using the pricing worksheet, a manager determines that the total direct and indirect cost for all management activities for that property is $2,500 per month. If the gross collectible income from the property is $50,000 per month and the manager needs an additional 30 percent of the direct costs to cover overhead and profit, what percentage fee should be charged?
   a. 5 percent
   b. 6.5 percent
   c. 8 percent
   d. 13 percent

10. A small management operation has direct costs of $35,000 and indirect costs of $20,000 annually. It can handle about 750 units and wishes to make a 20 percent profit. What is the minimum per unit fee that should be charged?
    a. $47
    b. $73
    c. $88
    d. $164

11. An apartment building with 50 units has a gross possible annual income of $300,000 per year and an estimated vacancy rate of 6 percent. The management firm has computed an adjusted per-unit fee of $300 for this property. What percentage management fee should be charged?
    a. 5 percent
    b. 6 percent
    c. 7 percent
    d. 8 percent

12. The MOST important operating record kept by the property manager is
    a. a personal expense account.
    b. quarterly and semiannual profit and loss statements.
    c. monthly report on cash flow.
    d. annual financial statement.

13. Which of the following is a nonrecurring variable expense?
    a. Ad valorem taxes
    b. Insurance premium
    c. Employee wages
    d. An addition to the building

14. For the final quarter of the year, all of the following tax forms concerning employees must be filed by the manager EXCEPT
    a. Form 941.
    b. Form W-2.
    c. Form W-3.
    d. Form 1099.

15. Which statement accurately describes income tax withholding forms?
    a. Each employee must complete Form 941.
    b. Form W-2 shows total wages contracted for by the employee.
    c. Form W-3 sets forth the number of tax exemptions claimed by an employee.
    d. Form W-4 is filled out by the employee, but the responsibility for obtaining it is on the employer.

16. A manager would most likely want a percentage of the collected rents in which of the following situations?
    a. Upscale apartment building with high demand
    b. Condominium community
    c. Rundown property that needs a lot of work
    d. Building with high turnover because of reputed illegal drug activity

17. Unemployment taxes are levied and must be paid when filing
    a. FUTA.
    b. FICA.
    c. Form I-9.
    d. Form 941.

18. A commercial property containing 35,000 square feet is rented at $6 per square foot. However, actual retail collections over the past year amounted to only $168,000. What occupancy rate should be used in the budget forecast for the next year?
    a. 48 percent
    b. 78 percent
    c. 80 percent
    d. 85 percent

19. An apartment building has fixed costs of $75,000 per year and a variable costs ratio of 25 percent. What is the break-even point for the property expressed in dollars per year?
    a. $68,750
    b. $75,000
    c. $100,000
    d. $300,000

20. The capitalization rate is
    a. a method to convert future income to present value.
    b. usually figured at 12 percent for investment properties.
    c. used to determine the return on investment.
    d. the ratio the appraised value of the property bears in comparison to other noncompeting properties.

CHAPTER TEN

FEDERAL AND STATE LAWS

■ KEY TERMS

Actual damages
Americans with
   Disabilities Act
   (ADA)
Antitrust laws
Blockbusting
Civil Rights Act of 1866
Civil Rights Act of 1968
Conciliation
Credit report

Equal Credit Oppor-
   tunity Act (ECOA)
Equal housing logo
Fair Credit Reporting
   Act (FCRA)
Familial status
Handicap
Lead-Based Paint
   Hazard Reduction Act
   (LBPHRA)

Megan's Law
Price-fixing
Protected classes
Punitive damages
Retaliation
Security deposit
Steering
Testers
Uniform Residential
   Land-lord and Tenant
   Act

■ LEARNING OBJECTIVES

At the end of this chapter, the student will be able to

1. state the reason for antitrust laws, and give an example of what not to discuss with competitors;

2. list seven protected classes under the Fair Housing Act of 1968;

3. give examples of illegal steering;

4. state the importance of displaying the equal housing poster and summarize steps to take to avoid fair housing violations;

5. explain why retail and office building managers must understand the Americans with Disabilities Act, and the necessity of negotiating the cost of removing barriers between the owner and the tenant;

6. list the protected classes under the Equal Credit Opportunity Act, prohibited requests, and the importance of using business reasons for denying credit;

7. explain the value of a credit report when qualifying a prospective tenant, and the restrictions on who can obtain the credit report;

8. relate the provisions of Megan's Law of which property managers should be aware;

9. describe the effects of lead poisoning;

10. state the three requirements of the federal Lead-Based Paint Hazard Reduction Act that apply to property managers and landlords; and

11. summarize the differences between the Uniform Landlord Tenant Law and the student's state law regarding security deposits, procedures for evictions, and landlord and tenant obligations.

■ OVERVIEW

The title of this chapter may appear to be misleading in that it covers relevant federal laws and only in passing mentions state laws. Federal laws cover everyone in every state. State and city-specific laws cover only a specific state or city. Federal laws set the minimum standard; states and cities can add but never delete protections. In many circumstances, individual states are encouraged to pass "substantially" similar laws, as in the case of fair housing, or state-specific as with Megan's Law. Consequently, managers must be aware of the federal laws but understand their responsibility to determine relevant city and state requirements.

Federal and state antitrust laws apply to property managers, real estate agents, steel and oil, and most interstate industries. As previously mentioned, managers must be careful that they do not even appear to be setting rents and fees in collusion with other managers.

Federal laws have been enacted to prohibit discrimination based on certain, defined protected classes when renting or buying real property (Fair Housing Act) and when applying for financing (Equal Credit Opportunity Act), whether for a loan to buy a house or for credit for a lease. Most states operate under the federal Lead-Based Hazard Reduction Act, although some states have enacted more detailed laws.

Credit reporting agencies are supervised under the Fair Credit Reporting Act (FCRA). FCRA limits what can be reported, how long information can be retained, and who has access to this information to protect consumer privacy.

In 1972, the model Uniform Landlord Tenant Act was written. Today nearly 30 states have adopted the basic law, with minor changes in each state.

Property managers must be well versed in each of the laws, and must pay special attention to the variations enacted by their home states. Judges and juries are no longer automatically sympathetic to landlords, and penalties can be quite expensive.

■ ANTITRUST LAWS

The purpose of federal **antitrust laws**, particularly the Sherman Antitrust Act, is to promote competition in an open marketplace. Price-fixing limits this competition and damages the consumer because the consumer no longer has choices. Property managers should be quite careful not to violate this law. Each manager has the right to set rental and management fees according to the needs and expenses of the property.

In order to determine market rates, managers want to have an idea of what is being charged for similar rental units in the area. However, managers should not directly call their competition to ask what the consumer is being charged and then discuss those rental rates. There is a fine line between simply gathering information and *appearing* to conspire to fix prices.

The safest way to obtain competitive information is to go out and get it, a practice known as "shopping the competition." Either the manager or a leasing agent-in-training can be the shopper, appearing as a well-qualified typical prospect for a particular unit. This can be both a training device and a method of obtaining competitive information. While looking at the unit and by asking pertinent questions, the shopper will learn not only the fees but also the amenities, both of which affect leasing values. These anonymous visits take more time, but are more effective and less likely to be misunderstood in the long run.

Any suspicion of **price-fixing** between management companies or managers can result in civil and criminal penalties. If the courts were to determine that price fixing had occurred, the manager(s) could spend time in a federal penitentiary in addition to paying huge fines. Managers should never discuss their rental rates with anyone other than the owner of the property and the tenants they are charging.

■ FEDERAL FAIR HOUSING LAWS

Federal fair housing laws (as well as state and city fair housing laws) are designed to guarantee everyone an equal opportunity to live wherever they can afford and choose to live. Fair housing laws will not eliminate discrimination, but they do prevent a property manager or owner from arbitrarily rejecting a rental application based on race, color, religion, national origin, sex, familial status, handicap, or other legally protected characteristic.

The two significant civil rights laws with which every property manager should be familiar are the Civil Rights Act of 1866 and the Fair Housing Act (Title VIII of the Civil Rights Act of 1968) and its amendments.

Civil Rights Act of 1866   Under the **Civil Rights Act of 1866,** "all citizens shall have the same rights as white citizens to inherit, purchase, lease, sell, hold and convey real and personal property." According to the U.S. Supreme Court, any manner of racial discrimination in real estate is a violation of the Civil Rights Act of 1866. There are no exceptions to this prohibition against discrimination based on race.

The Civil Rights Act of 1866 was held constitutional by the Supreme Court in the case of *Jones v. Alfred H. Mayer Company.* The case was decided in June 1968, shortly after the **Civil Rights Act of 1968** was passed that did permit racial discrimination in certain circumstances. According to the court, the Civil Rights Act of 1866 *"prohibits all racial discrimination,* private or public, in the sale or rental of real property." (Italics added.) Accordingly, there are no exemptions for anyone or any kind of property. Under no circumstances is it legal to turn people down simply because of race or color.

Fair Housing Act (Title VIII of the Civil Rights Act of 1968)   ■ The federal Fair Housing Act and its amendments prohibit discrimination in the sale, rental, or financing of housing based on *race, color, religion, national origin, sex, familial status, or handicap.* Originally, these categories were called *minorities,* but today, as a reflection of what they really mean, are referred to as **protected classes**.

A property manager or owner may not, for discriminatory reasons, do any of the following:

- Refuse to show, rent, or negotiate with a person for housing
- Discriminate in the terms or conditions of a lease
- Engage in discriminatory advertising
- Tell potential renters that a property is not available, if in fact it is
- Interfere with, coerce, threaten, or intimidate a person to keep him or her from taking advantage of the full benefits of the federal Fair Housing Act

Blockbusting

Blockbusting is the act of encouraging people to sell or rent by claiming that the entry of a protected class of people into the area will have some negative impact on property values. It is illegal to assert that the presence of certain persons (i.e., protected classes) will cause property values to decline, that crime and antisocial behavior will increase, or that the quality of schools will decline.

A message from the manager or rental agent that the property or neighborhood is "undergoing changes" because a "certain group" is moving in may be viewed as **blockbusting.** Another term for this activity is *panic selling*.

Steering

Property managers should be especially careful to avoid **steering,** which is the channeling of members of protected classes to buildings or neighborhoods that are already occupied primarily by members of those same classes and away from buildings and neighborhoods occupied primarily by members of other classes. Historically, managers were steering when they put all the white tenants in one building or on one floor and all the Asian Americans, the African Americans, or any nonwhites in another building or floor. A more current example of steering is congregating all families with children in one building or on one floor away from tenants without children.

Steering may also occur when the manager tells the prospect that there is no vacancy when, in fact, there is a vacancy. This misstatement, which is illegal when it is made on the basis of any of the protected categories, steers the prospect away from the manager's building.

Steering can be very subtle and difficult to detect, and it can also be unintentional. For instance, a property manager may not even be aware of his or her own discriminatory assumptions, as when a manager believes that an Asian American tenant would automatically wish to live with other Asian Americans. However, whether intentional or not, such behavior is unlawful. The law is clear that even if there were no intent to discriminate, if discrimination occurs there is a violation.

In 2010, an Orange City, FL landlord and his former rental manager agreed to pay $415,000 in monetary damages and civil penalties to settle a Fair Housing lawsuit alleging that they discriminated against African Americans and families with children. The landlord must hire an independent manager to manage the 42-unit complex in the future.

The initial complaint came from an African American woman who was discouraged from applying for an apartment and whose application stated: "ADULTS ONLY." When a local television station sent out applicants, it was clear that the landlord and his former manager were providing more information and better treatment to white applicants than to African Americans.

Figure 10.1 shows a prospect equal service report form, published by the National Association of REALTORS®. A property manager can use this form to document the quality of service given to a potential renter.

FIGURE 10.1

National Association of REALTORS® Prospect Equal Service Report

NATIONAL ASSOCIATION OF REALTORS®
Prospect Equal Service Report
Rentals

Date:	Agent:	Office:

PROSPECT INFORMATION

Name:	Name:
Address:	Address:
Home phone: work phone:	Home phone: work phone:
Race: *	Race: *

* For Affirmative Marketing purposes. Information on prospect race is sought to assist in the monitoring of the firm's commitment to equal professional service. Article 10 of the NATIONAL ASSOCIATION OF REALTORS® Code of Ethics states: REALTORS® shall not deny equal professional services to any person for reasons of race, color, religion, sex, familial status, handicap, or national origin. REALTORS® shall not be parties to any plan or agreement to discriminate against a person or persons on the basis of race, color, religion, sex, familial status, handicap, or national origin.

Prospect came to us as a result of	Prospect is ___ current tenant ___ previous tenant	___ Ad (source)	___ For rent sign	___ Referral (source)	___ Other
Prospect preferences	possession date	rent range	size and type of unit: # bedrooms other features:		

Does prospect desire information regarding Housing for Older Persons?
If so, is any member of prospect's household over 55?

Prospect requested locations:

SERVICE PROVIDED - PROPERTY SHOWN

Did the prospect initially request information on or ask to view any specific property(ies)?

If yes, list address for each request, include street address, unit #, and community.	Rent	Deposit	Was unit shown?	If shown, prospect's comments and preferences. If not, why not.	Application offered?

Did you offer to put the prospect on a waiting list for any property requested?

If so, indicate which properties

Were other properties offered to the prospect?

List properties offered or shown. Include community, address, & unit #.	Rent	Deposit	Was unit shown?	If shown, Prospect's comments and preferences. If not, why not.	Application offered?

Were qualifying questions asked prior to application? If yes, indicate information obtained	___ Income	___ Employment	___ Current Rent	___ Other

Was an application offered to the prospect?	Did the prospect complete and return the application? Keep application on file for reference

Application and credit check fees quoted to prospect

Disposition, contact dates and comments:

Use the back of this page to list additional information, including other properties shown.

Source: © National Association of REALTORS®, reprinted with permission.

Equal Housing Poster

Failure to post the equal housing opportunity poster may be considered *prima facie* evidence of discrimination. A copy of the poster is shown in Figure 10.2. A copy of the poster can be obtained from the U.S. Department of Housing and Urban Development. The **equal housing logo** should also be used in all display advertising and printed materials. As mentioned in Chapter 4, classified ads do not have to have the logo so long as the newspaper prints a fair housing nondiscrimination disclaimer at the beginning of the rental section as shown in Figure 4.1. In addition to the poster, HUD provides fair housing brochures in fifteen different languages;: Amharic, Arabic, Armenian, Chines, Farsi (Iran), French, Hmong, Khmer (Cambodian), Korean, Portuguese, Russian, Somali, Spanish, Tagalong, Vietnamense (*www.hud.gov/offices/fheo/promotingfh/lep.cfm*).

Discriminatory Advertising

Discriminatory advertising includes using references to race, color, religion, sex, national origin, familial status, or handicap in any advertising. Property managers should avoid using terms that imply integrated or segregated neighborhoods or buildings. It is also unlawful to use human models in advertising to indicate exclusiveness based on race, color, religion, sex, handicap, familial status, or national origin. When human models are used in advertising, the models should reasonably represent the majority and minority groups in the community, both sexes, and families with children.

In late 1991, 13 Oregon newspapers received notice from the U.S. Department of Housing and Urban Development of 130 alleged violations. If all complaints had been upheld, hundreds of thousands of dollars of fines would have been levied. All of the newspapers thought that their advertising was legal and correct. From that experience, the Oregon Newspaper Publishers Association authored an instructional kit, *Fair Housing Advertising Manual*. Property managers who write and place ads should obtain a copy of this self-instructional manual. The newspapers that accept the ads must ascertain that the ads contain legal information. Violations continue today.

In December 2007, the Department of Housing and Urban Development (HUD) found that a landlord had used discriminatory advertising by running an ad that stated "No kids, No pets." The award of $4,000 was paid to the plaintiff and additional civil penalties of $11,000 were paid to the U.S. government in addition to attorney fees and continued administrative remedies for the next three years.

In May 2007, the Fair Housing Rights Center in Southeastern Pennsylvania conducted a one-month study of Craigslist "Apt/Housing" Rental Ads. After analyzing more than 200 ads that contained language indicating a tenant preference based on one or more protected classes, the Center concentrated on 15 ads that had been posted by a real estate professional and/or if the statements were blatantly discriminatory, such as "No Kids" or "No SSI." After the Center contacted the listing parties and explained the law, 7 of 10 either rewrote or removed the ads. Several other newspapers have settled complaints and are now running the disclaimer found in Figure 4.1.

FIGURE 10.2

Equal Housing Opportunity Poster

U.S. Department of Housing and Urban Development

EQUAL HOUSING OPPORTUNITY

We Do Business in Accordance With the Federal Fair Housing Law

(The Fair Housing Amendments Act of 1988)

> ## It is Illegal to Discriminate Against Any Person Because of Race, Color, Religion, Sex, Handicap, Familial Status, or National Origin

■ In the sale or rental of housing or residential lots

■ In advertising the sale or rental of housing

■ In the financing of housing

■ In the provision of real estate brokerage services

■ In the appraisal of housing

■ Blockbusting is also illegal

Anyone who feels he or she has been discriminated against may file a complaint of housing discrimination:
   1-800-669-9777 (Toll Free)
   1-800-927-9275 (TDD)

**U.S. Department of Housing and Urban Development
Assistant Secretary for Fair Housing and Equal Opportunity
Washington, D.C. 20410**

Previous editions are obsolete

form HUD-928.1A(8-93)

Protected Classes and Exemptions

When the law was passed in 1968, only race, color, religion, and national origin were included. Later, the 1974 amendment added sex as a protected class. Some exemptions were included. Basically, the exemptions include a For Sale or Rent by Owner; an owner who occupies a very small apartment building (two to four units); certain religious organizations; and very small investors.

Nevertheless, none of these exemptions apply to an agent who is renting any residential property for an owner. The Civil Rights Act of 1866 supersedes the exemptions in 1968; thus, no one can discriminate by race or color at any time.

Advertising should describe the property, not the other tenants and the landlord. Words should be inclusive, not exclusive. For example, an ad specifying a certain number of people for a rental unit could be interpreted as discriminating against children. On the other hand, "great for a family" would be acceptable. "Great for active people" may indicate that a handicapped person is not wanted. Likewise, "must be employed" may discriminate against an unemployed handicapped person who has another source of income. Better and legal phrases include "verifiable income" or "credit check required."

In February 2010, in Kansas City, MO, the U.S. Department of Justice announced the second largest monetary settlement in the history of federal fair housing cases. A combined $2.13 million was paid out to plaintiffs for repeated and egregious racial discrimination in an apartment housing community.

Fair Housing Amendments of 1988

The Fair Housing Amendments of 1988 added two of the protected classes previously mentioned: **familial status** and **handicap.**

Familial status   The minimum for establishing familial status is the presence of at least one individual in the family who is younger than 18, or the presence of a pregnant woman, or one who has or is obtaining custody of children. Landlords may no longer refuse to rent to families with children. Condominiums and cooperatives may not exclude children from living in their communities, unless the community meets specific HUD requirements to qualify as elderly or near-elderly (see the following page).

Property managers must ensure policies and procedures apply equally to everyone in the building; rules, however fair they may sound, may not be implemented with only children in mind. Placing families with children in one building or on one designated floor, or imposing occupancy standards that place undue burdens on families with children (such as "one person per bedroom") are also unlawful.

The courts do not look kindly on rules that unduly restrict children's activities or managers who turn away apartment seekers with children. In September, 2009, an agreement was reached with the owners and managers of a mobile home community in Alabama. The managers told an applicant that she had too many children (3) to live there. Further investigation indicated that the current residents with children were charged extra monthly fees. The owners must pay up to $104,130 to individuals who were discriminated against and an additional $30,000 to the United States as a civil penalty.

While there is no federal occupancy law, the U.S. Department of Housing and Urban Development has indicated that occupancy standards more restrictive than two persons per bedroom are *too* restrictive and unfairly impact families with children. In 1991, then Attorney-General Frank Keating wrote a memorandum outlining the legitimacy of two persons per bedroom, taking into account the size of the rooms; rooms that while not called bedrooms could be used as such; local building codes; and making exceptions for infants. HUD adopted the Keating Memorandum as the official guidelines for occupancy standards.

Exemption to familial status An exemption to the prohibition against excluding families with children is housing that falls into the "housing for older persons" category. The definition for housing for older persons includes any of the following:

- Housing that is provided by a state or federal program designed to assist older persons

- Housing that is intended for and solely occupied by those 62 years or older

- Housing designed for older persons in which at least 80 percent of the housing is occupied by at least one person who is aged 55 or older

Falsely implying exemptions In October, 2009, HUD and a Connecticut city signed an agreement settling claims that the city denied housing opportunities to families with children. Under the settlement, the city agreed to not enact an ordinance restricting housing only for persons 55 and over; to refrain from retaliatory actions against any person who aided or participated in the investigation; to pay the owner's $3,000 legal bill; and to maintain records that demonstrate its compliance. The Assistant Secretary said it is important that housing opportunities are "open to everyone, including families with children," given today's shortage of affordable housing.

Handicap The addition of the handicapped into the group of protected classes includes both the physically and the mentally handicapped. A handicap is defined as a physical or mental impairment that substantially limits one or more of a person's major life activities. For example, those who cannot see, hear, walk, speak, or learn would be considered handicapped. Also protected are those with HIV or AIDS. Note that handicaps caused by current illegal drug use are not covered.

Generally, landlords are not required to modify their units built before March 13, 1991, to fit the special needs of the handicapped, although they must let their handicapped tenants make any necessary modifications. (These tenants may be required to return the premises to their original condition at the end of the lease term.)

However, any newly constructed multifamily building (with four or more units) that was ready for occupancy after March 1991 must allow access and use by handicapped persons (for example, by including wheelchair ramps and elevators). It is not sufficient to "build to the local code." The federal guidelines mandate design minimums that must be followed, even if the local codes differ. Not all architects are aware of the requirements, and building to ADA code does not always satisfy accessibility requirements for private dwellings covered by the Federal Fair Housing Act.

Multifamily property and asset managers should consult the *HUD Design Manual* available through HUD's Fair Housing Information Clearinghouse at 800-343-3442. They should stay informed through trade associations and fair housing Web sites. Enforcement may include financial penalties as well as remedial action on a nonconforming property. Federal fair housing laws require that owners and agents allow for reasonable accommodations and modifications for persons with a disability so they will have full use and enjoyment of their home.

Reasonable accommodations may include a change in rules, regulations, policies, or services which could include

- allowing a service animal even though the property has a no pet policy;
- allowing for accessible parking spaces; or
- apartment transfers.

Reasonable modifications include physical or structural changes to the apartment or common areas such as

- adding grab bars to showers or toilets;
- installing ramps at curbing; or
- removing or lowing cabinets for access from a wheel chair.

Property managers should be aware of the different requirements of the Americans with Disability Act (ADA) which applies to commercial properties and the Fair Housing Laws which primarily pertains to residential properties. Often the type of property determines who is required to pay for the modifications.

Seeing eye dogs and "fetch" dogs utilized by those in wheelchairs may not be considered pets as a method of keeping the blind or wheelchair-bound tenant out of the property. Remember, service animals are *not* considered pets and therefore cannot be held to any restrictive rules or deposits regarding pets. There is no requirement for any special training or certifications for service animals. Further, the

Department of Justice makes no distinction between service animals and comfort or companion animals. All that is required is either a visible or verifiable disability and the direct coloration between the disability and need for the animal.

In late 2009, HUD charged a university with housing discrimination for refusing to allow a student with epilepsy and partial blindness to live in a dormitory with her trained service animal. The student was transferred to an inaccessible and less desirable dormitory.

According to reports in the National Fair Housing Advocate, in 2003, the owners of a Nebraska retirement community paid $87,000 as settlement for banning motorized wheelchairs and scooters from common areas at the community and required that any resident using these assistive devices could only live on the first floor. In 2007, the Justice Department reached agreements with owners and managers of a Georgia apartment community who refused to rent to a visually impaired individual who used a guide dog. The defendants agreed to pay $35,000 to the tenant, a $20,000 civil penalty to the government, to establish and follow non-discriminatory tenancy procedures, and to attend more fair housing training.

Using Credit Reports

Note that fair housing laws require a management firm to utilize **credit reports** for all applicants if it is going to use them at all. In other words, a manager may not require one particular applicant to pass a credit report check if this is not required of all applicants. Also, the 1988 Fair Housing Amendments Act prohibits charging families with children and those with handicaps higher deposits or higher rents than other tenants.

Testers

Discriminatory practices are often difficult to prove, so fair housing advocacy groups often use **testers** to gather evidence for fair housing complaints. Two or more testers might represent themselves to landlords as prospective tenants and then take note of any differences in treatment.

For example, both a white tester and a nonwhite tester may seek an apartment in the same building. If the white tester is shown the apartment but the nonwhite tester is told that no units are available, this information will provide very convincing evidence of discrimination. The evidence gathered by testers, such as tape-recorded conversations between property owners and the testers, has proved to be invaluable in determining the presence of discriminatory behavior.

> However, it is important to remember that anyone may be a tester, not just a person who has been specially trained. As a matter of practice, managers should treat everyone equally, without exception, without regard to race, color, religion, national origin, sex, familial status, or handicap.

Filing a Complaint

A complaint may be filed directly with HUD, or, more commonly, with a local city or state human rights agency. Initially, attempts to bring the parties together will be made; this is called the **conciliation** period. If that fails, either the case will be heard by an *administrative law judge* or as a civil action in the appropriate U.S. district or state court. The burden of proof falls on the complainant who must prove that the discrimination occurred.

Conciliation Relief

When possible, conciliation attempts to provide any or all of the following:

■ Monetary relief in the form of damages, including damages caused by humiliation and embarrassment, plus attorney fees

■ Other equitable relief, possibly including access to the dwelling or comparable dwelling

■ Injunctive relief to eliminate the discriminatory practice affecting the aggrieved person

Civil Penalties

Not every complaint can be resolved in the conciliation process. When cases end up in court, fines may be levied: up to $11,000 for the first offense; up to $27,500 for the second offense in five years; and up to $55,000 for more than two offenses in a seven-year period. The time limitations pertain to real estate companies. In the case of individuals, there are no time limitations for multiple offenses. These civil penalties are paid directly to the United States, not to the aggrieved person. In certain cases involving a "pattern or practice" of unlawful discrimination, the U.S. Department of Justice has the authority to seek civil penalties of $50,000 for a first offense and $100,000 for each subsequent violation.

Actual Damages and Punitive Damages

An aggrieved person can obtain an award of **actual damages** and injunctive relief in either an administrative or federal court. An administrative law judge can also impose the civil penalties mentioned above. In a court action, however, a judge or jury can award unlimited **punitive damages** to the aggrieved party. Also, the prevailing party may be awarded reasonable attorney's fees and costs.

Statute of Limitations

The federal law permits a complaint to be filed with HUD up to one year after the alleged violation. The case must be filed in court within two years of the alleged violation. Note that these are the federal guidelines that often act as a safety net inasmuch as most states and cities have imposed briefer limitations.

Avoiding Fair Housing Violations

One of the best sources of current fair housing enforcement cases is subscribing to HUD's Fair Housing Newsletters that are published on a quarterly basis. Each issue is published in a PDF format to allow for easy downloading and distribution. Subscribe at *www.hud.gov/offices/fheo/library/newsletters.cfm*. Managers can use the reported cases in staff meetings to better train their personnel. Additionally, there are numerous steps property managers can take to avoid fair housing complaints, including the following:

- Prominently displaying the equal housing poster

- Developing a written fair housing office policy that contains a statement affirming the manager's commitment to equal housing opportunity and that requires all employees to be familiar with and comply with fair housing requirements

- Providing fair housing training for all employees who have contact with prospective tenants, including information on protected classes, the types of behavior considered discriminatory, penalties for violations, and procedures for providing equal service

- Designating someone in the office to be a "fair housing officer," to be responsible for training, keeping up with current fair housing laws, answering employees' questions, and keeping track of compliance with office fair housing policies

- Discussing fair housing objectives and requirements on a regular basis in staff meetings

- Making sure that tenant selection criteria is objective, relevant to fulfilling lease obligations, and applied uniformly (appropriate criteria include the tenant's rent-to-income ratio, credit record, and rent payment pattern)

- Keeping detailed, comprehensive records of each prospect and inquiry. Amendments are fairly broad in that the definition of handicap includes a mental as well as a physical impairment: recovering drug addicts, alcoholics, and people with AIDS are included in the definition of handicap. (Note that the 1988 amendment also strengthened the enforcement mechanisms of the act and removed the limitation on the amount of monetary damages that could be awarded in civil lawsuits.)

- Ensure that policy and procedures provide consistent services to all residences, comply with the law and are effectively communicated to staff and tenants.

State and City Laws

The manager should supplement information in this section with information from the city and/or state in which the manager works. These laws may add to the protected classes and may add to the penalties, but may never conflict with any of the basic rights outlined in the federal laws.

Role of the Property Manager

The manager can contact the local human rights organization for additional state and city information. Every attempt to remain current with the laws should be made, including attending seminars at trade shows and taking continuing education classes. The manager should constantly stress compliance at every opportunity with every employee, and keep copies on file of any training sessions held.

■ AMERICANS WITH DISABILITIES ACT (ADA)

ADA Protections   Since 1994 the **Americans with Disabilities Act (ADA)** has directed that no person may be discriminated against on the basis of disability in employment, transportation, public accommodations, telecommunications, and in state and local government services. The ADA requires any business or other facility open to the public to be accessible by the handicapped. This means that not only must physical barriers be removed whenever practical, but policies and standards must be changed to make businesses more accessible.

ADA Coverage   The ADA applies to all private entities with facilities open to the public, as long as the operation of the facility affects commerce. Examples of some of the types of businesses that are covered by the ADA include real estate offices, property management offices, hotels, restaurants, bars, concert halls, lecture halls, bakeries, clothing stores, hardware stores, shopping centers, banks, attorneys' offices, accountants' offices, gas stations, doctors' offices, and government facilities.

The ADA covers many of the tenants in retail space and office buildings; therefore, the facilities leased by these tenants must comply with ADA requirements. As well as ensuring that managed properties comply with the ADA, property managers must be aware that their own facilities must comply with the ADA. A property management office falls within the definition of a public accommodation under the ADA and, therefore, must be accessible to the disabled.

Note that discrimination against the disabled in the context of residential housing is covered by the Federal Fair Housing Act, previously discussed.

Additionally, a management company employing 15 or more employees may not discriminate when hiring. An employer may not ask applicants if they have a disability or inquire into the nature or severity of a disability. Employers may ask if the applicant can perform the essential job functions as described.

Disability Defined   A *disability* is defined as any physical or mental impairment that substantially limits one or more of the individual's major life activities, including caring for oneself, performing manual tasks, walking, seeing, hearing, speaking, and working.

Requirements   When readily achievable, ADA requires removal of structural architectural barriers and communication barriers to make goods and services accessible to individuals with disabilities. Other requirements include providing auxiliary aids and services to ensure that no individual with a disability is excluded, denied services, segregated, or otherwise treated differently than other individuals unless to do so would fundamentally alter the nature of the good, service, or accommodations, or result in an undue burden.

All commercial structures designed and constructed for first occupancy after January 26, 1993, must comply with the law. The only exception to providing access by individuals with disabilities to new or remodeled facilities occurs when the nature or purpose of the structure prevents any accommodations from being made, which is a difficult requirement to meet.

Existing barriers must be removed whenever this can be done at a reasonable cost. Following are some examples of how this can be done:

- A building with no elevator may have to install a buzzer or intercom at street level so that customers of a second-floor business may obtain assistance.

- A pay phone may have to be lowered to make it accessible to someone in a wheelchair.

- Automatic entry doors may have to be installed.

- Grab bars may have to be added to restroom stalls, which may also have to be made larger.

- Ramps must be installed to outside doors.

- Raised letters and braille markings must be added to elevator buttons.

- The direction in which doors open may have to be reversed.

Determining Who Must Comply

The parties to a lease may decide among themselves who is responsible for complying with the ADA, and the lease should stipulate which party is responsible. All such agreements should be in writing to prevent any misunderstandings. Failure to comply can result in heavy penalties, so managers should carefully follow through on any agreements to ensure that tenants have actually made the proper modifications. Property management firms are independently bound by the rules of the ADA if they are in a position to make decisions affecting building accessibility.

Property managers are not expected to be ADA legal experts, but they must be acutely aware of the necessity for strict compliance with the law and be able to recognize when there may be problems with compliance. The Building Owners and Managers Association (BOMA) recommends first doing a building survey. BOMA has published two books to guide property managers in complying with ADA's Title III: *Public Accommodations: ADA Compliance Guidebook,* and *The ADA Answer Book.*

Rules are so complex that whenever additions or renovations are being made, the manager should consult with very knowledgeable attorneys, architects, and engineers and should ascertain that these individuals are conversant with the law. Ignorance of the law is no excuse, and it can be very expensive to modify to comply.

■ EQUAL CREDIT OPPORTUNITY ACT

By the early 1970s it was apparent that lenders and other creditors were using a woman's sex and marital status as a means to deny her credit, instead of basing the decision on business terms, such as adequacy of income and lack of existing debt. **The Equal Credit Opportunity Act (ECOA)** was passed in 1974 to open borrowing doors to women. This paved the way for other complaints of discrimination, and shortly thereafter, the ECOA was amended to include a total of eight protected classes.

Protected Classes

Today, the Equal Credit Opportunity Act prohibits denying a person a loan simply because of his or her race, color, religion, national origin, sex, marital status, age, and receipt of income from public assistance. The law applies to applications to rent a dwelling, inasmuch as the lease is considered an extension of credit.

Evaluating Lease Applications

The property manager must evaluate each lease application on the same terms. The manager must base the decision to lease (extend credit) on sound financial reasons. Generally, the applicant must show proof of income, submit to a credit check, and not be excessively encumbered by debt. The manager may deny credit for many reasons, including the following:

■ Unverifiable credit references

■ Insufficient income

■ Temporary or irregular employment

■ Insufficient length of employment

■ Excessive debt

■ Too many unpaid bills

Prohibited Requests

It may seem humorous now, but it was not long ago that creditors (and landlords) required information about an applicant's birth control practices; marital status (single, divorced, widowed, married); race; color; religion; or national origin. Today, this information is not relevant to the loan process.

Nevertheless, applicants will be asked their race, color, and national origin on many loan applications. This information is asked in order to assist monitoring practices by governmental agencies. In fact, if the applicant does not answer the questions, the lender may be required to fill in the blanks based on what the lender sees and interprets. It is to everyone's benefit to comply, remembering that it is illegal to use this information to deny a loan.

Penalties

Penalties for violating the ECOA are severe; civil liability for damages includes up to $10,000 in addition to punitive damages. The aggrieved parties who file a class action suit in federal court can be awarded up to $500,000, or 1 percent of the creditor's net worth. The court can also award court costs and reasonable attorney's fees to the aggrieved applicant.

Property Manager's Responsibilities

The manager should use the same lease application form for every applicant. If the manager is going to require a credit report from one applicant, it should be required of all applicants. The manager should be consistent when considering income and acceptable debt. Actually, the manager should only see one color: green!

Many managers do not rely on credit reports only. In order to verify income and timely rent payments, they call previous owners or managers, ask to see W-2 forms and paycheck stubs, or request copies of canceled checks to verify recent rent payments. The guiding principle remains: what is done for one must be done for all. Under ECOA, applicants who are rejected for credit (i.e., lease) have the right to see their entire file in order to determine if they have been denied credit because of a protected category.

■ FAIR CREDIT REPORTING ACT (FCRA)

Historical Background

The **Fair Credit Reporting Act (FCRA)** became law in 1971 and was amended significantly in 1997. The intent of the law is to provide that the data contained in credit reports are correct. The law regulates consumer reporting agencies, those who use credit reports, and those who provide information to the consumer reporting agencies. Landlords and property managers use this information and often contribute to consumer files.

Purpose of Consumer Credit Reporting Agencies

Lenders know the payment histories of their own customers, but have no idea of how an applicant has treated other creditors. The basic concept behind these requests is this: If an applicant has made timely and full payments to another creditor, then this creditor may presume that the applicant will do the same for this loan. On the other hand, if the applicant has been negligent in making payments or is consistently late, the lender may turn down the applicant, fearing that the applicant might not repay the lender. Past history can be as important as current history.

Credit Report Information

A credit report is a history of how a person pays his or her bills. A report generally includes identifying information; a list of current and previous credit cards and loans; public record entries and collection activity, if any; and a list of creditors who have inquired and reviewed the credit file. The report may include information about past due accounts and the number of payments currently due and whether these payments have been made on time. Property managers often enter information about delinquent tenants and those who have "skipped," leaving behind dirty apartments and unpaid leases.

Credit reports do not contain any information not related to the lending process, such as medical information; driving records; checking, savings, or brokerage accounts; insurance policies; or comments related to job performance.

Consumers have a right to obtain a copy of their reports and should do so at regular intervals to make sure that no erroneous information has been entered. If the consumer has been denied credit, he or she can receive a free report within 60 days of the denial, upon request. Other consumers should contact their local credit bureau for a copy. The local bureau will access one or more of the three nationwide credit reporting agencies: Equifax Credit Information Services, Experian National Consumer Assistance Center, or Trans Union Consumer Relations. The federal law permits the credit bureau to charge no more than $9. Some states require a lower charge.

Credit Report Errors

According to an Arthur Andersen audit, fewer than two-tenths of 1 percent of credit reports had errors in them that led to a credit denial. This is out of an estimated two billion pieces of data sent each month. Still, this can be troublesome, especially if the applicant/tenant is sitting in front of the manager.

The Fair Credit Reporting Act (FCRA) entitles consumers to challenge, in writing, the accuracy of any information in their reports. The information must be verified in a timely manner, and then certified as correct, modified, or deleted. If the verifying party does not do so within 30 days, the information must be deleted. The consumer must be notified about the change within 30 days. However, should the dispute still exist, the consumer has the right to add up to 100 words of explanation that will be reported every time that the disputed information is reported.

Information on File

Accurate though adverse information will stay on file for seven years, except for bankruptcies, which stay for ten years. Usually, completed Chapter 13 bankruptcies are deleted after seven years. Just because a delinquent account has been brought up to date or paid off does not mean that it is deleted from the report, however. Creditors will consider the paid collection and late payment notation as part of the overall payment history when determining whether they will grant credit.

Persons Seeing the Credit Report

Landlords are increasingly turning to credit reports as a means to determine financial responsibility on the part of the lease applicant. This is the only reason why a landlord should look at the report. The FCRA provides civil and criminal penalties in the event a credit report is obtained illegally or used for any other purpose. Consumer reporting agencies and consumers have a civil cause of action against those who illegally access reports. Property managers should thoroughly review reporting procedures with only those in the office who should see the report. Emphasis should be made about the confidentiality of such reports.

Rejection Based on Credit Report

In the past, if a property manager were denying an application based on the applicant's credit report, only the name and address of the credit agency needed to be given to the rejected applicant. After September 30, 1997, however, a rejection letter must include the following:

1. The name, address, and phone number of all consumer credit reporting agencies that provided information

2. Notice that the credit agencies only provide information about credit history, take no part in the decision process, and cannot provide an explanation for the decision

3. Explain the applicant's right to obtain a free copy of the credit report, dispute its accuracy, and provide a consumer statement describing his or her position

Application for Criminal Checks

Congress regulates criminal background reports as part of the Fair Credit Reporting Act (FCRA). Landlords or employers may run a criminal background report if an employee or a prospective employee or prospective tenant consents in writing. If the information is negative, and the manager does not want to hire this person at least in part because of this report, the manager must inform the applicant and provide a copy of the report. FCRA permits the person to challenge any of the information in writing, and if found to be incorrect, it must be timely corrected.

To be consistent, the manager must ask for permission to run the reports on every prospective job applicant. One should not hire just on appearances anyway. If the manager neglects to check out references, he or she may hire an unfit person and the manager could be found liable for negligent hiring. The manager could face a lawsuit claiming that the manager failed to make reasonable inquiry into the applicant's background, that a reasonable inquiry would have discovered potential problems, or that the manager knew or should have known that this person was a risk to others.

As many employees have easy access to keys to many properties, every property manager should carefully consider all references. In today's world, spending an extra few bucks to run a criminal check could be a wise investment.

■ MEGAN'S LAW

Seven-year-old Megan Kanka of Hamilton, New Jersey, was raped and murdered in July 1994 by a convicted sex offender who had moved into the neighborhood unbeknownst to Megan's parents. The law was named in her memory and requires that information about certain sex offenders be released to the general public. After New Jersey passed the first "**Megan's Law**," the U.S. Congress enacted a federal version as part of the federal Violent Crime Control and Law Enforcement Act in 1996. Megan's laws have been challenged as unconstitutional in several states, but none of the challenges have invalidated any state Megan's Law.

Reporting Requirements

Prison officials are required to inform convicted sex offenders of their obligation to register with state law enforcement authorities and to reregister if they move to another state. The state agencies are in turn required to inform local law enforcement authorities (typically the local police department) of convicted sex offenders who reside in their jurisdiction. Also, the agencies are to inform the FBI about these addresses.

Local law enforcement agencies are then permitted to release collected information as necessary to protect the public or "for any purpose permitted under the laws of the state." Divulging this information varies from state to state, inasmuch as states were permitted to choose one of the following three options:

1. Notification to all (putting all names on the Internet, for example)
2. Notification to those most at risk (schools, day care centers, etc.)
3. Individual and address-specific (when specifically asked about each address)

Although registration is required, there is often no verification of the address upon registration. The address can easily be inaccurate, plus there is often no verification when the individual moves on. Moreover, most law enforcement people do not always provide the consumer with a printed informational sheet as of a specific date. The Dru Sjodin National Sex Offender Public Web site (NSOPW), coordinated by the U.S. Department of Justice, is a cooperative effort between jurisdictions hosting public sex offender registries—including the 50 states, Puerto Rico, Guam, the District of Columbia, and participating tribes—and the federal government.

State Laws and the Property Manager

Property managers may wish to institute a criminal background check as part of the hiring process for employees who will have keys and access to apartments, particularly if access is not always supervised. Consulting the sex offender registry open to the public should be part of the pre-employment checklist. Owners and managers should do everything possible so the key to a resident's home does not end up in the hands of a registered sex offender.

In other liability cases, courts have not expected owners and managers to do everything possible to secure a property. Instead, they have looked at reasonable measures taken and reasonable standards of care. As state laws vary, the property manager must become familiar with the local requirements and should consult with a local attorney for specific guidance on how much information the manager is responsible for relaying to a tenant. The answer will no doubt depend upon the manager's actual knowledge about the presence of a convicted sex offender, the particular provisions of the applicable state Megan's Law, and whether the tenant questions the manager about the presence of convicted sex offenders.

■ SEXUAL HARASSMENT

Claims of sexual harassment by employees concern every employer. It is important for the property manager to put into place a clear, written policy against sexual harassment, provide an employee-friendly procedure for investigating complaints, and conduct thorough and unbiased investigations that lead quickly to corrective action. Moreover, the multifamily housing industry faces two additional concerns: tenants' claims of harassment by owners and management employees and claims against management for behavior between tenants that may constitute sexual harassment.

Quid pro quo cases are the easiest to define; that is, lease terms may not be conditioned on submitting to sexual demands. It is hard to prove that the act was not pervasive and persistent. Defense on these grounds is risky, and owners and managers face the potential of huge awards and attorney's fees. In December 008, a Texas landlord was permanently barred from managing rental property and ordered to pay $275,000 to several agencies and six female tenants. The lawsuit alleged that the landlord made unwelcome and unwanted verbal and physical sexual advances, made or denied housing benefits in exchange for sexual favors, and denied rent based on the sex of a potential tenant.

The policy should include a zero-tolerance written policy for tenants as well. This policy should be publicized to every tenant and a means by which tenants can complain should be indicated. If a complaint is raised, property managers should act swiftly when investigation indicates a problem. Employees should understand that what appears to be personal matters between tenants could turn into liability claims against the company.

■ LEAD-BASED PAINT HAZARD REDUCTION ACT (LBPHRA) (TITLE X OF THE 1992 HOUSING AND COMMUNITY DEVELOPMENT ACT)

Lead is a heavy, soft, malleable, blue-gray metal found as a natural ore and/or as a by-product of smelting silver; once removed from the ground, lead is part of the human environment forever. Lead was banned from gasoline in the early 1970s and from paint in 1978.

Effects of Lead on Humans

Lead poisoning is not spread from person to person, but rather through ingesting and retaining high concentrations of lead. Lead is very slowly eliminated through the kidneys and gastrointestinal tract. Lead has no known use in the body.

Although high concentrations will affect anyone, children younger than six are particularly vulnerable. Lead poisoning is discovered through a blood test. Excessive lead can cause major health problems in children by damaging the child's brain, nervous system, kidneys, hearing, or coordination, causing headaches and behavior problems and affecting learning.

Sources for Lead Exposure

Major sources of exposure include paint, surface dust and soil, drinking water, air, and food. House and soil dust comes from the weathering and chipping of **lead-based paint.** Renovation efforts such as scraping or sanding help spread the dust, and it is easily carried by many sources: clothing, tools, pets, shoes, and so on. Raising and lowering windows disturbs the paint and also rubs the lead ballasts.

Chipping and peeling lead paint in the house can become airborne and widely spread through the use of an ordinary vacuum cleaner. Airborne lead lands on toys, and even fingers, which children tend to touch, suck on, and chew.

Target Housing

Any housing constructed prior to 1978 is affected. Exempt is housing for the elderly or persons with disabilities, unless children who are younger than six will be living in such a dwelling. Any zero-bedroom dwelling (no separation between living, eating, and sleeping areas) is affected. Exemptions also include rental property that has been inspected and certified to be free of lead-based paint; property leased for fewer than 100 days per year; property where renewal or extension cannot occur (summer rentals); and in cases where an existing lease is renewed once proper disclosure has been made.

Required Disclosures

There are three basic requirements for landlords and managers:

1. Disclose to the tenant the presence of any known lead-based paint or hazards (see Figure 10.3 in English and 10.4 in Spanish).

2. Provide tenants with copies of any available records or reports pertaining to the presence of lead-based paint and/or hazards.

3. Give the tenant a copy of the EPA lead hazard information pamphlet, "Protecting Your Family from Lead in Your Home," available from *www.epa.gov* in English, Spanish, Vietnamese, Russian, Arabic, and Somali.

Provisions must be included in the rental agreement to ensure that disclosure and notification actually take place. The wise manager will include a space for the tenant to acknowledge receipt of the disclosure. The EPA has begun monitoring files for review, to determine compliance with these rules. Copies of the lead warning statement must be retained for three years from the date of the lease. This

FIGURE 10.3
Lead-Based Paint Disclosure

Disclosure of Information on Lead-Based Paint and/or Lead-Based Paint Hazards

Lead Warning Statement

Housing built before 1978 may contain lead-based paint. Lead from paint, paint chips, and dust can pose health hazards if not managed properly. Lead exposure is especially harmful to young children and pregnant women. Before renting pre-1978 housing, lessors must disclose the presence of known lead-based paint and/or lead-based paint hazards in the dwelling. Lessees must also receive a federally approved pamphlet on lead poisoning prevention.

Lessor's Disclosure

(a) Presence of lead-based paint and/or lead-based paint hazards (check (i) or (ii) below):

    (i) _____ Known lead-based paint and/or lead-based paint hazards are present in the housing (explain).

    _____

    _____

    (ii) _____ Lessor has no knowledge of lead-based paint and/or lead-based paint hazards in the housing.

(b) Records and reports available to the lessor (check (i) or (ii) below):

    (i) _____ Lessor has provided the lessee with all available records and reports pertaining to lead-based paint and/or lead-based paint hazards in the housing (list documents below).

    _____

    _____

    (ii) _____ Lessor has no reports or records pertaining to lead-based paint and/or lead-based paint hazards in the housing.

Lessee's Acknowledgment (initial)

(c) _____ Lessee has received copies of all information listed above.

(d) _____ Lessee has received the pamphlet *Protect Your Family from Lead in Your Home*.

Agent's Acknowledgment (initial)

(e) _____ Agent has informed the lessor of the lessor's obligations under 42 U.S.C. 4852d and is aware of his/her responsibility to ensure compliance.

Certification of Accuracy

The following parties have reviewed the information above and certify, to the best of their knowledge, that the information they have provided is true and accurate.

Lessor	Date	Lessor	Date
Lessee	Date	Lessee	Date
Agent	Date	Agent	Date

FIGURE 10.4
Lead-Based Paint Disclosure (Spanish)

Declaración de Información sobre Pintura a Base de Plomo y/o Peligros de la Pintura a Base de Plomo

Declaración sobre los Peligros del Plomo

Las viviendas construidas antes del año 1978 pueden contener pintura a base de plomo. El plomo de pintura, pedazos de pintura y polvo puede representar peligros para la salud si no se maneja apropiadamente. La exposición al plomo es especialmente dañino para los niños jóvenes y las mujeres embarazadas. Antes de alquilar (rentar) una vivienda construida antes del año 1978, los arrendadores tienen la obligación de informar sobre la presencia de pintura a base de plomo o peligros de pintura a base de plomo conocidos en la vivienda. Los arrendatarios (inquilinos) también deben recibir un folleto aprobado por el Gobierno Federal sobre la prevención del envenenamiento de plomo.

Declaración del Arrendador

(a) Presencia de pintura a base de plomo y/o peligros de pintura a base de plomo (marque (i) ó (ii) abajo):

    (i) _____ Confirmado que hay pintura a base de plomo y/o peligro de pintura a base de plomo en la vivienda (explique).

_____

    (ii) _____ El arrendador no tiene ningún conocimiento de que haya pintura a base de plomo y/o peligro de pintura a base de plomo en la vivienda.

(b) Archivos e informes disponibles para el vendedor (marque (i) ó (ii) abajo):

    (i) _____ El arrendador le ha proporcionado al comprador todos los archivos e informes disponibles relacionados con pintura a base de plomo y/o peligro de pintura a base de plomo en la vivienda (anote los documentos abajo).

_____

    (ii) _____ El arrendador no tiene archivos ni informes relacionados con pintura a base de plomo y/o peligro de pintura a base de plomo en la vivienda.

Acuse de Recibo del Arrendatario o Inquilino (inicial)

(c) _____ El arrendatario ha recibido copias de toda la información indicada arriba.

(d) _____ El arrendatario ha recibido el folleto titulado *Proteja a Su Familia del Plomo en Su Casa.*

Acuse de Recibo del Agente (inicial)

(e) _____ El agente le ha informado al arrendador de las obligaciones del arrendador de acuerdo con 42 U.S.C. 4852d y está consciente de su responsabilidad de asegurar su cumplimiento.

Certificación de Exactitud

Las partes siguientes han revisado la información que aparece arriba y certifican que, según su entender, toda la información que han proporcionado es verdadera y exacta.

Arrendador	Fecha	Arrendador	Fecha
Arrendatario	Fecha	Arrendatario	Fecha
Agente	Fecha	Agente	Fecha

notification must also be made whenever a tenant renews a lease made prior to September 6, 1996.

If more than two square feet of painted area is likely to be disturbed in a dwelling built before 1978, the manager must make additional notifications. If the work will be contained in only one unit, only those tenants must be notified. If the work will be done in a common area, then all tenants must be notified that lead-based paint may be disturbed. The EPA has several training programs available for renovators. Essentially, managers and owners want to achieve the following:

- Protect both workers and tenants from exposure to lead-based paint-contaminated dust while work is being performed.

- Minimize the amount of lead-based paint contaminated dust and debris created.

- Contain the created lead-based paint dust and debris.

- Clean up lead hazards created by renovation or remodeling activities.

EPA published new lead laws in the form of modifications to the Toxic Substances Control Act (TSCA) Sections 402 and 406(b) rules previously published. The new rules specify who must be notified in housing when lead-based paint (LBP) is disturbed and the accreditations and training required for those firms (including property managers) doing work that disturbs known or suspect LBP. The Renovation, Repair, and Painting (RRP) rules are effective April 2010.

Under RRP, "de minimis" levels are 6 square feet of paint on an interior surface or 20 square feet of paint on an exterior surface. Also, window replacement work is automatically subject to RRP regardless of square footage as historically it has been one of the largest generators of lead dust. Work that disturbs less than these amounts of paint is not subject to the law.

The following requirements apply to renovation projects that disturb paint above the "de minimis" levels of paint:

- Brochure "Renovate Right" must be used to notify owners and occupants before renovations begin. "Protect Your Family from Lead in Your Home" will still be used for lease notifications under Section 1018 of Title X.

- Once accredited by the EPA, training providers may offer courses in safe work practices for "Certified Renovators."

- After October 2009: Renovation firms (including property management firms) may apply to EPA to become "Certified Firms" to perform renovations or dust sampling. In their applications they must prove they have a "Certified Renovator" on their staff to oversee renovation projects and/or dust tests.

- After April 2010: Firms conducting renovations must be certified by EPA. Renovation work disturbing known or suspect LBP above de minimis levels must be done by Certified Firms employing a Certified Renovator. Both Certified Firms and Certified Renovators must be recertified every 5 years.

- Certified Firm Responsibilities: All workers disturbing painted surfaces are either Certified Renovators or have been trained by a Certified Renovator. A Certified Renovator is assigned to each renovation and performs all certified renovator responsibilities. All renovations must be performed in accordance with work practice standards of the RRP program. Pre-renovation education requirements along with record keeping requirements are met.

- Certified Renovator Responsibilities: Use EPA approved test kits to confirm presence of LBP. Must provide on-the-job training on safe work practices to workers. Must be physically present when warning signs are posted, while containments are set and while work-area cleaning is performed. Must direct work by others to insure work practices are followed, containments are functional and dust/debris does not spread beyond the work area. Must perform project cleaning verification. Must have applicable certificates and records at the work site.

- All documents must be retained for three years after a renovation, including: Reports certifying LBP is not present. Confirmations of lead brochure distribution. Completed Compliance Checklists from EPA.

- Enforcement: EPA may suspend, revoke, or modify a firm's firm's certification if the firm is found to be in non-compliance. Non-compliant contractors may be liable for civil penalties of up to $25,000 for each violation. Contractors who knowingly or willfully violate this regulation may be subject to fines of up to an additional $25,000 per violation, or imprisonment, or both.

Penalties for Nondisclosure

There are 11 possible violations per lease. Failure to comply with these regulations could result in civil fines from $110 to $11,000 per violation in addition to any criminal fines and awards of triple damages that may be assessed. In April 2010, a New York City landlord was fined $20,000 for failing to properly inform residents in his 25 properties about the potential lead-based paint in their apartments through disclosure statements, warning statements, and failing to make them aware of records or reports that would alert them. A Connecticut property management company has agreed to pay a $276,000 penalty for violating the federal disclosure rules (February 2010).

Monitoring Files

Both the Department of Housing and Urban Development (HUD) and the EPA have awarded grants to advocacy groups to increase awareness of the requirements of Title X; moreover, a special $50 million fund has been created at the U.S. Department of Justice for stepped up enforcement of environmental violations.

Management Responsibilities

The public is becoming increasingly aware of the hazards of lead, and more and more blood testing is being done in young children. Awareness will result in increased testing for compliance with the disclosure notices, just as testing for fair housing is done.

Each regional EPA office has quarterly quotas to inspect office files. Officials will be randomly checking rental office files. If a complaint is received about nondisclosure, that property goes to the top of the list.

It is incumbent upon the owner and manager to properly maintain any property built before 1978, and to avoid chipping and peeling of paint. If repair and renovation activities go beyond routine maintenance, an employer must perform air sampling to monitor employee exposure unless it has objective data demonstrating that the lead dust levels are below any action level. The property manager should be sure that the resident manager and maintenance personnel are properly trained in lead-safe work practices and familiar with the various regulations pertaining to housing built before 1978.

> The manager should develop an operations and maintenance plan for any lead-based paint on the property. Such a plan may include representative dust testing to verify that clean-up practices following routine maintenance procedures are sufficient to eliminate lead dust hazards. Let tenants know that routine housekeeping on their part is essential to controlling any lead-containing dust that may be tracked or blown into their apartments from outside. Finally, the tenants should be encouraged to report any situation involving damaged or deteriorating painted surfaces.

■ UNIFORM RESIDENTIAL LANDLORD AND TENANT ACT

The Uniform Residential Landlord and Tenant Act, drafted in 1972 by the National Conference of Commissioners on Uniform State Laws, was designed to standardize and regulate the relationship between property owners and their tenants. Variations of the Uniform Act have been incorporated into the statutes of several states, so property managers should study and keep current with variations and modifications found in state and local laws. (The act covers only residential property.)

Each of the states that have adopted the uniform act have variations to the basic law, so the manager should carefully read his or her law and look for specific answers to the following uniform act provisions.

No Abrogation of Rights

Under the act, leases may not contain a judgment clause, a clause in which the tenant waives any rights or remedies, or any clause contravening the act. The tenant may not sign away his or her rights.

No Retaliation

If a tenant makes a complaint to the health department, fair housing board, or any other governing authority, the landlord is generally prohibited from summarily raising that tenant's rent or any other type of response that can be interpreted as retaliation or punishment.

Fair Dealings

If a legal dispute arises between owner and tenant, the court may refuse to enforce all or part of a lease that it finds grossly unfair. The act further stipulates that the owner and tenant should make a joint inventory detailing the condition of the premises and all rented furnishings and appliances within five days after the tenant takes possession. Both parties should sign and retain a copy of this inventory.

Estate from Period to Period

One of the more notable provisions of the Uniform Residential Landlord and Tenant Act is that unless otherwise specified, a tenant is considered to have an estate from period to period. A tenant who pays weekly rent holds tenancy from week to week, whereas all others hold an estate from month to month.

Effects of Unsigned Leases

If the owner or tenant signs and delivers a written lease and if either party pays or accepts rent, the lease is often considered binding, even without the other party's signature. The act also establishes standard lease termination procedures.

Security Deposits

Specific guidelines are established regarding **security deposits,** which have been one of the largest single sources of disagreement between owners and tenants. Security deposits are generally limited to an amount not exceeding one month's rent for unfurnished apartments and one and one-half month's rent for furnished units. Neither the tenant nor the manager should consider the security deposit the last month's rent; it is a deposit to be used for damages.

What to do with the security deposit and the interest it earns varies from state to state. Sometimes it may be forwarded to the owner; in other states, it must be deposited in a trust or escrow account, often within the state where the property is located. Some states require that deposits are made into interest-bearing accounts; others do not. The manager must learn local requirements.

Many states specify exactly what the landlord may do with the deposit at the end of the tenancy. Generally, the landlord may deduct money for unpaid rent and damage to the property. However, usually the landlord must itemize the deductions within a certain time frame, explaining why all the deposit is not being returned. Failure to do so may result in having to refund up to three times the amount wrongfully withheld. In some states, the tenant is required to ask for the security deposit at the end of the term.

Owner's Responsibilities

Although the rental agreement may limit the owner's liability for fire, theft, and damage in common areas, the act clearly establishes the owner's responsibility for keeping the premises safe and fit for habitation. The act authorizes the owner to establish building rules concerning use and occupancy, as long as they are reasonable and equitably enforced. These rules must be in writing, and the tenant must agree to them.

Owner's Right to Re-enter

The owner is given the right to enter rental units, after giving reasonable notice, to inspect, make repairs or improvements, supply services, or show the unit. Only in emergencies may the owner enter without prior permission from the tenant.

Tenant Use and Occupancy

The act covers only residential property. The tenant should use the premises for residential purposes unless there is an agreement to the contrary, and should not conduct any illegal activities on the property.

Tenant's Noncompliance

The tenant must comply with applicable laws and ordinances, use facilities and fixtures in a reasonable manner, avoid damage or destruction of the premises, and preserve other tenants' quiet enjoyment. If the tenant breaches the lease, the owner may give legal notice and force compliance. If the tenant does not respond within a specified time, the owner may terminate the lease and claim possession, rent owed, damages, and attorney's fees. The manager should read the governing state law very carefully to determine specific time frames to follow—what notice must be given and when and how, when to go to court, and the time frames the judge will follow. All these time frames vary from state to state.

Abandonment

A tenant who abandons a unit usually remains liable for the rent unless the unit is rerented or the owner releases the tenant from the obligation. The owner is required to make a reasonable effort to rerent the unit in cases of abandonment, if the owner seeks to recover rent for the unexpired term.

Tenant Remedies for Owner's Noncompliance

A tenant's remedies for the owner's noncompliance with the lease are also set forth in the act. If the owner does not begin a good faith effort to remedy the breach, the tenant may terminate the lease after giving notice. The tenant is entitled to the deposit plus any prepaid rent and may also sue for damages and attorney's fees. Should the owner fail to deliver possession or illegally exclude the tenant from the premises, the tenant may give legal notice and obtain the essential services, sue for damages, or vacate the premises.

Fire or Casualty Damage

If a unit is rendered uninhabitable by fire or other casualty, the tenant may give notice and terminate the lease immediately. If damage is partial, the tenant may reduce the rent proportionately.

■ SUMMARY

Federal laws set the standards. States and cities may add protections but may never take away protections offered by the federal law. The Fair Housing Laws and Megan's Law require that states enact state statutes with which the manager must become familiar.

Antitrust laws have been passed to prevent monopolies and price fixing. Managers should avoid discussions with competitors about fees and pricing.

The 1866 Civil Rights Act is the oldest civil rights law and prohibits discrimination based on race or color in the sale or leasing of real and personal property. It has been reaffirmed by the *Jones v. Mayer* Supreme Court decision.

The Civil Rights Act of 1968 as amended prohibits discrimination in the sale or rental of housing based on race, color, religion, national origin, sex, familial status, or handicap. Managers should avoid "steering," such as putting all families in one building or on one floor, or all Asian Americans in one area. A handicapped tenant may modify the property to accommodate his/her handicap, but may be required to replace or repair those modifications at the end of the tenancy.

A manager may not deny housing to families unless the community is designated elderly (all older than 65) or near-elderly (80 percent are 55 and older). Discriminatory advertising is prohibited, and consistency in renting is expected without regard to the protected classes.

The property manager should constantly emphasize obedience of the law and remind staff that housing discrimination can result in large fines. At the very least, every office should prominently display the Equal Housing poster.

The Americans with Disabilities Act (ADA) prohibits discrimination on the basis of disability in employment, transportation, public accommodations, telecommunications, and in state and local government services. The ADA applies to all private and government entities with facilities open to the public, so even property management offices have to comply. The ADA also applies to many of the tenants in retail and office buildings.

Property managers who are negotiating retail or commercial leases should seek to have a clear understanding as to who must modify the premises in order to comply with this act.

The Equal Credit Opportunity Act (ECOA) prohibits discrimination based on race, color, religion, national origin, sex, receipt of public assistance, age, and marital status with regard to applications for credit. If an applicant feels the denial was based on discriminatory reasons, other than business reasons, the applicant may ask to see the entire file.

Many managers require a credit report before making a decision to rent. A credit report summarizes the applicant's history of making payments. If the applicant has been timely and current, the landlord can rent to the applicant. If the applicant's payments have been sporadic or nonexistent, the landlord may presume that the applicant will be equally derelict and refuse to rent. The Fair Credit Reporting Act (FCRA) governs credit reporting bureaus, and which information may be given to which party. Criminal record checks may be consulted before hiring only with the applicant's permission. FCRA rules pertain to challenging the accuracy of any information in these reports.

The federal Megan's Law requires that certain sex offenders must register with local authorities upon release from prison. Each state law must be consulted to determine whether the property manager has any responsibility to notify tenants of any such person.

The federal Lead-Based Paint Hazard Reduction Act covers dwellings built before 1978. Managers and owners must notify tenants that such housing may have lead-based paint; moreover, they must give the tenant the federal booklet, "Protecting Your Family From Lead in Your Home." Such disclosures must be kept for three years. Similar disclosures must be made before major restoration work is started. Effective April 2010, those involved with renovation must be properly trained and certified when the work exceeds a certain level of disturbed space.

The Uniform Residential Landlord and Tenant Act is a model law that attempts to provide some uniformity and regulation of the landlord-tenant relationship. Variations have been made in each state that has adopted the law. Property managers must consult the local state law for specific details. The act applies in the absence of a written lease and governs clauses in written leases. Managers should definitely research how to handle security deposits. The law addresses several valid issues that should be considered in residential leases, even in areas where the act is not in effect, such as acting in good faith and prohibiting retaliatory acts.

■ CASE STUDY

THE COMPLIANCE MANAGER

June Wheeler is a brand-new resident manager of a building built in the 1940s. As she reads through the files, she doesn't see any lead-based paint disclosure forms. When she brings this up with the owner, he has no idea what she is talking about. When she explains what can happen with lead poisoning, he says, "Well, if we have to do any painting, at least we only have to do it on the ground floor, because that is where the previous manager put the kids."

1. Should June expect to see lead-based paint disclosure forms in the files of this building? Why or why not?
2. What should June do about the lead-based paint disclosure forms?
3. What legal issue is raised by the owner's remarks about all families with kids being on the ground floor?
4. What is June's responsibility to the owner of the property in this situation?

■ REVIEW QUESTIONS

1. *Jones v. Mayer* reaffirmed the Civil Rights Act of 1866 by prohibiting
   a. some racial discrimination.
   b. all racial discrimination.
   c. discrimination based on sex.
   d. discriminatory advertising.

2. A property manager had two vacancies. When a single parent and her child inquired about an apartment, they were told that the building was 100 percent occupied. This is an example of
   a. steering.
   b. blockbusting.
   c. redlining.
   d. a sound business practice.

3. According to the Fair Credit Reporting Act, a loan applicant may
   a. seek to correct errors on the report.
   b. not examine the credit report.
   c. ask that certain information not be given to lenders.
   d. not make any attempt to challenge incorrect information.

4. Under the federal Equal Credit Opportunity Act, the property manager who requires a credit report on a prospective tenant can do which of the following?
   a. Publish the report in the property manager's association's monthly newsletter
   b. Turn down the creditworthiness of the tenant because of his or her age
   c. Turn down the creditworthiness of the tenant because of the tenant's sex
   d. Evaluate the tenant based on income and debt ratios

5. The resident manager has decided to shop other properties in order to determine if her rental rates are competitive. She calls the manager of a nearby property, and finds out that the second manager is thinking about raising rates. The two of them decide to raise rates at the same time. This might be construed as an example of
   a. a good business practice since tenants won't move when both properties have the same rates.
   b. the illegal practice of price-fixing.
   c. the illegal practice of steering.
   d. a cooperative agreement.

6. Which of the following acts are permitted under the federal Fair Housing Law?
   a. Offer different terms and conditions to young adults and families with children
   b. Refuse to rent to a single woman
   c. Tell an African American man that the apartment is rented, when it is not
   d. Refuse to rent to an Asian American man because he has a poor credit history

7. If someone is found guilty of violating the Fair Housing Act of 1968, he or she may be liable for actual damages and maximum punitive damages of
   a. $11,000.
   b. $27,500.
   c. $55,000.
   d. an unlimited amount.

8. If a person feels that she or he has been discriminated against by a property manager, a complaint may be filed with
   a. the U.S. Supreme Court.
   b. a local magistrate.
   c. the real estate commission.
   d. the Department of Housing and Urban Development.

9. Which of the following laws requires credit bureaus to supply information to a person who has been denied credit?
    a. Equal Credit Opportunity Act
    b. Civil Rights Act of 1968
    c. Fair Credit Reporting Act
    d. Sherman Antitrust Law

10. Lead-based paint disclosure forms must be retained
    a. for one year.
    b. for three years.
    c. for five years.
    d. indefinitely.

11. Generally, if the tenant and landlord do not agree on the term of the tenancy, then the tenancy is a
    a. tenancy at will.
    b. tenancy for years.
    c. periodic tenancy.
    d. tenancy at sufferance.

12. When the tenant makes a complaint to a government agency about a housing code violation, the landlord can
    a. retaliate by raising the rent over fair market value to force the tenant out.
    b. decrease essential services to the tenant.
    c. bring court action against the tenant.
    d. correct the problem.

13. Usually, if a fire destroys part of a residential property, the tenant may
    a. vacate immediately.
    b. lose his prepaid rent and security deposit.
    c. sue the owner for damages.
    d. prorate the rent deducting the portion he cannot use.

14. The Landlord Tenant Act establishes
    a. base rents for apartments.
    b. the owner's responsibilities.
    c. minimum amenities required for commercial properties.
    d. maximum amount required for a security deposit.

15. How would a parent discover that a child has lead poisoning?
    a. Blood test
    b. Urine test
    c. Lung x-ray
    d. Unsatisfactory school reports

16. The lead-based paint disclosures must be made on a house that was built
    a. last year.
    b. between 1900 and 1940.
    c. between 1940 and 1978.
    d. any time before 1978.

17. Which law requires that sex offenders register their address with the police?
    a. Equal Credit Opportunity Act
    b. Megan's Law
    c. Uniform Landlord Tenant Act
    d. There is no law; once people serve their time, they are free.

18. The Uniform Landlord Tenant Act generally covers all of the following *EXCEPT*
    a. how to handle security deposits.
    b. when to declare the unit abandoned.
    c. removal of structural barriers.
    d. retaliatory behavior.

19. Which of the following requests may a property manager ask on the tenant application?
    a. Birth control practices
    b. Intent to get married
    c. Whether income is welfare money
    d. Other landlord references

20. All of the following may be required by the Americans with Disabilities Act *EXCEPT*
    a. install ramps to outside doors.
    b. someone to assist a wheelchair user in the restroom.
    c. grab bars added to restroom stalls.
    d. braille letters on elevator buttons.

CHAPTER ELEVEN

11

RESIDENTIAL PROPERTY

■ KEY TERMS

Cash flow analysis   Leasing agent   Resident manager
Cash flow report   Operating budget   Show lists
Curb appeal   Rental center   Triplex
Duplex

■ LEARNING OBJECTIVES

At the end of this chapter, the student will be able to

1. list at least four different types of residential multifamily properties and examples of who is likely to rent them;

2. explain why managing scattered-site housing is financially marginal;

3. state two reasons why a manager should prepare a residential market analysis and summarize the information required for this analysis;

4. discuss the importance of curb appeal and list at least three reasons for utilizing a show list;

5. review the differences between classified and display ads, give examples of each, and discuss for what properties each might be used;

6. summarize the importance of regular communication with tenants and discuss some issues that should be personally explained to tenants;

7. compare the responsibilities of the resident manager to those of the property manager; and

8. list three suggestions to improve cash flow and the negative consequences of each.

■ OVERVIEW

Residential rental housing ranges from single-family houses to huge apartment projects of several thousand units and includes mobile home parks, time-sharing resorts, government-assisted housing, institutional housing, apartment hotels, and retirement communities. As the greater portion of residential tenants live in apartment buildings, this chapter will emphasize the management of apartment buildings. While specific application of the property management techniques discussed in this chapter may have to be modified according to the circumstances, the basic principles here have universal application.

Property managers should research and follow the laws and regulations of the jurisdiction where the property is located. Compliance with fair housing laws, discussed in the preceding chapter, is of particular concern in residential management. In some parts of the country, rent control laws, laws limiting or prohibiting the construction of new units, and other laws and regulations have been passed that present unique problems, mainly in the areas of financial operation, rent raises, and eviction of tenants.

■ TYPES OF RESIDENTIAL PROPERTY

Different types of dwellings require unique management capabilities. This chapter discusses *scattered-site rentals*, that is, single-family residences, **duplexes, triplexes,** and large apartment communities. Multifamily properties, including condominium and cooperatives, low-income and government-subsidized housing and some manufactured home parks, are discussed in Chapter 12.

Scattered-Site Housing

Investing in single-family rental homes has been popular for some time, and many owners have built up large holdings of *single-family dwellings*. The owners often manage these homes if they live in the city where the homes are located; if not, the owners hire professional managers.

It may be unprofitable or impractical for a professional property manager who manages other types of property to manage one single-family home or a few duplexes and triplexes. The principal difference between managing single-family homes and managing apartment buildings centers on geography and time because scattered site rentals are often located in various parts of a city. Properly maintaining and showing property to prospective tenants may involve unproductive travel to and from various locations.

Another source of income to these managers is receiving a fee when the property is sold. The manager should consult state law to ascertain whether a real estate license is required to receive this commission, if the manager wishes to include the right to a commission in the management contract.

Even with the most skillful and well-organized management, the financial return on owning many small homes, duplexes, and triplexes is marginal at best, compared to alternate uses of investment funds. If interest rates on mortgages are high, cash flow may be negative. Further, many owners will agree to a below-market rent in exchange for a tenant who will take care of the property and remain in it for a long period of time.

Duplexes and triplexes with common areas including front, side and backyards require harmonious cooperation among occupants. Thus, the tenants must be compatible, a condition not usually as strong a factor when renting in larger communities.

Multifamily Properties

Multifamily properties are commonly defined as apartment buildings of five or more units. There are several classifications of apartments, based mainly on the architecture of the project, as described below.

Garden apartments   Garden apartment complexes are designed for family living, usually in a sprawling two-story building or buildings in a project containing predominantly two-bedroom and three-bedroom units. They are often are located in suburban areas or other regions where land is relatively inexpensive and large tracts are easily obtained.

Walkup building   Walkups usually are found in urban areas and in older, more concentrated sections of the suburbs. Generally preferred by couples and singles, most walkups include one-bedroom or two-bedroom apartments.

Multistory elevator buildings   These contain efficiency and one-bedroom units and are concentrated primarily on the edges of downtown areas of large cities, although they also are found in suburban locations. These are often favored by unmarried people who want to be close to their jobs.

High-rise luxury properties   These emphasize view, amenities, and prestigious addresses and are often located either near the central city or in more affluent outlying areas. Units in these buildings may have one, two or three bedrooms but all have relatively larger living areas than units in other types of apartment buildings. Common luxury high-rise tenants are generally higher-income families who seek security and the service and the comforts of a single-family home without the responsibilities of home ownership.

Loft conversions   Loft buildings are named because their interior floor space is not specialized. Starting in the 1950s, many large lofts on the fringe of central business districts became vacant as light industries moved to the suburbs. Some loft buildings in prime locations have been successfully converted into condominiums and apartments, as well as shopping malls, restaurants, and bars. These apartments are attractive to singles, young adults, artists, and older couples who are downsizing (Figure 11.1).

Other Alternatives and Services

Housing alternatives range from fully furnished units, where everything is supplied for the tenant, to unfurnished apartments equipped only with floors and walls, with the standard unit lying somewhere in between. Large multifamily complexes are referred to as *communities*. The larger the community, the more likely it offers recreational facilities such as swimming pools, tennis courts, patios, exercise rooms, and recreation rooms. These apartments usually have central air-conditioning, the newest appliances, off-street parking areas, and sophisticated security systems.

Luxury high-rise may offer doormen, window cleaning services, heated garages, grocery stores, banks, drugstores, and other conveniences located within the building. The walkup tenant probably receives the least in the way of extra services or facilities. Many walkups, garden, and multistory apartments include only water and trash removal as part of the monthly rent. The tenant is billed separately for all other utility services.

In any type of residential rental housing, the kind and number of facilities provided has a direct effect on the property manager's workload; swimming pools, laundry rooms, and parking areas increase the maintenance activities for the premises. These facilities and services affect the overall desirability and influence the rental structure of any type of residential rental complex, commanding more in rents to offset the extra maintenance activities.

■ RESIDENTIAL MARKET ANALYSIS

Market surveys of comparable residential properties and economic conditions in the immediate area are absolutely essential for two reasons:

1. To establish a rental schedule for the apartments or single family dwellings

2. To gauge the property's viability as an income-producing investment

FIGURE 11.1

Brochure

Source: The Seldin Company.

FIGURE 11.1 (CONTINUED)
Brochure

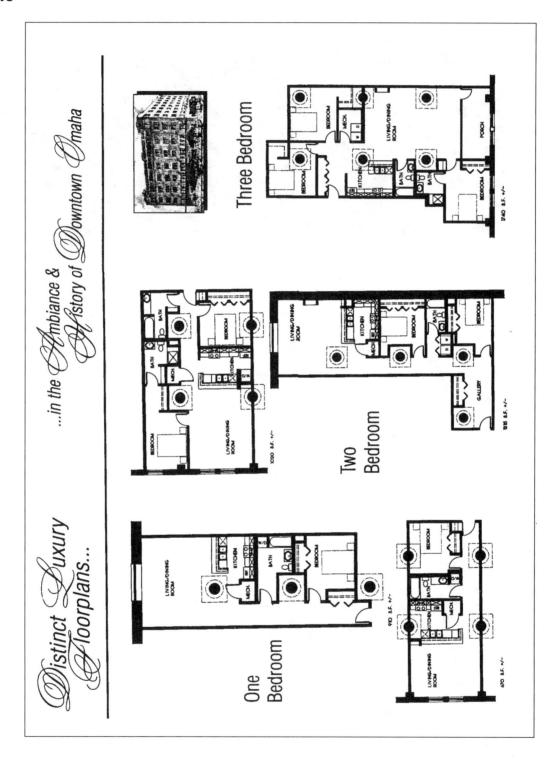

Establishing a Rental Schedule

As discussed in Chapter 2, the residential manager must analyze the rental values of comparable properties in the area. Many managers will shop other properties to see the space that is being rented, the amenities offered, and at what value. Reading the competitor's advertising is another way to learn of competing market market values.

This *comparative analysis* measures and records data such as size, location, amenities, and rental structures for buildings similar to the subject property (Figure 11.2). After the relative market value of the space is determined, a base rental can be established for each type of apartment. This base rate should be adjusted to reflect preferential location, view, exposure, size, or design. An increase in the base rate might also be justified if the occupancy level in the neighborhood is 95 percent or better, indicating a heavy consumer demand.

Employment and income data collected for the neighborhood should serve as a touchstone for setting the residential rental schedule. Because of rising costs, the increasing number of working couples, and the trend toward smaller families, many persons are willing to spend a higher percentage of their income on better living accommodations.

Gauging Profitability

Gathering demographic information can assist the manager in making recommendations to increase profitability. U.S. Census Bureau statistics can give the property manager a general idea of the population density within a particular neighborhood. However, it is not sufficient for the manager merely to be aware of the total number of persons in an area; he or she must also know the size of the average family to determine the type and number of housing units needed. For example, the financial prognosis for a high-rise complex composed of studio and one-bedroom units would be quite different in an area of small families than in a neighborhood of young singles or childless couples.

The manager must analyze current population shifts in terms of land use and income level. Such shifts may be caused by increased population mobility, unsettled economic conditions, changes in family size and structure, and extended longevity because of improved health care. The implications for the future of the neighborhood and for the manager's property are quite different between an increase that stems from an influx of middle-income families into an expanding community and one that is due to overcrowding in low-rent buildings.

■ MARKETING AVAILABILITY OF SPACE

Apartment and single housing space is a consumer good and as such can be marketed with the same promotional techniques used to sell cars or clothing. There are some differences, though.

FIGURE 11.2

Comparative Analysis

Name: _____ Address: _____ Date: _____

Management Co: _____ Number of Units: _____ Phone: _____

Subject Property: **Spruce Pointe**

			Est/Occ ___ %	Est/Occ ___ %	Est/Occ ___ %	Est/Occ ___ %	Est/Occ ___ %
			Date: ___	Date: ___	Date: ___	Date: ___	Date: ___
Unit Type	Sq. Ft.	No. Units	Rent Per S.F.	Rent Per S.F.	Rent Per S.F.	Rent Per S.F.	Rent. Per S.F.

General Information

Age: _____

Sec. Dep. _____

Pets   Y / N

Addt'l Dep: _____

App Fee: _____

Lease Terms: _____

Utilities   Heat   Electric   Water   Sewer   Trash

Own / Tenant   Own / Tenant   Own / Tenant   Own / Tenant   Own / Tenant

Marketing Information

Resident Referrals: _____

Resident Renewals: _____

Discounts, Etc. _____

Concessions: _____

Pricing Variables

W/D Conn $ _____

W/D $ _____

Fireplace $ _____

Pool/View $ _____

Vault/Cath $ _____

Balcony $ _____

Other $ _____

Extra Person $ _____

Kitchen

( )w/d or w/connections
( )Electric Range
( )Oven
( )Microwave
( )Dishwasher
( )Refrigerator ( )Icemaker
( )Double Sinks
( )Pantry
( )Disposal

Bathroom

( )Linen
( )Vent Fan/Heat Lamp
( )Vanity/Dressing Area
( )Double Sinks
( )Shower Doors ( )Curtain

Living Room

( )Fireplaces
( )Ceiling Fans
( )Miniblinds ( )Window Cov.
( )Cable
( )Wallpaper
( )Wet Bar
( )Dining Area
( )Vaulted Ceiling

Exterior

( )Covered Parking
( )Limited Access
( )Patio
( )Balconies

Amenities

( )Pool
( )Clubhouse
( )Tennis Court
( )Racquetball
( )Exercise Room
( )Jacuzzi/Hot Tub
( )Playground
( )Laundry
( )Garages $ _____
( )Storages $ _____

Signs and Curb Appeal   Proper signage and maintaining **curb appeal** are essential because many rental prospects come to the property as a result of searching the neighborhood. Curb appeal, the impression created when the building is first seen from the street, helps attract good tenants and maintain a positive attitude among the current residents.

> The basis for "curb appeal" is that one never has a second chance for a good first impression. Examples of curb appeal include litter-free grounds, well-trimmed lawns and attractive landscaping, and clean and maintained amenities such as the swimming pool and parking areas. The buildings should be free from peeling paint.

Price Adjustment   Sometimes market conditions may preclude the rental of some units. An alert leasing manager quickly realizes which units are renting rapidly or are not moving fast enough and either adjusts the price or changes the method of advertising and display.

An optimal price structure should assure the manager of a 95 percent occupancy level for all units. If each type of apartment is priced correctly, the different units will have the same rate of demand; that is, demand for studio, one-bedroom, and two-bedroom units will be equal. If a single house stands empty for any period, the manager will have to discuss with the owner reasons for the vacancy and solutions, which may include lowering the rent.

Show List   Compiling a **show list** is one effective method to establish a reasonable rental schedule. This list should itemize no more than three apartments of each type and size in the building that are available for inspection by prospects. When one unit is rented, it should be replaced by another vacant apartment that is ready for rental.

Properly utilizing a show list is advantageous for any number of reasons:

- The show list can be used as a control guide for the marketing program, and the traffic count of showings will serve as a source of feedback on its success or failure.

- The features of particular units can be itemized on the short and easy-to-read list so the manager can do a better and more informed selling job.

- The maintenance staff can more easily maintain 12 to 15 units on the list in top-notch condition rather than trying to maintain all building vacancies.

- The limited number of show units suggests that space is at a premium and that a decision must be made quickly.

The show list and traffic count should be reviewed weekly to determine which units are not moving. The manager should then inspect these units personally to find out why they are hard to rent. All curable flaws (worn carpeting, obsolete fixtures) should be corrected.

Advertising and Display

The building may still struggle with a high vacancy rate if prospective tenants are not actively attracted to view the premises. The manager must develop, implement, and monitor an advertising campaign as discussed in Chapter 4. There are specific types of advertising that are more appropriate when advertising residential property. Regardless of the type of advertising used, the manager should implement a tracking program to monitor the effectiveness of each type of marketing.

Classified ads   The major vehicle for renting apartments and single-family homes is newspaper classified advertising. The classified advertisement should address the needs of the prospective tenant. For example, if three-bedroom apartments are difficult to rent, an ad might appeal to a broader segment of the market if it is promoted as a two-bedroom apartment with a den.

It is time-efficient to include in the classified ad the amount of rent, size of the unit, address of the property, date available and the phone number of the manager. A typical small classified ad might read as does the one on the right.

> $675/month for sunny, large
> 1-bdrm. apt.; new carpet &
> drapes. Available 12-1.
> 1025 Webster/555-327-7083.

> **1025 Webster**
> ---
> Large 1-bedroom apt.
> New carpet & drapes
> Bright sunny living
> room. $675/Possession
> Dec. 1. To see, call:
>
> 555-327-7083

Depending on the budget, major amenities can be mentioned. Attention can be drawn to the ad by highlighting the location, size, and rent rate with varied typefaces and larger layouts. For example, the preceding ad could be redesigned for greater appeal to look like the sample on the left.

Display ads   More prestigious residential projects, especially when newly opened, often benefit from display advertisements. These larger ads attract immediate attention, appeal to potential tenants' pride, and point up the many amenities offered by the building. Although specifics of the rental schedule may be omitted in deference to the status of the prospective clientele, an indication of rent ranges is usually included. This will save management time as tenants are less likely to call on properties that are out of their price range.

Internet Web sites   More and more prospective tenants are using the Internet to find available units. In particular, job transferees often begin their apartment search on the Internet long before they visit the new city. At the very least, good Web sites should include pictures of the property, floor plans of typical units, and current availability to find different style and price range apartments. Many also include one-minute videos. You can often also click on "area maps" for an idea of where the property is located.

Property signage and display ads should direct prospects to this Web site. Newspaper classifieds often offer a complimentary site on the Web that allows for hyperlinks to the manager's Web site. The manager or leasing agent must respond to all e-mail inquiries promptly. However, most consumers today expect a response almost immediately, so someone who generally remains in the office should be designated to respond initially to these inquiries.

Apartment journals   In some parts of the country, prospective tenants consult local apartment journals as often as they read the newspaper. (For an example of one of these journals, see Figure 11.3.) These journals, published monthly and generally distributed free of charge, are available at retail and convenience store display stands or at sidewalk newspaper display-type boxes. Apartment journals list most apartments in the local area where they are published. A full-page ad in one of these publications may cost less than a weekend newspaper display ad. Leasing agents report that many prospects come to their offices with these journals in hand.

Federal and state laws   In addition to learning how to write an attractive and effective ad, managers must also follow certain state and federal laws. Many real estate regulatory bodies require that the name of the licensee or firm be in the ad. The federal fair housing law discussed in Chapter 10 requires that display ads carry the equal housing logo and that the newspaper include a general disclaimer at the beginning of for sale or rent classifieds. Also, the equal housing opportunity poster must be prominently displayed in the leasing office and rental center.

Furthermore, the consumer-oriented *Truth-in-Lending* law requires that certain disclosures be made if the ad contains any potentially misleading "trigger items." For example, perhaps the ad mentions a low monthly rent that is actually available only to tenants who sign a long-term lease. This is potentially misleading, so somewhere in the ad, the manager must mention the additional terms required for the lower rate.

Rental centers   A **rental center** is a special leasing area located in a real estate development typically found in complexes larger than 100 units. It includes a display area, furnished models, and an area that can be used to close lease transactions.

A center can shorten the rent-up time during the initial stage of a project's development. After rent-up is complete, the manager must decide whether there is a continued need for the center to sustain occupancy levels through replacement

FIGURE 11.3

Page From Apartment Finder

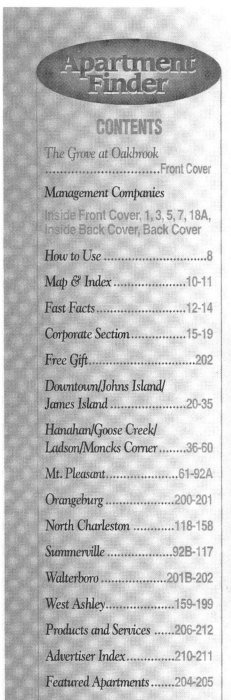

How to...
use this magazine

Apartment Finder is designed to help you find your ideal apartment home. Our easy-to-use format makes it simple to shop and compare different communities. Below you will see how to use our **Directory Pages** on individual communities. On pages 10 and 11 there is an **Area Map** that is color coded to match the color bar at the top of each Directory Page. Each listing's **Page Number** corresponds with the **Map Number** on the Area Map. This easy-to-use system makes it simple for you to find an apartment in the area of the city where you wish to live.

Our **Apartment Fast Facts** section on pages 12-14 is a quick reference guide if you are searching for specific amenities.

After signing a lease, don't forget to fill out the **Free Gift Coupon** on page 202 of this magazine and mail it. We will send you a free gift for using Apartment Finder to find your new apartment home.

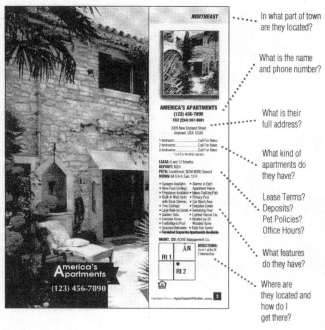

In what part of town are they located?

What is the name and phone number?

What is their full address?

What kind of apartments do they have?

Lease Terms?
Deposits?
Pet Policies?
Office Hours?

What features do they have?

Where are they located and how do I get there?

Get The Real Picture!
Color photos, specials, floorplans and featured amenities

PLEASE SAY YOU SAW IT IN APARTMENT FINDER!

Apartment Finder

8

WE'RE NATIONWIDE! For other areas call **Toll Free 1-800-222-3651**
Find Additional Photos, Floorplans & More @**ApartmentFinder.com**

Source: RELCON, Inc., a publication of the Chicago Tribune Company.

rentals. If, typically, only 50 apartments are vacant in any one year, a model apartment would serve the merchandising goal more cost-effectively. However, if 200 apartments must be rented each year, the need for a rental center would be indicated.

Leasing Agents

Managers of larger properties have come to recognize the benefits of using a **leasing agent** specialist. Good leasing agents are often compensated on the number of units rented, so they quickly learn how to present themselves and their properties most effectively. They are experts in learning the prospect's basic needs and desires, and how to handle and overcome objections in order to rent the apartment. This area is considered so important that the National Association of Home Builders Multi-Family Council offers a certification program for these specialists.

■ MANAGING TENANT RELATIONS

**Explaining the
Apartment Leases**

The basis of good tenant relations begins with selecting tenants who are able and willing to fulfill their obligations as stated in the lease agreement. By opening the lines of communication with tenants, the manager will build mutually satisfactory landlord-tenant relationships.

Many managers recognize that some tenants do not take the time to read the lease carefully, so these managers take the extra time to highlight key clauses, such as when, where, and how rent is to be paid, and the consequences for being late. They may emphasize other conditions such as parking arrangements, how long visitors can stay (days, weeks, or months), the need to be respectful of other tenants' rights (noise and loud music), reemphasizing penalties for unauthorized pets, and so forth. The house rules should be presented to the prospect very early in the process, hopefully avoiding problems before they are even contemplated. For a sample lease, see Figure 11.4.

Additionally, the manager should explain that the owner cannot and does not carry insurance on the tenant's personal belongings and that the tenant should obtain renter's insurance (see #31 in the lease). The manager can provide a list of three or four insurance agents in the area. Also, the manager should carefully explain that the tenant may not make any changes to the carpeting or wall coverings without explicit written permission of the manager and owner (see #16 in the lease).

**Regular
Communication**

One method of regularly communicating with residents is to publish a brief but informative monthly or semimonthly newsletter. If major changes are being contemplated, such as extensive renovation, the manager may hold a meeting to explain when these events will occur.

FIGURE 11.4

Sample Lease

CALIFORNIA
ASSOCIATION
OF REALTORS ®

**RESIDENTIAL LEASE OR
MONTH-TO-MONTH RENTAL AGREEMENT**
(C.A.R. Form LR, Revised 11/08)

Date _____, _____ ("Landlord") and
_____ ("Tenant") agree as follows:

1. **PROPERTY:**
   A. Landlord rents to Tenant and Tenant rents from Landlord, the real property and improvements described as: _____
      _____ ("Premises").
   B. The Premises are for the sole use as a personal residence by the following named person(s) **only:** _____
      _____
   C. The following personal property, maintained pursuant to paragraph 11, is included: _____
      _____ or ☐ (if checked) the personal property on the attached addendum.
2. **TERM:** The term begins on (date) _____ ("Commencement Date"), **(Check A or B):**
   ☐ **A. Month-to-Month:** and continues as a month-to-month tenancy. Tenant may terminate the tenancy by giving written notice
      at least 30 days prior to the intended termination date. Landlord may terminate the tenancy by giving written notice as
      provided by law. Such notices may be given on any date.
   ☐ **B. Lease:** and shall terminate on (date) _____ at _____ ☐ AM/☐ PM.
      Tenant shall vacate the Premises upon termination of the Agreement, unless: **(i)** Landlord and Tenant have extended this
      agreement in writing or signed a new agreement; **(ii)** mandated by local rent control law; or **(iii)** Landlord accepts Rent from
      Tenant (other than past due Rent), in which case a month-to-month tenancy shall be created which either party may
      terminate as specified in paragraph 2A. Rent shall be at a rate agreed to by Landlord and Tenant, or as allowed by law. All
      other terms and conditions of this Agreement shall remain in full force and effect.
3. **RENT:** "Rent" shall mean all monetary obligations of Tenant to Landlord under the terms of the Agreement, except security deposit.
   A. Tenant agrees to pay $ _____ per month for the term of the Agreement.
   B. Rent is payable in advance on the **1st (or ☐ _____) day** of each calendar month, and is delinquent on the next day.
   C. If Commencement Date falls on any day other than the day Rent is payable under paragraph 3B, and Tenant has paid one full
      month's Rent in advance of Commencement Date, Rent for the second calendar month shall be prorated based on a 30-day
      period.
   D. PAYMENT: Rent shall be paid by ☐ personal check, ☐ money order, ☐ cashier's check, or ☐ other _____,
      to (name) _____ (phone) _____ at (address)
      _____, (or at any other location
      subsequently specified by Landlord in writing to Tenant) (and ☐ if checked, rent may be paid personally, between the hours of
      _____ and _____ on the following days _____). If any payment is
      returned for non-sufficient funds ("NSF") or because tenant stops payment, then, after that: (i) Landlord may, in writing, require
      Tenant to pay Rent in cash for three months and (ii) all future Rent shall be paid by ☐ money order, or ☐ cashier's check.
4. **SECURITY DEPOSIT:**
   A. Tenant agrees to pay $ _____ as a security deposit. Security deposit will be
      ☐ transferred to and held by the Owner of the Premises, or ☐ held in Owner's Broker's trust account.
   B. All or any portion of the security deposit may be used, as reasonably necessary, to: **(i)** cure Tenant's default in payment of Rent (which
      includes Late Charges, NSF fees or other sums due); **(ii)** repair damage, excluding ordinary wear and tear, caused by Tenant or by a
      guest or licensee of Tenant; **(iii)** clean Premises, if necessary, upon termination of the tenancy; and **(iv)** replace or return personal
      property or appurtenances. **SECURITY DEPOSIT SHALL NOT BE USED BY TENANT IN LIEU OF PAYMENT OF LAST
      MONTH'S RENT.** If all or any portion of the security deposit is used during the tenancy, Tenant agrees to reinstate the total security
      deposit within five days after written notice is delivered to Tenant. Within 21 days after Tenant vacates the Premises, Landlord shall:
      (1) furnish Tenant an itemized statement indicating the amount of any security deposit received and the basis for its
      disposition and supporting documentation as required by California Civil Code § 1950.5(g); and **(2)** return any remaining
      portion of the security deposit to Tenant.
   C. **Security deposit will not be returned until all Tenants have vacated the Premises and all keys returned. Any security
      deposit returned by check shall be made out to all Tenants named on this Agreement, or as subsequently modified.**
   D. No interest will be paid on security deposit unless required by local law.
   E. If the security deposit is held by Owner, Tenant agrees not to hold Broker responsible for its return. If the security deposit is held
      in Owner's Broker's trust account, **and** Broker's authority is terminated before expiration of this Agreement, **and** security deposit
      is released to someone other than Tenant, **then** Broker shall notify Tenant, in writing, where and to whom security deposit has
      been released. Once Tenant has been provided such notice, Tenant agrees not to hold Broker responsible for the security
      deposit.
5. **MOVE-IN COSTS RECEIVED/DUE:** Move-in funds made payable to _____
   shall be paid by ☐ personal check, ☐ money order, or ☐ cashier's check.

Category	Total Due	Payment Received	...nce ...	Date Due
Rent from _____ to _____ (date)				
*Security Deposit				
Other _____				
Other _____				
Total				

*The maximum amount Landlord may receive as security deposit, however designated, cannot exceed two months' Rent for
unfurnished premises, or three months' Rent for furnished premises.

Tenant's Initials (_____)(_____)
Landlord's Initials (_____)(_____)

Reviewed by _____ Date _____

EQUAL HOUSING
OPPORTUNITY

LR REVISED 11/08 (PAGE 1 OF 6) Print Date

RESIDENTIAL LEASE OR MONTH-TO-MONTH RENTAL AGREEMENT (LR PAGE 1 OF 6)

Source: California Association of REALTORS®. Endorsement not implied.

FIGURE 11.4 (CONTINUED)

Sample Lease

Premises: _____   Date: _____

6. **LATE CHARGE; RETURNED CHECKS:**

   A. Tenant acknowledges either late payment of Rent or issuance of a returned check may cause Landlord to incur costs and expenses, the exact amounts of which are extremely difficult and impractical to determine. These costs may include, but are not limited to, processing, enforcement and accounting expenses, and late charges imposed on Landlord. If any installment of Rent due from Tenant is not received by Landlord within **5 (or ☐ _____) calendar days** after the date due, or if a check is returned, Tenant shall pay to Landlord, respectively, an additional sum of $ _____ or _____% of the Rent due as a Late Charge and $25.00 as a NSF fee for the first returned check and $35.00 as a NSF fee for each additional returned check, either or both of which shall be deemed additional Rent.

   B. Landlord and Tenant agree that these charges represent a fair and reasonable estimate of the costs Landlord may incur by reason of Tenant's late or NSF payment. Any Late Charge or NSF fee due shall be paid with the current installment of Rent. Landlord's acceptance of any Late Charge or NSF fee shall not constitute a waiver as to any default of Tenant. Landlord's right to collect a Late Charge or NSF fee shall not be deemed an extension of the date Rent is due under paragraph 3 or prevent Landlord from exercising any other rights and remedies under this Agreement and as provided by law.

7. **PARKING: (Check A or B)**

   ☐ **A.** Parking is permitted as follows: _____

   The right to parking ☐ is ☐ is not included in the Rent charged pursuant to paragraph 3. If not included in the Rent, the parking rental fee shall be an additional $ _____ per month. Parking space(s) are to be used for parking properly licensed and operable motor vehicles, except for trailers, boats, campers, buses or trucks (other than pick-up trucks). Tenant shall park in assigned space(s) only. Parking space(s) are to be kept clean. Vehicles leaking oil, gas or other motor vehicle fluids shall not be parked on the Premises. Mechanical work or storage of inoperable vehicles is not permitted in parking space(s) or elsewhere on the Premises.

   OR ☐ **B.** Parking is not permitted on the Premises.

8. **STORAGE: (Check A or B)**

   ☐ **A.** Storage is permitted as follows: _____
   The right to storage space ☐ is, ☐ is not, included in the Rent charged pursuant to paragraph 3. If not included in the Rent, storage space fee shall be an additional $ _____ per month. Tenant shall store only personal property Tenant owns, and shall not store property claimed by another or in which another has any right, title or interest. Tenant shall not store any improperly packaged food or perishable goods, flammable materials, explosives, hazardous waste or other inherently dangerous material, or illegal substances.

   OR ☐ **B.** Storage is not permitted on the Premises.

9. **UTILITIES:** Tenant agrees to pay for all utilities and services, and the following charges: _____ except _____, which shall be paid for by Landlord. If any utilities are not separately metered, Tenant shall pay Tenant's proportional share, as reasonably determined and directed by Landlord. If utilities are separately metered, Tenant shall place utilities in Tenant's name as of the Commencement Date. Landlord is only responsible for installing and maintaining one usable telephone jack and one telephone line to the Premises. Tenant shall pay any cost for conversion from existing utilities service provider.

10. **CONDITION OF PREMISES:** Tenant has examined Premises and, if any, all furniture, furnishings, appliances, landscaping and fixtures, including smoke detector(s).

    (Check all that apply:)

    ☐ **A.** Tenant acknowledges these items are clean and in operable condition, with the following exceptions: _____

    ☐ **B.** Tenant's acknowledgment of the condition of these items is contained in an attached statement of condition (C.A.R. Form MIMO).

    ☐ **C.** Tenant will provide Landlord a list of items that are damaged or not in operable condition within **3 (or ☐ _____) days** after Commencement Date, not as a contingency of this Agreement but rather as an acknowledgment of the condition of the Premises.

    ☐ **D.** Other: _____.

11. **MAINTENANCE:**

    A. Tenant shall properly use, operate and safeguard Premises, including if applicable, any landscaping, furniture, furnishings and appliances, and all mechanical, electrical, gas and plumbing fixtures, and keep them and the Premises clean, sanitary and well ventilated. Tenant shall be responsible for checking and maintaining all smoke detectors and any additional phone lines beyond the one line and jack that Landlord shall provide and maintain. Tenant shall immediately notify Landlord, in writing, of any problem, malfunction or damage. Tenant shall be charged for all repairs or replacements caused by Tenant, pets, guests or licensees of Tenant, excluding ordinary wear and tear. Tenant shall be charged for all damage to Premises as a result of failure to report a problem in a timely manner. Tenant shall be charged for repair of drain blockages or stoppages, unless caused by defective plumbing parts or tree roots invading sewer lines.

    B. ☐ Landlord ☐ Tenant shall water the garden, landscaping, trees and shrubs, except: _____

    C. ☐ Landlord ☐ Tenant shall maintain the garden, landscaping, trees and shrubs, except: _____

    D. ☐ Landlord ☐ Tenant shall maintain _____

    E. Tenant's failure to maintain any item for which Tenant is responsible shall give Landlord the right to hire someone to perform such maintenance and charge Tenant to cover the cost of such maintenance.

    F. The following items of personal property are included in the Premises without warranty and Landlord will not maintain, repair or replace them: _____.

Tenant's Initials (_____)(_____)
Landlord's Initials (_____)(_____)

Reviewed by _____ Date _____

LR REVISED 11/08 (PAGE 2 OF 6)

EQUAL HOUSING OPPORTUNITY

RESIDENTIAL LEASE OR MONTH-TO-MONTH RENTAL AGREEMENT (LR PAGE 2 OF 6)

FIGURE 11.4 (CONTINUED)

Sample Lease

Premises: _____ Date: _____

12. **NEIGHBORHOOD CONDITIONS:** Tenant is advised to satisfy him or herself as to neighborhood or area conditions, including schools, proximity and adequacy of law enforcement, crime statistics, proximity of registered felons or offenders, fire protection, other governmental services, availability, adequacy and cost of any wired, wireless internet connections or other telecommunications or other technology services and installations, proximity to commercial, industrial or agricultural activities, existing and proposed transportation, construction and development that may affect noise, view, or traffic, airport noise, noise or odor from any source, wild and domestic animals, other nuisances, hazards, or circumstances, cemeteries, facilities and condition of common areas, conditions and influences of significance to certain cultures and/or religions, and personal needs, requirements and preferences of Tenant.

13. **PETS:** Unless otherwise provided in California Civil Code § 54.2, no animal or pet shall be kept on or about the Premises without Landlord's prior written consent, except: _____.

14. ☐ (If checked) **NO SMOKING:** No smoking is allowed on the Premises. If smoking does occur on the Premises, **(i)** Tenant is responsible for all damage caused by the smoking including, but not limited to, stains, burns, odors and removal of debris; **(ii)** Tenant is in breach of this Agreement; **(iii)** Tenant, Authorized Guests, and all others may be required to leave the Premises; and **(iv)** Tenant acknowledges that in order to remove odor caused by smoking, Landlord may need to replace carpet and drapes and paint entire premises regardless of when these items were last cleaned or replaced. Such actions and other necessary steps will impact the return of any security deposit.

15. **RULES/REGULATIONS:**
   A. Tenant agrees to comply with all Landlord rules and regulations that are at any time posted on the Premises or delivered to Tenant. Tenant shall not, and shall ensure that guests and licensees of Tenant shall not, disturb, annoy, endanger or interfere with other tenants of the building or neighbors, or use the Premises for any unlawful purposes, including, but not limited to, using, manufacturing, selling, storing or transporting illicit drugs or other contraband, or violate any law or ordinance, or commit a waste or nuisance on or about the Premises.
   B. **(If applicable, check one)**
      ☐ **1.** Landlord shall provide Tenant with a copy of the rules and regulations within _____ days or _____.
      OR ☐ **2.** Tenant has been provided with, and acknowledges receipt of, a copy of the rules and regulations.

16. ☐ (If checked) **CONDOMINIUM;PLANNED UNIT DEVELOPMENT:**
   A. The Premises is a unit in a condominium, planned unit development, common interest subdivision or other development governed by a homeowners' association ("HOA"). The name of the HOA is _____. Tenant agrees to comply with all HOA covenants, conditions and restrictions, bylaws, rules and regulations and decisions. Landlord shall provide Tenant copies of rules and regulations, if any. Tenant shall reimburse Landlord for any fines or charges imposed by HOA or other authorities, due to any violation by Tenant, or the guests or licensees of Tenant.
   B. **(Check one)**
      ☐ **1.** Landlord shall provide Tenant with a copy of the HOA rules and regulations within _____ days or _____.
      OR ☐ **2.** Tenant has been provided with, and acknowledges receipt of, a copy of the HOA rules and regulations.

17. **ALTERATIONS; REPAIRS:** Unless otherwise specified by law or paragraph 29C, without Landlord's prior written consent, **(i)** Tenant shall not make any repairs, alterations or improvements in or about the Premises including: painting, wallpapering, adding or changing locks, installing antenna or satellite dish(es), placing signs, displays or exhibits, or using screws, fastening devices, large nails or adhesive materials; **(ii)** Landlord shall not be responsible for the costs of alterations or repairs made by Tenant; **(iii)** Tenant shall not deduct from Rent the costs of any repairs, alterations or improvements; and **(iv)** any deduction made by Tenant shall be considered unpaid Rent.

18. **KEYS; LOCKS:**
   A. Tenant acknowledges receipt of (or Tenant will receive ☐ prior to the Commencement Date, or ☐ _____):
      ☐ _____ key(s) to Premises,   ☐ _____ remote control device(s) for garage door/gate opener(s),
      ☐ _____ key(s) to mailbox,   ☐ _____,
      ☐ _____ key(s) to common area(s), ☐ _____.
   B. Tenant acknowledges that locks to the Premises ☐ have, ☐ have not, been re-keyed.
   C. If Tenant re-keys existing locks or opening devices, Tenant shall immediately deliver copies of all keys to Landlord. Tenant shall pay all costs and charges related to loss of any keys or opening devices. Tenant may not remove locks, even if installed by Tenant.

19. **ENTRY:**
   A. Tenant shall make Premises available to Landlord or Landlord's representative for the purpose of entering to make necessary or agreed repairs, decorations, alterations, or improvements, or to supply necessary or agreed services, or to show Premises to prospective or actual purchasers, tenants, mortgagees, lenders, appraisers, or contractors.
   B. Landlord and Tenant agree that 24-hour written notice shall be reasonable and sufficient notice, except as follows: 48-hour written notice is required to conduct an inspection of the Premises prior to the Tenant moving out, unless the Tenant waives the right to such notice. Notice may be given orally to show the Premises to actual or prospective purchasers provided Tenant has been notified in writing within 120 days preceding the oral notice that the Premises are for sale and that oral notice may be given to show the Premises. No notice is required: **(i)** to enter in case of an emergency; **(ii)** if the Tenant is present and consents at the time of entry or **(iii)** if the Tenant has abandoned or surrendered the Premises. No written notice is required if Landlord and Tenant orally agree to an entry for agreed services or repairs if the date and time of entry are within one week of the oral agreement.
   C. ☐ (If checked) Tenant authorizes the use of a keysafe/lockbox to allow entry into the Premises and agrees to sign a keysafe/lockbox addendum (C.A.R. Form KLA).

20. **SIGNS:** Tenant authorizes Landlord to place FOR SALE/LEASE signs on the Premises.

21. **ASSIGNMENT; SUBLETTING:** Tenant shall not sublet all or any part of Premises, or assign or transfer this Agreement or any interest in it, without Landlord's prior written consent. Unless such consent is obtained, any assignment, transfer or subletting of Premises or this Agreement or tenancy, by voluntary act of Tenant, operation of law or otherwise, shall, at the option of Landlord,

Tenant's Initials (_____)(_____)
Landlord's Initials (_____)(_____)

| Reviewed by _____ Date _____ |

LR REVISED 11/08 (PAGE 3 OF 6)

RESIDENTIAL LEASE OR MONTH-TO-MONTH RENTAL AGREEMENT (LR PAGE 3 OF 6)

FIGURE 11.4 (CONTINUED)

Sample Lease

Premises: _____   Date: _____

terminate this Agreement. Any proposed assignee, transferee or sublessee shall submit to Landlord an application and credit information for Landlord's approval and, if approved, sign a separate written agreement with Landlord and Tenant. Landlord's consent to any one assignment, transfer or sublease, shall not be construed as consent to any subsequent assignment, transfer or sublease and does not release Tenant of Tenant's obligations under this Agreement.

22. JOINT AND INDIVIDUAL OBLIGATIONS: If there is more than one Tenant, each one shall be individually and completely responsible for the performance of all obligations of Tenant under this Agreement, jointly with every other Tenant, and individually, whether or not in possession.

23. ☐ **LEAD-BASED PAINT (If checked):** Premises was constructed prior to 1978. In accordance with federal law, Landlord gives and Tenant acknowledges receipt of the disclosures on the attached form (C.A.R. Form FLD) and a federally approved lead pamphlet.

24. ☐ **MILITARY ORDNANCE DISCLOSURE:** (If applicable and known to Landlord) Premises is located within one mile of an area once used for military training, and may contain potentially explosive munitions.

25. ☐ **PERIODIC PEST CONTROL:** Landlord has entered into a contract for periodic pest control treatment of the Premises and shall give Tenant a copy of the notice originally given to Landlord by the pest control company.

26. ☐ **METHAMPHETAMINE CONTAMINATION:** Prior to signing this Agreement, Landlord has given Tenant a notice that a health official has issued an order prohibiting occupancy of the property because of methamphetamine contamination. A copy of the notice and order are attached.

27. MEGAN'S LAW DATABASE DISCLOSURE: Notice: Pursuant to Section 290.46 of the Penal Code, information about specified registered sex offenders is made available to the public via an Internet Web site maintained by the Department of Justice at www.meganslaw.ca.gov. Depending on an offender's criminal history, this information will include either the address at which the offender resides or the community of residence and ZIP Code in which he or she resides. (Neither Landlord nor Brokers, if any, are required to check this website. If Tenant wants further information, Tenant should obtain information directly from this website.)

28. POSSESSION:
A. Tenant is not in possession of the premises. If Landlord is unable to deliver possession of Premises on Commencement Date, such Date shall be extended to the date on which possession is made available to Tenant. If Landlord is unable to deliver possession within **5 (or ☐ _____) calendar days** after agreed Commencement Date, Tenant may terminate this Agreement by giving written notice to Landlord, and shall be refunded all Rent and security deposit paid. Possession is deemed terminated when Tenant has returned all keys to the Premises to Landlord.
B. ☐ Tenant is already in possession of the Premises.

29. TENANT'S OBLIGATIONS UPON VACATING PREMISES:
A. Upon termination of this Agreement, Tenant shall: **(i)** give Landlord all copies of all keys or opening devices to Premises, including any common areas; **(ii)** vacate and surrender Premises to Landlord, empty of all persons; **(iii)** vacate any/all parking and/or storage space; **(iv)** clean and deliver Premises, as specified in paragraph C below, to Landlord in the same condition as referenced in paragraph 10; **(v)** remove all debris; **(vi)** give written notice to Landlord of Tenant's forwarding address; and **(vii)** _____.
B. All alterations/improvements made by or caused to be made by Tenant, with or without Landlord's consent, become the property of Landlord upon termination. Landlord may charge Tenant for restoration of the Premises to the condition it was in prior to any alterations/improvements.
C. Right to Pre-Move-Out Inspection and Repairs: (i) After giving or receiving notice of termination of a tenancy (C.A.R. Form NTT), or before the end of a lease, Tenant has the right to request that an inspection of the Premises take place prior to termination of the lease or rental (C.A.R. Form NRI). If Tenant requests such an inspection, Tenant shall be given an opportunity to remedy identified deficiencies prior to termination, consistent with the terms of this Agreement. **(ii)** Any repairs or alterations made to the Premises as a result of this inspection (collectively, "Repairs") shall be made at Tenant's expense. Repairs may be performed by Tenant or through others, who have adequate insurance and licenses and are approved by Landlord. The work shall comply with applicable law, including governmental permit, inspection and approval requirements. Repairs shall be performed in a good, skillful manner with materials of quality and appearance comparable to existing materials. It is understood that exact restoration of appearance or cosmetic items following all Repairs may not be possible. **(iii)** Tenant shall: **(a)** obtain receipts for Repairs performed by others; **(b)** prepare a written statement indicating the Repairs performed by Tenant and the date of such Repairs; and **(c)** provide copies of receipts and statements to Landlord prior to termination. Paragraph 29C does not apply when the tenancy is terminated pursuant to California Code of Civil Procedure § 1161(2), (3) or (4).

30. BREACH OF CONTRACT; EARLY TERMINATION: In addition to any obligations established by paragraph 29, in the event of termination by Tenant prior to completion of the original term of the Agreement, Tenant shall also be responsible for lost Rent, rental commissions, advertising expenses and painting costs necessary to ready Premises for re-rental. Landlord may withhold any such amounts from Tenant's security deposit.

31. TEMPORARY RELOCATION: Subject to local law, Tenant agrees, upon demand of Landlord, to temporarily vacate Premises for a reasonable period, to allow for fumigation (or other methods) to control wood destroying pests or organisms, or other repairs to Premises. Tenant agrees to comply with all instructions and requirements necessary to prepare Premises to accommodate pest control, fumigation or other work, including bagging or storage of food and medicine, and removal of perishables and valuables. Tenant shall only be entitled to a credit of Rent equal to the per diem Rent for the period of time Tenant is required to vacate Premises.

32. DAMAGE TO PREMISES: If, by no fault of Tenant, Premises are totally or partially damaged or destroyed by fire, earthquake, accident or other casualty that render Premises totally or partially uninhabitable, either Landlord or Tenant may terminate this Agreement by giving the other written notice. Rent shall be abated as of the date Premises become totally or partially uninhabitable. The abated amount shall be the current monthly Rent prorated on a 30-day period. If the Agreement is not terminated, Landlord shall promptly repair the damage, and Rent shall be reduced based on the extent to which the damage interferes with Tenant's reasonable use of Premises. If damage occurs as a result of an act of Tenant or Tenant's guests, only Landlord shall have the right of termination, and no reduction in Rent shall be made.

33. INSURANCE: Tenant's or guest's personal property and vehicles are not insured by Landlord, manager or, if applicable, HOA, against loss or damage due to fire, theft, vandalism, rain, water, criminal or negligent acts of others, or any other cause. **Tenant**

Tenant's Initials (_____)(_____)
Landlord's Initials (_____)(_____)

Reviewed by _____ Date _____

EQUAL HOUSING OPPORTUNITY

RESIDENTIAL LEASE OR MONTH-TO-MONTH RENTAL AGREEMENT (LR PAGE 4 OF 6)

FIGURE 11.4 (CONTINUED)

Sample Lease

Premises: _____ Date: _____

is advised to carry Tenant's own insurance (renter's insurance) to protect Tenant from any such loss or damage. Tenant shall comply with any requirement imposed on Tenant by Landlord's insurer to avoid: **(i)** an increase in Landlord's insurance premium (or Tenant shall pay for the increase in premium); or **(ii)** loss of insurance.

34. **WATERBEDS:** Tenant shall not use or have waterbeds on the Premises unless: **(i)** Tenant obtains a valid waterbed insurance policy; **(ii)** Tenant increases the security deposit in an amount equal to one-half of one month's Rent; and **(iii)** the bed conforms to the floor load capacity of Premises.

35. **WAIVER:** The waiver of any breach shall not be construed as a continuing waiver of the same or any subsequent breach.

36. **NOTICE:** Notices may be served at the following address, or at any other location subsequently designated:
    Landlord: _____ Tenant: _____
    _____ _____
    _____ _____

37. **TENANT ESTOPPEL CERTIFICATE:** Tenant shall execute and return a tenant estoppel certificate delivered to Tenant by Landlord or Landlord's agent within 3 days after its receipt. Failure to comply with this requirement shall be deemed Tenant's acknowledgment that the tenant estoppel certificate is true and correct, and may be relied upon by a lender or purchaser.

38. **TENANT REPRESENTATIONS; CREDIT:** Tenant warrants that all statements in Tenant's rental application are accurate. Tenant authorizes Landlord and Broker(s) to obtain Tenant's credit report periodically during the tenancy in connection with the modification or enforcement of this Agreement. Landlord may cancel this Agreement: **(i)** before occupancy begins; **(ii)** upon disapproval of the credit report(s); or **(iii)** at any time, upon discovering that information in Tenant's application is false. A negative credit report reflecting on Tenant's record may be submitted to a credit reporting agency if Tenant fails to fulfill the terms of payment and other obligations under this Agreement.

39. **MEDIATION:**
    A. Consistent with paragraphs B and C below, Landlord and Tenant agree to mediate any dispute or claim arising between them out of this Agreement, or any resulting transaction, before resorting to court action. Mediation fees, if any, shall be divided equally among the parties involved. If, for any dispute or claim to which this paragraph applies, any party commences an action without first attempting to resolve the matter through mediation, or refuses to mediate after a request has been made, then that party shall not be entitled to recover attorney fees, even if they would otherwise be available to that party in any such action.
    B. The following matters are excluded from mediation: **(i)** an unlawful detainer action; **(ii)** the filing or enforcement of a mechanic's lien; and **(iii)** any matter within the jurisdiction of a probate, small claims or bankruptcy court. The filing of a court action to enable the recording of a notice of pending action, for order of attachment, receivership, injunction, or other provisional remedies, shall not constitute a waiver of the mediation provision.
    C. Landlord and Tenant agree to mediate disputes or claims involving Listing Agent, Leasing Agent or property manager ("Broker"), provided Broker shall have agreed to such mediation prior to, or within a reasonable time after, the dispute or claim is presented to such Broker. Any election by Broker to participate in mediation shall not result in Broker being deemed a party to this Agreement.

40. **ATTORNEY FEES:** In any action or proceeding arising out of this Agreement, the prevailing party between Landlord and Tenant shall be entitled to reasonable attorney fees and costs, except as provided in paragraph 39A.

41. **C.A.R. FORM:** C.A.R. Form means the specific form referenced or another comparable from agreed to by the parties.

42. **OTHER TERMS AND CONDITIONS;SUPPLEMENTS:** ☐ Interpreter/Translator Agreement (C.A.R. Form ITA); ☐ Keysafe/Lockbox Addendum (C.A.R. Form KLA); ☐ Lead-Based Paint and Lead-Based Paint Hazards Disclosure (C.A.R. Form FLD) _____
    _____
    The following ATTACHED supplements are incorporated in this Agreement: _____
    _____
    _____

43. **TIME OF ESSENCE; ENTIRE CONTRACT; CHANGES:** Time is of the essence. All understandings between the parties are incorporated in this Agreement. Its terms are intended by the parties as a final, complete and exclusive expression of their Agreement with respect to its subject matter, and may not be contradicted by evidence of any prior agreement or contemporaneous oral agreement. If any provision of this Agreement is held to be ineffective or invalid, the remaining provisions will nevertheless be given full force and effect. Neither this Agreement nor any provision in it may be extended, amended, modified, altered or changed except in writing. This Agreement is subject to California landlord-tenant law and shall incorporate all changes required by amendment or successors to such law. This Agreement and any supplement, addendum or modification, including any copy, may be signed in two or more counterparts, all of which shall constitute one and the same writing.

44. **AGENCY:**
    A. **CONFIRMATION:** The following agency relationship(s) are hereby confirmed for this transaction:
       Listing Agent: (Print firm name) _____ is the agent of
       (check one): ☐ the Landlord exclusively; or ☐ both the Landlord and Tenant.
       Leasing Agent: (Print firm name) _____ (if not same as Listing Agent) is the agent of (check one): ☐ the Tenant exclusively; or ☐ the Landlord exclusively; or ☐ both the Tenant and Landlord.
    B. **DISCLOSURE:** ☐ (If checked): The term of this lease exceeds one year. A disclosure regarding real estate agency relationships (C.A.R. Form AD) has been provided to Landlord and Tenant, who each acknowledge its receipt.

45. ☐ **TENANT COMPENSATION TO BROKER:** Upon execution of this Agreement, Tenant agrees to pay compensation to Broker as specified in a separate written agreement between Tenant and Broker.

Tenant's Initials (_____)(_____)
Landlord's Initials (_____)(_____)

LR REVISED 11/08 (PAGE 5 OF 6)

Reviewed by _____ Date _____

RESIDENTIAL LEASE OR MONTH-TO-MONTH RENTAL AGREEMENT (LR PAGE 5 OF 6)

FIGURE 11.4 (CONTINUED)
Sample Lease

Premises: _____ Date: _____

46. ☐ **INTERPRETER/TRANSLATOR:** The terms of this Agreement have been interpreted for Tenant into the following language: _____. Landlord and Tenant acknowledge receipt of the attached interpretor/translator agreement (C.A.R. Form ITA).

47. FOREIGN LANGUAGE NEGOTIATION: If this Agreement has been negotiated by Landlord and Tenant primarily in Spanish, Chinese, Tagalog, Korean or Vietnamese, pursuant to the California Civil Code, Tenant shall be provided a translation of this Agreement in the language used for the negotiation.

48. OWNER COMPENSATION TO BROKER: Upon execution of this Agreement, Owner agrees to pay compensation to Broker as specified in a separate written agreement between Owner and Broker (C.A.R. Form LCA).

49. RECEIPT: If specified in paragraph 5, Landlord or Broker, acknowledges receipt of move-in funds.

> Landlord and Tenant acknowledge and agree Brokers: **(a)** do not guarantee the condition of the Premises; **(b)** cannot verify representations made by others; **(c)** cannot provide legal or tax advice; **(d)** will not provide other advice or information that exceeds the knowledge, education or experience required to obtain a real estate license. Furthermore, if Brokers are not also acting as Landlord in this Agreement, Brokers: **(e)** do not decide what rental rate a Tenant should pay or Landlord should accept; and **(f)** do not decide upon the length or other terms of tenancy. Landlord and Tenant agree that they will seek legal, tax, insurance and other desired assistance from appropriate professionals.

Tenant agrees to rent the Premises on the above terms and conditions.

Tenant _____ Date _____
Address _____ City _____ State _____ Zip _____
Telephone _____ Fax _____ E-mail_____
Tenant _____ Date _____
Address _____ City _____ State _____ Zip _____
Telephone _____ Fax _____ E-mail_____

☐ **GUARANTEE:** In consideration of the execution of this Agreement by and between Landlord and Tenant and for valuable consideration, receipt of which is hereby acknowledged, the undersigned ("Guarantor") does hereby: **(i)** guarantee unconditionally to Landlord and Landlord's agents, successors and assigns, the prompt payment of Rent or other sums that become due pursuant to this Agreement, including any and all court costs and attorney fees included in enforcing the Agreement; **(ii)** consent to any changes, modifications or alterations of any term in this Agreement agreed to by Landlord and Tenant; and **(iii)** waive any right to require Landlord and/or Landlord's agents to proceed against Tenant for any default occurring under this Agreement before seeking to enforce this Guarantee.

Guarantor (Print Name) _____
Guarantor _____ Date _____
Address _____ City _____ State _____ Zip _____
Telephone _____ Fax _____ E-mail_____

Landlord agrees to rent the Premises on the above terms and conditions.

Landlord _____ Landlord _____
Address _____
Telephone _____ Fax _____ E-mail_____

REAL ESTATE BROKERS:
A. Real estate brokers who are not also Landlord under this Agreement are not parties to the Agreement between Landlord and Tenant.
B. Agency relationships are confirmed in paragraph 44.
C. COOPERATING BROKER COMPENSATION: Listing Broker agrees to pay Cooperating Broker (Leasing Firm) and Cooperating Broker agrees to accept: **(i)** the amount specified in the MLS, provided Cooperating Broker is a Participant of the MLS in which the Property is offered for sale or a reciprocal MLS; or **(ii)** ☐ (if checked) the amount specified in a separate written agreement between Listing Broker and Cooperating Broker.

Real Estate Broker (Listing Firm) _____ DRE Lic. # _____
By (Agent) _____ DRE Lic. # _____ Date _____
Address _____ City _____ State ____ Zip ____
Telephone _____ Fax _____ E-mail _____

Real Estate Broker (Leasing Firm) _____ DRE Lic. # _____
By (Agent) _____ DRE Lic. # _____ Date _____
Address _____ City _____ State ____ Zip ____
Telephone _____ Fax _____ E-mail _____

THIS FORM HAS BEEN APPROVED BY THE CALIFORNIA ASSOCIATION OF REALTORS® (C.A.R.). NO REPRESENTATION IS MADE AS TO THE LEGAL VALIDITY OR ADEQUACY OF ANY PROVISION IN ANY SPECIFIC TRANSACTION. A REAL ESTATE BROKER IS THE PERSON QUALIFIED TO ADVISE ON REAL ESTATE TRANSACTIONS. IF YOU DESIRE LEGAL OR TAX ADVICE, CONSULT AN APPROPRIATE PROFESSIONAL.
This form is available for use by the entire real estate industry. It is not intended to identify the user as a REALTOR®. REALTOR® is a registered collective membership mark which may be used only by members of the NATIONAL ASSOCIATION OF REALTORS® who subscribe to its Code of Ethics.

Published and Distributed by:
REAL ESTATE BUSINESS SERVICES, INC.
a subsidiary of the California Association of REALTORS®
525 South Virgil Avenue, Los Angeles, California 90020

Reviewed by _____ Date _____

LR REVISED 11/08 (PAGE 6 OF 6)

RESIDENTIAL LEASE OR MONTH-TO-MONTH RENTAL AGREEMENT (LR PAGE 6 OF 6)

Tenant Unions

Tenant unions have been formed, encouraged by the passage of landlord-tenant legislation in many states. Conflicts can be avoided, however, by implementing a plan that brings management and residents together quickly in a controlled environment for the purpose of joint problem solving.

A relatively easy strategy is to establish formal, regularly scheduled meetings with representatives of tenant groups. Once the tenants bring up a problem, they should be confident that management will be responsive, even if the answer is "no." A manager should avoid a win-lose atmosphere, with potentially destructive emotions, so that decisions can be made in a businesslike manner.

■ MAINTAINING THE APARTMENT BUILDING

The precise duties of all employees involved in maintaining a property depend on the size and facilities of the building, the condition of the premises, and the terms of the management contract. As pointed out in Chapter 8, maintenance duties may be carried out by a large staff that includes a resident manager, janitorial staff, on-site maintenance crew, and various outside service contractors. The resident manager for a smaller property may have to assume maintenance responsibilities with no on-site support whatsoever.

Maintenance Personnel

The manager's decision to hire full-time or contract services must be based on the amount of services required and the cost-effectiveness to the owner. Hiring decisions should be made on the experience and versatility of the applicant. Many on-site janitorial and maintenance personnel can quickly and adequately perform minor plumbing, electrical repairs, and painting touch-up work at great savings, thus saving the expense of a professional plumber or skilled electrician.

Resident Manager's Responsibilities

The resident manager is one of the most important team members on the management team as this may be the only person the tenant ever meets. As a result, the resident manager must possess a variety of skills: able to manage tenants and maintenance personnel, adept at accounting for money and supplies, aware of community issues and tenant concerns, all the while balancing the owner's wishes with the tenant's demands.

The resident manager is usually responsible for supervising all maintenance activities and, from time to time, being able to execute repairs. The resident manager also supervises housekeeping and maintenance of all common interior areas. Inspection reports can be designed to meet the requirements of the building and should be utilized in order not to forget something and to show continuity. The exterior inspection report form shown in Figure 11.5 illustrates some of the resident manager's typical concerns.

FIGURE 11.5
Exterior Inspection Report

Exterior Inspection Report			

Property _____   Date _____

Address _____

Item	Condition	Repairs Needed	Cost
Air-Conditioning			
Boiler/Furnace			
Exterior Walls			
Curbs and Gutters			
Elevators			
Grounds			
Windows			
Stairways			
Common Areas			
Plumbing			
Outdoor Lighting			
Parking Lot			
Roof			
Sidewalks			

Routine tasks should be scheduled on a daily, weekly, or monthly basis. High-traffic areas require daily attention, as do lawns and swimming pools. Recreation and laundry rooms, parking areas, rubbish cans, and so forth can generally be inspected and cleaned on a semiweekly or weekly basis. Monthly activities might include fertilizing the lawn, pest control, and inspecting the heating and ventilating plant.

Tenants should be encouraged to put their requests in writing. A written request documents the request and limits what will be done when the repairperson arrives. All oral or written requests for service should be entered on a three-copy form similar to that shown in Figure 7.3 or into the computer. The original and a copy, which should be left in the apartment on completion of the work, are assigned to the maintenance person answering the request. The third copy is kept by the manager until the job is completed.

The resident manager should visit the apartment with the new tenant using the checklist to avoid any misunderstandings as to the condition of the move-in. The resident manager should thoroughly inspect each apartment after tenants vacate the premises; at best, the unit will have to be cleaned before it can be shown to prospective tenants.

Property Manager's Responsibilities

Because the property manager is not usually in daily contact with each building, the resident manager should submit weekly reports on the condition of the property, the work performed, and jobs anticipated for the upcoming week. When coupled with monthly inspection tours, these reports reveal a lot about the resident manager's performance and attitude.

■ APARTMENT OPERATING REPORTS

Owners of apartment buildings have the same need for operating reports as owners of commercial and industrial properties. The reports described in Chapter 9 give the owner the raw data necessary to evaluate the property manager, determine the value of the investment, and decide on the best course of action.

Apartment Operating Budgets

Apartment occupancy rates are always subject to change because of economic conditions, such as employment cuts or the addition of new units to the market. As mentioned in Chapter 2, consumers have taken advantage of the low interest rates to buy their housing instead of renting. When preparing a budget, a property manager should determine if there are any predictable influences in the market for the coming budget year that might affect occupancy.

For example, long periods of low vacancy rates in a community often stimulate the construction of new apartments. So, in these periods of high occupancy, it is important to know what new projects are under construction and when they will be available for leasing. A study of lease expiration dates in such situations should also be made to analyze the vulnerability of the manager's apartments to losses from moveouts to newer units.

A sample **operating budget** for a medium-size apartment building appears as Figure 11.6. The manager should look for any significant deviations from the planned budget and be able to explain why these deviations occurred. In some circumstances, the manager can plan for fluctuations in the future, if she or he knows why they occurred in the past.

Additional Income

In addition to the rents, rental of videotapes, parking and storage fees, and vending and laundry machines can provide revenue. Laundry leasing companies will install washers and dryers on a percentage basis, the rate depending on the bargaining power of the manager and the overall expected revenue from the machines. An alternative is for the manager to buy laundry machines outright on behalf of the owner.

Operating expenses for apartment buildings can be allocated to four major categories, as shown in the sample monthly **cash flow report,** Figure 11.7. This is an alternative to the form presented in Chapter 9 and is consistent with the National Apartment Association (NAA) and the Institute of Real Estate Management (IREM).

Cash Flow Analysis

Cash flow projections really deal only with previously used data, as discussed in Chapter 9. The after-tax **cash flow analysis** allows the owner to analyze actual return on investment after taxes and decide whether it is economically more advantageous to keep the property, invest more money in it, refinance it, or sell it. Also, the owner may use the manager's operating reports, particularly the cash flow, as a "report card" or measure of the manager's performance by comparing ratios from period to period. Here is an example for calculating cash flow using a method employed by professional accountants.

An older apartment building has a reliable gross income of $100,000 per year. Its operating cost rate is 50 percent, including capital expenditures and reserves. At the beginning of the year, its depreciable tax base was $400,000; $5,000 was spent for capital improvements. Straight-line depreciation is computed based on an economic life of 27.5 years. For simplicity of illustration, assume that the owner is in a 28 percent income tax bracket and that the entire amount of capital expenditures is depreciable for one full year. When calculating taxable income, those capital expenditures for additions or other major repairs that extend the life of the property or markedly increase its value should be added to the basis of the property and depreciated over its life, rather than being currently deducted as an operating cost. The property carries a $300,000 first mortgage at a 10 percent constant rate, which includes a 1 percent principal payback. The after-tax cash flow analysis for this property is shown in Figure 11.8.

FIGURE 11.6

Operating Budget

Operating Budget		
Income		
4 Studio @ $550/month	$26,400	
6 One-Bedroom @ $650/Month	46,800	
7 Two-Bedroom @ $800/month	67,200	
Gross scheduled rental income	$140,400	
5% vacancy and rent loss	(7,020)	
Gross collectable rental income	$133,380	
Income from other sources	5,500	
Total Anticipated Revenue		$138,880
Expenses		
Real Estate Taxes	$12,960	
Salaries	22,550	
Utilities	9,990	
Supplies	2,700	
Maintenance and repairs	5,500	
Insurance	3,000	
Administrative	1,875	
Management @ 5% gross income	6,669	
Reserves	7,500	
Total Expenses		$72,744
Net Operating Income before Debt Service		$66,136
Debt Service ($200,000 @ 7% constant)	$14,000	

FIGURE 11.7

Cash Flow

<table>
<tr><th colspan="3">Cash Flow Report</th></tr>
<tr><th>Property: Garden Arms Apartments</th><th>Month:
February</th><th>Year:
2004</th></tr>
<tr><td>**Income**</td><td></td><td></td></tr>
<tr><td>Gross Potential Income</td><td>$30,000</td><td></td></tr>
<tr><td>less vacancy, rent loss, and delinquencies</td><td>2,500</td><td></td></tr>
<tr><td>**Effective Gross Income**</td><td></td><td>$27,500</td></tr>
<tr><td>**Other Income**</td><td></td><td></td></tr>
<tr><td>laundry</td><td>200</td><td></td></tr>
<tr><td>vending</td><td>200</td><td></td></tr>
<tr><td>parking</td><td>200</td><td></td></tr>
<tr><td>storage</td><td>300</td><td>900</td></tr>
<tr><td>**Gross Operating Income**</td><td></td><td>$28,400</td></tr>
<tr><td>**Expenses**</td><td></td><td></td></tr>
<tr><td>Wages</td><td></td><td></td></tr>
<tr><td>property manager</td><td>1,500</td><td></td></tr>
<tr><td>resident manager</td><td>700</td><td></td></tr>
<tr><td>staff</td><td>3,000</td><td>5,200</td></tr>
<tr><td>Variable Expenses</td><td></td><td></td></tr>
<tr><td>utilities</td><td>1,000</td><td></td></tr>
<tr><td>maintenance</td><td>800</td><td></td></tr>
<tr><td>professional fees</td><td>1,100</td><td>2,900</td></tr>
<tr><td>Fixed Expenses</td><td></td><td></td></tr>
<tr><td>property tax</td><td>650</td><td></td></tr>
<tr><td>insurance</td><td>500</td><td>1,150</td></tr>
<tr><td>**Total Operating Expenses**</td><td></td><td>$9,250</td></tr>
<tr><td>**Net Operating Income**</td><td></td><td>$19,150</td></tr>
<tr><td>Capital Expenditures</td><td></td><td></td></tr>
<tr><td>rugs</td><td>650</td><td></td></tr>
<tr><td>drapes</td><td>50</td><td></td></tr>
<tr><td>appliances and fixtures</td><td>1,000</td><td>1,700</td></tr>
<tr><td>**Debt Service**</td><td>8,000</td><td></td></tr>
<tr><td>**Less Capital Expenditures and Debt Service**</td><td></td><td>$9,700</td></tr>
<tr><td>**Cash Flow**</td><td></td><td>$9,450</td></tr>
</table>

In calculating total return, investors will often add in the equity buildup from the reduction of the mortgage. Total return for this property would thus be $19,288.

Investment properties are expected to yield a satisfactory cash return on the investment (as shown by the after-tax cash flow in the example) to ensure that the invested capital is not impaired, and to present the opportunity for value

FIGURE 11.8
After-Tax Cash Flow Analysis

Cash Flow Report

After-Tax Cash Flow Analysis

a.	Gross Annual Income		$100,000
b.	Operating Costs ($50,000 – $5,000)		(45,000)
c.	Net Operating Income (NOI)		$55,000
d.	Capital Expenditures		(5,000)
e.	Debt Service: ($300,000 @ 10% constant)		
f.	Interest Payment		(27,000)
g.	Principal (1% payback)		(3,000)
h.	Income Tax Payable	$55,000	
	Net Operating Income (c)	(27,000)	
	Less Interest Payment (f)	(14,742)	
	Less Depreciation Deduction*	$13,258	
	$13,258 × 28% (tax bracket)		(3,712)
i.	Net After-Tax Cash Flow Position		$16,288

Depreciation Deduction		
	$400,000	Initial Cost (Basis)
	+ 5,000	Capital Expenditures
	$405,000	New Basis
	× .0364	(See Chapter 9)
	$ 14,742	Annual Depreciation Deduction

---

enhancement. These are goals the owner will want to discuss with the manager when analyzing the cash flow statement and investigating economic alternatives to remedy unsatisfactory situations. If the cash return on the building in the previous example had not met the owner's expectations, the manager might have suggested that the owner refinance the property, raise the rents, or institute strict cost-accounting procedures to reduce costs.

Reducing Costs

It is unwise to increase present cash flow by deferring expenditures for real maintenance needs. Savings may sometimes be made through volume buying or through an energy conservation program, both of which are discussed in Chapter 8. Generally, an energy conservation program in apartment property cannot be carried out successfully without the cooperation of the building staff and tenants. However, the possibility for savings can be promising by installing automatic or computerized controls in many older apartment projects, particularly in the southern states.

Some common sense precautions can be exercised to hold a ceiling on rising operating costs. All utility firms have energy consultants with whom the manager can confer. (Utility rate schedules can be quite confusing to the uninitiated. Electric rates, for example, vary according to amount of power used, time of day, peak consumed at any one time, use to which the electricity is put, and cost of the fuel used to generate the electricity.) A *utility representative* can determine the optimal type of service for the property and suggest ways of reducing waste.

■ **Simple Cost Saving Suggestions**

- Installing timers—preferably photocell switches if possible—for hallway and outdoor lights
- Installing compact fluorescent lighting fixtures
- Installing storm windows
- Caulking around doorways and windows
- Adding insulation to protect against heat loss through transference
- Installing automatic heating controls
- Reducing heating hours

Final Choices

If the rents are as high as the market will allow, costs are pared to the bone, and if the property still does not show a satisfactory return, the owner is faced with final choices:

1. Subsidize

2. Make a major capital investment that will render the property more marketable

3. Refinance to reduce debt service

4. Sell

■ THE APARTMENT BUILDING STAFF

In general, the personnel guidelines set forth in Chapter 9 are fully applicable to the management of apartment projects. Because of round-the-clock involvement, the resident manager in particular occupies a key position in maintaining residential properties and dealing with tenants.

Resident Manager

The manager of residential property is much closer to tenants' personal lives than the manager of commercial property. Thus, the **resident manager** must possess versatility with dedication and fairness backed by training, strong selling and communication skills, good business judgment, tact and patience, and a working knowledge of record keeping. Several professional associations offer educational programs designed to develop the skills of a resident manager.

Good resident managers are not easy to find. Most often, the property manager will have to rely on referrals from other managers or on classified newspaper ads. In addition, a property manager can become acquainted with prospective resident managers through activity in local apartment associations. Long-time residents are another source of recruits.

A prospective manager should be required to fill out an employment application listing education, experience, and references. The ideal candidate should combine experience with a good employment history, a background compatible with that of the tenant population, a stable work record, and a mature approach to the job.

Some property managers employ resident managers under a comprehensive contract that clearly specifies the compensation rate (including any apartment concessions); the hours of work; and the duties to be performed. It is standard policy to insert a clause in such contracts setting a dollar limit on expenditures the resident manager may make without the property manager's approval. Other property managers prefer a simpler contract on the grounds that neither party can foresee contingencies. At a minimum, wages and hours should always be in writing.

■ The resident manager must have the respect of the tenants in order to successfully collect rents and deal with problems. The property manager should back up the resident manager whenever possible and cultivate goodwill by indicating that management appreciates his or her work. The property manager should ask the resident manager's opinion of any changes or improvements to be made on the premises or proposed changes in operating plans. If the resident manager's advice is not followed, a reasonable explanation from the property manager is common courtesy and a gesture of team spirit.

Leasing Agents

As mentioned earlier, leasing agents may be employed to assist in marketing and closing the prospect. Although some leasing agents prefer to stay in this role, others may be considered for assisting the resident manager or to become the resident manager. This is a traditional career path for many resident managers who sometimes move even further up the ladder to the position of property manager.

■ SUMMARY

Residential property may be broadly grouped into single family residences, duplexes and triplexes, and apartments, commonly called multifamily dwellings. Multifamily dwellings differ from one another in size, structure, location, and number of amenities provided. Garden apartments are common in the suburbs and are fairly large (two or three bedrooms) and offer some recreational facilities. Units in three-story walkup and multilevel elevator buildings usually are smaller and more modestly equipped. Multistory and high-rise buildings are concentrated near the downtown areas of large cities or in older more densely populated suburbs. These differences exert a direct influence on an owner's economic policies and on the advertising techniques used to market each type of space.

Each unit must be priced correctly for the market and the most effective advertising and promotional strategy used for the particular property. In establishing a rent schedule, the property manager should first survey the rental schedules of comparable properties in the area and analyze the overall supply and demand relationship for apartments in the neighborhood. If there is more demand for one type of unit than for another, the manager may have to adjust the basic rental schedule.

A show list of apartments available for inspection can be invaluable to a property manager's marketing program, particularly if a traffic count is incorporated in it. The show list fosters the impression that space is at a premium and enables the maintenance staff to concentrate its efforts on the apartments currently being shown. The show list should not include all vacancies, only two or three samples of each type of unit.

Newspaper advertising is most widely used for renting apartments. A conventional listing should be brief but informative, appealing to the needs of the prospective tenant. Display ads are usually limited to large, prestigious, or newly opened apartment complexes. Apartment journals are an important tool in many localities. Care should be taken to follow fair housing guidelines. Probably the most useful advertising tool today is the company's Web site.

The cost-effectiveness of permanent rental centers is determined by the size and location of the building, uniqueness of its services, market demand, and tenant turnover. They may be worthwhile if large numbers of apartments must be rented over an extended period of time, as is usually the case with a young, mobile tenant population. Otherwise, temporary rental centers or model apartments are more economical alternatives.

The resident manager often shares building management responsibilities with the property manager, who oversees the general welfare of several buildings at once. The resident manager is the most important member of the apartment building staff. Cooperation and respect between the property manager and the resident manager can do much to further their common goal of financially sound and trouble-free building operations. Because the resident manager occupies such a pivotal position in the overall operation of the building, dealing with both owner and tenant, formal job training in this field has become more popular and some community colleges offer such programs.

The manager of a smaller property with little or no on-site staff should be versatile enough to make minor repairs without calling in expensive skilled labor. The absent property manager relies heavily on maintenance reports from the resident manager. These should cover not only surface maintenance but upkeep of the building's vital plumbing and HVAC systems as well.

The property manager informs the owner of the property's financial status through the monthly cash flow reports and annual profit and loss statement. Funds should be conservatively budgeted in all four categories of expense: taxes, insurance, maintenance, and administration.

The manager's cash flow analysis enables the owner to evaluate the return on the property investment. If the owner is dissatisfied, the property manager should suggest alternatives to the current management program. The after-tax cash flow on a property can sometimes be improved by an energy conservation program or other techniques for shaving operating costs. In other cases, the property might have to be refinanced, altered, or even sold.

■ CASE STUDY
THE RESIDENTIAL MANAGER

Harriet Montgomery is the property manager of a large apartment complex. One of the tenants, Han, came to Montgomery's office with a complaint. Han told Montgomery that his bathtub did not drain properly, but Han's repeated requests to the resident manager, Fitzgerald, to have it repaired have been ignored. Han claimed that several of his friends, who are also tenants, had given Fitzgerald repair requests, and they had all been completed immediately. Han suspects that Fitzgerald is dragging his heels about Han's request because Han is Asian-American and Fitzgerald is discriminating against him.

1. How should Montgomery respond to Han's complaint? Is it a discrimination complaint?
2. What procedures can Montgomery implement to ward off complaints like this in the future?
3. What should Montgomery do about Fitzgerald?

■ REVIEW QUESTIONS

1. Which of the following types of apartment community is MOST likely to be located in downtown urban areas?
   a. Garden apartment complex
   b. Walkup apartments
   c. Multistory elevator building
   d. High-rise luxury property

2. A tenant receiving minimal services MOST likely lives in a
   a. garden apartment.
   b. walkup apartment.
   c. multistory elevator building.
   d. luxury apartment building.

3. Which of the following are generally less profitable because they require more management time?
   a. Scattered site housing
   b. Loft conversions
   c. Multifamily elevator building
   d. Garden apartments

4. Which is a special consideration when managing duplexes and triplexes?
   a. Showings to prospective tenants do not require many trips to the property.
   b. Tenants should have a high degree of compatibility.
   c. Return on investment is quite high.
   d. Repairs do not require much management time.

5. Neighborhood boundaries are important in a residential market analysis because
   a. they influence transportation facilities.
   b. they affect employment data.
   c. they dictate the type of construction by affecting zoning.
   d. economic conditions in the neighborhood may affect the rental schedule.

6. On which factor of the market analysis should rents should be based?
   a. Comparable value to other properties
   b. Age of the property
   c. Employment and income data
   d. U.S. Census Bureau statistics on population density

7. What is the basis for sound tenant relations?
   a. Numerous rules
   b. Open lines of communication
   c. Employing a public relations specialist
   d. Slow response to maintenance requests

8. Maintaining litter-free grounds and well-trimmed lawns are examples of
   a. show lists.
   b. a rental center.
   c. curb appeal.
   d. ready-to-rent.

9. An apartment building consists of ten one-bedroom apartments renting for $180; ten two-bedroom units renting for $210; and ten three-bedroom units that rent for $240. All of the units are rented except for four three-bedroom units. The vacancy rate of the three-bedroom apartments can be expected to decrease by 10 percent (one of the four vacant will rent) with a $10 rental cut. The property manager should establish which of the following rental schedules?
   a. One-bedroom units at $180; two-bedroom units at $210; three-bedroom units at $230
   b. One-bedroom units at $190; two-bedroom units at $220; three-bedroom units at $250
   c. One-bedroom units at $190; two-bedroom units at $220; three-bedroom units at $230
   d. Rental schedule should remain the same

10. The show list of apartments to be rented
    a. should include all vacant apartments.
    b. is designed for use by the manager.
    c. is for use by the owner.
    d. is updated monthly.

11. What tool can the manager use as a control for marketing and as a source of feedback on marketing success or failure?
    a. Ready-to-rent list
    b. Show list
    c. Maintenance supervisor's completed work order list
    d. Price list

12. Which is the *MOST* effective method of renting apartments?
    a. Classified ads
    b. Display ads
    c. Billboards
    d. Radio commercials

13. A manager who assumes maintenance responsibilities because there is no on-site help is most likely found in
    a. luxury high-rise.
    b. large garden apartments.
    c. medium-size garden apartments.
    d. small walkup apartments.

14. Which of the following should be carefully explained to tenants?
    a. When rental payments can be late
    b. Racial composition of the complex
    c. When and where rent must be paid
    d. How to unstop a toilet

15. Of the following, which is *MOST* likely to be prepared by the resident manager?
    a. Monthly income expense statement
    b. Semiannual balance sheet
    c. Operating budget
    d. Property condition, work performed, and jobs anticipated in the following week

16. Responsibility for controlling the daily operations of an apartment building rests with the
    a. on-site janitor.
    b. property manager.
    c. resident manager.
    d. on-site maintenance employee.

17. Preventive and corrective maintenance of residential units is generally coordinated by the
    a. maintenance supervisor.
    b. supervising property manager.
    c. resident manager.
    d. assigned maintenance person.

18. Specialists who can most effectively market the property are
    a. resident managers.
    b. leasing agents.
    c. manager's assistants.
    d. supervising property managers.

19. All of the following could be used as an additional revenue stream *EXCEPT*
    a. cleaning deposits.
    b. parking and storage fees.
    c. vending and laundry machines.
    d. deposits per child.

20. Although cash flow projections appear to be complex
    a. they are based on figures from the data already gathered.
    b. the property manager can get the owner's assistance in preparing them.
    c. they are simple in design and do not contribute to the owner's decision making.
    d. they are not complex, because they have no impact on tax returns.

CHAPTER TWELVE

SPECIALIZED HOUSING

■ KEY TERMS

Common elements
Condominiums
Cooperatives
Covenants, conditions,
  and restrictions
  (CC&Rs)
Management pricing
  worksheet

Manufactured home
  parks
Planned Unit
  Developments
  (PUDs)
Proprietary lease
REOs (lender owned)
Section 8

Section 202
TRACS
U.S. Department of
  Housing and Urban
  Development (HUD)

■ LEARNING OBJECTIVES

At the end of this chapter, the student will be able to:

1. explain the difference between cooperative, condominium, and planned
   unit development ownership and benefits and disadvantages of each;

2. discuss the importance of thoroughly explaining the CC&Rs to tenants
   and owners;

3. summarize the importance of building a sense of community in mobile
   home parks;

4. discuss the disadvantage of charging a percentage fee when managing multiowner communities and explain why charging a cost-per-unit, flat fee, or the use of a management pricing worksheet is better;

5. summarize the effect of government regulations on managing subsidized housing and the unique management qualities called for, and

6. describe accessibility modifications that must be made for housing for the elderly.

■ OVERVIEW

As land and construction costs become more expensive, people are turning to less expensive forms of housing such as cooperative and condominium forms of ownership, planned unit developments, and mobile home parks. Subsidized housing is still a fact of life as housing costs increase faster than wages. Baby Boomers are aging and will demand "older person housing," lower-cost housing, or both. All of these factors present management opportunities.

Cooperatives and condominiums are multiple-occupant properties in which the occupants of the premises have a vested interest in the building. Although there are retail, office, and industrial use condominiums, most cooperative and condominium projects are residential properties. Therefore, this chapter focuses on residential cooperatives and condominiums, and a variation called *planned unit developments (PUDs)*. PUD homeowners own their houses and land, but share ownership and responsibility in certain public areas. Management of PUDs is similar to that of condos and co-ops.

From a management perspective, these specialized forms of residential management share many characteristics of ordinary multiple-occupancy structures, but the form of ownership changes the manager's goals and objectives.

The apartment manager represents the building owner to the tenants of the owner's property, whereas the property manager of a cooperative or condominium works for a group of owner-occupants. Management is most concerned with administrative duties and maintenance of the common areas, because each owner is responsible for the condition and upkeep of the individual units. Unlike the apartment manager, the manager of a cooperative or condominium usually has no responsibility for maintaining occupancy levels.

Resort housing consists of single-family houses, condominium, or cooperative units. During the high season, the manager markets, approves short-term leases, and arranges cleaning and maid service; during the low season, he or she is concerned with maintenance and security. In multitenant properties, the manager must balance the owners' objectives with the overall rules of the community.

Subsidized housing projects have unique ownership structures and management requirements. Many of these properties are built in order to gain tax credits for the owners, often anonymous and absentee. These managers must be conversant with many additional local, state, and/or federal guidelines regarding income verification and tenant qualifying as well as tax code requirements. Several trade associations offer a designation in tax credit management as on-site compliance is one of the key risks involved with managing tax-credit properties discussed in Chapter 9.

Another area of opportunity involving property management skills is "REO sales." The REO is a property that has been repossessed and is now owned by the lender. Many lenders use a "listing agreement" that basically involves property management functions.

■ MANAGING COOPERATIVES

Some co-ops look like apartment buildings, and a cooperative community may look like any other suburban development, but differences in ownership affect responsibilities, liabilities, and maintenance. Co-op ownership is becoming popular with two groups who want the tax advantages of home ownership with the minimum responsibilities of maintenance and repairs: young people just entering the job market and retirees leaving the job market.

Structure of Cooperative Ownership

In **cooperative ownership** the apartment owner purchases shares in the corporation (or partnership or trust) that holds title to the entire apartment building. The ownership of the building can be either trust or corporate in nature. The principal asset of the cooperative is the building. The co-op shareholder receives a **proprietary lease** granting occupancy of a specific unit in the building. The cooperative owns the building and the shareholder owns a lease (personal property).

The owner occupies an apartment as a lessee under the terms of the lease but does not own it. Each lessee must pay a pro rata share of the corporation's expenses, which include any mortgage charges, real estate taxes, maintenance, payroll, and such. The owner can deduct a proportionate share of the taxes and interest charges for tax purposes (provided 80 percent of a cooperative's income is derived from tenant-owner rentals).

The success or failure of cooperative ownership depends on every lessee paying his or her pro rata share. Many cooperative associations reserve the right to approve or reject subleases and sales, which can delay transfer of ownership indefinitely.

Trust ownership Legal ownership of the building is placed in the name of a trustee, which may be a trust company. The trustee issues beneficial participation certificates, or memberships, in the amount of the purchase price of the property (total cost minus mortgage). Trustees of the trust share responsibility for managing the cooperative or hiring a professional property manager to assume these duties. An individual with a membership certificate is granted the right to occupy a unit in the building subject to specific rules and regulations.

Corporate ownership   Corporate cooperatives are established as corporations. The corporation then issues stock of a total value equal to the purchase price of the cooperative, again figured by subtracting the amount of the mortgage from the cost of the property. This stock is allocated among the units of the building according to their relative value. Purchasers of stock in the corporation are then granted the right to occupy a unit under a proprietary lease. A board of directors, elected by the shareholders, is in charge of the operation of the property. The board has the right to engage the services of a professional property manager, if it so desires.

Share/Proprietary Lease

The proprietary lease is inseparable from the share of stock and lasts for the life of the corporation or trust and is subject to rules and regulations established by the corporate charter and bylaws. Among these rules is the provision that the mortgage debt and the operating expenses for the property are divided among the occupants through monthly assessments.

Share allocation   The number of shares allocated to a unit could be equal, or more commonly, they are determined by the size of the unit, its location in the building, and its features. As part of the lease, the charges consist of a monthly assessment for operating costs based on the par value of the shares allocated to the unit plus that unit's proportionate share of the total mortgage debt for the property.

For example, in the case of a 20-unit building worth $800,000 and subject to a $400,000 mortgage, the equity base held by the corporation totals $400,000 and could be represented by 4,000 shares of stock worth $100 each. The purchaser of 5 percent of the stock, or 200 shares, would hold a proprietary lease for a unit valued at $40,000 subject to a mortgage debt of $20,000. If the total monthly mortgage payment for the building was $4,000 and operating costs, including payroll, property taxes, insurance, management fees, utilities, services, supplies, maintenance, and reserve funds, totaled $6,000 per month, the holder of this lease would be assessed $500 per month ($4,000 × .05 = $200; $6,000 × .05 = $300).

Covenants   Under a proprietary lease, the interior maintenance of each unit is the responsibility of the lessee, as are all utilities for the apartment except possibly water and sometimes heat. Corporate responsibilities include maintaining structural elements such as in-the-wall plumbing, electrical and ventilating systems; cleaning exterior and interior public areas; and ensuring efficient services and the smooth operation of the property.

The lease should also establish the lessee's liability for negligence and limit the lessor corporation's liability for damage and injury. The rental section provides for some token rental consideration, monthly assessments, and additional rent. Generally, the board of directors is empowered to adjust the monthly assessment as the need arises.

Default If some occupants are unable to meet their monthly assessments or if they contract for services for which they are unable to pay, the remaining shareholders must bear the extra costs. Otherwise, the trustee or corporation will default on the mortgage or a mechanic's lien might be filed against the title to the property. Hence, most proprietary leases provide remedies in the event of monthly payment defaults.

The ultimate penalty is usually cancellation of the lease and forfeiture of all shares. The corporation would then own the unit and could sell or lease it.

Reserve Funds and Right of First Refusal

Generally, a small amount is added to the monthly maintenance charge to maintain a reserve fund. Lessees usually receive an audited operating statement at the end of the year along with a forecasted operating budget for the next year. The lease also specifies that adequate insurance be carried on the entire property, a necessity for cooperatives.

To protect the financial integrity of the cooperative as a whole, most proprietary leases state that the right of possession of the unit may not be transferred without the consent of the board of directors. Others give the corporation the first right to purchase the stock or the certificate and lease of an occupant who wishes to sublet or sell out.

The Property Manager's Role

The cooperative property manager's first responsibility is to fulfill corporate aims on behalf of the shareholders. This usually includes maintaining the physical integrity of the property, ensuring ongoing services to the occupants, and submitting regular operating reports to the board of directors. The precise services rendered can range from a periodic consultation to full-time management services on a fixed-fee basis. The aims of the corporation and the services expected from the manager should always be spelled out in a detailed written contract.

Because the property manager must operate within the economic confines imposed by the board of directors, he or she must have some input when the operating budget for the coming year is drawn up. The manager will find the *Income and Expense Analysis: Condominiums, Cooperatives, and PUDs,* published by IREM, a valuable source for comparison with other associations when preparing a budget. The manager must make a realistic calculation of maintenance costs, one that provides for a contingency reserve fund to alleviate future increases in monthly payments.

Dealing with numerous resident owners on a day-to-day basis requires a great deal of skill on the part of a manager. Managing cooperatives has its downside; an inordinate amount of time must be spent attending monthly meetings, communicating with various tenant-owners, setting agendas and budgets, and most difficult of all, refereeing disputes between tenants.

The advantage of managing cooperatives (and condominiums) over apartment buildings is that members occupying their own units generally take more pride in their surroundings. Also, these tenants want to be more informed about management policies and practices. The manager should accommodate them and foster goodwill by providing information (including operational programs, progress, and annual reports); soliciting opinions both in person and through written questionnaires; and encouraging feedback. A monthly association newsletter for all owners is a valuable tool in this respect, and occupants should be encouraged to contribute items for publication.

Fractious differences of opinion among the owners may ultimately result in disgruntled shareholders or members, a stagnant corporation, needless expense, and reduced service. The property manager can avoid this pitfall of cooperative ownership. Acting with the approval of the board of directors, and responsible only to it, the manager can assume full responsibility for the operation of the property, including employment decisions, maintenance functions, accounting reports, administration of corporate policy, and transference and registration of corporate stock.

In the management contract, managers should suggest a provision to allow them to function as a nonofficer administrator of the governing association—the person in charge of preparing the agendas for all meetings of the directors and stockholders, recording the minutes of these sessions, and providing the members with copies. To fulfill these obligations, the manager must be familiar with corporate law and procedure and have an experienced attorney available for consultation.

Cooperative managers need copies of the incorporation documents, the corporate seal, the stock journal, the bylaws, and minutes of previous board meetings.

■ One note of caution: The cooperative form of organization occasionally has been used for discriminatory purposes. A property manager considering employment by a cooperative should avoid association with any group he or she suspects of discrimination. For more information on discrimination and fair housing laws, see Chapter 10.

■ MANAGING CONDOMINIUMS

The condominium has been a revolutionary and rapidly growing form of ownership in U.S. real estate ownership for more than four decades. From a successful beginning in Puerto Rico in the 1950s, condominium units have accounted for a notable percentage of all new housing starts because the condominium may often be priced lower than a single-family home. While the new co-op owner receives a proprietary lease—that is, personal property—the new condominium owner receives a deed to real property. Therefore, interest and ad valorem taxes are conveniently tax-deductible inasmuch as they are applied directly to each unit, as opposed to the co-op ownership, whereby the co-op owner *may* deduct a proportionate share under certain conditions.

Ownership Structure

Condominium ownership estates in real property consist of an individual interest in an apartment or commercial unit and an undivided common interest in the common areas in the condo project, such as the land, parking areas, elevators, stairways, and exterior structure. Each condominium unit is a statutory entity that may be mortgaged, taxed, sold, or otherwise transferred in ownership, separately and independently of all other units in the condo project. Units are separately assessed and taxed. While some condominium associations reserve the right of first refusal when a sale is proposed, and many restrict the right to rent out the unit, the individual owner has many more options than when owning a proprietary lease in a cooperative.

A condominium development is created by the filing of a condominium map or condominium plan. Sometimes, the investor will change the ownership structure of an existing building. In this case, each tenant purchases a unit plus a percentage of the common areas and the land from the present property owner or the investor, who acts as an intermediary. Most often, however, condominium projects are multifamily communities built by speculative developers for sale to individual buyers.

Covenants, Conditions, and Restrictions Declaration (CC&R Declaration)

Most state laws enable and regulate the formation and control of condominiums. The Articles of Incorporation sets up an owners' association (HOA), which follows appropriate state law and defines the property, common elements, easement, and type of ownership. This owners' association operates in the same way as a cooperative board of directors.

The rights, privileges, and limitations of the association directors are controlled by the bylaws set forth in the CC&R declaration. The board assesses fees for common areas maintenance and association operation costs. It typically authorizes the association to designate the insurance liability of the association and of the individual owners, prorate the common property tax bill among the units, regulate property use, establish a reserve fund for repairs and improvements, and maintain the common elements as described in the governing documents. The association is usually empowered to employ outside professional management.

The CC&Rs often provide for the sale, lease, or transfer of rights in the property. It is not uncommon to require that prospective tenants be qualified by the management company. Moreover, some prospective purchasers may have difficulty obtaining a mortgage if a high percentage of the building is tenant occupied.

In many states, condominium statutes, although similar to cooperative laws, are less demanding. Because each owner holds fee simple title to a unit, failure by one unit owner to pay a mortgage does not endanger the financing of the entire project, as it might with a cooperative project. It is for this reason that condominium ownership has become so popular.

The association may regulate the resale of individual units. Resales are often subject to the right of first refusal by the other owners, minimum credit and reference criteria for the purchaser, or approval by the owners' association. The regulation of resale of condominiums must not be used as a facade for discrimination. For this reason, the restriction of resale rights to condominiums has been severely curtailed by the courts.

The Property Manager's Role

The rapid expansion of the residential condominium market has opened new opportunities for property managers. Condominium management, like cooperative management, is concerned mainly with maintaining the integrity of the premises, ensuring ongoing service to occupants, and attaining other mutual goals of the owners. Before taking over an association, the manager should thoroughly read the CC&Rs, carefully study recent operating reports, and review the amounts in any reserve funds.

The manager is usually responsible for billing and collecting assessments and keeping accounting records. Generally, the manager maintains all common areas and advises the owners' association. The property manager usually provides the cost data necessary to draw up an operating budget and make individual assessments for maintenance and reserves, constantly balancing the owners' desires for lower maintenance fees against the need to spend money to preserve the property. A reserve fund is typically required by some financiers but definitely should be established to save for major repairs, keeping in mind that some very large expenses will be accrued when the property must be repainted and the parking lot repaved.

Before taking on condominium or cooperative management, the manager should closely study local and state law and governing documents. Legal structures vary even within the same state. For example, Florida now requires a Condominium Association Manager's license for anyone who manages an association that totals 50 units or has a budget or combined budgets of at least $100,000. Some states require condominium managers to hold property manager or real estate licenses. This trend towards increasing regulation and licensing requirements is likely to be followed by other states.

Like the board of directors of a cooperative, the owners' association is an elective body, not a permanent group. Thus, the manager is often given full control of building operations to ensure stability and continuity of operation.

In some areas of the country condominiums are predominantly used as second homes—that is, they are occupied by the owner for a portion of the year and then rented during the off-season. A year-round property manager may assume responsibility for leasing the owners' apartments during their absence, but as a separate and distinct duty outside association management.

Management Contract

The manager should insist on a written contract describing the rights and duties of each party. Areas that should be covered in detail are collection of assessments, accounting and budgeting, maintenance standards, personnel employment, legal status of the manager as an agent, emergency spending, and handling of owners' money. The management contract should also specify the amount of compensation and other terms of the agreement (hours, cancellation). The manager should negotiate a contract for a guaranteed and reasonably long period knowing that the owners' association governing board will change frequently.

The **management pricing worksheet** (Figure 9.2 in Chapter 9) is an excellent place to define the time and expense that goes into condominium management. Without such a guideline, the manager may never receive adequate compensation for the time and effort expended in managing the property. Note, however, that the initial agreement for a new condominium is drawn up between the developer, acting on behalf of the owners, and the property manager. Not until the board of directors is elected does control pass from the developer into the hands of an owners' organization. To prevent a developer from retaining control over the property when the owners' association should be functioning independently, many states have enacted legislation imposing a maximum allowable term for management contracts negotiated by developers.

Fannie Mae Requirements

On the national level, the secondary mortgage markets impose requirements when underwriting purchase loans. Fannie Mae regulations require that developers turn over a condominium association to the owners as soon as a specific percentage of units have been sold and that reserve funds for major repairs be established. Some lenders will not make loans to prospective purchasers if too many of the units are tenant-occupied.

Required Information at Time of Transfer

At the time that management responsibility is transferred to the manager, he or she will require the general types of information and records discussed in Chapter 3. Condominium managers need in addition copies of the covenants, conditions, and restrictions for the building's use; other controlling documents; and any warranties held by the developer and still in force.

Insurance

The owners' association usually purchases insurance to cover all the common elements. The individual unit owner must purchase a condominium policy to cover the owner's personal property and any additions or alterations made to the unit. This policy is often referred to as *HO-6*.

The property manager should continually emphasize to the individual owners and the association the importance of carrying adequate insurance. Insurance claims can get complicated—for example, a washing machine hose may disconnect and flood a top floor unit while the owner is on vacation. The occupants of the unit below, which also flooded, happen to be out of town on business. As a result the leaking water is not noticed for several days, at which time it is discovered that six units have water damage, several quite extensively. This scenario is not uncommon, unfortunately. The insurance companies of each unit and that of the association are involved in sorting out the liability.

MANAGING PLANNED UNIT DEVELOPMENTS (PUDS)

The **planned unit development (PUD)** is a highly popular concept in land development that is designed to produce a high density of building improvements and maximum utilization of open spaces. These neighborhoods often mix residential with common recreational areas. Owners not only own their own houses, but they have an interest in the community homeowners' association that manages the common areas. The common areas can be quite minimal or quite extensive, including parkland, pools and golf courses, clubhouse facilities, and jogging and biking paths.

Covenants, Conditions, and Restrictions (CC&Rs)

Usually, the developer creates the **covenants, conditions, and restrictions (CC&Rs)** to enhance the overall quality and desirability of the neighborhood and to keep up the values. Once the developer has sold out, he or she will turn over enforcement of the CC&Rs to the community association. The homeowners are bound by the CC&Rs. Some restrictions might include certain house colors, where to park a boat or recreational vehicle, prohibiting certain types of fences, number and kind of pets permitted, and so on.

Property Manager's Role

In practice, the management of a PUD is very similar to that of a condominium. The manager is expected to see that the common property is maintained while, at the same time, keeping fees as low as possible.

MANAGING COMMUNITIES

Education for the Manager

The Community Associations Institute (CAI) sponsors an extensive educational program including a professional management and development program consisting of courses of training in every aspect of condominium and homeowner association operation. Successful completion of the course, coupled with employment experience as a manager of a community association, earns the designation of Professional Community Association Manager (PCAM).

The CAI is an independent, nonprofit research and educational organization formed in 1973 to serve as a clearinghouse and research center on community associations. The CAI does not represent any one profession or interest group; rather, it supports the process of creating and operating a successful viable community association. Its membership is open to anyone involved with that process.

Marketing Cooperatives and Condominiums and PUDs

In general, cooperatives and condominiums are marketed in a manner similar to that used for prestige apartments and other luxury residences. Most developers use their own or outside sales agents for the initial sale of such properties, but the manager should be able to suggest marketing and publicity techniques when called on to maintain the occupancy level. Most large condominium and cooperative projects are advertised in newspapers and local magazines because media publicity can be a cost-effective means of presenting the project to the buying public.

Some cooperatives and condominiums are marketed toward a particular segment of the population. For the military market, for example, communities are established to cater primarily to retirees of a specific branch of the armed services; others target golfers or boaters; whereas still other projects are designed for the elderly. The property manager involved must be especially current with and follow fair housing marketing and management practices when catering to a special group.

Condominium and cooperative managers must modify the financial reports used by apartment managers, discussed in Chapter 9. They must prepare an annual operating budget, monthly income and expenditure statements, and yearly cash flow reports. However, the more complex system of ownership and the fact that the residents are also the owners creates unique budgeting problems for condominiums and cooperatives. Because there is technically no income in a not-for-profit association, specialized training, such as that provided through the CAI, is required of association managers.

Need for Professional Planning

On the whole, many condominiums and cooperatives suffer from a lack of long-range planning. A professional property manager can avoid the problems that often arise when a condominium or cooperative development chooses inadequate service contractors in a misguided attempt to cut operating costs. Emphasis should be on managing for value rather than for profit.

Importance of Accurate Budget Projections

In budget projections the manager should make allowances for inflation and increasing rates, because the cost of all forms of energy continues to rise. Reserve funds should be budgeted for contingencies and replacement of major items such as roofs and central heating and air-conditioning equipment. The amount should increase as the property ages and more repairs are needed. It is a disservice to the community as a whole to create inadequate budgets in response to pressure from the owners' association or to base any activity on internal political considerations.

Income

Condominium income comes almost entirely from assessments to members (owners of units), and income is budgeted to meet expenses.

Expenses

Most expenses relating to or arising from fee simple ownership of a unit are the sole responsibility of the owner. Some examples are utilities, interior decorating, interior maintenance, condominium homeowners' insurance covering occupant improvements, and appliance or fixture replacement. In some condominium projects, however, water supply and utilities for electricity, heating, and air-conditioning may not be metered separately to units. In that situation, a unit owner will pay a pro rata share of the total condominium expense.

Common elements The expenses of **common elements** of the project are allocated among the unit owners based on their percentage ratios. The common elements of a project include not only structural portions of a building such as foundation, walls, and roof; but common walkways, parking, and other areas for the use and benefit of all owners. Swimming pools, recreation and laundry rooms, storage areas, and the like are considered common elements.

Limited common elements In addition to the common elements, some condominiums establish limited common elements. These are areas such as porches, patios, or storage closets designated for the private use of the unit owner but not owned in fee simple as part of the unit itself. The unit owner must follow CC&R rules for these spaces as well.

Calculating pro rata share An owner's pro rata share for each unit is determined by state statute and/or the ratio the square footage of the unit bears to the total square footage of all units in the project. It is expressed as a percentage, such as 1.034 percent. This percentage is established in the original condominium declaration (called *unit ownership declaration* in many states) and is the basis for allocating expenses applicable to all units. The monthly pro rata charge is allocated to each unit for recurring budgeted items, which is based on the percentage set forth in the declaration, and billed to each occupant as a regular assessment. Reserves for replacement also should be calculated in and collected as part of the regular monthly assessment.

Capital expenditures If the need for an unbudgeted capital expenditure arises, a special assessment will be necessary, which must be levied by a vote of either the board of directors of the association or of the owners themselves, depending on the condominium declaration and bylaws. An experienced association manager will keep such surprise special assessments to a minimum by proper use of reserves. If reserve funds are inadequate, special assessments can run into the hundreds or thousands of dollars for each owner, depending on the total required for the expenditure. Such an occurrence can create severe problems for the condominium owners and for the association itself.

■ MANAGEMENT FEES

Cost-per-Unit or Pricing Worksheet

Condominium and cooperative management fees can be calculated using either the cost-per-unit method or the pricing worksheet explained in Chapter 9. Condominiums and cooperatives that contract only for an accounting or consulting service can be charged a minimum fee, but there should be an additional charge for attendance at more than one board meeting per year.

With the per-unit method, a surcharge should be added for the additional time spent satisfying a board of directors or an owners' association. The manager should also charge additional fees to cover the time expended on other specified duties such as attending board or association meetings or developing a newsletter for circulation to stockholders or owners.

Flat Fees

There is a compelling reason why the management figure should be a flat fee rather than a percentage of gross income, as is used for residential apartment fees. A percentage fee gives the residential manager incentive to raise rents and thereby gain extra profit. The revenue from cooperatives and condominiums comes not from rents but from monthly assessments to cover operating costs. Managers who contract for a percentage fee profit more by allowing operating costs to skyrocket because this increases the monthly assessments (total revenue) and thereby, the percentage management fee. They also profit from increases in real property taxes and reserve funds.

Because a percentage fee would place the owner and the manager in opposite camps, a flat fee should always be used when dealing with condominium and cooperative properties. In general, the manager also should quote a fee slightly higher than that on the estimate because any increase in the management fee will have to come from negotiation with the board or association, at which time competitive bids will usually be solicited.

■ LEASING COOPERATIVE AND CONDOMINIUM UNITS

Many condo and co-op units are not owner-occupied. Serious problems may arise if tenants are not carefully qualified or do not follow association mandates.

Rental may be handled individually by the owner, by a third-party manager, or by or through the owners' association, either on an individual unit basis or as part of a rental pool. Under a pool arrangement, all rental income from all units in the condominium is placed in a fund that is shared equally after management expenses. Thus, an owner with a unit that may not be attractive to prospective tenants can participate fairly with units for which there is higher demand.

In any event, the apartment rental principles discussed in Chapter 11 are applicable to renting condominiums and cooperatives. The only real difference is that the association declaration, bylaws, and resident rules and regulations take precedence over the terms of the lease. For this reason, a manager should secure legal assistance in drafting a clause, which should appear in each lease: Tenant occupying (the owner's unit) acknowledges that the premises are a condominium project governed by a condominium declaration, bylaws, and rules and regulations. A copy of these documents has been furnished to tenant. Tenant agrees to abide by these rules and regulations. Tenant understands that violation of any of them may be grounds for eviction.

■ MANAGING MANUFACTURED HOME PARKS

Manufactured homes (formerly referred to as "mobile homes") have changed a lot over the years. They are no longer trailer houses being pulled down the road or rusting exteriors next door to an automotive dump. However, these images have been hard to overcome. Today's manufactured home is efficient, practical, and affordable housing for 8 percent of Americans. Some are even luxurious.

Today, the **manufactured home park** is a combination of individual home ownership and homesite rental. It is usually an orderly, well groomed entity and sometimes is indistinguishable from a more traditional development. Once the manufactured home has been moved to the site, most are never moved again, as their value comes from the desirability of the community.

Inexpensive Housing

Manufactured housing can be purchased for far less than it costs to build a traditional home. This is appealing to those with lower incomes, including the elderly on fixed incomes. Today's manufactured home is larger than ever before; 83 percent of the manufactured homes have three or more bedrooms, and the average single-wide has been growing in size more than 2 percent per year. More than 1 million Californians live in manufactured homes and there are more than 2,000 manufactured home parks in New York state.

Near-Elderly Housing

Under the Fair Housing Laws, certain housing is exempt from the law requiring access to housing by families with children. The **U.S. Department of Housing and Urban Development (HUD)** defines "near elderly" as 55 and older and "elderly" as 62 and older. Once a community qualifies for this designation from HUD, it can refuse to rent to anyone with children, and many manufactured home parks do just that; in fact, some even market themselves as housing for the elderly. Marketing to these folks is financially sound: near-elderly ages 55 to 64 have the highest per capita income, and seniors age 65 and over have the most discretionary income.

Role of the Property Manager

Manufactured home park management requires a combination of the skills of managing apartment communities with those of managing condos and co-ops. A common task is making sure that the tenants clearly understand the rules and regulations of the park community. If the park consists of rented manufactured homes, then the manager collects rents for the units. In other situations, the home is owner-occupied, and the manager collects a rental fee for the site.

The duties of a property manager vary widely depending on the type of park being managed. In some communities, managers will do little more than show space, collect rents, and prepare reports for the owner. Those managing "seniors'" parks will no doubt perform these traditional duties in addition to scheduling community events that involve many of the members. In fact, creating and inspiring a community feeling is one of the best ways to foster referrals and waiting lists.

In any event, the manager generally is charged with minimally maintaining the value of the park, and often with increasing the value by improving condition and appearance. Every attractive, well-maintained property will attract sound tenants and sell for a higher price when put on the market, even when compared with a poorly maintained park bringing in the same amount of income.

The manager may be directed to track other sources of income from laundromats, vending machines, convenience stores, and the like. Computer software can help greatly. Anyone specializing in mobile park management should consult *Managing Mobile Home Parks*, a book published by the Institute of Real Estate Management (IREM).

■ MANAGING SUBSIDIZED HOUSING

Actual construction and operation of public housing projects for low-income families has traditionally been the responsibility of local governments. In 1965, Congress authorized the U.S. Department of Housing and Urban Development (HUD) to provide financial assistance to local housing authorities for the acquisition and operation of existing buildings or privately constructed new housing for low-income tenants. Under the 1968 Housing and Urban Development Act, the Federal Housing Administration (FHA), an agency of HUD, was authorized to encourage private participation in the development and construction of housing for low-income families through rental and mortgage insurance programs. FHA-insured mortgages and government subsidies were awarded to nonprofit cooperative groups for the construction of low-income housing.

In the late 1970s and early 1980s, housing funds were made available to private owners to build and manage affordable housing for the low, very low, and extremely low income population. These units are available throughout the country. Although owned and managed by private owners and agents, the units must adhere to strict HUD enforcement regarding verification of resident income and meet very high standards of physical condition.

Today, HUD is pushing for the privatization and project-based management of public housing. As there are 3,400 public housing authorities in the United States responsible for more than 1.3 million units, cooperating with HUD is a great opportunity for many property managers. These complex networks are in sharp contrast to private management, which often gives employees authority to make many decisions on-site.

Each government program comes with its own set of rules and criteria. This discussion will highlight certain elements common to each program, but the property manager truly becomes a specialist when managing subsidized housing.

Section 8 Housing Assistance Programs

Single family homes or apartments in public housing buildings covered under the HUD **Section 8** Housing Assistance Payments Program are rented on a subsidized basis. A low or very low-income family will pay up to 30 percent of its adjusted monthly income; HUD pays the landlord the difference between that and market rent. Income eligibility for occupants of public housing varies according to geographic area and the number of dependents in the family.

In 1996, HUD established the Real Estate Assessment Center (REAC) in order to assess the stock of private HUD housing in the United States. This set of stringent physical standards requires owners and agents to maintain HUD housing to the highest standards of safe, decent, and sanitary housing. REAC has been instrumental in changing HUD housing for the better.

Vouchers for Private Owners

In addition to public housing, the local housing authority in some cities contracts with private investors for housing for eligible recipients. Tenant screening is left up to the private landlord that chooses to accept the vouchers awarded to the resident by the local public housing authority. HUD has developed several standard lease forms to be used with public housing, and the property manager must use these forms and be familiar with their provisions.

Tenant Rental Assistance Certification System (TRACS)

HUD developed a computer system to improve the management of all assisted housing programs. The Tenant Rental Assistance Certification System (called **TRACS**) gives HUD a central information system used to verify subsidy calculations. TRACS has automated the collection of tenant data and provides HUD offices with an online database, significantly reducing HUD's paperwork. TRACS is already reducing fraud, speeding up the turnaround of information processing, and improving the management of and budgeting for subsidy programs.

Need for Professional Property Management

All subsidized public housing developments, of whatever type, have a common need for ongoing, competent management. Since its inception, low-income public housing has suffered from both inadequate property management and bureaucratic mismanagement. Effective January 31, 2010, all public and private affordable housing owners must use HUD's Enterprise Income Verification system (EIV). EIV provides data from TRACS and both the Social Security Administration and the Heath and Human Services New Hire database to ensure that residents are making a full and adequate disclosure of household income to landlords to reduce waste and fraud of HUD funding. This will allow more households to take advantage of available federal programs.

In an effort to stay solvent, properties are funded with many types of federal funding, each of which have specific rules and regulations and require great attention to detail to stay in compliance. Thus, the need for trained, affordable professionals is greater then ever.

Professional property managers who choose affordable housing as a career have a number of options for specific training and certification through local HUD offices and state finance agencies. Some of the available certifications follow:

- National Affordable Housing Management Association (HAHMA): Certified Professional of Occupancy (CPO), National Affordable Housing Professional (HAHP), National Affordable Housing Professional Executive (HAPH-e)

- National Apartment Association (NAA) in cooperation with NAHMA): Specialist in Housing Credit Management (SHCM)

- National Home Builders Association (NHBA): Housing Credit Certified Professional (HCCP)

HUD is attempting to correct the lack of trained management by conducting management courses, sometimes in connection with local colleges, and by certifying managers who have graduated from HUD-approved management courses. Additionally, most of the certification programs offered by trade associations contain specific courses in managing low-income housing.

Management Plan

Although low-income housing is managed in much the same way as other types of housing, the larger dwelling units and greater population density, typical characteristics of public housing, create heavy use and significantly higher maintenance costs. Tenant turnover, vacancy rates, rent loss, and collection costs are also higher.

The manager should outline specific problems in each housing project: for example, disadvantages of the neighborhood (such as vandalism); the physical condition of the interior and exterior of the premises; the quality of present building operation, administration, and staff; and the current state of tenant relations. Then the manager can decide which areas need personal attention and which areas can be delegated to a subordinate.

An economic study of the property's financing structure provides the data necessary to draw up a realistic and comprehensive budget. Existing rental rates should be compared to the rental income needed to meet projected expenses; then plans (such as an on-site program or a stricter rental collection policy) for meeting extra costs can be formulated. Each month the manager should measure actual progress against the prognosis and make appropriate adjustments.

Consistency with tenants   A consistent Tenant Selection Plan (TSP) for initial tenant screening helps to avoid later undesirable conduct. At a minimum, the TSP should include credit and criminal checks. Landlord references may uncover a history of property damage, noise complaints, or other problems. The manager should not tolerate nor cater to anyone abusing the system.

All residents should receive a copy of the building regulations, clearly establishing the expectations and obligations of both parties. The manager must firmly and reliably enforce those regulations, particularly those concerning pets, maximum number of residents per apartment, security precautions, trash handling, noise, and prompt rental payments.

Responsiveness   Residents want to live in a building that is efficiently operated and maintained, and they can often devise a better way of coping with a particular problem such as building security. An open dialogue shows the tenants that management is doing its best to keep the property safe and clean, encouraging their cooperation in these efforts. Repairs should be made quickly, as good repair service shows that management is sincere about maintaining the building.

Rent collection   The system for rent collection should be inflexible. If the rent is not paid within the specified period, appropriate legal action should be taken. This may sound harsh, but there are compelling reasons for management to insist on prompt rental payments.

If rent delinquencies are tolerated, payments on the mortgage and other expenses for the property will be delayed and late penalties incurred. Lax collection procedures are actually a disservice to delinquent tenants, because those tenants are thus allowed to build up a larger debt than they can afford to repay. The manager also is being unfair to residents who pay their rent promptly, for rental rates will eventually have to be raised to cover the delinquencies.

Building strong tenant/landlord relations   Rapport between tenants and management can be improved by hiring a person with skills or training such as those demonstrated by a social worker to handle tenant relations. This individual can act as a conduit of information from the residents to the manager and can assist with programs involving tenant participation. In many cases, a qualified representative can solve minor problems before they become large enough to require management's attention. Also, a manager and staff who are familiar with local public service organizations such as free legal aid societies, low-cost medical clinics, job placement centers, and religious or ethnic organizations can enhance landlord-tenant rapport and help the occupants solve their financial and domestic problems.

Occupant responsibility   Tenants should be educated about management procedures and policies and about their own responsibility in the maintenance of the building. Many of them will have to be shown how to care for the equipment in their apartments and how to report maintenance problems. They should be encouraged to take pride in their homes and to report disruptive or destructive behavior. As tenants become more responsible, they become less prone to vandalism.

Tenant Management Participation and Ownership

Groups advocating tenant ownership of public housing have become more active in recent years, joined by consumer and tenant rights organizations and charitable institutions interested in improving social and living conditions for those below the poverty level. Also, management by tenants has long been a dream of many tenant organizations, but only in a few locations has it become a reality. Often local governments are supportive as a means of relieving themselves of ownership and management problems.

When supported by the authorities and by owners, it can be a feasible alternative to nontenant management. In recognition of this fact, HUD has published a rule, "Resident Management in Public Housing," which appeared in the September 7, 1988, *Federal Register*. Many HUD offices have reprinted this issue of the *Register* and make it available for distribution to interested parties.

The first step for a property manager when approached by tenants desiring participation in management (or one interested in encouraging tenant participation in management) should be to obtain a copy of this rule. However, experience shows that professional management is still required even in buildings owned by the tenants.

Drug Abuse and Other Crime

Managers of many subsidized rental properties must cope with drug dealing and high crime rates. To help meet this challenge, Congress passed the Drug Free Workplace Act of 1988 as part of omnibus drug legislation. Based on the provisions in the act, public housing authorities (PHA) receiving grants, operating subsidies, or annual contributions are required to submit a drug-free workplace certification along with an authority's operating budget. All PHAs must also submit a certification with applications for funds.

Companies that contract with a PHA for goods or services in amounts of $25,000 or more must certify to the PHA that they will maintain a drug-free workplace.

These contractors or consultants must publish a statement on employee use of controlled substances in the workplace. They must establish a drug-free awareness program to inform employees of the dangers of drug abuse and of company policy with regard to drug use, the availability of drug counseling or other employee assistance programs, and the penalties that may be imposed for drug-abuse violations.

Contractors also must notify federal agencies of employees convicted of criminal drug statutes, and they must notify federal agencies that they are requiring satisfactory participation by convicted employees in drug-abuse assistance programs. Finally, they must provide a good-faith effort to maintain a drug-free workplace.

The term *drug-related criminal activity* means the illegal manufacture, sale, distribution, use, or possession with intent to manufacture, sell, distribute, or use a controlled substance. To assist in providing a drug-free climate within a project, HUD has written a model paragraph for leases to assist managers in removing tenants who deal in drugs or become involved in other criminal activities. The paragraph also serves to amend leases already in force; a 30-day notice must be given to tenants beforehand. The paragraph is as follows:

> The tenant, any member of the tenant's household, or a guest or other person under the tenant's control shall not engage in drug related criminal activity, on or near the Housing Authority's premises, while the tenant is a tenant in public housing, and such criminal activity shall be cause for termination of tenancy.

To further assist managers in their fight against crime, HUD has proposed new rules for allowing police and housing inspector searches in several instances: in emergencies, in common areas of public housing, in vacant apartments, and when consent is given. The proposal includes inserting a consent clause into standard lease documents, which would in effect make the consent to a search part of the lease agreement. This approach is controversial, and, while giving management more power to reduce crime, may encroach on low-income tenants' constitutional rights.

The Future of Subsidized Housing Management

In the early 1990s, subsidized housing was perceived as deteriorating and crime-ridden housing, but this image has changed over the last 20 years through the government program HOPE IV. Studies conducted in 2009 by the Urban Institute indicate that many of the former residents received Housing Choice Vouchers (HCV) or moved into mixed-income developments now live in better housing and in safer environments. Unfortunately, "hard-to-house" families—those with multiple issues that make them ineligible for mixed-income housing or unable to negotiate the private market with a Housing Choice Voucher—have often been shifted from distressed development to another. Both private and government involvement continue to be challenged to meet the needs of every member of society, even those with low incomes.

■ MANAGING HOUSING FOR THE ELDERLY

Americans are living longer. According to the U. S. Census Bureau, the population in the 55 to 64 age group will grow by 75 percent until the year 2020. Many will continue to live in their homes; still others will move into communities specifically designed with the older person in mind. As previously noted, many of the aging population have spendable income, and many of these are moving into manufactured home parks or upscale condo, co-op, or apartment communities.

Age-Restricted Housing

The senior housing industry defines five different types of senior housing. With proper planning, developers and managers can significantly carve out a niche specializing in senior housing, meeting the needs of the fastest growing population segment, those over 55. The description of each type of housing follows.

Active adult communities   Those in the 55–65 age group typically sell a larger home and move into an active, resort-oriented community offering single-family detached/attached housing. Residents are looking for a lifestyle, meaning that they want recreational amenities, security, and social functions. They will probably live there for 10–15 years. Many of these homes are condominium-owned, so there is a definite need for professional management, not only of the housing, but also of all of the associated amenities.

Independent living developments   The healthy 70–75 age group is willing to move down in size, quality, and range of recreational amenities. Recreational facilities, such as a gym, pools, and garden areas, are more important than golf courses and more active recreation. Many will purchase in condominium communities with ownership of zero-lot lines, courtyard homes, or attached townhouse units, all of which require professional management. Still others will seek out rentals in a multifamily facility with an on-site concierge or staff.

Congregate care communities   Elders live on their own with a minimum of assistance, but shelter, social, health care, and support services are provided in this contractual arrangement. Often, although residents may cook in their own units, they share common dining and social areas. Congregate care primarily serves those 75–80 years of age, usually single women and a few couples. Indoor social activities are far more desirable than outdoor recreational facilities, especially in colder climates. Congregate care management may offer services similar to those offered in hotels. Many of these communities are developed as cooperatives, retaining the right to purchase back the apartment, and developing waiting lists.

Assisted living facilities   Although not generally licensed as a nursing home, these facilities offer more personal care to the resident who needs assistance with daily activities, such as help with dressing, hygiene, and medications as needed, but does not require round-the-clock assistance. Usually, these facilities can more easily respond to acute medical emergencies and provide related medical services. The market consists primarily of women in their mid-80s. Most of these facilities are designed for singles and not double occupancy.

Nursing homes   Round-the-clock nursing home care is more similar to a hospital model than to typical rental situations, and therefore is more likely to be developed by nursing care specialists.

Living Arrangements for People with Differing Needs

Today, the aging baby boomers realize that they will no doubt live longer than their parents, and it is likely that they eventually will need some kind of assisted care. Some communities are planned and developed so that people can move in while they are still healthy and mobile and enjoy an active lifestyle, with the idea that as they need more care, they can receive it at the community. Although this is the age group that will eventually need more care, they are not eager to be mixed with those requiring that care. From a psychological and marketing viewpoint, it is easiest to mix congregate care housing with assisted living arrangements than independent living and congregate care.

Special Requirements

Housing for the elderly requires attention to the original design. Considerations include eliminating steps, if possible; modifying doorknobs and bathtubs; and including brighter lighting. Whenever possible, the manager who specializes in housing for the elderly should be involved from the beginning when rehabbing or constructing a new facility. Care must be taken to ensure that each unit is as accessible as it can be for those who are slower moving or otherwise limited in physical ability.

Section 202

Many of the elderly require housing assistance. Of the quarter-million applicants for federally assisted housing programs, more than a third are elderly persons. The profile is a frail woman in her mid-70s, living alone on less than $10,000 per year. Statistically, in public housing, 34 percent are elderly, under Section 515 (rural housing); 39 percent are elderly; and 42 percent of individuals living in Section 8 housing are elderly. Government program **Section 202** provides capital funding for new construction, rehab, or acquisition of nonprofit facilities for the very low-income elderly. Unfortunately, 202 funding to build 5 to 15 units is often viewed as too small to be self sustaining.

Property Management Skills

Managers of these facilities are called upon to facilitate social events, manage medical emergencies, provide most housekeeping, provide meals, and manage the traditional operating reports to owners. Marketing skills are needed here more than ever. As more communities are being built, there is increasing competition for these tenants. It goes without saying that such managers must have a real affinity for and care for the aging population.

■ SUMMARY

The manager of alternative forms of multifamily ownership such as cooperative, condominium, or planned unit developments (PUDs) works for a group of owner-occupants who have slightly different goals than either apartment building owners or tenants. Condominium management is concerned primarily with maintaining the physical integrity of the premises and achieving the mutual goals of the owners, and the manager has no responsibility for occupancy levels.

Under cooperative ownership a corporation or trust holds title to the property, and stockholders are granted proprietary leases that give them the right to occupy a unit of the building subject to rules and regulations. The purchaser in a condominium receives fee simple title to the unit, plus undivided common interest with the other residents in the common building elements and the land.

In both types of properties, a board of directors often hires a professional manager to preserve the major structural elements, maintain equipment, clean exterior and interior common areas, ensure operating efficiency, provide services to the occupants, and set up a reserve fund. The association or corporation should purchase enough insurance to cover all common areas and elements, and the tenants or unit owner must obtain the proper insurance to cover the occupant's personal property.

Financial reports for cooperatives and condominiums are basically modified versions of those used for apartment buildings. Either the per-unit method of computing management fees or the management pricing worksheet can be used for cooperatives and condominiums, but additional charges should be included for the extra time involved in communicating with and satisfying multiple owners.

Most subsidized housing is constructed with financial assistance from the U.S. Department of Housing and Urban Development (HUD). HUD requires the use of a computer system, TRACS, thus creating paperless reporting. Effective January 31, 2010, all public and private affordable housing owners must use HUD's Enterprise Income Verification system (EIV) to ensure that residents are making a full and adequate disclosure of household income to landlords to reduce waste and fraud of HUD funding. Managers who work directly for HUD have detailed procedural guidelines to follow and numerous records to keep. Actual physical operation of low-income housing is not substantially different from that of other residential properties. The key to success in managing subsidized housing lies in the ability to be firm, equitable, and responsive to tenants while instilling in them a sense of responsibility for the condition of the property.

As baby boomers age, there is an increasing demand for housing to meet the needs of the elderly by including handicap accessibility. Five types of senior housing are defined: active adult communities (55–65); independent living developments (70–75); congregate care (75–80); assisted living (typically mid-80s); and nursing homes. The first two mentioned often buy into condominium communities with professional management. The trend is to combine assisted living, partial care, and full nursing care in one facility, which may be a cooperative ownership arrangement with buybacks and waiting lists. Property managers specializing in senior housing face many different problems and definitely must care about and for seniors.

■ **CASE STUDY**

MANAGING A CONDOMINIUM

John Slocum has been hired by a condominium association to take over its management. The previous management company had written the contract so that it would be paid a percentage of the unit owners' monthly assessment fees. Consequently, those fees had more than doubled in the last few years although the unit owners felt that very little maintenance has been performed. Also, an elderly woman who needed a wheelchair was ready to file a complaint with fair housing officials because she was not given a ramp or a nearby parking space. Other owners had additional maintenance complaints. John sees a challenge.

1. What was wrong with the previous company's charging a percentage of monthly fees?
2. What form of management fee should John propose and why?
3. How should John tackle this project?

■ **CASE STUDY**

MANAGING SUBSIDIZED HOUSING

Judy Kelleher has recently taken over the management of a subsidized housing project. Unfortunately, drug dealing and crime in the project has reached such proportions that law-abiding tenants are being harassed and generally terrorized. Kelleher firmly believes in the principles of low-cost subsidized housing and is determined to improve the conditions of the housing project.

1. What can Kelleher do to reduce drug dealing and crime in the project?
2. How can Kelleher improve the social conditions of the project?

■ REVIEW QUESTIONS

1. Unlike a manager of an investor-owned apartment building, the manager of a cooperative or condominium has no responsibility for maintaining
   a. occupancy levels.
   b. common areas.
   c. communication with owners.
   d. administrative functions.

2. A PUD is similar in management to a(n)
   a. triplex.
   b. public housing development.
   c. condominium.
   d. investor-owned apartment project.

3. In managing condominiums and cooperatives, emphasis is on managing for
   a. value.
   b. profit.
   c. the short term.
   d. absentee owners.

4. The condominium legal structure has been more popular than the cooperative because
   a. more condominiums have been built.
   b. the occupant is responsible for the interior of the unit occupied.
   c. condominium owners do not risk losing their units in event of default of the owning association.
   d. condominium owners may hire professional property managers.

5. Generally, property taxes are assessed separately on each unit in a
   a. cooperative.
   b. condominium.
   c. limited partnership project.
   d. time-share project.

6. When managing a manufactured home park, income can come from all of the following sources EXCEPT
   a. providing nursing services.
   b. renting the site.
   c. renting the house.
   d. providing a laundromat on-site.

7. Developing a sense of community spirit is often useful in encouraging referrals in
   a. a loft building.
   b. subsidized housing.
   c. manufactured home parks.
   d. office parks.

8. In most states, the Articles of Incorporation
   a. are more stringent than rules and regulations for most cooperatives.
   b. establish owners' associations under most state laws.
   c. prohibit time-share arrangements.
   d. require independent professional management of the owners' association.

9. When a manager is concerned with the physical design of the property and who may have to handle social events and medical emergencies, he or she may be managing a
   a. condominium.
   b. cooperative.
   c. housing for the elderly.
   d. planned unit development.

10. The initial agreement for management of a new condominium is usually between the manager and the
    a. president of the owners' association.
    b. developer of the project.
    c. board of directors of the owners' association.
    d. mortgage company.

11. Condominium and cooperative managers generally use the same financial reporting system as that used by
    a. certified public accountants.
    b. treasurers of corporations.
    c. managers of apartment buildings.
    d. owners of single-family homes.

12. With regard to insurance, the condominium owner must
    a. buy separate flood insurance.
    b. provide extra liability insurance.
    c. be written in as a co-insured on the common elements.
    d. purchase an HO-6 condominium policy.

13. The management fee for a condominium generally is
    a. prorated among the occupants according to their interests in the property.
    b. expressed as a percentage of revenue.
    c. divided on a per-unit basis.
    d. greater on units sublet by their owners.

14. The initial sellout of cooperative and condominium properties is
    a. best done with television advertising.
    b. often handled by the first homeowners to buy units.
    c. usually accomplished through display and classified ads.
    d. first registered with the Securities and Exchange Commission.

15. Fannie Mae regulates condominiums
    a. through the Community Associations Institute.
    b. in cooperation with HUD.
    c. by prescribing standards for condominium mortgages that it purchases in the secondary market.
    d. by veto power over the actions of the board of directors.

16. Public housing projects for low-income families
    a. have traditionally been the responsibility of local government.
    b. include only newly built projects.
    c. do not involve participation with the private sector.
    d. were authorized by HUD in the 1940s.

17. The manager of low-cost housing should consider employing a person to handle tenant relations because
    a. tenants try to take advantage of management with their complaints.
    b. this person can save the manager time by screening tenant complaints.
    c. this person can provide extra service to the tenants and gain their cooperation.
    d. supervising maintenance is a full-time job for the manager.

18. Under HUD Section 8 housing,
    a. the tenant gets housing at no cost.
    b. housing is rented on a subsidized basis.
    c. the tenant pays up to 50 percent of his or her adjusted monthly income.
    d. the standards for eligibility based on income are the same throughout the United States.

19. Collection of rent from tenants in subsidized units
    a. should follow the same firm policy as in privately owned housing.
    b. may be flexible because of the subsidies being paid.
    c. is not of concern because subsidies paid will make up for any losses.
    d. should allow longer grace periods than a private project.

20. HUD contracts with property managers of subsidized housing
    a. vary widely from place to place.
    b. require the property manager to develop report forms.
    c. are generally for a term of years.
    d. are without regard to qualification for the work.

13

OFFICE PROPERTY

■ KEY TERMS

Absorption rate
Base rate
Base rent
BOMA office building
   classifications

Dominant portion
Facilities manager
Institute of Real Estate
   Management (IREM)

Rentable area
Shared tenant services
Usable area

■ LEARNING OBJECTIVES

At the end of this chapter, the student will be able to

1. explain how important regional and neighborhood analysis is to the property manager drawing up a management plan for an office building;

2. relate the differences between BOMA's office classifications;

3. identify several key factors tenants use to choose office space;

4. explain the difference between usable and rentable space;

5. discuss the difference between minimum rent and base rent in determining the rental schedule;

6. review the effectiveness of at least five different ways to market office space;

7. discuss the importance of properly qualifying the tenant regarding space needs;

8. explain the importance of determining a building standard and how to use it when negotiating concessions from the owner;

9. summarize the three maintenance requirements unique to managing office property; and

10. summarize the development and management tasks of "intelligent buildings."

■ OVERVIEW

The need for office space steadily increased as the majority of American people left agriculture and manufacturing for information technology. Although almost 75 percent of the U.S. workforce is engaged in occupations other than farming or industry, the growth in office space has slowed dramatically in the 21st century due to downsizing and outsourcing.

By definition, an *office* is a building or room in which a particular service is supplied as opposed to a facility where goods are manufactured, worked on, or sold. The *multistory office building* is the most common type of office space. However, as the inner cities have suffered economic decline, businesses have moved to suburban locations, sparking the growth of smaller, outlying office complexes.

Originally private investors owned most office property. Increases in the costs of construction, equipment, services, and labor, though, have made it virtually impossible for an individual or small corporation to finance and maintain an average-size office building in an urban area. As a result, many multistory office buildings are owned by investment syndicates: large institutional investors or large conglomerates with the financial ability to develop and sustain the building over the initial years when cash return on the investment is minimal. Many small developers, unable to compete with corporate giants, have built office space in the suburban market.

■ MARKET ANALYSES

Regional and neighborhood analyses are especially relevant to commercial properties. Current economic trends are at least as significant as present market conditions when assessing the supply and demand for office space in an area.

Regional Analysis

The regional analysis for an office building considers the growing sectors of the regional economy, which may draw national firms to relocate there or to open branch offices. Rates for office space reflect availability or scarcity, as determined by the cyclic nature of office building construction. The manager must not overlook the number of new businesses in the area, the quantity of space a typical new business demands, and the number and type of tenants who want to move from their present location into newer facilities.

Neighborhood Analysis

For office properties, the *neighborhood analysis* emphasizes transportation, parking, and proximity to businesses and services. The prestige of the address should be highlighted, as should improvements, renovations, and new construction in the area.

Absorption Rate

In analyzing demand for office space, the property manager must determine the **absorption rate,** or the number of square feet that have historically been leased in the market area. For example, if there are 3 million square feet of vacant office space in a city, and the absorption in recent years has been 750,000 square feet per year, the city is said to have a four-year supply of leasable office space.

Energy Efficiency

Energy costs cannot be ignored. In a triple net lease, under which the tenant pays all heat, air conditioning, electric, and gas bills, energy inefficiencies definitely impact the ultimate costs and overhead for the tenant. Even a well-located, 20- to 30-year-old building with modern appearances will be negatively impacted if its systems are substandard by today's standards.

BOMA Building Class Definitions

BOMA building class definitions provide subjective standards to discuss office markets, either within a local metropolitan area or an international office space market, considering properties in many metropolitan areas. The metropolitan base considers rent, building finishes, system standards and efficiency, building amenities, location and accessibility and market perception.

According to the BOMA.org Web site, the metropolitan base definitions include the following:

- *Class A*—Prestigious buildings competing for the best tenants with above average rental rates; high quality finishes, state of the art systems, excellent accessibility and distinct market presence.

- *Class B*—Buildings vie for wide range of tenants with average priced rents for the area; fair-to-good quality finishes and systems are adequate, but value is not as good as Class A for the same price.

- *Class C*—Buildings compete for tenants who require functional space priced below average rents for the area.

The market can be broken down into segments and buildings grouped according to rating and age, condition, location, facilities, amenities, and energy efficiency. Because these standards vary from city to city, any discussion with prospective clients should include an explanation of the area's accepted definition of these classifications. An average market vacancy rate of 12 percent is misleading unless the manager realizes that vacancies in newer buildings are as low as 2 percent, whereas older buildings have vacancy rates from 16 percent to 20 percent. Once the demand pattern for an area has been analyzed, the rent schedule for a specific building can be determined. Retrofitting a building may bump a property into a higher rated segment (for instance, from a C building to a B building).

The property manager can then market the property by emphasizing its advantages over competing properties. To avoid misinterpretation, the manager can prepare a simple one-page handout that outlines the area's accepted definition of the A, B, and C classifications qualifying the rent per square foot to give to each new prospective tenant and incorporated in any marketing package. This overview is especially helpful if the management company is not directly owned and operated by the builder/developer/owner, and even more helpful to those who are not used to the process of renting office space. Misunderstood definitions ultimately leads to poor success at marketing, resulting in a bad reputation for the management company.

Once the demand pattern for an area has been analyzed, the rent schedule for a specific building can be determined. Upgrading a building may bump a property into a higher rated segment (for instance, from a C building to a B building).

Site Selection

A survey published in the *Institute of Real Estate Management's* **(IREM's)** *Journal of Property Management* identified four key factors that influence the selection of office facilities. On the average, cost is the overriding concern for most respondents, followed by bus and highway accessibility, environment of the property, and labor market, in that order. Although cost is the first consideration in all three groups, larger firms place more emphasis on labor market and bus and highway accessibility than do smaller ones.

■ PROPERTY ANALYSIS

Property analysis gives the manager a basis for setting a rental schedule, estimating income and expense for the property, and anticipating the reactions of prospects. The first step in property analysis is to determine the exact size of areas to be rented. Basically, the manager must take outside and inside measurements and factor in the BOMA office classifications previously mentioned to arrive at the appropriate rent for that space.

The BOMA/ANSI Standard Method for Measuring Floor Area

BOMA has developed a standard method of floor measurement that measures construction, rentable, usable, and store areas in an office building. The BOMA Standard has been accepted and approved by the American National Standards Institute (ANSI).

Construction area   Sometimes called the *New York method*, the area is computed by measuring to the outside finished surface of permanent outer building walls. It includes the area of all enclosed floors of the building, basements, mechanical equipment floors, and penthouses.

Rentable area   The **rentable area** is computed by measuring to the inside finished surface of the dominant portion of the permanent outer building walls. The restrooms, janitor closets, and rooms such as electrical rooms, which are necessary to the operation of the building, are included.

Dominant portion   The **dominant portion** is the inside finished surface of the permanent outer building wall, which must be 50 percent or more of the vertical floor-to-ceiling dimension. If there is no dominant portion or if the dominant portion is not vertical, the measurement for area is the inside finished surface of the permanent outer building wall where it intersects the finished floor. Any major vertical penetrations of the floor, such as utility shafts, stairwells, and elevators, are excluded. No deductions are made for building columns or projections necessary to the building.

Usable area   The **usable area** is the number of square feet that can actually be occupied. It is computed by measuring from the finished surface of the office side of corridor and other permanent walls to the center of partitions that separate the office from adjoining usable areas, and to the inside finished surface of the dominant portion of the permanent outer building walls. Those portions of the building normally associated with the core of the building, such as corridors, lobbies, restrooms, major penetrations of the floor, and rooms containing equipment for the building are excluded.

Computing Rentable Area

In determining the *rentable area* of an office on a multiple-tenancy floor, the rentable/usable ratio (R/U ratio) for the floor is first computed. The conversion formula for computing the for a multiple-tenancy floor is as follows:

$$\frac{\text{Rentable area}}{\text{Usable area}} = \text{Rentable/usable ratio (R/U ratio)}$$

$$\text{Usable area} \times \text{R/U ratio} = \text{Rentable area (of an office on that floor)}$$

$$\frac{\text{Rentable area}}{\text{R/U ratio}} = \text{Usable area}$$

If an entire floor is rented to a single tenant, the rentable area is taken as the area chargeable to the tenant (restrooms and corridors on that floor are considered part of the tenant's space) and there is no necessity for conversion.

The ratio of rentable space to usable space is sometimes called the *loss factor*, a reflection of the efficiency of space utilization on a single-tenancy floor. On a multiple-tenancy floor, this relationship is referred to as the *load factor*.

The loss or load factor is figured into the cost of usable space. For example, if 22,000 rentable square feet are offered at $16 per square foot, but only 19,125 square feet are usable, the loss factor is 1.15 (22,000 ÷ 19,125 = 1.15). The real cost to the tenant per usable square foot is $18.40 ($16 × 1.15 = $18.40), or a difference of $2.40 per square foot from the rent quotation. The efficiency of space utilization should be considered when constructing the rental schedule for the building. Spaces with a high loss factor should compensate with a lower **base rent**.

Setting the Rent Schedule

Although the market ultimately will set the rent actually paid, a uniform and realistic rent schedule capitalizes on all the features tenants customarily consider part of rental value.

Minimum rents   The minimum rate is the absolute minimum that can be charged for economic survival. It does not take into account contingencies such as vacancy loss, and it does not bear any relation to the current market. Nonetheless, this computation can ensure that the base rental rate suggested by the market and property analyses is high enough to cover the basic costs.

The following formula may be used to calculate the minimum rental rate:

$$\frac{\text{Operating expenses + Mortgage payments + Owners' return on equity}}{\text{Rentable area of building}} = \frac{\text{Minimum}}{\text{rent}}$$

For example, an office building with a market value of $4 million contains 64,000 square feet of rentable space. The owner put 20 percent down on the property and has mortgage payments totaling $90,000 a year. Operating expenses are about $300,000 per year, and the owner needs to get at least a 10 percent return on the investment or equity. Follow the above formula for computing the minimum rental rate.

$$\frac{\$300,000 + \$90,000 + (10\% \text{ of } \$800,000 \text{ down payment})}{64,000 \text{ sq. ft.}} = \frac{\$7.34 \text{ per sq. ft.}}{\text{minimum rent}}$$

Establishing a base rate   The next step is to establish a realistic **base rate** per square foot for a typical space within the building. The base rate should be significantly higher than the minimum rate arrived at earlier and should reflect the features of the property and its current value relative to similar buildings in the area. Once the base rate has been established for typical office space in the building, a specific rental schedule for each type of space can be developed. Depending on its features, each office space is graded as above-standard or below the base rate.

Ultimately, the rental schedule will reflect variables such as height above street level, floor location relative to elevators, interior layout and decor, natural lighting, and view.

New York method   Another method of measuring and charging for office space is the *New York method,* under which all the construction area of a floor or building in a shopping center is used in determining the rent. For instance, if a building or floor measures 100 feet by 100 feet, the area that must be allocated to tenants in renting the space is 10,000 square feet. Rents will tend to be less per square foot than under the BOMA method, but the number of leased square feet will be higher, because areas that are excluded under other measurement methods are included here. This method is not popular in some areas, due to the difficulty of convincing prospective tenants that they should pay for stairwells and elevator shafts, space they cannot actually occupy.

■ MARKETING OFFICE SPACE

Marketing office space requires a systematic and continuing program to attract prospective occupants. Once the manager analyzes the prospects' space needs, the manager can show them units suited to their budgets and space requirements. Several points can be raised to convince prospects to relocate: a substantial price advantage, accessibility, environment, labor market, increased efficiency, prestige, and economy in a new location.

Before starting the campaign, the manager should research the area for specific or special needs and ask "does the building lend itself to special need use?" If the commercial district is surrounded by a large residential area with very few nearby medical and dental offices, the target market could be these professionals to move and upgrade their existing offices and/or open new branches.

The manager should then determine the special needs required by these prospective tenants. The management team can better advise the builder/developer/owner on marketing future improvements such as plumbing, electricity, and computer/internet wiring, as these uses often require more special types of improvements. Thus, the landlord has an opportunity to ask more for the rent due to the special improvements. The specialty tenants often make up a more dependable rent paying tenancy for longer periods of time.

The most commonly used methods of attracting prospective tenants to office buildings are signs, Web sites, brochures, display ads, direct mail, publicity and public relations efforts, referrals, canvassing, leasing agents, and rental centers. The property manager must decide which techniques are best suited to each type of office space and how to develop an advertising strategy that captures the prospect's interest and enhances the desire for the space.

Signs

During construction, with interest high, signs should be strategically placed to draw attention to the availability of space. After initial lease-up, a sign directing inquiries to the manager should be posted on all office buildings.

Web sites

Web sites advertise 24/7. They should be enticing, including pictures of the property as well as prices. The prospect should be able to see how to make inquiries via e-mail, phone, or mail. A properly maintained Web site will be constantly updated and changing. The investor or potential tenant can find a wealth of information, not just about local conditions but also information for properties worldwide.

Brochures

It is a good idea to give prospects a brochure after they have seen the space. They can take the brochure back to share with the other people who will be involved in making the "move" decision. Figure 13.1 is an example of an effective brochure.

Classified ads are rarely used to market office space, but well-placed institutional display ads can be effective. Such ads appeal to the decision makers and their influence groups within prospective tenant organizations, emphasizing the prestige and value of the space. Display advertisements in well-selected out-of-town target area newspapers or trade publications (including the *Wall Street Journal*) reach a select audience over a wide metropolitan or regional area.

Direct Mail

The quickest way to lease a large new building is to generate movement within the current market. Firms not actively looking for new offices are not generally influenced by signs, ads, or leasing agents, but they may be responsive to direct-mail pieces that offer a better value or location than their present office space. A list of potential tenants can be culled from sources like the *Dun & Bradstreet Reference Book*, which lists companies according to the nature of their business. *The Dunhill International List* provides names of law, accounting, and brokerage firms, as well as small businesses. Letters, with printed materials about the building and a reply card, should be mailed to potential tenants.

Public Relations

A well-executed public relations program can be a cost-effective supplement to advertising, direct mail campaigns and other marketing techniques, particularly when dealing with newly constructed multistory office buildings. News items like the one shown in Figure 13.2 are invaluable publicity for an office building.

Referrals

Goodwill is a powerful leasing tool, so current tenants are a good source of prospects. Local government officials and utility company representatives often are in a position to provide leads. An ambitious office building manager will cultivate these sources and become active in the local chamber of commerce, professional associations, and other service groups. As in all types of rental property, the manager should check state law to determine whether a fee or lease concessions can be paid to a tenant or anyone else who makes a referral that results in a lease.

FIGURE 13.1

Brochure

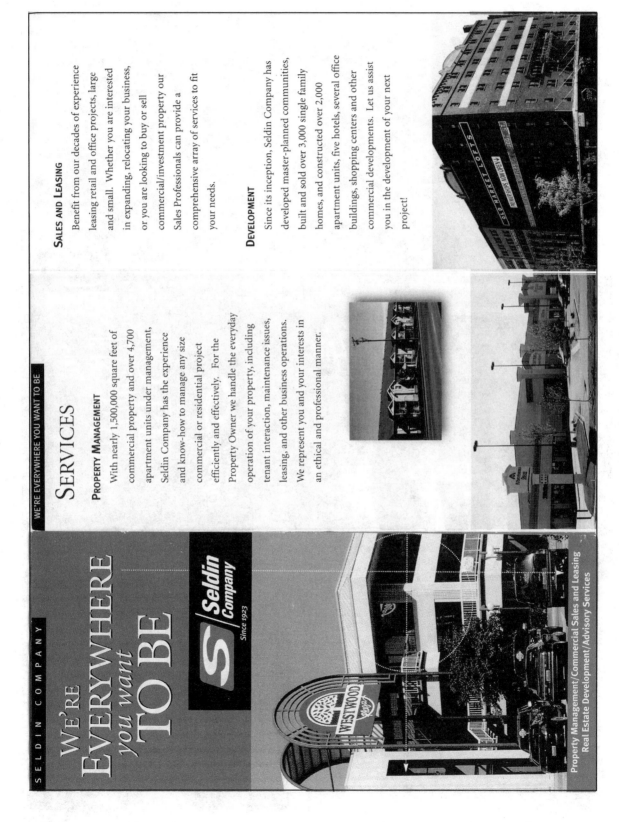

SERVICES

PROPERTY MANAGEMENT

With nearly 1,500,000 square feet of commercial property and over 4,700 apartment units under management, Seldin Company has the experience and know-how to manage any size commercial or residential project efficiently and effectively. For the Property Owner we handle the everyday operation of your property, including tenant interaction, maintenance issues, leasing, and other business operations. We represent you and your interests in an ethical and professional manner.

SALES AND LEASING

Benefit from our decades of experience leasing retail and office projects, large and small. Whether you are interested in expanding, relocating your business, or you are looking to buy or sell commercial/investment property our Sales Professionals can provide a comprehensive array of services to fit your needs.

DEVELOPMENT

Since its inception, Seldin Company has developed master-planned communities, built and sold over 3,000 single family homes, and constructed over 2,000 apartment units, five hotels, several office buildings, shopping centers and other commercial developments. Let us assist you in the development of your next project!

WE'RE EVERYWHERE YOU WANT TO BE

SELDIN COMPANY

WE'RE EVERYWHERE *you want* TO BE

S | Seldin Company
Since 1923

Property Management/Commercial Sales and Leasing
Real Estate Development/Advisory Services

FIGURE 13.1 (CONTINUED)

Brochure

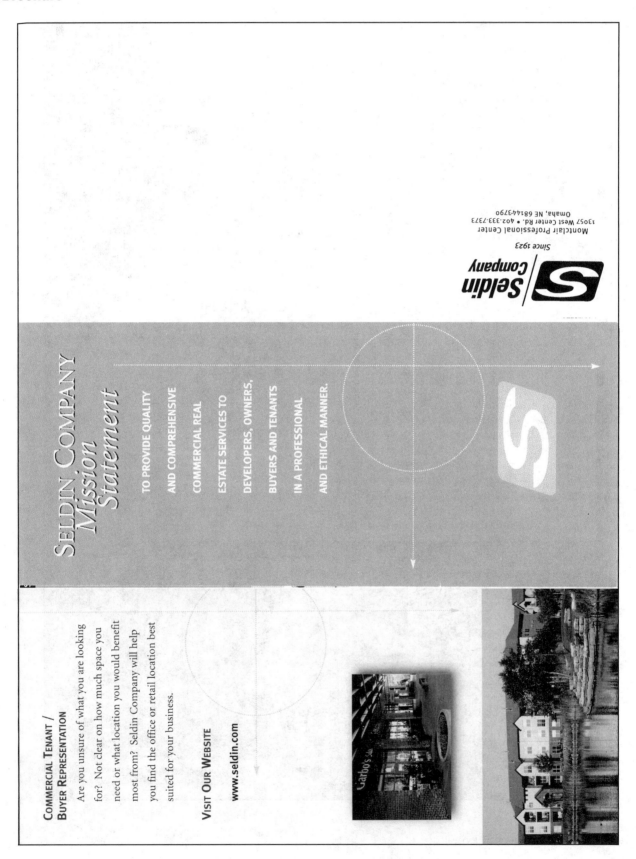

FIGURE 13.2
Publicity News Item

Rockbrook Village getting 'new look'

1-13-04

■ The 40-year-old shopping center will see a major overhaul with new tenants, a new plaza, and landscaping.

BY JOHN TAYLOR
WORLD-HERALD
STAFF WRITER

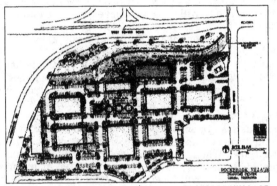

ROCKBROOK VILLAGE

THE WORLD-HERALD

Russell Daub found that if you start making changes to the familiar landscape of a longtime neighborhood shopping center, particularly one as entrenched as Rockbrook Village, you'd better be prepared to explain yourself.

When neighbors of the center on the southwest corner of 108th Street and West Center Road saw last month that machinery was chewing up Rockbrook's plaza and leveling the area, they were, in Daub's words, "almost in revolt."

As a result, he and his marketing director, Merrilee Miller, immediately mailed 6,000 postcards to residents in the vicinity, basically telling them not to worry. The cards announced "A new look for an old friend."

It said that replacing the old plaza would be a new one, complete with a community pavilion, colored concrete and greenery — about 57 trees.

But that's not the only change that Rockbrook is scheduled to undergo. As it happened, the postcards, also containing an overview of the new plaza, didn't have room to

explain all the improvements that the owners of Rockbrook, Daub and his wife, Sue, have planned.

By Sept. 11, in time for Rockbrook's popular art fair, these projects are expected to have been completed:

■ The Rockbrook creek channel, now an eyesore whose banks fill with weeds and small trees that block the view of the center from West Center Road, will be relocated and cleaned up. Water runoff from the cen-

ter will go into collector points all along the property to clean it before it spills into the creek. Retention ponds will be built on the five acres between the shopping center, and the entire area will be landscaped.

The site plan, above, for Rockbrook Village at 108th Street and West Center Road shows some of the new landscaping scheduled for the shopping center, which is undergoing extensive upgrading.

■ The retention ponds will be integrated with common areas, walkways and tenant areas.

■ A new plaza will be built for concerts, craft and art fairs and for merchant promotions.

See Shop: Page 2

ROCKBROOK VILLAGE

The rendering shows some of the additions planned for Rockbrook Village. Many of the improvements are scheduled to be completed by Sept. 11, in time for Rockbrook's popular art fair.

Source: Omaha *World Herald*, Omaha, Nebraska.

FIGURE **13.2** (CONTINUED)
Publicity News Item

Shop: Mall gets $6 million makeover

Continued from Page 1

■ Three new, free-standing buildings will be constructed overlooking the new creek, and space between two existing buildings will be filled in with another retail area. One of the three new buildings will have 15,050 square feet on each of two floors; a building containing a drive-through area will have 3,000 square feet; a new convenience store will have 2,800 square feet of space; and the connector building will have 1,800 square feet.

■ The existing convenience store on the corner of the center will be torn down. When all work is completed, the center, now at 149,909 square feet, will have 184,693 square feet of space.

■ Exteriors of current businesses will be remodeled through the use of bricks, tile, awnings, wood and columns of varying colors.

■ Space for 11 new merchants will be added, boosting the number to 55.

■ The number of parking spaces will be increased to 713 from 632.

■ A new right-turn lane for southbound 108th Street traffic will flow into a newly constructed entrance.

Daub estimated the cost of this latest investment at $6 million, to be borne by the owners.

His goal, he said, is simple. "I've got to continue to do things to overreact and overrespond to the needs of the people and the businesses that serve this neighborhood. I have to do it by providing more quality and more service and (a better) environment than the average real estate project in the city. If we do that, we stay competitive as a supplier of individual specialty merchant property."

According to Daub, Rockbrook has managed to stay competitive since it opened in 1964 by going against some established methods of operation. He believes, for example, that Rockbrook can remain healthy without having at least one large anchor store.

"If the proposition that a center needs a strong anchor to draw traffic were true," he said, "then Rockbrook would have closed long ago."

A shopping center can be successful if it contains "a large number and diverse mix of tenants that offer many products and services," Daub said. "They collectively equal the power of an anchor tenant."

Rockbrook has 18 retailers, 20 service providers and eight food locations in what Daub calls six "key categories — specialty stores, food/restaurants, home furnishings, sports and fitness, barber and hair salons and neighborhood services.

Daub also said the property has a history of being the place where thriving businesses got their start. It was the site of Godfather's first franchise outlet. Elan started there as Shelf Shop. The Garden Cafe began as a breakfast shop.

Rockbrook has suffered losses, he said, most of them the result of retailing moving to western parts of the city to larger malls or shopping centers, or because of the growth of big national discount stores.

"We're not going to have a discounter in here. We're locally (owned), and we're not going to have any category killers in here."

Typical of the shops at Rockbrook are Gloria's Custom Framing, which has been there 33 years, and Omaha Jewelry Co., a 10-year tenant.

Owners of both stores like the coming changes.

"I think it really is exciting," said Bob Krause, owner of Omaha Jewelry. "They're going to do a lot of neat things and change the center for the better."

Rockbrook is unique, he said, in that "it's like being in a small town."

"I think it is a wonderful addition," said Juanita Galvan, owner for the last 23 years of Gloria's and president of the Rockbrook Merchants Association. "It's kind of looking into the future for Rockbrook customers. It's a very welcome look for a shopping center and better usage of the plaza."

Galvan also helps run the annual art fair, now in its 33rd year, which she said draws 25,000 each of its two days.

The Spring Fever Craft Show, this year scheduled for May 1, draws 5,000 people; the Apple Day Craft Show, set for Oct. 2, attracts 7,500 people; and the family concerts held each Friday from June 4 through Aug. 27 will attract from 500 to 1,000 people each.

If all these activities don't generate a corresponding big increase in business for merchants — with the exception of food vendors — they do enhance the center's image as a busy place, Daub said.

"You've got to continue to convince the market that you're bringing them something more than just a cold place (to do business)," he said. "They must continue to identify your center as a place they want to be."

Canvassing

Canvassing is probably the best prospecting method for leasing office space and is most productive when the list of prospects has been prequalified. The Dun & Bradstreet directory and others published by the local chamber of commerce furnish the manager with names of firms that might be interested in the particular space being marketed. The financial section of the newspaper often contains articles on firms that are enjoying rapid financial growth, acquiring subsidiaries, or planning for expansion. Though time-consuming, phone calls to area firms can generate business from the inactive market as well as from companies with admitted space needs.

Canvassing efforts should begin in areas closest to the subject property and progress outward in concentric circles around the property. Managers of large office buildings often allow leasing agents or sales representatives to perform this function on their behalf.

Rental Centers

Like large residential developments, new multistory office buildings often use rental centers. The center should be attractively furnished, and space should be provided for private discussions with prospective tenants.

Despite what most say, many people cannot imagine how the space can be arranged, so the visual benefits of a "model office" can go a long way. When there are only a small number of tenants in a large project, a property manager might ask one of the tenants in place if their office can be used as a "model office" to demonstrate to potential tenants. Arrange to do this by appointment and offer this tenant a small break in the rent for his or her cooperation until the building is fully rented.

For specialty or new mostly vacant buildings, consider holding an open house, similar to a residential open house, except this is for the professional and business community, on a mid-week day. To attract attention and to encourage interest, use large signage as well as newspaper, radio, and targeted Internet advertising. Every commercial broker in the area should be invited because these brokers can account for a substantial amount of commercial leasing. Several management team members should be on-hand all day to pass out brochures in addition to light snacks and refreshments.

■ QUALIFYING THE PROSPECTIVE TENANT

Spatial Qualifying

Spatial requirements is one of the first areas of qualification, because if the space is not adequate for the prospective tenant, there is no further need to proceed. Therefore, it is wise for the manager or leasing agent to analyze prospects' space requirements before showing them any specific office areas. The manager should keep a permanent record of all the information obtained when qualifying a prospect.

The manager should find out the nature of the prospect's business, the types of staff positions it demands, the number of people in each position, and the tasks that each performs as these variables shape the space allocation plan. Office space varies according to need: the secretarial staff and managerial staff likely will be allocated different types and arrangements of space. From this information, the following four different categories of space usage will have been identified.

Single office space   This refers to enclosed or semienclosed areas serving a single occupant and including a circulation area to provide access to the office. Unit office spaces can vary in size from a private office of about 100 square feet, suitable for middle managers, to a 345-square-foot private office large enough to accommodate a company president.

Multipersonnel areas   Multipersonnel areas are open or closed work spaces for more than one person ranging from 55 to 90 square feet per person, depending on the status of the individual, company policy, and the number of workers sharing one closed space. In general, when a number of workers share a space, the square footage allotted to each may be reduced. These standards provide sufficient space so that workstations do not interfere with one another and traffic can circulate to and through the work area. Open-area requirements can range from approximately 45 square feet each for 15 or more workers to 80 square feet per person for six employees or fewer.

Special facilities   These work spaces are designed to accommodate the special equipment used by these workers in the course of their jobs. Standard space allotments are difficult to determine for special-use areas. Some guidelines have been established. For example, a conference room for four people requires about 200 square feet of space as does a reception area for three visitors and a receptionist. A lunchroom for four should contain 250 square feet.

Miscellaneous areas   Miscellaneous areas do not include permanently assigned work areas, such as filing space, traffic-flow allowances, libraries, supply rooms, mail rooms, vaults, and computer rooms. Corridors and other interior circulation requirements are often estimated at 15 percent of the total office area, whereas 5 percent is usually added for filing space. Access circulation needs can be determined later on a situational basis, with allowance for interior traffic flow.

Level of Quality Desired

The manager should also discover what quality of office space is desired, as the business image of the tenant firm will be influenced by the physical appearance of the space. The floor population and the clerical-executive mix also must be considered when exploring the quality of space that a prospect desires.

Because they are sensitive to the visiting clientele for the other tenants on the floor, most prestige-oriented business tenants want tenants of comparable status in close proximity, whether they are competitive firms or not. Ideally, each floor should be leased by tenants involved in different businesses but enjoying the same level of prestige.

> The best way to gauge a prospect's space requirements and other needs is to visit the space the firm is presently occupying and study its current operations, together with any changes or expansions the prospect desires. There is no substitute for this firsthand knowledge and the flexibility it can provide.

Additional Areas of Qualification

After determining the prospect's space requirements, the manager then proceeds to related information—motives for moving, rental budget, parking and transportation needs, preferences for amenities and alterations, projected moving date, and special lease clauses needed. It is also important to qualify the representative of the prospect firm with regard to that person's status in the company and authority to make decisions.

Sometimes an executive seeking space will not give a property manager all the information needed for proper qualification until the executive is interested in a particular property. In such cases, the manager must show space that corresponds to the prospect's stated specifications. When a suitable space is found, the manager must backtrack and qualify the prospect thoroughly to accommodate the firm's actual requirements.

The following questions should be asked of all prospective tenants:

- When does your present lease expire?
- How long have you been in your present space?
- What is your current rent?
- Are you interested in new space?
- Do you need more, less, or an equal amount of space?
- What is your budget for new space?
- What is your financial strength?
- Why do you want to move?
- When do you need the new space?
- How many employees will you move?
- What kinds of improvements and amenities are needed?
- How much parking is required? Is it paid by the company or the employee?
- Do you have any specific transportation needs?
- Who will make the decisions?
- Who can sign the lease? Where is this person located?
- Where do you want to locate? Why?
- When can you see the space?
- Are you interested in renting?

An information sheet that can be useful in recording basic specific information is illustrated in Figure 13.3. Additionally, the following questions should be asked of all prospective tenants:

- When does your present lease expire?
- How long have you been in your present lease?

Showing the Space

The space itself usually is the factor that transforms a prospect into a tenant. If the space is not skillfully presented and its advantages highlighted, preliminary advertising and qualification efforts will be wasted. It is essential that the management office be attractively furnished, for it is the first office the prospect will see.

The manager should begin with a description of the features of the building's locale, as brought out in the manager's area and neighborhood analyses. The manager should help prospects visualize their firms in the space and should listen carefully to each prospect's reactions to specific features and benefits. Client responses tell the manager what adaptations are needed to make the space suitable for the prospect. This information is indispensable as the merchandising process moves into its final and most critical stage—negotiation of the lease agreement.

When showing the space, good lighting is essential. When the space is new or the space is vacant, demonstrating the space with a flashlight is not really effective.

If the space is a large open space or undivided new space, then in addition to having it well-lighted, marking lines every ten feet with small chalk or spray paint helps delineate the area to make it easier for the prospective tenant to imagine his or her use of the space with walls, offices, hallways, meeting rooms, storage, and so on.

If the space has been previously occupied, but is now vacant, be sure there is no obnoxious smell or musty odor in the space. If so, find a remedy, as this is a real turn-off to most prospective tenants.

If there are any visible ceiling water stains or roof leaks, address these issues prior to the inspection. No tenant wants to deal with the possibility of a ceiling or roof water leak problem. If prior or old leaks were fixed, point it out to the prospective tenant. If there are visible current leaks, then it may be best to have the landlord represent that the issue will be repaired prior to occupancy.

Closing the Transaction

The manager can begin discussing lease terms after showing the office space. The manager should provide as much additional material as possible, such as a brochure, and follow up with phone calls or personal contact, especially if a prospect lacks the authority to negotiate terms or requires more time.

When dealing with an agent or branch office of a large corporation located in another city, the manager can expedite the transaction by offering to get

FIGURE 13.3
Office Space Leasing Information Form

Date: _____

Organization: _____ _____
Address: _____ Phone: _____
Service/Product: _____ Market Area: _____
Yrs. in Bus: _____ No. of Employees: _____ Hrs. Oper: _____
Decision Maker/Position: _____

Lease

Starting Date: _____ Length: _____ Options: _____
Price (per sq. ft.) _____ Month: _____ Year: _____
Other Expenses: _____

Location

Preferred Locations: (1) _____
(2) _____ (3) _____ (4) _____
Specific Locational Requirements (freeways, other businesses, etc.): _____
_____
Access to Public Transportation: _____
Other: _____

Facility

Type of Building: _____
Quality: _____ Total Sq. Ft.: _____
Specifications:
   reception _____ private offices _____
   open area _____ work area _____
   storage area _____ conf. room _____
   parking _____ other _____

Previous Viewing

space seen	shown by	date
(a) _____	_____	_____
(b) _____	_____	_____
(c) _____	_____	_____
(d) _____	_____	_____

Are you interested in new space?
If yes:
   When do you need to be in the new space? _____
   How many employees will you move? _____
   What kind of improvements do you require? _____
   Who will make the decision to move? _____
   Who can sign the lease? _____
   Will you buy? _____

Other Information

_____
_____
_____
_____
_____

all pertinent data to the decision maker in the home office. This might be accomplished by mailing the brochures, plans, and specifications to the decision maker; by discussing the matter over the telephone; or by traveling to the home office to present the benefits of the space in person. However, the manager must be sure that the local representative of the prospect is sold on the space and wants the manager to do so. The manager must help the local prospect, not go over his or her head.

■ NEGOTIATIONS AND THE LEASE

Written Contract

The object of negotiation is to achieve a signed lease that is beneficial to both parties, in the shortest time. The general rules for negotiation outlined in Chapter 6 include acting in a professional manner, inspiring confidence, cooperating with outside leasing agents, and excluding attorneys from initial negotiations. The manager must be knowledgeable concerning the property, the market, the owner's objectives, and the tenant's needs to strike a satisfactory agreement between the parties.

The office lease itself is subject to the requirements for a legal contract and should contain at least the basic clauses mentioned in Chapter 5. Because office leases generally are lengthy, space does not permit the reproduction of an entire lease in this book. A typical lease index, shown in Figure 13.4, illustrates the complexity and uniqueness of office building leases. Following the index, a few special clauses are included for illustration.

Office Lease Concessions

Concessions, or *inducements*, common in leasing office space, are simply negotiable points in the lease terms in favor of the prospective tenant. To be attractive, a concession must alleviate a basic problem or satisfy a particular desire of the prospect. When negotiating lease terms, the property manager must balance the wants and needs of the prospect with the owner's objectives in terms of the market situation. The manager must always remember that concessions mean money lost to the owner and affect the total economic value of the lease.

Negotiation is a process of give and take, and the first prerequisite of a successful negotiator is recognizing which concessions will be sacrificed by one party in return for others deemed of greater value. When leasing office properties, the manager will find that prolonged negotiations are the rule rather than the exception. The following items are usually open for negotiation:

- Escalation clauses
- Assigning and subletting
- Recapture clause
- Services by landlord

FIGURE 13.4

Index of Sample Lease

The index to a sample office lease that follows has been modified from Appendix 10 of the Management Simulation Source Book published by BOMI Institute, Arnold, Maryland, to supplement courses in their Real Property Administration designation program. It is used here by their permission.

1. LEASED PREMISES
   A. Premises and Building
   B. Parking
   C. Premises Less than 3,000 Rentable Sq. Ft.
   D. Environmental Hazards

2. TERM
   A. Duration
   B. Early or Late Possession
   C. Use of Premises

3. RENT
   A. Amount
   B. Late Charges
   C. Adjustment for CPI
   D. Additional Rent: 1. Direct Operating Expenses
      2. Tax Adjustment
   E. Additional Rent: Tax Adjustment

4. SECURITY DEPOSIT

5. SERVICES
   A. Customary
   B. Additional

6. QUIET ENJOYMENT

7. LEASE SUBJECT TO SUPERIOR RIGHTS

8. ESTOPPEL CERTIFICATE BY TENANT

9. RIGHTS RESERVED TO THE LANDLORD
   A. General
   B. Rules and Regulations

10. WAIVER OF CLAIMS
    A. Damage from Water and Similar Sources
    B. Damage from Other Causes
    C. Loss of Business, etc.

11. INSURANCE BY TENANT
    A. Property
    B. Liability
    C. Workmen's Compensation
    D. Tenant to Furnish Copies
    E. Waiver of Subrogation

12. ASSIGNMENT AND SUBLETTING
    A. Consent
    B. Sublease of More than 50 Percent of Premises
    C. Sublease of 50 Percent or Less of Premises
    D. Excess Rent
    E. Tenant Not Released

13. CONDITION OF PREMISES

14. OBLIGATION TO REPAIR
    A. Tenant's Obligation
    B. Landlord's Obligation

15. TENANT'S ALTERATIONS AND ADDITIONS

16. TENANT TO KEEP PREMISES FREE OF LIENS

17. LIABILITY

18. BANKRUPTCY

19. DAMAGE TO LEASED PREMISES
    A. Untenantable—Permanent
    B. Untenantable—Temporary
    C. Negligence of Tenant
    D. 30 Percent Damage
    E. Last 12 Months of Tenant's Term

20. CONDEMNATION

21. NOTICES

22. DEFAULT AND REMEDIES
    A. Default
    B. Remedies

23. LANDLORD DEFINED
    A. Definition
    B. Limitation of Assets Liable for Collection of Judgment

24. RECORDING LEASE PROHIBITED

25. PREVAILING PARTY IN LEGAL PROCEEDINGS

26. SEVERABILITY

27. HOLDING OVER

EXHIBIT "A" Commencement Date of Term of Lease

EXHIBIT "B" Building Rules and Regulations

ALTERNATIVE SAMPLE CLAUSES
   Expense Stop
      Contribution of Landlord to Building
         Operating Costs
      Taxes
      Landlord to Furnish Statement
      Payment Due after Termination
   Escalation
      Additional Rent: Utilities and Taxes
      Adjustment for Building Maintenance Cost Fluctuations

FIGURE 13.4 (CONTINUED)
Index of Sample Lease

Other Sample Clauses

Option
Agency
Option or Renewal Term Rent Based on
  Appraisal

ESTOPPEL CERTIFICATE

RENT AND ESCALATION

A. Amount

Tenant shall pay to Landlord as Base Rent, at Landlord's office, or as directed from time to time by Landlord's notice, the total base rent for the full term hereof, without prior notice, demand, or setoff whatsoever, the sum of _____ ($ _____) which shall be payable in advance in monthly installments of ($ _____) on or before the first day of each and every calendar month of the term hereof, except that the first month's rent shall be paid upon the execution hereof. Rent for any period during the term hereof which is for less than one (1) month shall be prorated according to the then current monthly rental, based upon a thirty (30) day month.

B. Late Charges

If rent or other payments due the Landlord hereunder are paid later than the tenth (10th) day of the month when due, a late fee of five percent (5%) of the amount due or Twenty-five Dollars ($25.00), whichever is the greater, shall be due and payable by the Tenant as additional rent. The parties agree that calculation of the exact costs which the Landlord will incur if the Tenant makes late payments would be difficult to determine but would include, without limitation, processing and accounting charges and late charges which may be imposed upon the Landlord by the terms of any mortgage or deed of trust constituting a lien upon the Building. The parties agree that the late fee provided herein is a fair and reasonable stimate of the costs the Landlord will incur. This provision, or payment by Tenant hereunder, or action taken by Landlord hereunder shall not diminish or abrogate Tenant's duty to pay rent when due, or Landlord's rights to declare default for late payment as provided elsewhere in this Lease.

C. Adjustment for CPI Fluctuation

The Base Rent provided in this lease shall be increased, commencing with the first anniversary of the Tenant's Commencement Date set forth in Exhibit _____ and annually thereafter on succeeding anniversary dates, by an amount equal to _____ (%) of the percentage increase, if any, in the cost of living average for the metropolitan _____ area as reflected by the _____ "Consumers Price Index for all Urban Consumers.

All items (1967 = 100) (city)" published by the U.S. Department of Labor, Bureau of Labor Statistics, by dividing the Base Index into the difference determined by subtracting the Base Index from the Anniversary Index. Any resulting positive number shall be deemed the percentage increase in the Fixed Minimum Rent. Landlord shall furnish Tenant with the computation of the additional rent, to be paid by Tenant for the lease year in question. As used herein, the following terms shall apply:

"Base Index" shall be the Consumer Price Index which is the most recently published prior to the Commencement of this Lease.

"Anniversary Index" shall be the Consumer Price Index which is the most recently published prior to the first anniversary month and succeeding anniversary months of this lease.

"Index" shall be the aforesaid Consumer Price Index. If said index is not published at any time during the term of this Lease, then another index generally recognized as authoritative shall be selected by the Landlord and applied pursuant to the intent of this Article _____.

Upon the first anniversary of the Commencement Date of this Lease, the Tenant shall pay in one lump sum an adjustment in accordance with the foregoing, attributable or occurring during said preceding lease year upon receipt of notice thereof from the Landlord, or, in the alternative in Landlord's sole discretion, an adjustment will be paid commencing with the first rental payment due for the then ensuing lease year. The Tenant shall pay one-twelfth (1/12th) of the increase, as determined by the Landlord aforesaid, with each succeeding regular monthly rent installment for the balance of that lease year and thereafter until the rent is subsequently increased in a similar fashion by written notice from the Landlord, in which event the Tenant shall again pay a lump sum payment to the Landlord on the anniversary of the Commencement Date hereof for the preceding year, and all succeeding monthly rental payments shall be increased according.

D. Additional Rent

Tenant covenants and agrees to pay as additional rental an amount equal to Tenant's proportionate share of any increase in the amount of "direct operating expenses" as said terms are hereinafter defined, over the total "direct operating expenses" payable by Landlord during the base year, as follows:

Base Year: Calendar Year _____ Fiscal
year _____ to _____

Comparison Year: Each calendar or fiscal
  year of the term after the Base Year.

FIGURE 13.4 (CONTINUED)
Index of Sample Lease

(1) Direct Operating Expenses

All direct costs of operation and maintenance determined by standard accounting practices, which shall include the following costs by way of illustration, but shall not be limited to: salaries, wages, hospitalization, medical, surgical, and general welfare benefits (including group life insurance) and pension payments of employees of Landlord engaged in the operation or maintenance of the Building of which the Premises form a part, payroll charges and/or taxes, workmen's compensation, insurance, electricity, lamps, fluorescent tubes, ballasts, steam, fuel, utility taxes, water (including sewer charges and/or rental), casualty and liability insurance, repairs and maintenance, building and cleaning supplies, uniforms and dry cleaning, window cleaning, management fees, service contracts with independent contractors, telephone, telegraph, stationery, advertising, equipment necessary for the maintenance and operation of the Building, and all other expenses paid in connection with the operation of the Building. ("Direct Operating Expenses" shall not include depreciation on the Building of which the Premises are a part of equipment therein, loan payments, or real estate brokers commissions.)

(2) Additional Rent: Tax Adjustment

Tenant shall pay to Landlord an amount equal to Tenant's proportionate share of the increase, if any, in the ad valorem taxes charged against the property and all improvements thereon in any Comparison Year over the Base Year. The term "ad valorem taxes" for the purposes of this Lease shall mean any and all real estate taxes and assessments or other similar charges on real property, whether general or special, for improvements, or other charges assessed, levied, imposed, or becoming a lien upon the said land, improvements, and appurtenances thereto imposed by the United States, Central State, or any local government or political subdivision thereof. If Landlord shall receive   refund for said ad valorem taxes for any Comparison Year for which Tenant may have paid its share to Landlord under this provision, then Landlord shall repay to Tenant, Tenant's proportionate share of such refund after deducting therefrom all costs and expenses of obtaining such refund. If this Lease should terminate on a date other than the last day of a calendar year, the amount of any such increase payable by Tenant during the calendar year in which this Lease terminates shall be prorated on the basis which the number of days which have elapsed from the beginning of said calendar year to and including said date on which this Lease terminates bears to 365. If the actual taxes for the year of termination have not been determined at the time the proration is made hereunder, then such proration shall be made upon the basis of the most recent assessments and mill levy. All prorations made in accordance with the provisions of the preceding sentence shall be final without regard to the amount of actual taxes later charged or assessed.

ALTERNATIVE EXPENSE STOP CLAUSE

A.   Operating Costs

Landlord herewith agrees to expend as its share of operating costs paid for and sustained by Landlord during any calendar year an amount not greater than _____ Dollars ($ _____). This sum shall constitute the maximum payable by Landlord as its contribution toward operating costs. Operating costs shall mean and include all general costs, expenses, and disbursements or whatsoever kind or nature which Landlord shall pay or become obligated to pay in respect to or in connection with the ownership, leasing, maintenance, repair, and operation of the Building (including the land upon which it is situated), including, without limitation amounts paid for electricity other than electricity furnished to and paid for by tenants in accordance with their separate meters; the amount paid for all hot and cold water other than that chargeable to tenants by reason of their extraordinary consumption of water; the amount paid for all labor and/or wages and other payments including the cost to Landlord of workmen's compensation and disability insurance, payroll taxes, welfare, and fringe benefits made to janitors, security personnel, employees, contractors, and subcontractors of Landlord involved in the operation and maintenance of the Building; sewer taxes and charges; managerial, administrative, and telephone expenses related to the Building; the total charges of any independent contractors employed in the care and operation, maintenance, and cleaning of the Building, including snow and trash removal and landscaping; the amount paid for all supplies, tools, equipment, and necessities which are occasioned by everyday wear and tear; accounting, legal, inspection, and consulting services; the cost of pest control; the cost of guards and other protection services; payments for general maintenance and repairs to the plant and equipment supplying climate control; and the payment paid for premiums for all insurance required or deemed desirable from time to time by Landlord or Landlord's mortgagee(s). Operating costs shall not, however, include interest on debt, capital retirement of debt, costs properly chargeable to capital account (except for capital expenditures which reduce operating expenses, in which case such expenditures shall be amortized over the life of the object for such capital expenditure), or any cost which is charged to and collected from any tenant of the Building on account of any negligent or willful act or omission of such tenant or for which such tenant may be liable, contractually or otherwise. The reference to "Building" in this subparagraph shall include all related facilities, including sidewalks, loading and/or parking areas in or around the Building. The provision or termination of such services or others and the degree thereof shall be determined by Landlord. Moreover, when Landlord causes services to be rendered by independent third parties, Landlord shall have no liability for the performance thereof or liability therefor.

FIGURE 13.4 (CONTINUED)
Index of Sample Lease

However, said sum as constituted for operating expenses shall not include real property taxes, ad valorem taxes, or personal property taxes.

B.   Taxes

Landlord herewith agrees to expend as its share of taxes paid for and sustained by Landlord during any calendar year an amount no greater than _____ Dollars ($ _____). Real Estate Taxes shall mean and include all general and special taxes and assessments levied upon or assessed against the Building and the Land upon which it is situated. If at any time during the term of this Lease, the method of taxation of real estate prevailing at the time of execution hereof shall be or has been altered so as to cause the whole or any part of the taxes now or hereafter levied, assessed, or imposed on real estate to be levied, assessed, or imposed upon Landlord wholly or partially as a capital levy or otherwise, or measured by the rents received therefrom, then such new or altered taxes shall be deemed included within the term "real estate taxes." This sum shall constitute the maximum payable by Landlord as its contribution toward real estate taxes, whether personal, property, and/or ad valorem.

ASSIGNMENT AND SUBLETTING

A.   Consent

Tenant will not sublet the premises or any part thereof or transfer possession or occupancy thereof to any person, firm or corporation, or transfer or assign this Lease, without the prior written consent of Landlord, which consent shall not unreasonably be withheld. No subletting or assignment hereof shall be effected by operation of law or in any other manner unless with prior written consent of Landlord.

B.   Sublease of More than 50 Percent of Premises

In the event Tenant desires to sublet all or more than fifty percent (50%) of the Premises, Tenant shall give to Landlord written notice of Tenant's desire to do so. Within ninety (90) days of receipt of said notice, Landlord shall have the right (i) to terminate this Lease on a date to be agreed upon by Landlord and Tenant; or (ii) with Tenant's consent, to terminate this Lease and to enter into a new lease with Tenant for that portion of the Premises Tenant may desire to retain upon terms to be mutually agreed upon; or (iii) to sublease from Tenant at the same rental rate then being paid by Tenant and subsequently to elet that portion of the Premises that Tenant desires to relinquish. If Landlord exercises its right to terminate this Lease or to sublet a portion of the Premises, Tenant agrees that Landlord shall have access to all or the affected portion of the Premises thirty (30) days prior to the effective termination or sublease commencement date for remodeling or redecorating purposes.

C.   Sublease of 50 Percent or Less of Premises

In the event Tenant desires to sublet fifty percent (50%) or less of the Premises, Tenant shall give to Landlord written notice of Tenant's desire to do so. Within sixty (60) days after receipt of said notice, Landlord shall have the right to sublet at the same rental rate then being paid by Tenant and subsequently to relet that portion of the Premises that Tenant desires to sublet. The effective date of such sublease shall be as agreed by Landlord and Tenant, and Landlord shall have access to the subleased area thirty (30) days prior to the effective sublease date for remodeling or redecorating purposes.

D.   Excess Rent

In the event Landlord does not exercise its right to terminate this Lease or to sublet a portion of the Premises from Tenant, and Landlord has granted its written consent, Tenant may sublet all or a portion of the Premises. Any rent accruing to Tenant as the result of such sublease which is in excess of the pro rata share of rent then being paid by Tenant for the portion of the Premises being sublet, shall be paid by Tenant to Landlord monthly as additional rent.

E.   Tenant Not Released

In the event of any subletting of the demised premises or assignment of this Lease by Tenant, with or without Landlord's consent, Tenant shall remain liable to Landlord for payment of the rent stipulated herein and all other covenants and conditions contained herein. Rent due from Tenant shall not be diminished or abated during any remodeling or redecoration period.

SERVICES BY LANDLORD

A.   Customary

Landlord shall provide at Landlord's expense, except as otherwise provided, the following services on Mondays through Fridays from 8:00 AM to 6:00 PM and until noon on Saturdays, except legal holidays celebrated by the United States Government:

(1) Reasonable quantities of water to lavatories, toilets and water fountains in or appurtenant to the premises.

(2) Reasonable amounts of electric current. If Tenant shall require electric current in excess of that usually furnished or supplied for use of the Premises as general office space, Tenant shall first procure the consent of the Landlord which consent Landlord may refuse. In the event Landlord shall approve Tenant's request for excess electric current, Landlord may cause an electric check meter to be installed in the Premises or Landlord shall have the right to cause a reputable independent

FIGURE 13.4 (CONTINUED)
Index of Sample Lease

electrical engineer or consulting firm to survey and determine the value of such excess electric current. The cost of any such survey or meters and installation, maintenance and repairs thereof shall be paid for by Tenant. Tenant agrees to pay Landlord promptly upon demand therefor, all such excess electrical current consumed plus any additional expenses incurred in keeping account of the excess electrical current so consumed. Tenant covenants and agrees that at all times its use of electrical current shall never exceed Tenant's proportionate share of the capacity of existing feeders to the building or the risers of wiring installation. Any riser or risers or wiring to meet Tenant's excess electric requirements, upon written request of Tenant, will be installed by Landlord at the sole cost and expense of Tenant, if in Landlord's sole judgment, the same is necessary and will not cause permanent damage or injury to the building or premises or cause or create a dangerous or hazardous condition or entail excessive or unreasonable alteration, repairs or expenses or interfere with or disturb other tenants or occupants.

(3) Heating and air conditioning reasonably sufficient to heat or cool the Premises, for normal office use.

(4) Janitorial services for general care and cleaning of the Premises. Landlord reserves the right to alter the hours during which the above services are to be provided during the term hereof stated, as may be necessary to comply with laws, ordinances or legal directives.

B.   Additional

Should Tenant require any additional work or service, including but not limited to the additional work or service described above, including service furnished outside the stipulated hours, Landlord may on terms to be agreed, upon reasonable advance notice by Tenant, furnish charges as may be agreed on, but in no event at a charge less than Landlord's actual cost plus overhead for the additional services provided. It is understood that Landlord does not warrant that any of the services referred to above, or any other services which Landlord may supply, will be free from interruption. Tenant acknowledges that any one or more such services may be suspended by reason of accident or of repairs, alterations or improvements necessary to be made, or by strikes or lockouts or by reason of operation of law, or causes beyond the reasonable control of Landlord. Any such interruption or discontinuance of service shall never be deemed an eviction or disturbance of Tenant's use and possession of the Premises, or any part thereof, or render Landlord liable to Tenant for damages by abatement of rent or otherwise, or relieve Tenant from performance of Tenant's obligations under this lease.

TERM AND POSSESSION

A.   Duration

This lease is for a term of _____ commencing _____ and expiring _____.

B.   Early or Late Possession

Should tender of possession of premises be later or earlier than the beginning date named above, for any reason, this Lease shall not be void or voidable, nor shall Landlord be liable to Tenant for any loss or damage resulting therefrom, but in that event, the beginning and ending dates of this Lease shall be adjusted by letter from Landlord to Tenant, to conform to date of such tender of possession just as if the same had been originally named as the beginning date, and this Lease shall run and be in full force and effect for its full term from the date of such tender of possession. Such failure to give possession on the date of such tender or commencement of the term shall not in any other respect affect the validity of this Lease or the obligations of Tenant hereunder. Upon Landlord's request, in event this lease does not begin on the date set forth in Paragraph 2A; the parties agree to execute a writing the form of Exhibit C attached hereto and incorporated herein by reference to record the commencement and expiration dates hereof.

C.   Use of Premises

Tenant covenants and agrees to occupy the Premises only as general office space and shall use them in a careful, safe, and proper manner. Tenant agrees to pay on demand for any damage to the Premises caused by misuse or abuse of said Premises by Tenant, its agents or employees, or by any other person entering upon the Premises under the express or implied invitation of Tenant. Tenant shall not conduct any activity or perform any act prohibited by the laws of the United States of America or the State of _____ or the ordinances of the city or county in which the Building is situated and shall not commit waste nor suffer waste to be committed, nor permit any nuisance on or in the Premises.

D.   Environmental Hazards

Tenant agrees that Tenant, its agents and employees shall not handle, use, manufacture, store or dispose of any flammables, explosives, radioactive materials, hazardous wastes or materials, toxic wastes or materials, or other similar substances, petroleum products or derivatives (collectively "Hazardous Materials") on, under, or about the Premises, without Landlord's prior written consent (which consent may be given or withheld in Landlord's sole discretion), provided that Tenant may handle, store, use or dispose of products containing small quantities of Hazardous Materials, which products are a type customarily found in offices and households (such as aerosol cans containing insecticides, paints, paint remover, and the like), provided further that Tenant shall handle, store, use and dispose of any such Hazardous Materials in a safe and lawful manner and shall not allow such Hazardous Materials to contaminate the Premises or the environment.

- Possession
- Remodeling
- Building standard

Escalation clauses   Because most office leases run for terms in excess of one year, an *escalation clause*, or *passthrough clause*, is usually incorporated into the terms of the agreement. Such a clause covers the unavoidable annual increases in real estate taxes and operating expenses in addition to keeping up with anticipated increases in market rents. Methods of computation vary greatly. Increases in taxes and expenses above the figures for the stipulated base year can be prorated, based on the tenant's percentage of the total space occupied, and billed and paid as a separate charge; in other cases, the base rental rate can be adjusted directly.

Some leases compute increases in reference to a base-year figure that has been adjusted to reflect full occupancy. This is most advantageous for the tenants, especially when the base year is the first year of a building's life, when leasing is still in progress. For example, if base-year expenses totaled $500,000 for a building only 50 percent occupied and the operating expenses from the first comparison year at 75 percent occupancy came to $1.25 million, the amount of increase prorated among the tenants would be $750,000. However, if the base-year figure is adjusted to $1 million to reflect full occupancy, the amount to be prorated after the first year would only be $250,000, a substantial savings for the tenants.

An alternate method of escalation, unique to office leasing practice, is the use of an *expense stop*. Under this method, the landlord is obligated to pay expenses up to a certain dollar figure per square foot per year; the excess is prorated to tenants.

Assignment and subletting   The right to assign or sublet the leased premises can be vital to a tenant. It protects the tenant from rapid expansion or collapse in business. The tenant's liability in no way decreases when the space is assigned or sublet, but the tenant may vacate the premises without major financial loss. Many leases provide that a tenant may sublet or assign the premises only after obtaining the landlord's written approval and giving sufficient notice. Some require that any increases of sublet rental rates over the tenant's rate be shared with the landlord. This allows the landlord to maintain control over the constituency of the tenant population while leaving the tenant an alternative.

Recapture clause   An office lease can include a recapture provision within the assignment and subletting clause. This provision gives the landlord the right to recover any space that the tenant is unable to occupy or sublease. The landlord can then release the space to another tenant. A tenant who sees a possibility of subleasing the space for a higher rent than that called for in the lease may object. On the other hand, the landlord is justified in keeping maximum control of the length of tenants' leases and the economic terms of tenancy agreements.

Services by landlord   The landlord's obligation to provide utility services should be explicitly stated. Some leases will specify that the landlord supply heating and air-conditioning during business hours only. The tenant may want heating and air-conditioning at a reduced but comfortable level during nighttime and weekend hours. After-hours heating and cooling are sometimes available to the tenant at cost; in these cases, the basis for the charges must be explicit in the lease. Some landlords supply electrical service up to certain specified limits and in other cases, electricity may be resold by the landlord to the tenants or each tenant may be separately metered and billed.

Possession   An office lease does not usually become void if the landlord fails to deliver possession of the premises on the date stated. Some leeway in meeting construction deadlines should be allowed due to the magnitude of the work involved in fitting an area to a particular tenant's needs. Tenants may insist, however, on a time limit on such delay. The tenant's cooperation is vital in the initial alteration of space. Some leases allow the landlord to accelerate the beginning of the rental obligation period if the tenant delays in delivering the firm's space utilization plans.

Remodeling office space   One area of negotiation that reflects economic conditions is initial tenant alteration and remodeling. In the past, when space was at a premium, incoming tenants bore the expense of altering an area to suit their needs. However, when the exodus to the suburbs began, many downtown office centers were left with vacancies and landlords became more willing to pay the cost of extensive tenant alterations to get tenants into their buildings.

■ Most large multistory office buildings have prescribed criteria for tenant alteration allowances, which may be expressed in terms of dollars per square foot.

Building standard   Prospective tenants should be aware only of the building standard, a specific combination of amenities and alterations that the owner is willing to make without charge for the incoming tenant. Tenants requiring alterations or additions beyond those itemized on the standards list must contract and pay for these services independently after receiving approval from the landlord. However, in some markets, the tenant may view their inclusion as a negotiable concession. In other words, the landlord may agree to pay for them.

The building standard might include any or all of the following items:

- Two coats of paint on walls and interior partitions
- One telephone jack for every 150 square feet of rentable space
- One double 115-volt electrical outlet per 100 square feet of rentable space
- Up to one linear foot of interior partitioning for each 15 square feet rented
- One door per each 30 linear feet of interior partitions

- Decorator venetian blinds on all windows

- Carpeting in enclosed areas; asphalt tile in open and high-traffic areas

- Acoustic-tile ceiling

- Air-conditioning

Many larger buildings with ongoing alteration and remodeling activity have their own construction crews or an administrative group that is responsible for contracting, coordinating, and supervising the work of engineers, architects, and construction workers for the remodeling project. In such cases, a schedule of cost estimates for the most frequent remodeling jobs can be made available to the tenant. Credit against excess construction costs will usually be given to the tenant for any of the building standard allowance not used. The tenant is also often given the option of amortizing the construction costs over the term of the lease.

Americans with Disabilities Act (ADA) Compliance

As discussed in Chapter 10, property managers must be careful to keep the requirements of the Americans with Disabilities Act in mind when discussing and planning for tenant improvements. Although not obligated to do so, property managers should also inform tenants of the existence of the ADA and that they may have compliance obligations along with the building management.

New leases should allocate responsibility for compliance with the ADA. If an existing lease does not contain a compliance clause stipulating which party is responsible for complying with new local, state, or federal regulations, the landlord and tenant should negotiate a clear understanding of ADA compliance obligations. The U.S. Department of Justice recommends that the parties include an indemnification clause to protect either party from costs resulting from the noncompliance of the other.

■ MAINTENANCE AND STAFFING OF OFFICE BUILDINGS

In general, building maintenance and operating personnel must fit into an efficient and cost-effective pattern. The need for permanent staff painters, window cleaners, carpenters, electricians, plumbers, garage keepers, and security guards will depend on the size of the building and the needs of the tenants. Many of these jobs can be performed more economically on a contract basis. In recent years, an increasing number of office buildings have been turned over to specialized contracting firms that perform all the janitorial work.

Preventing Turnover

Once the tenant has taken possession, the property manager should focus on maintaining good relations with the tenant. Efficient maintenance is the best way to keep a tenant population happy and thereby avoid the high costs of turnover. Proper maintenance also preserves the worth of the property, another of the owner's foremost objectives.

A comprehensive preventive maintenance program should be set up according to the procedures described in Chapter 8. Regular inspections and preventive maintenance can cut repair and replacement costs and ensure uninterrupted service to tenants. Inspection forms for both the interior and exterior of office buildings are available through IREM.

Unique Maintenance Requirements

Three areas of maintenance assume added significance when an office property is involved. Elevator operation, routine cleaning, and new construction in office properties differ from the same jobs in residential buildings. An additional consideration is that boilers and other large heating and air-conditioning units must be maintained by highly skilled personnel. Local building codes often require certain equipment to be attended to on a 24-hour basis.

Elevator operation   The two principal concerns of the office property manager are a satisfactory schedule of elevator service and the efficient movement of large numbers of people during morning and evening rush hours. A minimum summons interval between elevators can be established for each floor by regularly dispatching cabs from both the ground floor and the top of the shaft.

Elevators in office buildings travel more miles and require constant maintenance to ensure good service, safety, and cleanliness. Modern automatic elevator installations are so complicated and expensive that most office building managers contract the maintenance of the elevators, shafts, and machinery to an outside firm specializing in this type of work. The contractor is then responsible for maintenance functions, such as lubrication, cleaning, repair, and replacement.

Housekeeping   Unlike residential properties, office buildings endure heavy traffic during the day. Therefore, most public areas must be cleaned during night hours. Janitorial service is still needed during normal daytime hours to maintain washrooms, lobbies, corridors, and other public areas. In small buildings, the day janitor also can take care of minor repairs that tenants might request.

Management usually is responsible for having commercial tenants' interior spaces cleaned. Night janitors are charged with cleaning the individual offices if neither the manager nor the tenants have separate service contracts with outside firms for office cleaning. The night crew is also responsible for janitorial jobs that cannot be performed during the day, such as washing and waxing common areas and vacuuming or mopping the lobby and elevator cabs. Most office buildings will require two shifts of janitorial personnel, a supervisor for each shift, and a general maintenance superintendent to coordinate the efforts of all janitorial crew members. A chief engineer is usually engaged to care for the physical plant and equipment.

New construction   The office manager is faced with the prospect of new construction each time a tenant moves in, because most tenants require some special alteration of the space to suit their needs. Again, depending on which alternative is economically advantageous, the manager may choose either to contract out for such work or maintain a skilled on-site crew. In any case, time is often of the essence when preparing space to lease.

■ Many office managers supplement revenue from the property by selling construction and remodeling work to existing tenants. The services can be sold at a slight markup or provided at cost as an additional benefit to the tenant. Tenants appreciate the convenience for them to buy services through the manager's on-site crew or outside contracting firm.

■ THE INTELLIGENT BUILDING

Intelligent buildings, sometimes called *smart buildings,* have had tremendous publicity, leading many to believe it is a wholly new concept, although some of the components that identify an intelligent building have been in use for more than two decades. They are quickly becoming a fact of life.

Basic Information Services

An intelligent building incorporates several basic information services.

Automation systems   These systems described in Chapter 8 handle building controls, maintenance, and operation. Things such as HVAC operation, elevators, and control of lighting and life safety systems are included in this area. These applications were the first to come into common use.

Advanced telecommunications   This includes systems for voice communication only or systems that allow simultaneous voice and data transmission.

■ SECURITY AND LIFE SAFETY

Since 9/11, security and life safety have become increasingly important responsibilities of management for all types of property. Office buildings, particularly large structures, present unique problems because of the high concentrations of occupants above ground level. Security now factors into everyone's daily life. Identification badges must be worn and all visitors must sign in.

Emergency procedures must be prepared for earthquakes, fires, tornadoes, power failures, waterline breaks, explosions, bomb threats, and serious injuries to or heart attacks suffered by persons in the building. All these procedures and available security personnel must be coordinated with the building's electrical, mechanical, communications, and control equipment. Advances in safety and security devices are occurring daily, and the professional property manager needs to keep informed of developments in this critical area of responsibility. These subjects are more fully developed in Chapter 17.

■ MANAGEMENT ADMINISTRATION AND ACCOUNTING

Regardless of a building's size, a central office should be set up to oversee the management for the property. In small buildings, where a business office is not economically viable, tenants and others involved in the operation of the property should be told where to reach the superintendent and the property manager. In larger buildings, the business office should be centrally located, tastefully decorated, and adequately staffed, following the guidelines set out in Chapter 9. Administrative procedures for data recording, filing, and expense accounting should conform to the general patterns outlined in Chapter 9.

Facilities Manager

A **facilities manager** is an employee of a building occupant who is responsible for the internal arrangement and furnishing of the space leased by that employer-occupant and, in some cases, for maintenance of the leased space. The facilities manager may be present at the local level but could also be based at the occupant company's home office. This manager is a generalist who manages a team of specialists such as architects, designers, engineers, communications specialists, and others. General property management may be an included responsibility where a single tenant is the sole or majority occupant of a building.

Facility management is such a specialty that a separate trade association has formed—the International Facility Management Association (IFMA), with offices both in the United States and Europe. Its members can take classes leading to the Certified Facility Manager (CFM) designation. BOMI also offers several designations for the facilities specialist.

Specialized Accounting

BOMA International has developed one of the most comprehensive standardized systems of income and expense accounting available to the property manager. The advantage of this standard accounting method is that it discloses essential controls and facilitates intra-industry comparisons.

The BOMA chart of accounts provides a format for internal consistency of management accounting within a firm and facilitates comparison of the manager's operations with those of others, both locally and nationwide. BOMA also publishes an annual *Experience Exchange Report* containing local, regional, and national averages of operating income and expenses, plus other information, for office buildings of various sizes. Using the standard BOMA chart of accounts, the operating reports for a property can be checked against normative statistics compiled from industry experience. Property managers can then identify any areas of expense that seem too high and rate their own operating efficiency against that of other management operations.

■ SUMMARY

Multistory office buildings are usually owned by large institutional investors who are able to finance high construction and operating costs. Smaller developers build more modest office buildings of one to three stories in shopping centers, industrial parks, and suburban areas.

To set a valid rental schedule, the manager provides regional, neighborhood, and property analyses taking into consideration demand for space by new businesses in the area, the expansion rate of existing tenants, and the number and type of tenants who wish to move into newer facilities. Demand is also affected by the age of the building, its condition, special features, and competition.

An absolute minimum rent that covers expenses and provides a return on investment is first determined, Then, a base rent that is significantly higher than the minimum rent is computed. All office space in the building is graded as superior or inferior to the standard space, depending on individual features, and priced accordingly.

The BOMA method of measuring rentable space may be used to determine how much actual occupiable space a prospective tenant will be paying for. On a single-tenancy floor, the ratio of rentable to usable space is referred to as the loss factor; on a multiple-tenancy floor, this relationship is called the load factor.

Office space is marketed by an Web site, signs, brochures, display ads in newspapers and magazines, a direct-mail campaign, canvassing, and on-site rental centers. Public relations programs aimed at decision makers are often useful, as are referral networks including current tenants, business acquaintances, key contacts, and personal friends.

Before showing the property, the manager should qualify the prospect in terms of spatial requirements by considering the nature of the prospect's business, the types of staff positions in the firm, the number of persons in each position, and tasks that each performs. The four basic categories of space usage are single office space, multipersonnel areas, special facilities, and miscellaneous areas. Floor population, clerical-executive mix, and client image will determine the quality of space the prospect desires.

Office lease negotiations may include the right to assign or sublet the space, a recapture provision, office space remodeling, or alteration. Either the landlord, as a concession, or the tenant must absorb the cost of alterations beyond the ones itemized in the building standards. Both landlord and tenant must remember ADA requirements when planning and constructing tenant improvements and decide who will pay for those improvements.

Other negotiable items include providing heating, air-conditioning, and electrical service, especially during nonstandard office hours, and the method of calculating the escalation clause, if one is included. The lease should contain a clause that the contract is not void if possession is delayed for a short period. The lease should also have a clause requiring the tenant to deliver to the landlords space utilization plans so that the work involved in fitting up an area can be initiated in a timely manner.

A preventive maintenance program in the office building entails elevator operation, cleaning services, and new construction. Elevators in office buildings are more heavily used than their residential counterparts, so a satisfactory schedule of cleanliness, service, and efficiency must be ensured. A night shift of janitorial personnel is responsible for major cleaning of public areas and individual offices, whereas a day shift cleans the washrooms, lobby, and corridors.

The central office provides management, direction, and operating policies for the property. The format and accounting system developed by BOMA can help the manager prepare operating reports and can facilitate intraindustry comparisons. Under the BOMA chart of accounts, income is divided into rental income, service income, and miscellaneous income. The categories of expense include operations, alterations, fixed charges, and financial expenses.

■ CASE STUDY

THE OFFICE PROPERTY MANAGER

Jack Gonzalez has recently taken over managing Compton Place, a multistory office building located in an older part of a major city. It is near the recently completed renovation of the old railroad terminal where a number of farmers' markets have relocated. Ridership has increased due to this renovation. Compton Place has a high vacancy rate, and Gonzalez needs to address the situation.

1. What are some possible reasons for the high vacancy rate?
2. What is the first step Gonzalez should take to solve the high-vacancy problem?
3. After a thorough study, Gonzalez realized that setting a new rental schedule and increasing marketing efforts will be crucial to decreasing the vacancy rate. What can he do to market the property effectively?

■ REVIEW QUESTIONS

1. All of the following are useful when marketing office property *EXCEPT*
   a. brochures.
   b. signs.
   c. direct mail
   d. classified ads.

2. While longer lease terms are most desirable, to protect the owner from missing out on rising market rates, the lease should contain
   a. a recapture clause.
   b. right to assign clause.
   c. an escalation clause.
   d. right to sublet clause.

3. An employee of an office building tenant who is responsible for the internal arrangement and furnishing of the leased space is called a
   a. facilities manager.
   b. property manager.
   c. ADA manager.
   d. compliance officer.

4. One of the most effective methods to locate a new tenant for an office property is
   a. direct mail to businesses in a select ZIP code.
   b. canvassing a list of qualified prospects.
   c. a classified ad in a trade newspaper such as the *Wall Street Journal*.
   d. display ads in a local newspaper.

5. The absorption rate is determined
   a. from the property analysis.
   b. from the neighborhood analysis.
   c. from the class of the building (i.e., Class A, B, C, or D).
   d. by calculating the number of square feet that have historically been leased per year.

6. Which of the following factors was MOST important in the selection of office facilities, according to one survey?
   a. Cost
   b. Bus and highway accessibility
   c. Property environment
   d. Labor for building maintenance

7. Office space is designated Class A, B, C, or D on the basis of guidelines
   a. based on absorption rate.
   b. officially approved by law and published by BOMA.
   c. set by the local zoning boards.
   d. based on age, location, and market position.

8. The base rate for an office building
   a. should reflect the amenities of the space and competition in the area.
   b. is the lowest possible dollar-per-square foot figure.
   c. is set according to BOMA/ANSI criteria.
   d. should be calculated according to the New York method.

9. An older building, recently completely renovated, is located in a popular area amid several prestigious brand new buildings. By BOMA standards, the older building would be classified as
   a. A.
   b. B.
   c. C.
   d. D.

10. According to the BOMA method of measuring office space,
    a. rentable space includes elevator shafts and lobbies.
    b. columns used to support the building are deducted from the total area.
    c. a factor must be included giving weight to the availability of in-building parking.
    d. construction area is determined by a procedure similar to the New York method.

11. The New York method has not achieved wide acceptance because
    a. the measurement is too complicated.
    b. most property managers are suspicious of big-city innovations.
    c. it accounts for all of the construction area of a building and is difficult to "sell" to prospects.
    d. landlords resist it.

12. The ratio of rentable space to usable space is sometimes called the
    a. loss factor.
    b. BOMA method.
    c. lead factor.
    d. New York factor.

13. When preparing a market analysis on an office property, the manager should pay close attention to present market conditions and
    a. average vacancy rates.
    b. past economic trends.
    c. current economic trends.
    d. accessibility to public transportation.

14. Open or closed work spaces for more than one person are referred to as
    a. office space.
    b. special facilities space.
    c. miscellaneous areas.
    d. multipersonnel areas.

15. The manager measures all of the space on one floor. Then the manager subtracts the square footage for the restrooms, janitor closets, and elevator. The resulting square footage is called
    a. dominant area.
    b. construction area.
    c. usable area.
    d. rentable area.

16. If an office building lease does not prohibit assignment or subletting, the tenant may assign the space
    a. freely.
    b. only to an associated corporation.
    c. only with any increase being split with the owner.
    d. after hiring an attorney to obtain full rights to assign the lease.

17. Generally, the cost of tenant alterations and remodeling expenses above the building standard in an office property is the responsibility of the
    a. property manager who negotiated the lease.
    b. split equally between the lessee and lessor.
    c. lessor.
    d. lessee.

18. The purpose of a building standard is to
    a. ensure that the building is finished in compliance with fire codes.
    b. fix the amount the prospective tenant must pay, in addition to rent, for all alterations that need to be made to the space.
    c. fix insurance rates uniformly in any given state.
    d. list those amenities and alterations that a building owner will provide to an incoming tenant without charge.

19. A recapture provision
    a. is used by the IRS in assessing penalties for undeclared rental income.
    b. gives the tenant maximum control over space that may not be needed in the future.
    c. is for the benefit of the landlord.
    d. allows the tenant to sublease to a subtenant of his or her choice.

20. Proper maintenance of most office buildings differs from the maintenance of residential buildings in which of the following ways?
    a. Maintaining proper lighting
    b. Elevator operation
    c. Nighttime cleaning of tenant spaces
    d. Cleaning of common areas

CHAPTER FOURTEEN

RETAIL PROPERTY

■ KEY TERMS

Anchor tenants
Commercial strip centers
Community shopping
  centers
Mechanic's lien
Mixed use developments
  (MXD)

Neighborhood shopping
  centers
Percentage lease
Planned unit
  developments (PUDs)
Recapture clause

Regional shopping
  centers
Superregional shopping
  centers
Tax participation clause
Trade fixtures

■ LEARNING OBJECTIVES

At the end of this chapter, the student will be able to

1. identify and define five types of retail properties by size and number of families required to support the centers;

2. define anchor tenant and give examples of at least three patterns of retail centers, locating the anchor tenant in each;

3. contrast the difference between marketing to attract new tenants and marketing to attract shoppers to the shopping facility;

4. list examples of proper tenant mix, inappropriate tenant mix, and how to deal with parking;

5. summarize negotiating points regarding percentage leases and calculate three different forms of payments;

6. list five major rental income items, differentiating between preservation and income-producing capital expenditures; and

7. summarize the difficulties in determining risk liability and the importance for owners, tenants, and managers to carry adequate insurance.

■ OVERVIEW

Retail establishments are places where commodities are sold in small quantities directly to consumers. This chapter will focus on the predominant type of retail establishment—specialty and department stores—located in strip centers and malls.

Traditionally, retail merchants tended to congregate in areas accessible to a large number of people in a central urban business district located close to public transportation facilities. The larger metropolitan areas also supported secondary concentrations of retail stores at outlying transportation junctures.

As homes and businesses left the cities, investors and retailers built freestanding sets of stores with on-site parking that served as convenient retail outlets for the burgeoning residential neighborhoods on the fringes of the cities. By the 1950s, large retail and department stores began to follow customers to the suburbs. The emphasis in retailing shifted from merely satisfying neighborhood demands to catering to the merchandise needs of trade areas covering miles rather than blocks. The large regional shopping center became prevalent.

Today, retail property management runs the gamut from small neighborhood stores to large shopping complexes. Major regional shopping centers today offer one of the greatest challenges in property management. Much of this chapter is devoted to the broader aspects of shopping center management.

■ CLASSIFICATION OF SHOPPING CENTERS

Shopping centers are usually classified by market area, pattern, ownership, or merchandising. Traditionally, shopping centers have been grouped by market area: strip, neighborhood, community, regional, and superregional. Special kinds of centers, however, were developed that rely on a certain merchandising technique to draw customers.

Market Area Classifications

The size of the market area served by a shopping center determines the center's size. When leasing a retail location, the manager must find the tenant best suited to the available space, one that will enjoy the greatest chance of success. The following are only suggested guidelines; there are many variations.

Commercial strip centers   **Commercial strip centers** are also called *convenience centers* and are located on the edge of urban areas or in the suburbs. They are about 10,000 to 30,000 square feet (four to ten retail spaces) on a main thoroughfare and are primarily for convenience shopping. The typical design is a straight line of stores set back far enough from the street to allow for perpendicular parking. These strip developments often are owner-managed, even if the owner is not one of the occupants, which is also common.

Neighborhood center   The **neighborhood shopping center** is much larger, approximately 100,000 square feet, and must be supported by at least 1,000 families located within a 1.5-mile radius. It usually incorporates 15 to 20 stores located on about three acres of land and is often anchored by a supermarket and may contain a pharmacy, dry cleaner, and other small stores.

Community center   The **community shopping center** usually occupies about ten acres and includes from 20 to 70 stores, often anchored by a smaller local department store. The community center is normally from 150,000 to 300,000 square feet and draws customers from a five-mile trading radius. It depends on a minimum of 5,000 families for its support. Community centers usually include one or two supermarkets, a variety store, and small convenience stores in addition to the department store(s). In sparsely populated areas of the country, it may serve customers from a wider geographic area.

Regional center   The **regional shopping center** can house as many as six major department stores, accompanied by food stores, satellite stores offering a range of general merchandise, restaurants, and banks. It varies from 70 to 225 stores, serves a radius of 10 to 50 miles, and is supported by 50,000 to 150,000 families. Its size ranges from 300,000 to 800,000 square feet.

Superregional center   The largest type is called a **superregional shopping center.** It may house 1.5 million square feet or more of shops and appurtenant areas.

Pattern Classifications

Several basic design patterns, illustrated in Figure 14.1, have emerged during the evolution of the shopping center. Basic design patterns include the following:

- Neighborhood strip centers
- The *L-shaped center,* a spin-off from the straight strip center with anchor tenants (shown as shaded portions) usually located at each end of the L.

FIGURE 14.1

Shopping Center Pattern Classifications

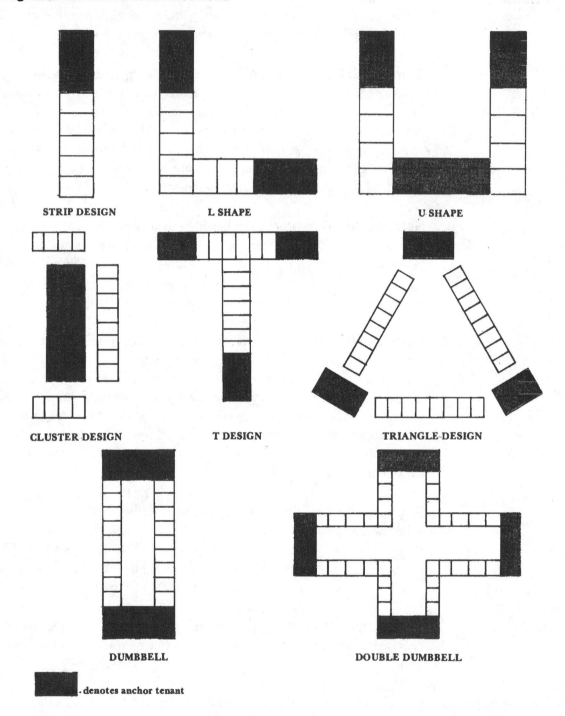

STRIP DESIGN

L SHAPE

U SHAPE

CLUSTER DESIGN

T DESIGN

TRIANGLE DESIGN

DUMBBELL

DOUBLE DUMBBELL

■ denotes anchor tenant

- The *U-shaped center*, another spin-off from the straight strip center that is formed by a line of stores at right angles to each end of the strip—because they are larger, U-shaped centers often serve entire communities and can have as many as three key tenants, one at each end of the U, with the major anchor store in the middle of the strip.

- *Cluster-design* shopping stores, which form a rectangle bounded by parking facilities on all four sides—the anchor store usually occupies one side of the rectangle and extends from the periphery to the center of the cluster. Cluster-design centers may be open or enclosed and may serve a local community or a region, depending on size.

- *T-design* or *triangle centers*, which can accommodate three anchor stores—both patterns provide for parking on all sides and can be either open or enclosed areas. They may serve a community or an entire region.

- *Dumbbell* or *double dumbbell* patterns, which consist of two strips of stores that face each other along a mall, with an anchor tenant at each end and parking on all four sides—the double-dumbbell center accommodates four key tenants. Dumbbell centers can be either single level or multilevel, open or enclosed. Split-level, enclosed double-dumbbell centers are now the preferred regional type.

Owner Classification

In the past, major stores were owned by individuals who created major buildings that were also architectural triumphs. Today, real estate development companies own and develop most shopping centers, especially malls. A shopping center can be owned by a single individual, by a group of persons forming a partnership, or by a corporation, and are financed by one or more long-term mortgages. The land, for instance, may be owned by one entity and the buildings by another.

Corporations and individuals are subject to different tax regulations; not all owners have the same overall financial objectives for their investments. Thus, it is essential for the manager to know the nature of the debt relationship, the type of ownership, and the implications these have for the operation of the center.

Merchandising Classifications

Shopping centers are often developed as a result of a specific merchandising approach, as follows.

Discount or factory outlets   Initially, many discount houses were simply factory outlets for surplus or bankrupt stocks of merchandise. They still remain. Others include the *closed-door discount house* that is open only to clientele who qualify on the basis of employment, such as government employees, or status, such as union membership; another type of closed-door store sells yearly memberships.

Off-price centers, *factory outlets*, and *discount malls* have enjoyed recent popularity and are usually found off major freeways outside small to medium-sized cities. The tenants usually are national and international firms selling discounted or "seconds" or irregular merchandise.

Specialty centers Specialty centers consist of specialty shops or boutiques, such as fashion malls. A flea market could be considered a special type of center. A *flea market* sells space to individuals who generally participate as a sideline or as a part-time occupation. The flea market may be indoors, often occupying older buildings that originally were discount houses, or outdoors, sometimes in property formerly occupied by drive-in theaters.

Power centers *Power centers* are generally large centers, from 300,000 square feet to in excess of 1 million square feet. These stores are mostly large national chain outlets that would be considered anchors in a conventional shopping center with a few adjoining small stores. Each merchant in a power center is dominant in its specialty, such as building supplies and material, toys, or imports. Such merchants are referred to as *category killers*, because it is feasible for only one of each merchandise classification to be in each complex. Power centers are popular with developers because the national credit status of the majority of tenants significantly assists in arranging financing.

Power centers advertise heavily as individual businesses, employing mass marketing and mass merchandising for their entire stock of goods, as opposed to featuring only certain items as loss leaders. Power centers are designed so that the customer may park in front of the main entrance of the destination store. The parking ratio is high, perhaps as many as six spaces per 1,000 square feet of gross leasable area (GLA).

Planned unit development Because conventional zoning lacks flexibility, the **planned unit development (PUD)** evolved, assigning various uses to a tract of land in accordance with a master plan and the particular terrain features of the tract. This flexibility frees developers from having to place a retail center only on a corner or on a major traffic artery of a multifamily or light office use development. The shops that are permitted in the PUD usually meet simple local needs, not serious shopping. Such shops could include convenience stores, dry cleaners, and perhaps small grocery stores.

Mixed-use developments The **mixed-use development (MXD)** is an expansion of planned unit developments. Generally, the MXD is a combination of retail, office, and residential areas, even sometimes including light industrial properties. By combining retail, office, and residential uses, MXDs rule out domination of one type of use, unless it was primarily designed as a shopping center or around a large office building development. Recently, hotels have been successfully integrated into mixed-use projects. For an example of this innovation see Figure 14.2.

The MXD allows people to live, eat, shop, conduct financial transactions, and partake of health and fitness facilities nearby, precluding the necessity for extensive automobile use. MXDs also meet the needs of large corporations who, when

FIGURE 14.2
Mixed Use Development

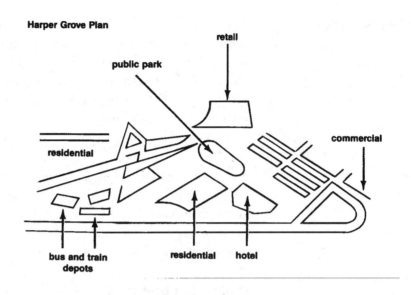

locating new corporate facilities, want to know where their employees can get housing, shopping, education, child care, and similar needs.

■ MARKETING RETAIL PROPERTY

Leasing is one of the retail property manager's most critical activities because each retail outlet in a shopping center depends on the traffic generated by other outlets. Percentage leases often are used, giving the owner a vested interest in the retailer's success, so quality tenants and the proper mix of types of stores are a must in retail space.

A sign on the property is probably the most cost-effective advertising. Retail space also is advertised by newspaper ads, radio spots, brochures, Web sites, direct mail campaigns, and personal contact with prospective tenants. Broker referral campaigns and in-house or outside leasing agents are other sources of qualified tenants. When deciding whether to hire a salaried on-site person for promotion or an outside advertising agency, the manager should remember the basic principle that advertising costs should not exceed 20 percent of the total operating budget for the center.

Anchor Tenants

Most centers have one or more **anchor tenants** or *key tenants*, large stores that through their own advertising will bring in shoppers. With the proper mix, both the large store and the smaller stores benefit. A shopper knows that once parked, he or she can locate several items at one time, or fulfill multiple tasks. For example, on the way home from work, the shopper can buy groceries, pick up dry cleaning, visit a toy store, and buy a dress, parking just once. Major marketing for other tenants is done after the anchor tenants have committed.

Customer Parking

The design of a center affects the type, placement, and accessibility of customer parking. Guidelines for the required number of parking spaces may be mandated by local ordinances and are usually based on the square feet of building or *gross leasable area* (GLA) in the center and are referred to as *parking ratio* or *parking index*. For example, one parking space for each 250 square feet is a common requirement. Different occupancies require different ratios: for example, a restaurant will have more demand for parking than will a dry cleaner.

Signage

Signage of retail space plays an important part not only of the initial lease-up efforts for the center and renting vacant space but also of the merchandising of the center. Merchants are very conscious of the value of signs. National or regional tenants want to be identified by their logos, which represent the reputations they have spent years building.

Preleasing phase   Billboards are usually used to announce the project, the spaces available, owner, leasing agent, and often the financing institution during the construction phase. Specific spaces can be indicated and marketed by window signs, informing of the size of space, a telephone number, and the name of a contact person. Because preleasing is a very important phase of launching the project, identify and publicize any committed tenants.

To stimulate even more interest, send postcard type invitations to all area commercial real estate brokers and agents. The marketing team should have already targeted certain retailers in the market area and invited them as well. A "moving allowance" could possibly be discussed with these existing business owners.

Established centers   When the center is up and running, permanent signage identifies the property; there may be a pylon sign advertising individual tenants if the tenants do not have distinctive signs on their individual premises; and there will be space identification signs. Mall centers, of course, have very little onstreet identification of individual stores other than of anchor tenants.

Merchants' associations   The merchants themselves are often responsible for certain common signage. Signs that advertise special sale days or special bargains in individual stores may be placed on signs that serve the center as a whole. These signs may be as simple as those with plastic removable letters or they may be complicated electronic signs, changeable by computer. These signs are run either as profit centers for the shopping center or as revenue for the merchants' association, whose members buy time or space on these signs as their needs arise. (Merchants' associations are discussed later in this chapter.)

Display Advertising

For retailers, display ads are generally used to promote the businesses, not to find tenants. (The tenants will drive around to find the site, so in that sense signs are better.) Display ads usually are placed in the financial section of metropolitan papers to promote large retail properties or in selected periodicals and trade journals. A large new regional shopping mall, for example, might run display ads in the regional issues of newsweeklies to create a prestigious image that will attract potential tenants.

Even more to the purpose is display advertising in the trade journals read by tenants, owners, and managers. This kind of advertising is most useful during the initial lease-up of a newly developed center. Spots aired over local radio stations are a viable advertising method for very large commercial developments.

Brochures

A concise, readable, and tastefully designed brochure should be distributed to a select group of potential tenants. It may highlight a single property or an entire shopping center. Location maps and layout diagrams will interest leasing agents as well as potential tenants. Lease terms should not be spelled out for fear of leading a prospect to a premature judgment before understanding the property's advantages.

Direct Mail

Direct mailings to companies most likely to become tenants are a popular vehicle for advertising large retail centers, although cost may limit or prohibit their use for small properties. Names can be obtained from the local Yellow Pages or from a more sophisticated source such as the *Dun & Bradstreet Reference Book* or the *Retail Tenant Prospect Directory* published by the National Mall Monitor.

Personal Contact

Personal contact solicitation is probably the most effective method of finding shopping center tenants, especially for small properties. The property manager of any center should build up a file of prospects and make regular cold calls on merchants in the trade territory of the shopping center, calling on those whose particular line of merchandise is needed in the center. The shopping center manager should keep a record of the termination dates of leases of competitive space and start canvassing for prospects a year or two before leases expire. Good prospects are aggressive, successful merchants who are tenants in centers that are not well maintained.

Publicity and Public Relations

The success of a retail store or shopping complex is dependent on ongoing promotional efforts. Many leases provide for the establishment of a merchants' association, and tenants must pay a membership fee based on square footage and spend a percentage of gross sales on joint advertising for the center.

Advertisements by an individual merchant or a group of merchants in one shopping center draw attention to that center. The added exposure gained from these ads increases sales for existing tenants and enhances the property's appeal to prospective tenants.

Newspaper Pull-Out Sections

Some regional shopping centers publish their own newspaper sections as supplements to local papers or as direct mail to consumers. Under the terms of the lease, the tenants have to periodically advertise in these sections. This newspaper advertising is more affordable and enlarges the trade area, and the shopping center reaps the benefits of free publicity.

Promotional Efforts

Promotional programs for large regional centers often are under the control of a salaried on-site director who may organize flower and plant shows, art exhibits, antique shows, car and boat shows, and seasonal events held in the shopping center as a means of attracting customers. While all regional centers require the need for organized, full-time promotion, the smallest type of center that can afford sustained or joint promotional programs is the community center.

Leasing Agents

Many retail property management firms use in-house leasing agents in the initial rent-up of a new development. The leasing agents are usually salaried and spend much of their time contacting proprietors of prosperous shops in the area and canvassing for other desirable tenants. The manager can encourage key commercial space brokers in the area to bring prospects to the center by offering a commission split or other financial incentive. Broker referral campaigns such as this can increase the property's exposure in the market.

■ LEASING RETAIL PROPERTY

Shopping center leases, like office building leases previously mentioned, have grown in length and complexity over the years. All of the basic clauses of a lease must, of course, be included, but some clauses are unique to retail leases. Space does not permit reprinting an entire shopping center lease, but Figure 14.3 shows some of those clauses that are exclusive to shopping center leases.

Qualifying Retail Prospects

Retail merchants must be qualified in much the same manner as office tenants are screened. The prospect firm must be financially solvent and compatible with other tenants in the center.

Tenant Mix

The mix of tenant types and locations is a prevailing concern. Stores should be placed so that traffic generated by one benefits the others and so that competition is not a detriment. In many cases, two or more businesses of the same kind in a center stimulate competition and add to the total volume of business transacted. On the other hand, if customer traffic is merely divided between the two retail

FIGURE 14.3
Shopping Center Lease

Shopping Centers, Inc.

Retail Premises Lease

Between SHOPPING CENTERS, INC., LESSOR and _____
_____ LESSEE
This LEASE is made and entered into this _____ day of _____, 19 _____ by and between
SHOPPING CENTERS, INC., a _____ corporation, hereinafter called LESSOR, and
_____
_____ hereinafter called LESSEE.

   WITNESSETH: That for and in consideration of the rentals hereinafter provided, and the covenants and agreements hereinafter contained, LESSOR leases unto LESSEE the following described premises, which premises LESSOR warrants it has good right to lease, to wit:

referred to hereinafter as "Leased Premises." A diagram of said premises, for purpose of reference and illustration only, is attached hereto and made a part hereof as "Exhibit A."

The Leased Premises are part of LESSOR'S property known as "BIG REGIONAL SHOPPING CENTER," and in which center other retail space is leased by LESSOR to other LESSEES. All areas in the Center other than retail space, including but not limited to, walks, parking lots, open areas, public facilities, etc., are designated "common areas" as used in this lease. All common areas are under the complete and exclusive control of LESSOR.

LESSOR and LESSEE further covenant and agree as follows:

1.   TERM OF LEASE. This lease shall be for a term of _____
(_____) years, commencing upon the _____ day of _____, 19 ___, and ending ___ day of

_____, 19 ___.

2.   RENTAL. LESSEE agrees to pay to LESSOR, its successors and assigns, as rental for said Leased Premises, the following:

   (a)   Base Rent. LESSEE shall pay, as base rent, the sum of _____
DOLLARS (_____) annually, in twelve installments of _____   _____
DOLLARS (_____) on the first day of each month during the term of this lease.

   LESSOR acknowledges the receipt of _____ DOLLARS ($ _____) as advance payment of the first and last months' rent for the above term of this lease, and as earnest money assuring LESSEE will enter into possession as agreed under the terms of this lease.

Source: Floyd M. Baird, Temple, Texas.

FIGURE 14.3 (CONTINUED)
Shopping Center Lease

(b) <u>Tax and Insurance Allocation, Ratio, and Adjustment.</u> In addition to the base rent above provided, and as additional rent, LESSEE shall pay its proportionate share of all taxes, general and special, assessed against every part of the entire real property of which the Leased Premises are a part, and also its proportionate share of the cost of all fire, windstorm and other hazard insurance carried upon the entire real property of which the Leased Premises are a part. LESSEE'S proportionate share of taxes and insurance costs shall be in the ratio that the floor area leased to LESSEE bears to the total floor area of the entire property of which the Leased Premises are a part, which ratio shall be applied to the total taxes assessed and insurance costs to determine LESSEE'S proportionate share. LESSOR shall estimate for the period from the effective date of this Lease to January 1st next following, the amount of LESSEE'S proportionate share of taxes and insurance costs, as provided above, based upon taxes and insurance premiums paid during the previous year. This proportionate share shall be the proportionate share of the LESSEE for the full year multiplied by the ratio that the number of months of this Lease prior to January 1st next following the execution of this lease, bears to twelve. LESSEE shall pay the amount so determined to LESSOR, in equal installments concurrent with payment of the base rental, commencing with the first day of the first full month of the term of this Lease, and ending with the rental payment due December 1st next following the effective date of this Lease. On or before January 1st next following the effective date of this Lease, and on or before each succeeding January 1st thereafter, LESSOR shall estimate LESSEE'S prorata share of the taxes and insurance costs for the succeeding calendar year, as provided above, and shall notify LESSEE of the amount of said estimate. LESSEE shall pay to LESSOR monthly thereafter during the ensuing calendar year, concurrent with the payment of the base rental, 1/12th of the amounts so estimated.

LESSOR shall keep annual records of the amount of taxes assessed and insurance costs paid and shall compute LESSEE'S pro rata share thereof. Within a reasonable time after January 1st of each year following the effective date of this Lease, LESSOR shall notify LESSEE of said LESSEE'S proportionate share of the taxes and insurance costs. If the monthly payments previously made by LESSEE are not sufficient to pay said LESSEE'S proportionate share of the taxes and insurance, LESSEE shall pay to LESSOR, within thirty (30) days after receipt of notice of said deficiency, the amount by which the actual costs of said LESSEE'S proportionate share of taxes and insurance exceed the estimated amount paid by LESSEE. If the estimated amount paid by LESSEE exceeds the LESSEE'S share of the taxes assessed and the cost of insurance, LESSOR shall credit said excess to LESSEE and shall reduce the estimated amount to be paid by LESSEE for the ensuing year by that amount. LESSEE shall have the privilege of examining records and computations upon which charges are made under these provisions.

(c) <u>Percentage Rent.</u> In addition to the payment of the Base Rent and all other rents and payments required hereunder, LESSEE shall pay to LESSOR, annually, the amount, if any, by which _____ percent (___ %) of the gross sales of merchandise (as hereinafter defined) during each Lease Year exceeds the aggregate amount of base rent paid by LESSEE to LESSOR attributable to said lease year, the method of computation and manner and time of payment of said percentage rent being more fully set forth hereinafter.

(d) <u>Statement of Revenue.</u> LESSEE shall submit to LESSOR, at the close of each month or within 10 days thereafter, a statement, signed by LESSEE and the manager of the store, showing the "gross sales of merchandise" for each day of said month.

(e) <u>Gross Sales of Merchandise Defined.</u> The term "gross sales of merchandise," as used in this Lease, is hereby defined to mean and include all sales of merchandise of every kind and character, and to include all revenues from all departments and services and sources made from the Leased Premises, for both cash and credit, including all orders taken and merchandise sold from the Leased Premises and filled or delivered from or to any other store or place, excluding taxes and refunds.

FIGURE 14.3 (CONTINUED)
Shopping Center Lease

(f) <u>Computation and Payment of Percentage Rent.</u> Concurrently with the furnishing of the monthly statements of gross sales of merchandise as hereinafter provided, LESSEE shall pay to LESSOR, as an installment payment to apply on the percentage rent due hereunder, any amount by which the percentage listed in (c) above multiplied by the gross sales of merchandise as shown on the monthly statement exceeds one month's Base Rent at the then current rate. Said percentage rent shall be computed at the close of each month or within 10 days thereafter, and shall be payable monthly as aforesaid. However, such percentage rent shall be annualized and subject to adjustment at the end of each Lease year. Within 60 days after the close of each Lease Year hereunder, LESSEE shall submit to LESSOR its statement showing the gross sales of merchandise for such Lease Year. Concurrently therewith, LESSEE shall pay LESSOR the amount of the percentage listed in (c) above multiplied by the gross sales of merchandise as shown upon the statement for the Lease Year less the aggregate monthly installment payments of percentage rent as heretofore provided for which have been paid for the Lease Year. If the aggregate monthly installment payments on percentage rent exceed the annual percentage rent due the excess shall be applied on future annual percentage rents due hereunder and any unapplied balance shall be refunded at the end of the term of this lease.

(g) <u>Lease Year Defined.</u> For all purposes under this lease, the term "Lease Year" shall mean the period from the commencement date of the term of this lease to the anniversary date of the first day of the month in which the commencement date of the term of this lease occurs and each 12 months period thereafter.

(h) <u>Books and Records.</u> LESSEE shall keep, in the Leased Premises, a permanent and accurate record in accordance with generally accepted accounting principles, consistently applied, showing "gross sales of merchandise" for each day during the term hereof, which record shall include all supporting and allied records, including but not limited to cash register receipts and sales tax reports. All such records shall be open to LESSOR at all reasonable times for the purpose of determining and verifying the percentage rent due. LESSEE shall retain and preserve all sales slips, cash register receipts and all other records pertinent to "gross sales of merchandise" for at least one year following the close of each Lease Year.

(i) <u>Audit.</u> LESSOR may at any reasonable time audit the records of LESSEE. If LESSOR audits the records of LESSEE and such audit reveals a greater amount of "gross sales of merchandise" than LESSEE has reported to LESSOR, LESSEE shall immediately pay the full and true amount of percentage rental due and shall pay all costs of the audit after notice thereof. If "gross sales of merchandise," as shown by the audit, do not exceed those reported by LESSEE to LESSOR, the audit shall be at the expense of LESSOR.

3. <u>CHANGE OF BASE RENT DUE TO COST OF LIVING (CPI).</u> Base rent as provided herein shall be adjusted in the same proportion as the fluctuation in the U.S. Department of Labor's Consumer Price Index published by the Bureau of Labor Statistics. For the purposes of this paragraph, the base month will be the month next preceding the first full month of the term of this Lease and the monthly rental commencing with the 13th month of this Lease will fluctuate in the same proportion that said Consumer Price Index is higher or lower than such base month on a cumulative basis. Such proportion will be computed annually for the first month following the completion of each twelve (12) months of the Lease, and the new rent derived from such computation shall be in effect for the next twelve months. In no event however will an adjustment be made which would reduce the Base Rental rate to an amount less than the rate set forth in this Lease. The necessary calculation for the adjustment required herein will be made as quickly as possible but in the event a rent paying date occurs before the adjustment can be calculated an amount equal to the then current unadjusted Base Rental rate will be paid by LESSEE to LESSOR on the rent payment date and as soon as the calculation of the adjustment has been made an additional payment will be immediately paid by LESSEE to LESSOR or a reduction on the next due Base Rental payments will be made, whichever is appropriate in order to cure any underpayment or overpayment of Base Rent.

FIGURE 14.3 (CONTINUED)
Shopping Center Lease

4.   PARKING. LESSEE agrees to cause its employees to park only in such places as provided and designated by LESSOR for employee parking. Upon written request from LESSOR, LESSEE will within five days furnish the state automobile license numbers assigned the cars of all employees.

5.   LIGHTING. LESSEE shall keep the display windows in the Leased Premises well lighted from dusk until 10:00 o'clock P.M. (local time) during each and every day of the term of this lease, and shall pay its portion of the cost of electric current and maintenance resulting from exterior lighting of the building and parking lot, based upon the ratio set out in 2(b) above.

6.   MERCHANTS ASSOCIATION. Should there be an association of the merchants in the shopping center of which the Leased Premises are a part, LESSEE shall belong to such association and pay reasonable dues assessed by a majority of the members of the association. The obligation to pay such reasonable dues shall be an obligation under this Lease.

7.   MAINTENANCE.
     (a)   Exterior. LESSOR shall be responsible for the maintenance of the exterior of the outside walls and Common Areas of the building, parking lot, roof, walkways, stairways, walks, drives, streets, alleys, yards, and other areas common to the premises of which the Leased Premises are a part. The pro-rata cost of such maintenance shall, however, be paid monthly as billed, by the LESSEE to LESSOR in the ratio that the square footage of the Leased Premises bears to the square footage occupied by all tenants of the premises of which the Leased Premises are a part.

     (b)   Interior. LESSEE shall maintain and keep in good repair the interior of the Leased Premises and all electrical and plumbing fixtures and equipment in the interior, including but not limited to, exposed installations on floors, walls and ceilings, all installations of any kind made by LESSEE, all hardware, interior painting and decoration of every kind, and all doors, windows and screens. LESSEE shall replace all broken or damaged glass on the Leased Premises at LESSEE'S sole cost. LESSEE will maintain and keep clear all floor drains and drain lines of all kinds in or upon the Leased Premises to their juncture with public sewer main.

     (c)   Heating and Air Conditioning. Heating and air-conditioning equipment, and hot water heaters, where present, shall be and remain the property of LESSOR. Where such equipment is installed by LESSEE, said equipment shall remain upon the Leased Premises at the termination of this Lease, and become property of LESSOR. LESSOR shall not be responsible for maintenance, repair or replacement of any such equipment, or damage caused by or because of such equipment. LESSEE shall hold LESSOR harmless from any damage caused by or because of such equipment, and in the event damage to the Leased Premises or the premises of which the Leased Premises are a part occurs by or because of such equipment, LESSEE shall immediately, and at LESSEE'S sole cost, repair and restore the damaged premises to their original condition. In the event of LESSEE'S failure, for a period of five days, to begin such restoration, LESSOR may make the necessary repair and restoration and LESSEE shall reimburse LESSOR the cost thereof.

8.   HOURS OF BUSINESS. LESSEE shall conduct its business in the Leased Premises during the regular and customary hours of such type of business and on all business days, and will conduct said business in a lawful manner and in good faith to the end that LESSOR may during the term of this lease receive the maximum amount of rental income reasonably to be anticipated from the conduct of said business.

9.   AWNINGS AND WINDOW COVERINGS. LESSEE shall not install awnings or other fixtures on the exterior of the building without prior written consent of LESSOR. In the event the Leased Premises have any exposed windows not used for merchandise display, LESSEE will install, at LESSEE'S cost, venetian blinds or other window coverings specified by LESSOR. LESSEE shall keep and maintain all awnings, venetian blinds, and other window coverings in a state of repair satisfactory to LESSOR.

FIGURE 14.3 (CONTINUED)
Shopping Center Lease

10. <u>SIGNS.</u> LESSEE is privileged to provide a store identification sign of its choice subject to consent and approval of LESSOR as to the type, design, construction, material used, and method of mounting. Any sign shall be installed and maintained by LESSEE so as to prevent all exterior water from entering the Leased Premises. LESSEE is responsible for securing any necessary permits and the payment of any fees in connection with erection of said sign. Damage to persons or property as a direct or indirect result of LESSEE'S sign is an exclusive risk of the LESSEE.

11. <u>TRADE FIXTURES.</u> LESSEE may install such trade fixtures as are reasonable and proper in carrying out the business which LESSEE is authorized to conduct in the Leased Premises. If LESSEE is not in violation of any of the terms or conditions of this Lease at the termination thereof, or any extension thereof, LESSEE shall remove all trade fixtures, including signs, from the Leased Premises and restore said premises to their original condition, all at LESSEE'S expense, except for any alterations, additions or improvements as provided for in Paragraph 14 of this lease. If LESSEE is in violation of any terms or conditions of this Lease, however, such trade fixtures shall remain on the Leased Premises and shall be subject to the terms of the Landlord's lien hereinafter contained.

12. <u>ADDITIONAL BUILDING.</u> LESSOR reserves the right at any time to build additional stories on the building occupied by LESSEE and to any building adjoining the same, and reserves the right to close any skylights and windows (except display windows) and to run necessary pipes, conduits and ducts through the herein Leased Premises. LESSOR further reserves the right to use and lease such additional space in such manner as LESSOR, at its sole option, may choose.

13. <u>NOT A PARTNERSHIP.</u> Nothing contained herein shall be deemed or construed by the parties hereto, or by any third party, as creating the relation of principal and agent or of partnership or of joint venture between the parties hereto, it being understood and agreed that neither the method of computation of rent, nor any other provision contained herein, nor any acts of the parties hereto, shall create any relationship between the parties hereto other than the relationship of LESSOR and LESSEE.

outlets, it is possible that neither profits. For example, if a strip center already has one grocery store, a second supermarket located in that center might possibly fail. A dry cleaning establishment or laundromat might do much better.

Industry statistics compiled by the International Council of Shopping Centers show the percentage of total shopping center space typically allotted to each type of store (department store, drugstore, women's specialty shop, tobacco shop, shoe store). For example, more than 7 percent of the total space in most regional shopping centers is used by food stores, about 23 percent by clothing stores, 6 percent by shoe stores, and 4 percent by gift and specialty shops. These figures can guide the retail manager in selecting the tenant population and the best tenant mix.

Location

Location of the vacant space within the shopping center also has an impact on tenant selection. In a large regional center, a men's clothing store is more suitably situated between a men's shoe store and a tobacco shop than between an ice cream parlor and a women's dress shop. Customers attracted to the shoe store, the tobacco shop, or the clothing store will overflow into the other two outlets, increasing sales for all three merchants.

Prospect's Needs

The manager should be certain that the prospect is the best possible merchant for the particular space and that the prospect will do the highest possible volume of business at that location. The prospect will be concerned about the adequacy of the parking facilities, gross amount of available leasable space, and suitability of the customer market for the prospect's type of business. The tenant must be financially solid enough to pay for or obtain financing for tenant alterations, fixtures, inventory, advertising, rent, percentage rent, insurance, maintenance, and other operating expenses.

Percentage Leases

The advantage of a **percentage lease** from the tenant's point of view is that it is a long-term lease with a fair minimum rental, obligating the tenant to pay additional amounts only when business volume justifies an increase. From the manager's and owner's perspective, the percentage lease implies that any new business is due to the tenant's location and the marketing efforts of the owners and the manager. The owner is allowed to share in the increasing value of the business volume and the location.

Because it is difficult to forecast future rental value, a percentage lease is utilized when leasing retail space for more than three or five years. There are several types of percentage leases: straight percentage, variable scale, and maximum, or a combination. Most percentage leases require payment of either a fixed minimum rental or a percentage rent based on gross sales, whichever is greater.

All percentage lease agreements should include provisions to verify the accuracy of the gross income reported by the tenant. If the threshold for the percentage rent to take effect is too low and/or if the percentage increase over the threshold is too high, some owners may "cook the books" and stay marginally under the threshold amount for rent increases.

Straight percentage   Under a straight percentage lease, the rental rate is based solely on a percentage of the gross income of the business, with no minimum guaranteed rent. This type of lease is uncommon and is employed only in unusual circumstances, such as for distressed property or for interim or seasonal occupancy.

Overage leases   Overage leases are sometimes called minimum-guaranteed percentage leases and are more beneficial to the owner. Although payments of overage rent may be made monthly, they usually are adjusted on an annual basis. The adjustment may be either on the tenant's lease anniversary or on a calendar year basis. To carry forward with the previous example, if yearly gross sales are less than $120,000, base rent paid for the year will still be $6,000. If, however, annual sales volume reaches $220,000, the tenant will pay a base rent of $6,000 plus overage rent of $5,000 or a total of $11,000 ($220,000 × 0.05 = $11,000 − $6,000 = $5,000).

■ By fixing a minimum rent, the owner is assured of a certain level of income, no matter how the tenant fares. For example, if the fixed monthly minimum rental is $500 and the percentage is 5 percent of annual gross sales, the tenant who has a yearly sales volume of $100,000 will pay only base rent ($6,000) for that year.

Combination   Many leases are a combination of calculations. For example, on a percentage lease calculated monthly, if the fixed minimum rental is $500 per month and the percentage rent is 5 percent of gross sales, a tenant who has a sales volume of $12,000 will pay $600 rent for that month ($12,000 × 0.05 = $600). However, if gross sales fall to $8,000 in the following month, the tenant will pay the $500 minimum rent, because 5 percent of $8,000 in gross sales is only $400. If in the third month, however, sales are $15,000, the tenant will pay $250 overage rent in addition to base rent.

Variable scale lease   Under a variable scale lease, the percentage rental rate changes according to the volume of business done. If, for example, the percentage rate is 6 percent of the first $10,000 income per month and 4 percent of all income over that amount, the lease is on a decreasing variable scale. Conversely, a lease might specify a rental schedule of 5 percent on sales up to $10,000 and 5.5 percent on sales over $10,000. This increasing variable schedule reflects the fact that a retailer's costs do not necessarily increase in proportion to sales volume. It allows the lessor to share in the extra profits of higher gross sales.

Maximum percentage lease   A maximum percentage lease has a clause setting a ceiling on the amount of rent they will pay over the course of the year, arguing that they are also adding to the pot, as it were, because of their advertising and ability to draw in customers.

Negotiating the Lease

The percentage lease contains most of the standard rights and obligations of landlord and tenant stipulated in other lease forms. The negotiation process usually centers around the computation and method of rental payment. The amounts of the minimum and percentage rentals; the definition of gross sales; methods of reporting sales and paying percentage rentals; geographical restrictions on business operations; requirements as to business hours, inventory, and personnel; and a recapture provision are all open for discussion during the negotiation of a percentage lease.

It is important to remember that the landlord's representative is looking at and working with leases everyday, and what might appear as an insignificant item to the representative could be substantially more significant to the prospective tenant. The representative should always endeavor to attempt to reach out and show concern about tenant issues. This will help to maintain prospective tenant interest.

Setting Rental Rates

The first step in the negotiation process is to arrive at an acceptable minimum rental based on rates for comparable space in the area market. The minimum rental must then be related to the percentage rental rate.

Calculating space   Areas used for retail stores in an office building are measured by the definition of store area. The number of square feet in a ground floor store area is computed by measuring from the building line in the case of street frontages and the inner surface of corridor and other permanent partitions to the center of partitions that separate the premises from adjoining rentable area. No deductions are made for vestibules inside the building line or for columns or projections necessary to the building. No additions are made for bay windows extending outside the building line.

Percentage of rental rate to business volume   Every type of business has a different percentage ratio of rental rate to business volume. This ratio is determined by each industry's cost of doing business, profit margin, and stock turnover rates. In general, slow turnover indicates lower business volume and higher profit margins, as with a jewelry store. Rapid turnover of stock is accompanied by high volume of sales and a low profit margin, as in a discount store or a supermarket. Accordingly, the percentage rental for a jeweler would be higher than for a grocer, because the sales volume is lower.

A general guide when negotiating lease terms is the percentage lease tables published by the International Council of Shopping Centers, the Urban Land Institute, and other real estate management organizations. Tables such as the one in Figure 14.4 display a range of percentage rents applicable to particular types of business throughout the country.

Tax participation clause   Many landlords include **tax participation clauses** in their percentage leases to provide more income stability. With property taxes rising so rapidly, long-term leases generally require the tenant to pay any increases in taxes or assessments above the rates for a specified base year.

The tax participation clause sometimes allows excess taxes paid by the tenant to be credited against the total percentage rental due for the lease year. The landlord may agree to this concession depending on the amount of the minimum rent and the percentage of gross sales to be paid. The parties usually agree on a gross sales total that must be reached before a credit is given. Similar participation provisions are sometimes included in large regional shopping center leases to cover escalating costs of insurance, common area maintenance, security services, contributions to a merchants' association, or joint promotional efforts.

Gross sales   The principal disadvantage is the difficulty of defining tenant sales and obtaining a complete and accurate reporting of those sales. The standard definition of gross sales most often acceptable to both parties is "the gross amount of all sales made on, from, or at the leased premises, whether for cash or on credit,

FIGURE 14.4

Percentage Lease Ranges

Automobile Dealers	1–3%
Automobile Accessories	2–5
Automobile Parking	40–70
Barber Shops	8–10
Beauty Shops	6–10
Books and Stationery	5–8
Candy Shops	6–10
Cigar Stores	6–10
Department Stores	2–3
Drugs—Independent	4–6
Drugs—Chains	2–4
Electrical Appliances	3–6
Florists	7–10
Furniture	4–6
Furriers	6–8
Hardware	3–6
Jewelers	6–10
Liquor Stores	3–6
Men's Clothing	4–8
Theaters	8–12
Restaurants	5–10
Shoes—Retail	5–8
Shoes—Repair	8–10
Sporting Goods	5–8
Women's Wear	4–8

after deducting the sales price of any returned merchandise where a cash refund is given."

The tenant must maintain records of all transactions subject to the percentage rate and furnish monthly statements of gross sales. At the expiration of the lease, the tenant may have to submit a statement of gross income for the entire lease term prepared by an independent certified public accountant. However, many leases provide that the owner/management company may audit the financial records to verify accurate sales reporting.

Financial audits   The lease should specify the owner's right to have the tenant's financial records audited during business hours. Because of the cost, most managers audit only the tenants of whom they are suspicious, and then only once a year. If an audit shows a tenant's records of gross sales to be accurate, most leases will make the landlord pay for the audit. However, if the audit discloses that the tenant owes rent in excess of a specified percent of the amount that was actually paid for that period, the tenant must pay for the audit as well as the amount of rent due as determined by the audit. An owner can request completion of an IRS Form 4506 so that tax returns could be requested if there are any questions on the information furnished.

Method of payment   Most percentage leases, including the sample in Figure 14.4, require gross sales to be reported by the tenant in writing on a monthly basis, with any amount due to be paid within ten days of the report. Many businesses are seasonal, though, and tenants with great seasonal variations in gross sales will insist on some type of adjustment provision. A luggage outlet, for example, which might have very low sales for the first ten months of the year, probably will have to pay the minimum rent because it is a higher figure than the percentage of income. In November and December, when business flourishes and more than compensates for the previous lack of revenue, the tenant is expected to pay a percentage of this overage income.

The most common method of adjustment requires the appropriate minimum or percentage rate to be paid each month, with the additional provision that if the total rent paid during a 12-month period exceeds the agreed-on percentage of total volume when computed over the entire year, the tenant will receive a refund or credit for the excess rent paid. Other leases provide that the percentage amount be paid only at the end of each lease year, while still others establish payment periods based on the expected variations in volume.

Non-Compete Clause

To protect their percentage of gross sales from erosion by sales from a branch store, most owners will not allow a tenant to open another store within a certain radius. Clauses like this sometimes do not hold in court, so they are becoming obsolete.

Regulating Tenant Operations

Other provisions in the percentage lease also are aimed at regulating tenant operations that affect gross sales volume. Tenants must be encouraged to expand their businesses as much as possible if the owner is to receive maximum profits from their use of the property.

If a tenant in an open mall agrees to extend its hours of operation beyond the normal business day to increase sales volume, thereby incurring added overhead costs, the landlord might consider a slight reduction in the percentage rental. If the percentage rate is decreased, however, the minimum rental should be raised proportionately to guarantee the owner adequate compensation despite the percentage reduction.

For security purposes, tenants in enclosed malls may not remain open after mall hours or on days when the mall is closed. Each lease should at least specify that the tenant will not close before the normal mall closing time (uniform hours). Depending on the tenant's reputation and financial status, lease covenants may stipulate its business hours, its staff composition, and the size of its inventory to ensure maximum gross sales. The tenant may be asked to spend a certain portion of income on advertising, as mentioned earlier.

Certain inherent representations are made by the landlord about the advantages of the market place created by the center, whether it is large or small. So when renting space during adverse economic conditions, the market representative, in concert with the landlord, needs to be careful about lowering the rent as compared to the existing tenants. Often, it is better to give the new tenant concessions such as the landlord paying for more of the tenant improvements or the first month of free rent types instead of lowering the price per square foot. Lowering rents generally angers existing tenants, and the practice also sets a pattern for lower rents in the future. If the process is continues to a large extent, existing tenants might bring a class action lawsuit against the landlord.

Recapture Clause

The **recapture clause** permits the landlord to retain the right to terminate a percentage lease at the end of an acceptable period of time if gross sales have not reached the level anticipated during negotiations. Another reason that landlords include recapture clauses is that they are concerned that an anchor may "go dark" rather than terminate a lease, in order to prevent competitors from leasing the space. The tenant may request a further provision that keeps the lease in effect by increasing the minimum rent to the amount the owner would have received had the expected sales volume been achieved.

This type of recapture clause must not be confused with the recapture provision mentioned in Chapter 13 in discussing an assignment and subletting clause. Each is used in a different situation.

Tenant Improvements

Retail and industrial space is generally rented with a minimal building standard, often as a bare building shell with central heating, ventilating, and air-conditioning systems. The tenant then pays for wall finishing, partitions, and other construction and decorating costs.

Some large commercial and industrial building owners may offer a plan for financing tenant alteration costs by amortizing the total cost of the improvements, plus interest at a reasonable rate, over the entire lease term. However, the total adjusted rent, including the improvements, can add up, sometimes to a price per square foot equivalent to as much as fifty percent above the going marketplace rent. This can be problematic during more difficult economic times.

Consider the consequences if the improvement amortization costs the tenant an additional $1.00 per square foot and the store is 4,000 square feet, and the agreement for the amortization requires the payment for the first five years of the lease term (i.e., $240,000). If the tenant sells the business or otherwise releases the space after two years, the landlord must consider who is going to pay the balance of the $144,000. Many new tenants are unwilling to pay the the improvement premium from the previous tenant.

Mechanic's lien   When the tenant makes improvements, it is important for owners to protect themselves from a **mechanic's lien** if the tenant does not fully pay for the improvements. The manager should check with state statutes. One method is to record the lease, thereby serving constructive notice that the tenant has possession; another way is filing a "notice of nonresponsibility."

Trade fixtures   Many tenants, particularly those with national recognition, will bring in and firmly attach shelves, counters, and other decorations. These improvements are called **trade fixtures**, and although they are attached, they do not become the property of the owner; instead, they remain personal property of the tenant. The tenant has the right to remove them up to the end of the lease, although the tenant may be responsible for repairing any damage that their removal causes.

In older centers, it may be difficult to differentiate between expenses for deferred maintenance and building improvements that correct deferred maintenance or increase the inherent value of the property itself and the alterations that accrue to the tenant's advantage only. The lease should be very specific about who is paying for what.

Tax advantages for improvements   Negotiations often center on the independent value and tax advantages of the improvement for both parties. If the owner performs the work and can prove that it is being done for a particular tenant only with no salvage value for future tenants, the owner can expect a short-term tax write-off for depreciation during the lease term. However, because it is not easy to prove that new flooring is for the sole benefit of the present tenant, the owner usually has to allocate this and other improvement costs to increasing the capital value of the property, thereby lengthening the period for depreciation write-off.

Tenants encounter fewer problems in verifying their right to depreciate their improvements over the term of a lease. The fact that tenants ordinarily garner a greater tax break from improvements than does the owner must be considered during negotiations. Regardless of who actually pays for the improvements, an amount should be added to the base rent to compensate for taxes or insurance costs resulting from them.

Insurance for Shopping Centers

Before any insurance can be purchased, the owner's legal liabilities must be clearly distinguished from the tenant's. Although the land or buildings for the center may have different owners, they function as a single entity; a loss in one owner's section may impede operations in another's.

Roadways, sidewalks, and parking areas also may have more than one owner and may be within an area leased by a specific tenant. These facilities are available to shoppers as a group, with no demarcation of different ownership interests. Thus, it is often difficult to determine the liability for a personal injury claim arising from an accident in a public area.

A good general rule for the manager to follow in securing public liability coverage for the center is to have all owners and tenants named as coinsureds on all policies even remotely affecting their interests. For added protection, the property manager and merchants' association should also be named as insureds on liability policies. Insurance policies should be purchased to cover all the major areas of risk outlined in Chapter 10. Plate glass insurance should be the responsibility of the tenant.

Each merchant in the shopping center will want to carry adequate insurance on inventory and improvements, plus product liability insurance, general liability insurance, workers' compensation, and other policies suited to the type of business.

Again, the owner, manager, and merchants' association should be named as coinsureds on public liability insurance purchased by the tenants. The two most expensive types of policy are general liability insurance and fire and extended coverage. The cost of the former has skyrocketed, especially for retail properties.

■ MAINTENANCE OF RETAIL PROPERTY

The retail property manager's maintenance duties depend on the center's size and the tenant's share of the common area maintenance. Strip centers usually require maintenance only of the exterior of the building, its structural elements, and parking facilities. Enclosed regional centers, with their common areas and central utility system, demand more of the manager's attention.

An enclosed center is actually one multiple-occupancy building, in which the obligations of the landlord, co-owners, and tenants overlap. Customarily, these overlapping obligations are set forth in the basic documents establishing the center, primarily in the reciprocal easement agreement. It usually is lengthy, but accompanying plats help to clarify the rights among the various tenants. The manager must understand the implications of any reciprocal easement agreements between the prime owner of the center and other owners, such as major department stores.

Like any manager of a large multitenant building, the retail center manager must be familiar with the heating, air-conditioning, utility distribution, waste disposal, and electronic security systems. The manager need not know how to maintain these systems personally but must know enough about them to set up maintenance procedures and to hire contractors or building employees to perform the work. If maintenance work is performed exclusively on a contract basis, at least one person is usually employed full-time by a large center to act as a liaison agent. This person should also be able to handle routine maintenance jobs that are costly when done by an outside contractor on a one-time basis.

Preventive maintenance programs and routine inspections of the building, grounds, and equipment are especially important for retail properties because of the heavy use they endure. A full set of physical inspection checklists can be obtained from the International Council of Shopping Centers (ICSC). These lists, entitled *Library of Shopping Center Forms for Management and Operations,* resemble those previously seen for apartment building inspection. A small strip center can be checked easily by the manager. Large regional centers, however, may require experts to examine their more complex operating equipment.

■ SECURITY AND LIFE SAFETY OF RETAIL PROPERTY

Security and life safety measures necessary for the protection of a shopping center will vary according to the size of the center. In a small strip center, the merchants generally will handle such problems; however, in larger centers, the on-site manager may be the sole security, although reinforced during busy shopping seasons by the addition of one or more security officers.

In a large mall center, a security director with a force of security officers will be in direct charge of security and life safety measures, but ordinarily the security director will report to the mall manager. (Security and life safety is covered in more detail in Chapter 17.) A decision must be made as to whether the security force will wear uniforms or distinctive blazers, which may be more in keeping with the tone of the center.

Today, malls have the added concerns of gang activity, drug dealing, and even kidnappings. Additionally, since 9/11, owners and managers must deal with the possibility of a terrorist attack and/or release of poisons as well. There are no easy responses. Constant vigilance and judicious use of cameras are all necessary to prevent crimes before they happen. Each center must clearly indicate evacuation routes.

The International Council of Shopping Centers recognizes that there is no one easy method for controlling these concerns. As a result, it is sponsoring ongoing seminars and conferences to assist in sharing of ideas. For example, businesspeople in the United States are taking their cues from Israeli businesspeople who have long allocated a substantial portion of their budgets to hiring and maintaining armed presences in their businesses.

Also, control of solicitation by organized charities, political organizations, and individuals in public areas of shopping centers has become an issue of increasing concern in recent years. Property managers should establish guidelines for the control of such activities and enforce them uniformly. An attorney experienced in this matter should be consulted and asked to draw up these guidelines based on local ordinances, and state and federal laws.

■ The National Multi-Housing Council's
Guidelines for Property Managers

The events of September 11, 2001, focused attention on the importance of building and property security. Concerns have also been voiced about the possibility of rented property being used to warehouse and conceal dangerous chemicals and explosives.

The National Multi-Housing Council (NMHC) has produced a guidance document for apartment owners and managers to help them respond to heightened security concerns. This document outlines procedures that property managers can use to supervise and monitor tenants and property, such as inspecting property routinely and closely interviewing prospective tenants.

Additional recommended steps include

■ expanding daily property-wide tours to include a viewing of all building perimeters;
■ inspecting occupied units immediately upon terrorist alerts and/or warning as per local laws, providing notice where laws require notice;
■ inspecting all vacant units regularly to make sure they are secured and vacant;
■ verifying identification of prospective residents;
■ verifying prior work history, visa information, and prior addresses; and
■ regularly updating school registration information if renting to students.

The free guidance memo for apartment owners is posted on NMHC's Web site at *www.nmhc.org/Content/ServeContent.cfm?ContentItemID=2489.*

Commercial property managers are also advised to increase security, including adding access controls, alarms, closed-cable TV monitoring, patrols, staff awareness training, policies and procedures, contingency plans, perimeter fortifications, window glazing, and other fortification.

Reprinted with permission from Deborah Long, *Real Estate Investment Fundamentals* (Dearborn Real Estate Education, 2004).

■ ADMINISTRATIVE RESPONSIBILITIES

The retail property manager's administrative responsibilities are governed by the owner's objectives. When a large corporation or association is the owner-employer, its objectives and the manager's responsibilities are clearly spelled out in the organization's bylaws. In other cases, the corporate owner of one or more shopping centers may sign a management contract delegating all authority to the manager, who becomes the primary decision maker for the property. The manager then must formulate a plan for attaining the owner's goals.

In either case, the manager must formulate a plan to meet the owner's goals. The manager must consider the tax consequences of decisions and their effect on the owner's income. The manager need not know the intimate details of the prime owner's income, but channels for reporting financial data must be set up and maintained if the owner's objectives are to be met and the manager is to receive adequate direction.

Industry Statistics

Managers can benefit by using a standardized system of accounting following the format of *Dollars & Cents of Shopping Centers*, the industry-wide compilation of financial reports on shopping centers published every three years by the Urban Land Institute (ULI). From this survey, the retail property manager can identify new trends and determine how well the shopping center is doing compared to similar centers. *Income/Expense Analysis: Shopping Centers*, published by IREM, is also helpful. Also, the International Council of Shopping Centers offers a wealth of statistical information at *www.icsc.org*.

Financial reports   It is impossible to establish a uniform system of financial reporting for retail properties because of variations in shopping center size, function, layout, ownership, and tenancy. It is possible, though, to classify and describe common reports in general terms. Basically, the owner wants two types of information about the property—its current financial status and its economic future. *A Standard Manual of Accounting for Shopping Center Operations*, published by the Urban Land Institute (ULI), provides retail property managers with a standardized system for reporting income and expense. The method is adaptable to both large and small centers and permits intraindustry cost comparisons. This accounting system is similar to BOMA's standardized method for office building accounting.

Major rental income items   Under the standardized accounting method for shopping centers, there are five major rental income items:

1. Minimum rental guaranteed by the tenants' leases

2. Overage rent based on percentage clauses

3. Rental income from rent escalation clauses

4. Income from sale of services to tenants

5. Income from sale of utilities

Actual income   Income items should be realistic estimates of actual income, with the rent loss and vacancy factors built in. The most difficult source of income to predict is the overage rental income based on percentage or escalation clauses. Overage income information must be gathered whenever the retail property manager prepares a forecast, budget, or financial statement.

The manager should obtain a statement of sales volume from all tenants at the times specified in their leases. Then the manager should compare each tenant's figures for the current period with its past performance and determine the percent of increase or decrease for the current year. Conferences with store managers may reveal sales projections for the coming year. The historical record of each tenant's performance permits comparison of one tenant with another and with the group as a whole. Obviously, such reports are most helpful during the lease renewal negotiations.

Expense items   Under the standard method of accounting for retail property, expense items are charged to one of the following categories: building maintenance, public area maintenance, utilities, office area maintenance, financing, advertising and promotion, real estate taxes, insurance, or administrative costs. Building maintenance expenses include employee wages and supplies for all retail space within the shopping center. Public area maintenance (e.g., parking lot, mall, and grounds) and office area maintenance are in separate categories. Utility expenses include the cost of all forms of energy, as well as the labor involved in supplying heat, lighting, and air-conditioning to tenants.

Financing costs are simply the interest on outstanding loans, because any amount applied to reduce the loan principal should not be expensed. Insurance costs include insurance against fire and other damage, boiler and equipment insurance, liability insurance, rental value insurance, and employee bonds. Management fees, the building office payroll, other office expenses, and professional fees are considered administrative expenses.

Operating Budget

The format of a retail center operating budget is similar to that used for other forms of income property. The major difference is that capital expenditures must be broken out and listed in a separate budget.

Another significant aspect of the retail property operating budget is its rigidity, as the major expense is for the real estate taxes.

Capital expenditures   The capital expenditures budget includes income from the sale of assets, payments on the principal of a mortgage or other debt, and yearly expenses for repairs or additions that will be depreciated over several years. The capital expenditures budget must be prepared along with the operating budget, because the two reports are closely interrelated. However, the manager must adopt a different frame of reference when preparing the capital budget.

> Unlike the operating budget, the capital expenditures budget must look several years into the future. Capital expenditures can be divided into two major categories governed by different economic principles: preservation, and income-producing capital expenditures.

Preservation   Money spent for preservation is not meant to generate new income but to protect the facilities already in existence. Repairing the asphalt surface of a shopping center parking lot would be classed as a capital expense for preservation. Tenants often absorb some of the cost of such an expense through a common area maintenance charge.

Income-producing capital expenditures Income-producing capital expenditures either produce more gross income or increase present net income by reducing operating expenses. For example, capital expenditures for expansion or for installation of a more efficient heating plant could be considered income producing. Before incurring any expenses of this nature, the manager should prepare a detailed cost analysis of the proposed investment to determine if the initial cash outlay will be recovered in the long run.

Monthly Cash Flow Forecast

After the owner has approved the annual budget, the manager should prepare a monthly forecast of cash flow to serve as a reference point for fiscal management in the upcoming year. For this report, cash flow is simply the difference between money received and money spent each month (total income minus operating expense and debt service).

The monthly forecast is necessary because of the uneven flow of cash during the year. Peaks in expenses must be anticipated so that there is cash on hand when the bills fall due. To some degree, income also fluctuates due to vacancies and the fact that percentage rents are not payable on a single time schedule. These variables are reflected in Figure 14.5.

To prepare the monthly forecast, the manager must estimate when total annual income will be received and expenses paid out. The estimates are then indexed by month and broken down into the standard income and expense categories contained in the operating budget. The forecast should be reviewed in depth at least quarterly. If obvious discrepancies are found, the manager should adjust the forecast for the remainder of the year or identify the reason for the discrepancies and try to remedy them.

Monthly Operating Income (Loss) and Cash Flow Statement

The frequency with which the manager must submit operating reports will depend on the owner's needs and the size of the shopping center. The monthly cash flow statement should compare the income and cash flow for the month with the cash flow forecast for that month. The statement should make a running tabulation of actual income and expenses for the year to date and should compare these figures with the budgetary allotment for this period. The ULI form, shown in Figure 14.6, illustrates this process.

FIGURE 14.5

Monthly Cash Flow Forecast

Dates

Property:	January	February	March	April	May	June	July	August	September	October	November	December
Income												
Minimum rental income	$100,000	$100,000	$100,000	$90,000	$60,000	$70,000	$80,000	$90,000	$98,000	$100,000	$100,000	$100,000
Overage rent	20,000	18,000	18,000	17,000	18,000	18,000	18,000	20,000	30,000	25,000	30,000	40,000
Rental Income from escalation	1,000	1,000	1,250	1,500	1,800	2,200	2,500	2,750	3,000	3,300	3,600	4,000
Services to tenants	9,000	9,000	9,000	9,000	9,000	9,000	9,000	9,000	9,000	9,000	9,000	9,000
Sales of utilities	7,000	7,000	7,000	7,000	7,000	7,000	7,000	7,000	7,000	7,000	7,000	7,000
Other income	1,000	1,000	1,500	1,500	2,000	1,500	1,500	1,500	1,500	1,000	1,000	1,000
Total	$138,000	$136,100	$136,750	$126,000	$97,800	$107,700	$118,000	$130,250	$148,500	$145,300	$150,600	$161,000
Expenses												
Building maint.	$1,000	$1,000	$1,000	$12,000	$2,000	$2,000	$2,000	$2,000	$1,000	$1,000	$500	$500
Public area maint.	9,000	9,000	9,000	9,000	9,000	9,000	9,000	9,000	9,000	9,000	9,000	9,000
Utilities	6,000	6,000	5,000	5,000	5,000	6,000	6,000	6,000	5,000	6,000	6,000	6,000
Office area maintenance	1,000	1,000	1,000	1,000	1,000	1,000	1,000	1,000	1,000	1,000	1,000	1,000
Financing and payments on loan principal	48,000	48,000	48,000	48,000	48,000	48,000	48,000	48,000	48,000	48,000	48,000	48,000
Advertising and promotion	1,500	1,500	1,500	1,000	1,000	1,500	1,000	1,500	1,500	1,000	1,500	1,500
Real estate taxes	—	—	—	—	—	72,000	—	—	—	—	—	72,000
Insurance	—	—	4,000	—	—	4,000	—	—	4,000	—	—	4,000
Administrative	5,500	5,500	5,500	4,600	4,100	4,600	4,600	5,100	6,100	6,000	6,100	6,300
Miscellaneous	5,000	5,000	5,000	5,000	5,000	5,000	5,000	5,000	5,000	5,000	5,000	5,000
Total	$77,000	$77,000	$80,000	$75,600	$75,100	$153,100	$76,600	$77,600	$80,600	$77,000	$77,100	$153,300
Cash Flow	$61,000	$59,100	$56,750	$50,400	$22,700	($45,400)	$41,400	$52,650	$67,900	$68,300	$73,500	$7,700
Cumulative Cash Flow	$61,000	$120,100	$176,850	$227,250	$249,950	$204,550	$245,950	$298,600	$366,500	$434,800	$508,300	$516,000

FIGURE 14.6

ULI Report of Operating Income (Loss) and Cash Flow

	Current Month			Year to Date		
Month Of _____	Plan	Actual	Over (Under) Plan	Plan	Actual	Over (Under) Plan
Income						
01 Rental Income—Minimum Rent						
02 Rental Income—Overages						
03 Rental Income—Rent Escalation Charges						
07 Income for Common Area Services						
08 Income from Sales of Utilities						
09 Miscellaneous Income						
TOTAL INCOME						
Expenses						
10 Building Maintenance						
20 Parking Lot, Mall, and Other Public Areas						
25 Central Utility Systems						
30 Office Area Services						
40 Financing Expense						
50 Advertising and Promotion						
60 Depreciation and Amortization of Deferred Costs						
70 Real Estate Taxes						
80 Insurance						
90 General and Administrative						
TOTAL EXPENSES						
NET INCOME (LOSS)						
Add: Depreciation and Amort. of Deferred Costs						
Deduct: Mortgage and Other Loan Principal Payments						
NET CASH FLOW						

Source: Reprinted with permission from *Urban Land Institute*, 1025 Thomas Jefferson Street, N.W., Suite 500W, Washington D.C. 20007-5201.

Profit and Loss Statement

Besides correlating actual results with forecasted amounts, the year-end profit and loss statement should supply any supplementary information needed for the owner's tax returns, such as depreciation charges, capital improvement costs, and the total amount of debt reduction. The data may be displayed in three columns:

1. The budgeted amount

2. The actual figures

3. The variance between budget estimates and real costs

An additional column showing the figures for the preceding year could be included as a frame of reference for the owner.

■ SUMMARY

The retail property management field ranges from centers with only a few retail outlets to large regional complexes. Small centers usually require only exterior maintenance from the manager, whereas major shopping complexes, with their sophisticated equipment and large common areas, test the executive and administrative skills of the most experienced manager.

Shopping centers can be classified according to market area, pattern, and ownership. The strip center consists of 4 to 10 stores and has the smallest market area. The neighborhood center includes from 15 to 20 stores and is designed to provide convenience shopping for customers within a 1.5-mile radius. The community center (from 20 to 70 stores) usually has a junior department store and draws customers from a five-mile radius. Regional centers can vary from 70 to 225 stores, but all have at least one major department store as their key tenant and draw customers from 10 to 50 miles.

Basic design patterns accommodate key and subsidiary tenants. These patterns include linear strip centers, L-shaped centers, U-shaped centers, clusters, T-design groups, or triangles.

Retail space is advertised through signs, ads, brochures, and direct-mail pieces. Broker referral campaigns, leasing agents, and publicity efforts also can increase the exposure of the property.

The manager's objective is to find the merchant who will do the largest volume of business in each retail location. The manager must assess that prospect's financial capabilities, compatibility with existing tenants, spatial and parking needs, preferences in amenities, and customer requirements.

Location within a shopping center has a great effect on the success or failure of the business. Competitors should not be situated next to each other, but allied businesses or services should be grouped together so that each benefits from the customer traffic to and from the neighboring stores.

A percentage lease is often used for leases for more than three or five years. A minimum guaranteed percentage lease requires periodic payments of either a fixed minimum rent or a percentage rent based on gross sales, whichever is greater. The other three types of percentage leases are straight, variable scale, and maximum percentage leases.

The lease must specify most of the standard rights and obligations of landlord and tenant, the amounts of the minimum and percentage rentals, the definition of gross sales, and methods for reporting sales and paying percentage rentals. Other provisions open to negotiation include any of the following: tax and insurance participation clauses, recapture provision, geographic restrictions on business operations; requirements as to business hours, inventory, and personnel; and extent of tenant alterations.

Physical maintenance of retail properties depends on the center's size, geographic location, and the tenants' share of common area maintenance. Shopping centers demand rigorous preventive maintenance programs and routine inspections of the physical structure, grounds, interior, and equipment. Housekeeping and routine cleaning of common elements are major expense items in the maintenance budget. Security is another major expense item.

It is impossible to establish a uniform system of financial reporting that meets the needs of every type of retail property. However, the owner generally wants two types of information about the property—its current financial status and predictions of events likely to influence the future of the shopping center.

Shopping centers need protection against all the major risks covered in Chapter 16. Retail property insurance is complicated by the fact that shopping centers, which function as a single entity, often are owned by more than one person, group, or corporation. Thus, it is often difficult to determine liability for a personal injury claim arising from an accident in a public area.

The manager should have owners, tenants, the manager, and the merchants' association named as coinsureds on all liability policies even remotely affecting the interests of any other party. The manager should also require each tenant to name all owners, the manager, and the merchants' association as coinsureds on liability insurance taken out by the individual tenant.

■ **CASE STUDY**

THE RETAIL PROPERTY MANAGER

Henry Palmer, owner of Palmer Properties Associates, asked Bud Lowe, a property manager, to review the management of a Palmer Properties shopping center. After a brief analysis of the property, Lowe gave Palmer a preliminary report, stating that the shopping center needed a facelift to remain competitive with newer malls. He also discovered that no escalation clauses had been included in the leases to cover increases in taxes and insurance. Other problems included insufficient maintenance contributions, nonenforced percentage rates, and noncoordinated promotional efforts.

1. Assuming that the shopping center is a one-story straight brick wall structure in a U-shaped configuration with a canopy running the full length of the building, what are some options for renovations?

2. Is there anything Palmer or his property manager could do about the lack of escalation clauses?

3. How could the property manager try to solve some of the other problems mentioned?

■ REVIEW QUESTIONS

1. Before the advent of shopping centers, retail merchants tended to congregate
   a. in scattered neighborhood centers.
   b. along major roads leading into town.
   c. in a central business district near major public transportation junctions.
   d. in no particular pattern.

2. Which of the following is typical of a neighborhood center?
   a. Incorporates shopping for about 100,000 people
   b. Serves an area approximately three miles in diameter
   c. Contains about 10,000 to 30,000 square feet
   d. Anchored by a junior department store

3. Most regional shopping centers are
   a. U-shaped.
   b. cluster-design.
   c. T-shaped.
   d. dumbbell-shaped.

4. Which type of shopping center draws customers from a five-mile radius?
   a. Neighborhood
   b. Regional
   c. Community
   d. Strip

5. Which of the following businesses require the greatest number of parking places?
   a. Fabric store
   b. Bike shop
   c. Dry cleaners
   d. Restaurant

6. A mixed-use development encompasses
   a. single-family, duplex, and multifamily housing in one subdivision.
   b. a mixture of light, medium, and heavy industry in a single development.
   c. tenants of various ethnic backgrounds.
   d. a combination of two or more types of uses, such as retail, office, and residential in the same complex.

7. Most prospective tenants interested in retail space find it by
   a. looking for leasing sites in the classified ads.
   b. responding to canvassing by the property manager.
   c. driving through the area in which they wish to locate.
   d. getting referrals from brokers.

8. In general, persons looking for retail property to rent
   a. read classified ads.
   b. look for signs.
   c. listen to the radio.
   d. respond to display ads.

9. The MOST effective method for finding shopping center tenants is
   a. brochures.
   b. personal contact.
   c. direct mail.
   d. use of public relations firms.

10. Large retail properties are promoted through display ads usually placed in
    a. newspaper pullout sections.
    b. the real estate advertising section of newspapers.
    c. ads in the classified section of the local newspaper.
    d. the financial section of metropolitan newspapers.

11. The prevailing concern in leasing retail space in a shopping center is the
    a. business experience of the tenant.
    b. financial qualifications of the tenants.
    c. requirement of an equal mix between regional chains and local firms.
    d. mix of tenant types.

12. Studies of tenant mix with regard to percentage of space allocated to various types of stores, based on their merchandise line, have been made by
    a. Building Owners and Managers Institute.
    b. International Council of Shopping Centers.
    c. Institute of Real Estate Management.
    d. National Association of Corporate Real Estate Executives.

13. When evaluating a prospective tenant in terms of tenant mix, the manager should look at a variety of the tenant's needs, including the tenant's need for
    a. access for the disabled.
    b. parking facilities.
    c. less expensive rent.
    d. good manager-tenant relations.

14. A merchant signs a lease that sets a minimum monthly rental rate of $600, or 6 percent of gross sales. If rent is computed on a monthly basis, what is the total amount of rent paid in the fourth quarter if gross sales were $8,000 in October, $11,000 in November, and $12,000 in December?
    a. $1,860
    b. $1,800
    c. $1,920
    d. $1,980

15. A variable scale percentage lease sets the monthly rental rate at 6 percent of gross sales up to and including $15,000, plus 5 percent of gross sales in excess of $15,000 but not in excess of $30,000, plus 4 percent of gross sales in excess of $30,000. What would the rental payment be if gross monthly sales were $42,000?
    a. $1,650
    b. $2,070
    c. $2,130
    d. $2,250

16. Overlapping obligations of landlords, co-owners, and tenants are customarily set forth in
    a. the property manager's rules and regulations for tenant conduct.
    b. franchise agreements.
    c. reciprocal easement agreements.
    d. Library of Shopping Center Forms for Management and Operations.

17. A recapture clause in a shopping center lease
    a. is the same as one in an office lease.
    b. refers to assignment and subletting.
    c. allows the landlord to terminate a percentage lease if a certain level of gross sales has not been achieved.
    d. refers to provisions in the Internal Revenue Code.

18. Negotiations for tenant improvements are the MOST complex in
    a. newly opened centers.
    b. centers where a long-term tenant has vacated.
    c. triple net lease negotiations for a freestanding building.
    d. buildings where there is little deferred maintenance.

19. The *Standard Manual of Accounting for Shopping Center Operations* is published by the
    a. Urban Land Institute.
    b. Institute of Certified Public Accountancy.
    c. International Council of Shopping Centers.
    d. Building Owners and Managers Institute.

20. Accounting statistics of centers may be compared to other centers by referring to the
    a. Experience Exchange Report.
    b. International Council of Shopping Centers' *Standard Marketing for Shopping Centers*.
    c. reports of the National Association of Certified Public Accountants.
    d. *Dollars & Cents of Shopping Centers*.

CHAPTER FIFTEEN

15

INDUSTRIAL PROPERTY

■ **KEY TERMS**

Building-employment
  density
Corridor development
Foreign trade zones
  (FTZs)
Industrial parks
Labor-oriented industries
Land-employment
  density

Market-oriented
  industries
Ministorage centers
Net lease
Private industry councils
  (PICs)
Rent factor

Research and
  development (R&D)
  centers
Resource-oriented
  industries
Sale leaseback
Structural density
Tax incentives

■ **LEARNING OBJECTIVES**

At the end of this chapter, the student will be able to

1. identify and explain key factors that distinguish industrial real estate from any of the other types of real estate: plant size and features, land-use patterns, and industrial development incentives;

2. explain a sale leaseback arrangement and the advantages to each party;

3. list and describe at least three incentives utilized by brokers and communities to lure industry to their areas;

4. discuss and identify the need for effective marketing techniques for the manager who specializes in industrial real estate to cooperate with other brokers and community development groups when marketing the space and describe other forms of advertising;

5. describe the industrial tenant's qualifications, and unique issues encountered in showing property and negotiating the lease;

6. summarize the complexity of negotiating long industrial leases and the advantages of longer leases;

7. explain rent factor and compare the advantages to the owner of the net lease versus the gross lease that the tenant may want;

8. define *ministorage* and explain why it has become so popular; and

9. summarize the job description of the resident manager for a ministorage facility and discuss how computer software can improve record keeping;

■ OVERVIEW

Industrial real estate includes all land and buildings used or suited for use by industry. Industry includes all activities involved in the production, storage, and distribution of *tangible goods* as opposed to intangible services. It refers to the transformation of raw materials or components into finished products and extends to packaging, warehousing, distributing, and transporting these finished products.

■ NATURE OF INDUSTRIAL REAL ESTATE

Classification by Use of Site

An industrial site is any location where industrial activity occurs. Depending on their adaptability, industrial land and buildings can be classified as general purpose, special purpose, or single purpose. The unique features of industrial real estate have a direct bearing on the management of such property.

General-purpose buildings have a wide range of alternate uses. These properties can be used for storage or adapted for light manufacturing or assembly plants. *Special-purpose buildings* have certain physical characteristics that limit the scope of their use. Buildings suitable for only one type of operation, or even one firm, are called *single-purpose industrial properties*.

Heavy Capital Investment

Industrial properties generally require heavy investment capital. Although many large corporations prefer to locate a site and build a plant to meet their exact specifications, these activities can tie up a substantial portion of the firm's operating funds.

Investor's Risk

The specialized nature of some industrial buildings and the large size of others make industrial property a slow-moving commodity in the real estate market. The nonliquidity of the property increases the owner's investment risk, which in turn leads the owner to place more demands on the industrial tenant.

Sale-Leaseback

Because many corporations prefer to invest their capital in their own business operations rather than in real estate, they will seek an investor who wants to put money into a property with a guaranteed long-term lease. The corporation will then sell the chosen site to the investor and simultaneously execute a long-term lease. This is called a **sale-leaseback** agreement: The corporation gets back its capital investment so that the funds can be reinvested in the business. Because this arrangement is profitable for both parties, industrial real estate is often investment property with the manufacturer-tenant paying rent to the investor-owner.

The value of industrial property is closely intertwined with the profitability of the firm renting the space. The integration of the property with the machinery and inventory of the tenant firm makes it difficult for the manager to distinguish between the value of the owner's facilities and the tenant's equipment. Once the equipment is installed, the customized quality of the property makes the functioning of the tenant's machinery an indispensable part of the owner's capital investment.

Functional Obsolescence

Technological changes make heavy or specialized industrial facilities susceptible to rapid *functional obsolescence*, i.e., the building is intact but the use is out-of-date. This threat increases the owner's investment risk and requires careful planning to minimize the chances of structural or functional obsolescence of the building or its tenants. Warehouses and storage space are an exception to this rule because they require less customization. Tenants in warehouses and distribution facilities tend to relocate more frequently; hence, the investment risk of such property is lower and the liquidity higher.

Most industrial tenants have comparatively long lease terms, ranging from 10 to 25 years or more. The high cost of moving heavy machinery and maintaining large inventories is not conducive to frequent changes in location, so the selection of a suitable site is critical. Because industrial tenants are not expected to be experts in the real estate market, the responsibility for matching tenant and property rests largely on the shoulders of the industrial property manager.

■ THE INDUSTRIAL REAL ESTATE MARKET

Trends in the Industrial Real Estate Market

Despite the high cost of relocation, more firms are leaving the traditional bastions of industrial activity in the northeastern United States for locations in the Southwest, South Central, and Southeast, and even overseas. A number of factors—lower property taxes, a better labor market, lower pay scales for workers, fewer unions, lower construction costs, and a better climate—have fostered this trend.

There is also a countertrend to the movement of industrial firms from the older industrial cities to new regions. Because older industrial communities have already paid for the infrastructure—roads, highway networks, ample utilities, and good sewage systems—industry can sometimes find competitive offers from older areas. High unemployment rates caused by employers closing or moving industrial business has caused some unions to soften some union requirements in an effort to re-establish jobs in the older industrial cities.

Industry Classification by Location Preference

Three major categories of industry can be identified, based on the criteria for selecting space.

Market-oriented industries   Market-oriented industries sell to private or industrial consumers. Industries of this type rely on a large consumer population and are sensitive to growth trends or shifts in the marketplace. They tend to be located near points of distribution to reach their customers more quickly and economically. Today, however, all of this is changing. In the current marketplace, goods can easily be shipped over vast distances, and then taken directly to the distribution center. A good example of this is the Wal-Mart distribution center located in Bentonville, Arizona.

Resource-oriented industries   Resource-oriented industries need to be located near their source of raw materials or supplies to minimize materials transportation costs. An example is a steel plant, because it needs to be located close to its fuel or bulky raw materials, such as iron ore.

Labor-oriented industries   Labor-oriented industries, especially if they use unskilled workers, are concerned with the availability and cost of the labor pool. An automobile manufacturer will center itself in an area market that offers semiskilled and unskilled workers. Also, firms have located on the U.S.–Mexican border to take advantage of cheap labor-intensive operations conducted in Mexico with final assembly or packaging in the United States.

Market and Property Analyses

Although general industrial trends provide a useful frame of reference, the industrial property manager's objective is to match a particular property with a specific firm. This process requires a detailed study of the physical aspects of the property, local supply and demand, and each prospect's needs.

The demand for industrial properties is not an independent factor but relies on consumer demand for the product of the industrial process. To determine the market demand for a particular type of industrial property, the manager must know something about the nature of industrial processes and the character of local industrial growth and development. The first step in advertising, showing, leasing, and managing an industrial property is to study its features and the prospect's reactions to them. The manager should keep a written record of such information, perhaps on a form similar to the one shown in Figure 15.1.

Site selection criteria   To interpret the demand for industrial space accurately, the manager must know why industries select one location over another. When selecting plant sites, an industrial firm will try to minimize production costs

FIGURE 15.1
Building Information Form

Industrial Building Information

Size _____ Dimensions _____

Location _____

Date Available _____ Monthly Rent _____

Ground Area _____ Parking _____

Lot Dimensions: Frontage _____ Depth _____

Zoning _____ In City _____ Out of City _____

Type Construction _____ Stories _____

Floor Load Capacities _____

Elevators _____ Capacity (Tons) _____

Electric Power (Quantity) _____ Natural Gas _____

Roof Construction _____ Truck Docks _____

Office Space (Describe) _____

Restrooms _____ Heating _____

A.C. _____ Sprinklers _____

Column Spacing _____ Drains _____

Clearance (Minimum Constant) _____ Taxes _____

Tax District _____ Topography _____

Rail Access _____ Labor Force _____

Distance from Highways _____

Source: Floyd M. Baird, Temple, Texas.

(rent, wages, utilities, and taxes) and transportation costs for both raw materials and finished goods. The firm will also assess the site's profitability, perhaps by comparing demand and income factors in the local market. In a highly competitive market, the location with the lowest transportation and production costs may not be the most profitable. Profit may be determined by the location of competitors, the importance of customer proximity, the extent of the market area, and the responsiveness of product demand to price changes.

Speculative building   Because the planning, financing, and construction of industrial property requires a long lead time, developers in many areas where demand is heavy have been successful in building speculative shell buildings in the most popular sizes. After signing a lease with a tenant, investors can finish a building in a short time, usually no more than 90 days.

If the market for the heavy industrial space softens, these speculative industrial building shells are easily converted to lighter industrial use or commercial space. The nature of these building shells allows the developer to be able to install more extensive tenant improvements should this be a requirement of a more commercial tenant who will take the industrial space.

Required Local Market Information

An industrial firm looking for space will usually want factual data about the economic base of the community and the population, including family size and composition, average age, income level, predominant occupations, and education. Potential industrial tenants will request data on local transportation services and on the skills, training, and turnover rate of the local labor force.

The market survey should look into the availability, price, and source of utilities and fuel, as well as into the financial stability, services, and attitude of local government. Income tax rates (federal and local) and assessment policies, municipal services, and zoning ordinances are vital pieces of information to prospective industrial tenants. The information is available to the property manager through public sources such as the U.S. Census Bureau, local tax rolls, and the local unemployment office. Other data can be gathered from the files of banks, local development groups, municipal agencies, utility companies, and university departments of social research and urban studies.

The market analysis should include information about any special available financing such as the availability of tax-free industrial revenue bonds or tax abatement programs and whether or not the chamber of commerce or a similar group has organized an industrial park. These organizations typically subsidize the sale of land for industrial plants at prices well below market rates to attract new industries to the city. In such cases, private investors may not be able to compete.

Transportation Considerations

Changes in the nation's transportation patterns have encouraged new factories and branch facilities to locate in suburban areas. The freight trucking industry has emerged as the primary mover of goods due to construction of interstate highways and expressway systems. Industrial firms are no longer forced to locate near rail facilities and have left congested metropolitan areas. The labor force, once dependent on urban transportation systems, can now drive to work in outlying areas. These factors, combined with the lower cost of suburban land, have been a catalyst for the construction of industrial developments in outlying areas.

Plant Size and Feature   Industrial firms relocating in outlying areas tend to prefer one-story buildings with very high inside clearance. The reasons are simple: There is more total usable space in a one-story building and the cost of construction is generally lower. Also, the single-level plant provides flexibility of spatial layout and ease in moving goods to and from the plant. Thanks to pallet storage and forklift moving equipment, goods can be moved more quickly on one level than they could in multilevel building elevators.

Shipping and receiving facilities   Technological changes in materials handling, from delivery of raw materials to shipment of finished products, have mandated the redesign of shipping and receiving facilities of industrial properties. Standard-sized shipping containers have increased the capacity and flexibility of materials handling operations. Plants using this new method require specialized docking and loading facilities, another need that the industrial property manager must try to accommodate.

Advantages of multiple tenancies   Industrial property managers should be aware of alternatives for industrial properties, especially that of multiple tenancies. Although most firms would prefer to reserve an entire building for their use, the economic advantages of multiple tenancies can be attractive to small and young enterprises. When establishing multiple tenancies, managers should give some thought to the rental schedule and tenant compatibility.

Multiple tenancy uses are a good mix when very large much older inner city type factories and mills are being redeveloped. Often, these older buildings have a variety of shapes and sizes that can best suit a variety of tenancies. Areas of concern include energy costs, parking, and loading dock facilities. The functionality and designs of these features were much different when they were built.

Land-Use Patterns   **Industrial parks**   An industrial park is simply a suburban industrial subdivision designed to offer land in outlying areas with good accessibility to comparatively small businesses. They attract businesses that formerly occupied lofts because they allow the tenant to combine office, manufacturing, and storage space in a one-story building. Some were located in cities, and although still used, the term "industrial park" has become outmoded.

Business parks   As occupancy and use in industrial parks changed, first to office-warehouse and sometimes to complete office use, industrial parks came to be called *office parks*; later, the term business park was coined and is now in almost universal use. Occasionally, however, some developers retain the older term.

In many cases, the land is sold to an industrial concern, which then builds its own plant. Many cities have areas where there is a concentration of office-warehouse buildings, consisting of one-story units with easy access to the interstate highway system. Quite often, developers will build several of these buildings on a speculative basis and sell them to individual owners. The multiple owners often hire professional management to maintain the quality, look, and feel of the business park.

Corridor development   Another phenomenon is **corridor development**, which results from the establishment or growth of two large industrial or business centers at some distance from each other on an interstate highway or other major traffic artery. As these two centers expand geographically, allied businesses and plants that service or feed off the large plants locate along the major arteries that connect them.

Regional cooperation   *Regional cooperation* is growing among individuals and organizations responsible for economic development. No longer do neighboring towns and cities compete strongly for industry. Instead they feel that an industry established anywhere within a reasonable distance of their location will benefit industry in all cities in the area.

Industrial Development Incentives

Industrial areas have been made possible in large part through liberalized zoning ordinances in growing communities. Many are the result of community efforts to raise funds to purchase suitable land to make available to new industry. In the last few years, many surplus military facilities were, and are being, converted to industrial use through such efforts.

Industrial revenue bonds   Industrial revenue bonds enjoy a special tax status, making them attractive to investors. Social and economic changes can affect the desirability of such bonds.

Special tax incentives   Many states and cities view industry as a source of employment, income, and tax revenue. To encourage companies to locate to their city and/or state, they are willing to pass legislation that provides favorable tax incentives to industry.

Foreign trade zones (FTZ)   In addition to revenue bond legislation, federal law also encourages another incentive, the **foreign trade zone (FTZ)**. An FTZ allows a company to import finished goods or component parts and to warehouse them duty-free until shipped. FTZs were created for the purpose of moving foreign or domestic goods in and out of a state without going through U.S. Customs. U.S. quota restrictions, duty, and bonding do not apply in FTZs.

Imports can be stored, graded, repacked, assembled, processed, or fabricated (sometimes qualifying for lower freight charges) without payment of customs duty until the goods leave for the U.S. market. No duty is paid on goods to be exported. Goods may be stored indefinitely in the zones to await the best market conditions, satisfy quota limitations, or take advantage of discount or seasonal prices. Manufacturing in these zones can be extremely advantageous, especially for companies that produce goods from domestic and foreign materials and then export the finished goods.

Research and development centers   Designed to bridge the gap between an industry engaged in high technology and the educational resources of its state or locality, **research and development (R&D) centers** provide assistance through facilities engineers and scientists at research universities. They also assist with product marketing and may offer low-cost, on-campus, or off-campus incubator spaces to house new product development groups or start-up operations. They are often supported by other businesses, grants, and tax revenues because they provide more than just space. They attract people who often spawn additional business opportunities.

Private industry councils (PICs)   Private industry councils (PICs) employ federal funds to operate employment and training programs. Hundreds of employers across the country have benefited financially from PICs on-the-job training programs and by hiring PIC graduates. Endorsed and assisted by the National Alliance of Business, PIC programs train the workforce to meet employment needs.

Miscellaneous other incentives   *Fixed-asset financing, land write-down, Urban Development Action Grants (UDAG)*, and *tax abatement financing* are just some of the many other incentives to industry to locate in a community. Under a fixed-asset financing assistance program, competitive financing is made available through Small Business Administration and other guaranteed loan programs, revenue bonds, and other financing mechanisms.

In a land write-down, the local government will, in appropriate circumstances, assemble and subsidize the purchase of land to be sold at a lower-than-acquisition price, hence the term write-down. Sometimes the community may arrange appropriate long-term land leases to fit the needs of the appropriate prospect.

UDAG grants are sponsored by the U.S. Department of Housing and Urban Development, which permits a city to apply for grants that will go to either private concerns as gap financing for a portion of a project or local government for public improvements. Enterprise zones have been established in some states in economically depressed areas to encourage the establishment of businesses, including industry, in those zones. The incentives are in the form of ad valorem tax abatements for a period of time for each new job located in the zone.

Many states offer customized job training as part of their economic development programs. In California, for example, the Employment Training Panel coordinates, organizes, and pays for training an industry's workers. It reimburses employers for training expenses incurred in starting up, restructuring, or retooling vocations.

■ MARKETING INDUSTRIAL SPACE

Industrial Advertising and Promotion

The industrial manager should present all the information about the property on the company's Web site in addition to developing brochure containing a picture of the premises and brief copy highlighting its special features. The Web site URL should be included on all signs. The brochure, along with an area map, should be mailed to all area industrial brokers and customers and suppliers of industrial firms in the area. The manager should also consider inviting a select group of prospective tenants to an open house featuring luncheon type food and beverages along with guided tours of these large facilities.

Dun & Bradstreet and other directories are helpful in compiling prospect lists. The *Standard Industrial Classification Manual* is another valuable reference tool that groups related industries and firms. By looking up one company that is particularly suited for a property (such as a previous tenant), the manager can find related firms with similar equipment, space, and location requirements. These firms might be interested in the vacant space and should be added to the direct mail list.

Specialized industrial brokers   The most distinctive feature of industrial space marketing is its specialization because industrial tenants are most interested in the utility of the property, not its amenities or prestige. They usually ground their decisions firmly in economic facts. Often the marketing and leasing of an industrial property are accomplished before the property manager becomes involved in the transaction. If this is not the case, the industrial manager should develop a mailing list of key brokers.

Most industrial managers and firms rely heavily on outside leasing agents, called industrial brokers, to market or locate properties. The industrial property manager and broker must be in command of technical knowledge about properties and about industries that may be good prospects for them. Professional organizations such as the Society of Industrial and Office REALTORS® can act as referral networks. Likewise, the National Association of Industrial and Office Parks (NAIOP) is an association of professional developers, owners, and managers of industrial and office parks that provides interchange of experience and professional training for its members through programs and seminars.

Regional development councils   Other sources of referrals are local, state, and regional *industrial development councils*, sometimes called *economic development commissions*. Local councils are generally sponsored by or are part of the local chamber of commerce. Regional cooperation of such efforts is growing. For example, the American Industrial Real Estate Association of Los Angeles is active in a five-county area. Other organizations, such as the Southern Industrial Development Council, may operate over several states. Industrial property managers should associate themselves with the councils in their respective areas.

FIGURE 15.2

Industrial Requirements Worksheet

Date _____

Address _____

Company _____

Type of Business/Mfg _____   Dist. _____ Employees _____

Area _____   N/S to _____ E/W to _____

Timing_____   Lease Expiration _____

Zoning Needs _____   Hazardous Materials? _____

Warehouse

Area _____ sq. ft. Dim _____   Expanded to _____

Clg. Hgt. _____   Concrete _____   Concrete Block _____   Steel _____   Other _____

Clear Span: y ❑ n ❑ Posts _____ ft. centers Skylights: y ❑ n ❑   Crane: y ❑ n ❑ _____ ton

Floor Drains: y ❑ n ❑ Sprinklers Required:y ❑ n ❑ Desirable: y ❑ n ❑

Rail Spur: y ❑ n ❑ No. of Spots _____

Parking _____ spaces Employees _____   Visitors _____

Floor Load: Normal _____   Heavy _____ lbs/sq. ft. _____

Elec. Power: 110V _____   240V _____   480V _____   single/3 phase _____ Amps

Heat: y ❑ n ❑ Number _____   BTUs _____

Light: Normal _____   Heavy _____   Foot Candles _____   Fluorescent: y ❑ n ❑

Front Truck Doors: DI _____   DH _____   Rear Truck Doors: DI _____   DH_____

Side Truck Doors: DI _____   DH _____   Truck Wells: y ❑ n ❑

Office

Total Area _____ sq. ft. A/C: y ❑ n ❑   Mess.: y ❑ n ❑ _____ lbs sq. ft.

Private Offices_____   Sizes_____

Conference _____   x _____   Lunchroom _____ x_____ft.

Reception _____   x _____   Other _____ x_____ft.

Restrooms _____   Ladies Lounge _____

Heat: F/A _____   Wall _____   ADT_____

Yard

Area _____ sq. ft.   Paved_____

Fenced_____ L.F.   Expansion _____ sq. ft.

L/B Ratio _____   Landscaping_____

Miscellaneous

Lease Term _____   Option _____

Parent Company_____   Address _____

Phone _____   Contact _____

Budget _____   Net Worth_____

Interstate Highway Distance Requirement _____

Dun & Bradstreet: y ❑ n ❑ Date _____

Foreign Trade Zone Needed?

Dun & Bradstreet: y ❑ n ❑ Date _____

Environmental Considerations: If client handles hazardous material or has special waste disposal requirements, attach a brief summary.

Other _____

_____

_____

Tenant Qualification

After attracting industrial prospects, the manager must assess their space, transportation, and labor needs. As suggested in Figure 15.2, a sample industrial client requirements worksheet, the manager should pursue several avenues when qualifying an industrial prospect.

One of the most important inquiries is the exact zoning status required by a prospect. This determines whether the available zoning will fit tenant needs or whether some special-use permit or action by the local board of zoning adjustment must be obtained. For example, with industries handling hazardous materials, the availability of *hazardous material disposal* sites also may be a critical factor.

Total land area required   A plant site includes the total land area within the property boundaries, both open acreage and the area covered by buildings, parking lots, landscaping, docks, and so forth. Custom-service, market-oriented industrial firms generally require fewer than 10 acres of land. These industries rely heavily on their proximity to a concentration of manufacturers that serve as potential consumers for their special products, such as precision tools and electronic components. On the other hand, heavy industries, such as automobile or aircraft manufacturers, may need 100 acres or more. Industries requiring large amounts of land tend to be resource or labor oriented.

Land-employment densities   Land-employment density is expressed as the ratio of the number of principal shift employees to total land area. Employment density assists in determining the prospective tenant's parking needs. However, because it is based only on the number of workers on the key shift, the figure must be adjusted to allow for shift overlap, which swells the number of vehicles on the premises. In general, the manager can figure that vehicle storage will account for 60 percent of the total space needed for parking, with the other 40 percent allowed for traffic flow.

Industries with a low ratio of employees per acre (ten or fewer) usually require plant facilities with a large area. These are called *labor-extensive industries*, most of which process raw materials. A chemical plant is a good example of this type of industry.

Labor-intensive industries, on the other hand, show a high concentration of employees per acre. Electronics firms and other operations using highly skilled professional personnel may have as many as 75 workers per acre.

Building-employment density   Though it is virtually impossible to forecast a prospective tenant's total floor area needs by the nature of its business alone, some generalizations can be made about **building-employment density**. Labor-intensive industries employing highly skilled personnel—drug manufacturers, for instance—usually require 25,000 square feet of floor space or less. Labor-extensive industries, however, often need more than 100,000 square feet of area to accommodate their activities.

Gross floor area is the total of all floor space within the exterior walls of the building with no allowance made for structural projections. To be classified as part of the gross floor area, a space must have a ceiling height of at least 7.5 feet. Unenclosed areas, such as loading platforms, should not be included in the gross floor area.

Structural density   The ratio of the total ground-floor area of a building to the total land area is called **structural density**. For example, a 100,000-square-foot site on which a plant with a ground floor of 25,000 square feet is located has a structural density of 25 percent. Standard structural density ratios have been decreasing steadily since 1945, when sites in the central city had ratios as high as 80 percent. The average density for a general purpose industrial building in today's market is between 25 percent and 33 percent.

Transportation access   Manufacturers in heavy industry usually require direct access to major trucking routes, air cargo transport, railroads, or even deep-water ports. Major thoroughfares to residential areas inhabited by the workforce are also crucial. Wholesalers and distributors need access to trucking routes and to major street systems capable of handling traffic flow for incoming goods and outgoing deliveries.

Beautiful industrial areas have stayed semi-developed for years because big companies will not risk bringing their trucks over inadequately raised overpasses, narrow winding roads, and small inferior bridges. Often, the developer can work on a plan with the city, county, state, or railroad company to make the required specific improvements upfront with the developer weaving in a tenant assessment on a per square foot basis payment as the space is leased.

Financial capability   As with commercial tenants, the property manager should study an industrial tenant's past profit records, financial resources, and backing to be sure that the firm will become a viable, productive tenant. Industrial tenants who want a sale-leaseback arrangement must demonstrate a strong fiscal position before a developer will become involved in the transaction as the owner-lessor; the property manager working for another type of owner should be no less careful.

■ Once an industrial tenant leases and takes possession of property, it is difficult to remedy any problems that arise if the tenant is not suited to the space or does not have the operating capital to be successful there.

Environmental Issues   The potential for environmental contamination is greater in industrial property than in any other type of property. For this reason, the property manager must make a thorough inquiry into the possibility that the prospect may be involved with handling hazardous material in the leased premises. Also, there must be provisions in the lease for the proper disposal of waste materials. The cost of cleanup of hazardous waste improperly disposed of on the premises by a tenant can far exceed the value of the owner's property. This subject is addressed more fully in Chapter 16.

Periodically monitoring the operation of any industrial tenant is a critical responsibility of the property manager to determine whether hazardous activity has been started or is being improperly handled.

Showing the Property

If a property is not zoned for the type of industrial activities the prospective tenant engages in or if the utility service is below the minimum needs of the firm's operation, then it may be a waste of time to bring the prospect to the site. The manager should simply explain the situation and try to build a rapport with the prospective tenant so that groundwork can be laid for placement in another property at a later date.

Prequalifying By knowing the firm's actual needs and willingness to make building modifications, the manager can save time and facilitate completion of the transaction. If the prospective tenant's land area, space, density, and other requirements match the specifications of the property, the manager can feel more secure about the prognosis for the firm's economic success at the location and thus should show the space. Prequalifying also provides information to the manager that will be useful when answering questions and fielding objections at the site.

Stress benefits When showing industrial space, the manager should remember to stress features and benefits that are important to the industrial prospect. Such benefits can include an adequate sprinkler and fireproofing system, covered truck docks, adaptability of layout, and, often, high ceilings.

Group presentations The industrial property manager often has to show a building to a group. Invariably, members of the group will split up to explore their separate concerns. Because the manager cannot follow everyone and note individual responses, he or she should accompany the person in charge. It is likely that subordinates will voice any objections to the decision maker, giving the property manager opportunity to respond to their remarks, too. If the property manager will arrange an appropriate debriefing session after the tour over coffee or at a lunch, there will be opportunity to answer all objections raised by members of the group.

Follow-through The manager must take the initiative in contacting the prospect, obtaining further information, and making follow-up presentations to all involved parties. By diplomatically overcoming minor problems and following through on the transaction, the manager will arrive at the final step in the marketing process—negotiating the lease for the premises.

Lease Negotiations

The industrial lease shown in Figure 15.3 includes a description of the premises, lease term, rent, security deposit, use of the premises and the legal responsibilities and remedies of both parties—all typical provisions of residential, office,

FIGURE 15.3

Net Industrial Lease

Parties	AGREEMENT OF LEASE, made as of the _____ day of _____, 19 _____, between _____ a corporation organized under the laws of the state of _____, with its principal place of business at _____ _____ hereinafter referred to as Lessor, and _____, a corporation organized under the laws of the state of _____, with its principal place of business at _____ _____, hereinafter referred to as Lessee.

WITNESSETH:

Leased Premises	1. Lessor hereby leases to Lessee and Lessee hereby hires from Lessor the land and all buildings erected thereon, known as _____ _____, and more particularly described as set forth on Exhibit A attached hereto, subject to all matters set forth on Exhibit B attached hereto.
Term	2. This lease is for a term of _____ years, commencing and terminating _____.
Cash Rental	3. Lessee covenants and agrees that it will pay to Lessor at the address herein specified, or to such other person or at such address as Lessor may from time to time designate by written notice to Lessee, an aggregate rental of $_____ for the term, payable in lawful money of the United States of _____ day of _____, 19 _____. Lessor shall have the right to assign its interest in the lease and in the rentals payable by the Lessee hereunder.
Taxes and Assessments	4. As additional rent, Lessee agrees and covenants to pay and discharge, before they become delinquent, all ad valorem taxes, general and special assessments and other taxes levied or assessed against the leased premises or arising in respect to the occupancy, use or possession of the leased premises, and which are assessed or become a lien or become due and payable during the term of this lease. This obligation of Lessee shall include the obligation, imposed by any law, ordinance or regulation now in existence or hereafter enacted or adopted, to pay any taxes, assessments or charges for public improvements or services levied or imposed in whole or in part as a capital or other levy against the leased premises or on the rents hereunder, or in substitution for ad valorem taxes, charges or assessments for public improvements or services as now imposed by law, but Lessee shall not be required to pay any income, gross receipts, corporate franchise or any inheritance, transfer, estate or succession taxes of Lessor. Lessee shall, within thirty (30) days following the last day on which any such taxes or assessments may be paid without incurring any interest or penalty, furnish to Lessor receipts or other evidence demonstrating payment thereof. There shall be an apportionment of all such taxes between Lessor and Lessee with respect to the first and last year of the term hereof. Lessee may, in good faith and in a lawful manner and upon giving notice to Lessor of its intention so to do, contest any tax, assessment or charge against the leased premises, but all costs and expenses incident to such contest shall be paid by Lessee and in case of an adjudication adverse to Lessee, then Lessee shall promptly pay such tax, assessment or charge. Lessee shall indemnify and save Lessor harmless against any loss or damage arising from such contest and shall, if necessary to prevent a sale or other loss or damage to Lessor, pay such tax, assessment or charge under protest and take such other steps as may be necessary to prevent any sale or loss.
Maintenance and Repair	5. Lessee agrees to keep and maintain the buildings and all other improvements on the leased premises, and parking areas and ways used in connection with the leased premises, in as good a state of repair as the same are turned over to it, ordinary wear and tear excepted, and in a clean, safe and

FIGURE 15.3 (CONTINUED)
Net Industrial Lease

sanitary condition, and agrees to make all necessary repairs, interior, exterior and structural, to said building and other improvements, and to pay and hold Lessor free and harmless from bills or assessments for light, heat, water, gas, sewer rentals or charges, vault taxes or rentals and any other expenses arising out of or incidental to the Occupancy of said leased premises. Lessee further releases and agrees to save Lessor harmless from any and all damages and liability which may occur to the contents of any portion of said leased premises during the term of this lease. Lessee agrees to repair and restore all improvements on the demised premises following any damage to or loss or destruction of the premises or any part thereof from any cause whatsoever, at Lessee's expense and without cost to Lessor.

Offsets

6. No claim the Lessee may have against the Lessor for any reason shall be offset against the rentals due from Lessee to Lessor.

Lessee's Improvements

7. Lessee, during the full term of this lease, shall have the right, at any time and from time to time, at its own and sole expense and liability, to place or install on the leased premises such improvements, buildings and fixtures it shall desire, all of which shall be and remain, from the time of construction or installation, the property of Lessor, without payment or offset; provided that Lessee shall first obtain the prior written consent of Lessor if any such improvements or buildings shall involve any structural changes in the improvements existing at the commencement of this lease, and provided further that upon the termination of this lease for many reason Lessee shall, if required by Lessor, promptly remove all such improvements, buildings and fixtures and place the leased premises in the same condition as at the commencement of the term of this lease, and provided further that no such installation or construction shall violate any lawful rule or regulation, plat or zoning restriction or other law, ordinance or regulation applicable thereto, and shall be done and performed in a good and professional manner. All costs of any such improvements shall be paid in cash by Lessee and Lessee shall allow no liens for labor or materials to attach to the leased premises by virtue thereof. If the estimated costs of such buildings or improvements shall exceed $ _____, Lessee shall submit drawings and specifications to Lessor for Lessor's approval, and no work shall be commenced until Lessor has approved such drawings and specifications and the contracts, contractors, performance and payment bonds and the sureties thereon.

Insurance

8. The Lessee agrees to pay as additional rental all premiums required during the term hereof to provide and keep in force policies of:

a. Fire and extended coverage insurance in some insurance company or companies authorized to do business in the state of _____ in an amount not less than _____ percent of the full insurable value of the buildings and other improvements now constructed or to be constructed on the said leased premises, and in any event not less than an amount sufficient to prevent the insured from becoming a coinsurer under any applicable coinsurance clause, and to keep such insurance in full force and effect for and during the time any buildings and improvements are located on the leased premises, or are being constructed on the leased premises and thereafter during the term of this lease. For the purposes hereof "full insurable value" shall mean the replacement cost of the improvements without allowance for depreciation but excluding footings, foundations and other portions of improvements which are not insurable. A determination of full insurable value shall be made at least once every 3 years at Lessee's expense by a firm of qualified fire insurance appraisers satisfactory to Lessor and to fire insurance companies generally. Lessee may provide policies containing a _____ percent coinsurance clause. Such policy or policies shall insure Lessor and Lessee and, so long as an institutional investor holds a first lien on the premises under a mortgage, shall contain a standard mortgagee clause providing for payment of proceeds to such mortgagee.

b. Public liability and property damage insurance with limits of not less than $_____ for injury or death of any one person, $_____ for injury or death in any one accident or occurrence and property damage in the amount of $_____ insuring Lessor and Lessee.

c. Such other types of insurance, and in such amounts, as Lessor may reasonably require, provided such other insurance is commonly carried in connection with properties similar to the leased premises or businesses similar to that being conducted on the leased premises.

FIGURE 15.3 (CONTINUED)

Net Industrial Lease

All policies required by this paragraph shall be carried in such companies and upon such forms as both parties hereto from time to time approve. No policies shall be subject to cancellation or material modification except after ten (10) days' written notice to Lessor and Lessor's mortgagee and each policy shall so provide. All policies required to be furnished hereunder (or certificates in the event insurance is provided under a blanket policy) shall be deposited with Lessor prior to the commencement of the term hereof, and renewals thereof or evidence of the payment of premium to continue the coverage in force shall be deposited with Lessor not less than 30 days prior to the date on which such insurance would expire.

Restoration Following Loss

9. Upon the occurrence of any loss, Lessee will give written notice thereof to Lessor and promptly commence and will diligently complete, or cause to be commenced and diligently completed, the repair and restoration of the premises so that, insofar as possible, upon the completion of such repair or restoration the improvements will constitute an entire architectural unit that will have a commercial value at least as great as prior to the damage or loss. If the estimated cost of repair or restoration shall exceed $ _____, Lessee shall submit to Lessor for Lessor's approval the drawings and specifications and all contracts, contractors, performance and payment bonds and the sureties thereon shall be subject to Lessor's prior approval. If the loss, damage or destruction results from a casualty covered by a policy or policies of insurance, the insurance proceeds recovered shall be paid to Lessee to reimburse it for its expenses incurred in repairing and restoring the premises upon submission by Lessee of evidence of completion of and payment for the work. In the event such proceeds are inadequate to reimburse Lessee for the cost of such repair or restoration, Lessee shall pay any additional amounts required from its own funds. Any sums remaining after such repair or restoration shall be the property of the Lessor.

Compliance with Laws, etc.

10. The Lessee's obligations to pay rent and to perform all of the other covenants and agreements which Lessee is bound to perform under the terms of this lease shall not terminate, abate or be diminished during any period that the premises or any part thereof are untenantable, regardless of the cause of such untenantability, except as provided in Paragraph 19 hereof.

Compliance with the Americans with Disabilities Act

11. Lessee, in the use and occupancy of the leased premises, and in the prosecution and conduct of its business and activities, shall at its own cost and expense secure and maintain all necessary licenses and permits required for the conduct of its business, and shall at all times comply with all laws and ordinances and all lawful rules and regulations issued by any legally constituted authority, and with the applicable orders, regulations and requirements of any Board of Fire Underwriters, and observe all plat and deed restrictions of record, including in such compliance any required changes in the improvements, structural or otherwise, but may, within such limits, use the leased premises for any lawful purpose.

Lessee's Environmental Responsibility

12. Lessee, at its sole cost and expense, shall be responsible for full compliance with the Americans with Disabilities Act of 1990, as amended, including, without limitation, Title III thereof and the regulations promulgated thereunder (collectively ADA), with regard to the leased premises and Lessee's business and conducted therein.

13. Lessee shall not permit or conduct any activity on the premises which would violate, or cause Lessor to be in violation of applicable laws, statutes, ordinances, rules, regulations, policies, orders and determinations of any governmental authority pertaining to health or the environment (collectively the Applicable Law), including, but not limited to, the Comprehensive Environmental Response, Compensation and Liability Act of 1980, as amended, the Resource Conversation and Recovery Act of 1987, as amended, and the (Appropriate State Laws), as amended, nor which would cause the presence of any substance or the existence of any condition, or the threatened release of any substance in, on, or under the surface of the premises, or the occurrence of any event in which any substance has been disposed of or released on, in or from the premises in any manner not permitted under Applicable Law such that Applicable Law would require (i) a report or other notice of such condition or event to any federal, state or local governmental agency or (ii) remodel, treatment, or other procedures or remedial action with respect to such condition or event in order to bring the premises into compliance with all Applicable Law or (iii) contribution by any current or former owner or operator of the premises toward removal, treatment or other procedures or remedial action required by or that may be brought under Applicable Law with respect to the premises or any other site or location affected by such condition or event.

FIGURE 15.3 (CONTINUED)
Net Industrial Lease

Waste; Use; Liens	14. Lessee agrees not to do nor suffer any waste to the leased premises, nor cause, suffer or permit any liens to attach to or to exist against the leased premises by reason of any act of Lessee or by reason of its failure to perform any act required of it hereunder. Provided, however, Lessee shall not be required to pay or discharge any lien against the leased premises so long as Lessee has given Lessor notice of its intent to contest such lien and Lessee is in good faith contesting the validity or amount thereof and has given to Lessor such security as Lessor has requested to assure payment of such lien and to prevent the sale, foreclosure or forfeiture of the leased premises by reason of nonpayment. On final determination of the lien or claim for lien Lessee will immediately pay any judgment rendered, and all costs and charges, and shall cause the lien to be released or satisfied. Lessee will not use or permit the use of the leased premises in any manner which would result, or would with the passage of time result, in the creation of any easement or prescriptive right.
Lessor's Performance of Lessee's Duties	15. If lessee should default in the performance of any covenant on its part to be performed by virtue of any provision of this lease, Lessor may, after any notice and the expiration of any period with respect thereto as required pursuant to the applicable provisions of this lease, perform the same for the account of Lessee, and Lessee hereby authorizes Lessor to come upon the leased premises and while on the leased premises to do anything necessary to accomplish the correction of such default. If Lessor, at any time, is compelled to pay or elects to pay any sum of money by reason of the failure of Lessee, after any notice and the expiration of any period with respect thereto as required pursuant to the applicable provisions of this lease, to comply with any provision of this lease, or if Lessor is compelled to incur any expense, including reasonable attorneys' fees, in instituting, prosecuting or defending any action or proceeding instituted by reason of any default of Lessee hereunder, the sum or sums so paid by Lessor, with all interest, costs and damages, shall be deemed to be additional rental hereunder, and shall together with interest thereon at the rate of 6 percent per annum be due from Lessee to Lessor on the first day of the month following the incurring of such respective expense, except as otherwise herein specifically provided.
Notice to Mortgagee and Right to Cure Lessor's Default	16. So long as there remains of record a first mortgage of Lessor's interest in the premises, and Lessee has been given written notice of the identity and address of such mortgagee, no notice provided for herein shall be deemed to have been given unless a copy thereof is given to such mortgagee at the same time and in the same manner as the original was given to the other party to this lease. Lessee agrees that if in any notice to Lessor the performance of some act is required or compliance with some provision hereof is requested and Lessor does not, within the allotted time, perform such act or comply with such provision, Lessee will so notify the mortgagee and mortgagee shall have sixty (60) days after receipt of such notice in which to perform such act or comply with such provision for and on behalf of Lessor, and Lessee shall have no right to terminate this lease if the mortgagee shall perform and comply as and within the time herein provided. In the event the act or thing to be complied with is of such a nature that it cannot be performed or complied with within said 60-day period, mortgagee shall be deemed to have complied herewith in the event it commenced the performance or compliance within said 60-day period and there-after completes the same with due diligence. The granting to the mortgagee of additional time in which to comply shall not be deemed in any manner to release or relieve Lessor from the obligations of Lessor under this lease. The said mortgagee is hereby authorized to enter upon the leased premises and while on the leased premises to do anything necessary to correct such default.
Covenant of Peaceful Possession	17. Upon performance of all of the conditions, covenants and agreements herein contained on the part of the Lessee, Lessor shall provide Lessee quiet and peaceful possession of the leased premises during the full term hereof, without hindrance or molestation from anyone claiming rights or interest therein through or against the Lessor.
Assignment and Subletting	18. Lessee shall not assign, mortgage or encumber this lease nor sublet the leased premises, or any part thereof, without the written consent of the Lessor, provided, however, that such consent shall not be arbitrarily nor capriciously withheld. Lessee shall in any event continue to be liable hereunder following any assignment or subletting.

FIGURE 15.3 (CONTINUED)
Net Industrial Lease

Condemnation	19. In the event all of the leased premises, or so much thereof as to cause the premises not taken to be unsuitable for Lessee's purposes even after restoration and repair, are permanently taken or condemned for a public or quasi-public use, this lease shall terminate. Lessee's interest in any award made with respect to such taking shall be subordinate to the extent of an amount, if any, which when added to the amount to which Lessor is entitled to receive is necessary to pay fully the then unpaid balance of any first mortgage on the leased premises.

In the event less than all of the leased premises are taken or condemned for a public or quasi-public use and the portion of the premises not taken may be made reasonably suitable for Lessee's use by repair or restoration, this lease will not terminate. Lessee shall, in such event, promptly commence and diligently complete the repair and restoration of the premises so that upon completion the premises will constitute a complete architectural unit with an appearance, character and commercial value as nearly as possible equal to the value of the premises immediately prior to the taking. There shall be an abatement of rental after such taking, and during the balance of the term hereof, in the proportion that the floor area of the building taken bears to the total floor area of the building immediately prior to such taking. Lessee shall be reimbursed for its costs of repair and restoration to the extent of the amount of the award received on account of such taking. In repairing and restoring the leased premises, the drawings and specifications, contracts, contractors, bonds and the sureties thereon, shall all be subject to Lessor's approval. Any award remaining after Lessee has been fully reimbursed for its costs of repair and restoration shall be the property of the Lessor.

Lessor Indemnified	20. Lessee agrees to indemnify and save Lessor harmless from any and all liability, damage, expense, cause of action, suits, claims or demands (unless due to the acts, omissions, negligence or fault of the Lessor) arising from injury to persons or damage to property on the leased premises, or upon the abutting sidewalks or curbs, and to save Lessor harmless from any and all liabilities arising from Lessee's failure to perform any of the terms, conditions and covenants of the lease required to be performed by Lessee.
Inspection of Premises	21. Lessee agrees to permit Lessor and its agents, and any mortgagee of the leased premises, to come upon and inspect the premises at all reasonable times, and to come upon the premises if necessary to perform any act which Lessee has failed to perform, as provided in Paragraph 15 hereof.
Defaults and Remedies	22. If one or more of the following events (herein called defaults) shall happen and be continuing, namely:

a. default shall be made in the punctual payment of any rent herein agreed to be paid and such default shall continue for a period of fifteen (15) days after written notice is given Lessee by Lessor of such default;

b. Lessee makes an assignment for the benefit of creditors;

c. Lessee files a petition in bankruptcy or for relief under the Federal Bankruptcy Law or any other applicable statute, or makes an assignment for the benefit of creditors;

d. an attachment or execution is levied upon the Lessee's property in or interest under this lease, which is not satisfied or released or the enforcement thereof stayed or superseded by an appropriate proceeding within thirty (30) days thereafter;

e. an involuntary petition in bankruptcy or for reorganization or arrangement under the Federal Bankruptcy Law is filed against Lessee and such involuntary petition is not withdrawn, dismissed, stayed or discharged within ninety (90) days from the filing thereof;

f. a Receiver or Trustee is appointed for the property of Lessee or of Lessee's business or assets and the order or decree appointing such Receiver or Trustee shall have remained in force undischarged or unstayed for thirty (30) days after the entry of such order or decree;

FIGURE 15.3 (CONTINUED)
Net Industrial Lease

Defaults and Remedies	g. Lessee shall vacate or abandon the leased premises, or shall fail to perform or observe any other covenant, agreement or condition to be performed or kept by the Lessee under the terms and provisions of this lease, and such failure shall continue for thirty (30) days after written notice thereof has been given by Lessor to the Lessee; then and in any such event Lessor shall have the right, at the option of the Lessor, then or at any time thereafter while such default or defaults shall continue, to elect either (1) to cure such default or defaults at its own expense and without prejudice to any other remedies which it might otherwise have, any payment made or expenses incurred by Lessor in curing such default with interest thereon at 6 percent per annum to be and become additional rent to be paid by Lessee with the next installment of rent falling due thereafter, or (2) to re-enter the leased premises by force or otherwise, without notice, and dispossess Lessee and anyone claiming under Lessee by summary proceedings or otherwise, and remove their effects, and take complete possession of the leased premises and either (i) declare this lease forfeited and the term ended, or (ii) elect to continue this lease in full force and effect, but with the right at any time thereafter to declare this lease forfeited and the term ended. In such re-entry the Lessor may, with or without process of law, remove all persons from the premises, and Lessee hereby covenants in such event, for itself and all others occupying the leased premises under Lessee, to peacefully yield up and surrender the leased premises to the Lessor. Should Lessor declare this lease forfeited and the term ended, the Lessor shall be entitled to recover from Lessee the rental and all other sums due and owing by Lessee to the date of termination, plus the costs of curing all of Lessee's defaults existing at or prior to the date of termination, plus the worth as of the termination of the lease of an amount equal to the then value of the excess, if any, of the aggregate of rent and charges equivalent to rent reserved in this lease for the balance of the term over the then reasonable rental value of the leased premises for the balance of the term, discounted at a rate of 4 percent per annum. Should Lessor, following default as aforesaid, elect to continue this lease in full force, Lessor shall use its best efforts to rent the premises on the best terms available for the remainder of the term hereof, or for such longer or shorter period as Lessor shall deem advisable. Lessee shall remain liable for payment of all rentals and other charges and costs imposed on Lessee herein, in the amounts, at the time and upon the conditions as herein provided, but Lessor shall credit against such liability of the Lessee all amounts received by Lessor from such reletting after first reimbursing itself for all costs incurred in curing Lessee's defaults and in re-entering, preparing and refinishing the premises for reletting, and reletting the premises.

No re-entry by Lessor or any action brought by Lessor to oust Lessee from the premises shall operate to terminate this lease unless Lessor shall give written notice of termination to Lessee, in which event Lessee's liability shall be as above provided. No right or remedy granted to Lessor herein is intended to be exclusive of any other right or remedy, and each and every right and remedy herein provided shall be cumulative and in addition to any other right or remedy hereunder or now or hereafter existing in law or equity or by statute. In the event of termination of this lease, Lessee waives any and all rights to redeem the premises either given by any statute now in effect or hereafter enacted. Any holding over by Lessee after the termination of this lease shall create a tenancy from month to month, on the same terms and conditions and at the same rental as herein provided applicable during the term hereof, and such tenancy may be terminated by Lessor on sixty (60) days' written notice to Lessee. |
Condition of Premises upon Termination	23. Upon termination of this lease, Lessee covenants and agrees to remove all of its property from the premises, and Lessee shall also remove any improvements made by Lessee upon the premises (which, prior to removal, shall be the property of the Lessor) if such removal is requested by Lessor, and Lessee shall repair any damage caused by the removal thereof, and shall leave the premises in good and clean condition and repair.
Successors and Assigns	24. The obligations and responsibilities shall be binding upon and the rights and benefits shall inure to the successors and assigns of the parties hereto; but the liabilities of any successor to the interest of the Lessor hereunder shall be limited to the performance of those obligations which arise and accrue during the period of ownership of the leased premises by any such successor.
Notices	25. Any notices or inquiries regarding this lease shall be delivered to Lessor at _____ _____ or to such other address as the parties may designate in writing. Notice may be given by registered or certified mail, and in such event the date of service shall be the date on which notice is deposited in a United States post office properly stamped and addressed.

FIGURE 15.3 (CONTINUED)
Net Industrial Lease

No Oral Agreements	26. It is expressly agreed between Lessor and Lessee that there is no verbal understanding or agreement which in any way changes the terms, covenants and conditions herein set forth, and that no modification of this lease and no waiver of any of its terms and conditions shall be effective unless made in writing and duly executed by the authorized officers of the necessary parties or party.
Subordination to Mortgage; Nondisturbance of Lessee	27. This lease shall be, at the election of the holder of any first mortgage, subject and subordinate to that mortgage, whether now existing or hereafter placed upon the leased premises and to all renewals, modifications, consolidations, replacements and extensions thereof, and Lessee will, at the request of the holder of such mortgage, promptly execute any instrument or instruments for delivery to any such mortgagee or mortgagees, specifically providing for such subordination, but such subordination is and shall be on the condition that so long as Lessee pays all rentals and performs all other obligations imposed upon it in this lease, in the time and manner specified, neither Lessee's use and occupation of the leased premises nor the continuance of this lease shall in any way be terminated, affected or prejudiced by the holder of such mortgage, by foreclosure proceedings or otherwise, and neither the Lessee nor the mortgagee shall have the right to terminate this lease following foreclosure of the mortgage.
No Implied Waiver	28. The failure of Lessor to insist, in one or more instances, upon the strict performance by Lessee of any of the provisions of this lease shall not be construed as a waiver of any future breach of such provisions. Receipt by Lessor of rent with knowledge of the breach of any provision hereof shall not be deemed a waiver of such breach.
Warranties of Lessee	29. Lessee warrants to and for the benefit of any mortgagee of the leased premises that as of the date of execution of this lease it neither has nor claims any defense to this lease nor any offset against the rentals payable or other obligations required of Lessee hereunder, and Lessee warrants that it has not paid any rental in advance for a period of more than one month and covenants that it will not, without such mortgagee's written consent, at any time during the term hereof prepay any rental for a period longer than one month.
Maintenance of Corporate Existence and Assets; Merger and Consolidation	30. Lessee covenants that it will maintain its corporate existence and that it will not during the term hereof sell, transfer or assign all or substantially all of its assets, or merge into or consolidate with any other corporation unless the surviving corporation shall have a net worth at least equal to the net worth of Lessee immediately prior to such merger or consolidation and unless such surviving corporation shall execute and deliver to Lessor and to any mortgagee of the leased premises a written assumption of the obligations of Lessee under this lease.

and commercial property leases. However, the terms and conditions involving taxes, insurance, maintenance, and other legal matters are highly individualized in industrial leases and must be negotiated separately between each landlord and tenant. Then an attorney must formalize the agreement.

Net Lease

As discussed in Chapter 5, a net lease requires the tenant to pay some or all of the basic property expenses, such as real estate taxes and assessments, insurance, utilities, and maintenance costs. Of all types of leases, these are typically the longest, and often the tenant has either built the structure or the landlord built the structure per the tenant's requirements. In this type of situation, landlords protect their interests by passing on the increased costs of taxes, assessments, insurance, utilities, etc. to the tenant. This is in contrast to a short term lease in which the landlord will accept the risk and pay the expenses in exchange for a chance to increase rents.

In theory, there are three standard forms of net lease:

1. The *straight net lease* requires the tenant to pay for some or all of the real estate taxes and assessments in addition to the rental obligation.

2. Under a *net-net lease* the tenant must generally pay the taxes and assessments plus the insurance premiums set forth in the lease agreement.

3. The *net-net-net* or *triple-net lease* holds the tenant liable for taxes and assessments, insurance premiums, and the cost of repairs and maintenance work stipulated in the lease terms.

Conflicting financial interests   A cost-conscious prospect will prefer a gross lease. The landlord, wanting safety, stability, and a reasonable level of income, will press for a net lease. Very few industrial leases are gross leases; the landlord and tenant usually compromise on some form of net lease agreement. Many owners prefer to retain the obligation to pay taxes and carry fire insurance (but with reimbursement by the tenant in many cases) so that they know their property will not be taken for unpaid taxes or destroyed by fire without reimbursement. Such leases should carry a *tax participation* clause and a clause directing the tenant to share in increasing insurance premiums.

Calculating annual rates   The annual rental rate for an industrial property is usually based on the owner's **rent factor**, which is calculated using the percentage of gross return the owner wants to earn on the investment. If the owner paid $600,000 for the building and wants a 10 percent return, the rental rate will be around $60,000 per year. Naturally, this figure is then modified by concerns such as the economic pressure on the owner, the desirability of the tenant, the urgency of the tenant's need for suitable quarters, competition, the specifics of the lease, and general market conditions. The total annual rental amount is then broken down into a dollar-per-square-foot figure for the tenant's analysis during negotiations.

Payment patterns   The manner of rent payment varies greatly under industrial leases. Rent may be paid monthly, quarterly, semiannually, or annually, at either the beginning or end of the lease period. Payments may be equal throughout the lease term or subject to adjustment at dates specified in the lease. The amount of rent and the method of payment are negotiable items. Neither the rent factor nor the per-square-foot rental figure is stated in the lease. It usually specifies only the total amount of rent to be paid and the rental rate over the term of the lease.

Longer terms, option clauses, and building modifications also are open to negotiation. The impact of these factors on the outcome of the transaction will depend on the manager's skill in assessing the position of each party and the issues on which each is willing to compromise to gain on another front.

For example, a prospective tenant's demand for additional dock space and a sprinkler system might be satisfied by a small rent reduction. Likewise, the tenant's willingness to sign a longer lease might encourage the landlord to lower the rent factor. The longer period gives the landlord more time over which to amortize the mortgage on the property, thereby reducing monthly loan payments and decreasing the annual cost of the property. If the yearly gross return on the investment increases, it is in the owner's best interests for the manager to adjust the rent factor on the property. It is the manager's job to know these facts and to bring owner and tenant to mutually satisfactory terms. Although much time and effort are spent negotiating industrial leases, they have relatively long terms and provide a very worthwhile financial return.

■ MAINTENANCE OF INDUSTRIAL PROPERTY

The manager of industrial property is most involved in leasing space and enforcing the terms of the lease agreement. Under the various forms of net lease, the tenant assumes some or all of the maintenance responsibilities for the property. The tenant's upkeep of his or her equipment accounts for much of the interior building maintenance that might otherwise fall to the manager. Many tenants hire their own janitorial crew to maintain the premises as stipulated in the lease. Others, especially those located in industrial parks, contract with a professional service agency for maintenance work at their plant.

Often, the only maintenance tasks of the property manager involved the upkeep of the grounds and the building's exterior. The vigilant property manager will inspect the property periodically for lease violations and to ensure that the owner's investment is being protected.

■ SECURITY OF INDUSTRIAL PROPERTY

Security of office-warehouses and small freestanding industrial buildings is provided during business hours by the presence of the tenant and by security alarm systems when the buildings are closed. Large industrial complexes and plants, which may occupy hundreds of acres, will have a separate security force, which may resemble the police department of a small city. Security of industry on this scale is generally a separate department of the industrial organization responsible for the facility.

■ SPECIALIZED INDUSTRIAL PROPERTY: MINISTORAGE CENTERS

Lifestyle changes such as births, deaths, marriages, and divorces and business expansion and contraction all create storage problems. Ministorage has captured markets in every major city and many smaller ones.

Choice of Name

Initially called miniwarehouses, a name still in use in some areas, self-service storage facility managers have adopted the term **ministorage**, a name change that came about because of the liability inherent in the use of the word warehouse. Under common and statutory law, someone who runs a warehouse where goods are stored for the general public is fully responsible for those goods. Because self-storage businesses simply are landlords renting space controlled by their tenants, ministorage has become the term of choice.

Ministorage centers fulfill a latent need within the real estate market by providing secure storage units for individuals and small businesses. Units range in size from 5′ × 5′ to 10′ × 20′ (often larger for commercial users) and usually can be rented either monthly or annually. This space gives homeowners convenient storage for surplus possessions and businesses a place for old records that would otherwise occupy more expensive office space.

Different Types of Storage Centers

The traditional ministorage complex consists of separate rows of concrete block buildings with driveways between them. Each building is from 20 to 30 feet wide with access doors on both sides. When this type of structure is not feasible in some market areas, such as older large urban areas, particularly northeastern industrial cities, creative property managers are adapting older fireproof buildings on the fringe of downtown areas for self-storage purposes.

Also, ministorage centers can be developed on odd property configurations often located in areas of zoning boundaries. This property can be purchased at a more reasonable price, so it allows for a little higher capitalization rate for the developer. Recently developed ministorage facilities are often air-conditioned and heated and are used by businesses for computer backup storage. Site location, directions, and signage are important for these types of sites.

Managers should emphasize to the tenant that goods are not insured by the storage facility. Generally, the manager should be able to supply names of insurance carriers. Tenants should receive a written document itemizing goods that should not be stored, including live animals, perishables, liquids, explosives, flammable liquids and fuels, and toxic materials. Fuel should be drained from gasoline engines before they are stored.

Resident Manager Job Description

An apartment and office for a resident manager is usually part of the complex. Job descriptions for these managers include regular and routine office activities, such as marketing and showing space, leasing, maintaining the grounds, maintaining tenant relations, monitoring the usage to which the space is put, and providing additional security. Professional property managers are hired when the owner does not have the skill to keep track of irregularly scheduled rental and mortgage payments and handle rental delinquencies and other tasks created by the high tenant turnover in a ministorage operation.

Ministorage managers face different problems from those managing tenant occupied properties. This is because the tenant leaves property in the storage areas. Problems develop when the contents are abandoned or if the tenant does not pay the rent. The manager must learn the legalities of state statutes before disposing of the property to recover back rent. The law will determine if and how the manager can sell the stored items.

Specialized Computer Software

Software has been developed to assist the manager in maintaining records. After determining which features the manager wants to track and follow, the manager can compare features from competing packages. Because security is so important, it is also useful for this software to interface with security and access systems.

Basically, the manager may want to use a program that has the following features:

■ Tracking of information specific to the customer or the unit

■ Maintenance tracking

■ Ease in making updates and changes

■ Availability of technical support

Also, consider how well the program tracks the following:

■ Multiple billing dates and proration of rents

■ Multiple rental items per customer

■ Billing of recurring charges other than rent (i.e., insurance)

■ Nonstorage rentals, such as RV parking or mailboxes

■ Nonrent sales, such as locks, boxes, etc.

■ SUMMARY

Industrial sites include all land and buildings where activities related to the production, storage, and distribution of tangible goods take place. Industrial sites fall into three major classifications, based on their adaptability to other uses. General-purpose buildings have a wide range of uses but are most often adapted for light manufacturing or assembly plants. The physical characteristics of special-purpose buildings limit their use. Buildings suitable for only one purpose and incapable of being converted readily to any alternate use are called single-purpose properties.

In general, industrial properties require heavy investment capital, move slowly in the real estate market, and are susceptible to rapid functional obsolescence. Industrial tenants are relatively stable, restricted from frequent changes in location by the high cost of moving their equipment and inventories. It is essential that the manager match tenant and location by analyzing the market and qualifying prospective tenants.

Planned industrial parks are often located in suburban industrial subdivisions, and offer land in outlying areas with good accessibility to comparatively small businesses.

To determine the demand for a particular type of industrial property and to assess its suitability for a specific tenant, the manager must be familiar with the nature of various industrial processes and the character of local industrial growth and development. Industries that prefer to be located near consumers or users are market-oriented. Industries that locate near their major supplier or source of raw materials are resource-oriented. Labor-oriented industries are concerned with the existence and cost of a sufficient labor pool.

Marketing demands much more technical and specialized knowledge than marketing commercial or residential space. Most marketing is accomplished with signs and brochures, and through industrial brokers. Negotiations are usually prolonged and complex, but because industrial leases are long term, leasing efforts need not be made frequently.

Industrial firms looking for space want detailed facts about the economic base of the community; a profile of its population; data on the skills, education, and turnover rate of the local labor force, and data on local transportation facilities, utilities, taxes, zoning, and other government regulations. The property manager must qualify the prospect firm in terms of space, transportation, and labor needs.

Industrial leases are generally net leases requiring the tenant to pay some or all the basic expenses of the property. Although the standard industrial lease includes many typical provisions of other leases, the terms and conditions involving real estate taxes and assessments, insurance premiums, and maintenance costs responsibilities are highly individualized and must be negotiated separately between each manager and tenant. Under a net lease, the tenant usually assumes most or all of the maintenance responsibilities for the property; those not assumed by the tenant become the responsibility of the property manager.

Ministorage areas avoid the common law implications associated with the word warehouse. Not only are many new facilities being built, but also many older buildings are being converted into self-storage areas. These facilities are used by homeowners to store personal belongings and by businesses to store business records and sometimes even inventory. Modern ministorage areas are heated and air-conditioned storage areas. To enhance security, the manager often lives on-site and tracks payments.

■ CASE STUDY

THE INDUSTRIAL PROPERTY MANAGER

Ron Yu is looking for tenants for a business park he manages. The business park is located in an outlying area and is made up of relatively small tenant spaces (five acres to ten acres). There is no direct access to air cargo transport or railroads, but there is easy access to trucking routes and residential areas.

1. What kind of tenants should Yu be looking for?
2. What qualities in a tenant should Yu screen for?

■ REVIEW QUESTIONS

1. Industrial real estate is classified according to
   a. nonconvertibility.
   b. adaptability.
   c. distribution factor.
   d. services provided.

2. What is the term used to describe a building built for use as a warehouse but adaptable to light manufacturing?
   a. General-purpose
   b. Special-purpose
   c. Limited-purpose
   d. Single-purpose

3. A building is still quite useable and in fairly good condition. However, the supporting pillars are placed only ten feet apart and the walls are solid. It is nearly impossible to thread computer cable in the walls. This property is
   a. currently unmarketable.
   b. physically obsolete.
   c. functionally obsolete.
   d. technically depreciated.

4. An industrial company has just completed building a factory to exact specifications. Now it wants to pull its equity out to use for other business purposes. Which of the following would MOST likely be utilized to realize this objective?
   a. Contract for deed
   b. Installment sale
   c. Sale-leaseback
   d. Purchase money mortgage

5. Speculative construction of shell industrial buildings
   a. permits tenants rapid occupancy to their specifications once their lease is signed.
   b. has not been successful in areas experiencing rapid population growth.
   c. works best if the building is designed for special-purpose use.
   d. is not permitted under local building codes.

6. Which of the following is a characteristic of storage space?
   a. High investment risk due to tenant instability
   b. Greater liquidity than light assembly plants
   c. Limited demand in cold weather
   d. Greater need for remodeling than office space when leases are renewed

7. Of the following, which method is particularly suited to marketing industrial space?
   a. Classified ads
   b. Display ads
   c. Direct mail
   d. Radio commercials

8. What is the primary objective of the industrial manager?
   a. Developing planned industrial parks
   b. Arranging for a compatible tenant mix
   c. Finding a location with the lowest transportation costs
   d. Matching a particular property with a specific firm

9. Showing industrial space to prospects
   a. often involves showings to several persons at the same time, each interested in a different aspect of the property.
   b. does not differ from showing office property.
   c. involves local chamber of commerce officials.
   d. should be done by a broker who is a member of the SIOR.

10. In addition to regular duties, the manager of a mini-storage area may also be required to furnish
    a. remodeling.
    b. utilities.
    c. additional security.
    d. social activities.

11. A labor-intensive industry
    a. is generally unionized.
    b. does not require plant facilities with a large parking area.
    c. has a high ratio of employees per acre.
    d. requires few in-plant facilities for workers.

12. All of the following are used as incentives to entice industry to an area *EXCEPT*
    a. special taxes levied on new businesses.
    b. private industry councils.
    c. special tax incentives.
    d. industrial revenue bonds.

13. A one-story plant occupying 200,000 square feet is located on a site containing 600,000 square feet. What is the structural density of the property?
    a. 30%
    b. 33%
    c. 40%
    d. 12%

14. What is the gross floor area of a one-story plant with a constant ceiling height of 11 feet and the following floor plan?

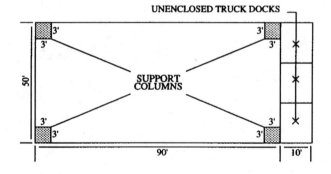

    a. 4,500 sq. ft.
    b. 4,464 sq. ft.
    c. 5,000 sq. ft.
    d. 43,964 sq. ft.

15. Which of the following leases describes a common industrial lease?
    a. A gross lease puts most of the basic property expense on the tenant.
    b. A straight percentage lease requires the tenant to assume real estate tax and assessment payments in addition to the rental payment.
    c. A simple-net lease requires payment of the mortgage in addition to taxes in addition to rent.
    d. A triple-net lease requires the tenant to pay taxes, assessments, insurance, and maintenance in addition to the rent.

16. How is the rent factor for industrial property expressed?
    a. Dollars per square yard per month
    b. Dollars per cubic foot per year
    c. Percentage of gross return on the leased property
    d. Dollars per square foot per year

17. An industrial building of 11,000 square feet cost $370,500, and the owner wants a 12% annual return on the investment. The minimum rent per square foot the manager should obtain for the space is
    a. $2.22.
    b. $4.04.
    c. $6.23.
    d. $7.37.

18. If an industrial tenant will sign a longer lease, the owner may be more inclined to
    a. amortize the mortgage over a shorter term.
    b. lower the rent.
    c. withdraw concessions.
    d. increase the rent.

19. Which of the following typifies the property manager's role in industrial property maintenance?
    a. Leases are generally gross leases, so there is little requirement for the property manager's involvement.
    b. Few tenants hire professional cleaning crews, so the property manager must arrange for daily cleaning of tenant space.
    c. Tenants provide much of the interior maintenance required for their own space through their own facility operations, so property managers generally need not be concerned with maintaining tenant space.
    d. Maintenance steps differ significantly from residential, office, or commercial property.

20. Smaller living quarters and the increasing need to store many business records have led to the popularity of
    a. mixed use developments.
    b. planned use developments.
    c. foreign trade zones.
    d. ministorage areas.

CHAPTER SIXTEEN

16

RISK AND ENVIRONMENTAL ISSUES

■ KEY TERMS

Asbestos
Building-related illness
  (BRI)
Carbon monoxide (CO)
Chlorofluorocarbons
  (CFC)
80 percent coinsurance
Environmental
  assessments
Environmental Impact
  Statement (EIS)

Environmental
  Protection Agency
  (EPA)
Flood insurance
Formaldehyde
Hazardous substance
Hazardous waste
Lead-based paint
Mold(s)
Polychlorinated
  biphenyls (PCBs)
Radon

Replacement cost
  insurance
Risk management
Risk management
  workers' compensation
Sick building syndrome
  (SBS)
Underground storage
  tanks (USTs)
www.epa.gov

■ LEARNING OBJECTIVES

At the end of this chapter, the student will be able to

1. identify four methods of risk management and the implications of each—avoid, control, retain, or transfer the risk;

2. identify at least five types of insurance policies that the owner should carry, and discuss the need for and coverage of each;

3. list at least three types of insurance that a property manager should carry and explain the reasons for carrying each;

4. summarize air quality issues and identify building systems that may be checked and improved;

5. contrast the difference between a Phase I environmental audit and an environmental impact statement;

6. plan employee information and training for dealing with hazardous substances;

7. list environmental laws and give a simple explanation of each;

8. describe the efforts of at least two governmental agencies concerned with workers and the environment; and

9. name at least five environmental hazards and describe ways that the property manager can minimize their effects.

■ OVERVIEW

In addition to all the other tasks and duties discussed in preceding chapters, the manager handles office records as well as the principal's funds and important documents. Insurance against loss of these documents or the property itself during the routine performance of the manager's duties is valuable protection for both parties and should be purchased by the manager as a good business investment. The property owner may consult the manager, but the final decision about any property insurance should be made by the owner after consulting with his or her own insurance agent.

Although the manager has no insurable interest in the property itself, he or she should be named as a coinsured on all liability insurance policies that the owner holds on the premises. The usual form of a manager's general liability insurance policy does not cover accidents arising because of the management of properties.

Environmental concerns require an increasing amount of management time and attention and may affect the availability of insurance as well. This is especially true regarding moisture claims and flood insurance. And after paying out huge settlements for mold-related claims, many insurance companies are now excluding mold damage in the policies.

With the proliferation of federal and state laws and increasing local regulation and enforcement, the area of environmental concerns has become a major responsibility of the property manager. Property managers are not expected to be experts in all the disciplines called on to operate a modern building properly. They are, however, expected to be knowledgeable in many diverse subjects, most of which are technical in nature, and environmental concerns fall into the technical category.

The property manager may manage structures containing hazardous materials or be called on to arrange an environmental audit of a property under consideration for purchase. If hazardous wastes are produced by the manager's employer or tenants, the manager must see that they are properly disposed of. Even the normally nonhazardous waste from an office building must be controlled to avoid violating laws requiring segregation of types of wastes. In areas where recycling is becoming the norm, the property manager must provide recycling facilities and see that tenants sort their trash properly.

■ RISK MANAGEMENT AND INSURANCE

One of the most critical areas of responsibility for a property manager, because of the potentially great dollar and personal losses, is the field of **risk management** and insurance. The property manager should have a working knowledge of casualty, liability, and special lines of insurance and an understanding of the whole insurance field—its theories, principles, and practices. Insurance has expanded from its beginning several centuries ago as a pooling of risks by merchants to its present-day sophistication in which the professional insurance administrator is now called a risk manager.

Premiums have skyrocketed, in large part because of lawsuits over the presence of mold. While the manager cannot prevent naturally occurring catastrophes, such as hurricanes or earthquakes, the manager can adopt risk prevention and risk reduction policies to minimize their financial effects.

Risk Management Theories

The risk manager is concerned with both the financial and humanitarian consequences of unforeseen events, and in taking steps to reduce those consequences. Risk management principles can be examined and implemented in the following ways:

- Identifying the risk and measuring its frequency and financial severity

- Avoiding the risk or discontinuing the loss-causing activity

- Controlling the risk with safety programs, loss reduction plans, and emergency preparedness

- Retaining the risk and internally funding loss consequences

- Transferring the risk to insurers or to third parties

- Monitoring the results and ongoing fit of the risk management strategies implemented

- Have tenant pay for or share extra costs for dealing with unusual risks or paying for specialized insurance

Identifying and measuring the risk   The risk manager begins the process with a survey of the physical structure, the operating equipment, and the tasks performed by personnel, particularly during maintenance. Contractor's insurance certificates should be reviewed.

The property manager can access additional sources to assess various risks. For example, the Internet, public records, and libraries can provide sources of weather, flood, and earthquake probabilities. Local fire departments may allow access to their information and offer suggestions on measuring fire hazards. Independent loss-control firms conduct hazards audits, and some insurers offer professional loss-control consultations.

Property replacement costs and actual depreciated values should be obtained. Current contracts and leases and inactive contracts with remaining indemnities should be discussed with legal counsel.

Avoiding the risk   The property manager should determine which risks can be avoided and which cannot. Windstorms, floods, and earthquakes cannot be avoided; they are known risks assumed by the owner. Icy sidewalks can be expected. Fires occur and are sources of property damage, loss of income, and injuries to employees, tenants, and the public.

Property managers can, however, avoid some identified risks by not managing hazardous properties and by eliminating dangerous equipment and hazardous operations. Avoiding risk can be as simple as removing a diving board or replacing wood shingles with noncombustible materials; or as complex as arranging environmental assessments and removing pollutants. Also, the manager should hire only contractors who can provide evidence of insurance for workers' compensation, and commercial or automobile liability.

Controlling the risk   Some risk cannot be avoided. The property manager should consider ways to reduce the likelihood of the loss event occurring and to reduce its impact (measured in terms of financial cost and human suffering). Emergency preparedness and adequate crisis response plans should be developed and regularly updated by the property manager.

Installing fire sprinklers and signs and physical barriers to warn people of hazards on the premises are examples of controlling physical hazards. Other examples include off-site backup computer records and installing security services to prevent some losses and sound the alarm in others. Drivers can be asked to provide satisfactory motor vehicle records. Property maintenance equipment should be kept in safe working order, and the operators can be carefully trained and required to wear protective clothing and equipment.

Recently mold has become a larger responsibility and liability issue, so buildings of all types should be periodically tested with mold detection units in order to prevent any surprise issues. Outside contractors can be used for annual or semi-annual testing. The results should be kept on file. If a problem is identified, it should be remediated before a major expensive situation arises.

Loss control can contribute directly to savings in insurance premiums. For example, workers' compensation, automobile and commercial liability, and multiple location property insurance agreements are individually loss experience rated by insurers. The well-managed risk is more desirable to underwriters and premium credits can be substantial—up to 40 percent in some situations.

Retaining the risk   After the principal risks have been avoided or reduced where possible, remaining risks require funding if the financial consequences of losses are to be absorbed. Internal funding either by cash or borrowing is nearly always the most economically efficient. With proper planning, reasonably expected loss costs such as dented fenders, broken windshields, minor vandalism, and plate glass breakage can be retained and paid for as ordinary business expenses. Increasing the insurance deductible is another way of retaining some of the risk; usually, the higher the deductible, the lower the premiums.

Transferring the risk   Risks that cannot be avoided or internally funded must be transferred. Transfer techniques include

- shifting the hazardous activity to professionals with satisfactory insurance;
- contractually shifting the legal liability to others by written indemnities to the owner/property manager; and
- transferring the risk, partially or wholly, to insurers.

Shifting the hazardous activity to others may include hiring contractors to provide security, swimming pool chemicals, maintenance, and roof repair. Of course, the property manager still has supervisory duties.

Contractually shifting legal liability to others is rarely a complete transfer of risk. Contractual indemnities must be funded by the indemnitor; therefore, the owner must rely on the indemnitor's financial worth and insurance coverage.

Transferring the risk to insurers, partially or wholly, is one technique for funding risks that cannot otherwise be retained, avoided, or transferred to others. Insurance is not a perfect transfer, however, because not all risks are insurable. For example, standard policies exclude loss caused by nuclear contamination, asbestos contamination, enemy invasion, and war.

Monitoring decisions   The property manager must continually monitor areas of risk to determine whether changes must be made to improve the effectiveness of the risk management plan. New operations or properties also must be evaluated for risk management. Property values must be updated at least annually and when improvements are underway.

> Constant vigilance of insurance certificates on the part of owners, their subcontractors, and tenants is a vital part of risk management. The property manager should set up ongoing compliance suspense files.

Property Manager as a Claim Adjuster

Inevitably, every property manager will experience a loss covered by insurance. This may be as simple as a dented fender on a maintenance truck. However, it could involve extensive physical damage to buildings from fire, windstorm, or other disaster. In most cases, the property manager will be responsible for arranging preservation of the property and later negotiating with insurance company representatives, such as claims adjusters, to obtain fair settlement.

The objective in any claim settlement is to compensate the owner for damages suffered in accordance with the terms and conditions of the insurance policies. For this reason, managers should have a thorough knowledge of coverage and limits and establish a good working relationship with their insurance agents.

Adjustment of claims is an area that requires a great deal of expertise and experience. Adjusters representing insurance companies, particularly independent adjusting companies, may be intent on trying to minimize the amount of claims paid rather than making a fair settlement. If a property manager is not well versed in claims adjustment, an experienced attorney or well-established independent claims adjuster should be consulted.

Before any disaster, the property manager should be prepared by doing the following:

- Have easily available the names of the insurance company for each property and the policy numbers of the policies that cover the managed properties
- Know the phone number of the agent that handles the policies
- Have the number for the claim department of the insurance company
- Have the phone number to call in the event of a catastrophe, as the number may be different than a regular claim number
- It is helpful to have the insurance company inspector conduct an annual visual inspection in order to avoid surprises or conflicts

In the event of serious damage, the renter and/or property manager should call in the claim as soon as possible and take pictures of the damage. Then, either or both should arrange for temporary repairs to prevent additional damage, keeping all receipts. The property owner should be notified as soon as possible.

■ TYPES OF INSURANCE

The basic purpose of insurance is to reduce loss caused by unforeseen misfortunes. Both property owner and manager are exposed to the consequences of loss or accidents and need the protection offered by various types of insurance. One term to remember is *insurable interest*. No one can buy insurance on something or even someone unless he or she has a reason to be involved with that entity or person. For example, the owner of the building can buy insurance to cover the building in case of a loss, but tenants will have to purchase their own insurance to cover what belongs to them.

Owners' Hazard Insurance Policies

A property owner wants to obtain the best insurance coverage against as many risks as possible at the most reasonable rate. Because different localities and conditions demand varied forms of coverage, the owner often relies on the experience and judgment of the property manager. Although the property manager should have a working knowledge of insurance and can make recommendations, ultimately, the owner should make insurance decisions based on recommendations from the owner's own insurance broker.

As a representative of the policy buyer, the insurance broker must determine the risks involved, shop the market for the best and most economical coverage, and then purchase the required policies on behalf of the owner. Homeowners who have moved out of their homes converting the home to a rental should be advised that their homeowner's policy must be changed. A home must be owner-occupied to qualify for the homeowner's policy. The landlord's policy offers less protection.

As discussed earlier, the property manager should consider several insurance covers. At a minimum, considerations should include the following:

- Property insurance, including fire, lightning, windstorm, vandalism, and malicious mischief
- Flood insurance
- Loss of income following damage to structures or their contents
- Additional costs for temporary premises that are required following a loss
- Rental value of leased premises that must be replaced by more expensive leases
- Workers' compensation and employers' liability for injury to workers
- Commercial automobile liability, including hired and nonowned automobiles, to cover injury and damage by vehicles
- Commercial general liability, including liability for contractors, completed operations, product, and contractually assumed liabilities

Standard fire insurance   Several standard forms for fire insurance policies are available. *Multiperil policies* have been designed especially for each type of property: apartments, office buildings, warehouses, row houses, and fireproof structures. Multiperil policies usually contain related covers such as loss of income and premises liability.

The policies contain four parts:

1. The insurance agreement
2. Policy exclusions, limitations, and reductions
3. Policy conditions and warranties, if any
4. Policy territory

The agreement section describes the named insured(s), property and locations insured, premiums charged, the period of coverage, hazards and perils insured, and any endorsements altering or extending the contract. The second part of the policy lists exclusions, limitations, and reductions. Provisions in this section state that the policy is voided if the insured concealed material facts concerning the risk when applying for insurance.

Suspending insurance   Many standard fire policies include a clause suspending or restricting insurance if the chance of fire is increased in any manner within the control of the owner. Some policies are suspended when buildings are unoccupied, have not been winterized, or sprinkler or alarm systems are inoperable.

The insurer also must be notified of ownership and occupancy changes. New owners or interests are not insured until the insurer has agreed to assume the new interest because underwriters rely on the good faith of the insureds and reserve the right to refuse the risk if ownership changes.

Event of loss   Other clauses in the standard insurance policy will specify the procedure to be followed in the event of loss. The pro rata amount of liability, the rights and interests of the mortgage holder and coinsureds, the insurance company's options for repair or replacement of the property, and the time within which a settlement will be made in case of loss are usually outlined in the standard forms.

The annual premium for a basic insurance policy is computed by multiplying the amount of the insurance by a rate per $100 of insurance. It is imperative that a property be adequately insured, particularly as labor and construction costs rise. The owner should obtain a current estimate of the physically depreciated value of the building and replacement costs.

Replacement versus actual depreciated value   Replacement cost **insurance** should be compared to *actual depreciated value* insurance. (Note that neither of these terms is related to *market value*.) *Actual cash value* insurance can be a problem on older buildings because partial losses will be reimbursed on a depreciated basis while repairs are at replacement costs. Replacement cost insurance guarantees that partial damage to old, depreciated property will be fully replaced by new construction.

Consider a ten-year-old roof destroyed or damaged by windstorm. If the property is insured for its actual cash value (physically depreciated value), the policy reimbursement will be the value of a ten-year-old roof. A replacement cost policy will reimburse the cost of a new roof. This is an especially important consideration because the most likely loss is a partial loss.

Cost of demolition after partial losses, should it become necessary, must be considered. For older buildings, insurance for additional expenses necessary to meet revised construction codes must be included if the building would need to be reconstructed.

> The property manager should make sure that the owner carries adequate coverage and that coverage is increased annually to cover the increased value of the improvements.

80 percent coinsurance   The coinsurance provisions of an insurance policy are critical and often misunderstood. In the typical situation, the owner/manager has promised the insurer two things in return for a lower premium:

1. Above-ground property will be insured to 80 percent of its full physical replacement cost or actual value cost.

2. Insured will maintain insurance coverage on that property at 80 percent of the value insured basis.

The responsibility for maintaining insurance to 80 percent of the replacement value or actual cash value rests with the owner/manager. Every property manager should track inflation and construction costs and at least annually review the property and liability limits of the insurance, property by property.

The premium for $50,000 of insurance on a building without coinsurance is about equal to the premium for $80,000 of insurance on a $100,000 building using an **80 percent coinsurance** clause. Insurers are reluctant to assume what they consider underinsured risks.

If there is a loss of $40,000 on the $100,000 building insured for $80,000 with **80 percent coinsurance,** the insurer will pay the entire loss of $40,000. If there is a loss of $100,000, the insurer will pay $80,000. But if the value of the building has increased through inflation to $200,000, and the insurance remains at $80,000, then a partial loss of $40,000 will be determined according to the following formula:

$$\frac{\text{Amount of insurance}}{\text{80\% of what it should have been insured for}} \times \frac{\text{Partial}}{\text{loss}} = \frac{\text{Insurer}}{\text{payment}}$$

$$\frac{\$80,000}{\$160,000 \ (80\% \text{ of } \$200,000)} \times \$40,000 = \$20,000 \text{ Insurer payment}$$

Had the loss been a total loss, the insurer would have paid the policy limit of $80,000. The owner who has failed to keep the property insured to 80 percent of the value would suffer a loss of $120,000, if the $200,000 building were a total loss.

For properties valued at $1 million or more, insurers may consider an "agreed amount" clause. Such a clause eliminates the possibility of a coinsurance penalty. In return, however, the insurer usually demands total insurance to value.

Compared to all-risks insuring agreements   Standard fire insurance policies cover loss caused by fire and lightning. Adding extended coverage includes causes of loss described as explosion, windstorm, tornado, hurricane, hail, riot, civil strife, falling aircraft, and smoke. Vandalism and malicious mischief perils can be added by endorsement. Some of the newer causes of loss forms combine all-risks coverage on some subjects and specific perils on other subjects of insurance.

All-risks coverage, instead of specifying the insured causes of loss, promises to insure all causes of loss except those excluded.

Machinery and equipment insurance   Boiler explosions have been the source of catastrophic loss of life. Standard fire insurance policies do not cover boiler explosion as a result of internal breakdown. Boiler and machinery insurance combines both risk of transfer to insurers and loss control by insurers' engineers. Boiler and machinery policies cover direct loss to the machinery, damage to property of others caused by boiler explosions, and bodily injury to persons injured in boiler explosions. The insurance can also be written to include loss of income and costs of expediting repairs.

Machinery breakdown coverage is important for air-conditioning and refrigeration equipment necessary to the use of the property or for preservation of food, furs, or chemicals. For example, retail stores often maintain freezers for food storage. Most multitenant buildings (residential or commercial) are obligated to provide heat. Any vehicles such as trucks, forklifts, or cars used in the operation of a property also must be insured, especially if numerous units are garaged together.

Loss of income and loss of occupancy   Loss of income insurance might include loss of rents, profits, and commissions after an insured loss. Extra expense insurance covers additional costs to rent temporary space after an insured loss. Loss of rental value compensates the owner for those properties occupied at favorable rents—often the case with long-term leases. These insurance policies may be a wise choice for properties with small profit margins and heavy debt loads.

Flood Insurance

No homeowners, renters, or building insurance policies cover water damage as a result of rising waters, nor can an endorsement be added. The policies must be purchased separately and subsidized policies are available to any property owner located in a community participating in the National Flood Insurance Program (NFIP). Flooding can be caused by heavy rains, melting snow, inadequate drainage systems, or failed protective devices such as levees and dams, as well as by tropical storms and hurricanes. For a complete description, consult *www.app1.fema.gov/nfip/*.

FDIC-insured lenders must require **flood insurance** on their collateral if the property is located in a Special Flood Hazard Area zone (SFHA). If the lender's loans are not adequately covered, the FDIC can impose fines and penalties and even cancel the lender's FDIC insurance. Even if flood insurance is not required by the lender, every property owner should still consider buying a policy. About 20 to 25 percent of all claims are from owners whose property is not located in a SFHA.

A preferred risk policy (PRP) can be written in non-special flood hazard areas *if* the property has never had a loss. PRP has lower rates than the standard flood policies. However, it is not eligible for properties located in the special flood hazard area (SFHA).

Flood insurance does have upper limits of coverage. Private insurers can write policies for the excess coverage. See Table 16.1 for Policy Forms and Coverage Maximums.

Owners are encouraged to buy the policy through their own insurance agents, so that if there is a disaster, they only have to work with one adjuster. The policy generally covers the dwelling, detached garage, a properly anchored manufactured home, and, if purchased, personal property. Deductibles are treated differently under flood insurance. Consider a $500 deductible. Most property policies carry a single deductible, so the insured pays $500 as the deductible against the entire loss. Flood policies carry a split deductible. For example, a $500/$500 deductible means that the insured pays $500 as a deductible for the building and then pays another $500 deductible for the contents.

Compare the flood insurance policies of the following. The apartment complex owner can buy $250,000 maximum building coverage with $100,000 contents coverage. But the condominium association can buy $250,000 per unit and up to $100,000 for the commonly owned contents. Then, finally, the coverage for a

FIGURE 16.1
Policy Forms and Maximum Coverage

	Policy Form	Building Coverage Minimum	Contents Coverage Maximum	Eligible for PRP
Single Family Home	Dwelling Form	$250,000	$100,000	Yes
24 Family Building	Dwelling Form	$250,000	$100,000	Yes
Single Family Unit in 24 Family Building	Dwelling Form	$250,000 per unit	$100,000 per unit	Yes
Condo Unit Owner	Dwelling Form	$250,000	$100,000	No
Condo Unit Renter	Dwelling Form	Not available	$100,000	No
Apartment Renter	Dwelling Form	Not available	$100,000	No
Apartment Building Owner	General	$250,000	$100,000	No
Manufactured (Mobile) Home Residential	Dwelling Form	$250,000	$100,000	Yes
Manufactured (Mobile) Home Non-Residential	General Property Form	$500,000	$500,000	No
Condominium Association	Residential Condominium Building Association Form	$250,000 times the number of units or Replacement Cost, whichever is less	$100,000 for commonly owned contents	No
Non-Residential Buildings	General Property Form	$500,000	$500,000	No

nonresidential building has an upper limit of $500,000 and up to $500,000 contents coverage.

Other Types of Insurance

Commercial, general, and auto liability insurance   Under the common law of negligence, the property owner has a duty to act in a manner, and to maintain the property in such a condition, that others will not be injured on the premises. Failure to act in a responsible manner can result in fines, imprisonment, or a judgment decree for damages and penalties.

Commercial general liability insurance usually covers legal responsibility and costs of defense for damage to real and personal property of others, including loss of use of the damaged property. Policies can be amended to include personal injury lawsuits alleging invasion of privacy, false arrest, libel, or slander by the insured or the insured's agents and representatives. The policy may be broadened to cover some contractually assumed liabilities as well as liability for the insured's products and completed operations. All of these covers may be necessary for the property owner. A *completed operations risk* may exist if a management company repairs the property of others. Owners and management companies also have *products liability* if they sell or rent property or equipment to others.

Pollution liability insurance   Although excluded under commercial general and auto liability policies, pollution liability insurance is required by law for underground storage tanks, hazardous waste storage or disposal sites, and transportation of hazardous wastes. Even though specialty insurers are willing to assume liability for unintentional pollution hazards, the policies are expensive and limited in scope. Further, nearly all of them are written on claims-made forms, meaning only those claims bought within the policy period are covered. Thus, the policies must be continued or extended for a time after the pollution risk has terminated or the polluted property has been sold or is no longer in use.

Workers' compensation insurance   State statutes and federal laws (on federal property) require workers' compensation insurance. Workers' compensation policies are standard forms covering the worker benefits prescribed by law (excluding fines or penalties) and are available from private insurers, state funds, and assigned risk pools. States consider both injuries and diseases related to the workplace as compensable. A person suffering a hearing loss, for example, may be compensated in many states.

Managers need to be sure that companies with a number of lower-pay employees are paying workers' compensation insurance to the full amount for all employees. A problem can arise when the company pays some employees on the books and others off the books. A major claim against this tenant could financially impact the business and lead to missed rental payments. Typically, this is an issue with smaller size companies and not larger or national companies.

Employer liability insurance   The manager/owner of commercial properties may have duties and risks over and above those covered by statutory workers' compensation insurance. These risks arise under tort liability and may be insured against by the purchase of *employer liability insurance*, plus purchase of coverage B of the standard workers' compensation and employer liability insurance policy.

When employee injuries or diseases are ruled noncompensable by the workers' compensation courts, employees may sue under ordinary negligence laws. Occasionally, employee family members sue the employer for wrongful death or loss of consortium. This type of insurance may also defend claims brought by employee family members who allege pollution brought home by employees from the workplace. Employers' liability insurance covers claims brought for unsafe workplace injuries.

Third-party-over suits   Employees injured by a product often sue the manufacturer for negligence. If the employee prevails in such a lawsuit, the manufacturer may try to pass this negligence award back to the employer. The basis for such suits against the employer, called *third-party-over suits,* is that the product that injured the employee was modified, misused, or poorly maintained by the employer, or that the employer did not properly train the injured employee. Another source of lawsuits under this cover are employer-producer situations where the employee is injured while using a machine or product manufactured or modified by the employer. The growing number of third-party-over suits against employers mandates the purchase of employer liability insurance.

Special considerations A growing trend in law expands the responsibility of employers of workers and independent contractors. Often, workers' compensation courts will rule that subcontractors are in fact employees for the purpose of compensation claims. Also, under no-fault laws, workers and subcontractors are nearly always considered employees, regardless of the contract for hire.

Managers must not neglect to obtain contractors' certificates of insurance for workers' compensation. The property owner's insurer will assess full workers' compensation premiums of uninsured contractors.

■ INSURANCE FOR THE TENANT

As a standard practice, the property manager should notify, in writing, all tenants—residential, commercial, and industrial—that they must obtain renter's insurance to protect their personal belongings. It may help to explain *insurable interest,* stating that the landlord cannot buy coverage if he or she does not own the property.

Business tenants renting a commercial building can obtain their own business or commercial policy. They can obtain business insurance through their own insurance agents. They would not require building or dwelling coverage as they are only renting.

Families or individuals who are renting an apartment, house, or condominium need an HO-4 or renter's policy. These policies are offered through the personal lines marketplace and insure the tenant's personal property. They can also obtain flood insurance to cover their personal belongings.

■ INSURANCE FOR THE MANAGER

The manager, as both a custodian and a contracting businessperson, may hire employees or contractors; handle client funds, documents, and records; and maintain an office and files. Common sense dictates that the manager should insure office contents, equipment, and supplies, as well as computers and software.

The manager should also purchase employee dishonesty insurance to cover money, merchandise, and any other property for which the manager may be held accountable. Loss of valuable records, theft, holdup, and messenger robbery insurance should be carefully considered. The manager should also carry *errors and omissions insurance* (with limits of at least 10 percent of the total annual collections) to protect against possible accounting mistakes or other oversights, including *failure to act*.

■ ALLOCATING COST OF RISK MANAGEMENT BETWEEN MANAGER AND OWNER

Property managers must be aware of the risks they assume when they agree to manage a property. Most property owners feel that they are hiring an expert when they hire a property manager and are paying for that manager's expertise. Thus, owners believe that the manager should protect the owner from any liability that may arise from management activities. However, few property managers can afford to be exposed to the kind of liability that could result from their management activities.

Limit Management Responsibilities

There are several ways for a property manager to control or limit his or her liability. To begin with, the manager can try to control liability by limiting management responsibilities. For example, when using outside companies such as janitorial services or security, the contract should be between the third party and the owner, whenever possible. The property owner's name should appear on the contract with the manager listed only as the agent.

Bid Bonds

Service and construction contractors should be required to post bid bonds from a reputable surety/insurer before work begins. Bid bonds are ordinarily furnished by the surety company without premium charge. The manager thus knows that the contractor awarded the work will be able to furnish a performance bond guaranteeing completion of the work and payment of suppliers and workers.

Named Additional Insured

In addition to carrying his or her own insurance, the property manager should ask to be named additional insured by the property owner's liability and property insurers. Ordinarily there is no extra premium charge to the owner. The manager should also ask that the owner's property, liability, and workers' compensation insurers waive their rights of *subrogation* against the property manager.

Property managers should require certificates of insurance from the owner's insurers evidencing these endorsements and each insurer's promise to notify the manager if the policies are canceled, nonrenewed, or materially changed.

Indemnity Clause

Another way to manage risk is the *indemnity clause*. An indemnity clause in the management agreement can require the property owner to indemnify the manager for any damages not caused by the manager's own negligence or willful misconduct. This would help protect the manager even in cases where damages occur where there is no negligence on anyone's part. Any indemnity required from the manager to the owner should be worded so that the owner is protected only against foreseeable damages caused by the manager's negligence or willful misconduct that occur during the course of management duties.

The property manager should include in the management contract a clause that the manager is responsible only for his or her best effort in coordinating outside services, and is not responsible for the work performed by contractors beyond ordinary supervision or products supplied by vendors.

Managers should also consider putting a dollar cap on the amount for which they would be responsible. For example, the manager may include a clause that states he or she will be responsible for damages caused by negligence or misconduct up to the dollar amount of all compensation earned to date.

■ MANAGING ENVIRONMENTAL ISSUES

Myriad federal, state, and local environmental laws affect property managers in connection with acquiring, owning, managing, or disposing of real estate. Managers must work to ensure the health and safety of their own employees and their tenants, and for the community at large. Keeping up with current law, regulation, and legislative trends will be critical to the success of property managers for the foreseeable future.

Familiarity with the background and history of environmental legislation is helpful, and knowledge of specific hazardous substances and hazardous waste is essential. The terms *hazardous substances* and *hazardous waste* are often used interchangeably, but they are not synonymous. A **hazardous waste** is generally a by-product of a manufactured item which itself may not be subject to environmental law or regulation. A **hazardous substance**, however, is broader in scope and may include everyday items such as household cleaning products and paint.

Not all property managers must be aware of all of the following laws. Some will be more relevant to residential, others to commercial and industrial. Additional information can be obtained by going to the Environmental Protection Agency's home page: *www.epa.gov.*

Environmental Legislation

If the owner of real estate uses it in a manner that unreasonably interferes with another person's enjoyment of nearby property, the law provides a remedy in the form of suits to abate nuisances. Nuisance actions, however, were not designed to deal with serious pollution problems, which require a strong overall solution. To meet this need, governments at all levels had passed laws to abate air and water pollution by the late 1950s and early 1960s. Increased concern in the 1970s over the quality and future of the environment produced new laws and further demands for action from the public.

A brief review of principal federal laws concerning the environment follows, but property managers are reminded that additional state and local laws—many of which go beyond federal requirements and are more stringent—should be examined. One of these, the Lead-Based Paint Hazard Reduction Act, is discussed in Chapter 10.

The National Environmental Policy Act   The National Environmental Policy Act (NEPA), which went into effect in 1970, requires the preparation of an **environmental impact statement (EIS)** in advance for every major federal action that would significantly affect the quality of the environment. An environmental impact statement must

- set forth the environmental impact of the proposed action;

- evaluate impacts that cannot be avoided;

- evaluate alternatives to the proposed action;

- distinguish between short-term and long-term impacts; and

- list any irreversible consequences to natural resources.

Government agencies at all levels and interested citizens are allowed to comment on the potential environmental impact of the action, and citizens may go to court to force compliance with environmental law. It is important to note that states and some local governments have similar environmental impact laws that require EISs for major public and private developments.

The Environmental Protection Agency   The Environmental Protection Agency (EPA) was established in 1970 to centralize the federal government's environmental responsibilities. Congress has charged the EPA with enforcing the legislation covering air and water pollution, toxic pesticides, waste disposal, etc. Initial efforts were aimed at obvious pollution problems—those that could be seen, smelled, or tasted—but as controls regulating those areas were implemented, the focus changed to problems that were less visible but even more dangerous, such as those posed by toxic substances.

Clean Air Act   The Clean Air Act of 1970 established a comprehensive approach for combating air pollution by requiring the EPA to set national air quality standards for major pollutants that have an adverse impact on human health. Ambient air quality standards are prescribed in two levels: primary standards, designed to protect human beings from harm, and secondary standards, designed to protect the environment itself.

The Clean Air Act also directs the EPA to regulate the emission of toxic air pollutants, and under this authority, EPA has set standards for a number of pollutants. New stationary sources, such as factories and power plants, must install the most effective technology available for reducing air pollution. The EPA's published regulations, *National Emission Standards for Hazardous Air Pollutants (NESHAP)*, guide matters involving air pollution. Property managers of industrial property will have more concern in this area than those who manage commercial property. They should review local ordinances as well.

In 1991, the Clean Air Act was amended to include laws to protect the stratospheric ozone layer. Since then, refrigerants must be properly recovered from air conditioning and refrigeration equipment. Environmental and financial penalties can be assessed of up to $25,000 per day, per violation of the Act (see CFCs section).

Clean Water Act   The 1972 Clean Water Act Amendments to the original 1948 law were as all-encompassing in the water pollution field as the Clean Air Act was in air pollution. The amendments contain two basic goals:

1. To achieve water clean enough for swimming and recreational uses and for the protection of fish and wildlife
2. To have no discharges of pollutants into the nation's waters

Although neither goal was reached by 1994, an EPA report did cite dramatic improvements in the conditions of water sources in most parts of the country. There may also be state regulations under this act that control apartment project pools and chemical usage.

Safe Drinking Water Act   In 1974, Congress passed the Safe Drinking Water Act to protect and improve the quality of drinking water. The EPA sets primary drinking water standards to provide minimum levels of quality for water to be used for human consumption. A program governing the injection of wastes into wells was included. The primary responsibility for complying with federally established standards lies with the states.

Amendments passed in 1995 set up new programs for technical assistance, operator training, restructuring, and capacity development to aid homeowners' associations and other nongovernmental entities to comply with the monitoring and treatment requirements of the Safe Drinking Water Act. States were also given authority to redirect federal funds to support administration of the drinking water program.

Ocean pollution   A permit system regulating the dumping of all types of materials into ocean waters was set up by the Marine Protection, Research and Sanctuaries Act of 1972. The EPA has the responsibility for designating disposal sites and establishing the rules governing ocean disposal, including incineration of hazardous material at sea.

Resource Conservation and Recovery Act of 1976 (RCRA)   This is a management program intended to regulate the handling, storing, and disposal of hazardous substances. The EPA issues regulations that implement RCRA. In general, EPA regulations establish record keeping, reporting, inspection, and other technical requirements for hazardous substance businesses, violations of which can bring fines and imprisonment. Again, this is important for industrial managers and some commercial managers.

Toxic Substances Control Act of 1976 (TSCA)   The EPA is permitted to determine which substances are likely to pose health hazards to human beings or to the environment and impose controls on the testing, manufacture, and distribution of such substances. A notorious example is polychlorinated biphenyl (PCB), an extremely toxic oil additive used in electrical transformers and other equipment during the 1960s and 1970s. Use of PCB has been banned and is now being eliminated in a phaseout program.

Asbestos Hazard Emergency Response Act of 1986 (AHERA)   AHERA amended TSCA, and mandates that all elementary and secondary schools be inspected within established time frames and abatement action to be implemented where exposure to asbestos is likely. Because regulations that govern schools and other buildings may be expanded in the future in one form or another to private property, property managers should keep abreast of developments under AHERA.

Comprehensive Environmental Response, Compensation and Liability Act of 1980 (Superfund)   The Comprehensive Environmental Response, Compensation and Liability Act of 1980 (CERCLA) is the famous Superfund law, named because two trust funds were created to help finance cleanup projects and payment of property damage claims. CERCLA establishes a body of remedies available to state and federal governments, as well as private parties, for action against the release or threatened release of hazardous substances into the environment. Petroleum is not included as a hazardous waste for purposes of requiring CERCLA cleanup because federal regulations specifically exclude "wastes associated with the exploration, development or production of crude oil (or) natural gas." Other laws govern that area.

Superfund Amendments and Reauthorization Act of 1986 (SARA)   CERCLA was modified in 1986. SARA gave the federal government a lien on contaminated property subject to a federal government cleanup action, subordinate to all previously perfected security interests. SARA also limits liability for damages caused by normal application of pesticides registered under the Federal Insecticide, Fungicide and Rodenticide Act (FIFRA) of 1972. Current and past owners may be liable for cleanup, so it is imperative that property managers monitor usage and storage of hazardous materials or anything containing oil or gasoline.

State and local laws   Federal courts have discretion to exercise exclusive jurisdiction over state environmental law interrelated with federal law. The exact role played by local laws and governments in the management of hazardous matter is not yet well defined.

A thorough environmental evaluation should be performed before the sale, lease or transfer of real property. Before any action, any comprehensive cleanup plan should also be submitted to the appropriate enforcement agency.

Typical Hazardous Substance

The property manager must understand typical hazardous substances with which he or she will come in contact and how they may affect a property under management or consideration for purchase or sale. Those generally most relevant to property managers are mold, asbestos, radon, carbon monoxide, chlorofluorocarbons (CFCs), underground storage tanks, PCBs, and lead paint.

Molds   Probably the number one environmental concern today is the presence of **molds** in office buildings and residential units. Molds are not new, but awareness of possible health effects is. Insurance companies, contractors, sellers, landlords, property managers, and real estate brokers have all faced huge lawsuits. As a result, many insurance companies now exclude any coverage for mold problems.

Molds are biological pollutants that require a cellulosic food source and moisture to grow. Since they are devoid of chlorophyll, they do not require light to survive. Indeed, they grow best in dark, damp places. Molds can grow on almost any surface—behind wallpaper, underneath bathtubs and flooring, in air conditioning systems, and in sheetrock or drywall.

■ Buildings sealed to prevent heat or cooling loss host the perfect mold-growth environment: limited air flow, continued condensation, poorly installed stucco, and poor drainage. Once water gets inside, it is trapped. Molds also like temperatures between 40 and 80 degrees and a relative humidity of about 55 percent—exactly the conditions in which humans also thrive. As a result, indoor air quality may be 10 to 200 times worse than the outdoor air.

Some molds such as the green-black *stachybotrys* are toxic. But even those that are not toxic may produce spores that cause allergic and respiratory problems in some people, particularly those with asthma or other respiratory illnesses. Thus, not all family members will respond in exactly the same way.

The number one prevention technique is moisture control. Property managers should encourage tenants to immediately report any water intrusion: from water pipes, air conditioners, humidifiers, etc. Kitchen and bathroom fans should be cleaned regularly and all carpeting removed from bathrooms. If there is a flooding situation, carpeting should be removed as quickly as possible and dried outdoors. Mold inhibitors can be added to paints to further discourage mold growth.

Property managers should have certain procedures in place before a tenant ever reports indoor air quality health problems. First, management should carefully discuss mold issues with their insurance carrier(s) and carefully document all maintenance procedures. Building files should contain written records of how management responded to any prior complaints. Legal counsel should review all procedures and managers should use the services of an environmental consultant to conduct air quality measurements. For more information, consult *www.epa.gov/iaq/*.

Carbon monoxide   Many buildings today are built nearly airtight to be more energy-efficient. These airtight buildings can allow a dangerous buildup of many combustion pollutants, particularly the deadly carbon monoxide gas. **Carbon monoxide (CO)**, a colorless, odorless, tasteless gas, is one of the most common and deadly poisons in our environment. CO is a by-product of incomplete burning of fossil fuels, such as gas, oil, coal, and wood used in engines, oil burners, gas fires, water heaters, open fires, etc.

Even small amounts of CO can displace oxygen cells in the bloodstream, affecting the functions of the heart, brain, and neurological reactions, and while not causing death, may affect normal activities. Many problems arise when tenants use portable space heaters without adequate ventilation. Whole apartment and office buildings have been sickened by faulty water heaters and inadequately vented furnaces.

At the beginning of every heating season, the property manager should have the heating system and water heaters inspected. Regular inspections should be scheduled to check all appliances and furnace flues, and to see that the unit has adequate ventilation. Flues and chimneys should be inspected and cleaned at least once a year. Tenants should be discouraged from using space heaters or the kitchen oven for heating.

Even if not required by law, landlords and property managers should install carbon monoxide detectors in every rental unit and test the detectors monthly following manufacturer's instructions. It is important to remember that carbon monoxide detectors do not function as smoke detectors, and vice versa.

Chlorofluorocarbons (CFC)   Chlorofluorocarbons (CFCs, or Freon™) are manufactured, inert, nontoxic, nonflammable chemical gases used primarily as refrigerants in motor vehicle air conditioners (MVACs), building air conditioning units, refrigerators, and freezers. They are also used as industrial cleaning solvents. Unfortunately, once released from their original containers, CFCs float into the stratospheric atmosphere where they may survive from 2 to 150 years. A single molecule of CFC can destroy 100,000 molecules of ozone. These "holes" in the ozone layer allow harmful ultraviolet (UV) radiation that can lead to skin cancer, eye damage, and weakened immune systems.

New air conditioners are using a different product, CFC 134a, which is chemically similar but breaks down more quickly and thus does not reach the stratosphere. In the meantime, many of the older appliances are still leaking CFCs and must be properly disposed of in order to prevent additional leakage. The property manager should consider upgrading the appliances to use the newer environmentally friendly products. New appliances will also be more energy efficient.

All appliances, such as air conditioning units and refrigerators, must be properly disposed. The EPA recommends that the following be done:

- Contact the local public works department and ask about home appliance recycling or CFC-HCFC recovery programs.

- Contact local home appliance retailers about their refrigerator and home appliance collection program or the availability of refrigerant-recovery services.

- Inform the local hauler or serviceperson about the problem, the law, and the penalties, up to $27,500 fine per day, per violation.

Only EPA-certified technicians who have passed the EPA-approved exam should do any work on a refrigeration system, as they know how to remove CFCs without releasing them into the atmosphere. The EPA has approved both the Air-Conditioning and Refrigeration Institute (ARI) and Underwriters Laboratories (UL) to certify recycling and recovery equipment. Approved equipment will carry a label reading: "This equipment has been certified by ARI/UL to meet EPA's minimum requirements for recycling and recovery equipment. . ."

Polychlorinated biphenyls (PCBs)   Polychlorinated biphenyls (PCBs) are more than 200 chemical compounds not naturally found in nature. Because they are flame resistant, they were used in many consumer products: transformers, lubricating oils, caulking compounds, electrical motors in refrigerators, even in cereal boxes and bread wrappers. Between 1930 and 1970, over 1.4 billion pounds of PCBs were manufactured in the United States alone.

Even though PCBs are no longer commercially produced in the United States, high levels of the chemicals remain in various parts of the country as a result of leakage of old equipment, leaching from landfills, and from previously contaminated sediments. Unfortunately, they remain in the food chain accumulating in the fatty tissues in fish and animals. The EPA has classified PCBs as reasonably carcinogenic. In addition to being cancer-causing, high levels can shorten lifespan, lower fertility, and cause reproductive problems. About the only way that they can be destroyed is by burning them in a closed environment with a temperature of higher than 2,400 degrees.

The commercial or industrial property manager is most likely to deal with PCBs. The manager should definitely require the services of an environmental consultant before taking on any project where there might be a possibility of the presence of PCBs. Transformers containing PCBs can be identified by an electrical utility. Although this type of electrical equipment is being phased out of use, the property manager should investigate transformers and electrical equipment for which they are responsible and obtain the services of local electrical utility experts to remove them. The penalties are expensive, should the PCBs leak into the environment, and they are expensive to destroy.

Asbestos   Asbestos management and control was an important concern for commercial property managers in the 1990s, but is lessening today. There are several reasons for this.

Asbestos-containing material (ACM), applied by spray as a surfacing, fireproofing, and insulating material, is present in many public and private buildings throughout the country. The use of ACMs was banned in the late 1970s. Other asbestos-containing materials such as floor tile, tile adhesives, roofing, and siding were installed well into the 1980s (asbestos cement waterpipe is still in use in some areas). Renovation, remodeling, and demolition of buildings requires proper removal of any asbestos disturbed during those processes.

A thorough audit should be made to identify location, type, and condition of asbestos-laden substances in a building. This audit or survey should include drawings, quantities, and the like so an *asbestos management plan* can be developed, reviewed, and approved by building management and ownership before removal by professionals can take place on an as-needed basis.

Several actions can be taken to manage asbestos. The first is *encapsulation*, a process that leaves the asbestos in place but encloses it with an adhesive that will permanently immobilize the asbestos fibers, preventing their release into the air. The second method, *enclosure*, simply erects an airtight barrier (which must be impermeable) between the asbestos, which is left in place, and the balance of the space. The third and most drastic—and therefore most expensive—method is *removal*, which must be handled only by an authorized contractor under the supervision of qualified engineers.

Radon   Radon is an invisible, odorless, and tasteless radioactive gas that occurs in small amounts almost everywhere. Its presence in the interior environment of homes and other enclosed structures has been found to cause lung cancer. Of all the environmental risks, radon is the easiest to mitigate by sealing the property and installing PVC pipes. A fan at the top of the PVC pipe will "suck up" vapors in the soil, including radon, and then disburse them outside.

Underground storage tanks   The most common use for **underground storage tanks (USTs)** is storage of petroleum products. The principal danger from USTs comes from leaking of toxic products. If the liquid in the tank gets into groundwater, it can contaminate a wide area. If more than 10 percent of the tank is below grade, it is considered an underground storage tank.

Property managers of real estate with automobile service stations or shopping centers with service stations or car care centers will be those most concerned with underground storage tank regulation. Industrial users such as chemical plants, metal plating companies, and paint manufacturers also use underground storage tanks to store a variety of toxic liquids, which means that industrial property managers must also be alert to the presence of tanks on their properties.

The federal government regulates the registration of underground storage tanks. Legislation requires owners and operators of these tanks to demonstrate their financial ability to be responsible for potential damage from leaking tanks. Removal of a tank and cleanup of the contaminated soil below and around it can become a very expensive process. A number of states have set up funds to assist in removing tanks and cleaning up sites that may have been contaminated by underground storage tanks. State regulations also exist in almost every state, and in many places, the removal procedure is administered by state agencies.

Formaldehyde   The best known of the *volatile organic compounds (VOCs)*, **formaldehyde** is implicated as a cause of many indoor air quality complaints. Formaldehyde is a colorless, organic chemical that usually has a very strong, pronounced odor. Originally considered harmless, formaldehyde was widely used as an inexpensive preservative and bonding agent (used in home insulation and pressed wood particles). It is a component of finishes, plywood, paneling, fiberboard, and particleboard in furniture and cabinets. Urea Formaldehyde Foam Insulation (UFFI) is now legal, but rarely used.

Formaldehyde is an irritant to the eye, nose, and throat, and symptoms such as headache, wheezing, coughing, fatigue, and skin irritation may be experienced at concentrations found in nonoccupational environments. The EPA has classified it as a "probable human carcinogen." Formaldehyde is found extensively throughout buildings, particularly newly constructed ones, both residential and commercial.

The easiest and least expensive solution to reducing exposure to formaldehyde is to increase ventilation, particularly during renovation and installation of new carpeting and furniture. In extreme circumstances, removal may be necessary. Renovation projects should be done in the spring or summer when the manager can open windows to allow maximum ventilation.

Lead-based paint   Until 1978, when **lead-based paint** was banned, many paints contained lead as a primary ingredient. When absorbed by humans, excessive lead levels can cause damage to the brain, kidneys, or nervous system. Doses that would have little effect on a grown-up may have serious consequences for a young child. Residential property managers are the most likely to be affected by this potentially dangerous substance. The Lead-Based Paint Hazard Reduction Act (LBPHRA) is discussed in Chapter 10. Any manager of any residential property built before 1978 should be well-versed on this law.

Potentially Responsible Parties

Of particular concern to commercial and industrial managers is the issue of who has to pay to clean up a problem. CERCLA, discussed above, imposes liability on persons and organizations responsible for creating environmental hazards. Liability is imposed on *potentially responsible parties (PRPs)* without regard to fault, and any responsible party may be held liable for all costs and expenses associated with the cleanup of a contaminated facility. Current statutes define four categories of PRPs subject to liability for cleanup costs:

1. The present *owner* or *operator* of a facility contaminated by hazardous substances or hazardous wastes

2. Any person who, at the time of disposal of hazardous substances or hazardous wastes, owned or operated a facility at which the hazardous substances or hazardous wastes were disposed

3. Any person who generates hazardous substances or hazardous wastes or who has arranged with another person for the disposal or treatment of the hazardous substances or hazardous wastes

4. Any person who accepts hazardous substances or hazardous wastes for transport to disposal or treatment facilities

The first category, owner or operator, is of critical importance to property managers. Although statutory law does not define a standard of liability, courts have interpreted liability to be strict and joint and several. *Strict liability*, as defined in law, generally means that intent or fault is not an element of the act; the act (of being an "owner or operator") is sufficient in and of itself. *Joint and several liability* means that all such persons, as a group and individually, have complete responsibility for the entire loss, damage, or expense. The government may, therefore, recover the full cost of cleanup from the present owner or operator even though that entity did not own the site or participate in the activity that led to contamination.

The *innocent owner* (or *innocent purchaser*) is a defense that an owner may use against a claim for liability. An owner may not be held liable if it can be shown that the release or threat of release of a hazardous substance and the damage resulting therefrom were caused solely by an act of God, an act of war, or an act or omission of a third party who is not an employee or agent of the owner-defendant. An act or omission that occurs in connection with a contractual relationship, whether direct or indirect, however, is not excluded.

For example, a contractual relationship exists between the grantor and grantee of real property unless the real property is acquired by the defendant after the hazardous waste has been disposed of. The defendant must show that he or she did not know, and had no reason to know, that any hazardous substance was disposed of on the property.

In order for the defendant to show such lack of knowledge, or that the defendant had no reason to know that any hazardous substances had been disposed of on the property, an environmental professional must perform an environmental site assessment that establishes that there is no contamination on the property. If the site assessment finds that the site is not contaminated, the purchaser may rely on the innocent owner defense.

A property manager can establish policies concerning management or purchase of property in order to avoid CERCLA liability. However, attorneys specializing in environmental law should be consulted at every step in the process.

Environmental Assessments

An **environmental site assessment (ESA)**, often called "due diligence," is an evaluation to determine if there are any environmental hazards or concerns that could affect the use of the property or impose future financial liability. If a property manager observes environmental concerns, then the manager should suggest hiring a professional to conduct an ESA. Unfortunately, no standard guidelines exist for environmental assessments, although many follow those developed by the American Society for Testing and Materials (ASTM). References should be thoroughly evaluated before any hiring. Also, the manager can recommend that owners work with environmental lawyers as well.

Fannie Mae defines an *environmental professional* as an individual or an entity managed or controlled by such an individual who, through academic training, occupational experience, and reputation (such as engineers, environmental consultants, and attorneys), can objectively conduct one or more aspects of a Phase I environmental assessment. Typically, a Phase I assessment includes a review of the records, site reconnaissance, interviews with current owners and operators, and an evaluation and report preparation.

If the Phase I environmental assessment discloses the presence or likely presence of a release or threatened release of hazardous substances on the real property to be managed or acquired, the property manager should recommend further action to confirm the absence of such release or threatened release. In such a case, the manager must arrange for a qualified environmental engineer to conduct a Phase II environmental assessment that consists of sampling, testing, and evaluation of substances found on the property.

When a separate subdivision of a lot out of a large development project has a high potential for environmental and ground pollution, the parcel should be owned by a separate legal entity in order to help protect the land developer or landlord.

Air Quality Issues

Air quality issues rank quite high among all building management and design problems, even higher than security, parking, and inadequate work space. While there is no precise definition for *inadequate air quality*, it generally includes two recently identified conditions, *sick building syndrome* and *building-related illness*.

■ Sick Building Syndrome

Sick building syndrome (SBS) was first described in the 1970s, and is used to describe a situation in which reported symptoms among the population of building occupants can be temporarily associated with their presence in that building. Usually, this is an office building. Some of the key symptoms include lethargy or fatigue, headache, dizziness, nausea, irritation of mucous membranes, and sensitivity to odors. In 1991, as many as 24 percent of U.S. office workers perceived air quality problems in their work environments, and 20 percent believed that their work performance was hampered.

Building-related illness   Building-related illness (BRI) is a clinically diagnosed condition that is caused by toxic substances or pathogens. Unlike SBS, BRI persists when an occupant leaves the building. Symptoms of BRI include hypersensitivity, pneumonitis, asthma, and certain allergic reactions.

An investigation and analysis of the implicated building should be undertaken by the appropriate individuals: employer, building owner or manager, building investigation specialists, and sometimes state and local health authorities. In particular, the design and operation of the heating, ventilation, and air-conditioning systems should be looked at. It may not be clear what exactly is causing the problem, but possible culprits include poor design, maintenance, or operation of the building ventilation system.

Other contributing factors may include contamination by specific pollutants such as molds, humidity, poor lighting, and temperature extremes. Also suspect are *volatile inorganic compounds* (chemical emissions from products such as paints, adhesives, cleaners, pesticides, fixtures, and furnishings); microorganisms (fungi, bacteria, viruses, pollen, and mites); and particulate (dust and dander).

Both SBS and BRI have become more prevalent in recent years because of higher energy-efficiency standards. Energy-efficient buildings are more airtight with reduced ventilation rates. Reduced ventilation means that the agents causing the contamination cannot be easily dispersed. If building occupants are suffering from these two syndromes, increasing ventilation often will improve their condition. Also, replacing interior products such as carpeting, furniture, and paint with newer versions helps, because manufacturers are constantly reformulating their products with safer materials.

■ MANAGING HAZARD CONTROL

The Occupational Safety and Health Act (OSHA) requires all businesses that manufacture or handle toxic or otherwise potentially hazardous chemicals to evaluate and label them for the protection of their employees.

Under certain conditions ordinary chemicals—including cleaning compounds commonly used by property management, maintenance, and building service companies—may be flammable, caustic, toxic or otherwise dangerous to human health. Thus, OSHA has prescribed appropriate warning labels to apprise employees of all hazards to which they are exposed at the workplace. Label information should include relevant symptoms and recommended emergency treatment plus conditions and precautions for safe use or exposure.

Hazard Warnings

Producers of chemicals or chemical by-products are required to evaluate chemical hazards, to label containers according to a *hazardous material identification system* (HMIS), and to provide material safety data sheets (MSDSs) to serve as hazard warnings to purchasers of their products.

Material safety data sheets may be kept in any form, including operating procedures, and may be designed to cover groups of hazardous chemicals in a work area where it may be more appropriate to address the hazards of a process rather than individual hazardous chemicals. However, the employer must ensure that in all cases the required information is provided for each hazardous chemical and is readily accessible during each work shift to employees in their work area(s). Material safety data sheets must be made readily available upon request to OSHA representatives.

■ The term *hazard warning* means any word, picture, symbol, or combination thereof that conveys the hazard(s) of the chemical(s) in the container(s). Appropriate hazard warnings are to be put on container labels, and requirements have been broadened to cover all employers and include requirements for a hazard communication program, labeling of in-plant containers, training workers, and providing access to MSDSs. If buying in bulk, i.e., large containers, the manager should ensure that similar warnings are placed on the smaller containers to which the product is transferred.

Employee Information and Training

Employers must provide employees with information and training on hazardous chemicals in their work area at the time of their initial assignment and whenever a new hazard is introduced into their work area.

Employee training must include methods and observations that may be used to detect the presence or release of a hazardous chemical in the work area (such as monitoring conducted by the employer, continuous monitoring devices, visual appearance or odor of hazardous chemicals when being released); physical and health hazards of the chemicals in the work area; and measures employees can take to protect themselves from these hazards (including specific procedures the employer has implemented to protect employees from exposure to hazardous chemicals, such as appropriate work practices, emergency procedures, and personal protective equipment to be used). Training shall also include details of the hazard communication program developed by the employer, including an explanation of the labeling system and the material safety data sheet and how employees can obtain and use the appropriate hazard information.

Written Hazard Communication Program

With these standards in mind, most property managers will find they have a responsibility to publish and implement a *Hazard Communication Standard Plan* for their buildings. Employers must maintain copies of the required material safety data sheets for each hazardous chemical in the workplace and ensure that they are readily accessible during each work shift to employees in their work area(s).

Under OSHA rules, a written hazard communication program must be developed and implemented for each workplace. Current written hazard communication program requirements include a provision that requires employers also to provide hazard information to on-site contractor employers who have employees who may be exposed to the hazards generated by the employer.

Federal Community Right-to-Know Act

In 1986, the Superfund Amendments and Reauthorization Act, mentioned earlier, became law, part of which is Title III, the Emergency Planning and Community Right-to-Know Act. The act encourages and supports emergency planning efforts at the state and local levels and provides citizens and local governments with information concerning potential chemical hazards present in their communities. Employers required under the OSHA 1970 regulations to prepare or have available material safety data sheets for hazardous chemicals in their workplaces must also submit chemical hazard information to state and local governments. In addition, they must submit an emergency and hazardous chemical inventory form to state emergency response commissions, local emergency planning committees, and local fire departments.

■ SUMMARY

One of the major concerns of a property owner is obtaining insurance coverage against as many risks as possible at the most reasonable rate. As risk managers for the owner, property managers examine potential risks to see which should be avoided, retained, controlled, and transferred through the purchase of insurance. They may be called on to adjust claims for insured property losses. Property managers may advise the owners, but a final insurance decision should be made by the owner after consulting with his or her own insurance broker.

The most common types of insurance needed by property owners are the standard fire insurance policy; extended coverage and collateral fire lines; machinery and equipment insurance; consequential loss, use, and occupancy coverage; and commercial general liability, auto liability, and workers' compensation coverage. As representatives of policy buyers, managers shop the market for the most comprehensive and economical coverage.

As both an agent and a contracting businessperson, the manager engages employees and contractors; handles client funds, documents, and records; and maintains his or her own office and files. Extended fire coverage is a must for the manager's offices, as are floater insurance on office contents, errors and omissions insurance, bond coverage, valuable records replacement and theft insurance, general liability policies, and workers' compensation. The manager should also be named as coinsured on all of the owner's liability insurance policies.

Business nonemergency standard procedures instituted by property managers must follow strict government guidelines and regulations with regard to environmental standards and procedures. One procedure mandated by the 1970 National Environmental Policy Act (NEPA) requires the preparation of an environmental impact statement (EIS) prior to every major federal action significantly affecting the quality of the environment. This procedure is overseen by the Environmental Protection Agency (EPA). Congress has passed laws that address air and water pollution and dumping of hazardous substances.

Air quality issues are also on the rise with the increasingly common occurrences of the two air quality-related conditions, sick building syndrome and building related illness. The current issue is mold, which can be prevented by quickly containing water intrusion and reducing indoor humidity. Also, better ventilation and products that contain fewer contaminants are other solutions to these problems.

The Occupational Safety and Health Act (OSHA) charges property managers with familiarizing themselves with potentially hazardous substances—asbestos, radon, toxic leaks from underground storage tanks, urea formaldehyde, PCBs, and lead paint.

In addition to federal restrictions, an increasing number of environmental protection guidelines and restrictions are enacted by state legislatures. Mandated procedures include thorough environmental evaluations of real property every time it is leased, sold, or transferred.

■ CASE STUDY

THE RISK MANAGER

Nelson Rockford is about to sign a management agreement with Harold Stern, owner of Hartford Business Park. Rockford recently read that a property manager was sued because a tenant's employee was injured due to the negligence of the employee of a security company hired to patrol the premises. Rockford is understandably worried about his own liability. He is also acutely aware that today's society has become very litigious. He wants to minimize his risks.

1. What can Rockford do to limit his liability for acts of third parties?
2. Before Rockford can successfully limit his own liability, he must at lease partially alleviate Stern's fears about being held liable for Rockford's negligence. How can he do so?
3. What can Rockford do to limit his liability in general?

■ REVIEW QUESTIONS

1. Installing fire sprinklers is an example of
   a. avoiding the risk.
   b. controlling the risk.
   c. retaining the risk.
   d. measuring the risk.

2. All of the following are examples of avoiding risk *EXCEPT*
   a. hiring contractors who show evidence of insurance for workers' compensation.
   b. removing the diving board from the swimming pool.
   c. arranging environmental assessments.
   d. managing hazardous properties.

3. Which of the following would protect the property manager from damages not caused by the manager's own negligence or misconduct?
   a. Standard fire policy
   b. Employer liability clause
   c. Workers' compensation
   d. Indemnity clause

4. When the property manager lowers an insurance premium by increasing the deductible, the manager is making an effort to
   a. avoid risk.
   b. retain part of the risk.
   c. control the risk.
   d. identify the risk.

5. A building has a physically depreciated cash value of $200,000. The property manager must remember that
   a. if coinsurance coverage of $160,000 is taken out, the cost will be about equal to "straight" insurance of $100,000.
   b. "straight" coverage of $50,000 will cost about the same as 80 percent coinsurance.
   c. in the event of a loss of $40,000 under an 80 percent coinsurance policy, the insurer will pay $32,000.
   d. under an 80 percent coinsurance policy, if the building is a total loss the insurer will pay $190,000.

6. What type of insurance protects the owner against loss for damage to other persons or their property?
   a. Extended coverage insurance
   b. Eighty percent coinsurance
   c. Business interruption insurance
   d. General liability and workers' compensation insurance

7. Which statement is *TRUE* concerning the insurance available to independent property managers?
   a. Multiperil insurance protects equipment and supplies.
   b. The manager should be named as an additional insured under the owner's liability policy.
   c. Errors and omissions insurance protects against loss of rent because the property manager failed to check a tenant's credit thoroughly.
   d. Employee dishonesty insurance is never necessary.

8. Which of the following hazards can generally be greatly reduced through proper ventilation?
   a. Asbestos
   b. Lead-based paint
   c. Radon
   d. Polychlorinated biphenyls (PCBs)

9. Which of the following is recommended to alleviate mold problems?
   a. Increase humidity
   b. Decrease humidity
   c. Follow the advice of the insurance company
   d. Regularly conduct mold testing

10. Environmental impact statements for major public and private developments may be required by
    a. the federal government only.
    b. state governments only.
    c. local governments only.
    d. all levels of government.

11. In order to survive and thrive, mold requires a food source and
    a. moisture.
    b. strong light source, such as sunshine.
    c. chlorophyll.
    d. extreme temperatures.

12. The Comprehensive Environmental Response, Compensation and Liability Act of 1980 (CERCLA) provided remedies against hazardous substances in the environment and is popularly known as the
    a. Education and Recovery Act.
    b. Superfund Law.
    c. Federal Insecticide and Rodenticide Regulation.
    d. Hazard Emergency Rule.

13. Which of the following poisons could result from an incorrectly vented space heater?
    a. Radon
    b. Carbon monoxide
    c. Mold
    d. Asbestos

14. How much of a petroleum tank must be buried to cause the tank to be classified as "underground"?
    a. None; any petroleum tank is considered dangerous
    b. 10 percent
    c. 50 percent
    d. 100 percent

15. The Environmental Protection Agency has recognized that the least hazardous way to deal with asbestos that is in place in a building is to
    a. remove it.
    b. ignore it.
    c. manage it in place.
    d. analyze it.

16. The standard insurance policy will NOT cover damages from
    a. fire.
    b. hail.
    c. tornadoes.
    d. flooding.

17. Federal law now requires that only certified technicians may handle which of the following hazardous materials?
    a. Chlorofluorocarbons
    b. Formaldehyde
    c. Radon
    d. Lead-based paint

18. Which of the following hazards could be leaking from a landfill?
    a. Chlorofluorocarbons
    b. Radon
    c. Polychlorinated biphenyls (PCBs)
    d. Asbestos

19. How long is the manager required to retain lead-based paint disclosure records?
    a. One year
    b. Three years
    c. Five years
    d. Indefinitely

20. The property manager should insist that the landlord buy all of the following types of insurance EXCEPT
    a. flood insurance.
    b. all risks insurance.
    c. renter's insurance.
    d. fire insurance.

CHAPTER SEVENTEEN

LIFE SAFETY ISSUES

■ KEY TERMS

American Society for
   Industrial Security
   (ASIS)
Emergency spokesperson
Evacuation drills
Intrusion alarms
Life safety control center
   operator

Life safety officer (LSO)
Low flame spread rating
National Burglar
   and Fire Alarm
   Association (NBFAA)
Paging system

Sprinkler system
Tenant emergency
   procedures manual
Tenant wardens

■ LEARNING OBJECTIVES

At the end of this chapter, the student will be able to

1. design a program to manage life safety utilizing personnel, equipment, and procedures to reach four important goals: preventing an emergency, detecting a breach, containing the damage, and counteracting the damage;

2. discuss the importance of preventing criminal activity on the property; and

3. identify key tasks to be accomplished in the event of an emergency and assign to key individuals.

■ OVERVIEW

The management of life safety and security is a special management concern that is increasingly becoming more complex and sophisticated. We no longer think solely in terms of *security* for office buildings, shopping centers, and other properties but instead in terms of the total environment and the protection of those in that environment from harm caused by criminal acts, natural disasters, and hazardous materials.

Building security no longer simply means the presence of a night watchman. Security is a 24-hour-a-day, 365-days-a-year responsibility, and the modern approach to dealing with emergencies such as fire and natural disasters focuses on prevention and safety. Hence, the term *life safety* has come into favor.

■ MANAGING LIFE SAFETY AND SECURITY

Security officers are now called **life safety officers.** Their responsibilities have increased commensurably with technical advances and the changing needs of building owners. Adequate security, as defined by the courts, is that security necessary to protect life and property under the circumstances existing in the building and the neighborhood of the property in question. Owners who have failed to maintain adequate security have been subjected to lawsuits with judgments often running into millions of dollars.

■ Four Goals of Any Program

A program to deal with emergencies threatening life and property is based on four goals:

1. *Preventing* emergencies or security breaches
2. *Detecting* a breach as early as possible and sounding an alarm
3. *Containing* or *confining*
4. *Counteracting* the damage by prompt and proper action, such as extinguishing a fire or arresting an intruder

Post "9/11"

Historically, owners of buildings wanted to keep their restroom facilities private, or perhaps they were concerned with minor theft. However, in post 9/11/01, everyone has a sense of required heightened security. One of the effects of the attacks on the World Trade Center is the sense that many facets of public life have been changed forever. Not only do people wait in long lines at the airport to check in, but they must now register and be recognized in many office buildings as well.

Building the Smart [and Safest] Building

Americans have a history of recognizing and utilizing broad applications from one program to another. For example, the space program of the 1960s not only furthered advances in flight technology but also in fire and safety standards. Medics in Vietnam developed procedures that kept many soldiers alive, during and after the battles.

Today, real estate developers, architects, insurers, and business owners are scrambling to cover contingencies as they try to learn from the 9/11 disaster. The first bombings a few years earlier were only precursors to the actual disaster in 2001. The owner of the World Trade Center quickly learned that reading the insurance policy is extremely important, and architects are now searching for building alternatives that could provide a safer environment.

In a March 14, 2004, *New York Times* article, James Glanz discusses the issues involved when "designing the safest building in history for the scariest address on earth." According to Glanz, the concerns being tested in computer simulations include

"mass evacuations as emergency personnel rush up the stairs, fires and smoke that sweep through multiple floors, blasts and impacts that knock out huge steel structural supports, and internal damage that leaves some of the water sprinklers unable to function."

Architects on the new construction at "the scariest address" are redesigning critical areas: cable structure, core stairwells, the external shell, lighting, fire safety, elevators, and communication within the building. As the best defense is to prevent the original disaster, intense security efforts will also be implemented.

In fact, the new designs are so extensive that the building may set higher industry standards. The end results are sure to trickle down to less prestigious buildings and even those not considered terrorist targets. Everyone in the property management field will no doubt be affected by these changes.

Utilizing Personnel, Equipment, and Procedure

Generally, a good life safety and security program is a three-pronged approach that incorporates skilled use of equipment, personnel, and procedure. Each property manager must tailor a life safety and security program to the tenants' needs, whether the property is commercial, industrial, or residential. The discussion that follows will not be wholly applicable to all types or sizes of properties.

■ EMERGENCY EQUIPMENT AND TECHNOLOGY

New and improved equipment to assist with life safety and security is constantly coming on the market. The property manager can stay informed of all such developments by regularly reviewing security trade magazines and, if possible, attending trade shows. Concerned property managers will continually expand their knowledge of life safety and security technology by independent inquiry.

Modern security technology is available in the form of advanced electronic equipment (intercommunication networks, automated fire protection and security systems, access control, and closed-circuit television), which in many buildings is integrated with lighting and temperature control devices. The property manager must plan carefully to coordinate all of these elements into an effective integrated system; individual features must be selected with care and then fitted into the overall system.

New buildings are constructed with state-of-the-art electronic devices, but property managers of older structures must retrofit their buildings to provide these same services. Often this is best done on a phase-by-phase basis. A particularly good opportunity to install electronic equipment is between occupancies, but this is not always necessary as most electronic installations are similar to changing telephone or electric outlets and thus impose no serious disruptions of tenant services.

Building Systems

The design concept of present-day emergency equipment is to discover and report a fire or other emergency before it further threatens life and property. The focal point of up-to-date emergency response systems is a master central control panel in a life safety control room that automatically monitors smoke detectors, water flow switches for the sprinkler system, and manual fire alarm pull stations located throughout the building.

For example, if a smoke detector or sprinkler water flow switch detects a fire, an annunciator is activated on the fire panel in the life safety control room, prompting the operator to summon the fire department. If fire is discovered by a building staff member or a tenant before one of the emergency fire devices signals the fire control panel, manual fire pull stations can be used, as well as telephones or two-way radios placed strategically throughout the building to alert the life safety control center operator that an emergency exists.

The fire control panel in the life safety control room starts fans, which pressurize stairwells to prevent the entry of smoke and unlock stairway doors to provide unlimited access for evacuation. The latest fire alarm systems will even cause the smoke to be vented out of the building through the HVAC system. The fire control panel contains a speaker system, which can play prerecorded evacuation instructions or broadcast live instructions on any floors or combination of floors to warn of a fire.

■ Telephones or telephone jacks should be located next to each exit door and in the elevator lobbies for intercommunication between the floor of the emergency and the control room. These communication devices are useful to firefighters, maintenance personnel, and security staff.

Elevators The danger in using elevators during a building fire comes from heat and smoke or toxic gases accumulated in the elevator shaft. Elevator shafts running throughout the building create a *chimney effect*, causing an updraft of air and filling them with gas and smoke, which can be poisonous to elevator occupants. When a fire occurs in a high-rise building equipped with the latest electronic safety devices, elevators in the fire zone will not respond to a call from the call button, forcing use of the stairwells to get to another floor, and will move elevators to the ground level.

Once the elevators are captured and returned to the ground floor, they cannot be operated without an elevator control key. Thereafter, only trained personnel at the direction of the building manager or fire officials may use the elevators, a measure that prevents unauthorized personnel from using the elevators and risking injury to themselves and others.

Provisions must be made to evacuate physically impaired persons from floors affected by emergencies. Thus, a life safety officer or tenant warden (discussed later in this chapter) must capture an elevator and take it to a safe floor closest to the fire. Responding personnel must then disencumber the disabled person from wheelchair or crutches and carry the individual down the stairwell to a waiting elevator or a safe location.

Smoke detectors   Smoke detectors, which will indicate danger by flashing a light on the detector housing panel, should be located on each floor. In a centralized system, a charged smoke detector will prompt a local alarm or an alarm in the fire control room. Smoke detectors usually reset automatically once they have been cleared of smoke. Smoke detectors may also make a loud sound to attract attention. The manager should ensure that the detectors are tested regularly.

Sprinkler system   Water flow detectors signal the fire panel when a sprinkler head is discharging water, a pipe has broken, or another plumbing malfunction has occurred. Valve tamper alarms are available for sprinkler valves to indicate whether the sprinkler valve has been closed, to prevent the sprinklers on that floor from discharging water in the event of a fire. Sprinkler water flow switches reset automatically when water ceases to flow through the **sprinkler system**.

Paging system   A **paging system** should be installed on each floor to permit broadcast of emergency messages, which in some cases may be pretaped. If tied into the music system, an override switch will permit paging to any number of selected floors. In some systems, emergency response personnel (including the fire or police department) can communicate with the control center by use of intercom connector outlets on each floor using plug-in handsets.

Intrusion alarms   Security intrusion detectors (intrusion alarms) are quite sophisticated. They can be activated by sound or motion and send wireless signals to a control panel that can identify the exact area of intrusion. The sound-detection devices can be activated by running water, alerting security personnel to broken water pipes, or other abnormal water flow.

Monitoring Tenant Equipment

Extensive remodeling frequently alters the life safety protection requirements of an area of a building, such as exit routes and alarms, and fire protection and tenant notification systems. Therefore, remodeling plans should be reviewed by the property manager with the assistance of experienced life safety personnel to ensure that remodeling efforts meet current life safety, fire, and security provisions. In addition to building code review, some cities require that the fire department inspection bureau review plans and facilities.

Fire codes generally dictate that finishing materials (carpeting, draperies, wall coverings, and ceiling tile) have a **low flame spread rating**. Building management should make every effort to ensure that any new materials placed in the buildings conform to those standards—especially along common paths of travel that lead to exits.

A difficult and often politically sensitive challenge is to control type and quality of tenant-installed furnishings and the finish on new products. Every effort should be made to avoid use of any form of plastics which when burned produce toxic gases that are hazardous to all tenants. Tenants should be encouraged to use noncombustible or fire-retardant-treated furniture and self-extinguishing upholstery and materials. Draperies should be of glass fiber or other flameproof material, and carpeting and carpeting padding must have a relatively low flame spread and *smoke-developing rating* (obtained from the manufacturer); a flame spread, smoke-developing, and fuel contributing rating of 25 or less is desirable.

■ ROLE OF PERSONNEL IN LIFE SAFETY

Employee Training Procedures

To protect employees and company assets, employees must be provided with a safe working environment. Management must provide training programs for each employee, including training with each type of equipment the employee will be using and applying all the safety measures required for its operation. Safety guidelines are based on applicable rules and regulations of federal, state, and local governments, as well as established policies of the building ownership and management. Training programs should be written, reviewed, and approved by management.

Employees should not be assigned duties for which they are not properly trained or physically capable of performing. Duties requiring a specific license or permit are assigned only to employees holding valid licenses or permits. Employees must work from written operating procedures and safety regulations applicable to their duties.

Two organizations are working to advance the professional standing of life safety and security personnel:

1. The *American Society for Industrial Security (ASIS)*, which has developed a designation program, Certified Protection Professional (CPP) based on its training courses

2. The *National Burglar and Fire Alarm Association (NBFAA)*, which provides a certification course for security installations personnel

Protect Human Life

The first priority of a life safety and security program is to protect human life. During an emergency, members of the building staff will be expected to help combat the danger and protect human life, but under no circumstances must any person undertake unnecessary risks that would endanger themselves or other building occupants. A life safety program is for the protection of all persons in the building, staff members included.

It is impossible to determine in advance exactly how an emergency will occur, so systems to mobilize, deploy, and protect personnel must be designed to provide a wide range of responses to any emergency. Each member of the building staff must be well informed about how the system works and the problems that may be encountered in handling an emergency.

Central Base of Operations

The key to dealing with all emergencies is to establish a central headquarters, or base of operations. In buildings with small staffs, this may be the manager's office or the information desk. Large complexes establish an elaborate *life safety control center,* fully staffed 24 hours a day and usually located on the ground floor or on a floor below grade. Although the following discussion describes procedures for a larger complex, the manager of a smaller property should have no trouble adapting the principles to that property.

All communications should come from a designated person in the life safety control center. Specific duties should be assigned to the various personnel of the property management staff, such as the roving officer, the property maintenance manager, mechanical technicians, life safety control center operator, chief of security, and the building manager. They should report in person to the control center or inform the control center that they are at their assigned posts.

The property maintenance manager and mechanical technicians should be in charge of all mechanical functions on the floor where an emergency occurs, reporting to the life safety control operator on conditions existing there. If possible, they will try to deal with an emergency—for example, extinguishing fires with portable fire extinguishers—until the arrival of trained emergency personnel, after which they should assist and act as advisers. For instance, they should be responsible for ensuring that activated sprinkler systems will not be turned off prematurely by unauthorized personnel. All personnel on the emergency floor must exercise great caution to avoid placing themselves in danger unnecessarily.

Outside the building, pedestrian and automobile traffic should be the responsibility of the police department. Building personnel who do not have specific emergency assignments should report to a central point for assignments, and all emergency personnel should be directed from a central location on ground level. From a legal standpoint, emergency crews—police, fire, and other nonmanagement crews—are in control as soon as they enter the building.

Tenant Wardens

The most modern equipment and the best devised emergency procedures will be useless unless the property manager and staff are well trained and disciplined to act effectively and calmly, the tenants respond to staff orders, and everyone follows routines as set out in the procedures. This is best accomplished by organizing a cadre of *tenant wardens*, employees of tenant companies who are schooled in emergency procedures by the building staff to direct their fellow employees during routine drills and actual emergencies.

Many tenants may have skills or training that would be of critical assistance in an emergency. Some may even have been previously employed as firefighters or police officers or have pertinent military experience. The property manager should locate and qualify these people through the tenant warden organization by requesting response to a questionnaire such as that appearing in Figure 17.1.

> Special clothing, such as red baseball caps, should be provided to tenant wardens for use during drills and actual emergencies. Recognition of the tenant warden team by holding regular monthly training sessions and other activities will increase their visibility and creditability and make them an effective supplement to the building staff during emergencies. A tenant employee should be selected to lead the warden team.

Personnel Assignments

The following descriptions of the roles played by various building personnel in an emergency assumes a sizable building staff available for assignment to life safety and security duties in addition to daily occupational routines. The functions illustrated, however, are typical of the needs to be met in an emergency, regardless of the number of on-site employees. Even in a smaller building, the property manager should see that all the areas are covered, although sometimes one person may be responsible for more than one task. For an example, see Figure 7.2.

Emergency spokesperson In the event of a major emergency, such as a fire, explosion, or natural disaster, the first priority is always the safety of employees, tenants, and the public. In an emergency, an authorized spokesperson, designated in advance, must be available constantly to represent management on the scene and provide immediate factual information on personnel casualties to employees' families. To the extent possible, the **emergency spokesperson** refrains from giving out information on personnel casualties before families have been notified. The property manager is responsible for notifying the property owner as soon as possible.

Life safety control center operator It is the responsibility of the **life safety control center operator** to notify the fire department and building personnel and provide communication throughout the emergency. A list of personnel in the building who should be contacted in case of emergency and the order in which they are to be notified should be maintained in the center. Also a list of all known disabled occupants and their usual workstations should be maintained in the control center, to immediately provide to roving life safety officers. The center

FIGURE 17.1

Employee Qualification Form

Emergency Information Form
EMPLOYEE QUALIFICATIONS
(If more space is needed, use reverse of this form)

Name: _____

Department: _____

Building Location: _____

Home Address: _____

Home Phone: _____   Office Phone: _____

TRAINING

MEDICAL

❑   First Aid — Ability Level

_____

❑   CPR — Ability Level

_____

FIREFIGHTING

❑   Military   ❑   Experienced Firefighter   ❑   Volunteer   ❑   Other _____

LAW ENFORCEMENT

❑   Military   ❑   Former Police Officer   ❑   Security Guard   ❑   Other _____

COMMUNICATIONS

❑   Ham Operator   ❑   Telephone Operator   ❑   Other _____

❑   Foreign Languages _____

EXPERIENCE

CONSTRUCTION

❑   Electrical   ❑   Plumbing   ❑   Carpentry

MECHANICAL

❑   Auto Repair   ❑   HVAC   ❑   Other _____

EMERGENCY SITUATIONS

(Please explain type of experience, if any) _____

RESOURCES

TEMPORARY SHELTER

Can you provide shelter for others?   ❑   Yes   How Many? _____

Location _____

EMERGENCY VEHICLES

Vehicles available for use in an emergency

❑   Motorcycle/Bike   ❑   4-Wheel Drive   ❑   RV/Van

❑   Pickup Truck   ❑   Station Wagon

Other: ❑   If you have any special training not listed above, please check here and detail on reverse side.

Source: Floyd M. Baird, Temple, Texas.

control operator assists the fire department through the communications system and advises them of current information coming into the control center.

Upon notification of an emergency condition by an alarm on the control panel, the control center operator begins notifying the personnel on the communications list and assigning life safety personnel. After making sure the service elevators are called and waiting at the ground floor for arrival of the emergency response teams, the operator, through the emergency paging system, notifies occupants of the floors affected of the need to evacuate in the event a taped message is not operational.

Life safety officer (LSO)   The responsibility of a roving LSO is to assist tenant evacuation and enforce safety precautions. It is also the officer's responsibility to provide an elevator (or alternate means) for evacuation of the disabled. To do so, the officer goes directly to the ground level using whatever means necessary, remembering that elevators in the affected zone will probably not be available for use.

Mechanical technician   The property maintenance manager and one mechanical technician must report to the emergency scene to take charge of the mechanical functions on the floor, including fire-extinguishing devices. If two mechanical technicians are on duty, one should meet the fire department with information about the building's mechanical systems.

Property manager   The property manager reports to the control center to assist the emergency crews and directs the action of all building staff.

Chief of security   The senior security officer on duty reports to the building's main entrance (or to a designated alternate location if the entrance is inaccessible). He or she coordinates assignments of all nontechnical building employees.

Unassigned personnel   It is the responsibility of all building employees with no specific assignment to report to a central point for instructions. Assistance requested by emergency crews will be supplied through the manpower at this location.

■ PROPERTY MANAGEMENT PROCEDURES

Each property manager responsible for life safety and security is charged with the development and implementation of procedures that emphasize employee training, fire and accident prevention, good housekeeping, equipment maintenance, and safety of tenants, customers, employees, and the community. Procedures must meet requirements of the Occupational Safety and Health Administration (OSHA) and other applicable laws.

Life Safety Procedures   These are generally organized into two parts:

1. In-house (or internal) procedures

2. Hazard detection and emergency evacuation procedures

Internal procedures   In-house procedures concern only building management and its employees and are circulated only on a need-to-know basis. That is, procedures that concern only one group of employees are given only to that group, whereas procedures for the guidance of tenants are often distributed to every employee of every tenant.

Hazard detection and emergency evacuation   Hazard detection and emergency evacuation procedures are of particular concern in older structures. Newer projects are equipped with state-of-the-art security and fire detection equipment and building operating systems. Older structures have to be retrofitted with adequate safety features and building operating systems as the need is determined and as their physical structures permit. Often, because the physical structure of an older building does not permit installation of some of the more modern technology, managers of older structures depend more on management procedures than on technology in managing life safety.

Disaster planning   A disaster procedure (or emergency response) plan, an expansion of emergency procedures designed for handling severe damage, calls for setting up an off-site command post and a chain of command. Prior arrangements must be made on a standby basis with suppliers of emergency items or necessary repair material.

For instance, after a hurricane, there is usually an immediate shortage of plywood. Although it would not be feasible for a building owner to stockpile extensive quantities of plywood on the chance that a hurricane or tornado would require its use, arrangements must be made with the wholesale lumber trade for immediate confirmed purchase and delivery of plywood. This arrangement would require extensive coordination by life safety personnel, the accounting department, and other involved parties.

Emergency supplies   If space and budget permit, it is good practice to stockpile a small quantity of emergency supplies. In a hurricane zone, for example, large plastic tarps and enough plywood could be kept on hand to board up all ground-floor windows. In an area subject to earthquakes or hurricanes, a 72-hour food and water supply should be maintained. Additionally, if a building does not have a standby or auxiliary electricity source, a generator with ample fuel supply should be kept available.

Evacuation drills   Evacuation plans should be developed for all buildings and **evacuation drills** should be regularly scheduled. The tenant warden organization should be actively involved in planning and executing such drills as a means of testing the building emergency organization, equipment, and tenant indoctrination. Buildings that are higher than the local fire department are equipped to reach—generally seven stories—may require more elaborate emergency evacuation planning and drills.

Emergency Preparedness Procedures

At a minimum, emergency response plans should include fire, explosion, bomb threat, evacuation, and elevator emergency procedures. In certain geographic areas, planning should include responses to earthquake, tornado, hurricane, or other severe weather.

A well-trained emergency organization comprised of building management and staff must be in place to respond to emergencies using the plans as a guide. It is recommended that tenant wardens be included in the emergency organizations to aid in evacuation, if necessary. An emergency coordinator, normally the building property manager, should head up the emergency team.

Written procedures detailing emergency organization members' duties should be provided to each member and periodic training sessions held to test emergency response. Managers must develop and keep current emergency plans for their properties.

Inspection Procedures

Protection of tenants. company assets, and the general public depends on minimizing hazards at each property. Many potential emergencies can be detected and minimized by instituting a thorough life safety inspection procedure.

Fire protection systems must be inspected on a regular basis and repairs made immediately. In addition, walk-through inspections for safety hazards and housekeeping problems should be conducted by building management at least twice annually, with more thorough inspections annually.

Structural inspections should be a day-to-day practice of the maintenance technicians, and if defects are found, a structural engineer should be engaged to make an inspection. Because electrical problems can cause fires and plumbing breaks can cause major damage, it is very important that an inspection schedule for each of these systems be regularly scheduled and a preventive maintenance program adopted. Most state laws require that properties with boilers be inspected by a licensed boiler inspector.

Documentation of all inspections should be retained in management files for a period of at least two years, along with documentation of repairs of defective or damaged equipment discovered during inspections. Insurance companies require ongoing inspection of the facilities they insure and will issue recommendations based on the inspections.

These inspections are designed to assist property management personnel in the area of fire protection and to gather underwriting data about the property. Upon completing the inspection, inspectors meet with the property manager to outline recommendations and resolve questions.

Communicating with Tenants and the Media

In any building emergency—from a partially flooded floor due to a plumbing breakdown to a total conflagration—it is imperative that the property manager make immediate contact with each tenant. The manager should contact the landlord's legal counsel as soon as possible in order to discuss suggested dialogue with tenants, the media, and others. An inaccurate or wrongly recorded statement could potentially be very damaging to the property owner and the management company.

In a large building, the property manager may delegate assistants to make a preliminary visit to assure tenants that the property manager will contact them as soon as the emergency has been brought under control. An open, sympathetic, and understanding manner is essential, and the property manager would do well to prepare a written statement that could be used as a guideline so that all points will be covered, particularly if the manager is unable to contact each tenant personally.

Tenants should be advised of the steps management is taking to handle the emergency, what reconstruction is planned, and any other item pertinent to the immediate situation. Tenants should be reminded to contact the insurers that cover their personal property and office equipment. Although the building insurance may take care of some damage, most leases provide that the landlord is not responsible under certain circumstances, and in these cases the tenant's insurance coverage is critical.

During an emergency, news media may seek access to the area to cover the event, and to the extent possible, the property manager should cooperate fully with media, authorities, and other segments of the public but retain the authority and control necessary to deal with the emergency. Factual information should be provided as quickly as facts can be verified, but admissions of liability or speculations about the cause of an accident or damage to property of others should be avoided.

Although reporters and photographers may be admitted to emergency areas within the limits of safety, no estimates of damage or construction costs should be made until they can be accurately assessed. Decisions related to special employee or community relief or reconstruction should be released to the media as soon as possible, along with data emphasizing the owning and managing companies' safety record and the continuing precautions taken to avoid accidents. Every available means of communication should be used to present factual information that will offset rumors or misstatements. All those affected by the incident, which may include employees' families, suppliers, dealers, and members of the community, must be informed fully as soon as possible.

Tenant Emergency Procedures Manual

The property manager should make a printed booklet available to tenant management detailing the emergency organization, workday procedures and telephone numbers, and after-hours procedures. Building management should maintain an up-to-date list of permanently and temporarily handicapped occupants of each business building, along with procedures for their evacuation.

Because action to be taken by tenants and systems operation affecting occupants must be set out clearly, written procedures for dealing with various building emergencies can become quite lengthy. This documentation is necessary, but it should be condensed and published in a distinctively colored brochure for each building occupant. Usually called an Emergency Procedures Guide, the **tenant emergency procedures manual** should include, at a minimum, procedures for the following emergency situations:

- Accident or illness
- Tornado or hurricane
- Earthquake
- Fire drill
- Bomb threat
- Elevator emergencies (including building or floor evacuation and special emergencies)
- Criminal activity

Accident or illness   In the event of an employee or visitor illness or accident, the guide directs tenants to call the life safety control room to report the location of the incident and other available details. They are instructed not to move the injured or ill persons but to try to make them comfortable. Many tenants will have skilled first aid and CPR-trained employees. They should be identified before an emergency so that they can be located quickly if and when there is an emergency (as discussed previously in connection with Figure 17.1).

When outside help, such as medical personnel, have been summoned to the building, one person should be dispatched to the building entrance to act as guide for the emergency crew.

Tornado or hurricane   This section of the booklet should include definitions of a tornado watch and a tornado warning. A tornado watch is a report from National Oceanic and Atmospheric Administration officials that weather conditions are conducive to the creation of a tornado. A tornado warning is an alert by the National Weather Service that confirms a tornado sighting and its location. Winds during tornadoes can be 300 mph or more. Detailed instructions are included for self-protection for those persons in various parts of the building (exterior offices, corridors, lobby).

In the event a tornado watch is changed to a tornado warning and official emergency sirens are sounded, a message similar to the one below is broadcast on the emergency paging system:

> *May I have your attention, please. May I have your attention, please. This is the Life Safety Department. The U.S. Weather Bureau has issued a tornado warning for this building's immediate area. Building occupants should move away from all windows. Proceed to inside offices, corridors, restrooms, or stairways until the danger has passed. Do not leave the building. The Life Safety Department will keep you advised.*

Hurricane procedure, essential for properties along the Atlantic and Gulf coasts, is similar for that followed in tornadoes, although hurricanes can be much more destructive, with winds over 75 mph, accompanied by heavy rainfall. The area of destruction covers a much wider area than the swath cut by a tornado. High waves and possible tidal waves must always be expected along beachfront properties. However, there is always more advance warning, because hurricanes are tracked by weather forecasters, and the location is broadcast frequently by the authorities.

Managers of single-family homes and small apartment buildings should decide on what kind of followup they should make as the hurricane advances towards the mainland. It is not always safe to assume that all tenants are listening to the news. In 1989, during Hurricane Hugo, one property manager received a call from a tenant who asked, "The water is rising here in the house. What should I do?"

Earthquake   Usually there are warnings for tornadoes and hurricanes, allowing the manager some time to prepare the office and tenants. There is usually no warning for an earthquake. It happens. If the damage is not too severe, it can be dealt with from the building. Under severe conditions, however, rescue and recovery operations must operate from a location outside the building. Because earthquakes vary in intensity, procedures for tenant action and dealing with the consequent damages must provide for alternatives ranging from no damage to complete destruction. In any event, messages must be broadcast to persons in the building. Typical announcements for various consequences of earthquakes are shown in Figure 17.2.

The building manager should consult with local fire and police departments when writing earthquake procedures. For large complexes, it may be advisable to hire consultants specially trained in disaster response.

Fire drill   Most tenants will remember fire drill procedures from their school days. Good fire emergency procedure, based on more sophisticated versions of these exercises, will appear in the guide. In buildings with a large number of occupants, the designation and equipping of wardens should include something visual so that they will be known to the evacuees. This is most important.

FIGURE 17.2
Earthquake Announcements

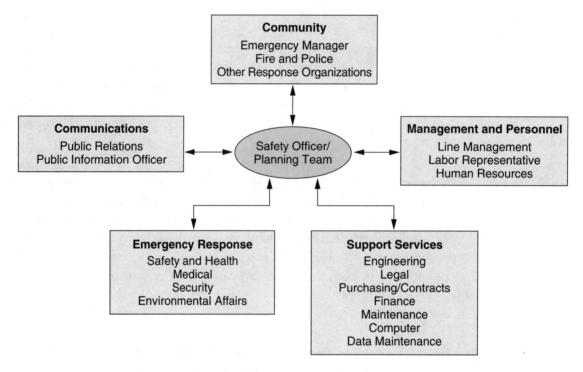

Source: Reprinted from *Emergency Management Guide for Business and Industry* sponsored by a public partnership with the Federal Management Agency (FEMA).

Bomb and poison threat Bomb threats, although not common, must be taken seriously. One variation is the threat that a poison will be released in the air. These threat procedures should be reviewed with each new tenant and periodically with tenant representatives. Usually, the person receiving a bomb threat is a clerical employee in the building who routinely answers the phone. A bomb threat checklist, included in the emergency procedures guide kept at each employee's desk, should be completed immediately after the call is received. The bomb threat checklist (see Figure 17.3), is quite extensive and includes descriptions for the caller's voice, speech, language, accent, and so forth.

Elevator emergencies These are not uncommon, so continuing emphasis needs to be placed on how they are to be handled. These procedures can be obtained from the company who installed the elevators.

Emergency special provisions These provisions complete the guide and cover general items, such as the use and location of portable fire extinguishers, and elevator operation and exit stairways.

FIGURE 17.3
Bomb Threat Checklist

Bomb Threat Checklist

Write out the entire message exactly as received: _____

_____

_____

_____

Notify Life Safety—555-8090—and complete this portion of the Checklist.

Time of Call _____   Caller's Identity _____

Male-Female _____   Estimated Age _____

Caller's Location

Local _____   Phone Booth _____   Long Distance _____

From within building _____

Check all appropriate choices.

Caller's Voice   Speech

___ Loud   ___ Soft   ___ Fast   ___ Slow
___ High Pitch   ___ Deep   ___ Distinct   ___ Distorted
___ Raspy   ___ Pleasant   ___ Stutter   ___ Nasal
___ Intoxicated   ___ Other   ___ Slurred   ___ Other

Language   Accent

___ Excellent   ___ Good   ___ Local   ___ Not Local
___ Fair   ___ Poor   ___ Foreign   ___ Regional
___ Foul   ___ Other   ___ Race   ___ Other

Unusual use of words (explain)   Explain

_____   _____

_____   _____

Manner   Background Noise

___ Calm   ___ Angry   ___ Office Machines   ___ Airplanes
___ Rational   ___ Irrational   ___ Factory Machines   ___ Trains
___ Coherent   ___ Incoherent   ___ Bedlam   ___ Voices
___ Deliberate   ___ Emotional   ___ Animals   ___ Party
___ Righteous   ___ Laughing   ___ Quiet   ___ Music
                                       ___ Mixed   ___ Atmosphere
                                       ___ Street Traffic   ___ Other/explain

                                                               _____

Date _____   Your Name _____

Company _____

Bomb Threat Checklist

Criminal activity   Planned responses include drills wherein the police are called as available security personnel scour the subject building in order to report on where the activity is located. When police arrive, the security personnel are there to direct them to the scene.

Minimizing Post-Emergency Damage

The first consideration after a disaster has damaged a building is the safety of personnel who may need to gain access to the premises, especially critical in major structural damage, such as that caused by earthquakes. A structural engineer should be immediately engaged together with the assistance of the fire department and building code enforcement officials to determine just how safe the damaged structure is and what sort of access can be allowed. If the structure is severely damaged, total demolition will be necessary.

It is in the best interest of the owner for the property manager to take immediate steps to prevent further damage, not only to prevent further loss but to meet insurance requirements. In fact, insurance policies provide reimbursement to the owner for expenses incurred to prevent loss beyond initial damage, over and above the amounts payable for the damage itself. Measures that may prevent additional damages include boarding up windows, placing tarpaulins over furniture or inventory, installing a temporary building cover, and the like.

Utility lines and equipment must be inspected and protected. One often-overlooked aftereffect of building damage in cold weather is the freezing of exposed pipes. The property manager must be aware that the insurer will not pay for additional damage that occurs that reasonably could have been prevented.

Business interruption insurance is designed to alleviate financial losses from suspension of rent. It is very simple to compute lost rent, but the dollars-and-cents effects of collateral costs, such as loss of customers, are intangible and thus difficult to measure and quantify. Many fallout costs may not be recoverable from insurance.

Restoration operations   Emergency planning must not overlook the restoration phase. Matters to consider regarding postdisaster (or postaccident) restoration operations include providing protective clothing and breathing apparatus for employees who assist utilities in establishing power through the building and salvaging personal property and equipment. Fire protection equipment must be brought to a *ready status* as soon as possible, and tests must be conducted for hazardous chemicals that may have spilled or been released into the air.

High-speed reconstruction   Resuming operations as soon as possible can minimize losses from business interruption, and there are construction companies that specialize in speedy disaster repair. As part of an emergency preparedness plan, a forward-looking property manager will seek out such companies and learn their capabilities. In the event of a widespread catastrophe, these specialists will be in high demand, so that having prior acquaintance with these contractors and contingent arrangements for their services helps to ensure their availability if disaster strikes.

High-speed reconstruction companies employ nonroutine methods, materials, and techniques, but because they are familiar with insurance claims submission, they prepare their cost estimates to conform to the requirements of insurers and use only stock materials and equipment. Their special techniques include using rapid-curing cement, thus reducing the time required for concrete to become strong enough to support further building. Similar time savings can be effected in many other ways, and these specialty contractors are expert in their application.

Disaster aftershocks   Effects of serious disaster damage on a building include aspects other than visible destruction, as demonstrated by reports from Hurricanes Hugo and Andrew and the 1989 San Francisco and 1994 Los Angeles earthquakes. Many businesses in New York City suffered for months following the 9/11 attacks on the World Trade Center.

What everyone learned after 9/11 is just how everyone relies on the availability of electricity and phone service. Retail stores obviously lose business while they are closed because customers must satisfy their needs elsewhere, a loss that may continue after reopening because many patrons will have formed new shopping patterns and may never return. However, there were other problems. Many retailers had customers but could not process credit card payments.

The power outage that engulfed several states in the summer of 2003 also illustrated serious flaws. Many tenants were locked out of their walkup apartments in New York City because they could only enter using an electronic key, which was ineffective without electricity. Likewise, many hotels were not prepared for the loss of electricity, so many hotel guests ended up sleeping on the pavement. Not only could the guests not enter their rooms, it was also very unsafe to have people in the building without adequate fire protection. Restaurants had to deal with rotting food that also had to be properly disposed.

In a shopping center that has received overage rent, the resulting sales losses can be a serious financial blow. Also, landlords may lose tenants as a consequence of lease clauses that permit cancellation in the event of destruction of the premises. On top of this, leasing programs for new space or space soon to have been vacated must be suspended, causing prospective tenants wanting to open by a certain date to seek alternate locations. For nonretail businesses, the loss of a central office or a key facility (such as a manufacturing plant or distribution center) will cause massive internal disruption.

An after-action review committee, composed of representatives of the owners, managing company, and pertinent others, should meet subsequent to a disaster, accident, or emergency drill to evaluate the response of building management and all other parties to the accident, disaster, or emergency drill. An after-action report with appropriate recommendations should be written. The completed report should be circulated to the owner and to management for any necessary corrective action.

■ MANAGING CRIMINAL ACTIVITY ISSUES

A critical safety issue is protection from criminal acts. According to the U.S. Department of Justice, a violent crime is committed every 17 seconds somewhere in the United States. Vandalism, theft, and other crimes against property occur even more frequently—as often as every two seconds. Crime has recently become the number one problem for many Americans, and certainly for many property managers. In fact, homicide has become the second leading cause of death across the nation and is the leading cause of death for women in the workplace.

Increasing Management Liability

Not only are crimes occurring in or on properties managed by professional property managers, but those property owners and managers are increasingly being held accountable for those crimes by courts. For example, a shopping center owner in Los Angeles was ordered to pay $3.5 million to the parents of four teenage girls who were murdered during a 1991 robbery in a store where two of the girls worked. The parents of a New York woman who was murdered in a clothing store where she worked sued two security firms, among others, for her death. In light of these facts, property managers must take an active role in making sure the premises they manage are as secure as possible.

Preventing Criminal Activity

Because prevention is a basic ingredient of any life safety and security program, proper technical equipment—appropriate locks and keys, access control, and visible security devices—is essential to deter criminal activity. Strategically placed cameras allow one guard to monitor many areas, and central intercommunication systems, capable of broadcasting to specific areas, assist in control.

A complete survey of building security by a trained and experienced security consultant is vital to the success of a life safety program. The consultant should be brought in early, during the planning stage of the new building or during the drafting of major remodeling. Crime prevention sections of the local police department may offer crime prevention and safety seminars at low or no cost.

As with any building expenditure, the property manager must heed budgetary restrictions. However, prices of electronic devices continue to decrease as more suppliers enter the market with new mechanisms that outperform the old.

Criminal Theft Procedures and Requirements

Managers and landlords should require that tenants do not readily display or make visible any costly items. This is not necessarily applicable to retail centers wherein there is usually optimum security. It is more applicable to large industrial and commercial complexes, which have little to no evening traffic and much less security manpower per given area. For example, a flat-screen television manufacturer shouldn't be allowed to showcase its wares on the walls in the office reception area that is easily visible through office windows and glass doors. Good thieves will be in and out, even with alarms, before anyone can stop the theft.

All tenants in these large developed areas should be required to have at minimum, a security system that notifies a security company and the on-site security officer. Part of the life safety issue is that many of the theft rings are well-armed so civilian casualties cannot be ignored if the thievery is not thwarted by preventative measures. Sign postings that security is armed are another helpful deterrent. If there are security cameras in place, then sign postings warning criminals of this may also prevent unwanted activity.

Hiring Security Personnel

Property managers may choose to hire their own security personnel or contract with a security firm. If property managers hire their own personnel, they must take special care to properly train and supervise those personnel. And if they contract with a security firm, they must choose that firm carefully.

To properly train security personnel, the building security supervisor must first identify the skills, procedures, and duties the personnel must know (including the management of physical confrontations). Next, the supervisor has to determine how often personnel should review these procedures and duties. High-priority skills generally receive more emphasis in the training process. Then the supervisor must devise a plan to train security personnel in these procedures, maintain a regular schedule of training, and provide adequate feedback.

In order to choose a competent security firm, a property manager must have clearly defined standards and then carefully evaluate the quality of the services offered. The manager must decide what duties will be required of the security personnel, what equipment will be needed, who will provide insurance coverage, and who will provide supplies, such as uniforms. The manager must then carefully screen the firms by thoroughly checking all references and investigating their hiring, training, and supervision policies.

Watch Programs

Community watch programs are becoming a popular way to reduce crime and the effects of crime, including costly repairs, vacancies, declining property values, and lawsuits. Community watch programs are based on cooperation—using the joint efforts of police and tenants to combat crime. While traditionally used by residential neighborhoods to reduce crime, watch programs are effective for all types of properties. Community watch programs are currently being used in apartment complexes, shopping centers, and commercial properties.

Community watch programs often include monthly meetings between management, local police, and tenants on various security issues; a telephone chain among tenants to alert them of possible criminal activity; and a fax network between tenants to share information and safety tips. Security officers on the property may also be in touch with a police officer by means of a police-type radio, which can be used to call for police help when necessary.

To set up a community watch program, property managers should contact local law enforcement offices, get advice and support from already existing groups, and get their tenants involved. As tenants begin to look out for suspicious activities, they get to know each other, and often overall satisfaction begins to rise; a very nice side benefit and a way to cut back on turnover.

Working to Control Illegal Drug Activity

Illegal drug activity and crime often go hand in hand. In order to reduce other types of crimes, property managers must often work to reduce or eliminate illegal drug activities first. Illegal drug activity is predominantly a problem for residential properties. Additionally, the U.S. Drug Enforcement Agency takes a zero-tolerance approach to the presence of drugs on the property, and the owner could see the building forfeited if no action has been taken to stem drug usage and trafficking.

Make repairs   Property managers can take several steps to create a drug-free property. First, the manager should make sure all maintenance and repairs are completed. For example, sending repair crews to fix broken fences and windows can help eliminate means of access to the property and disrupt the drug dealers' business. Publicizing these repairs and improvements throughout the community (via local newspaper articles, flyers, and word of mouth) can change the image of the property, thus discouraging drug activity.

Involve other tenants   Calling regular meetings of the tenants and discussing problems, as well as identifying tenant and management responsibilities for the solutions, is also an effective tool. Encouraging resident activities (such as exercise classes, tenant patrols, and co-op day care) also fosters a new attitude among residents that discourages drug activity. Educating staff members to recognize signs of drug use and working closely with the police are also important tools.

Focus on potentially hazardous locations   Some areas of a property are more susceptible to criminal activity and require extra care. The parking lots of shopping centers, for example, are prime locations for criminal and gang activity. Many improvements can be made:

- The landscaping could be changed so as not to provide hiding places near cars or deserted walkways.
- Lighting could be improved to increase customer confidence.
- The number of patrol vehicles (and the vehicles themselves can be made more visible with brightly colored markings) could be increased.
- Customer service booths could be installed at strategic places in the parking lot.

Make use of technology   Various devices are now available to help with security issues. These include closed circuit television using high-tech, low-light cameras, which can pick up considerable detail at great distances. Robot patrols are available that come equipped with video surveillance, smoke detectors, and odor-sensing and heat-sensing devices. A touchpad radio can be used as either a radio or a telephone and can be used to summon the police from any location. Caller ID and audiotaping systems can be used on security telephones to help trace calls and verify the caller's message.

■ **Review Lease Clauses**

While landlords cannot be completely protected from liability for injuries and damages caused by crime, lease provisions can be used to minimize liability. Property managers should consult competent, experienced attorneys to determine if their standard lease clauses should be changed to help protect themselves and property owners from excessive liability.

Stop employee crime   Property managers should also be aware that they may be held liable for any crimes committed by their employees. For example, if a resident manager breaks into the apartments he or she is supposed to be overseeing, the property manager who hired the manager and provided a master key to the apartments may well be held liable. This kind of liability is based on the argument that the property manager made an improper hiring decision.

To minimize this kind of liability, property managers should thoroughly screen job applicants. If a security guard who has a criminal history of breaking and entering burglarizes an apartment building, the property manager likely will be held liable on the basis of hiring someone who posed a threat to the tenants. After hiring all personnel, the property manager must carefully supervise them—property managers should never allow employees to engage in conduct that endangers others. If a property manager learns that an employee is behaving recklessly or criminally and fails to take corrective action, that manager can be held liable for any damage caused by that employee.

■ **SUMMARY**

A life safety plan should be based on four goals: prevention; detection of the problem and sounding an alarm; containment of damage; and counteraction of damage.

In large buildings, a central headquarters must be set up and staffed by a life safety control center operator.

The property manager should designate specific responsibilities to all building staff. Trained tenant wardens and preidentified tenants who possess useful skills or training should assist with the care and evacuation of occupants.

During a building emergency, it is imperative that the property manager make immediate individual contact to advise each tenant of the crisis and how it is being handled. A second priority is to cooperate with the news media authorities and the public while retaining the control necessary to deal with the emergency.

A disaster-procedure plan should be developed for all buildings regardless of their size. Procedures must meet the Occupational Safety and Health Act (OSHA) and other applicable laws. The plan should be designed for handling severe damage and for setting up an off-site command post. If space and budget permit, a minimum of emergency supplies should be stored as part of this plan.

An emergency-procedures guide, distributed to all tenants, should outline emergency response plans for accident or illness, severe weather (including earthquake, tornado, or hurricane), fire, bomb threats, and elevator problems. Building owners should be encouraged to acquire business interruption insurance to alleviate financial losses stemming from emergencies.

Following a disaster, the property manager must concentrate on preventing further damage and to minimize the loss. Resuming normal operations as quickly as possible is the best way to keep sales and leasing losses at a minimum.

Increased and well-trained security personnel, community watch programs, and high-tech security devices can all be used to increase safety and decrease criminal activity. Property managers must be especially careful to watch for and work to eliminate illegal drug activity.

■ CASE STUDY

THE LIFE SAFETY MANAGER

Susan Kim manages a small business park. Several of the tenants have been complaining about a recent crime spree in the park. Several businesses have been burglarized, and one tenant's employee was mugged in the parking lot. Also, the local newspaper has published several articles on the increased danger of flooding in the area, due to increased building in the nearby watershed. Tenants have asked Kim to increase security, reduce crime, and develop an emergency plan should the business park flood next spring.

1. Should Kim hire a security firm and if so, what should Kim look for?
2. What are some of the ways that Kim can reduce crime?
3. What elements should be included in Kim's emergency procedures guide?

■ REVIEW QUESTIONS

1. A good life safety and security program is based on a coordinated approach including
   a. electronic techniques and a trained security force.
   b. the skillful use of equipment, personnel, and procedures.
   c. management expertise and independent consultants.
   d. detectors, alarms, and centralized control.

2. Of the following essential elements in a good security program, which is the MOST important?
   a. Emergency prevention
   b. Problem detection
   c. Loss confinement
   d. Damage control

3. A modern emergency response system will do all of the following EXCEPT
   a. discover and report a fire.
   b. call the fire department.
   c. vent the smoke out of the building.
   d. monitor tenant-installed improvements.

4. During an emergency, handling pedestrian and vehicle traffic outside the building is the responsibility of the
   a. property manager.
   b. chief of security, who reports to the main entrance and is in charge during an emergency.
   c. first available LSO (life safety officer).
   d. local police department.

5. Plastics used in furnishings and finishings may be
   a. fire retardant.
   b. noncombustible.
   c. dangerous because of toxic gases.
   d. self-extinguishing.

6. Which of the following statements is the MOST accurate concerning electronic life safety and security systems?
   a. Most older buildings that can accommodate them are equipped with electronic communication systems.
   b. They can be installed readily by available on-site maintenance personnel.
   c. Their purchase should not be hampered by budgetary restrictions because lives are at stake.
   d. Experienced consultants should be used early in their planning.

7. The news media may be interested in reporting emergency situations. The manager should
   a. permit access if safety is not a factor.
   b. give details on losses and admit liability.
   c. not be concerned with rumors because they cannot be confirmed.
   d. lock out reporters because they never get the story right.

8. The number one priority in a major emergency is to
   a. notify next of kin of those injured.
   b. alert the owner to the nature of the disaster.
   c. ensure safety of employees, tenants, and the public.
   d. arrange for an emergency spokesperson.

9. Preventive maintenance inspections
   a. are required by all insurance companies.
   b. cannot be expected to detect plumbing problems.
   c. do not include structural inspections.
   d. can identify potentially hazardous defects in electrical systems.

10. Which statement is *TRUE* concerning emergency procedures?
    a. Bomb threats are no longer taken seriously.
    b. Building or floor evacuation routines should be rehearsed on a regular basis.
    c. There is no way to anticipate a hurricane.
    d. Procedures for tornadoes and earthquakes are quite different.

11. Emergency communication with tenants and the media should be
    a. in writing.
    b. deferred until the emergency is over and full information is available.
    c. through an authorized spokesperson.
    d. released expeditiously as soon as it is learned to avoid delay incurred by verification.

12. The primary purpose of life safety and security technology is to
    a. turn on the sprinkler system.
    b. discover and promptly report an emergency.
    c. broadcast evacuation instructions.
    d. prohibit access to elevators.

13. One effective method to combat illegal drug activity is to
    a. organize community watch programs.
    b. hire off-duty police to act as security guards.
    c. require a drug test of every occupant as part of the lease qualification.
    d. refuse to rent to anyone younger than 30.

14. Which of the following disasters generally offers enough time in advance to issue warnings?
    a. Tornadoes
    b. Hurricanes
    c. Bomb threat
    d. Earthquake

15. Which of the following cannot be used during a fire emergency?
    a. Stairwells
    b. Window exits
    c. Hallways
    d. Elevators

16. Elevators can be deadly during a fire because
    a. the shafts create a chimney effect allowing updrafts of dangerous materials.
    b. the elevator might tear loose and fall to the basement.
    c. there is no way to reach trapped occupants.
    d. they are automatically turned off as part of containing the fire.

17. Why is it important for the property manager to take steps to minimize post-emergency damage?
    a. Shows the owner that the manager is a responsible worker
    b. Reassures the tenants that they can quickly resume their occupancies
    c. Required by insurance companies
    d. Required by the terms of the management agreement

18. What value, if any, is there in cultivating a relationship with reconstruction companies before an emergency?
    a. They may be more available to someone with whom they have a relationship.
    b. There is no value unless the manager can provide some kind of "make do" work.
    c. The manager can expect lower prices after the disaster.
    d. There is no value as the manager can expect many choices for workmen after a disaster.

19. The manager of which of the following properties should develop disaster preparedness plans?
    a. Large high-rise properties
    b. Commercial properties
    c. Scattered site housing
    d. All of the above

20. What is one of the aftershocks of a disaster?
    a. Tenants loyally return to the damaged property.
    b. Consumers will retain shopping patterns.
    c. Tenants are not permitted to terminate leases.
    d. Consumers form new shopping patterns and may not return.

INTERNET RESOURCES

Following is a list of associations that may be of interest to property management professionals or those interested in learning more about the property management field. It is selective and not exhaustive.

American Society for Industrial Security (ASIS)
1625 Prince Street
Alexandria, VA 22314-2818
Voice: 703-519-6200
Fax: 703-519-6299
Web: *www.asisonline.org*

Education: Certified Protection Professional (CPP)
Publication: *Security Newsbriefs* (daily)

American Society of Civil Engineers (ASCE)
World Headquarters
1801 Alexander Bell Drive
Reston, VA 20191-4400
Voice: 703-295-6300
Fax: 703-295-6222
Faxback: 703-295-6444

ASCE/Washington Office
1015 15th Street NW, Suite 600
Washington, DC 20005
Voice: 202-789-2200
Fax: 202-289-6797
Web: *www.asce.org*

Publications: *ASCE News, Civil Engineering*, Journals

Building Owners and Managers Association International (BOMA)
1201 New York Avenue NW, Suite 300
Washington, DC 20005
Voice: 202-408-2662
Fax: 202-371-0181
Web: *www.boma.org*

Education/Designations: Continuing education courses for designers
Publications: *Experience Exchange Reports;* Monthly *Skylines*

Building Owners and Managers Institute (BOMI)
1521 Ritchie Highway
Arnold, MD 21012
Voice: 410-974-1410
Fax: 410-974-1935
Web: *www.bomi.org*

Education/Designations: Real Property Administrator (RPA); Facilities Management Administrator (FMA); Systems Maintenance Administrator (SMA); System Maintenance Technician (SMT), etc.

Community Associations Institute (CAI)
1630 Duke Street
Alexandria, VA 22314
Voice: 703-548-8600
Web: *www.caionline.org*

Education/Designations: Accredited Association Management Company (AAMC); Association Management Specialist (AMS); Certified Manager of Community Associations (CMCA); Professional Community Association Manager (PCAM); Reserve Specialist (RS)

Commercial Investment Real Estate Institute (CIREI)
430 N. Michigan Avenue, Suite 800
Chicago, IL 60611-4092
Voice: 800-621-7027; 312-321-4460
Fax: 312-321-4530
Fax-on-demand: 800-839-2387
Web: *www.ccim.com*

Education/Designation: Certified Commercial Investment Member (CCIM)
Publication: *Commercial Investment Real Estate*

CoreNet Global
260 Peachtree Street, NW, Suite 1500
Atlanta, GA 30303
Voice: 1-800-726-8111
Fax: 404-589-3201
Web: *www.corenetglobal.org*

Education/Designation: Board Certified in Corporate Real Estate (BCCR); Professional Certificates: Master; Professional; Advanced Professional; Publication: *Corporate Real Estate Leader*

Housing and Urban Development (HUD)
HUD's Housing Counseling Service Locator: 800-569-4287
HUD's National Multifamily Clearinghouse: 800-685-8470
Office of Inspector General (OIG: to report fraud and waste): 800-347-3735
Office of Fair Housing and Equal Opportunity: 800-669-9777
Web: *www.hud.gov*
Publication: Fair Housing Newsletters (*www.hud.gov/offices/fheo/library/newsletters.cfm*)

International Council of Shopping Centers (ICSC)
New York Office
665 5ᵗʰ Avenue
New York, NY 10022
Voice: 212-421-8181
Fax: 212-486-0849

London Office
Caroline House, 5ᵗʰ Floor
55-57 High Holborn
London WC1V6DX
United Kingdom
Voice: 011-44-171-727-3935
Fax: 011-44-171-727-6081

Asia Office
95 South Bridge Road
Pidemco Centre 11-15
Singapore 058717
Voice: 011-65-532-3722
Fax: 011-65-532-7355
Web: *www.icsc.org*

Education/Designations: Certified Shopping Center Manager (CSM); Certified Leasing Specialist (CLS); Certified Marketing Director (CMD); Senior Level Certified Shopping Center Manager (SCSM); Accredited Shopping Center Manager (ASM); Senior Level Certified Shopping Center Marketing Director (SCMD); Accredited Marketing Director (AMD)
Publications: *Shopping Centers Today; Government Relations Report; Asia-Pacific Retail Real Estate Report*

International Facility Management Association (IFMA)
1 E. Greenway Plaza, Suite 1100
Houston, TX 77046-0194
Voice: 713-623-4362
Fax: 713-623-6124
Web: *www.ifma.org*

Education/Designation: Certified Facility Manager (CFM)
Publication: *Facility Management Journal*

Institute of Real Estate Management (IREM)
430 N. Michigan Avenue
Chicago, IL 60611-4090
Voice: 312-329-6000
Fax: 312-410-7957
Web: *www.irem.org*

Education/Designations: Certified Property Manager (CPM); Accredited Residential Manager (ARM); Accredited Management Organization (AMO)
Publication: *Journal of Property Management*

Manufactured Housing Institute (MHI)
2101 Wilson Boulevard, Suite 610
Arlington, VA 22201-3062
Voice: 703-558-0400
Fax: 703-558-0401
Web: *www.mfghome.org*

National Affordable Housing Management Association
526 King Street
Alexandria, VA 22314
Voice: 703-683-8630
Fax: 703-683-8634
Web: *www.nahma.org*

Education/Designations: Certified Professional of Occupancy (CPO); Housing Credit Certified Professional (HCCP) (with NAHB)

National Apartment Association (NAA)
201 N. Union Street, Suite 200
Alexandria, VA 22314
Voice: 703-518-6141
Fax: 703-518-6191
Web: *www.naahq.org*

Education/Designations: Certified Apartment Supervisor (CAPS); Certified Apartment Manager (CAM); Certified Apartment Maintenance Technician (CAMT); National Apartment Leasing Professional (NALP); Certified Apartment Supplier (CAS)
Publication: *Units*

National Association of Home Builders (NAHB)
NAHB's Multifamily Services Division
1201 15th Street, NW
Washington, DC 20005
Voice: 202-861-2138; 800-368-5242, Ext. 138
Fax: 202-861-2120
Web: *www.nahb.com*

Education/Designations: Registered in Apartment Management (RAM); Senior RAM; Certified Leasing Professional (CLP)

Publications: *Multifamily Hotline Newsletter; RAM Digest*

National Association of Housing and Redevelopment Officials (NAHRO)
630 Eye Street, NW
Washington, DC 20001
Voice: 202-289-3500
Fax: 202-289-8181
Web: *www.nahro.org*

Publications: *Journal of Housing and Community Development; NAHRO Monitor*

National Association of Industrial and Office Parks (NAIOP)
2201 Cooperative Way, Third Floor
Herndon, VA 20171
Voice: 800-666-6780
Fax: 703-904-7942
Web: *www.naiop.org*

Publication: *Development*

National Association of Real Estate Investment Trusts (NAREIT)
1875 Eye Street NW, Suite 600
Washington, DC 20006
Voice: 202-739-9400
Fax: 202-739-9401
Web: *www.nareit.org*

Publications: *REIT Report; REITWatch; Journal of Real Estate Investment Trusts; FaxBrief*

National Association of Residential Property Managers (NARPM)
PO Box 1554
Lake Oswego, OR 97035
Voice: 800-782-3452
Fax: 503-635-6508
Web: *www.narpm.org*

Education/Designations: Professional Property Manager (PPM); Master Property Manager (MPM)

National Fair Housing Advocate
835 W. Jefferson Street, Room 100
Louisville, KY 40202
Voice: 502-583-3247
Fax: 502-583-3180
Web: *www.fairhousing.com*

Publication: *National Fair Housing Advocate*

National Investment Center for the Seniors Housing and Care Industries (NIC)
705 Melvin Avenue, Suite 201
Annapolis, MD 21404
Voice: 410-267-0504
Fax: 410-268-4620
Web: *www.nic.org*

Oregon Newspaper Publishers Association
7150 SW Hampton Street, Suite 111
Portland, OR 97223
Voice: 503-624-6397
Fax: 503-639-9009
Web: *www.orenews.com*

Society of Industrial and Office REALTORS® (SIOR)
700 11ᵗʰ Street, NW Suite 510
Washington, DC 20001-4511
Voice: 202-737-1150
Fax: 202-737-8796
Web: *www.sior.com*

Education/Designations: Specialist, Industrial and/or Office Real Estate (SIOR)
Publication: *Professional Report*

Urban Land Institute (ULI)
1025 Thomas Jefferson Street NW, Suite 500W
Washington, DC 20007-5201
Voice: 202-624-7062
Fax: 202-624-7140
Web: *www.uli.org*

Education/Designation: Real Estate Development Certification, Real Estate Development Financing Certification
Publication: *Urban Land*

ANSWER KEY

■ CHAPTER 1
Professional Property Management

POSSIBLE RESPONSES TO CASE STUDY: The Professional Property Manager

1. Advantages to working as an employee manager include the security of a paycheck and the freedom from having to solicit clients and properties to manage; a disadvantage is being confined to working for someone else. Advantages to working as a third-party manager include the freedom of running one's own business (although the property owner's goals must always be fulfilled); disadvantages include the work (and insecurity) of finding new clients and new buildings to manage.

2. Owners hire managers for a variety of reasons: the owner may lack the time required to manage properly; the owner may lack the required expertise to manage properly; the owner may want to deduct the cost of professional management from the property's income for tax purposes; or the owner may want a more objective viewpoint about how the property should be managed.

3. A property manager should always operate ethically for several reasons: ethical behavior is the right way to conduct business; ethical behavior is the best way to avoid any legal difficulties; ethical behavior is the best way to build up and preserve a reputation for professionalism and good service; and compliance with an ethical code is required for membership in most professional organizations.

Review Questions

1. a The structural advantages of the steel frame building, coupled with the perfection of the electric elevator, made it possible to build tall buildings on small parcels of urban land, which in turn led to the development of multifamily apartment buildings that required professional property management.

2. c The traditional downtown concentration of commerce became decentralized because the population moved to the suburbs, and large shopping centers were built to accommodate their needs.

3. a The growth of shopping centers has been fueled by the expansion of public transportation and increase in automobile ownership enabling young couples to buy homes in the suburbs.

4. a The primary functions of a property manager are to generate income while achieving the owner's objectives, always preserving or increasing the value of the property. The manager may not always achieve 100 percent occupancy.

5. a BOMA was formed in 1921; the others were created in the 1930s and later.

6. b Spaces in research parks may include spaces for beginning companies, called incubator spaces.

7. d Special-purpose properties are buildings designed for a special business or organiza-

tional undertaking that dictates the design and operation of the buildings themselves, such as nursing homes, hospitals, and schools.

8. d   Residential real estate is the largest source of demand for the services of professional property managers.

9. d   Although the owner usually wants to realize the most amount of income while preserving the value of the property, it is imperative that the manager understand what the owner wants to achieve with a specific property.

10. c   Rising construction costs and a decrease in the availability of usable land have resulted in the growing popularity of multifamily developments such as town homes, condominiums, and cooperatives.

11. d   Income-producing properties that provide services are office parks and business parks.

12. a   The success or failure of retail property, particularly a shopping center, often hinges on the property manager's ability to assess the market, to conduct sales promotion and public relations, and to act swiftly and decisively.

13. a   The primary purpose of ministorage units is to provide extra storage space for homeowners and apartment dwellers, but businesses also rent space to store files, extra supplies, and surplus equipment.

14. b   Enterprise zones are created under state statutes and are predominantly warehousing, light manufacturing, or assembly zones.

15. b   Motels, hotels, theaters, schools, and places of worship are considered special-purpose because the activity in these buildings is a special business or organizational undertaking that dictates the design and operation of the buildings themselves.

16. a   Manufactured home parks offer a combination of home ownership and site rental. Few manufactured homes are moved a second time.

17. c   Concierges offer both business and personal services in office buildings, condominium developments, shopping centers, and apartment complexes.

18. d   Asset management refers to financial management of a sizeable number of investment properties rather than directly managing an individual property or properties in a particular area.

19. b   The prudent course of action is to terminate the management agreement if the property manager will suffer increased exposure to liability based on an owner's refusal to comply with such laws.

20. b   Business ethics are a kind of business version of the Golden Rule and refer to fidelity, integrity, and competency.

■ CHAPTER 2   Property Management Economics and Planning

POSSIBLE RESPONSES TO CASE STUDY: The Property Manager as Economist-Planner

1. Real property is subject to the same economic trends as the general business economy, and it is important for the property manager to be able to forecast what is ahead. By doing so, the property manager can plan the best way to stay competitive and operate the property effectively. For example, local economic information is an important indicator of the supply and demand for housing, which will affect the rental rates that can be charged.

2. The shutdown of the local defense factory means that unemployment in the community will rise. This, in turn, may well mean that residential vacancy rates will increase as workers leave the community in search of new jobs. It could also mean a higher rate of evictions and noncollection of rent as people have trouble making ends meet. As it is likely that vacancy rates will go up, the managers of competing properties may lower rental rates to attract new tenants.

This means that Charles will have to look very carefully at current rents to make sure they are competitive when evaluating current and potential income and operating costs.

3. An overall decrease in property values can be both negative and positive for Charles and his new employer. On the one hand, a decrease in property values means that the residential properties Charles is managing will become less valuable and that Charles will have to work hard to stay competitive and make sure that the properties generate enough income to keep up with maintenance and repairs. On the other hand, if Charles's employer has additional capital to invest, this would be a good time to buy up competing properties at bargain prices, and give them to Charles to manage effectively.

Review Questions

1. a The expansion phase is when the country is working at near full employment level, wages and consumer purchasing power climb to their highest point, and demand for goods increases.

2. a When supply meets and begins to surpass the demand for products and services, recession occurs and the economy contracts because there is less demand for goods.

3. b Long-term movements reflect the overall direction the economy is taking. Population growth and shifts, technological breakthroughs, and other political, bureaucratic, and contingency factors influence a nation's growth rate.

4. b Real estate activities occur on local levels at irregular intervals and may be shorter (five to ten years) than those in the general economy.

5. b During the contraction phase, vacancy rates are high and property owners must compete for tenants, resulting in a drastic reduction in rent.

6. b Reserve funds cover the "unexpected expenditures that may be expected." Therefore, any budget forecast, whether an operating budget or a five-year projection, should provide for reserve funds under the expense category.

7. b Technical oversupply results when there are more spaces than tenants who want the spaces.

8. d The property manager who represents the owner is responsible for identifying the major economic trends and their effect on the value of a specific property in that particular market level. This is true regardless of what type of property it is, whether large retail mall, business park, or residential.

9. d The objective in a market analysis is to arrive at the optimum price for a standard unit of that type within the market area. From this figure the expected base income for the property can be calculated.

10. d The terms of the lease will disclose the amount and durability of rental income.

11. d Residential property managers will be most concerned with population demographics such as the size of family units, the median income level, population trends, and current employment rates for a neighborhood market survey.

12. c Economic oversupply results when tenants cannot afford the rents.

13. a High occupancy rates indicate a shortage of space and therefore suggest the possibility of rental increases.

14. b Prospective tenants form their initial impressions of the premises based on what they see as they approach the building, the "curb appeal."

15. a Evaluation of the comparables provides information about the operating costs and estimates of the capital expenditures needed to make the property competitive.

16. d   Step one in the formulating management plan is to determine an operating budget; step two is the five-year forecast, and step three is the comparative income and expense analysis.

17. c   By assisting the owner in establishing written goals, the property manager can make a real contribution to the owner and may determine that alternative use should be explored.

18. c   Cash flow is the amount of money available for use after paying expenses and the debt service from the expected gross effective income.

19. b   Although the property and neighborhood analyses and five-year forecast are important, the owner's objectives will ultimately determine the acceptance or rejection of the management plan.

20. c   The owner's objectives will determine the acceptance or rejection of the management plan.

■ CHAPTER 3   Owner Relations

POSSIBLE RESPONSES TO CASE STUDY: The Owner Relations Manager

1. Having learned from his previous experience, Doug can try to devote the large part of his time to maintaining sound owner relations. For instance, he can send each client a personal letter along with each monthly report. Also, Doug can set aside a regular time to telephone each owner and deliver monthly reports in person (for instance, over lunch at a restaurant that is convenient to the client). Doug can plan to use the management agreement in Figure 3.1 but modify it to suit the requirements of the customer (for example, tailoring his flexible computer-reporting system to the needs or wishes of each owner).

2. Doug can form a transitional team to oversee the acquisition of specific new properties. Doug can also implement a proven owner relations activity: he can photograph the properties as they are

at the time of takeover and then again at yearly intervals to send to the owners. Doug can also use these pictorial histories as a marketing tool to obtain new accounts.

Review Questions

1. b   An agent has a fiduciary relationship to his or her principal, a confidential relationship marked by trust and confidence that requires the highest degree of loyalty on the part of the agent. The agent must always put the property owner's interests first, above his or her own interests.

2. a   An agent has certain duties imposed by common law in the fiduciary relationship with his or her principal. Common law duties implicit in this relationship include the duties of care, obedience, loyalty, accounting, and disclosure.

3. b   In lieu of a formalized contract between employer and employee, a written authorization to sign leases should be given to the employee. This authorization is sometimes limited in the dollar amount or length of lease.

4. b   The management agreement between the owner and the manager defines the relationship between the parties, serves as a guide for the operation of the property, and provides a basis for settlement of any future disputes.

5. d   The name on the contract should be the same as on the title or deed to the property. If the property is owned by a partnership, each partner's name should be stated in the management agreement. If corporately owned, the corporate name should appear on the contract.

6. d   As a rule, the property manager's employees who handle funds should be covered by a surety bond, obtained at the manager's expense.

7. a   The manager who exerts a considerable initial effort to lease the premises and set up a management system will desire sufficient

protection as compensation for extra effort and will usually seek a minimum one-year contract.

8. c An agent may terminate early when the owner causes the agent damages or liability, but termination by the agent due to an owner's illegal acts does not release the owner from his or her obligations under the contract terms.

9. d Notice of cancellation may be served in person or by registered mail, with "Return Receipt Requested," to the address listed on the contract. Cancellation is effective when the notice is deposited in the mail.

10. d As common practice, the agent should not advance his or her own funds to cover a deficiency. The amount of the reserve fund should be proportional to the size of the property.

11. b The manager who is responsible for the work done by employees should also have the power to hire and supervise them. Employees often develop greater loyalty to a manager they can look upon as the prime authority figure.

12. a The property manager should seek protection through a clause stating that employees are the responsibility of the owner, not the property manager. This clause should explicitly set forth the owner's obligations to pay all settlements, damages, etc. in the event of litigation or investigations arising from alleged or actual violations of labor laws.

13. c A flat-fee arrangement is different from a percentage fee, which would be based on a percentage of gross income.

14. b The percentage fee is a wonderful incentive for an agent, as it is based on gross collectible income and can result in significant increase in revenue, although the management fees will decrease if the building revenue drops.

15. a The manager should pay close attention to the accounts payable ledger, and the owner and the manager need to agree in the management agreement on each party's specific liabilities for expenses.

16. b A note with the monthly earnings report demonstrates continuing personal interest in the property and can explain unusual items in either the expense or income columns, or that operations were normal.

17. b A flat fee arrangement is most appropriate when managing condominiums. These owners want management to contain expenses, not increase them.

18. b The person most responsible for the property should be the primary contact with the owner to avoid confusion that can arise when several people take problems and conflicting opinions to the owner.

19. a The agent can demonstrate continuing personal interest in the property by including a note or letter with each monthly report. The note can indicate that operations are normal, or explain deviations from the owner's expectations.

20. b Any information that may pertain to the fiscal affairs of the property, such as serving an eviction notice, should be noted to the owner monthly.

■ CHAPTER 4   Marketing

POSSIBLE RESPONSES TO CASE STUDY: The Marketing Manager

1. Depending on local custom, the following media should be effective in both decreasing vacancy rates and improving the project's image.

   a. Tasteful signs posted on the property will identify the type of space available and the person to contact. If the project has its own office, the directory should list it prominently.

b. Newspaper advertisements are the most effective way to advertise residential property; classified ads are inexpensive and effective, and a well-designed display ad would help improve the project's image.

c. A brochure could be developed to give to interested prospects. For a residential property, the brochure would have to be fairly inexpensive to design and produce to be cost-effective. It would, however, have to look professional to increase the prestige of the project.

2. Following are some marketing ideas Jon could use to improve the project's image:

   a. Start an intensive advertising campaign (as discussed in question 1).

   b. Generate publicity for the project with a series of press releases on any newsworthy events connected to the project.

   c. Develop a direct-mail marketing campaign aimed at reputable brokers and agents who can provide referrals or actual tenants.

   d. Ensure that showings are made in a professional manner and that the units shown are in excellent shape.

3. Whether a rental center is appropriate for this project will depend mostly on the size of the project. Because rental centers are expensive to maintain and run, the project must be fairly large to justify the cost. Often rental centers are appropriate when a project is new or recently converted and needs many new tenants in a short period of time. As Jon has lived in this project for several years, the project is not new and is unlikely to need a large influx of new tenants. Therefore, a rental center may well be an unjustified expense.

Review Questions

1. b   The principal responsibility of a property manager is to make sure that a property generates income. Unless potential tenants are actively attracted to the property and the space is skillfully shown, it is unlikely that many tenants will be willing to sign leases or pay rent.

2. d   Recommendations from satisfied tenants are the best and least expensive method of renting property.

3. c   The amount budgeted for advertising and promotion gives the manager all the data necessary to select the best techniques for reaching the most prospects at the least cost.

4. d   When a good product is backed with a complete marketing effort, it should rent faster and at a higher price that its average competition. The marketing effort should include 1) advertising campaign strategy and methods, 2) promotional efforts, and 3) personal selling activities.

5. c   If there is a low vacancy rate in a stable market, a well-planned promotional effort can enhance the prestige of the building and generate consumer demand to support a higher rental schedule.

6. b   Each type of property determines the specific method of advertising to reach the greatest number of potential tenants.

7. b   Classifieds are relatively inexpensive per line of copy and are the most prevalent method of advertising residential properties.

8. c   The most effective advertising brochure will have a central theme and will not try to cover every conceivable point about the property.

9. a   Billboards are most effective when advertising larger industrial and commercial properties because industrial users often drive around to observe buildings in the area they prefer.

10. c   For Rent signs are useful in front of residential properties and in vacant store windows and should state type of unit presently vacant and person to contact, if this is a common practice in the area.

11. a   Most regional magazines and trade journals are reliable vehicles for advertising commercial as well as industrial and residential real estate and accept both classified and display ads. Industrial and commercial property owners and managers are most likely to use direct mail.

12. c   Using in-house leasing agents allows the property manager more control.

13. d   Networking with professional organizations for real estate practitioners builds a cooperative referral network.

14. d   The manager must be familiar with the space so as to answer questions, overcome objections, and point out relevant features to the prospective tenant.

15. a   The manager's task is to convince the consumer that the space is the most advantageous as the consumer has already expressed some interest in the property.

16. d   The model space, as part of the rental center, can be made available for rent in one of the least attractive areas and, and when leased, another less appealing area can be decorated as the rental center and subsequently rented.

17. c   Rental centers can be prohibitively expensive as they usually include a display area, furnished models, a closing area, and sometimes a manager's office. They are more appropriate for large developments.

18. c   The radio ad is least expensive, costing $10 per prospect only (five are needed to lease). The cost per prospect per lease is how the expense of marketing is often figured.

19. a   Before lowering the rent rather than spending more on advertising, the manager must determine how decreasing the rent may affect similar space in the building.

20. b $30 × 2 days ÷ 7 prospects = $8.57 per prospect.

■ CHAPTER 5   Leases

POSSIBLE RESPONSES TO CASE STUDY: The Lease Manager and Record Keeper

1. The lease form should always contain all of the lease terms, even if it means extra legal fees. Otherwise, as happened here, confusion may result if the property or the lease changes hands or a dispute as to the additional terms arises.

2. Patti should try to convince the property owner to have an amended lease form drawn up at once with the altered maintenance agreement terms, so that everyone is sure what the agreement is and all the lease terms can be found in one place, i.e., the lease agreement.

3. If the owner insists on using a standard lease form, it should at least be a current form to comply with all current legal requirements. For example, the Americans with Disabilities Act requires certain provisions be included in all leases. Laws are becoming more protenant, and a 1989 lease agreement may no longer pass muster with the courts should a conflict arise. It is imperative that clauses pertaining to such things as security deposits, habitability, and termination procedures comply with current state laws.

4. Patti should insist that an attorney draft several provisions that could be added to the outdated lease, such as the ADA clause and an illegal drug activity clause. Also, any clauses in residential leases that may violate the Fair Housing Act (for instance, a clause restricting children) should also be changed to comply with current laws and regulations.

Review Questions

1. a   A tenancy for years has a definite beginning and definite end. Most leases begin as estates (or tenancies) for years and then convert to period to period.

2. c   Estates from period to period run week to week, or month to month, or year to year; notice is often equal to the period.

3. c   Generally, net expenses include utilities and taxes; net-net would include those expenses plus insurance, and triple net would include net-net expenses plus maintenance.

4. a   Residential leases are usually gross leases and the tenant pays a fixed amount of rent.

5. d   Net leases are common with industrial property in which the tenant is responsible for most, if not all, of the expenses.

6. b   Retailers consent to a percentage lease because they pay more only as indicated by their sales. The owner shares in the risk.

7. b   An oral lease of less than one year is usually legally enforceable (Statute of Frauds), while a lease for more than one year must be in writing to be enforceable.

8. a   A valid lease should clearly identify the property. The lease does not have to be acknowledged, on a standard form or in compliance with the Uniform Residential Landlord Tenant Act.

9. a   The apartment number and the street address of the building are usually sufficient identification in an apartment lease.

10. a   Automatic cancellation may occur if the tenant is denied use of the property because it has been appropriated or condemned by a government agency.

11. d   The lease is between the property owner and the tenant; power can be delegated to the property manager, as the owner's agent, to execute leases.

12. a   The option to renew is an owner's concession and gives the tenant the right to extend the lease for an additional period on specified terms. To take advantage of this option, the tenant merely gives sufficient notice of intent.

13. c   The lease should prohibit subletting without the owner's prior, written consent to ensure that the owner has stable and financially secure tenants occupying the property.

14. d   The answer is $402.25. Add three months and multiply by 2.5 percent. $5,270 + $4,500 + $6,320 × 2.5 percent = $402.25.

15. a   Constructive eviction is a result of the landlord's being unable to supply such services as heat or water or repair major material defaults that render the premises unusable.

16. c   The index used in an index lease must be reliable and published on a regular and continuing basis by an independent, reputable agency, such as the Consumer Price Index and the Wholesale Price Index.

17. a   A lease may be assigned without either party's prior written approval unless the terms of the lease prohibit otherwise.

18. a   The owner is transferring only a portion of the remainder of the lease; hence, it is a sublet. This would be an assignment if the new tenant were assuming ALL of the remainder of the lease.

19. d   Federal bankruptcy laws and court decisions interpreting them change, so a property manager should review bankruptcy clauses in leases with an attorney.

20. a   A lease clause or legal statement may bind an owner, so the manager's or owner's attorney should advise the parties about leases and riders.

■ CHAPTER 6   Lease Negotiations

POSSIBLE RESPONSES TO CASE STUDY: The Lease Negotiator

1. Aimes could try to negotiate a solution with at least two of the three tenants. Because all the tenants want more space, Aimes could release one tenant from his or her lease obligations and

lease the vacated space to one or both of the other two tenants.

2. Releasing one tenant should also help solve the parking problem, because one business and its employees will be leaving the building. However, the remaining tenants will probably expand to create the same parking problem, and Aimes may have to give each tenant fewer parking spaces in future lease negotiations.

3. Aimes needs to institute some new procedures for finding tenants. First, he needs to be more careful when qualifying prospective tenants. It is imperative that each tenant be suitable for the available space in terms of both size and cost. Second, Aimes needs to be a little tougher in negotiating lease terms. He should set a firm rental schedule and then stick to it. Remember, it may be better to have a vacant space than to rent it at an unprofitable rate. A free-rent concession is a better way to attract tenants in a tough market. Other concessions, such as additional alterations or help with moving costs, are also attractive to prospective tenants.

Review Questions

1. b   The tenant does not have to be concerned with who else is looking at the property. The tenant should be concerned with "is this the best location," space, price, and the usefulness of the concessions to the tenant.

2. a   The manager may need to summarize the benefits repeatedly throughout the showing and closing process to reassure an indecisive prospect that the space is ideal.

3. c   All activities involved in marketing rental space are directed toward a single goal—the signing of a lease.

4. b   The stability of the tenant's rental history will influence the manager's final decision.

5. d   The tenant is asking for a noncompeting restriction, fearing that customers will be confused with two shops in such close proximity; some competition is good—too much is a detriment.

6. d   The property manager is responsible for coordinating all activities and decisions, even with third party interests.

7. d   The attorney's task is to formalize the agreement by translating it into legal terms properly; the manager's task is to control negotiations and strike an agreement between the parties.

8. a   It is in the property manager's best interest to try to secure an agreement on basic terms and conditions of the lease before the lease goes to the respective attorneys.

9. d   A prospect's financial condition is a factor in qualifying a tenant, not a factor in negotiation.

10. c   A concession should be granted reluctantly to increase the value of a concession in the eyes of a tenant. In addition, a concession granted to one may have to be given to all.

11. b   A temporary rental concession is often offered at the back end of a lease. Temporarily lowering the rent may not cost the owner as much as lowering the rent over the term of the lease.

12. b   A commercial property manager will try to negotiate a long-term lease in order to recover expenditures made to alter the space for a particular tenant.

13. c   It is critical to evaluate the concessions, because every concession costs the owner money and affects the total economic value of the lease to the owner.

14. c   The manager must consider not only the type of alteration required but also the total expense to the owner. Negotiation usually involves trade-offs for certain items.

15. b   There is less need to grant a concession for an expansion clause in more fully tenanted commercial or industrial property because most of the space will already be leased or under option to other tenants.

16. d   The law does not care who pays for the ADA required alterations, simply that they are made; so whoever agrees to make the alterations is responsible for the payment. The written lease should be specific.

17. a   Many landlord-tenant misunderstandings can be avoided if the manager establishes clear guidelines from the beginning when negotiating the lease terms.

18. c   The property manager usually performs the residential tenant concessions. All concessions granted should be in writing to prevent misunderstandings.

19. d   A building standard is a set of amenities that are included in the basic rent and usually include a specific number of outlets, light fixtures, windows, etc. The tenant is then expected to pay for anything over the provided basics.

20. a   A large shopping mall should not have noncompeting tenant restrictions in the leases as the total effect of many similar shops in large retail centers is to stimulate business and encourage competition.

■ CHAPTER 7   Tenant Relations

POSSIBLE RESPONSES TO CASE STUDY: The Tenant Relations Manager

1. Chin should take the time to review the rent payment policies with White and emphasize the importance of timely payment. For example, if White realized that Chin would not be able to give White a good reference, making it difficult for him to get another apartment, this might be another incentive to pay on time. (If Chin has not already done so, she might consider revising future lease documents to include a provision for a late penalty that would encourage tenants to pay the rent on time.)

2. Chin should spend some time with Samuals going through his lease and explaining what repairs and maintenance he can reasonably expect during his tenancy and why. If Samuals has a clear idea of what requests will be acted on and why others will be rejected, he may become less combative. Also, Chin should increase her personal contact with the other tenants to foster good relations. If the other tenants feel comfortable with Chin and with the level of service they are receiving from her, they are unlikely to get worked up to a state of discontent by Samuals.

3. Chin should immediately meet with Juarez to discuss her comment in detail. The fact that Juarez has been a model tenant for five years makes her failure to renew her lease and her dissatisfaction with management a serious issue. She may offer valuable insights into problems with the complex or problems with Chin's management style. It is important that Chin approach Juarez with a genuine desire to improve the management of the apartments and without defensiveness. It is possible that if Chin and Juarez have a constructive exchange of ideas, Juarez may change her mind and decide to renew her lease after all. If she does not renew, her comments can be used to improve future practices.

Review Questions

1. a   A high tenant turnover means greater expense for the owner in terms of advertising, redecorating, and uncollected rents.

2. c   Managers should keep these records of lease renewal dates so they can anticipate expiration and retain good tenants who otherwise might move when their leases expire.

3. b   Joint inspection by the landlord and tenant before move-in can determine whether promised repairs or alterations have been made or are in progress and alleviate many misunderstandings.

4. b   At the time of the move-in inspection, the manager and residential tenant should mutually agree to the condition of the premises and note any exceptions. Both sign forms and should have copies.

5. a   The manager's personal efforts will do more than amenities themselves to establish friendliness and loyalty among the tenant population.

6. c   From the outset, the manager should be clear as to when rent is due, where it is to be paid, and the penalties for being late or not making payment.

7. d   A prerequisite for enlightened property maintenance, a system should be developed to quickly and effectively channel service requests to the appropriate parties.

8. c   If the service request will be denied, the manager should be honest with the tenant and explain why. The fastest way to alienate a tenant is to allow him or her to expect something and then to procrastinate and evade the issue if delivery becomes impossible.

9. b   An effective property manager will establish a good communication system with tenants, ensure that maintenance and service requests are attended to promptly, and enforce all lease terms and building rules.

10. a   The manager should ascertain if the decision to move was prompted by an oversight on the part of management, and if the situation can be corrected to retain a valuable tenant.

11. b   The critical factor in determining whether to raise rents is total net increase after accounting for move-outs due to the increase.

12. c   If the manager can provide reasonable explanations for the rental increase, the tenant's attitudes toward the increases often change dramatically.

13. c   200,000 sq. ft. × $8.70 × .95 = $1,653,000; 200,000 sq. ft. × $8.50 × .97 = $1,649,000; 200,000 sq. ft. × $8.20 × 1.00 = $1,640,000; 200,000 sq. ft. × $8.90 × .91 = $1,619,800

14. b   The net increase is $1,200 a month and will increase again as soon as the departed tenants are replaced. $600 × 75 = $45,000; $660 × 70 = $46,200

15. b   The requirements for prompt payment of rent and the provisions for default should be reviewed when the tenant signs the lease.

16. d   There should be a predetermined, fixed, reasonable period of time between the due date and the announcement of legal action for delinquency that in most cases should not exceed three to five days.

17. b   The manager's file should contain the record of the notice so the manager will know when to contact the attorney to file the notice in court.

18. c   The post-occupancy inspection should be conducted with the tenant after the tenant has removed all personal items.

19. d   The manager should use the same form used for move-in for the move-out to determine if any damage has been done to the property and if the unit is in reasonable condition.

20. b   Generally, in most states, the property manager must provide the tenant with a written statement of deductions; failure to follow this procedure can result in severe criminal and civil penalties.

■ CHAPTER 8   Maintenance and Construction

POSSIBLE RESPONSES TO CASE STUDY: The Maintenance Managerr

1. Blake should carefully examine his maintenance staff to make sure that it is cost-effective. Perhaps he could replace two employees with one employee with more varied skills or use outside services to do the work of two or more employees. Blake should also contact utility and fuel companies to seek ways to economize on fuel consumption. Blake can institute a bulk purchasing program for supplies that are used in volume or that store well. Blake should also look at his security system to make sure that valuable supplies are protected from theft.

2. Areas of ADA concern include: parking, passenger loading zones, drinking fountains, elevators, stairs, parking lots, curb ramps, doors, toilet stalls and urinals, and telephones.

Review Questions

1. a   Although the property manager is responsible for the hiring and firing of maintenance personnel, the manager should welcome the resident manager's opinion when screening or terminating employees.

2. d   A property may be more profitable if kept in top condition and operated with full tenant services because it can command premium rental rates.

3. b   Regular maintenance activities and routine inspections (preventive maintenance) of the building and equipment will disclose structural and mechanical problems before major repairs become necessary, hopefully eliminating or reducing corrective maintenance costs.

4. d   This type of new construction is called *upgrading* and is closely tied to leasing and tenant relations.

5. b   Deferred maintenance is not strictly a type of maintenance, but a stock term in the property management business referring to a condition when obvious repairs are not made when needed (deferred) and the building begins to lose value (depreciate).

6. d   After determining the work to be done and the time and expense involved, the property manager will make the decision on which is most cost-effective for the owner.

7. d   Cost is a critical factor in deciding whether to use on-site maintenance personnel or hire outside services.

8. d   A manager must determine to either act as a general contractor or hire a prime contractor.

9. d   In a negotiated contract situation, contractors know that they have the manager's commitment to use their services if the price is acceptable, so they will often do their best to shave costs.

10. b   Fast-track construction is a development in the area of negotiated contracts that allows the contractor to begin work before the final plans are completed; this should only be used when the parties trust one another.

11. b   It is customary to withhold a certain percentage until after the work has been completed in case additional service is necessary.

12. b   The first step in a preventive maintenance program is to make a complete inventory of the equipment and include such information as date and place of purchase, warranties, and when each system needs to be serviced or overhauled.

13. d   Many potentially serious problems can be averted by regular inspections, which should include checklists of the building features to be examined and the maintenance personnel responsible for each task.

14. d   Retrofitting is an extensive measure to reduce operating costs by replacing or upgrading equipment.

15. b   Some of the greatest savings can be realized by simple, inexpensive measures to conserve energy, such as properly maintaining equipment, reducing size and number of lights, weatherstripping, and caulking.

16. b   Life-cycle costing is done to compare the total cost of one type of equipment with that of another. A higher-priced energy-efficient appliance may be the least expensive product due to its lower operating costs.

17. b   Numerous software packages can assist the manager with all kinds of maintenance activities including integrating maintenance information into the financial reports.

18. c   Each floor (loft) has nonspecialized interior floor space and is a single open area, divided only by the support columns for the building.

19. a   The ADA applies to businesses or facilities open to the public, not to single-family dwellings.

20. c   A performance bond protects the owner from the losses resulting from a contractor not finishing the job. The bonding company will arrange for other contractors to finish the work.

■ CHAPTER 9   Managing the Office and Reports

POSSIBLE RESPONSES TO CASE STUDY: The Office Manager

1. The primary element of a good filing system is ease of use—staff must be able to file and access information quickly. Separate files should be set up for leases, including lease documents and tenant information; correspondence; work estimates and bids; financial data, including canceled checks, budgets, profit and loss statements, and income and expense reports; legal documents, including property management agreements and mortgage and title information; and employee and independent contractor information. Emerson should discuss the system with the clerical staff to determine the best way to set up files. For example, one type of information may be more easily accessed by date, another by alphabetical order.

2. To be competitive in any business in today's economic climate, computerization is a must. Emerson needs to educate his boss on the increased efficiency and accuracy of computer systems, especially in the basic functions of accounting and word processing. He could determine how much time the overworked clerical staff could save on simple tasks (such as mailouts) and quickly compute the dollar savings. It is possible that office staff could be reduced while still achieving increased efficiency. He can also present her with safety facts, such as the backup systems available, to alleviate her fears of losing data.

3. Emerson should investigate computer software being used by other property management companies. He can do this by attending trade shows or local association meetings. He will want to show his boss the reports that can be generated. Computers are getting less expensive, so his boss may be more receptive than she might have been in the past.

Emerson's list should include a database program, a word processing program, and an accounting program. He should shop carefully, not only to get the best prices but also to get a system that can be easily upgraded as the need to expand the system arises. He also might think about purchasing a system that includes on-site training, to help the staff retrain and familiarize his boss with computers and their ease of use. Depending on the size of the office staff, he may wish to purchase a system with a local access network (LAN) for speed and ease of interoffice communication. Once Emerson's boss becomes acquainted with what property management software can do in respect to lease/profitability analysis, marketing, maintenance and inventory management, and ADA compliance, Emerson may end up spending more time with computers than he ever imagined.

Review Questions

1. b   Even if a manager has a home office elsewhere, a small office to be used for specific functions is often set up on the property.

2. d   Five filing categories are appropriate for whatever size the office.

3. a   Documents pertinent to the property itself such as management contract, mortgage, and title information; labor contracts; and insurance policies are kept in the permanent file.

4. c   On-the-spot maintenance and repairs, along with price, are probably the most important considerations when purchasing a computer system.

5. d   The cost of specific management personnel at the specific building would most likely be a direct cost.

6. d   As this is a crucial function, the executive property manager in a smaller operation will usually assume the responsibility of a comptroller.

7. a   The field manager reports to the property management executive and is over the on-site manager.

8. c   The per-unit-cost method of computing fees is derived from the operating budget for the management organization and will represent the minimum per unit fee that must be obtained.

9. b $2,500 (costs) + [.30 (for overhead and profit) × $2,500] = $3,250 ÷ $50,000 = 6.5 percent. Formula: Monthly management fee ÷ gross collectible income = percentage fee.

10. c $35,000 + $20,000 = $55,000 ÷ 750 (units) = $73.33 × .20 (profit) = 14.66. $73.33 + $14.66 = $88. Formula: Management fee divided by number of units firm is capable of handling plus percentage for profit = Minimum per unit fee

11. a $300 (fee) × 50 (units) = $15,000; $300,000 (possible gross annual income) × .06 (vacancy factor) = $282,000 (gross collectible income). $15,000 ÷ $282,000 = 5 percent. Formula: Adjusted per unit fee divided by gross collectible income = percentage management fee

12. c   The most important operating record is the monthly report, which indicates to the owner the sources on income and expenses, net operating income, and net cash flow.

13. d   Nonrecurring variable expenses may or may not occur in any given year, such as a building addition, for example.

14. d   The 1099 form is issued to independent contractor vendors, not to employees.

15. d   The government charges the employer with the responsibility for obtaining the W-4 certificates.

16. a   A manager would want a percentage of the collected rents from an upscale apartment building with high demand, as the rents are most likely regularly paid and increase on a regular basis. A flat fee would be more

appropriate for managing a condominium community or a property that is going to require extra work either in maintenance or changing the tenant population.

17. a   The FUTA must be filed by every employer of one or more persons who work for some portion of a day for 20 weeks during the year or earn at least $1,500 during the year.

18. c   The same percentage that was realized this year, 80 percent, should be used in the budget forecast for the next year as it is preferable to use present rental rates for the estimates.

19. c $BE = \$75,000 \ (FC) \div 1.00 - .25 \ (VCR) = \$100,000$.

20. a   The capitalization rate is a number assigning a relationship between income and value.

■ CHAPTER 10   Federal and State Laws

POSSIBLE RESPONSES TO CASE STUDY: The Compliance Manager

1. Because the building was built prior to 1978, the disclosure forms should be there.

2. Certainly, the first time that a lease is renewed after September 6, 1996, she must make the first disclosure. She must make the disclosures to those tenants who have renewed since then. She must also make the disclosure to each new tenant. She should also inspect the property for chipping and peeling paint; and if she finds such disrepair, she should let the owner know that they need to repaint and contain.

3. If the previous manager was not making other space available, the owner may be open to a fair housing complaint. June should show all available apartments to everyone, and families with children should have the option to rent on other floors. Additionally, June should put up the Equal Housing Poster, institute fair housing education for the office staff, and thor-

oughly document her compliance with showing apartments equally to all applicants, including families with children.

4. June needs to educate her owner about the Lead-Based Paint Hazard Reduction Act and its required disclosures, as well as the Fair Housing Act of 1968. She should also be concerned that some liability for these omissions will accrue to her personally. Thus, she should thoroughly document and date her efforts to bring the building into compliance.

Review Questions

1. b   The 1866 Civil Rights Act prohibits racial discrimination. In 1968 the Supreme Court case of *Jones v. Mayer* reaffirmed that no exemptions would be allowed for racial discrimination.

2. a   Telling a prospect there are no vacancies when there are in fact vacancies is a form of illegal steering as the manager is steering the prospect away from the building.

3. a   Consumers may challenge the accuracy of any information in the report and the information must then be verified. If the dispute still continues, the consumer may attach an explanation to the credit report.

4. d   The manager may evaluate the tenant on the basis of the income-to-debt ratio. The manager may not consider the tenant's race, color, religion, sex, source of income, age, or marital status.

5. b   Managers who are competitors should not discuss rental rates so that there will be no suspicion of price-fixing, which is in violation of antitrust law.

6. d   The manager is permitted to deny credit to anyone based on their credit history, as long as the credit criteria are consistently applied to all applicants.

7. d A judge or a jury can award unlimited punitive damages to the aggrieved party in a court action for violation of the Federal Fair Housing Law.

8. d Most fair housing complaints can be made directly to HUD.

9. c If a person has been denied credit, he or she can receive a free report within 60 days of the denial, upon request per the Fair Credit Reporting Act.

10. b Signed copies of the lead warning statement must be retained for three years from the date of the lease.

11. c Under the Uniform Residential Landlord and Tenant Act, a tenant is considered to have an estate from period to period unless otherwise specified.

12. d The landlord should correct the problem. If a tenant makes a complaint to a government agency, the landlord is generally prohibited from retaliatory reactions, such as summarily raising a tenant's rent or any other type of response that can be interpreted as punishment.

13. d If damage is partial, generally, the tenant may reduce the rent proportionately, per the Uniform Residential Landlord and Tenant Act.

14. b The Act clearly establishes the owner's responsibilities for keeping the premises safe and fit for habitation, and authorizes the owner to establish building rules concerning use and occupancy.

15. a Lead poisoning is discovered through a blood test.

16. d The law requires disclosure when renting or selling any residential property built before 1978.

17. b Megan's Law requires that certain sex offenders register with local police who are empowered to release information as appropriate.

18. c The ADA requires the removal of barriers. The Uniform Residential Landlord and Tenant Act references retaliatory behavior, security deposits, and abandonment.

19. d Under the Equal Credit Opportunity Act, it is legal to request landlord references, but illegal to ask a credit applicant about birth control practices, intent to get married, and welfare money as income.

20. b The ADA does not require businesses to provide personal services to handicapped persons. It does require that barriers be removed, whenever this can be done at a reasonable cost, to make services accessible to individuals with disabilities.

■ CHAPTER 11 Residential Property

POSSIBLE RESPONSES TO CASE STUDY: The Residential Manager

1. Han's complaint is a serious one, and Montgomery should respond accordingly. Montgomery should personally see that Han's repair request is completed in a timely manner. She should assure Han that she will investigate the matter immediately and thoroughly. Montgomery should also make a note of Han's complaint and record the actions that she takes to look into and correct the situation. For example, Montgomery should examine all the records kept on repair requests and their completion to see if there is any evidence of a discriminatory pattern. If any corrective action is taken (i.e., against the resident manager), Han should be so informed.

2. Montgomery should make fair housing compliance an immediate priority. She should examine her office policies to make sure they comply with fair housing rules and emphasize her office's commitment to nondiscriminatory practices. If she has not already done so, she should institute training sessions on fair housing laws and bring up the topic regularly at staff meetings. Selecting someone in her office to be a compliance

officer is a positive step. Making sure that all her employees, including resident managers, are up-to-date on fair housing laws and cognizant of the importance of obeying them is an important part of her job. She can subscribe to the *National Fair Housing Advocate* and discuss published cases with her staff.

3. If Montgomery does not believe that the resident manager's failure to respond to Han's repair was discriminatory, she could decide to keep him in the position, but she should make sure that he is thoroughly trained in fair housing laws. She should oversee his activities more carefully for the next several months to make sure the problem does not recur. Even if the resident manager's failure to complete the repair was due to some other reason, he is not performing his job properly. Montgomery may want to screen and supervise future resident manager applicants more carefully. If Montgomery suspects that there was some discriminatory intent on the resident manager's part, she should proceed with the disciplinary proceedings mandated by her office policies.

Review Questions

1. d   A high-rise luxury property will more likely be located in a downtown urban area or any area where land is scarce and expensive. The building goes *up*, not *out*.

2. b   Walkup apartments are usually found in urban areas and the tenant probably receives the least in the way of extra services and facilities.

3. a   The principal differences between managing scattered sites (single-family homes) and managing apartment buildings centers on geography and time. Because homes are located in various locations, showing property to prospective tenants generally involves unproductive travel to and from each location.

4. b   Tenants must be compatible, especially if duplexes and triplexes are in buildings with front, side, and backyards that must be maintained. These common areas require harmonious cooperation among occupants.

5. d   Economic conditions in the neighborhood will definitely affect the rental schedule.

6. a   The comparative analysis measures and records data such as size, location, amenities, and rental structures for buildings similar to the subject property. The relative market value of the space then can be set and base rental established for each type of apartment.

7. b   The manager will build mutually satisfactory landlord-tenant relationships by opening the lines of communication with tenants.

8. c   Curb appeal not only helps attract good tenants, it helps to maintain a positive attitude among current residents.

9. c   An occupancy rate of 100% for the one-bedroom and two-bedroom units could justify a rent increase, with the three-bedroom units then having a rent reduction of $10 each.

10. b   The manager uses this list to show specific apartments available for inspection by prospects.

11. b   The show list can be used as a control guide for the marketing program. If a traffic count of showings is kept in conjunction with this list, it will also serve as a source of feedback on its success or failure.

12. a   Because of its wide audience, newspaper classified advertising is the major vehicle for renting apartments.

13. d   The manager of a smaller property with little or no on-site staff should be versatile enough to make minor repairs.

14. c   Because many tenants do not take the time to carefully read the lease that they are signing, many managers will take the extra

time to highlight key clauses such as when, where, and how rent is to be paid.

15. d   Because the property manager is not usually in daily contact with each building, the resident manager should submit weekly reports on the condition of the property, the work performed, and jobs anticipated for the upcoming week.

16. c   The resident manager is responsible for the daily physical operation of the building, whereas the property manager oversees the general welfare of several buildings.

17. c   The resident manager is usually responsible for supervising all maintenance activities.

18. b   Leasing agents are experts in learning the prospect's basic needs and desires, and how to handle and overcome objections in order to rent the apartment.

19. d   The answer is deposits per child. The fair housing laws prohibit charging deposit fees based on the number of children who will occupy the dwelling.

20. a   Cash flow projections appear to be complex, but they deal only with previously used data to show the effect that the investment property has on the owner's income in terms of tax benefits.

■ CHAPTER 12   Specialized Housing

POSSIBLE RESPONSES TO CASE STUDY:
Managing a Condominium

1. Charging a percentage of monthly fees is typically seen in apartment renting. It is meant to encourage the manager to raise rents, convince tenants to pay the higher rate, and then share in the increased income. It is inappropriate in this situation inasmuch as the occupants own their units, and they want the monthly assessment as low as possible or at least visibly tied to maintenance and repairs. It is possible that the previous

company was increasing the monthly assessment simply to increase its own fees.

2. John should utilize a management pricing worksheet (Figure 9.2 is an example) to help determine the time it takes to manage the condominium association. He can base his fee on that outcome.

3. In the beginning, John will probably have to spend time at meetings with residents to hear complaints and to explain plans for changes. He should immediately look into the elderly woman's need for a handicapped parking space and provide that quickly. He can provide "maintenance request forms" so that all maintenance requests are in writing. He should walk the property to see any noticeable problems. That and hearing from the residents can help him develop a work plan. Finally, he will want to continue communication with the residents via a monthly newsletter keeping them informed about progress.

POSSIBLE RESPONSES TO CASE STUDY:
Managing Subsidized Housing

1. Kelleher can install a crime-stopper telephone line to solicit tips for special police units. Any tenants housing drug dealers or otherwise engaging in illegal drug activity can be evicted immediately. Kelleher can invite the police to attend special meetings with the tenants to improve tenant-police relationships, open communications, and build trust. Kelleher can make sure that physical repairs (such as broken windows or faulty security systems) are completed and outside lighting is installed or increased to discourage drug activity. Kelleher can provide special training to her staff to enable them to better detect drug activity and learn how to deal with it.

2. Kelleher can appoint a staff member to coordinate public and private social services, such as welfare, child care, and medical assistance. A food bank and clothing bank to serve needy tenants can be established. Kelleher can request local schools to report unexcused absences of

tenant children to her office, so she can help provide necessary counseling for the parents and children involved. She can set up volunteer tutoring centers and initiate scholarships and school attendance prizes. She can also arrange to have local parent-teacher conferences held at the project instead of on the school grounds to encourage parent participation.

Review Questions

1. a   The property manager of a cooperative or a condominium works for a group of owner-occupants and therefore has no responsibility for maintaining occupancy levels.

2. c   Managing a PUD is very similar to managing a condominium, in that the property manager is expected to see that the property is maintained while at the same time keeping fees as low as possible.

3. a   Condominium and cooperative management is concerned mainly with maintaining the integrity of the premises.

4. c   Condominium owners own their units in fee simple, and the financial failure of any one owner will not affect the others. On the other hand, a cooperative is owned by a corporation and is dependent on every lessee's paying his or her pro rata share.

5. b   Condominium owners finance their own units and real estate taxes are assessed on an individual basis.

6. a   A manager of a manufactured home community is unlikely to provide nursing services.

7. c   Creating and inspiring a community feeling is one of the best ways to foster referrals and waiting lists in a manufactured home park.

8. b   Laws in most states enable and regulate the formation and control of condominiums.

They define the property, common elements, easements, and type of ownership.

9. c   Managers of housing for the elderly must have a real affinity for the aging population and are called upon to facilitate social events, medical emergencies, provide most housekeeping, and provide meals as well as manage the traditional operating reports to owners.

10. b   The initial agreement for a new condominium is drawn up between the developer, acting on behalf of the owners, and the property manager. Not until the board of directors is elected does control pass from the developer into the hands of an owners' organization.

11. c   Condominium and cooperative managers must prepare an annual operating budget, monthly income and expenditure statements, and yearly cash flow reports, but these reports are modifications of the financial reports used by apartment managers due to the complex system of ownership and that the residents are also the owners.

12. d   The condominium owner must purchase a condominium policy, commonly called HO-6.

13. a   The board of directors or owners' association may allocate to each resident a prorated amount of the management fee, which should be a flat fee and not a percentage fee. This prorated amount is based on the occupant's share of ownership in the property.

14. c   Most large condominium and cooperative projects are advertised in newspapers and local magazines because that form of media publicity can be a cost-effective means of presenting the project to the buying public.

15. c   Fannie Mae prescribes standards that must be met before condominium mortgages may be sold on the secondary market. Fannie Mae regulations require, for example, that developers turn over a condominium

association to the owners as soon as a specific percentage of units have been sold and that reserve funds for major repairs be established.

16. a   Although public housing projects have traditionally been the responsibility of local governments, under the 1968 Housing and Urban Development Act, the FHA was authorized to encourage private participation in the development and construction of housing for low-income families.

17. c   Rapport between tenants and management can be improved by hiring a person with skills or training such as those demonstrated by a social worker to handle tenant relations. This individual can act as a conduit of information from the residents to the manager and can assist with programs involving tenant participation.

18. b   Under HUD Section 8, housing is rented on a subsidized basis, with the tenant paying up to 30 percent of his/her adjusted monthly income. Income eligibility for occupants varies according to geographic area and number of dependents in the family.

19. a   The system for rent collection in subsidized units should be as inflexible as in privately owned housing. If delinquencies are tolerated then mortgage and expense payments on the property could be delayed, in addition to rental rates eventually having to be raised to cover the delinquencies.

20. c   Managers who work as independent contractors for HUD usually are employed under a contract for a term of years and duties include taking over the property, preparing repair specifications, and submitting financial reports.

■ CHAPTER 13   Office Property

POSSIBLE RESPONSES TO CASE STUDY: The Office Property Manager

1. Reasons for a high vacancy rate can include the age of the building; improvements are in poor condition; poor location (inaccessibility, far from labor market, location has little prestige); poor environment; high rents; poor management; and inadequate maintenance.

2. First of all, Gonzalez should complete a thorough market analysis. This will give him information on economic trends in the region, the local supply and demand for office space, number of new businesses in the area, absorption rate in the area, rental rates of competing properties, and the vacancy rates for similar types of properties. Gonzalez must have this information before he can determine what the typical vacancy rate is for similar properties and what the demand is for the property. He could discover that the property's vacancy rate is typical for that type of property, which would mean that to decrease the vacancy rate, the owner would have to make substantial improvements. On the other hand, if the vacancy rate for Compton Place is unusually high for the type of property, Gonzalez can then determine the other factors that are causing the problem.

3. Gonzalez needs to institute a thorough marketing plan. It should include placing signs on the property that direct inquiries to Gonzalez. He can prepare attractive brochures, detailing the advantages of the building, to give to interested parties. Newspaper and trade publication ads can also be effective. Publicity is an excellent advertising tool that costs nothing yet can dramatically increase the prestige of a building and its management. Also, Gonzalez should not neglect current tenants for referrals, direct mail to local businesses, and canvassing growing businesses that may need new, expanded offices.

Review Questions

1. d Brochures, signs, and direct mail are useful when marketing office property. Classified ads are more useful when marketing residential property.

2. c An escalation clause protects the owner who has entered into a long-term lease by raising the rents to keep pace with the unavoidable annual increases in real estate taxes and operating expenses in addition to keeping up with anticipated increases in market rents.

3. a A facilities manager is an employee of a building occupant who is responsible for the internal arrangement and furnishing of the space leased by that employer-occupant, and in some cases, for maintenance of leased space.

4. b Canvassing is probably the best prospecting method for leasing office space and is more productive when the list of prospects has been qualified to some extent. Sources such as the Dun & Bradstreet directory and others published by the local chamber of commerce will furnish the manager with some names of firms that may be interested.

5. d When analyzing demand for office space, the property manager must determine the absorption rate, or the number of square feet that have historically been leased in the market area.

6. a A survey conducted by the Journal of Property Management found that, on the average, cost was the overriding concern for most respondents, followed by bus and highway accessibility, environment of the property, and labor market, in that order.

7. d Office space is often referred to as Class A, B, C, or D, based on unofficial guidelines published by the Building Owners and Managers Association International, and is determined by three major factors: age, location, and market position (rental rates).

8. a The base rate should be significantly higher than the minimum rate and should reflect the features of the property and its current value relative to similar buildings in the area.

9. b This is a Class B building: older, fully renovated to modern standards, prime location, high occupancy, competitive rates.

10. d The construction area is computed by measuring to the outside finished surface of permanent outer building walls and is sometimes called the New York method.

11. c The New York method is not popular in some areas, due to the difficulty of convincing prospective tenants that they should pay for stairwells and elevator shafts, space they cannot actually occupy.

12. a The ratio of rentable space to usable space is sometimes called the loss factor, a reflection of the efficiency of space utilization on a single-tenancy floor.

13. c Current economic trends are as significant as present market conditions when assessing the supply and demand for office space in an area.

14. d Multipersonnel areas are open or closed work spaces for more than one person, as opposed to single office spaces, which are meant to serve a single occupant.

15. c The usable area is the number of square feet that can actually be occupied. It excludes portions of the building normally associated with the core of the building, such as restrooms, janitor closets, and rooms containing equipment for the building.

16. a A tenant may assign the space freely unless the lease contains a provision requiring the landlord's written approval and sufficient notice for subletting or assignment.

17. d   Tenants requiring alterations or additions beyond those itemized on the building standard list must contract and pay for these services independently.

18. d   The building standard outlines the amenities and alterations that the landlord furnishes as part of the rent. Tenants (lessees) requiring alterations or additions beyond those itemized on the building standard list must contract and pay for these services independently.

19. c   A recapture provision gives the landlord the right to recover any space that the tenant is unable to occupy or sublease and gives the landlord maximum control of the length of tenants' leases and the economic terms of tenancy agreements.

20. c   Management is usually responsible for cleaning tenants' interior spaces. They must clean at night because the offices are used and occupied during the day.

■ CHAPTER 14   Retail Property

POSSIBLE RESPONSES TO CASE STUDY: The Retail Property Manager

1. Some possibilities include painting the structure, replacing the canopy with awnings, installing a mansard, and making all signage uniform.

2. Palmer can only renegotiate the leases to include escalation clauses as they expire. Escalation clauses are an important way to keep the rents in line with increases in expenses, and unless this can be done, the other problems (such as the need for repairs or renovations) might have to await resolution because the owner may not be able to afford the solutions.

3. The property manager should make sure each lease is rigorously enforced as to maintenance contributions. Also, he or she should examine the leases to see which revenue possibilities that are not included in the lease could be put

in place through the merchants' association (for example, renting sign space). Income due from tenants should be collected and audited if necessary to ensure proper rental payment. Also, promotional efforts by the merchants' association should be started (for example, putting together flyers to insert into local newspapers).

Review Questions

1. c   Before the advent of shopping centers, retail merchants tended to congregate in areas accessible to a large number of people, and the result was the establishment of a central urban district located at the focal point of public transportation facilities.

2. b   The neighborhood shopping center, approximately 100,000 square feet, is designed to provide for customers within a 1.5 mile radius, or 3 miles in diameter.

3. d   The stores in shopping centers are generally placed in dumbbell or double dumbbell patterns.

4. c   The community shopping center draws customers from a 5 mile radius, on about ten acres, and includes from 20–70 stores.

5. d   A restaurant will have the most demand for parking because there are more customers who stay longer.

6. d   A mixed-use development generally includes a combination of retail, office, and residential areas.

7. c   Most prospective tenants interested in retail space find it by driving around an area and looking for signs.

8. b   A sign on the vacancy is the most cost-effective advertising to attract prospective tenants to the premises.

9. b Personal contact solicitation is probably the most effective method of finding shopping center tenants, especially for small properties.

10. d Display ads are usually placed in the financial section of metropolitan papers to promote large retail properties.

11. d The mix of tenant types is a prevailing concern when leasing retail space in a shopping center because stores should be placed so that traffic generated by one benefits the others and so that competition is not a detriment.

12. b The International Council of Shopping Centers has compiled industry standards to show the percentage of total shopping center space typically allotted to each type of store.

13. b Adequacy of the parking facilities should be considered when evaluating a prospect's needs.

14. d The answer is $1,980. ($800 × .06) = [$480] $600; ($11,000 × .06) = $660 + ($12,000 × .06) = $720.

15. c The answer is $2,130. ($15,000 × .06) = $900 + ($15,000 × .05) = ($750 + $12,000) × .04 = $480.

16. c These overlapping obligations of the landlord, co-owners, and tenants are set forth in the basic documents establishing the center, primarily in the reciprocal easement agreement.

17. c The recapture clause in a shopping center lease is a right by the landlord to terminate a percentage lease if gross sales have not reached the level anticipated during negotiations and does not refer to assignment or subletting.

18. b In older centers, when a new tenant moves into a previously occupied space, negotiation of tenant improvement expenditures is complicated. It is difficult to differentiate between those improvements that accrue to the tenant's advantage only and those that correct deferred maintenance or increase the inherent value of the property itself.

19. a The *Standard* is published by the Urban Land Institute and provides retail property managers with a standardized system for reporting income and expense.

20. d The *Dollars & Cents of Shopping Centers* publishes the industry-wide compilation of financial reports on shopping centers from which a property manager can determine how well the shopping manager is doing compared to similar centers.

■ CHAPTER 15 Industrial Property

POSSIBLE RESPONSES TO CASE STUDY: The Industrial Property Manager

1. Because the tenant spaces are relatively small and there is no direct access to major transportation facilities, Yu should concentrate on prospecting for custom-service, market-oriented tenants, and tenants who are labor-intensive (who will appreciate the easy access to workers from the residential areas).

2. Yu needs to qualify tenants as to their space requirements (remember the five-acre to ten-acre limitation); parking needs (which are especially important for labor-intensive tenants); floor area requirements; financial capability; and environmental qualifications.

Review Questions

1. b Depending on their adaptability, industrial land and buildings can be classified as general purpose, special purpose, or single purpose.

2. a A warehouse that can be used for storage or adapted for light manufacturing or assembly plants is called a general-purpose building.

3. c   This property is functionally obsolete. Although it is physically intact and can be used for some purposes, the fact that the support pillars are so close together and that it is difficult to "hide" computer cables may induce prospective tenants to seek a building with a more modern design.

4. c   In a sale-leaseback arrangement, the corporation gets back its capital investment so that the funds can be reinvested in the business.

5. a   After signing a lease with a tenant, investors can finish a building in a short time, usually no more than 90 days. This system has been particularly successful in areas experiencing a rapid increase in population.

6. b   Storage space, or buildings that are general purpose, require less customization and have tenants who tend to relocate more frequently. As a result, the investment risk of such property is lower and the liquidity higher.

7. c   Brochures marketing industrial property include a picture of the premises, brief copy highlighting the property's special features, and an area map, and are sent to a select group of prospective firms.

8. d   Because of the nature of industrial property, it is essential that the manager match tenant and location by analyzing the market and qualifying prospective tenants.

9. a   The industrial property manager often has to show a building to a group, and invariably, members of the group will split up to explore their separate concerns.

10. c   An apartment and office is often provided for a resident manager of a ministorage facility, and the manager often needs to provide additional security in addition to marketing and showing space, leasing, maintaining the grounds, maintaining tenant relations, and monitoring the usage to which the space is put.

11. c   A labor-intensive industry, using highly skilled personnel, will have a higher concentration of employees per acre than a labor-extensive industry.

12. a   Levying a special tax on a new business would discourage an industry from moving to an area. Special tax incentives, private industry councils, and industrial revenue bonds are all designed to encourage an industry to locate to a given locale.

13. b   The answer is 33 percent. 200,000 sq. ft. (plant site) ÷ 600,000 sq. ft. (land site) = 33 percent structural density.

14. a   The answer is 4,500 sq. ft. Area = 90′ (length) × 50′ (width)= 4,500 sq. ft.

15. d   A lease for an industrial tenant is most often a triple net lease under which the tenant pays the taxes, assessments, insurance, and maintenance in addition to the rent. The gross lease puts most of the expense on the landlord and is generally used for residential leasing. Percentage leases are used in retail and the tenant would not make a mortgage payment for the landowner!

16. c   The annual rental rate for an industrial property is usually based on the owner's rent factor, which is calculated using the percentage of gross return the owner wants to earn on the investment.

17. b   The answer is $4.04. $370,500 × .12 (desired annual return) = $44,460 ÷ 11,000 sq. ft. building = $4.04 per sq. ft.

18. b   As a negotiating point, the tenant's willingness to sign a longer lease might encourage the landlord to lower the rent factor.

19. c   The steps involved in the upkeep of industrial property are basically the same as those for residential, office, or commercial property. However, because tenants assume some

or all of the maintenance of their interior spaces, industrial property managers generally only need to maintain the grounds and building exterior.

20. d   Ministorage units fulfill a latent need within the real estate market by providing space for homeowners to store surplus possessions and businesses a place for old records that would otherwise occupy more expensive office space.

■ CHAPTER 16 Risk and Environmental Issues

POSSIBLE RESPONSES TO CASE STUDY: The Risk Manager

1. There are several things Rockford can do to limit his liability for the acts of third parties. First, Rockford can make sure that any service contracts are signed by Stern, the property owner. Rockford can try to include a clause in the management contract stating that Rockford is only responsible for administering third-party contracts and is not responsible for any negligent acts committed by third parties. He can also include an indemnity clause in the contract, stating that the property owner will indemnify for any damage caused by anything other than Rockford's negligence or willful misconduct.

2. Like most property owners, Stern is likely to protest the inclusion of the indemnity clause discussed above. However, Rockford can point out that he, Rockford, will be responsible for his own negligence or willful misconduct. In fact, a parallel indemnity clause spelling this out can also be included. To limit his liability, Rockford can try to limit his exposure to a certain dollar figure. In any event, Rockford should obtain errors and omissions insurance to cover the risk of loss in this area.

3. It is imperative that Rockford be familiar with all the various types of insurance that both he

and Stern should have, including fire; machinery and equipment; consequential loss, use, and occupancy; commercial general liability; automobile; employer liability; worker's compensation; fidelity bond; and errors and omissions insurance. There are also other things Rockford can do to reduce risks, such as inspect both his own office and Hartford Business Park for dangerous conditions and, once found, repair or eliminate them.

Review Questions

1. b   Installing fire sprinklers is an excellent risk controlling example. No one wants a fire, but having the sprinklers installed will put it out faster, thus reducing the overall damage.

2. d   One effective way to avoid risk is to avoid managing properties on which there are hazardous substances.

3. d   The indemnity clause in the management contract can require the property owner to "protect" the manager from any damages not caused by the manager's own negligence or willful misconduct.

4. b   A higher deductible on an insurance premium means the property manager is retaining part of the risk, which should reduce the premium amount.

5. a   The premium for a building with 50 percent coverage ($100,000) under a "straight" insurance plan will be about the same as the premium for a policy with an 80 percent coinsurance clause ($160,000).

6. d   General liability insurance covers the legal responsibility for damage to real and personal property of others and for those injured on the premises. Workers' compensation insurance covers employer's liability for injury to workers.

7. b   Ordinarily, there is no extra premium charge to the owner for adding the manager as additional insured, and this added coverage protects the property manager in addition to the manager's own insurance.

8. c   Radon mitigation consists of sealing the property and then installing fans to take the air out of the property to the outdoors.

9. b   The best method for dealing with mold is to prevent it in the first place by decreasing humidity. The manager should not wait for a "problem" and then depend on the insurance company.

10. a   The National Environmental Policy Act (NEPA), which went into effect in 1970, requires the preparation of an environmental impact statement (EIS) in advance for every major federal action that would significantly affect the quality of the environment.

11. a   In order to survive and thrive, mold requires a food source and moisture. As it lacks chlorophyll, it does not require sunshine.

12. b   CERCLA is commonly referred to as the Superfund law, so named because of the two trust funds created to help finance cleanup projects and payment of property damage claims.

13. b   Carbon monoxide is a by-product of incorrectly burning fossil fuels and one of the reasons that all heaters must be properly vented.

14. b   If 10 percent of a tank is below grade, it is considered "underground."

15. c   The Environmental Protection Agency (EPA) has recognized that the least hazardous way to deal with asbestos that is in place in a building is to manage the asbestos by either sealing it (encapsulation) or by enclosing it.

16. d   The standard insurance policy will not insure damages as a result of flooding. Flood insurance must always be purchased separately.

17. a   Only an EPA certified techician, who has passed the EPA-approved exam, should do any work on a refrigeration system, since they know how to remove CFCs without releasing them into the atmosphere.

18. c   Polychlorinated biphenyls (PCBs) do not break down in the environment and may be leaking from a landfill.

19. b   Federal law requires that lead-based paint disclosure records must be maintained for three years.

20. c   The landlord cannot buy renter's insurance since the landlord does not have an insurable interest in the renter's property.

■ CHAPTER 17   Life Safety Issues

POSSIBLE RESPONSES TO CASE STUDY: The Life Safety Manager

1. It appears that Kim should hire a security firm. Kim should screen the firms she is interested in carefully; she should check their references and their hiring policies and learn about their training and supervision policies. Kim must be aware that if an employee of the security firm is negligent in his or her duties, or actually harms a tenant, Kim and the property owner may be liable. Of course, Kim should also make sure that the rates of the firm selected are competitive and that the equipment they use is up-to-date.

2. Kim can examine the premises to determine if any improvements can be made to discourage crime. For example, increasing the lighting in the parking lot and making sure that landscaping does not offer a place for a mugger to hide would help improve the safety of the parking lot. Kim could also start a community watch among the tenants. Getting the tenants involved would

make everyone more aware of the problem, and thus more careful; provide more eyes for policing; and increase the effectiveness in responding to a crime should another one occur. Kim should also make sure that her life security facilities use current technology to improve deterrence, detection, and response time.

3. Kim should include procedures to follow in the case of any major type of emergency, including illness, accident, tornado, hurricane, earthquake, fire, bomb threat, and, of course, flooding. Because her tenants are especially concerned about flooding, she may want to call a special meeting just to discuss what to do in the event of flooding. Getting in touch with each tenant individually, discussing individual concerns, and getting each tenant to appoint a special contact person would also help alleviate her tenants' fears. Kim may want to send each tenant information on flood insurance as well.

Review Questions

1. b   A life safety and security program must be tailored to the tenant's needs, whether the property is commercial, industrial, or residential, and is a three-pronged approach that incorporates skilled used of equipment, personnel, and procedures.

2. a   A program to deal with emergencies threatening life and property is based on four goals, the first and most important of which is prevention. Detection, confinement, and damage control are the other three goals.

3. d   A response system installed in a building cannot control tenant-installed furnishings. These systems can discover and report a fire and vent the smoke out of the building. Tenants need to be encouraged to avoid certain products which can be hazardous.

4. d   Outside the building, pedestrian and auto traffic should be the responsibility of the police department. The personnel of the property management staff, including the property manager, the LSO, and the chief of security, should be assigned specific duties regarding emergencies at the location itself.

5. c   Neither the landlord nor tenant should use any form of plastics for furnishings or finishing materials, as they produce toxic gases that are hazardous to all tenants. Noncombustible and fire-retardant materials are safer.

6. d   New and improved equipment is constantly coming on the market and concerned property managers will expand their knowledge of life safety and security technology by consulting with experts to ensure that all elements are carefully coordinated into an effective integrated system.

7. a   The property manager should cooperate fully with media but retain the authority and control necessary to deal with an emergency. Admissions of liability or speculations about the cause of an accident should be avoided. Every available means of communication should be used to present factual information that will offset rumors.

8. c   In the event of a major emergency such as fire, explosion, or natural disaster, the first priority is always the safety and protection of human life. An authorized spokesperson should be designated in advance to represent management on the scene and provide factual information.

9. d   Structural, plumbing, and electrical systems should all have preventive maintenance inspection programs to identify problems before they become hazardous.

10. b   Emergency preparedness procedures should include evacuation plans and periodic training sessions should be held to test emergency responses.

11. c   The property manager should prepare a written statement that can be used as a guideline so that all points will be covered by an appointed spokesperson when communicating with tenants or the media in times of emergency.

12. b   The design concept of present-day emergency equipment is to discover and report a fire or other emergency before it further threatens life and property.

13. a   One of the most effective methods of combating illegal drug activity is to involve the tenants in organizing community watch programs.

14. b   Hurricanes are spotted and tracked several days before they hit the mainland, leaving time for managers to prepare for the onslaught of wind and rain. Tornadoes, earthquakes, and bomb threats generally provide little or no time for preparedness.

15. d   Elevators cannot be used in an emergency. The shafts create a chimney effect allowing updrafts of dangerous materials.

16. a   Elevators can be deadly during a fire because the shafts create a chimney effect allowing updrafts of dangerous materials.

17. c   Most insurance companies will not cover damages that could have been prevented if proper steps to secure the damage had been taken immediately after the disaster.

18. a   The property manager should cultivate a relationship with reconstruction companies before an emergency as they will be in high demand later. Any relationship might assist in getting work done sooner.

19. d   All managers of ALL types of property should develop disaster preparedness plans.

20. d   One of the aftershocks of disaster is that consumers often form new shopping patterns and may not return to the stores they once frequented.

GLOSSARY

absorption rate When analyzing demand for office space, the total number of vacant square feet of office space in the market area divided by the square footage historically leased per year. For example, for 750,000 square feet leased per year divided by 3 million square feet of available vacant office space in a city, the absorption rate is 4.

Accelerated Cost Recovery System (ACRS) A mandatory method of calculating depreciation for tax purposes passed into law in 1981 and revised in 1986.

actual damages In the event of a breach of contract, the award of money to compensate for the actual loss caused by the failure of the non-breaching party. Unpaid rent or a bill for a hole in the wall could be considered actual damages. The Uniform Landlord Tenant Law generally requires that the landlord document actual damages when deducting from the security deposit.

actual eviction Forcible removal of a tenant from a property by an officer of the court after a judgment decree of possession has been issued in favor of the owner.

advertising Purchased space in a newspaper, magazine, or other medium used to attract public attention to a commodity for sale or lease.

agent An individual who is legally empowered to act on behalf of another.

Americans with Disabilities Act (ADA) A law that requires that property that is open to the public include features that facilitate access to the building. The ADA is designed to eliminate discrimination against individuals with disabilities by providing equal access to jobs, public accommodations, government services, public transportation, and telecommunications.

anchor store, anchor tenants Major department store in a shopping center. Also called *key tenant*. This tenant is important as it is meant to draw in many customers who may also shop at the smaller stores.

antitrust laws Laws designed to preserve free enterprise of the open marketplace by making illegal certain private conspiracies and combinations formed to minimize competition. Most violations of antitrust laws in the real estate business involve either *price-fixing* (brokers or managers agreeing to set fixed compensation rates) or *allocation of customers or services* (brokers or managers agreeing to limit their areas of trade or dealing to certain areas or properties).

asbestos A mineral fiber, classified as a carcinogen. Found in asbestos containing materials (ACMs), it is often found in older properties where it was used in insulation, shingles, siding, concrete, floor and ceiling tiles, plasters, and more.

assessment (1) A monthly fee paid by cooperative and condominium members to cover maintenance costs for the property. (2) A special real estate tax levied by the government to finance improvements in the area.

asset management services The assembly, management, and disposition of a portfolio of investment properties.

assignment Transfer of a tenant's remaining rental rights in a property to a third party. The tenant can transfer rights but not responsibilities unless agreed to by the landlord.

base rate Rent, per square foot for typical space in building. It is higher than the minimum rate and reflects features of property and its current value relative to similar buildings in the area.

blight correction Rehabilitation of residential properties that have deteriorated significantly.

blockbusting The illegal practice of inducing homeowners to sell or apartment dwellers to move out by making representations regarding the entry or prospective entry of persons of a particular race or national origin into the neighborhood. Sometimes referred to as *panic selling*.

bond coverage Insurance protecting individuals or firms against default in the performance of their duties.

break-even point Occupancy level at which gross income for a property equals the total fixed and variable operating costs.

broker cooperation Working with outside licensed real estate brokers who have prospective tenants. In many states, it is legal to pay a referral fee or to split a commission.

building-employment density An estimate of the spatial requirements of a prospective tenant based on number of employees.

building-related illness (BRI) A clinically diagnosed condition that is caused by toxic substances or pathogens that persists when an occupant leaves the building. Symptoms include hypersensitivity, pneumonitis, asthma, and certain allergic reactions.

building standard The specific set of amenities and alterations a landlord is willing to make free of charge for an incoming commercial tenant.

bulk purchasing A method of cutting operating costs for a property in which supplies are purchased in large quantities and stored for later use. Also called *volume buying*.

business cycle A wavelike movement of increasing and decreasing economic prosperity consisting of four phases: expansion, recession, contraction, and revival.

business park A development or subdivision allocated to office-warehouse or similar use. Also known as an *office park*. An outgrowth of industrial parks.

cancellation option A lease clause granting the tenant the option to cancel at the end of a predetermined term.

capital improvement A cash expense to the property that increases the value of the property, including tenant alterations, or extends the life of a building component.

capitalization rate A method of relating a property's value, its net annual income, and rate of return on the owner's investment, computed as follows:

$$\text{Capitalization rate} = \frac{\text{Income}}{\text{Value}} \times 100\%$$

carbon monoxide (CO) An air pollutant that is a colorless, odorless, poisonous gas that is a byproduct of incomplete combustion of burning fossil fuels such as gasoline, kerosene, wood, and oil.

cash flow An item in a property's financial operating reports that represents the net operating income minus all additional disbursements such as debt service and capital improvements.

cash flow report A financial report showing the property's net operating income minus all additional disbursements such as debt service and capital improvements and the amount remitted to the owner.

chlorofluorocarbons (CFC) A family of inert, nontoxic, nonflammable chemicals used in the manufacture of aerosol sprays, blowing agents for foams and packing materials, as solvents, and as refrigerants. They are extremely injurious to the stratospheric atmosphere and their use and disposal is highly regulated.

Civil Rights Act of 1866 A federal law that guarantees that citizens of all races have the same rights as white citizens to inherit, purchase, lease, sell, hold, and convey real and personal property. Reaffirmed by the *Jones v. Mayer* decision in 1968.

Civil Rights Act of 1968 Federal law, Title VIII, often called Fair Housing law, prohibits discrimination in the sale, rental, or financing of housing based on race, color, religion, national origin, familial status, and handicap.

classified ads Inexpensive line ads, most widely used when advertising residential property.

closing techniques The process by which the manager guides the prospect to accepting the space and signing the lease. The best leasing agents use a variety of techniques to "close" a prospect.

Code of Ethics A set of guidelines on good business conduct, which often requires the agent to act beyond the letter of the law.

coinsurance clause A common provision in property insurance policies that limits the liability of the insurance company to that proportion of the loss that the amount of insurance bears to a percentage of the value of the property.

collectible income Gross income from a property minus vacancy and other types of rent loss. Also called *gross adjusted income*.

commercial property Income-producing properties; public accommodations.

common elements Parts of a property that are necessary or convenient to the existence, maintenance, and safety of a condominium or are normally in common use by all of the condominium residents. Each condominium owner has an undivided ownership interest in the common elements.

community center, community shopping center A shopping center of about 100,000 to 250,000 square feet (20 to 70 retail spaces) providing convenience shopping to about 5,000 families within a 1.5-mile radius.

comparables Properties used in the market analysis that are substantially similar to the subject building or apartments.

comparative income and expense analysis A financial study of the projected income from a property in as-is condition versus financial returns from that property if suggested capital improvements were implemented. Property managers use the analysis to demonstrate to owners the return on proposed capital expenditures.

competitive bids Work estimates submitted to the property manager by service contractors, suppliers, tradespeople, or construction contractors.

Comprehensive Environmental Response Compensation and Liability Act (CERCLA) A 1980 federal law created to impose liability on people or organizations responsible for environmental damage and to facilitate financing of asbestos cleanup projects and property damage claims.

concession A negotiable point in a lease, often requiring the landlord to give up something in the prospective tenant's favor.

concierge services A trend in the property management field that provides personal, secretarial, catering, or other services to the occupants of office or residential buildings.

conciliation agreement Successful result of mediation between the parties in a discrimination complaint.

condominium A form of property ownership in which each occupant of a multiunit building owns his or her dwelling unit separately and an undivided interest with other owners in the property's common elements (lobbies, hallways, etc.).

conservation Minor repair, renovation, and restoration of residential buildings that have substantial economic use remaining. Also called *blight prevention*.

constructive eviction A situation in which a tenant must abandon the premises because of the landlord's negligence in providing essential services.

contraction A phase of the business cycle characterized by decreasing production.

contract services Maintenance tasks performed by outside laborers on a regular basis for a specified fee.

cooperative A residential multifamily building whose title is held by a trust or corporation that is owned by and operated for the benefit of persons living within the building, who are the beneficial owners of the trust or stockholders of the corporation, each possessing a proprietary lease that gives them the right to occupy a certain unit in the building.

corporate cooperative Cooperative in which legal ownership of a building is held by a corporation created for that purpose.

corrective maintenance Actual repairs necessary to keep a property in good condition and operating smoothly.

corridor development Growth of businesses or plants along major arteries connecting two large industrial or commercial centers some distance from each other.

cost-plus A method of paying construction contractors in which the contractor furnishes a preliminary estimate for the proposed job and is paid the actual cost of the work plus a percentage for profit.

covenants, conditions, and restrictions declaration (CC&Rs) A set of private restrictions on the use of a specific parcel of real property; often used with a condominium development.

credit rating Numeric financial rating of commercial or industrial companies utilized internationally by Dun & Bradstreet. Composite credit ratings and estimated financial strength range from a high of 5A/1 to a low of HH/4.

credit report A report issued by a service bureau detailing an individual's past and current accounts and history of making payments. Each account is numbered from a high of 1 to a low of 9.

curb appeal The impression gained, good or poor, of a property when it is first seen, usually from the street while driving, hence "curb" appeal.

cyclical fluctuation *See* business cycle.

declining balance depreciation A method of computing accelerated depreciation that adjusts the straight-line depreciation rate according to a percentage factor.

default Nonperformance of a duty; failure to meet an obligation when due.

deferred maintenance Physical depreciation or loss in value of a building resulting from postponed maintenance to the building.

depreciation Loss of value due to physical deterioration, functional obsolescence, or economic obsolescence; to an appraiser, loss in value from any cause.

direct management costs (direct costs) Expenses that can be attributed directly to the operation of a management firm or department.

disability Any physical or mental impairment that substantially limits one or more of an individual's major life activities, including caring for oneself, performing manual tasks, walking, seeing, hearing, speaking, and working.

discount department store A specialized type of shopping center or large single store with emphasis on lower prices as a merchandising technique. The "closed door" discount house is open only to qualifying members; the "open" discount house is open to the general public.

display ads Newspaper ads that cost more than classified ads offering graphics and more elaborate designs. Display ads may be a quarter-page or more in size and are used to market all types of real estate.

dispossess proceedings A suit brought by a landlord to evict a tenant for defaulting on the terms of the lease. Also known as *unlawful detainer actions* or *dispossess proceedings*.

Dun & Bradstreet A credit reporting agency that publishes credit ratings for many corporations and businesses.

duplex Two-apartment building.

economic oversupply A market condition in which available rental space is priced beyond the financial capabilities of potential tenants.

80 percent coinsurance Insured promises insurance company that above-ground property is insured to 80 percent of its full physical replacement cost or actual value.

employee A worker whose work is directed and controlled by the person for whom he or she works. The employer controls when, where, and how the work is done as well as defining the desired end result of the work. Usually the employer withholds taxes and pays a portion of the employee's contribution into the Social Security retirement fund.

employer The individual or company who pays people to work for them. State laws determine the minimum number of persons hired, total amount of wages paid, and working conditions that must exist to classify as an employer.

Enterprise Income Verification system (EIV) A HUD data base of information gathered from TRACS, the Social Security Administration and the Heath and Human Services New Hire database to ensure that residents are making a full and adequate disclosure of household income to landlords to reduce waste and fraud of HUD funding.

environmental assessments An investigation of a property to determine if there are any environmental hazards or concerns that could affect the use of the property or impose future financial liability. Preliminary research should be done prior to purchase in order to protect the seller, buyer, lender and property managers.

Environmental Impact Statement (EIS) Analysis of impact on environment of proposed action. Required for every major federal action that would significantly impact quality of environment.

Environmental Protection Agency (EPA) A federal organization created by the National Environmental Policy Act. The EPA's purpose is to centralize government's environmental responsibilities.

Equal Credit Opportunity Act (ECOA) The federal law passed to protect borrowers when applying for a loan. The lender (or property manager) can deny a borrower credit based only on reasonable business reasons, not because of the borrower's race, color, religion, national origin, sex, receipt of public assistance, age, or marital status.

equal housing logo A picture of a house containing an equal sign. This logo should be included in all display ads, brochures, and other forms of advertising indicating to the public that the landlord/manager will not discriminate against individuals based on their race, color, religion, national origin, sex, familial status, or handicap.

equity An owner's interest in a property over and above any liens or financial encumbrances against it.

errors and omissions insurance A type of coverage that protects property managers and real estate brokers from loss due to errors, mistakes, and negligence.

escalation clause A lease clause providing that the rental rate will increase or decrease according to a selected index of economic conditions, such as the consumer price index.

estate for years A leasehold estate that continues for a specified period of time. It is not ordinarily terminated by death of either party or by the sale of the property.

estate from period to period A leasehold estate that is automatically renewed for successive periods of time until either party gives notice to the other.

ethics A system or code of professional behavior.

evacuation drills Practice of testing the building emergency organization, equipment, and tenant indoctrination.

eviction notice A landlord's legal notice to a tenant explaining the tenant's default under the terms of the lease and informing him or her of a pending eviction suit.

eviction suit Legal process by which landlord can recover possession of the property; precise procedures are state-specific.

expansion A phase of the business cycle characterized by increasing production.

expansion option A lease clause granting a tenant the option to lease additional adjacent space after a specified period of time.

facilities manager Commercial property specialist who is responsible for managing a team of other specialists, for furnishing and maintaining leased space.

Fair Credit Reporting Act (FCRA) The Act regulates the action of credit bureaus and the use of consumer credit information.

Fair Housing Act (Title VIII of the Civil Rights Act of 1968) A federal law that prohibits discrimination in the sale, rental, or financing of housing based on race, color, religion, national origin, sex, familial status, and handicap.

familial status A class of people protected by the Federal Fair Housing Act, which is defined as the presence of at least one individual in the family who is younger than 18 or the presence of a pregnant woman.

fast-track construction A method under which construction of a building begins under a negotiated contract before all plans and specifications have become final. Construction proceeds as plans come off the drawing board.

feasibility study A report on the potential profitability of a proposed real estate project. It includes considerations such as land area, physical features of the land, requirements of the project, and estimated cost.

Federal Housing Administration (FHA) An agency of the U.S. Department of Housing and Urban Development authorized to provide rental and mortgage insurance and subsidies to developers of low-income housing.

Federal Insurance Contributions Act (FICA) A federal regulation requiring employers to pay retirement fund taxes (Social Security) for employees.

Federal Unemployment Tax Act (FUTA) A regulation requiring employers to file federal unemployment tax returns for employees.

fiduciary The relationship between an agent and his or her principal, which requires the utmost loyalty and good faith.

fiduciary duties The duties of an agent to the principal to maintain the greatest trust and confidence generally including care, obedience of lawful instructions, accountability, loyalty, and disclosure of material facts.

five-year forecast A long-term projection of estimated income and expense for a property based on predictable changes.

fixed expense An expense item in a property's operating budget that does not fluctuate with rental income.

fixed-fee bids Also called *flat-fee bids*, the contractor estimates his/her costs including profit and submits one fee to do the job. Most construction contracts are negotiated on this type of fee.

flame spread Possible rate and spread of fire throughout a building once a fire has started; can be slowed by products that are low flame spreading.

flat (or fixed) fee A property management fee expressed as a dollar amount per year or per month.

flea market A large building or open area in which space is sold to individuals for the sale of merchandise, usually used or of a collectible nature.

flood insurance Insurance that compensates for physical property damage resulting from flooding. Rising water damage usually is not covered by other insurance, and generally must be purchased separately.

foreign trade zone (FTZ) An area designated under federal law that permits manufacture, shipping, or storage of goods duty-free.

formaldehyde A colorless, organic chemical with a strong pronounced odor. One of the indoor air pollutants that contributes to sick building syndrome.

gross collectable rental income Income determined by multiplying available space by the base rental rate, and then subtracting the percentage of probable loss resulting from vacancies, tenant defaults, and turnover.

gross floor area A method of measuring industrial space in which area is the total of all floor space within the exterior walls of the building, with no allowance made for structural projections and with a required minimum ceiling height of 7.5 feet.

gross lease A common residential lease under which the tenant pays a fixed rental and the landlord pays all operating expenses for the property.

gross sales The total sales made by a retail tenant at a leased premises. A proportion of gross sales is charged as rental consideration under a percentage lease.

ground lease A type of net lease, usually used with industrial real estate, under which the owner of a tract of land leases the property to a tenant who constructs his or her own building on the site. Also called a *land lease*.

handicap A handicap is a physical or mental impairment; an impairment that substantially limits one or more of an individual's major life activities. Persons who have AIDS are protected by the fair housing laws under this classification, as are those participating in addiction recovery programs, but current users of illegal drugs are not. For example, a landlord may lawfully discriminate against a cocaine user, but not against a member of Alcoholics Anonymous.

hardware The physical parts of the computer that can be seen and touched, including the keyboard, printer, and display screen, or terminal.

hazard communication standard plan An OSHA-mandated plan to be compiled by property managers detailing protective measures to be implemented when handling hazardous chemicals. See *Occupational Safety and Health Administration (OSHA)*.

hazardous substance Any material designated by the EPA to be a threat to human health and/or the environment, often including products that are ignitable, corrosive, toxic, or explosive.

hazardous wastes Solid wastes that have been listed by the EPA and are ignitable, corrosive, toxic, or reactive.

income and expense report A financial report showing the property's net operating income subtracting depreciation and interest expense and adding back any capital improvement expenses.

incubator space A building located in an industrial park and divided into small units of varying sizes to accommodate young, growing companies that want to combine office and industrial space at one location.

independent contractor Workers who control when, where, and how they perform their own jobs and who are responsible for paying their taxes into the Social Security system.

index lease A lease containing an escalation clause that is tied to an index.

indirect management costs (indirect costs) Expenses in the budget of a real estate agency or parent company that are partially attributable to the operation of the management department.

industrial park A suburban industrial subdivision designed to offer comparatively small firms land in outlying areas with good accessibility to transportation; now often called a *business park*.

industrial property The type of property that converts raw materials into finished products for storage and distribution of goods.

infrastructure The man-made physical features of an urban area, such as roads, highways, sewage and drainage systems, and utility facilities necessary to support a concentration of population.

institutional property Office buildings owned and occupied by the same corporation.

insurable interest Insurance term for the economic interest suffered in the event of a loss, usually an ownership interest.

intrusion alarms Sounds or notice made if someone enters the property.

key tenant A major department store in a shopping center. Also called *anchor store*.

labor-extensive industry A business with a low concentration of employees per acre.

labor-intensive industry A business with a high concentration of employees per acre.

labor-oriented industry A business that tends to locate near a low-cost labor pool.

land-employment densities In industrial properties, expressed as a ratio of the number of principal shift employees to total land area. Those that process raw materials often require fewer employees, while electronics firms and others utilizing highly skilled workers will have a higher ratio. This impacts on parking needs, for example.

Lead-based Paint Hazard Reduction Act (LBPHRA) The federal act that seeks to control exposure to lead-based paint hazards, specifically mentioning protecting children younger than six. It requires that landlords of properties built before 1978 make certain disclosures before entering into a lease.

lease A written or oral contract between a landlord (lessor) and a tenant (lessee) that transfers the right to exclusive possession and use of the landlord's real property to the lessee for a specified period of time and for a stated consideration (rent). Most state laws require that leases over more than a certain amount of time must be in writing to be enforceable.

lease assumption A concession whereby a property owner agrees to take over the balance of payments on a prospective tenant's current lease if he or she rents space in the owner's property.

leasehold estate A tenant's right to occupy real estate for a specified period of time in exchange for some form of compensation.

lease renewals After the lease expires, signing a new lease with the existing tenant. Topics up for renegotiation may include a new rental rate, repairs or alterations, expansion, or contraction of space.

leasing agent Salespeople who are skilled in communications and telephone techniques, on-site customer qualifying, merchandising themselves and their properties, and closing techniques.

liability insurance Insurance protecting a property owner or manager in case of damage to the person or property of another due to the owner's or manager's negligence.

life safety and security A trend in property management that provides for the management of the total physical protection of tenants. A typical life safety and security program consists of prevention, detection, containment, and counteraction.

life safety control center A security center found most often in large complexes, responsible for handling various emergencies impacting complex workers. See *life safety* and *security*.

life safety control center operator Person, in the event of an emergency, who is responsible for notifying the fire department and building personnel, and for providing communication.

life safety officer (LSO) In the event of an emergency, the person who is responsible for assisting tenant evacuation and enforcing safety precautions.

load factor The ratio of rentable space to usable space on a multiple-tenancy floor of an office building.

local access network (LAN) A method of linking together personal computers within the same office to allow communication between the computers.

loft A low-rent, multistory building located in the central business district, originally used for a combination of manufacturing, office, and storage space.

loss factor The ratio of rentable space to usable space on a single-tenancy floor of an office building.

maintenance request A request from the tenant for repairs. A key to tenant satisfaction, it should be in writing, and the tenant should be told when the repair will be made or why it will not be.

management contract The contract between an income property owner (principal) and a management firm or individual property manager (agent) that outlines the scope of the manager's authority, owner's responsibilities, and compensation.

management plan The financial and operational strategy for the ongoing management of a property. It is based on market analyses, a property analysis, and the owner's goals and consists of an operating budget, a five-year forecast, and sometimes a comparative income and expense analysis.

management pricing worksheet A method of computing management fees by itemizing management activities, calculating the direct cost to the firm, and adding a percentage for profit. This method is most appropriate when managing condominium communities.

manufactured home park A popular, expanding form of residential living consisting of permanently or semipermanently situated manufactured homes. The ground only, the home, or both may be rented from the owner.

market analysis Regional and neighborhood study of economic, demographic, and other information made by the property manager to determine supply and demand, market trends, and other factors important in leasing and operating a specific property.

market-oriented industry A business that tends to locate near industrial users and consumers of its products.

maximum percentage lease A type of percentage lease that sets a ceiling on the amount of rent to be paid.

mechanic's lien (mechanics' liens) A statutory lien created in favor of contractors, laborers, and materialmen who have performed work or furnished materials in the erection or repair of the building.

Megan's law Federal and state laws requiring that certain sex offenders register with local law enforcement agencies.

merchants' association An organization of shopping center tenants intended to facilitate joint advertising, promotion, and other activities beneficial to the center as a whole.

minimum-guaranteed percentage lease A type of percentage lease that requires the tenant to pay either a fixed minimum rental or a percentage of gross sales, whichever is greater.

ministorage (center) Small, secure storage units rented to individuals and small businesses.

mixed-use development (MXD) A development in the use of property combining retail, office-residential, or industrial-office residential development.

mold, molds Simple, microscopic living organisms that exist both indoors and outdoors requiring a food source and moisture to thrive. An indoor air quality issue because they produce airborne spores that may be toxic or cause allergic reactions and respiratory symptoms in some people.

National Environmental Policy Act (NEPA) A federal act passed in 1970 that requires the processing of environmental impact disclosures for major federal action affecting the environment.

negotiated contract A joint proposal of costs based on collaboration among the plumbing, electrical, hardware supplier, and other tradespeople which often leads to a lower price than if the manager solicited bids individually from each contractor.

neighborhood analysis A part of formulating the management plan; an assessment of five factors in the neighborhood market area of the subject rental property—boundaries and land usage, transportation and utilities, economy, supply and demand, and neighborhood amenities and facilities.

neighborhood center, neighborhood shopping center A shopping center of about 30,000 to 100,000 square feet (15 to 20 retail spaces) on about 3 acres. Often anchored by a supermarket and small stores that serve about 1,000 families.

net lease A common industrial lease form requiring the tenant to pay rent plus certain costs incurred in the operation of the property. Generally, straight net leases require the tenant to pay rent, utilities, real estate taxes, and assessments. Net-net leases require the tenant to pay rent,

utilities, real estate taxes, assessments, and insurance premiums. Net-net-net or triple-net leases may require the tenant to pay all of the above expenses plus agreed-on items of maintenance and repair.

net operating income Gross collectible income from a property minus all fixed and variable operating expenses.

noncompeting tenant restriction A lease clause granting a retail tenant an exclusive right to operate without competition on the property.

nonrecurring variable expense A type of variable property expense (e.g., capital improvements) that occurs only once.

Occupational Safety and Health Administration (OSHA) A federal organization empowered to prescribe and legislate the use of potentially toxic chemicals and compounds, and other safety rules for the workplace.

office park See *business park*.

office property A type of income-producing commercial property from which a particular service is rendered.

off-price center A specialized type of shopping center recognized by the Urban Land Institute; a variation of the discount department store concept.

on-site job program Employment of tenants occupying low-cost residential buildings to perform maintenance work in these buildings.

operating budget A projection of income and expense for the operation of a property over a one-year period.

operating costs A calculation of yearly costs of operation based on operating expenses from comparable properties and the maintenance needs of the subject property; used in preparing an annual operating budget.

optimum rents The ideal rent for a specific type of unit in a defined market area that may need to be adjusted to reflect specific advantages and disadvantages of the subject property.

option to renew A lease provision giving the tenant the right to extend the lease for an additional period of time on specified terms.

overage A percentage of gross sales over a certain amount paid to an owner in addition to a minimum base rent; often required in percentage leases.

partial eviction A situation in which the landlord's negligence renders all or part of the premises unusable to the tenant for the purposes intended in the lease.

participation certificate Proof of membership in a trust cooperative granted in a particular amount, usually with the right to occupy a unit in property owned by the trust.

percentage fee A property management fee expressed as a percentage of the gross collectible income from a property.

percentage lease A common retail lease requiring the tenant to pay a percentage of its gross income as rental consideration.

periodic costs A type of fixed property expense (e.g., property taxes) that occurs on a regular but infrequent basis.

per-unit-cost method A method of computing management fees based on the management firm's capabilities and the direct cost of managing a specific number of units.

Planned Unit Development (PUD) A planning concept in the development of property, principally employed in housing development to produce a high density of dwellings and maximum utilization of open spaces.

polychlorinated biphenyls (PCBs) Now banned, synthetic, toxic industrial chemicals used in paint and electrical transformers.

press release A news release written by the manager or professional advertising agency highlighting specific features of the rental property sent to local papers or real estate trade journals. A press release can lend more credibility than paid advertising and provide valuable, inexpensive advertising.

preventive maintenance A program of regularly scheduled maintenance activities and routine inspections of the interior and exterior of the buildings, equipment, and grounds. Its objective is to preserve the physical integrity of the property, eliminate corrective maintenance costs, and ensure uninterrupted service to the tenants.

price-fixing A violation of antitrust laws whereby brokers or managers conspire to fix (set) rental or compensation rates.

prime contractor A construction supervisor who contracts with the property manager to oversee a job and then sublets the work to various skilled tradespeople.

principal (1) An individual who designates another as his or her agent. (2) The original amount of a loan.

private industry councils (PICs) Using federal funds, groups operate employment and educational programs to train the workforce to meet employment needs.

profit and loss statement An annual financial report of a property's actual net profit before taxes.

property analysis A study made to familiarize a property manager with the nature and condition of a building, its position relative to comparable properties, and its estimated income and operating expenses.

property management A branch of the real estate profession that seeks to preserve or increase the value of an investment property while generating income for its owners.

proprietary lease The right of a member of a cooperative to occupy a unit in the building subject to certain conditions.

protected classes Any group of people that can be identified by a characteristic designated as such by the U.S. Department of Housing and Urban Development (HUD) in consideration of federal and state civil rights legislation. States may add groups for protection, but may not delete any group designated by the federal laws.

publicity Editorial space in a newspaper, magazine, or other medium that is not paid for but serves to attract public attention to an individual, firm, or commodity.

punitive damages In the event of fraud, damages awarded to one party to punish the other party for his/her dishonest conduct to deter others from committing the same offense.

qualifying process Determining the prospect's spatial needs, urgency to move, motives, and financial ability in order to determine if the manager has a space appropriate for the prospect.

radon A naturally occurring, odorless, colorless, radioactive gas that is a known carcinogen which has been found in every state and territory. Buildings with levels above the EPA action level of 4 should be mitigated.

real estate cycle A sequence of strengths and weaknesses that occurs in the real estate segment of the general business economy; phases of the cycle are influenced by, but are not identical to, those of the business cycle.

Real Estate Investment Trust (REIT) An unincorporated trust set up to invest in real property.

real property The earth's surface extending downward to the center and upward into space, including all things permanently attached thereto, by nature or by human hands.

recapture clause A provision in a percentage lease that grants the landlord the right to terminate the lease at the end of a certain period if gross sales have not reached the level anticipated during negotiations.

recapture provision A clause within an assignment and subletting lease clause giving the landlord the right to recover any space that the tenant is unable to occupy or sublease.

recession The peak of the business cycle; the point at which supply equals and begins to surpass demand.

recurring variable expense A type of variable property expense (e.g., redecorating costs) that occurs repeatedly on an irregular basis.

regional center, regional shopping center A large shopping center containing from 70 to 225 stores and more than 400,000 square feet of leasable area housing up to six major department stores and numerous satellite stores and supported by 50,000 to 150,000 families.

regional market analysis Used when drafting the management plan, a report detailing demographic and economic information on the regional or metropolitan area in which the subject property is located and used to interpret economic trends.

regularly recurring cost A type of fixed property expense (e.g., cleaning costs) that occurs consistently each month.

rentable area According to BOMA, the floor area of an office building minus allowances for stairs, elevator shafts, duct work, and other areas not available to the tenant.

rental center A special leasing area located in a real estate development. It includes a display area, furnished models, and a closing area.

rental history A record of the prospect's previous rental patterns that can influence the manager's decision to rent or not rent. Considerations include frequent moves, expensive modifications, and future expansion requirements.

rent factor A multiplier used to establish the rental rate for industrial properties, based on the rate of return the owner desires on the investment.

replacement cost insurance The type of insurance that guarantees that partial damage to old, depreciated property will be fully replaced by new construction.

research and development (R&D) center Provides assistance to facilities engineers and scientists at research universities, can assist with product marketing, and may provide incubator space for startup companies.

reserve funds An expense category in the operating budget, monies are set aside for replacement expenditures not covered by insurance, such as roof or furnace repairs.

resident manager A manager who resides at the managed property who coordinates and executes maintenance operations for the building, and in some cases, interfaces regularly with tenants.

residential property The type of property where people live. It includes privately owned dwellings as well as government and institutional ownership, and provides the greatest demand for professional property management.

resource-oriented industry A business that locates near suppliers or raw materials necessary for its operations.

restrictive clause A clause in a deed or lease that limits the way that the real estate ownership or possession may be used.

retail property Commercial property from which goods are sold.

retaliation Under the Uniform Landlord Tenant Law, landlords are not permitted to *get even* with a tenant who files a complaint with a government agency. Prohibited examples include singling out the tenant for a rental increase, unnecessary and frequent property inspections, and removing a parking space.

retrofitting An energy-saving program that calls for replacing or upgrading heating and air conditioning equipment, often at great expense.

return on investment (ROI) A measure of profitability of a property, computed either before or after income taxes, as follows:

$$\text{return on investment} = \frac{\text{(before-tax)(after-tax)}}{\text{equity}} \times 100\%$$

revival The lowest point, or nadir, of the business cycle; the point at which demand equals and begins to surpass supply.

risk management That portion of property management that deals with minimizing or allocating risk of damage, such as utilizing insurance policies to transfer the risk of loss to a third party.

routine maintenance Regular upkeep aimed at finding structural and mechanical problems before major repairs are necessary.

sale (and) leaseback An arrangement whereby an investor purchases real estate owned and used by a business and then leases it back to that business.

seasonal variations Changes in the economy that recur at least once a year.

Section 8 A federal subsidized housing program administered by HUD whereby a tenant pays up to 30 percent of his or her adjusted monthly income and HUD pays the difference between that figure and market rent. Income requirements vary regionally, and owners are not required to participate.

Section 202 A federal subsidized housing program providing capital for new construction, rehab, or acquisition for very low-income elderly.

security deposit A payment by a tenant, held by the landlord during the lease term and kept (wholly or partially) on default or destruction of the premises by the tenant. Individual states set forth rules for holding, retaining, or returning security deposits.

shared tenant services When permitted by local utilities, building management can provide telephone and data transmission services to two or more unrelated tenants.

show list A short list of up to three available apartments ready for inspection at any given time. As one is rented, another is made ready and added to the list for showing and renting. Analysis of the show list can serve as a control guide for the marketing program.

sick building syndrome (SBS) A physical condition caused by substances within a building that causes symptoms that disappear when the occupant leaves the building.

slum clearance The razing of substandard and unsalvageable residential buildings for redevelopment.

special-purpose property Hotels, resorts, nursing homes, theaters, schools, places of worship, and other businesses or organizations whose specialized needs dictate the design and operation of the building.

specific cycle A wavelike movement, similar to the business cycle, that occurs in certain sectors of the general economy.

sprinkler system Water flow system designed to discharge water to put out a fire.

stabilized budget Part of a five-year projected budget, arrived at by averaging income and expense items over a five-year period.

standard fire insurance A basic form of insurance protecting a property against direct loss or damage.

statute of frauds That part of state law that requires certain instruments, such as deeds, real estate contracts, and certain leases, to be in writing to be legally enforceable.

steering The directing of members of protected classes to buildings or neighborhoods that are already occupied primarily by members of those same classes and away from buildings and neighborhoods occupied primarily by members of other classes.

step-up clause A lease clause providing for rental rate increases of a definite amount at specific times over the term of the lease.

straight-line depreciation A method of computing depreciation that assumes that the wearing-out process proceeds at a stable rate over the useful life of a building.

$$\frac{100\%}{\text{life of building}} = \text{depreciation rate}$$

straight percentage lease A type of percentage lease that bases rental rate solely on gross sales.

strip centers Also known as *convenience centers*, shopping centers located on the edge of urban areas or in the suburbs, consisting of about 10,000 to 30,000 square feet, four to ten retail spaces. They usually include parking spaces in front of the shops, and are often owner-managed.

structural density The ratio of the total ground floor area of a building to the total land area of the site on which it is built.

subletting Partial transfer of a tenant's right in a rental property to a third party.

subsidized housing Residential developments for low-income families that are insured or (indirectly) financed in part by a government agency.

Superfund Amendments and Reauthorization Act of 1986 (SARA) The umbrella title given to various amendments to CERCLA. Amendments limit pesticide liability and provide for government reclamation of contaminated property.

superregional shopping centers Largest type of shopping center, housing as much as 1.5 million square feet of shops and appurtenant areas.

supply and demand The principle that follows the interrelationship of the supply of and the demand for real estate, recognizing that real property is subject to the influences of the marketplace just as any other commodity.

tax incentives Inducements by states and cities to encourage companies that are a source of employment, income, and tax revenues to locate in their areas.

tax participation clause A lease provision requiring the tenant to pay a pro-rata share of any increase in real estate taxes or assessments in addition to the basic rental.

technical oversupply A market condition in which available rental space exceeds tenant demand.

tenancy at sufferance A rental situation in which a tenant who originally obtained possession of the premises legally continues to occupy the property after the expiration of the leasehold interest and without the consent of the owner.

tenancy at will An estate that gives the tenant the right of possession for an indefinite period until the estate is terminated by either party or the death of either party.

tenant alteration costs Construction, remodeling, and alteration expenses for work needed to make the premises usable by the tenant. These costs may be assumed by the tenant or the owner or both and are a major point of negotiation.

tenant emergency procedures manual Printed booklet outlining emergency organization, workday procedures, telephone numbers, and after-hours procedures during an emergency.

tenant mix The combination of retail tenants occupying a shopping center; must be considered carefully to achieve maximum profit for each merchant and the center as a whole.

tenant union A local organization of residential tenants working for their common interests and rights.

tenant wardens Employees of tenant companies who are schooled in emergency procedures by the building staff to direct their fellow employees during routine drills and actual emergencies.

testers People used to gather evidence for fair housing complaints.

time-share condominium Ownership in vacation area residential property for an assigned period, usually two weeks. Also called *interval ownership*.

TRACS An online computer system being developed by HUD to help administer subsidized housing.

trade fixtures A fixture installed by a commercial or industrial tenant under the terms of the lease and removable by the tenant before the lease expires.

triplex A three-unit apartment building.

trust cooperative A cooperative in which legal ownership of a building is held by a trust company.

underground storage tanks (USTs) One or more combinations of tanks, including the piping, used to contain an accumulation of regulated substances, and is 10 percent or more underground. If a tenant's tanks leak petroleum products or hazardous or toxic materials, the landlord may be all or in part responsible for the cleanup.

Uniform Residential Landlord and Tenant Act A model law drafted in 1972 by the National Conference of Commissioners on Uniform State Laws. It serves as a model statute for standardization and regulation of the residential landlord-tenant relationship.

urban renewal Renovation, rehabilitation, and redevelopment of substandard urban residential properties.

U.S. Department of Housing and Urban Development (HUD) A government agency authorized to construct and provide financial assistance to housing developments for low-income tenants. HUD also works with Fair Housing complaints and violations.

usable space Floor area of an office building that can be used for tenant office space.

variable costs ratio A method of expressing variable costs for a property as a percentage of total rental income

$$\text{Variable costs ratio} = \frac{\text{actual annual variable costs}}{\text{gross collectible income}} \times 100\%$$

variable expense An expense item in a property's operating budget that increases or decreases with the occupancy level of the building.

variable scale percentage lease A type of percentage lease in which the percentage rental rate increases or decreases according to the volume of business done by the tenant.

volume buying See *bulk purchasing.*

worker's compensation insurance (worker's compensation) Laws that require an employer to obtain insurance coverage to protect his or her employees who are injured in the course of their employment.

work order bids Work estimates filed according to the property involved providing important comparison data when considering future projects.

INDEX